HANDBOOK OF BEHAVIORAL MEDICINE

HANDBOOK OF BEHAVIORAL MEDICINE

EDITED BY

W. Doyle Gentry
University of Virginia Medical School

THE GUILFORD PRESS
New York • London

Library of Congress Cataloging in Publication Data

Main entry under title:

Handbook of behavioral medicine.

   Bibliography: p.
   Includes index.
   1. Medicine and psychology.   2. Medicine, Psychosomatic.
I. Gentry, W. Doyle (William Doyle), 1943–   . [DNML:
1. Behavioral medicine—Handbooks.   WB 39 H236]
R726.5.H34 1984   616.08   84-4566
ISBN 0-89862-636-6

To my children,
Rebecca and Christopher,
for bringing such joy and happiness
into my life

CONTRIBUTORS

Robert Ader, PhD, Department of Psychiatry, University of Rochester School of Medicine and Dentistry, Rochester, New York

W. Stewart Agras, MD, Department of Psychiatry, Stanford University School of Medicine, Stanford, California

Nicholas Cohen, PhD, Department of Microbiology (Immunology), University of Rochester School of Medicine and Dentistry, Rochester, New York

John W. Farquhar, MD, Stanford Heart Disease Prevention Program, Stanford University, Stanford, California

Susan Folkman, PhD, Department of Psychology, University of California, Berkeley, Berkeley, California

W. Doyle Gentry, PhD, Department of Behavioral Medicine and Psychiatry, University of Virginia Medical School, Charlottesville, Virginia

David C. Glass, PhD, Department of Psychology, State University of New York at Stony Brook, Stony Brook, New York

Mary Gutmann, PhD, Department of Psychiatry, University of Wisconsin School of Medicine, Mount Sinai Hospital, Milwaukee, Wisconsin

J. Alan Herd, MD, Sid W. Richardson Institute for Preventive Medicine, The Methodist Hospital, Houston, Texas; Baylor College of Medicine, Houston, Texas

Irving L. Janis, PhD, Department of Psychology, Yale University, New Haven, Connecticut

Suzanne C. Ouellette Kobasa, PhD, Department of Psychology, The Graduate Center, City University of New York, New York, New York

David S. Krantz, PhD, Department of Medical Psychology, Uniformed Services University of the Health Sciences, Bethesda, Maryland

Richard S. Lazarus, PhD, Department of Psychology, University of California, Berkeley, Berkeley, California

Howard Leventhal, PhD, Department of Psychology, University of Wisconsin–Madison, Madison, Wisconsin

Nathan Maccoby, PhD, Stanford Heart Disease Prevention Program, Stanford University, Stanford, California

Douglas S. Solomon, PhD, MPH, Stanford Heart Disease Prevention Program, Stanford University, Stanford, California

S. Leonard Syme, PhD, Department of Biomedical and Environmental Sciences, University of California, Berkeley, Berkeley, California

Jay M. Weiss, PhD, Laboratory of Behavioral Biology, The Rockefeller University, New York, New York

Rick Zimmerman, PhD, Department of Sociology, University of Miami, Coral Gables, Florida

PREFACE

I, along with 19 fellow educators and researchers representing a variety of biomedical and behavioral–social science disciplines, was fortunate to participate in the now historic Yale Conference on Behavioral Medicine, co-hosted by Yale University and the National Heart, Lung and Blood Institute on February 4–6, 1977. This conference emphatically heralded the beginning of a major shift in health research away from a "single-discipline tradition," typifying the past several decades, toward a more "integrated and interdisciplinary tradition," which would characterize research activity in the 1980s. The Yale Conference offered various parent disciplines (medicine, psychology, psychiatry, epidemiology, sociology) a challenge for increased collaborative dialogue; this, it was hoped, would lead to increased evidence of collaborative research. The conference also offered individual researchers and educators a similar challenge of, as Neal Miller put it, developing "two skills in one skull."

The further elucidation, clarification, and amendment of the Yale Conference's definition of "behavioral medicine" (to emphasize the concept of *integration* more explicitly) at a meeting held at the Institute of Medicine, National Academy of Sciences, on April 10–11, 1978; the simultaneous founding of the *Journal of Behavioral Medicine* that same year; the formation of the Academy of Behavioral Medicine Research; and the establishment of a permanent Study Section on Behavioral Medicine for peer review of research and training grants within the National Institutes of Health—all these developments have served to reaffirm the basic conclusions of the Yale Conference. These conclusions are as follows:

1. It is possible to arrive at a general definition of behavioral medicine that will serve as a guide to future research activity and that will be acceptable to researchers operating in virtually all biomedical and social–behavioral sciences.
2. It is possible to create a matrix of research issues dealing with human health and illness that highlights the contributions of a broad spectrum of disciplines to problems of mutual concern.
3. It is possible to establish a forum for collaborative, integrated, and interdisciplinary communication both "within the covers of a single journal" and at the annual meeting(s) of a national professional society.

Unquestionably, the key to the progress made thus far in shifting away from the intellectual confines of a "single-discipline tradition" in health research lies in the fundamental wisdom of those participating in the Yale Conference, who unanimously agreed that behavioral medicine should *not* be defined in terms of or dominated by the theories, tools, or empirical findings of any one discipline or subdiscipline (e.g., internal medicine, behavioral psychology, social epidemiology). Rather, behavioral medicine was intended from the outset to be open-ended with respect to contributing fields of study; inclusive rather than exclusive with respect to content and methodology; and, generally speaking, free of intellectual dogma and resistant to scientific fads and special-interest needs of individuals and groups whose research activities fall under this rubric.

It was in this spirit—that is, a need for greater integration of ideas, methodology, and empirical data among and between biobehavioral scientists—that I embarked on the challenging task of editing a *Handbook of Behavioral Medicine,* a task that has absorbed much of my thinking and energy over the past several years. My goal in organizing the *Handbook* was to provide readers with a broader perspective on prevention, etiology, pathogenesis, diagnosis, treatment, and rehabilitation of physical disease than they might otherwise obtain from their own single-discipline readings and research experience. (This is the same basic goal I have had for the past 6 years as editor-in-chief of the *Journal of Behavioral Medicine.*) My own knowledge base, approach to research, and conceptualization of how, when, where, and why various individuals fall prey to illnesses such as essential hypertension, coronary heart disease, and cancer have indeed been altered and enhanced as a result of organizing and editing this *Handbook.* My hope is that this will also be true for each reader, including those who are only newly acquainted with the concept of behavioral medicine, as well as those seasoned investigators whose work is chronicled herein.

This volume, in my estimation, is unlike most other texts published recently dealing with the same topic. That is, I believe it represents the first systematic and serious effort to embrace state-of-the-art research conducted by biomedical *and* social–behavioral scientists on the matrix of research problems targeted by the Yale Conference. Other texts have instead restricted their focus *exclusively* on the application of "behavioral treatment and behaviorism" to persons ill or at risk for various types of physical disease. As such, much of the content of this *Handbook* will not appear in these other works, and thus will not add to the redundancy that already appears to characterize the latter.

This *Handbook* is intended as a source book for researchers and educators who truly seek to comprehend the interactive nature of biomedical and social–behavioral factors influencing illness and illness behavior; its focus is on complexity rather than simplicity, or, in statistical terminology, on "interaction effects" as contrasted with simple "main effects." While the coverage and treatment of relevant literature are indeed broad, and intentionally so, every effort has been made to give a critical evaluation of "what we know so far" in terms of prevailing scientific considerations. In essence, we have not tried to sacrifice depth for breadth. Of course, the reader will be the final judge as to whether or not we have succeeded in this regard.

I am especially indebted to Seymour Weingarten, editor-in-chief of The Guilford Press, for his continuing patience in seeing this project through to completion and his general support and confidence throughout as regards its merits. I am most grateful to all chapter authors; their hard work, willingness to delay gratification, and forbearance have made this volume a reality of which we can all be proud. Finally, I am thankful for the continuing support and encouragement of my wife, Catherine, who often over the past 5 years has had to remind me that behavioral medicine is not an affliction!

CONTENTS

Behavioral Medicine: A New Research Paradigm

W. Doyle Gentry
University of Virginia Medical School

REVIEW OF HISTORY AND TERMINOLOGY

The term "behavioral medicine," as far as we can ascertain, was first used publicly by Birk (1973) to describe the merits of biofeedback in treating medical disorders such as asthma, epilepsy, tension and migraine headaches, and Raynaud disease. Birk noted that

> it is perhaps not an exaggeration to point out that a new "behavioral medicine", biofeedback, now still in its infancy, may in fact represent a major new developing frontier of clinical medicine and psychiatry. (p. 362)

In a similar though somewhat broader vein, Blanchard (1977) next defined behavioral medicine as

> the systematic application of the principles and technology of behavioral psychology to the field of medicine, health and illness. By behavioral psychology I mean primarily experimental, or at least empirical, psychology which has its roots in the psychology of learning, social psychology, and to a lesser degree physiological psychology. (p. 2)

Shortly thereafter, behavioral medicine served as the focal point of discussion at the now historic Yale Conference on Behavioral Medicine (Schwartz & Weiss, 1978b), held February 4–6, 1977. Participants at this conference collectively defined the concept as follows:

> Behavioral medicine is the field concerned with the development of behavioral science knowledge and techniques relevant to the understanding of physical health and illness and the application of this knowledge and these techniques to prevention, diagnosis, treatment and rehabilitation. Psychosis, neurosis, and substance abuse are included only insofar as they contribute to physical disorders as an endpoint. (Schwartz & Weiss, 1978b, p. 7)

About this same time, writers (Schwartz & Weiss, 1977) began to distinguish between such terms as "behavioral medicine" and "psychosomatic medicine," a term already in use since the early 19th century (Laman & Evans, 1980), and to distinguish further between different uses of the term "behavioral medicine." For example, the field of psychosomatic medicine was viewed as evolving primarily from the biomedical sciences and being more concerned with basic research issues of disease etiology and pathogenesis, whereas behavioral medicine was seen as evolving more from the behavioral sciences (e.g., psychology, sociology) and being more concerned with treatment and prevention of physical disease. Schwartz and Weiss (1977, p. 378) were quick to point out that "ideally there should be no conflict between them"; rather, they should complement each other, as "understanding etiology and pathogenesis is essential for rational treatment and prevention." These writers also noted that obvious differences were emerging between the use of the term "behavioral medicine" by proponents of the Yale Conference definition and the earlier use by Birk (as well as Blanchard). Already it was clear that the question "What is behavioral medicine?" is presumptuous and misleading, in that it implies a consensus among users that in fact does not exist (Gentry, 1982).

At a second meeting of biomedical and behavioral scientists (many of whom had attended the Yale Conference), held at the Institute of Medicine, National Academy of Sciences, on April 10–11, 1978, the concept of "behavioral medicine" was further elucidated and amended to highlight more explicitly the concept of *integration of thought and technology*. This redefinition of the term by Yale Conference proponents was as follows (Schwartz & Weiss, 1978a):

> the interdisciplinary field concerned with the development and integration of behavioral and biomedical science knowledge and techniques relevant to health and illness and the application of this knowledge and these techniques to prevention, diagnosis, treatment and rehabilitation. (p. 250)

From this point on, events have occurred in rather rapid fashion to reify the concept(s) and definition(s) outlined above. Proponents of the Yale Conference definition set about to form a *Journal of Behavioral Medicine* as a primary outlet for interdisciplinary research and communication (Gentry, 1978a, 1980), and they established an Academy of Behavioral Medicine Research to promote ongoing face-to-face interdisciplinary education of members at annual meetings (Weiss, Herd, & Fox, 1981). They have also succeeded in setting up a permanent Study Section on Behavioral Medicine within the National Institutes of Health for peer review of research and training grants (Weiss & Shields, 1980), which has resulted in a much greater expenditure of federal research funds for biobehavioral research. Behavioral medicine branches have also been established as part of the National Heart, Lung and Blood Institute and the National Cancer Institute, in both instances to reinforce the general principles set forth in the Yale Conference.

Similarly, proponents of the ''behaviorism'' definition of behavioral medicine have continued to emphasize the vital, albeit rather restricted, role of behavioral psychology in determining assessment and treatment parameters within this field of activity; at the same time, they have extended the application of the term ''behavioral medicine'' far beyond the boundaries of biofeedback, as suggested by Birk (1973). To illustrate this extension, Pomerleau and Brady (1979) have defined ''behavioral medicine'' more succinctly as

> (a) the clinical use of techniques derived from the experimental analysis of behavior—behavior therapy and behavior modification—for the evaluation, prevention, management, or treatment of physical disease or physiological dysfunction; and (b) the conduct of research contributing to the functional analysis and understanding of behavior associated with medical disorders and problems in health care. (p. xii)

These same individuals have formed a Society of Behavioral Medicine, a professional organization closely affiliated with the Association for Advancement of Behavior Therapy (AABT), which currently serves as an educational forum for members of that ''camp'' (Pinkerton, Hughes, & Wenrich, 1982). They have also been quite productive in a short period of time as regards written testimony to the merits of behavioral medicine, as they have chosen to view it; for example, the Society of Behavioral Medicine has established *Behavioral Medicine Update*, an informal journal for the membership, as well as *Behavioral Medicine Abstracts*. Similarly, a number of books have appeared in the past 5 years that embrace this concept of behavioral medicine: Daitzman (1983), Davidson and Davidson (1980), Doleys, Meredith, and Ciminero (1982), Ferguson and Taylor (1980a, 1980b, 1981), McGrath and Firestone (1983), McNamara (1979), Melamed and Siegel (1980), Pinkerton, Hughes, and Wenrich (1982), Pomerleau and Brady (1979), Turk, Meichenbaum, and Genest (1983), and Williams and Gentry (1977).

Along the way, there have been critics of the term ''behavioral medicine''—namely those who scoff at the *newness* of the concept and/or its distinction from classic psychosomatic medicine (West & Stein, 1982) and suggest that the ''label . . . itself may misdirect the future growth and character of the field'' (Millon, Green, & Meagher, 1982). Still others argue that the ''essential nature'' of behavioral medicine remains elusive and will ultimately be defined by future activities of researchers and clinicians who choose to identify with the term (Doleys *et al.*, 1982; Pinkerton *et al.*, 1982). There is even some disagreement as to whether ''behavioral medicine'' refers to a field of scientific activity (Weiss, 1979) or a discipline (Surwit, 1982). Finally, there are those who would ignore the term altogether and instead prefer use of the term ''biopsychosocial'' (Engel, 1977) to describe an integrated approach to clinical research and medicine that simultaneously attends to psychological, social, and biological factors as regards etiology, pathogenesis, and treatment.

We agree with Blanchard (1977), Weiss (1979), and Agras (1982), however, that behavioral medicine is *an idea whose time has come*. More than that, we believe that "behavioral medicine" refers to a mandate for a new, different approach to scientific inquiry within the domain of human health and illness—one that generates and rewards interdisciplinary research activities and puts a premium on collaborative research expertise. We view it as an active effort on the part of researchers and funding agencies alike to shape links between the biomedical and social–behavioral sciences, rather than merely a passive descriptor of research activity that may come to pass. In fact, history has shown that collaborative research, involving more than one discipline, is the exception rather than the rule (cf. Hull, 1977; Matarazzo, Carmody, & Gentry, 1981) in decades past. As Miller (1981) has pointed out, academic bureaucracy has evidenced a strong tendency to reward "disciplinary conformity" and is unlikely to "waste" resources on scientists who stray from the single-discipline fold. Behavioral medicine, in essence, represents that "crack between disciplines" that heretofore presented a dilemma for researchers operating on the outer boundaries of their parent disciplines.

THE ESSENTIAL NATURE OF BEHAVIORAL MEDICINE

Regardless of how one chooses to define behavioral medicine, especially since virtually all proponents will to some extent apply their own idiosyncratic views (cf. Agras, 1982; Blanchard, 1977), one is quick to realize that the essential ingredient, the sine qua non, of behavioral medicine is an integration of empirical knowledge stemming from interdisciplinary research efforts. The essence of this interdisciplinary thrust is graphically illustrated in Figure 1.1. As Weiss and Schwartz (1982) suggest, we might think of behavioral medicine as a conceptual *crucible* that provides a forum for many disciplines and subdisciplines to undertake a process of joint exploration targeted on health issues of mutual concern. In other words, it is a "pooling of talent and diverse perspectives" (Weiss & Schwartz, 1982), a type of "holistic" problem solving (Gentry, 1982), an "emerging network of communication among an array of disciplines not previously well connected" (Agras, 1982), and a synthetic "systems theory" model for understanding the complexities of human disease (Schwartz, 1980).

A second, and as yet less appreciated, element of behavioral medicine is its recognition of the *reciprocal* nature of relationships between human biology and human psychology and sociology. That is, personality, coping styles, and membership in various social and ethnic groups can influence illness morbidity and mortality; conversely, poor health or wellness can influence the way in which one perceives the world (stress), how one copes with adversity, and so forth. If anything, behavioral medicine appears to have given a disproportionate amount of attention to the first of these influences at the

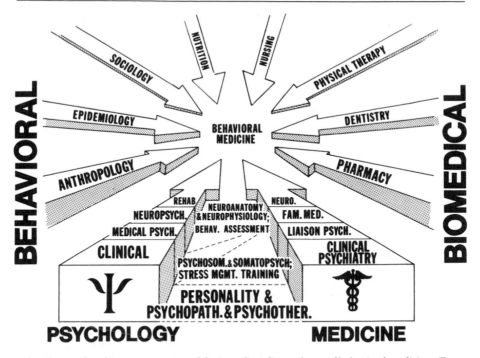

FIGURE 1.1. Graphic representation of the interdisciplinary thrust of behavioral medicine. (From Masur, F. T. An update on medical psychology and behavioral medicine. *Professional Psychology*, 1979, *10*, 259–264. Reprinted by permission.)

expense of the second. Psychosomatic medicine and/or the biopsychosocial approach (Engel, 1977; Weiner, 1977), on the other hand, have tended to focus on the second influence (i.e., the influence of biological processes on human behavior) more often than not. This difference in directionality of research focus is, of course, understandable, given the fact that biomedical and behavioral science researchers have different points of departure (e.g., medicine vs. psychology) from which they can expand their respective view(s) of the interplay between "man the biological machine" and "man the behaving, social creature" (Brady, 1981).

BEHAVIORAL MEDICINE: WHY NOW?

One might well ask, "Why has behavioral medicine so recently surged to the forefront as regards a paradigm for either empirical research or clinical application?" What accounts for this rather drastic change in *Zeitgeist* (Blanchard, 1977), which increasingly favors the conduct of interdisciplinary, collaborative research on and/or treatment of persons afflicted by or at risk for physical illness? No one factor or set of circumstances, to be sure, is responsible; rather, as Miller (1981) and Agras (1982) point out, it is the result of a confluence or convergence of several factors, which include but are not necessarily limited to the following:

- The fact that biomedical and behavioral researchers operating independently have been unable to explain satisfactorily in any "all or nothing" way why some persons become ill and others remain well.
- The fact that most of the challenges of modern-day medicine have to do with the diagnosis and treatment of *chronic,* rather than acute, illness, which is highly influenced by behavioral or life style factors (e.g., personality).
- The general maturity of research in the social and behavioral sciences (e.g., in experimental and social psychology), as well as advances in behavioral epidemiology (Sexton, 1979).
- The growth of interest in prevention of illness, public health, or what Matarazzo (1980) has called "behavioral health," in large part spurred by drastically increasing costs of medical care.
- The reemergence and rapid growth of medical psychology (Gentry & Matarazzo, 1981; Matarazzo *et al.*, 1981), which has added a dimension of applied clinical science previously lacking in psychosomatic medicine (Agras, 1982; Schwartz & Weiss, 1977). The role of medical or health psychologists appears to be somewhat unique in catalyzing increased interest in behavioral medicine, due (1) to the emphasis on learning as applied to disease etiology and illness behavior; and (2) to the capacity of psychologists, as compared to other types of behavioral scientists (e.g., sociologists and anthropologists), to intervene in ways that serve to interrupt the expected risk relationship between stress and illness (e.g., stress management training) and/or to actively reduce morbidity and mortality after disease has been diagnosed (e.g., modification of Type A behavior(s) in persons following survival of acute myocardial infarction).

Together, these factors have provided a "point of departure" (Schwartz & Weiss, 1978b)—an impetus for crossing a conceptual and empirical threshold (Gentry, 1978b) beyond which the "integrative ideal" (Eiser, 1982) of behavioral medicine might yet be fully achieved.

A WORD ABOUT CONCEPTUAL MODELS

At this point, a few words about conceptual models seem in order. First, it is important to emphasize, as does Schwartz (1982), that behavioral medicine necessitates a "systems theory" or *organistic* model of thinking about disease etiology, pathogenesis, and treatment. That is, researchers in this field *must* from the outset consider behavior *and* disease as being multidetermined—that is, as subject to the additive or interactive influence(s) of genetic, biological, psychological, sociocultural, and ecological factors. The type of "either–or" thinking that has so long characterized single-discipline research (e.g., defining risk for cardiovascular disease in terms of whether one has evidence of coronary heart disease *or* not in one's family history, whether *or* not one smokes cigarettes, exercises *or* not, is obese *or* not, or is Type A *or* not) does not apply here.

Second, the matrix approach suggested by the Yale Conference on Behavioral Medicine (Schwartz & Weiss, 1978b), which emphasizes the respective contributions of various disciplines (see Figure 1.2) to targeted problems in the field, now seems rather in conflict with the true spirit of behavioral medicine research. That is, the discipline axis of the matrix suggests that each specified single discipline (psychology, medicine, sociology, anthropology, psychiatry, epidemiology, physiology) contributes equally to the ultimate knowledge base of behavioral medicine in parallel, as opposed to integrative, fashion. This model, as shown, does not mandate collaborative research efforts; rather, it offers a framework (or perspective) for integrating information generated by single-discipline researchers.

Also, the matrix approach reinforces to a large extent the belief that different parent disciplines "own" a specific knowledge set (e.g., psychology), as well as scientific techniques for deriving same, and that contributions to that particular part of the behavioral medicine "whole" (matrix) can only be made by member researchers of that discipline. As Schwartz (1982) has noted, this notion of ownership is not only without merit; it violates the initial intent of the Yale Conference participants that behavioral medicine should by its very nature be inclusive rather than exclusive in fostering the "development and integration of behavioral and biomedical science knowledge and techniques relevant to health and illness" (Schwartz & Weiss, 1978a). Hull (1977) provides an excellent example of the fact that, while different disciplines tend to focus on certain categories of research variables (e.g., psychologists most often focus on emotional traits as they influence susceptibility to illness, while sociologists concentrate their attention on factors such as age, sex, ethnicity, and marital status), there is considerable overlap between disciplines.

The "systems theory" model of Schwartz (1982), on the other hand, more aptly captures the spirit of behavioral medicine by specifying various levels of analysis within the system and then the disciplines and subdisciplines that might logically contribute to each level. For example, psychology, ethology, and zoology all contribute to our understanding at the level of the organism, sociology at the level of groups, and physiology, cardiology, and neurology at the level of organs and organ systems. In a similar vein, Margolis, McLeroy, Runyan, and Kaplan (1983) have employed an "ecological model" to clarify more fully the development and function of Type A (coronary-prone) behavior, a major risk factor for coronary heart disease in humans. In doing so, they have speculated on the role played in the development of Type A by achievement striving, social comparison processes, attribution, and social learning at the intrapersonal level; competition and social support at the interpersonal level; role demands and reward systems at

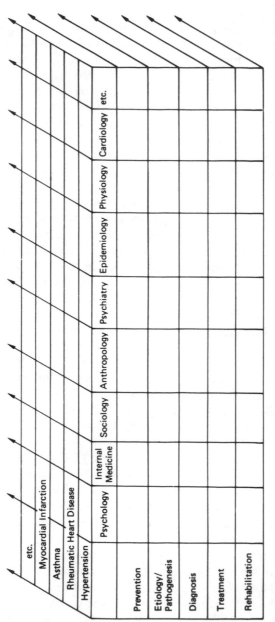

FIGURE 1.2. Matrix of problems in behavioral medicine. (From Schwartz, G. E., & Weiss, S. M. Yale Conference on Behavioral Medicine: A proposed definition and statement of goals. *Journal of Behavioral Medicine*, 1978, *1*, 3–12. Reprinted by permission.)

the institutional level; and, finally, time orientation and industrialization at the cultural level. They have also addressed the issue of relationships between and among levels in suggesting that Type A intervention efforts directed at only one level (e.g., intrapersonal or interpersonal) may fail because of influences from other levels (e.g., institutional or cultural). This same point was made earlier by Mettlin (1976) in discussing the feasibility of Type A intervention.

GOALS AND ORGANIZATION OF THIS VOLUME

This volume is a logical extension and outgrowth of the Yale Conference on Behavioral Medicine (Schwartz & Weiss, 1978b) and the subsequent meeting of researchers at the Institute of Medicine, National Academy of Sciences, on this same topic. Like the *Journal of Behavioral Medicine*, the newly formed National Institutes of Health Study Section on Behavioral Medicine, and the Academy of Behavioral Medicine Research, its basic goal is to foster the ideal of integrated and interdisciplinary thinking as regards issues of human health and illness and to facilitate the ultimate realization of this ideal through collaborative research. As such, the *Handbook* quite naturally is not representative of any particular single-discipline constituency, disciplinary doctrine, or methodology. Rather, it attempts to capture for the reader a rich diversity of research perspective and empirical findings on a number of problem areas initially targeted by Yale Conference proponents for special attention. These topic or problem areas include the following:

- *Etiology*—Discussion of how critical life (stress) events, behavioral traits, and personality predispose an individual to physical illness.
- *Host resistance*—Discussion of how resistance resources, including personality traits, social support, and coping style(s), can mediate the untoward effects of stress on health.
- *Disease mechanisms*—Discussion of how human physiology is altered by stress (i.e., that resulting from maladaptive behavioral tendencies), with special attention being directed at the immune system, gastrointestinal disease, and cardiovascular disease and hypertension.
- *Patient Decision Making*—Discussion of the process whereby individuals make decisions about avoiding health hazards, choosing appropriate medical or behavioral therapies, and adhering to treatment regimens.
- *Compliance*—Discussion of biomedical, behavioral, and self-regulative perspectives on the problem of medical compliance, with particular attention given to the practitioner–patient relationship, differential expectations, social roles, and cultural values.
- *Intervention*—Discussion of the efficacy of health education and behavioral treatment in altering unhealthy life styles (smoking, dietary abuse) and in directly reducing illness and/or illness behavior (e.g., asthma, ulcer, hypertension, headache, insomnia, Raynaud disease) at the level of individuals and communities.

Unlike most other volumes dealing with behavioral medicine, the *Handbook* does not limit itself to a discussion of "behavior" as typically defined by behaviorists, behavior therapists, or general psychologists (Schwartz, 1981); rather, "behavior" here is meant to encompass the activities of individuals at several levels, but also that of such systems as communities and cultures. The focus in the *Handbook* is not chiefly or entirely on clinical application; however, it does provide the reader with a sound basis for targeting intervention efforts (e.g., on facilitating utilization of resistance resources so important in mediating stress–illness relationships) and for deciding at what level(s) intervention should be directed if meaningful health outcome(s) are to be achieved (e.g., intrapersonal vs. institutional). The *Handbook* is not organized, as noted above, along the lines of specific disorders (e.g., asthma, pain, headaches, obesity, hypertension) or clinical techniques (e.g., systematic desensitization, cognitive therapies, biofeedback); rather, it is addressed to larger problems (e.g., compliance, decision-making mechanisms) that have relevance to all such diseases and disorders. Finally, and perhaps most importantly, the *Handbook* contains contributions from researchers in the fields of epidemiology, psychology, psychiatry, biology, and medicine, all obviously knowledgeable about the respective ideas and findings of fellow biobehavioral investigators; we hope that this approach will leave the reader who digests the *Handbook* in its entirety with a refreshing new interdisciplinary view of the complexities of human health—how to achieve it and how to maintain it.

REFERENCES

Agras, W. S. Behavioral medicine in the 1980s: Nonrandom connections. *Journal of Consulting and Clinical Psychology*, 1982, *50*, 797–803.

Birk, L. (Ed.). *Biofeedback: Behavioral medicine.* New York: Grune & Stratton, 1973.

Blanchard, E. B. Behavioral medicine: A perspective. In R. B. Williams & W. D. Gentry (Eds.), *Behavioral approaches to medical treatment.* Cambridge, Mass.: Ballinger, 1977.

Brady, J. P. Behavioral medicine: Scope and promise of an emerging field. *Biological Psychiatry,* 1981, *16*, 319–332.

Daitzman, R. J. (Ed.). *Diagnosis and intervention in behavior therapy and behavioral medicine.* New York: Springer, 1983.

Davidson, P. O., & Davidson, S. M. (Eds.). *Behavioral medicine: Changing health lifestyles.* New York: Brunner/Mazel, 1980.

Doleys, D. M., Meredith, R. L., & Ciminero, A. R. (Eds.). *Behavioral medicine: Assessment and treatment strategies.* New York: Plenum, 1982.

Eiser, J. R. (Ed.). *Social psychology and behavioral medicine.* New York: Wiley, 1982.

Engel, G. L. The need for a new medical model: A challenge for biomedicine. *Science,* 1977, *196*, 129–136.

Ferguson, J. M., & Taylor, C. B. (Eds.). *The comprehensive handbook of behavioral medicine* (Vol. 1, *Systems intervention*). Jamaica, N.Y.: Spectrum, 1980. (a)

Ferguson, J. M., & Taylor, C. B. (Eds.). *The comprehensive handbook of behavioral medicine* (Vol. 2, *Syndromes and special areas*). Jamaica, N.Y.: Spectrum, 1980. (b)

Ferguson, J. M., & Taylor, C. B. (Eds.). *The comprehensive handbook of behavioral medicine* (Vol. 3, *Extended applications and issues*). Jamaica, N.Y.: Spectrum, 1981.

Gentry, W. D. About the *Journal of Behavioral Medicine. Journal of Behavioral Medicine*, 1978, *1*, 1–2. (a)

Gentry, W. D. On the threshold of behavioral medicine. *Contemporary Psychology*, 1978, *23*, 857–858. (b)

Gentry, W. D. Developing a new journal in the area of medicine: An editorial perspective. *National Forum*, 1980, *60*, 33–35.

Gentry, W. D. What is behavioral medicine? In J. R. Eiser (Ed.). *Social psychology and behavioral medicine.* New York: Wiley, 1982.

Gentry, W. D., & Matarazzo, J. D. Medical psychology: Three decades of growth and development. In L. A. Bradley & C. K. Prokop (Eds.), *Medical psychology: A new perspective.* New York: Academic Press, 1981.

Hull, D. Life circumstances and physical illness: A cross disciplinary survey of research content and method for the decade 1965–1975. *Journal of Psychosomatic Research*, 1977, *21*, 115–140.

Laman, C., & Evans, R. I. Behavioral medicine: The history and the past. *National Forum*, 1980, *60*, 13–18.

Margolis, L. H., McLeroy, K. R., Runyan, C. W., & Kaplan, B. H. Type A behavior: An ecological approach. *Journal of Behavioral Medicine*, 1983, *6*, 245–258.

Masur, F. T. An update on medical psychology and behavioral medicine. *Professional Psychology*, 1979, *10*, 259–264.

Matarazzo, J. D. Behavioral health and behavioral medicine. *American Psychologist*, 1980, *35*, 807–817.

Matarazzo, J. D., Carmody, T. P., & Gentry, W. D. Psychologists on the faculty of United States schools of medicine: Past, present and possible future. *Clinical Psychology Review*, 1981, *1*, 293–317.

McGrath, P. J., & Firestone, P. (Eds.). *Pediatric and adolescent behavioral medicine: Issues in treatment.* New York: Springer, 1983.

McNamara, J. R. (Ed.). *Behavioral approaches to medicine.* New York: Plenum, 1979.

Melamed, B. G., & Siegel, L. J. *Behavioral medicine: Practical applications in health care.* New York: Springer, 1980.

Mettlin, C. Occupational careers and the prevention of coronary-prone behavior pattern. *Social Sciences and Medicine*, 1976, *10*, 367–372.

Miller, N. E. An overview of behavioral medicine: Opportunities and dangers. In S. M. Weiss, J. A. Herd, & B. H. Fox (Eds.), *Perspectives on behavioral medicine.* New York: Academic Press, 1981.

Millon, T., Green, C., & Meagher, R. (Eds.). *Handbook of clinical health psychology.* New York: Plenum, 1982.

Pinkerton, S., Hughes, H., & Wenrich, W. W. *Behavioral medicine: Clinical applications.* New York: Wiley, 1982.

Pomerleau, O. F., & Brady, J. P. (Eds.). *Behavioral medicine: Theory and practice.* Baltimore: Williams & Wilkins, 1979.

Schwartz, G. E. Behavioral medicine and systems theory: A new synthesis. *National Forum*, 1980, *60*, 25–30.

Schwartz, G. E. A systems analysis of psychobiology and behavior therapy: Implications for behavioral medicine. *Psychotherapy and Psychosomatics*, 1981, *36*, 159–184.

Schwartz, G. E. Testing the biopsychosocial model: The ultimate challenge facing behavioral medicine? *Journal of Consulting and Clinical Psychology*, 1982, *50*, 1040–1053.

Schwartz, G. E., & Weiss, S. M. What is behavioral medicine? *Psychosomatic Medicine*, 1977, *39*, 377–381.

Schwartz, G. E., & Weiss, S. M. Behavioral medicine revisited: An amended definition. *Journal of Behavioral Medicine*, 1978, *1*, 249–252. (a)

Schwartz, G. E., & Weiss, S. M. Yale Conference on Behavioral Medicine: A proposed definition and statement of goals. *Journal of Behavioral Medicine*, 1978, *1*, 3–12. (b)

Sexton, M. M. Behavioral epidemiology. In O. F. Pomerleau & J. P. Brady (Eds.), *Behavioral medicine: Theory and practice*. Baltimore: Williams & Wilkins, 1979.

Surwit, R. S. Behavioral treatment of disease: Introduction. In R. S. Surwit, R. B. Williams, A. Steptoe, & R. Biersner (Eds.), *Behavioral treatment of disease*. New York: Plenum, 1982.

Turk, D. C., Meichenbaum, D., & Genest, M. *Pain and behavioral medicine: A cognitive–behavioral perspective*. New York: Guilford Press, 1983.

Weiner, H. *Psychobiology and human disease*. New York: Elsevier, 1977.

Weiss, S. M. Behavioral medicine: An idea. In J. R. McNamara (Ed.), *Behavioral approaches to medicine*. New York: Plenum, 1979.

Weiss, S. M., Herd, J. A., & Fox, B. H. (Eds.). *Perspectives on behavioral medicine*. New York: Academic Press, 1981.

Weiss, S. M., & Schwartz, G. E. Behavioral medicine: The biobehavioral perspective. In R. S. Surwit, R. B. Williams, A. Steptoe, & R. Biersner (Eds.), *Behavioral treatment of disease*. New York: Plenum, 1982.

Weiss, S. M., & Shields, J. L. The National Institutes of Health and behavioral medicine. *National Forum*, 1980, *60*, 30–32.

West, L. J., & Stein, M. (Eds.). *Critical issues in behavioral medicine*. Philadelphia: J. B. Lippincott, 1982.

Williams, R. B., & Gentry, W. D. (Eds.). *Behavioral approaches to medical treatment*. Cambridge, Mass.: Ballinger, 1977.

CHAPTER 2

Sociocultural Factors and Disease Etiology

S. Leonard Syme
University of California, Berkeley

The prevention of disease ultimately rests upon the identification of risk factors that increase the probability of developing disease. The list of risk factors for various diseases now increasingly includes references to sociocultural factors. This chapter (1) reviews the evidence that has led to this development, (2) summarizes current research findings in this field, and (3) suggests new avenues for future research.

THE RATIONALE FOR STUDYING SOCIOCULTURAL FACTORS

Differences in Disease Rates

The first modern argument for the inclusion of sociocultural factors in studies of disease etiology was that offered by Emile Durkheim in his classic research on suicide. His book, *Le Suicide*, was published in France in 1897, but was not translated into English until 1951 (Durkheim, 1951). Durkheim's work is among the very first modern examples of the systematic and organized use of the statistical method to further the sociocultural investigation of disease. In this research, Durkheim noted that while suicide is one of the most individualistic acts imaginable, it can be understood only in terms of the social setting within which it takes place. At the time Durkheim wrote, it was known that suicide rates varied among different groups and among different time periods. Suicide rates were seen to be higher for Protestants than for Catholics, higher for the unmarried than for the married, higher for soldiers than for civilians, higher for noncommissioned officers than for enlisted men, higher in times of peace than in times of war and revolution, and higher in times of both prosperity and recession than in times of economic stability.

Durkheim acknowledged that there were many different individual reasons for committing suicide (e.g., economic problems, sickness, personal failure); he pointed out, however, that suicide rates differ among social groups, even though individuals come and go. These differences in rates among groups persist over time and cultural settings, even though individual problems vary within the groups. To explain this difference in group rates, Durkheim argued, one must refer to sociocultural factors. He reasoned that if different groups have different suicide rates, there must be something about the social organization of the groups that encourages individuals to commit suicide or deters them from it. Durkheim's research led him to conclude that the major factor affecting suicide rates was the degree of social integration of groups. He suggested that the extent to which the individual was integrated into group life determined whether he or she would be motivated to commit suicide. As soon becomes clear, this emphasis on the importance of social ties is a theme that emerges from current research also. Aside from Durkheim's substantive contribution regarding suicide, however, is the important epidemiological observation that systematic, patterned differences in disease rates among groups must be explainable in group terms. This idea continues to be the major rationale for sociocultural research in disease etiology.

This rationale can be illustrated in the case of current research on coronary heart disease (CHD). Findings from long-term community studies in the United States among several thousand middle-aged men show that high serum cholesterol levels, high blood pressure, and cigarette smoking are important risk factors for CHD (Inter-Society Commission for Heart Disease Resources, 1970). Men with all three of these risk factors have over six times the chance of developing a first major coronary attack than men with none of the risk factors have; the relative risk for men having one or two of the risk factors is 2.4 and 4.5, respectively.

On the other hand, as Marmot and Winkelstein (1975) have shown, only 14% of the men with all three of the risk factors were observed to develop CHD during the 10 years of observation in these community studies; 86% of these men did not have coronary events. Of men with one or two risk factors, only 5% and 9%, respectively, had events in the 10-year period of study. Thus, even though the risk factors are associated wth a clearly increased relative risk, few men with the risk factors actually develop disease. Looked at another way, of all the people who developed CHD in these community studies over the 10-year follow-up, only 17% had all three risk factors, and only 58% had two or more risk factors. It is clear from these figures that many people develop CHD for reasons not explainable by the three risk factors. While this observation should not lead one to deemphasize the importance of the three established risk factors, it does suggest that other risk factors are also importantly involved in the etiological process.

The search for other risk factors has been stimulated by the observation that CHD rates vary among population groups and countries. This observation has led to the suggestion that genetic factors may be involved. Research is now under way to explore this possibility (Feinleib, Garrison, Fabsitz, Christian, Hrubec, Borhani, Kannel, Rosenman, Schwartz, & Wagner, 1977). It is not likely, however, that the genetic hypothesis can be the entire explanation for geographic variations in CHD rates because of findings from migration studies. These studies have shown that when migrants move from low-CHD areas to high-CHD areas, their CHD experience tends to approximate that of the area to which they move. Of course, it is possible that migrants are a genetically select group. As is discussed later, however, evidence is available to suggest that the disease experience of migrants is more readily explained with an environmental rather than with a genetic hypothesis.

Some of the interesting differences in disease rates that have been observed among countries and population groups include the fact that CHD rates generally are highest among English-speaking countries of the world (with Finland as a major high-rate exception); higher among urban industrialized states in the United States; higher among men; higher among those in lower socioeconomic groups; and higher among those single, widowed, or divorced. Considerable research has been devoted to the understanding of these differences and much of it has focused on the possible role of various psychological, social, and cultural factors. Much of what is now known about these factors has come from the study of differences in disease rates among population groups.

Levels of Analysis

In studies of disease etiology, it is clear that we must deal with a complex web of causation in which many risk factors interact to produce disease (MacMahon & Pugh, 1970; Susser, 1973). Efforts to understand etiological processes must address three questions: (1) How do the various risk factors act alone or together to produce disease within a given person? (2) Why does one person get sick instead of another? (3) Why are rates of illness higher in one group than in another? It is entirely possible that the answers developed in the study of any one of these questions will not address the other two questions. There are different levels of analysis in any science; each level of analysis develops methods and concepts suitable to that level. The findings from one, however, should not contradict findings from the other.

An example may be useful. One can study factors associated with geographic, racial, or occupational differences in disease rates; one can study personal and interpersonal characteristics distinguishing people with and without disease; and one can study the metabolic, biochemical, and molecular processes set in motion when someone is becoming ill. Each sphere of study may be independent, but the findings from one should not contradict those from another. Indeed, it may be hoped that findings from one level stimulate the development of hypotheses at another level. Thus, observation of geographic differences may lead to exploration of life style differences between geographic areas and to the study of biological consequences of differences in life style. Conversely, differences observed at the cellular or interpersonal level may lead to studies of geographic variations in disease occurrence. Note that in this perspective, one research approach is not "best"; all interact, and each approach enriches the other.

Quality of Evidence

During the last 30 years, research evidence has accumulated regarding the role of sociocultural factors in disease etiology. While this research evidence is now vast in quantity, it is also variable in quality (Jenkins, 1971, 1978). The reason for this variation in quality is not so much that investigators are poor researchers, as it is that this type of research is extraordinarily difficult to do well. Consider the following difficulties: (1) A very long list of possible risk factors exists for all of the major causes of morbidity and mortality; for diseases such as mental illness, cancer, CHD, and accidents, the list of risk factors could easily include several dozen possibilities. (2) These risk factors operate in very different ways to produce disease; some are important in early life, some later; some initiate disease while others promote it; some act directly, others indirectly; and so on. (3) The risk factors interact with one another in complex ways. If one were to make a list of possible risk factors for any specific disease, it is likely that any one of the factors on the list would be related to almost all of the other factors on the list. In many cases, not only does factor A affect factor B, but factor B affects factor A.

This situation is particularly problematic because, in most cases, experimental research is not possible. In most research on sociocultural factors, the investigator is forced to study the world as he or she finds it. While this is a major strength of social epidemiology, it also represents a methodological weakness. Thus, rates of disease must be observed in various geographic, occupational, socioeconomic, or religious groups, as these groups exist at the time of study. Rarely do people randomly allocate themselves to these groups for the researcher's convenience. A classic example of how this problem affects results is the study of CHD among bus drivers and conductors on London's double-decker buses (Morris, Heady, Raffle, Roberts, & Park, 1953). The study of this group was initiated to take advantage of the fact that conductors continually run up and down steps collecting fares, while drivers are less physically active. The hope was that this occupational group would permit a test of the CHD–physical activity hypothesis. It was found that drivers developed CHD at twice the rate observed for conductors. A second report from this study, however, noted that drivers weighed considerably more than conductors on their first day of employment—before any of the employees had yet driven or conducted (Morris, Heady, & Raffle, 1956). Obviously, employees had not allocated themselves to occupational categories at random. When we study the world as we find it, it is almost certain that we will find people in various groupings for nonrandom reasons.

Since so many risk factors are involved in the etiology of disease in such complex and interrelated ways, and since we must do observational rather than experimental studies, it is not surprising that the quality of research in this field is problematic. In this circumstance, where no one study can be regarded as definitive and free of flaws, it may be necessary to look instead for consistent patterns of findings among various studies. Instead of settling an issue with one conclusive research project, it may be that we have to "surround" the issue with several different, imperfect projects. While each of these projects may be imperfect, the fact that so many different approaches yield the same pattern of findings should merit our attention.

With this caveat regarding quality of evidence, I proceed to a review of current research findings on the relationship of sociocultural factors to disease etiology.

CURRENT RESEARCH ON SOCIOCULTURAL FACTORS

Of all the research done in the area of sociocultural factors and disease etiology, three themes can be identified that are supported by a relatively large body of consistent empirical evidence. This selection of a few themes is obviously subjective and judgmental, and surely omits findings that others would regard as important. The selection offered here is only one perspective. One person's "consistent pattern of evidence" is another's "miscellaneous collection of unrelated findings."

Sociocultural Mobility

In an early study conducted in North Dakota in 1957 (Syme, Hyman, & Enterline, 1964), CHD rates were found to be two times higher among men who had experienced several lifetime job changes and geographic moves than among men with no such changes. Further, CHD rates were three times higher among men who were reared on farms but who later moved to the city to take white-collar jobs, compared to men who either stayed on the farm or took blue-collar jobs in the city. These findings were based on the study of the 203 men, 35 to 64 years of age, who developed CHD in a six-county area in 1 year, in comparison to an age-matched group of 406 men free of CHD, drawn at random from the population from which the cases came. These findings were not attributable to differences between cases and controls in diet, smoking habits, physical activity, obesity, blood pressure, or familial longevity.

Following this study of mobility in a rural area, a second study was conducted in the more urban state of California (Syme, Borhani, & Buechley,

1965). The rationale for conducting this second study was to see whether mobility would continue to be a risk factor in an area where life changes were more frequent. Again, CHD rates were found to be higher among those with frequent job and residence changes, and among those who exhibited discrepancies between their culture of upbringing and their current sociocultural situation. As in North Dakota, cases had CHD two to three times more frequently than controls—a difference that was not explained by differences in such other risk factors as parental longevity, cigarette smoking, relative weight, and physical activity. Following these early studies, similar findings were reported among such groups as Southern rural workers who moved to industrial jobs (Cassel & Tyroler, 1961) and college-trained monks from lower-class origins (Caffrey, 1970). In a follow-up study conducted in Evans County, Georgia, between 1960 and 1969, Kaplan and his associates (Kaplan, Cassel, Tyroler, Cornoni, Kleinbaum, & Hames, 1971) found twice the prevalence of CHD among lower-status persons who had moved upward in social status during the period, as compared to those who remained at the same level.

Shekelle, Ostfeld, and Paul (1969) conducted a study at the Western Electric Company in Chicago, in which CHD was studied prospectively over a 5-year period among 1,472 persons aged 42 to 57 years. It was found that inconsistencies in social status assessed at the beginning of the study were associated wth a subsequent increased risk of CHD. Men with four or five inconsistencies had six times the risk of CHD that men with no inconsistencies had. Again, these findings were not explained by the effect of such other risk factors as serum cholesterol, blood pressure, blood glucose, education status, relative weight, or cigarette smoking.

While most of the findings regarding sociocultural mobility have developed in the study of CHD, other diseases have also been studied. Haenszel, Loveland, and Sirken (1962) observed a higher rate of lung cancer among men raised on farms who, as adults, had moved to the city (compared to those who remained on the farm); this difference was independent of cigarette-smoking behavior. Similarly, Terris and Chaves (1966) reported a higher rate of sarcoidosis among persons who had migrated from rural and urban areas. Other studies and reviews supporting these findings have been reported by Bruhn, Chandler, Miller, Wolf, and Lynn (1966), Bakker and Levinson (1967), Smith (1967), Marks (1967), Jenkins (1971), and House and Jackman (1979).

On the other hand, several studies have failed to find increased rates of disease among mobile persons. Sociocultural change only infrequently has been associated with increases in blood pressure levels (Syme & Torfs, 1978). Hinkle, Whitney, Lehman, Dunn, Benjamin, King, Plakum, and Flehinger (1968) and Williams (1968) found no relationship between occupational advancement and CHD among employees of industrial firms. As Lehman (1967) and Kaplan *et al.* (1971) have pointed out, however, industrial firms may not be appropriate settings for the study of sociocultural mobility.

Haynes, Levine, Scotch, Feinleib, and Kannel (1978) recently studied various types of mobility in the community setting of Framingham, Massachusetts, and reported no statistically significant associations between CHD and occupational mobility, educational mobility, or status incongruity for the overall sample of men and women in various age groups. In addition, one study has recently reported an absence of deleterious health consequences associated with rapid social change. In this study of oil development in the Shetland Islands (Suzman, Voorhees-Rosen, & Rosen, 1980), residents exposed to massive economic and industrial changes did not experience an increase in mental or physical illnesses. It was suggested in this study that such changes need not lead to ill health if the community is well integrated prior to change, if the changes are anticipated and planned for, and if the changes bring more benefits than deficits.

A major test of the hypothesis of sociocultural mobility was undertaken in the study of Japanese migrants to the United States (Syme, Marmot, Kagan, Kato, & Rhoads, 1975). In that project, Japanese were studied in Japan, Hawaii, and California, using comparable study methods. A gradient in CHD morbidity (Marmot, Syme, Kagan, Kato, Cohen, & Belsky, 1975) and mortality (Worth, Kato, Rhoads, Kagan, & Syme, 1975) was observed in this group, with the lowest rates in Japan, with the highest rates in California, and with intermediate rates in Hawaii. This gradient was not explained by differences in these populations in serum cholesterol, diet, blood pressure, or cigarette-smoking patterns; thus, the major CHD risk factors did not account for most of the increase in CHD rates among migrants. However, in a special study of Japanese living in California (Marmot & Syme, 1976), two subpopulations were observed. One subpopulation, migrants who had adopted Western life styles and were considered "acculturated," had CHD rates 2.5 to 5 times higher than the second group of migrants, who had retained traditional Japanese ways. These data are shown in Figure 2.1. While acculturation was assessed in several ways in this study, the particular measure used in Figure 2.1 represents a combination of two items: (1) childhood upbringing, measured by determining whether the child was raised in traditional Japanese circumstances (including living in a Japanese neighborhood) and whether the child played with Japanese friends and attended Japanese language schools; and (2) adult commitment to the Japanese community, assessed by determining whether the person chose a Japanese doctor, lawyer, and dentist when such professional services were required.

Findings from the Japanese-American study suggest that mobility per se does not increase CHD rates, since those migrants who retained Japanese life styles exhibited rates very similar to those of Japanese living in Japan. Thus, this group of migrants seemed relatively immune from the effects of sociocultural mobility, even though they experienced a major change in geographic and cultural circumstances.

The ways in which sociocultural mobility might affect the incidence of

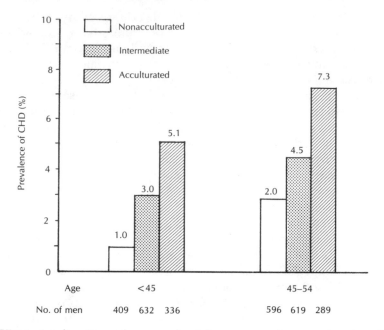

FIGURE 2.1. Acculturation and coronary heart disease among Japanese-Americans living in California. (Adapted from Marmot, M. G., & Syme, S. L. Acculturation and coronary heart disease in Japanese-Americans. *American Journal of Epidemiology*, 1976, 104, 225–247.)

disease is not clear. Few data are available as to whether disease risks increase because of the changes necessitated by mobility, because of the situation into which the mobile person moves, or because of characteristics predisposing certain persons to become mobile. The Japanese data suggest that mobility by itself is not a major factor.

One study has been done, however, indicating that change can influence disease rates even when individuals remain in place. Tyroler and Cassel (1964) studied the trend of mortality rates among residents of rural counties in North Carolina as some of these counties became urbanized. They found that CHD mortality rates increased among the residents of those counties that had experienced the most urbanization. Two possible explanations for this finding—differences in diagnostic custom with increasing urbanization, and selective migration—were shown to be unlikely. One interpretation of these findings is that rates of disease can increase when social change occurs, even though people stay put.

Clearly, the links between sociocultural mobility and disease are complex and require further study. Nonetheless, it seems reasonable to conclude that sociocultural mobility is somehow involved in disease etiology. The majority of studies done suggest a consistent increase of disease rate associated with occupational, geographic, intergenerational, and situational mobility. No one of these studies is flawless. Nevertheless, the overall pattern of findings is impressive, because many different investigators have independently come up with similar findings, even though they have used different approaches and methods in different population groups. Exceptions to the pattern have been noted. These exceptions represent either differences due to study methodology or serious contradictions that challenge the hypothesis. Only continued study will shed light on this question.

Type A Behavior Pattern

A second major theme that has emerged concerns the relationship between a particular behavior pattern (Type A) and CHD. This behavior pattern is said to be exhibited by individuals engaged in a relatively chronic and excessive struggle to obtain an unlimited number of things from the environment in the shortest period of time and/or against the opposing efforts of other persons or things (Dembroski, 1977).

For over 20 years, Friedman, Rosenman, Jenkins, Brand, and their colleagues have published a series of papers showing an increased rate of CHD among men characterized by this behavior pattern. The most compelling evidence from this group is based on the study of 3,524 men in the Western Collaborative Group Study (WCGS). This study is a prospective investigation and involves an 8½-year follow-up of these men. In this project (Rosenman, Brand, Jenkins, Friedman, Straus, & Wurm, 1975), it was found that men with Type A behavior pattern were found to have experienced twice as much CHD as those without it had, as shown in Table 2.1. In a multiple-

TABLE 2.1. Behavior Pattern and Coronary Heart Disease after 8½-Year Follow-Up

AGE	BEHAVIOR PATTERN	TOTAL SUBJECTS	SUBJECTS WITH CHD	CHD RATE[a]
39–49	Type A	1,067	95	10.5*
	Type B	1,182	50	5.0
50–59	Type A	552	83	18.7*
	Type B	383	29	8.9

Note. Adapted from Rosenman, R. H., Brand, R. J., Jenkins, C. D., Friedman, M., Straus, R., & Wurm, M. Coronary heart disease in the Western Collaborative Group Study: Final follow-up experience of 8½ years. *Journal of the American Medical Association*, 1975, 233, 872–877.

[a]Average annual rate per 1,000 subjects at risk.

*$p < .001$.

logistic analysis of these data (Brand, 1978), Type A subjects were seen to have a CHD risk 2.37 times the risk of Type B subjects before adjustment for other risk factors. When major CHD risk factors (age, systolic blood pressure, cigarette smoking, and serum cholesterol) were taken into account simultaneously, the estimated relative risk was reduced to 1.97. Thus, the apparent relative risk of about 2 persists after adjustment for these risk factors. Results from the Framingham Study, using a different method of assessing the behavior pattern, are generally consistent with results from the WCGS (Haynes et al., 1978). In that investigation, however, Type A behavior was significantly associated with CHD among men and women in the 45- to 64-year age group, but not among older age groups.

Many other studies have been done that tend to implicate striving, diligence, ambition, and perfectionism as risk factors for CHD (Jenkins, 1971, 1978). However, almost all of these studies were done on persons who already had CHD, and it has not been clear whether the behavior pattern preceded or followed the occurrence of disease. However, this problem of time sequence is not involved in findings from the two prospective studies that have been done, and far greater confidence can be placed in their data.

Some have criticized research on the Type A behavior pattern, because much of it is based on the use of a relatively subjective clinical interview to determine the pattern. It is true that behavior pattern interviewers are required to use considerable judgment in evaluating individual responses to specific questions; interviewers must undergo special training to learn the technique. Several approaches have been attempted to develop more objective assessment methods, including a self-administered questionnaire (Jenkins, Zyzanski, & Rosenman, 1971) and a laboratory-administered performance test (Bortner & Rosenman, 1967), but only the questionnaire is considered to be useful in yielding data approximately equivalent to that of the interview.

In spite of these methodological concerns, it is impressive that a relatively simple classification of people into two behavioral types permits the subsequent prediction of CHD, independently of other recognized risk factors. These results clearly suggest that something of importance is going on. The next research challenge is to gain increased understanding of the psychological and personality attributes of the Type A behavior pattern, as well as of the biological mechanisms linking the behavior to the occurrence of CHD. Of further interest will be the study of the Type A behavior pattern in relation to other disease outcomes, in addition to CHD.

Almost all of the research done on the Type A pattern has been done among employed, middle-class white men living in Western industrialized countries (including Australia, the Netherlands, Israel, and Sweden). It has been suggested that enhanced understanding of the behavior pattern would be gained if it were studied among men and women living in other sociocultural circumstances and environments (Dembroski, 1977; Review Panel on Coronary-Prone Behavior and Coronary Heart Disease, 1981). One such study, done by Cohen and colleagues (Cohen, Syme, Jenkins, Kagan, & Syzanski, 1979) among Japanese-Americans living in Hawaii, is quite instructive in this regard. In that study, Type A behavior as measured by the Jenkins Activity Survey (JAS) was only moderately related to the occurrence of CHD. The JAS had been developed in the WCGS (Jenkins *et al.*, 1971) and included three independent dimensions of Type A behavior: (1) hard-driving and competitive behavior, (2) job involvement, and (3) speed and impatience. In the Japanese-American cohort, these factors were no longer independent. A new factor analysis revealed three different dimensions: (1) hard-driving, competitive behavior, together with speed and impatience; (2) job involvement; and (3) hard-working behavior. Factor 1 represents a more Westernized competitive style, while the other two are composites of Western Type A behavior, together with the Japanese response (i.e., strong job commitment and an emphasis on hard work for its own sake).

An examination of Type A behavior in this new cultural setting makes it possible to see that certain aspects of the behavior pattern are simply reflections of Western life styles. In the Japanese cohort, it is easier to see that competitive, hard-driving, impatient behavior is more closely related to CHD than are hard work and job commitment. These latter behaviors are valued in the Japanese community in their own right and do not necessarily imply an ambitious, competitive orientation, as might be true in more Western settings. These findings are shown in Figure 2.2, where the relationship of these three new factors and CHD are analyzed in relation to extent of Westernization. In this figure, it can be seen that those Japanese men who scored highest on the most "Western" dimension of Type A behavior—the hard-driving, competitive, speed-and-impatience dimension—had higher rates of CHD than did men who scored high on the more traditionally Japanese dimensions. It can be seen also that men who exhibited this most Westernized aspect of Type A behavior and who were most Westernized in other life styles had the highest rates of CHD.

Studies of the Type A behavior pattern in other sociocultural circumstances might provide additional understanding. Thus, one aspect of the behavior pattern might be related to CHD in a particular population group, while other aspects might not be. If studies of this kind were done among women, among persons in lower socioeconomic groups, and among other racial and ethnic groups, it might be possible to observe an aspect of the behavior pattern that is common to all groups. In a way, this approach might lead to the detection of an "essence" of Type A behavior, independent of cultural embellishments.

Stressful Life Events

A third theme now emerging in the sociocultural literature concerns the relationship of "stressful life events" to the etiology of disease. Holmes and Rahe (1967) have developed a Social Readjustment Rating Scale to record

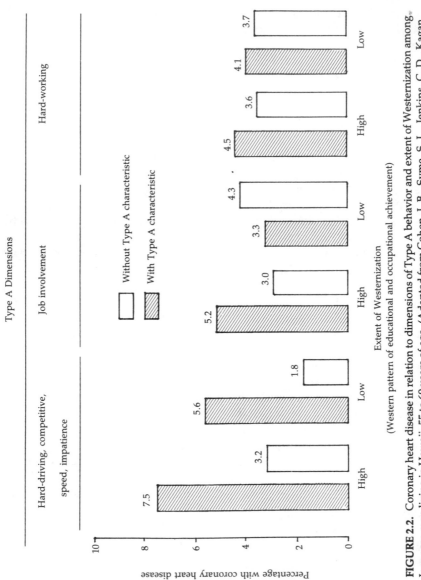

FIGURE 2.2. Coronary heart disease in relation to dimensions of Type A behavior and extent of Westernization among Japanese men living in Hawaii, 55 to 69 years of age. (Adapted from Cohen, J. B., Syme, S. L., Jenkins, C. D., Kagan, A., & Syzanski, S. J. Cultural context of Type A behavior and risk for CHD: A study of Japanese-American males. *Journal of Behavioral Medicine*, 1979, 2, 375–384.)

such life events as change in residence, injury, job changes, death of loved ones, and birth of children. Over the years, various suggestions have been offered to refine this scale and increase its usefulness (Dohrenwend & Dohrenwend, 1974). From the use of the scale in one form or another, a relatively large body of data has developed that suggests an association between a wide variety of life events and a broad array of disease outcomes, including eczema, tuberculosis, CHD, childhood illnesses, and complications of pregnancy. Much of this research, however, has been retrospective: Persons who have already experienced an illness are asked to identify stressful life events within a year or so prior to their illness. People who have become ill often attempt a retrospective reconstruction of past events to explain their current situation. It is possible that these people would be more likely than healthy persons would be to recall and report life events to account for their state of ill health.

Prospective studies of life events and illness have been reported by Parens, McConville, and Kaplan (1966); Thurlow (1971); Spilken and Jacobs (1971); and Rahe, Mahan, and Arthur (1970). However, most of these studies deal with the incidence of relatively minor diseases (such as upper respiratory infections, gastrointestinal upset, and skin problems) among people who have come to physicians for help. The people who have been studied in these investigations generally have been willing to seek help for conditions that clearly allow personal discretion. It may be that those motivated to report life event problems may also be more motivated to seek medical aid for such minor health problems. Thus, these prospective data showing a relationship between life events and illness may be more a function of illness reporting than of true differences in incidence rate.

These methodological problems are not an issue, however, in bereavement studies, such as that conducted by Parkes, Benjamin, and Fitzgerald (1969). In that research, the investigators followed 4,486 widowers, 55 years of age and older, for 9 years after the death of their wives. Of these men, 213 died during the first 6 months of bereavement, a rate 40% higher than would have been expected for married men of the same age. After the first 6 months, the mortality rate gradually fell to that of married men and remained at that lower level. Similar findings have been reported by Jacobs and Ostfeld (1977), Maddison and Viola (1968), and Rees and Lutkins (1967). Jacobs and Ostfeld (1977) conclude that the attributable risk of death for people losing spouses may be as high as 50%. There are studies that fail to show health consequences associated with bereavement, but most of these deal with small samples (Heyman & Gianturco, 1973; Parkes, 1970; Parkes & Brown, 1972) or, in one case, with an older group of bereaved people (Clayton, 1974). In general, the most impressive evidence regarding bereavement is found among males at younger ages, and among those experiencing unexpected widowhood. Other clear-cut life events that have been shown to be associated with subsequent illness include unemployment (Cobb & Kasl, 1977; Gore, 1978; Kasl & Cobb, 1970) and abnormalities of pregnancy (Gorsuch & Key, 1974; Nuckolls, Cassel, & Kaplan, 1972).

It seems reasonable to conclude from the available evidence that the experience of certain life events leads to an increased rate of disease. That this relationship does not fit a simple cause–effect model, however, is suggested by the work of Nuckolls *et al.* (1972). In that study, complications of pregnancy and delivery were studied among 107 white married primiparae of similar age and social class, all of whom were delivered in the same medical facility. Women reported on life changes both before and during pregnancy, as well as on the presence or absence of social supports. Among women who experienced both (1) low social support and (2) high life changes before and during pregnancy, 90% had one or more complications of pregnancy. As shown in Figure 2.3, all other groups of women experienced far lower rates of complications, ranging from a low of 33% to a high of 56%. It may be hoped that continued research on life events will be directed toward a clearer specification of intervening links in the causal chain, as well as to the study of biological mechanisms that connect life changes to the occurrence of disease.

A NEW DIRECTION FOR RESEARCH ON SOCIOCULTURAL FACTORS

Three sets of empirical evidence have been presented to illustrate ways in which sociocultural factors can influence the etiology of disease. The three themes selected do not exhaust the data available on this topic, but they do

FIGURE 2.3. Complications of pregnancy by life change score and level of social support. (Adapted from Nuckolls, K. B., Cassel, J., & Kaplan, B. H. Psychosocial assets, life crises, and the prognosis of pregnancy. *American Journal of Epidemiology*, 1972, *95*, 431–441.)

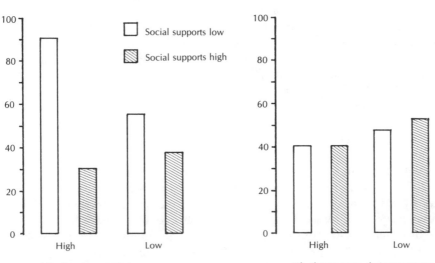

represent an increasingly important body of evidence. In thinking about the direction that future research ought to take, therefore, it certainly is reasonable to suggest that more work be done to clarify or specify the concepts of sociocultural mobility, Type A behavior pattern, and stressful life events. Some suggestions have already been offered regarding needed research on these topics. However, the evidence accumulated to date also suggests another alternative to guide future research.

Cassel (1976), in a classic paper, has noted the diverse disease consequences associated with alterations in social environment. He noted that this phenomenon characterized people who developed tuberculosis, schizophrenia, or alcoholism, or who had numerous accidents or committed suicide. He suggested that the common denominator underlying all of these circumstances was that these individuals had been "deprived of meaningful social contact." Cassel expressed surprise that others had not previously observed this wide variety of outcomes associated with similar life circumstances. He felt that this was probably due to the fact that each investigator was concerned with one disease entity, so that common features tended to be overlooked.

The concept of "deprivations of meaningful social contact" can also be seen as an underlying common denominator for all of the evidence presented here. Thus, changes in job or residence certainly involve interruptions in social relationships, as do virtually all other forms of mobility. Most of the items contained in the inventory of "stressful life events" (e.g., death of loved ones, job loss, divorce) involve disruptions of this kind. It also seems reasonable to suggest that those persons characterized as exhibiting Type A behavior experience less meaningful social contact. Rosenman (1979) has indicated that persons with this behavior pattern probably devote less time to the cultivation and maintenance of interpersonal relationships, since the establishment and continuation of such relationships requires substantial energy and commitment, the investment of which may be regarded as "unproductive" by Type A persons.

The hypothesis that meaningful social contacts are related to the etiology of disease was recently tested in a study of residents of Alameda County, California (Berkman & Syme, 1979). In that investigation, an increased mortality rate was observed among persons previously identified as having fewer friends and social relationships. This study was conducted among a random sample of 6,928 adults whose mortality experience was monitored for 9 years following the baseline interview. Social ties were assessed in terms of marital status, contacts with friends and relatives, church membership, and organizational affiliations. As may be seen in Figure 2.4, those persons with more social ties had lower mortality rates than those with fewer ties had. This relationship existed in all age groups and for both sexes. The relative risks for these various age and sex groups ranged from 2.1 to 4.6. These relative risks were reduced after account had been taken of relative weight, cigarette smoking, alcohol consumption, physical activity, health practices, and health status at baseline, but still remained at between 2 to 3.

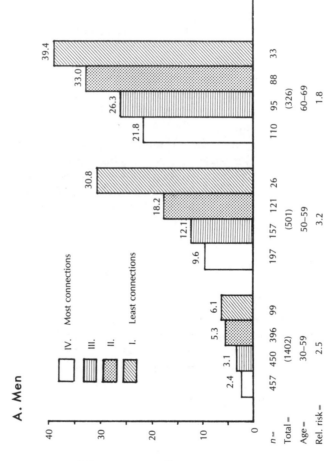

A. Men

Percentage died from all causes

	IV. Most connections
	III.
	II.
	I. Least connections

n =	457	450	396	99	197	157	121	26	110	95	88	33
Total =	(1402)				(501)				(326)			
Age =	30–59				50–59				60–69			
Rel. risk =	2.5				3.2				1.8			

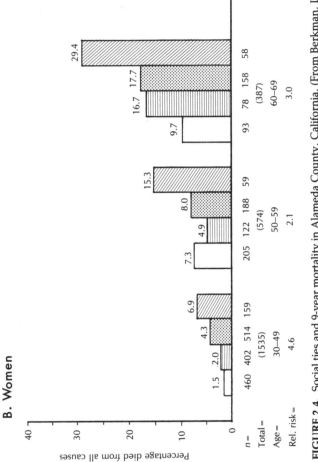

FIGURE 2.4. Social ties and 9-year mortality in Alameda County, California. (From Berkman, L. F., & Syme, S. L. Social networks, host resistance, and mortality: A nine year follow-up study of Alameda County residents. *American Journal of Epidemiology*, 1979, *109*, 186–204. Reprinted by permission.)

One of the most likely explanations for these findings is that people with fewer social ties at the time of interview were already sick and, for that reason, were less active socially and were more likely to die. This is a plausible hypothesis that was indirectly tested in two ways in the Alameda County data. First, it was found that those with fewer social ties did not in fact report more illnesses at the time of interview. This finding is not entirely convincing, however, since people were reporting about doctor-diagnosed diseases that had occurred at some time in the past. Second, it was reasoned that if those with fewer social ties were already ill, their higher death rates would be observed in the first year or two after the interview. In fact, the data revealed a higher death rate among those with fewer social ties throughout the entire 9-year follow-up period, with no excess in the first few years. These data, although indirect, suggest that ill health at the time of interview was not the explanation for the higher death rate observed among those with fewer social ties.

These findings from Alameda County have recently been replicated by House and his colleagues, studying the town of Tecumseh, Michigan (House, Robbins, & Metzner, 1982). In that study, 2,754 adults were studied in 1967–1969 and followed for 9 to 12 years. After adjustment for age and other relevant risk factors, men with more social relationships at baseline were significantly less likely to die during the follow-up period. Trends for women were similar but were not as striking. These findings not only provide independent support for the Alameda County results, but also provide new, stronger information regarding the influence of prior health status. In the Tecumseh study, all subjects were medically examined at the time of interview, and it was possible therefore to determine directly whether those with fewer social ties were already sicker. The findings were identical to those in Alameda County: The relationship between social ties and subsequent mortality was not due to preexisting illness.

As discussed previously, Japanese migrants to California exhibited lower rates of CHD when they retained traditional Japanese life styles, but it was not clear why this was so (Marmot & Syme, 1976). Traditional Japanese-Americans did not differ from more Westernized Japanese in their diets, smoking, blood pressure, or physical activity patterns. However, they had been raised as children in Japanese neighborhoods with Japanese friends, and as adults, they had maintained close ties to the Japanese community. It was reasoned that these Japanese might be enmeshed in a whole set of close and frequent relationships with family, friends, and others. Certainly, Japanese in Japan have much less job and residential mobility than Americans have, and they surely also experience fewer such life events as divorce and job loss. The maintenance of close social ties is of paramount value in Japanese culture, as is exemplified by the Japanese saying that "a rolling stone gathers no moss." In the United States, this saying is meant to convey the idea that a person "on the move" is more highly valued than a person "stuck in a rut." In Japan, the opposite meaning is intended. In Japan, moss is a highly treasured plant, and a stone with moss is highly regarded. The only way one can acquire moss (value) is to stay put and remain in place. It may be, therefore, that those Japanese-Americans in California who retained traditional life styles also had more intimate and meaningful social ties than those who had become more Westernized had. This possibility has recently been examined by Joseph (1980). In her study, Joseph found that those Japanese men who were most isolated had CHD twice as frequently as those with more social relationships did, even after the effect of other CHD risk factors (age, serum cholesterol, blood pressure, smoking, family history, and physical activity) had been removed.

It is always dangerous to search the literature in hopes of finding empirical support for a favored hypothesis. It is dangerous because it is virtually certain that such support will be found. Unfortunately, searches of this kind tend to give more important weight to findings that support the hypothesis and less weight to those that do not. Cassel's (1976) suggestion that disrupted social ties may be related to the etiology of disease was supported in Alameda County and is consistent with a substantial quantity of data on mobility, life events, and behavior patterns. This hypothesis certainly is consistent with data on the Japanese. It is also consistent with the fact that married persons have lower disease rates than those who are single, widowed, or divorced have (Ortmeyer, 1974). Looked at in this way, it may be said that the hypothesis of social ties provides a parsimonious explanation for a diverse set of empirical observations. Nevertheless, the only responsible conclusion that should be drawn from this recitation is that the concept of disrupted social ties is a plausible hypothesis that deserves further exploration and testing.

There are several key issues that should be addressed in future research on this hypothesis. One issue is to clarify the meaning of terms such as "social ties," "social supports," and "meaningful social contacts." It is possible to conceptualize these relationships in terms of (1) the number of contacts a person has; (2) whether or not these contacts are intimate or superficial; (3) whether they are important to the individual; and (4) whether they provide instrumental, informational, or emotional support (Satariano & Syme, 1981).

A second issue for future research is to develop a better understanding of the function that social relationships serve for people. The data suggest that people involved with other people have lower rates of disease; one implication from these data is that people somehow benefit from the presence of others. On the other hand, while it may be important for people to do something for an individual, it may also be important for that individual to do something for others. The work of Langer and Rodin (1976) among elderly persons in nursing homes underscores the possible importance for health of people taking responsibility themselves for aspects of their lives, rather than having them looked after by others. In that study, nursing home residents were assigned to two groups; both groups were alike on socioeconomic factors and on physical and psychological health status. Each of the first group of elderly persons was given the sole responsibility for looking after a plant; members of the other group also were given plants but were told that the staff would look after the plants for them. Eighteen months later, a lower mortality rate was observed among those who had responsibility for the plants: About half as many people in the "responsibility" group had died as in the other group. It may be hoped that future research will provide clarification of these and other dimensions of the concept of social ties as they affect health and disease. Antonovsky (1979) has explored this issue recently in great depth and with an imaginative approach.

One of the more useful ways of gaining such clarification is to gain a better understanding of the mechanisms linking social ties to disease processes. There are two general approaches to this issue. One approach is to view social ties and social supports as buffers or mediating agents between risk factors and disease. The second approach is to view disrupted social ties as risk factors themselves and as direct etiological agents. This is a complex issue that probably will not be resolved easily. However, it should be noted that the increase in disease rates associated with interrupted social ties involves a very diverse group of diseases and conditions. In the Alameda County project, all causes of death were higher among those with fewer social contacts. Married persons have lower rates of diseases for virtually all causes of death. The list of diseases associated with mobility and other life events is long and includes such different diseases and outcomes as CHD, cancer, infectious disease, sarcoidosis, schizophrenia, and accidents. It is possible that interrupted social ties affect host resistance to disease, increasing vulnerability to a wide range of pathological processes (Antonovsky, 1979; Cassel, 1976; Syme, 1967). In this perspective, whether a vulnerable person develops one or another specific disease would be dependent on the concurrent presence of disease-specific risk factors, including particular viruses, bacteria, serum lipids, air pollutants, cigarette smoking, and so on.

At the risk of oversimplifying a very complex issue, these concepts are graphically displayed in Figure 2.5. At the top of the figure are shown a variety of risk factors that impinge upon people. Some of these risk factors are ubiquitous, even though only some of us succumb to them and only occasionally. For example, Boyce and colleagues (Boyce, Jensen, Cassel, Collier, Smith, & Ramey, 1977) have reported that 30% of a school-age population can harbor group A streptococci without developing symptoms, that 75% of preschool children infected with *Mycoplasma pneumoniae* remain asymptomatic, and that as many as 42% of upper respiratory tract cultures from well children yield pneumococci. On the other hand, only some of us are exposed to other risk factors, such as air pollution, toxic industrial wastes, and so on. Whether risk factors are always present or only occasionally so, most disease risk factors only infrequently result in disease, suggesting that variations in host

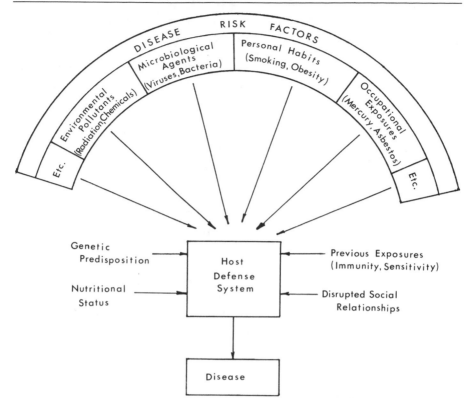

FIGURE 2.5. Hypothetical relationship among risk factors, host resistance, and disease.

susceptibility mediate the risk factor–disease relationship. Of course, some risk factors are so overwhelming that people exposed to them will almost always become ill. If a measles virus were introduced into a population that had not previously been exposed to it, almost everyone would get measles.

Also shown in the figure are some of the factors that may influence host resistance. While precise knowledge of these factors remains primitive, it is suggested that factors such as those listed influence the body's defense system, either favorably or unfavorably. While there seems little doubt that genetic factors influence immunological functioning, it seems clear also that other factors must be considered. Thus, the research evidence shows that disease occurs in a given individual in relation to specific changes in life style and circumstance, even when that person's genetic makeup remains unchanged. It is suggested that disease occurs when (1) a disease risk factor is present and (2) the body's defense system to that factor is compromised. The specific disease that results from this interaction may be a function of the particular risk factor present and of the way the body's defense system deals with the challenge.

This two-stage model of disease etiology has two advantages: (1) It accounts for the fact that certain psychosocial and sociocultural factors seem related to so many different diseases involving many organ systems, and (2) it accounts for the fact that most disease-specific risk factors have only a modest relationship to specific diseases.

Enhanced understanding of the mechanisms linking social ties to disease will be of great value in clarifying the meaning and possible importance of the concept of social ties. Whether social ties affect disease processes directly or indirectly, or whether they are involved in a two-stage etiological model, is an important issue that deserves specific and focused attention.

SUMMARY

Systematic, patterned differences in disease rates exist among population groups. These differences in rates are most usefully explained by studying differences in group characteristics. Many of these differences involve sociocultural factors. Of all the research done on the relation of sociocultural factors to disease etiology, three themes can be identified that are supported by a relatively large body of consistent empirical evidence. These themes are sociocultural mobility, behavior patterns, and stressful life events. A common denominator underlying these themes may be the concept of disrupted social ties. Future research should be directed toward clarification of this concept and of the mechanisms linking it to disease etiology.

R E F E R E N C E S

Antonovsky, A. *Health, stress, and coping: New perspectives on mental and physical well-being.* San Francisco: Jossey-Bass, 1979.

Bakker, C. B., & Levinson, R. M. Determinance of angina pectoris. *Psychosomatic Medicine,* 1967, *29,* 621–633.

Berkman, L. F., & Syme, S. L. Social networks, host resistance, and mortality: A nine year follow-up study of Alameda County residents. *American Journal of Epidemiology,* 1979, *109,* 186–204.

Bortner, R. W., & Rosenman, R. H. Measurement of Pattern A behavior. *Journal of Chronic Diseases,* 1967, *20,* 525–533.

Boyce, W. T., Jensen, E. W., Cassel, J. C., Collier, A. M., Smith, A. H., & Ramey, C. T. Influence of life events and family routines on childhood respiratory tract illness. *Pediatrics,* 1977, *60,* 609–615.

Brand, R. J. Coronary prone behavior as an independent risk factor for coronary heart disease. In T. M. Dembroski, S. M. Weiss, J. L. Shields, S. G. Haynes, & M. Feinleib (Eds.), *Coronary-prone behavior.* New York: Springer-Verlag, 1978.

Bruhn, J. G., Chandler, B., Miller, M. C., Wolf, S., & Lynn, T. N. Social aspects of coronary heart disease in two adjacent ethnically different communities. *American Journal of Public Health,* 1966, *56,* 1493–1506.

Caffrey, B. A multivariate analysis of sociopsychological factors in monks with myocardial infarctions. *American Journal of Public Health,* 1970, *60,* 452–458.

Cassel, J. The contribution of the social environment to host resistance. *American Journal of Epidemiology,* 1976, *104,* 107–123.

Cassel, J., & Tyroler, H. A. Epidemiological studies of cultural change: I. Health status and recency of industrialization. *Archives of Environmental Health,* 1961, *3,* 25–33.

Clayton, P. J. Mortality and morbidity in the first year of widowhood. *Archives of General Psychiatry,* 1974, *30,* 747–750.

Cobb, S., & Kasl, S. V. *Termination: The consequences of job loss* (DHEW Publication No. (NIOSH) 77-224). Washington, D.C.: U.S. Government Printing Office, 1977.

Cohen, J. B., Syme, S. L., Jenkins, C. D., Kagan, A., & Syzanski, S. J. Cultural context of Type A behavior and risk for CHD: A study of Japanese-American males. *Journal of Behavioral Medicine,* 1979, *2,* 375–384.

Dembroski, T. M. (Ed.). *Proceedings of the Forum on Coronary-Prone Behavior* (DHEW Publication No. (NIH) 78-1451). Washington, D.C.: U.S. Government Printing Office, 1977.

Dohrenwend, B. S., & Dohrenwend, B. P. *Stressful life events: Their nature and effects.* New York: Wiley-Interscience, 1974.

Durkheim, E. *[Suicide: A study in sociology]* (G. Simpson, Ed. and trans.). Glencoe, Ill.: Free Press, 1951.

Feinleib, M., Garrison, R. J., Fabsitz, R., Christian, J. C., Hrubec, Z., Borhani, N. O., Kannel, W. B., Rosenman, R., Schwartz, J. T., & Wagner, J. O. The NHLBI twin study of cardiovascular disease risk factors: Methodology and summary of results. *American Journal of Epidemiology,* 1977, *106,* 284–295.

Gore, J. The effect of social support in moderating the health consequences of unemployment. *Journal of Health and Social Behavior,* 1978, *19,* 157–165.

Gorsuch, R. L., & Key, M. K. Abnormalities of pregnancy as a function of anxiety and life stress. *Psychosomatic Medicine,* 1974, *36,* 352–362.

Haenszel, W., Loveland, D. B., & Sirken, M. G. Lung-cancer mortality as related to residence and smoking histories: I. White males. *Journal of the National Cancer Institute,* 1962, *28,* 947–1001.

Haynes, S. G., Levine, S., Scotch, M., Feinleib, M., & Kannel, W. B. The relationship of psychosocial factors to coronary heart disease in the Framingham Study: II. Prevalence of coronary heart disease. *American Journal of Epidemiology,* 1978, *107,* 384–402.

Heyman, D. K., & Gianturco, D. T. Long-term adaptation by the elderly to bereavement. *Journal of Gerontology,* 1973, *28,* 359–362.

Hinkle, L. E., Whitney, L. H., Lehman, E. W., Dunn, J., Benjamin, B., King, R., Plakum, A., & Flehinger, B. Occupation, education and coronary heart disease. *Science,* 1968, *161,* 238–246.

Holmes, T. H., & Rahe, R. H. The Social Readjustment Rating Scale. *Journal of Psychosomatic Research,* 1967, *11,* 213–218.

House, J. S., & Jackman, M. F. Occupational stress and health. In P. I. Ahmed & G. V. Coelho (Eds.), *Towards a new definition of health.* New York: Plenum, 1979.

House, J. S., Robbins, C., & Metzner, H. L. The association of social relationships and activities with mortality: Prospective evidence from the Tecumseh Health Study. *American Journal of Epidemiology,* 1982, *116,* 123–140.

Inter-Society Commission for Heart Disease Resources. Primary prevention of the atherosclerotic diseases. *Circulation,* 1970, *42,* A55–A95.

Jacobs, S., & Ostfeld, A. An epidemiological review of the mortality of bereavement. *Psychosomatic Medicine,* 1977, *39,* 344–357.

Jenkins, C. D. Psychologic and social precursors of coronary disease. *New England Journal of Medicine,* 1971, *284,* 244–255, 307–317.

Jenkins, C. D. Behavioral risk factors in coronary artery disease. *Annual Review of Medicine,* 1978, *29,* 543–562.

Jenkins, C. D., Zyzanski, S. J., & Rosenman, R. H. Progress toward validation of a computer-scored test for the Type A coronary-prone behavior pattern. *Psychosomatic Medicine,* 1971, *33,* 193–202.

Joseph, J. G. *Social affiliation, risk factor status and coronary heart disease: A cross-sectional study of Japanese American men.* Unpublished doctoral dissertation, University of California, Berkeley, 1980.

Kaplan, B. H., Cassel, J. C., Tyroler, H. A., Cornoni, J. C., Kleinbaum, D. G., & Hames, C. G. Occupational mobility and coronary heart disease. *Archives of Internal Medicine*, 1971, *128*, 938–942.

Kasl, S. V., & Cobb, S. Blood pressure changes in men undergoing job loss: A preliminary report: *Psychosomatic Medicine*, 1970, *32*, 19–38.

Langer, E. J., & Rodin, J. The effects of choice and enhanced personal responsibility for the aged: A field experiment in an institutional setting. *Journal of Personality and Social Psychology*, 1976, *34*, 191–198.

Lehman, E. W. Social class and coronary heart disease: A sociological assessment of the medical literature. *Journal of Chronic Diseases*, 1967, *20*, 381–391.

MacMahon, B., & Pugh, T. F. *Epidemiology: Principles and methods.* Boston: Little, Brown, 1970.

Maddison, D., & Viola, A. The health of widows in the year following bereavement. *Journal of Psychosomatic Research*, 1968, *12*, 297–306.

Marks, R. U. Factors involving social and demographic characteristics: A review of empirical findings. *Milbank Memorial Fund Quarterly*, 1967, *45*, 51–108.

Marmot, M. G., & Syme, S. L. Acculturation and coronary heart disease in Japanese-Americans. *American Journal of Epidemiology*, 1976, *104*, 225–247.

Marmot, M. G., Syme, S. L., Kagan, A., Kato, H., Cohen, J. B., & Belsky, J. Epidemiological studies of coronary heart disease and stroke in Japanese men living in Japan, Hawaii and California: Prevalence of coronary and hypertensive heart disease and associated risk factors. *American Journal of Epidemiology*, 1975, *102*, 514–525.

Marmot, M., & Winkelstein, W., Jr. Epidemiologic observations on intervention trials for prevention of coronary heart disease. *American Journal of Epidemiology*, 1975, *101*, 177–181.

Morris, J. N., Heady, J. A., Raffle, P. A. B., Roberts, C. G., & Park, J. W. Coronary heart disease and physical activity of work. *Lancet*, 1953, *ii*, 1053–1057.

Morris, J. N., Heady, J. A., & Raffle, P. A. B. Physique of London busmen: Epidemiology of uniforms. *Lancet*, 1956, *ii*, 569–570.

Nuckolls, K. B., Cassel, J., & Kaplan, B. H. Psychosocial assets, life crises, and the prognosis of pregnancy. *American Journal of Epidemiology*, 1972, *95*, 431–441.

Ortmeyer, C. E. Variations in mortality, morbidity and health care by marital status. In C. E. Erhardt & J. E. Berlin (Eds.), *Mortality and morbidity in the United States.* Cambridge, Mass.: Harvard University Press, 1974.

Parens, H., McConville, B. J., & Kaplan, S. M. Prediction of frequency of illness from the response to separation: A preliminary study and replication attempt. *Psychosomatic Medicine*, 1966, *28*, 162–176.

Parkes, C. M. The first year of bereavement: A longitudinal study of the reaction of London widows to the death of their husbands. *Psychiatry*, 1970, *33*, 440–467.

Parkes, C. M., Benjamin, B., & Fitzgerald, R. G. Broken heart: A statistical study of increased mortality among widowers. *British Medical Journal*, 1969, *i*, 740–743.

Parkes, C. M., & Brown, R. J. Health after bereavement: A controlled study of young Boston widows and widowers. *Psychosomatic Medicine*, 1972, *34*, 449–461.

Rahe, R. H., Mahan, J. L., & Arthur, R. J. Prediction of near-future health change from subjects' preceding life changes. *Journal of Psychosomatic Research*, 1970, *14*, 401–406.

Rees, W. D., & Lutkins, S. J. Mortality of bereavement. *British Medical Journal*, 1967, *iv*, 13–16.

Review Panel on Coronary-Prone Behavior and Coronary Heart Disease. Coronary-prone behavior and coronary heart disease: A critical review. *Circulation*, 1981, *63*, 1199–1215.

Rosenman, R. H. Personal communication, 1979.

Rosenman, R. H., Brand, R. J., Jenkins, C. D., Friedman, M., Straus, R., & Wurm, M. Coronary heart disease in the Western Collaborative Group Study: Final follow-up experience of 8½ years. *Journal of the American Medical Association*, 1975, *233*, 872–877.

Satariano, W. A., & Syme, S. L. Life changes and diseases in elderly populations: Coping with change. In J. L. McGaugh & S. B. Kiesler (Eds.), *Aging: Biology and behavior*. New York: Academic Press, 1981.

Shekelle, R. B., Ostfeld, A. M., & Paul, O. Social status and incidence of coronary heart disease. *Journal of Chronic Diseases*, 1969, *22*, 381–394.

Smith, R. Factors involving sociocultural incongruity and change: A review of empirical findings. *Milbank Memorial Fund Quarterly*, 1967, *45*, 23–37.

Spilken, A. Z., & Jacobs, M. A. Prediction of illness behavior from measures of life crisis, manifest distress and maladaptive coping. *Psychosomatic Medicine*, 1971, *33*, 251–264.

Susser, M. *Causal thinking in the health sciences: Concepts and strategies of epidemiology*. New York: Oxford University Press, 1973.

Suzman, R. Z., Voorhees-Rosen, D. J., & Rosen, D. H. *The impact of North Sea oil development on mental and physical health: A longitudinal study of the consequences of an economic boom and rapid social change*. Paper presented at the annual meeting of the American Sociological Association, New York, 1980.

Syme, S. L. Implications and future prospects. *Milbank Memorial Fund Quarterly*, 1967, *45*, 175–180.

Syme, S. L., Borhani, M. O., & Buechley, R. W. Cultural mobility and coronary heart disease in an urban area. *American Journal of Epidemiology*, 1965, *82*, 334–346.

Syme, S. L., Hyman, M. M., & Enterline, P. E. Some social and cultural factors associated with the occurrence of coronary heart disease. *Journal of Chronic Diseases*, 1964, *17*, 277–289.

Syme, S. L., Marmot, M. G., Kagan, A., Kato, H., & Rhoads, G. Epidemiologic studies of coronary heart disease and stroke in Japanese men living in Japan, Hawaii and California: Introduction. *American Journal of Epidemiology*, 1975, *102*, 477–480.

Syme, S. L., & Torfs, C. P. Epidemiologic research in hypertension: A critical appraisal. *Journal of Health and Human Stress*, 1978, *4*, 43–48.

Terris, M., & Chaves, A. D. An epidemiological study of sarcoidosis. *American Review of Respiratory Disease*, 1966, *94*, 50–55.

Thurlow, H. J. Illness in relation to life situation and sick-role tendency. *Journal of Psychosomatic Research*, 1971, *15*, 73–88.

Tyroler, H. A., & Cassel, J. Health consequences of culture change: II. Effect of urbanization on coronary heart mortality in rural residents. *Journal of Chronic Diseases*, 1964, *17*, 167–177.

Williams, C. A. *The relationship of occupational change to blood pressure, serum cholesterol and specific overt behavior patterns*. Unpublished doctoral dissertation, University of North Carolina at Chapel Hill, 1968.

Worth, R. M., Kato, H., Rhoads, G. G., Kagan, A., & Syme, S. L. Epidemiologic studies of coronary heart disease and stroke in Japanese men living in Japan, Hawaii and California: Mortality. *American Journal of Epidemiology*, 1975, *102*, 481–490.

CHAPTER 3

Personality, Behavior Patterns, and Physical Illness: Conceptual and Methodological Issues

David S. Krantz
Uniformed Services University of the Health Sciences

David C. Glass
State University of New York at Stony Brook

INTRODUCTION AND HISTORICAL BACKGROUND

The notion that personality traits and psychological characteristics play a role in the etiology of physical disease has its roots in pre-Cartesian medicine and philosophy (Alexander, 1950; McMahon, 1976). Early physicians believed that intense emotions had the potential to produce acute imbalances in bodily function, which culminated in various forms of organ pathology. In the first half of this century, emphasis was placed on the role of chronic emotional conflicts in the etiology of physical disorders (Alexander, 1939). Based on observations of clinical groups, correlations between particular diseases and personality types were described. Dunbar (1943), for example, reported striking psychological similarities among patients suffering from the same organic disease. These similarities were formulated into a series of personality profiles, and characteristic types were linked to specific disorders, such as coronary heart disease (CHD), peptic ulcer, arthritis, and asthma. Other trait approaches (e.g., G. L. Engel, 1968; Nemiah, Freyberger, & Sifneos, 1976; Schmale, 1958) subsequently suggested that certain dispositions, such as giving up, depression, and inability to express feelings, were related to general susceptibility to illness.

Concepts derived from work on the physiological effects of emotional states also fostered the notion that traits, coping dispositions, or personality factors could influence the development and course of disease (Alexander, 1950; Lipowski, 1977). Cannon (1929) noted that the sympathetic nervous system is activated in terms of "flight or fight," and that strong emotions such as anger, rage, or fear lead to increased cardiac output, enhanced muscle blood flow, and increased adrenomedullary activity. Early workers in psychosomatics proposed that these emotional tensions, if chronically elicited, might produce physical alterations that become manifest as organ diseases.

Considerable research has since been directed toward validating early psychosomatic hypotheses concerning the causal role of emotional dispositions and psychological characteristics in the etiology of illness. However, much of the early work in this area has been justifiably criticized for over-emphasizing the role of trait predispositions, without taking into account physiological, genetic, and situational factors that interact in predisposing an individual to a particular disorder (Weiner, 1977). This research was characterized by attempts to correlate or describe psychological factors that were associated with disease states. Psychological variables were often poorly defined and/or borrowed from psychodynamic theories of mental health. Moreover, few attempts were made to advance understanding beyond the correlational level by exploring basic mechanisms linking behavioral processes to disease states.

The scope of research relating psychological variables to disease states has since been expanded to place increased emphasis on events in the social environment, as well as on the physiological mechanisms linking psychosocial factors to the onset, course, and outcome of illness (Lipowski, 1977). Most current conceptions of mechanisms linking psychosocial stimuli to physical disorders in some way invoke the concept of stress as a precipitating factor. We use the term "stress" here in a psychological sense to refer to an internal state of the individual who is perceiving threats to physical and/or psychic well-being (Cox, 1978; Lazarus, 1966). There is increasing evidence that a number of different psychological processes mediate or modify the possible relationship between stress and disease, and that personality characteristics, including traits, coping dispositions, beliefs, and attitudes, constitute one important category of mediating variable. Other variables include biological factors (e.g., genetic susceptibility); aspects of the immediate context in which the stressor occurs (e.g., whether the stressor is perceived as controllable or uncontrollable); and various sociocultural factors (e.g., the amount of social support from other people and/or the health care system). Recent reviews by F. Cohen, Horowitz, Lazarus, Moos, Robins, Rose, and Rutter (1982), Krantz, Glass, Contrada, and Miller (1981), and the chapters in this volume by Lazarus and Folkman (Chapter 8) and Syme (Chapter 2) provide a comprehensive discussion of these issues.

The present chapter critically examines the literature on the role of personality traits and/or behavior patterns in physical illness. The review is, of necessity, selective and focuses on major conceptual and methodological issues. The reader is referred to Fox (1978), Graham (1972), Jenkins (1971, 1976), Matthews (1982), and Weiner (1977) for detailed reviews of the literature regarding specific diseases. We begin by presenting a conceptual outline of the ways in which personality characteristics have been related to disease processes. Next, we discuss several major psychological formulations that have been proposed to account for these relationships. The chapter then directs special attention to the literature linking traits and behavior patterns to CHD, essential hypertension (EH), and cancer, since these disorders have been the subject of considerable research in recent years. Significant progress has been made in establishing the association between a behavior pattern called "Type A" and CHD; we therefore emphasize this area as an exemplar of research on behavior patterns and physical illness. The chapter concludes with a critique of issues and difficulties associated with the study of individual differences and illness, and with an outlook on directions for future investigation.

CONCEPTUAL APPROACHES

A number of perspectives have been taken in studying the relationship of personality to illness. These perspectives make different assumptions about the points in time at which personality traits influence disease processes, and about the mechanisms linking these psychological characteristics to illness. Most research presumes that traits play a causal role in illness; however, the effects of illness and/or factors associated with treatment on personality dispositions have also been examined.

Personality as a Causal Factor in Disease

Research assuming that personality plays a causal role in disease can be divided into two categories. The first category assumes that personality is causally involved in the etiology of disease before symptoms are manifest. Usually this implies that traits in some way are involved in producing pathogenic alterations in tissue function via neuroendocrine or other physiological responses.

A second approach places emphasis on the role of psychological factors on the course and outcome of illness once disease is manifest. Most research in this category conceptualizes illness as a stressor and presumes that the way in which the individual appraises and reacts to illness can mediate or affect the subsequent clinical course of disease. This model adopts the view that physiological reactions to the stress of illness are affected not only by biological factors such as general state of health, but also by psychosocial factors; these include the extent to which the individual views illness as threatening or harmful, and his or her felt ability to cope or take action to reduce the threat (F. Cohen & Lazarus, 1979; Krantz, Glass, Contrada, & Miller, 1981). Here again, it is assumed that the success or adequacy of coping can influence the course of illness by altering *physiological* processes involved in the progression of disease or recovery. However, psychological attributes might also influence the course of illness by altering *behavioral* reactions to illness; for example, individuals who use denial as a coping strategy may ignore physicians' advice or fail to comply with medical regimens.

Alternatives to a Causal Role for Personality

In contrast to viewing personality characteristics as causal in either the etiology and/or clinical course of illness, a third approach to personality and illness has been proposed. This approach minimizes or negates the causal role of personality; instead, factors associated with illness are thought to alter psychological attributes (Barofsky, 1981; Fox, 1978; Haney, 1977). These factors include characteristics of the treatment received, or experiences with the health care system. The notion that treatment experiences can affect personality is plausible, since much of the research linking traits and illness consists of cross-sectional and retrospective studies.

A related perspective presumes that a set of traits characterizes those individuals who are most likely to notice symptoms and/or to seek medical care. Therefore, associations between personality and certain illness categories are seen as resulting from factors involving symptom perception or the tendency to use health care facilities. This is in contrast to presuming that personality directly influences biological disease states. Still another perspective considers the fact that behaviorally relevant neurological, endocrine, and metabolic changes may occur even prior to the point that disease becomes manifest (Elias & Streeten, 1980; Shapiro, 1978; Sklar & Anisman, 1981). There is some evidence that these preclinical biological changes can affect psychological functioning; hence "premorbid" psychological traits may reflect underlying correlates of disease processes.

Within each of the categories described above, a number of formulations of trait–illness relationships have been proposed and subjected to empirical study. Several of the more prominent models and examples are discussed in the following sections of this chapter. Throughout our review, we refer to the three perspectives presented in this section as means for directing attention to some of the mechanisms that might link personality and related individual-difference variables to illness. The distinctions are also useful for making explicit the scope and assumptions of particular models of traits and disease.

PERSONALITY AND THE ETIOLOGY OF ILLNESS: MAJOR FORMULATIONS

Nuclear Conflict Theory

The "nuclear conflict theory" of Alexander and colleagues (e.g., Alexander, 1950) is an early and influential proposal that unconscious conflicts and the emotions they produce are associated with the onset of specific diseases. According to Alexander, the conflicts are involved both in predisposing an individual to a disorder and in the initiation of the disorder. Thus, when specific psychological conflicts are "activated" by precipitating situations, they generate such emotions as anger, depression, and anxiety. These emotions, in turn, result in autonomic and endocrine responses that serve to initiate the disease. Descriptions are proposed for distinct emotional conflicts presumably underlying a variety of psychosomatic or psychophysiological disorders, including asthma, duodenal ulcer, migraine headache, and EH. For example, suppressed rage and hostility are thought to underlie EH, and frustrated oral and dependency needs are viewed as the basis of duodenal ulcer.

Alexander was willing to consider that these latent conflicts could be present but remain unactivated by appropriate situations; similarly, particular conflicts might be expressed by different overt behaviors. However, the tendency was to describe the constellations of underlying conflicts in language conducive to the interpretation of these constellations as personality traits or types that are independent of eliciting situations. In addition, the psychodynamic descriptions of particular conflicts proposed by nuclear conflict theory are difficult to translate into standardized techniques of objective psychological assessment that could be subjected to rigorous testing by researchers.

Considered as a whole, only some aspects of Alexander's formulations have received support. For example, in a study of duodenal ulcer, Weiner, Thaler, Reiser, and Mirsky (1957) were able to identify individuals who were hypersecretors of serum pepsinogen (a substance thought to predispose individuals to duodenal ulcer) solely by means of a psychological test battery designed to tap concepts relevant to the "ulcer-prone" conflict. On the basis of this categorization, they could further identify those subjects who either had ulcers at the onset of the study or subsequently developed them.

However, nuclear conflict theory does not indicate the mechanisms by which a particular emotional state may be translated into pathophysiological processes predisposing to one disease, rather than another (Weiner, 1977). While it is possible to argue that some of Alexander's descriptive categories have been validated in controlled experimental studies, the ultimate utility of the theory must rest on its ability to account for psychophysiological processes that play a role in the etiology of disease. In this regard, nuclear conflict theory has proven less than satisfactory. Alexander's theory, like other approaches proposing that certain traits predispose individuals to specific disorders, must deal with the still unresolved question of whether different emotions are associated with specific patterns of physiological responses (Lang, 1979; Lang, Rice, & Sternbach, 1972).

The Specificity-of-Attitude Hypothesis

Graham and colleagues (Grace & Graham, 1952; Graham, 1972) have attempted to account for the development of disorders related to autonomic nervous system function by examining the *specific attitudes* of patients at the time of symptom appearance. These attitudes were originally obtained from clinical interviews centering on life situations associated with the time of occurrence of attacks of the patients' symptoms. This model is, therefore, relevant not only to etiology, but also to the clinical course and possibly to the progression of disease. Graham described specific attitudes—that is, statements about what patients felt was happening to them at the time of symptom onset and what they wanted to do about these difficulties. A series of interview studies with hospitalized patients (Grace & Graham, 1957; Graham, Lundy, Benjamin, Kabler, Lewis, Kunish, & Graham, 1962) was conducted to establish associations among 10 diseases (e.g., EH, asthma, duodenal ulcer, eczema, hyperthyroidism, rheumatoid arthritis, etc.) and particular attitudes. Table 3.1 presents a representative sample of these attitudes and the disease predicted to be associated with each.

The initial study by Grace and Graham (1952) was essentially descriptive in nature; it did not report the methodology or criteria used to deter-

TABLE 3.1. Psychophysiological Disorders and the Attitudes Said to Be Associated with Them

DISORDER	SPECIFIC ATTITUDE
Acne	The person feels he or she is being ''picked on'' and wants to be left alone.
Asthma	The individual feels left out, unloved, or ignored, and wants to screen out another individual or the situation, and not have anything to do with them.
Hypertension	The person feels threatened with being harmed by an ever-present danger. As a result, he or she feels the need to be on guard, and prepared to meet all threats.
Hives	There are feelings of taking a beating (or being mistreated) and being helpless to do anything about it.
Raynaud disease	The person wants to take some hostile physical action (such as hitting) but does not know what the actual act should be.
Migraine	The individual feels that something has to be accomplished or achieved or some goal reached. The person then relaxes after the effort is exerted.
Duodenal ulcer	The individual feels deprived of what is due him or her (i.e., what is owed or promised) and wants to seek revenge or get even.
Rheumatoid arthritis	The person feels tied down, restrained, or restricted and wants to restore freedom of movement.
Hyperthyroidism	The individual feels he or she might lose a loved person or object, and takes care to prevent such a loss by holding on or possessiveness.
Low back pain	The person wants to run away, walk out, or escape from the situation.

Note. Adapted from Graham, D. T., Lundy, R. M., Benjamin, L. S., Kabler, J. D., Lewis, W. C., Kunish, N. O., & Graham, F. K. Specific attitudes in initial interviews with patients having different ''psychosomatic'' diseases. *Psychosomatic Medicine*, 1962, 24, 257–266.

mine the link between these attitudes and the disorders or procedures (if any) used to guard against experimenter bias. A second validating study (Graham, Lundy, Benjamin, Kabler, Lewis, Kunish, & Graham, 1962) involved 20 patients with 10 diseases, as noted. Half were interviewed by an experimenter who was blind to the hypotheses, and the remaining 10 patients (matched for disease) were interviewed by an individual who was aware of the hypotheses. Edited transcripts of the interviews were submitted to a panel of judges, who indicated for each patient the three most applicable attitudes selected from a list of 18 attitudes submitted to the judges. The study reported that judges chose the predicted attitude at frequencies significantly above chance.

Several experimental studies were then conducted to test mechanisms presumed to mediate associations between attitudes and illness. In one study, attitudes supposedly linked to particular disorders were suggested to hypnotized subjects, while measures were taken of variables relevant to those disorders (Graham, Kabler, & Graham, 1962). For example, the hypertension attitude (see Table 3.1) was induced by giving subjects suggestions about ''being threatened by harm and needing to be on guard.'' Results indicated that this attitude was associated with an increase in diastolic pressure. In another study (Graham, Stern, & Winokur, 1958), hypnotized subjects were given suggestions of attitudes specific to hives or to Raynaud disease. In the case of Raynaud disease, the actual skin temperature is low; for hives, it is high. Results of the study indicated that manipulated attitudes produced the skin temperature changes appropriate to each disorder. However, a subsequent attempt by Peters and Stern (1971) to replicate these findings for hives and Raynaud disease was not successful. These investigators found that when subjects high in hypnotic susceptibility were hypnotized, the attitudes associated with both Raynaud disease and hives *both* produced a decrease in skin temperature.

Critiques of the specificity-of-attitude theory (Buss, 1966; Gatchel, Baum, & Lang, 1982; Mears & Gatchel, 1979) have noted that this approach is an improvement upon previous psychodynamic formulations in several ways. Specific attitudes can be operationalized, albeit with some difficulty; and dependent measures, such as psychophysiological responding to the induction of the attitudes, can be measured. However, as noted above, the evidence supporting the theory has been inconsistent. Furthermore, the notion that the large number of attitudes listed by Graham and colleagues will each be associated with a physiological response pattern relevant to the development of a unique disorder is difficult to accept without additional supporting data (Buss, 1966). This is particularly true since many investigators have encountered considerable difficulty in differentiating physiologically among subtle emotional states (e.g., depression, anxiety, anger; cf. Lacey, Kagan, Lacey, & Moss, 1963; Lang et al., 1972; Schachter & Singer, 1962).

The specificity-of-attitude theory also does not consider the role of biologically determined individual differences in physiological responses to similar emotional stimuli—a concept known as "individual-response stereotypy" (B. T. Engel & Bickford, 1961; Lacey, 1967). Thus, some individuals tend to respond in such a way that maximum activation occurs in the same physiological function (e.g., heart rate, blood pressure), even when the individuals are exposed to a variety of stressors and emotions (B.T. Engel & Bickford, 1961; Lacey & Lacey, 1958).

Helplessness–Hopelessness: The "Giving-Up-Given-Up Complex"

The approaches described so far propose that there are psychological traits that predispose individuals to specific physical disorders. In contrast, G. L. Engel, Schmale, and their coworkers (G. L. Engel, 1968; Schmale, 1972) have advanced a "generality" position, which argues that a set of psychological characteristics influences susceptibility to illnesses of many types. They propose that in individuals who are biologically predisposed, a variety of illnesses may occur in response to situations that involve psychological feelings of loss and/or bereavement. The psychological state of helplessness or hopelessness is described as a general precursor of illness. This state of helplessness, called the "giving-up-given-up complex," is said to involve a sense of psychological impotence and a feeling that one is unable to cope with changes in the environment. Although the occurrence of a loss situation is described as an external precipitating event, it seems that what is involved is the individual's perceived inability to cope in the face of negative events—hence the characterization of this helplessness model as a trait approach.

Most proponents of the helplessness–hopelessness approach acknowledge that this psychological state alone is not sufficient to result in illness; the person must be predisposed to disease (see reviews by F. Cohen, 1979; Weiner, 1977). However, there has not been extensive research documenting the physiological mechanisms or conditions that would constitute these biological predispositions. G. L. Engel and Schmale believe that prolonged states of helplessness and/or depression are accompanied by a "conservation–withdrawal reaction," characterized by a predominance of parasympathetic nervous system activity and relative sympathetic inactivity. Their notion is that the conservation–withdrawal reaction is an adaptive physiological mechanism that functions as a way of screening out an unfavorable external environment.

As presented by G. L. Engel and Schmale, the mechanisms involved in the giving-up-given-up response and their precise linkages to disease remain vaguely specified. Most of the evidence these investigators present is descriptive and anecdotal, and focuses on behavioral manifestations of helplessness rather than on physiological processes (G. L. Engel & Schmale, 1972). However, it has been noted that there is a literature on responses to separation, loss, and bereavement in humans and animals that is relevant to the Engel–Schmale hypothesis (cf. Weiner, 1977).

Associations of Bereavement and Disease

There are relatively few studies of morbidity following loss experiences, separation, or bereavement; moreover, many of these studies are either descriptive or subject to such methodological limitations as inadequate control groups. In those studies that are well controlled, measures of individual perceptions and attitudes are rare. Thus, the relevance of this research to the focus of this chapter—individual traits—is difficult to assess. In one retrospective study, Maddison and Viola (1968) found that widows reported an excess of minor symptoms, but there was little change reported in the severity or frequency of major diseases. Clayton (1974) found that widows reported increased grief-related psychological symptoms, but did not indicate more frequent visits to physicians.

Several morbidity and mortality studies have focused specifically on either cancer or CHD, rather than examining the incidence of a variety of disorders. Again, most of these studies are retrospective, and it is to be expected that patients with diagnosed serious illness would report increased expression of helplessness or hopelessness as a consequence of life-threatening disease (F. Cohen, 1979).

Studies of psychological antecedents of sudden coronary death provide some support for the helplessness–hopelessness hypothesis. Although research findings have produced contradictory results in this area (Jacobs & Ostfeld, 1977; Rowland, 1977; Stroebe, Stroebe, Gergen, & Gergen, 1981), it appears that death of a close relative increases the likelihood of death in next of kin, particularly as a result of coronary disease (Cottington, Matthews, Talbott, & Kuller, 1980; Parkes, Benjamin, & Fitzgerald, 1969). G. L. Engel (1971) reviewed anecdotal evidence and case studies suggesting that rejection by a loved one or a loss in self-esteem may sometimes precede sudden coronary death. Other evidence supportive of a helplessness–death relationship comes from a retrospective study of 26 male patients who died suddenly from CHD (Greene, Goldstein, & Moss, 1972). Data were obtained from medical records and from direct interviews with the surviving next of kin. Results indicated that up to 50% of the patients were reported to have had clinical symptoms of depression for periods varying from a week up to several months prior to death. A sudden state of arousal (either brought about by positive or negative emotions) would seem to have precipitated the acute coronary event in many cases.

Greene *et al.* (1972) and G. L. Engel (1971) suggest that the sequence of depression followed by acute arousal is most likely to lead to sudden death in individuals with advanced atherosclerotic heart disease. It is further suggested that rapid affective changes between depression and arousal are accompanied by shifts between parasympathetic and sympathetic effects on the heart, thereby precipitating arrhythmia and ventricular fibrillation.

Another recent study of patients who experienced cardiac arrhythmias revealed a high percentage of acute psychological disturbances during the 24 hours preceding the arrhythmic episodes (Reich, DeSilva, Lown, & Murawski, 1981). In contrast to the speculations of Greene et al. (1972), as well as data prevalent in the cardiology literature (e.g., Verrier, DeSilva, & Lown, 1983), regarding the presumed presence of underlying coronary artery disease as a predisposing factor, patients in the Reich et al. (1981) study who experienced antecedent psychological disturbances included a disproportionate number with no detectable coronary artery disease. It also was not clear that these acute stress situations specifically involved loss or helplessness; however, loss events were highly represented in the descriptions of the precipitating events given in the study. Relevant to this point, Luborsky, Doherty, and Penick (1973) have noted that the onset of symptoms in a broad range of physical disorders is preceded or accompanied by a variety of psychological symptoms and complaints. Therefore, it is not clear that feelings of helplessness per se rather than general psychological symptoms are unique precursors of the onset of illness.

Mechanisms Linking Helplessness and Disease

The Engel–Greene hypothesis proposes that feelings of loss and the grieving process are accompanied by pathophysiological processes inimical to general physical health. In support of this notion, psychological states of loss and bereavement have been shown to alter body biochemistry and possibly immune functions in a manner that could predispose individuals to disease. Consider, for example, studies of parents of leukemic children who were faced with the impending death of the children (Hofer, Wolff, Friedman, & Mason, 1972a, 1972b). Parents who coped with these impending losses by experiencing intense grief, sadness, distress, or guilt showed higher urinary levels of 17-hydroxy-corticosteroid than did those parents who were able to overcome their grief. Similarly, cortisol levels were shown to covary positively with states of depression and despair, and negatively with the effectiveness of coping, in women who were about to undergo breast biopsy (Katz, Ackman, Rothwax, Sachar, Weiner, Hellman, & Gallagher, 1970). Other recent reports (Schleifer, Keller, McKegney, & Stein, 1980) indicate that there are measurable alterations in immune function in individuals who are experiencing bereavement.

G. L. Engel (1971) and Greene et al. (1972) implicate rapid shifts in autonomic function between states of depression and arousal as mechanisms in the relationship between death of a significant other and sudden coronary death. However, several other mechanisms have been suggested. Some investigators (Jacobs & Ostfeld, 1977; Rowland, 1977; Stroebe et al., 1981) propose that a deceased significant other and a deceased subject may both have been exposed to the same unhealthy environment, or that they may both have been constitutionally unhealthy. Another explanation suggested by Matthews and colleagues (Cottington *et al.*, 1980) concerns the health-impairing changes in life style that occur during bereavement or, presumably, during states of helplessness or depression. Documented life style changes during bereavement include increased consumption of cigarettes, alcohol, and drugs (Maddison & Viola, 1968; Parkes & Brown, 1972).

We have noted that many of the studies designed to validate the help-lessness–hopelessness hypothesis may be criticized for their retrospective nature. A study of psychological correlates of cancer outcomes overcomes some of these problems. Schmale and Iker (1971) tested women about to undergo biopsy for cervical cancer because of prior evidence of suspicious cell growth derived from a Pap smear. These women, who showed no gross evidence of cervical disease at the time of testing, were interviewed and given standardized psychological tests before the results of their biopsies were known. Thus the problem of retrospective bias was minimized. Based on the interviews, patients were classified as high or low in hopelessness according to their reports of experiencing feelings of low self-esteem, inability to cope, or self-blame in the 6 months prior to the first (abnormal) Pap smear. Results indicated that about three-quarters of the women could be correctly categorized as having or not having cancer, based on interview classifications; women with diagnosed cervical cancer were classified as significantly higher in hopelessness. Psychological test results did not reveal significantly higher Minnesota Multiphasic Personality Inventory (MMPI) depression (*D*) scores or lower ego strength scores in the women with cancer, although trends in the expected direction were obtained for these measures.

Schmale and Iker (1971) did not present any evidence for physiological mechanisms that could mediate the association between psychological state and cancer diagnosis in women with precancerous cells. A complex literature (see Chapter 5 by Ader & Cohen, this volume) has subsequently demonstrated that psychological and behavioral stimuli, including states of bereavement and loss, are associated with alterations in immune processes that could conceivably affect cancer growth and progression. An adequate understanding of these presumed physiological mechanisms would require intensive examination of them in conjunction with the psychological states of helplessness reported by patients in the aforementioned study (see Schleifer *et al.*, 1980).

It has been noted (F. Cohen, 1979; Fox, 1978; Sklar & Anisman, 1981) that the study by Schmale and Iker (1971) may be more aptly considered as retrospective rather than predictive, since all subjects were initially diagnosed as having some abnormality. Data exist indicating that the pathological process in cancer may cause psychological changes, such as neurological and/or psychiatric symptoms, before the disease becomes clinically manifest (F.

Cohen, 1979; Davies, Quinlan, McKegney, & Kimball, 1973; Fox, 1978; Sklar & Anisman, 1981). The existence of these behavioral changes prior to or concurrent with the appearance of disease provides support for conceptual approaches (described in a later section) presuming that psychological trait differences among groups of patients may be secondary products of disease processes, rather than primary causal factors.

Two prospective studies have yielded results that would appear to contradict the pattern predicted by the Engel–Schmale hypothesis. Dattore, Shontz, and Coyne (1980) obtained MMPI records at a time when subjects were apparently healthy. Scores were then compared between a group of patients who subsequently developed a variety of cancers and a group of patients who developed other disorders, including EH, benign tumors, and ulcers. The results indicated that those who developed cancers scored *lower* on an MMPI D scale and *higher* on repression–sensitization (R–S). A 30-year prospective study (Gillum, Leon, Kamp, & Becerra-Aldama, 1980) found no relationship between MMPI scores and subsequent morbidity or mortality linked to cardiovascular problems, cancer, and other chronic diseases.

On the other hand, a third recent prospective study (Shekelle, Raynor, Ostfeld, Garron, Bieliauskas, Liu, Maliza, & Paul, 1981) found that increased MMPI D scores were positively associated with incidence of cancers in men during 17 years of follow-up. Moreover, this relationship persisted after the investigators controlled for known cancer risk factors, such as age, smoking, and family history. The conflicting patterns of results obtained in prospective studies make it difficult to draw firm conclusions about relationships between psychological depression as a premorbid precursor of chronic disease.

It can be argued that the helplessness–hopelessness hypothesis refers to the psychological state of individuals at a time period preceding, but relatively close to, the *onset* of illness. Thus, the giving-up-given-up syndrome might be seen as a proximal cause of clinical symptomatology, rather than as a long-term precursor of illness. It also is possible that any psychological vulnerability exhibited by subjects requires appropriately stressful loss events to elicit illness. No such events were measured in the two MMPI studies described above; the various populations may therefore have differed in frequency of occurrence of loss. If it is necessary to measure loss events proximal to appearance of clinical symptoms, the helplessness–hopelessness complex makes it difficult to test the hypothesis without the confounds of retrospective bias or contamination of the patients' psychological state by the biological correlates of disease.

It also should be noted that most of the research conducted by G. L. Engel, Schmale, Greene, and colleagues has not included adequate control groups (e.g., Greene, Moss, & Goldstein, 1974). A particular problem with such studies is the inability to determine the frequency with which depression, loss, or helplessness experiences occur in individuals who do not develop disease. Loss events such as failure, death of loved ones, divorce, and so on are inevitable throughout the life cycle, yet only a minority of individuals suffer lasting adverse effects (F. Cohen, 1979; Krantz, Glass, Contrada, & Miller, 1981).

Temperament, Mental Health, and Physical Illness

Another approach presuming that personality traits predispose individuals to general susceptibility to disease has examined psychological variables thought to be more biologically based. In a prospective study of medical students, Betz and Thomas (1979) derived a measure of "temperament," defined as "a dispositional tendency, a given at birth, with variance among individuals, but constant over time for a single individual" (p. 81). They considered temperament to be an affective rather than a cognitive variable, and based their conceptualization on previous work by Gesell and Ilg (1943). Prospective psychological data from 45 subjects were divided into three types, based on "careful perusal of the objective data in each subject's record" and criteria outlined by Gesell and Ilg (1943). The three types were "slow/solid" (or "alpha"), characterized by cautiousness and self-reliance; "rapid/facile" (or "beta"), characterized by coolness, spontaneity, the ability to adapt to situations, and articulateness; and "irregular/uneven" (or "gamma"), characterized by over- or underreactiveness, moodiness, and confusion. The gamma types were more likely to develop a range of medical disorders—most notably benign tumors—over the next 30 years. Since the initial sample size was very small, more objective criteria were developed to distinguish the three types, and the analysis was applied to prospective data acquired from 127 subjects. Once again, the highest morbidity was found among the gamma subjects, with major cancers and coronary occlusion (but not hypertension) accounting for the largest differences among the groups. It should be noted, however, that there was no control for any of the other risk factors for the major diseases. Moreover, little discussion is given to the mechanisms that might account for the observed effects.

Difficulties with the Betz and Thomas (1979) temperament typology include vagueness and imprecise definition. Nevertheless, the gamma category seems, at least descriptively, to reflect less mentally healthy individuals. Insofar as this is true, the Betz and Thomas (1979) results are similar to the prospective findings of Vaillant (1979), who has reported that poor mental health is related to midlife deterioration in physical health. The mechanisms for the presumed linkage between mental health and physical health are not well specified, but Vaillant (1979) has suggested that good mental health is associated with mature and well-developed abilities to cope with life stresses.

Behavior Patterns and Coronary Heart Disease: Type A Behavior

Associations with Coronary Disease

A broad array of psychological and social variables have been associated with CHD in clinical and epidemiological studies. Comprehensive reviews of this research can be found in Jenkins (1971, 1976). Psychological differences most frequently examined include anxiety and neuroticism, life dissatisfaction, and the Type A behavior pattern. By far the most extensive support and the widest acceptance has been obtained for the Type A pattern, a complex set of behaviors described by M. Friedman and Rosenman (1959). Type A behavior is characterized by excessive competitive drive, impatience and hostility, and accelerated speech and motor movements. A contrasting Type B pattern is defined as the relative absence of these characteristics and a different style of coping with challenges and stress. No sharp division exists between the two behavior patterns; instead, the Type B person is a generally more relaxed and easy-going person who exhibits little aggressive drive and who is relatively devoid of time-urgent characteristics. The Type A concept does not refer to the conditions that elicit such behavior, nor to the responses per se, nor to some hypothetical personality trait that produces them. It refers, instead, to a set of behaviors that occur in susceptible individuals, given appropriately stressful and/or challenging conditions.

People who are competitive, achievement-oriented, time-urgent, and hostile have long been suspected of being at higher risk of clinical CHD (Osler, 1892). However, the major impetus for research validating this hypothesis comes from the work of cardiologists M. Friedman and Rosenman. In the past 20 years, several studies conducted by Rosenman, M. Friedman, Jenkins, and others indicate that Type A individuals show a substantially higher incidence and prevalence of CHD than do Type B's. This large body of research has been reviewed extensively elsewhere (Cooper, Detre, & Weiss, 1981; Dembroski, Weiss, Shields, Haynes, & Feinleib, 1978; Glass, 1977; Matthews, 1982), and we present a selective overview of this vast research area.

Rosenman and M. Friedman have developed a structured interview (SI), which constitutes the major tool for the diagnosis of Type A (Rosenman, 1978). In the SI, speech stylistics and behavioral mannerisms are heavily weighted by the interviewer in arriving at a behavior pattern assessment, although response content is also considered to a lesser extent (Glass, Ross, Contrada, Isecke, & Rosenman, 1982; Krantz & Durel, 1983; Matthews, Krantz, Dembroski, & MacDougall, 1982; Scherwitz, Berton, & Leventhal, 1977; Schucker & Jacobs, 1977).

Two self-administered questionnaires have also been developed as a means of detecting Type A. The Jenkins Activity Survey for Health Prediction (JAS) includes questions designed to mimic the content of the structured interview (Jenkins, Zyzanski, & Rosenman, 1971). The Framingham Type A scale, although not deliberately patterned after the SI, also contains questions that appear to measure Type A traits (S. G. Haynes, Feinleib, & Kannel, 1980). Comparisons among the three methods of assessment indicate only a moderate degree of concordance (Chesney, Black, Chadwick, & Rosenman, 1981; S. G. Haynes, Levine, Scotch, Feinleib, & Kannel, 1978; MacDougall, Dembroski, & Musante, 1979; Matthews *et al.*, 1982). Therefore, the SI and questionnaire techniques are probably measuring different facets of the behavior pattern. More important, however, are findings demonstrating each technique to have predictive validity for the occurrence of clinical CHD (S. G. Haynes *et al.*, 1980; Jenkins, Zyzanski, & Rosenman, 1974; Rosenman, Brand, Jenkins, Friedman, Straus, & Wurm, 1975). Nevertheless, recent comparative work indicates that the SI may be somewhat superior to questionnaire approaches in predicting clinical CHD (Brand, Rosenman, Jenkins, Sholtz, & Zyzanski, 1978), and in relating to physiological endpoints (see Krantz & Durel, 1983, and Matthews, 1982, for discussion).

Although several studies have documented an association between Type A and CHD, the most convincing evidence comes from two large-scale prospective studies. In the Western Collaborative Group Study (WCGS) (Rosenman *et al.*, 1975), an 8½-year follow-up showed that subjects exhibiting Type A behavior at the study's inception were about twice as likely as Type B individuals to develop CHD (i.e., angina pectoris or myocardial infarctions). This twofold differential in risk remained when statistical procedures were used to control for the influence of other risk factors, such as cigarette smoking, serum cholesterol, and high blood pressure. This research has also linked Type A to sudden cardiac death (M. Friedman, Manwaring, Rosenman, Donlon, Ortega, & Grube, 1973) and recurrent myocardial infarctions. Since Type A is linked to progression of CHD, it is considered also in our discussion of individual differences linked to the clinical course of disease.

An 8-year follow-up of data from the Framingham Heart Study indicated that the Type A pattern is predictive of CHD in both men and women, although for male subjects the enhanced risk appeared only among white-collar workers (S. G. Haynes *et al.*, 1980). The prospective association of Type A with CHD in the WCGS and the Framingham Study constitutes strong evidence for its independent pathogenic influence.

There may also be an association between Type A and coronary atherosclerosis. Supporting evidence has been obtained through the use of coronary angiographic techniques that make it possible to quantify the extent of coronary artery disease in living patients (e.g., Blumenthal, Williams, Kong, Schanberg, & Thompson, 1978). The evidence for the association between Type A and coronary atherosclerosis is not unequivocal (Dimsdale, Hackett, Hutter, & Block, 1980; Krantz, Arabian, Davia, & Parker, 1982), and the relationship between Type A and coronary artery disease among patients referred for angiography may not be robust (see Dembroski, MacDougall, Williams, & Haney, 1983).

It is important to note that unlike any other individual-difference variable studied in conjunction with illness, Type A behavior meets most of the stringent criteria used by epidemiologists to establish a cause–effect relationship (cf. Cooper *et al.*, 1981; Dembroski, Weiss, Shields, Haynes, & Feinleib, 1978; Jenkins, 1978). Among these criteria are the strength of association of Type A with clinical CHD; the consistency, persistence, and reproducibility of findings; the fact that Type A precedes CHD, rather than being caused by it; and the fact that the Type A–CHD link is plausible in light of biomedical knowledge of how CHD develops (Jenkins, 1978).

The available techniques for assessing Type A seem able to predict CHD as well as any of the standard physical risk factors considered alone does. However, the SI may be said to lack epidemiological specificity. A large proportion of the population is typically classified as Type A via the SI technique; estimates range from 15% in some populations to as high as 70% in others (Chesney *et al.*, 1981; J. B. Cohen, Syme, Jenkins, Kagan, & Zyzanski, 1979; Matthews *et al.*, 1982). At the same time, the incidence of CHD among Type A's is relatively low, albeit significantly greater than among Type B's. These observations suggest that not all facets of the behavior pattern confer risk, since they appear in all Type A's rather than in only those who develop CHD. It is of importance, therefore, to separate the behavior pattern into its coronary-prone and non-coronary-prone components. It is also necessary to understand the psychological and/or psychobiological mechanisms that give rise to and sustain Type A behaviors (particularly those that enhance cardiovascular risk), and the physiological mechanisms mediating associations between Type A and CHD.

In an item analysis of a subsample of interviews from the WCGS, Matthews, Glass, Rosenman, and Bortner (1977) found that only some elements of the Type A pattern significantly predicted incidence of CHD. Attributes reflected in these items included competitive drive, impatience, vigorous voice stylistics, and potential for hostility. The importance of the hostility trait as a risk factor is consistent with recent work (Williams, Haney, Lee, Kong, Blumenthal, & Whalen, 1980) indicating that both Type A behavior defined by an interview and scores on an MMPI measure of interpersonal hostility were, independently of each other, related to extent of coronary atherosclerosis.[1]

There is also suggestive evidence that different facets of the Type A pattern may be specifically associated with different clinical manifestations

1. Further research, conducted since the completion of this chapter, has reinforced the finding that measures of hostility derived from components of the SI are correlated with coronary angiographic findings. There have also been additional reports that have failed to report significant correlations between global Type A and coronary atherosclerosis.

of CHD. For example, Jenkins, Zyzanski, and Rosenman (1978) found that responses to the JAS questionnaire items were characteristically different among those men who developed acute myocardial infarctions, angina pectoris, and clinically unrecognized or "silent" myocardial infarctions. The conclusions of this study are in accord with other studies in the epidemiological literature dealing with standard and psychosocial risk factors, indicating that myocardial infarctions and angina pectoris might well have different physiological and psychosocial antecedents (Lebovitz, Shekelle, Ostfeld, & Paul, 1967; Medalie, Snyder, Groen, Neufeld, Goldbourt, & Riss, 1973). This finding also is consistent with data reported by S. G. Haynes and Feinleib (1982) indicating that the association between the Framingham Type A scale and later development of CHD was largely accounted for by cases of angina pectoris, rather than cases of myocardial infarction.

Psychophysiological Mechanisms

The epidemiological evidence reviewed above suggests that Type A behavior may contribute to the atherosclerotic process itself, and/or may be involved in precipitating the clinical complications of coronary artery disease (Herd, 1978; Williams, 1978). An adequate explanation of pathophysiological mechanisms mediating these associations must consider the psychophysiology of stress, as well as the role of specific environmental circumstances in eliciting the Type A response.

Recent research indicates that Type A persons, compared to Type B's, show evidence of elevated sympathetic nervous system arousal when confronted with certain situations that may be characterized as appropriately stressful or challenging. Hemodynamic reactions and neuroendocrine responses have received the most attention. A series of studies indicate that while Type A and Type B individuals do not differ in baseline levels, Type A's respond to laboratory challenges with greater elevations in blood pressure and heart rate (e.g., Dembroski, MacDougall, Shields, Petitto, & Lushene, 1978). This increased cardiovascular *reactivity* in Type A subjects has been reported in a variety of subject populations, including male and female college students, working-class adults, and coronary patients (see Krantz, Glass, Schaeffer, & Davia, 1982, for review).

Studies of neuroendocrine function also suggest excess sympathetic arousal in Type A subjects. Extreme Type A's, for example, show more rapid blood-clotting times and a smaller decrease in platelet aggregation in response to exogenous norepinephrine challenges. Of greater significance, perhaps, are the findings that Type A's show greater elevations of plasma levels of catecholamines during a harassing and stressful social competition (e.g., Glass, Krakoff, Contrada, Hilton, Kehoe, Mannucci, Collins, Snow, & Elting, 1980). The catecholamines, epinephrine and norepinephrine, have several physiological effects that may contribute to the pathogenesis of coronary heart disease. These include facilitation of platelet aggregation, possibly leading to coronary thrombosis; increases in blood pressure and heart rate, which increase cardiac demand for oxygen; elevation of lipids; acceleration of the rate of damage to the inner layers of the coronary arteries over time; and provocation of ventricular arrhythmias (Herd, 1978).

A notable feature of psychophysiological research on Type A behavior is the measurement of reactivity in response to stress, as distinct from the observation of basal or resting levels of physiological variables. By observing such changes in response, which are not detected by basal risk factor measurements, it is possible to examine potentially pathogenic states within the context of their psychosocial antecedents.

It should be emphasized that cardiovascular and neuroendocrine responses among Type A's are most pronounced under particular situational circumstances. For example, a study by Glass, Krakoff, Contrada, Hilton, Kehoe, Mannucci, Collins, Snow, and Elting (1980) revealed that the greater catecholamine response of Type A's in a competitive situation requires the additional instigation of harassment by a competitor. Situations also must involve a certain degree of environmental "challenge," and physiological reactivity is elicited in its most pronounced form by psychological rather than by purely physical demands. To demonstrate this, one study (Dembroski, MacDougall, Herd, & Shields, 1979) manipulated the instructions given to subjects exposed to tests of cold-water immersion and reaction time in order to vary the degree of psychological challenge inherent in the task. Results indicated only minimal A-B differences in the condition where instructions were not challenging, and considerably larger differences when subjects were sternly told that the tasks were difficult and exhorted to do well. In accord with the notion that A-B differences in physiological response are most pronounced under challenging environmental circumstances, naturalistic research has demonstrated differences between extreme Type A's and Type B's in excretion of urinary catecholamines during the working day, but not at night when subjects were home at rest (M. Friedman, Rosenman, & Carroll, 1958).

Further understanding of the possible motivational basis of Type A is based on an examination of the situational factors that elicit Type A behavior. The results of a series of controlled laboratory experiments by Glass and colleagues (Glass, 1977) suggest that Type A behavior may be a characteristic style of coping with stressful events that threaten the individual's sense of environmental control. In this view, the competitiveness, hostility, and time urgency exhibited by Type A individuals reflect an effort to assert and maintain mastery over uncontrollable events. The initial reaction of Type A's to uncontrollable stressors is one of behavioral hyperresponsiveness, whereas prolonged exposure to such situations brings about a pattern of hyporesponsiveness, or helplessness. Repeated alternation of this behavioral sequence is believed to be associated with physiological responses that mediate the link between Type A and CHD (Glass, 1977). A recent study (Contrada, Glass, Krakoff, Krantz, Kehoe, Isecke, Collins, & Elting, 1982) provides some evidence that an experimental situation where subjects could exert efforts to control an aversive stimulus elicited increased plasma norepinephrine secretion among Type A's.

Recent research suggests that there may be underlying biological or psychobiological factors that mediate both the expression of Type A behavior and the link between Type A and CHD. (See Krantz & Durel, 1983, for a review.) Two recent studies of patients undergoing coronary artery bypass surgery reveal that Type A patients evidence greater intraoperative increases in systolic blood pressure, even though patients are under general anesthesia (Kahn, Kornfeld, Frank, Heller, & Hoar, 1980; Krantz, Arabian, Davia, & Parker, 1982). Since these A-B differences occur entirely during surgery (with conscious mediation minimized), these findings suggest that Type A behavior may, in part, reflect an excessive sympathetic response to environmental stressors. Although studies have generally not indicated that Type A has a strong genetic component (Matthews & Krantz, 1976; Rahe, Hervig, & Rosenman, 1978), recent data suggest at least a modest genetic contribution to certain Type A components (Matthews, Rosenman, Dembroski, Harris, & MacDougall, 1983). It is also possible that excessive or repetitive elicitation of sympathetic responses over the course of a lifespan may both enhance the expression of Type A behavior and predispose to clinical CHD as well.

Another recent study (Krantz, Durel, Davia, Shaffer, Arabian, Dembroski, & MacDougall, 1982) has yielded evidence compatible with the notion of a psychobiological substrate for Type A behavior. Coronary patients who were either medicated or not medicated with the beta-adrenergic blocking drug propranolol were compared on intensity of Type A behavior. The effect of propranolol is to selectively reduce sympathetic nervous system responding. Results indicated that even after controlling for relevant medical and demographic variables, the patients on propranolol were rated lower on Type A characteristics by SIs. The effects of the drug were to reduce Type A "speech stylistic" components in the SIs, suggesting that these aspects of Type A might reflect an underlying sympathetic response to environmental events (see Krantz & Durel, 1983). However, the interplay of *both* cognitive/psychological *and* physiological processes must be considered in understanding the underpinnings of Type A behavior and its components.

A word of caution must be introduced here. All of the evidence bearing on physiological mechanisms underlying a Type A–CHD relationship is as yet preliminary. Conclusive results must await future research. It would be premature to argue, for example, that elevated production of catecholamines serve as the mediating processes whereby stress and the Type A behavior enhance the risk of CHD. On the other hand, it is probably reasonable to assume that the mechanisms in question are related to sympathetic nervous system and pituitary–adrenocortical activity. For example, studies comparing

CHD cases and healthy controls have demonstrated that patients who display overt symptomatology of ischemic heart disease (myocardial infarction and angina pectoris) have elevated hemodynamic and neuroendocrine responses to challenge and stress (Corse, Manuck, Cantwell, Giordiani, & Matthews, 1982; Dembroski, MacDougall, & Lushene, 1979; Schiffer, Hartley, Schulman, & Abelmann, 1976). However, there is no direct evidence in humans that hemodynamic reactivity per se is a mechanism that predisposes individuals to coronary atherosclerosis (Krantz, Schaeffer, Davia, Dembroski, MacDougall, & Shaffer, 1981). Promising research using animal models (e.g., Manuck, Kaplan, & Clarkson, 1983) will be useful in providing an understanding of these mechanisms.

The Hypertensive Personality

EH is a condition in which blood pressure shows chronic elevations. When the disorder becomes developed fully, elevated pressure is usually due to increased resistance to blood flow in the peripheral vasculature (Page & McCubbin, 1966). The causes of high blood pressure are believed to involve complex interactions among genetic, sociocultural, behavioral, and physiological processes. The conflicting patterns of results obtained in the study of this disorder have led Weiner (1977) to conclude, in an exhaustive review, that there is a consensus among researchers about only three characteristics of the disease: Blood pressure is elevated; peripheral resistance is increased in the later stages of the disease; and genetic factors are involved in the predisposition to the disorder. No area in the study of EH is more fraught with conflicting findings than is the study of personality correlates. Before considering research on personality and EH, however, it is necessary to describe the physiological bases of the disorder.

Heterogeneity of the Disorder and Physiological Mechanisms

The study of the etiology of EH is complicated by the fact that it is not a single, homogeneous disease (Weiner, 1977). In the development of the disorder, blood pressure is thought to progress over a period of years from moderately elevated or "borderline" levels to more appreciably elevated levels, called "established" hypertension. Several pathogenic mechanisms may bring about blood pressure elevations, and different physiological and/ or behavioral mechanisms are implicated at various stages of the disorder. For example, individuals with borderline hypertension are commonly observed to have elevated levels of cardiac output but to show little evidence of increased peripheral resistance. This physiological pattern is consistent with increased activation of the sympathetic nervous system, which is the body's initial reaction to psychological stress. However, in older individuals with more established high blood pressure, cardiac output is either normal or depressed, while the vascular resistance is elevated (Julius & Esler, 1975).

In addition to cardiovascular adjustments and changes, the physiological mechanisms of high blood pressure probably involve the interaction of the central and autonomic nervous systems, the endocrine system, and the kidneys. The enzyme renin, which is released by the kidney, is involved in a physiological regulatory process (the renin–angiotensin–aldosterone mechanism), which leads the kidney to increase water reabsorption and expand the volume of blood, thus raising the blood pressure (Kaplan, 1980). The process of renin release normally should be dampened whenever the blood pressure is raised, but in a subcategory of individuals with EH, the level of renin in the blood is inappropriately high.

Accordingly, behavioral factors such as psychological stress and personality characteristics might conceivably play a role in the etiology of EH via a number of physiological pathways (Kaplan, 1980). For example, emotional stress leads to a discharge of the sympathetic nervous system and to increases in catecholamines. High levels of blood and tissue catecholamines have been found in some hypertensive humans and animals (Julius & Esler, 1975). Such elevations could lead to increased blood pressure via increased heart rate and force of heart action; constriction of peripheral blood vessels; and/or activation of the renin–angiotensin–aldosterone system, which constricts the vasculature (Kaplan, 1980) and regulates the volume of blood.

Genetic–Environment Interactions

The prevalence of EH in the United States usually increases with age, and below 50 it occurs with less frequency in women than in men (Weiner, 1977). Evidence from animal research and studies of human twins indicates that genetic factors play a role in the etiology of the disease (Pickering, 1967). This evidence suggests that many genes are involved in susceptibility to high blood pressure, and it is likely that in humans, sustained elevations in blood pressure are produced by an interaction of a variety of environmental and genetic factors. Consider that epidemiological studies reveal a difference in the prevalence of high blood pressure among various social and cultural groups—a difference that cannot be accounted for by genetic factors alone (Henry & Cassel, 1969). For example, in the United States, hypertension is more common among blacks than among whites, but the prevalence of high blood pressure is greater in poor than in middle-class black Americans (Harburg, Erfurt, Hauenstein, Chape, Schull, & Schork, 1973). Animal research similarly reveals examples where environmental factors (such as dietary salt intake or environmental stress) lead to sustained blood pressure elevations only in certain genetic strains (Dahl, Heine, & Tassinari, 1962; R. Friedman, & Iwai, 1976; Lawler, Barker, Hubbard, & Allen, 1980).

The Suppressed-Hostility Hypothesis

As we have noted, psychosomatic researchers have proposed that emotional dispositions or personality traits are predisposing factors for EH (cf. Harrell, 1980). Many researchers (e.g., Alexander, 1950; Sapira, Scheib, Moriarty,

& Shapiro, 1971) have suggested that the hypertensive patient is characterized by chronic yet inhibited hostility, together with a degree of anxiety and neuroticism. It has further been suggested that over a period of time the continued inhibition of hostile impulses leads to neuroendocrine and cardiovascular responses (e.g., norepinephrine and acute blood pressure increases), which culminate in a chronic elevation of the blood pressure (Shapiro, 1978). Later research (Hokanson, 1961) has demonstrated that blood pressure rises in response to a variety of frustrations, and will return to normal levels more quickly if the individual has an opportunity to act aggressively against the perpetrator of the frustration than if he or she is provided no opportunity to act aggressively. This provides support for a hypothesized link between suppressed anger or hostility and transient blood pressure increases. On the basis of these data, it has been suggested that more frequent, greater-magnitude, or longer-lasting blood pressure increases in individuals might lead to chronic blood pressure elevations.

The physiological mechanism most frequently invoked for this hypothesized process involves the baroreceptors—pressure-sensitive receptors located primarily at the bifurcation of the carotid artery and the arch of the aorta (cf. Fahrion, 1981; Harrell, 1980). The baroreceptors initiate an important central nervous system reflex that slows heart rate and reduces peripheral vascular resistance as blood pressure increases. With increases in blood pressure, these receptors "reset," becoming less sensitive, with the result that peripheral resistance and blood pressure remain at higher and higher levels. Indeed, the range and threshold of the baroceptors appear to be altered in chronic hypertension (McCubbin, Green, & Page, 1956).

However, there are gaps and inconsistencies in the literature on personality, psychophysiological processes, and EH. These difficulties have led critical reviewers to question both the role of personality in the etiology of EH and the sequence of events involving hostility-induced blood pressure elevations as a major explanatory mechanism for the development of the disorder. (See Fahrion, 1981; Goldstein, 1981; Graham, 1972; Harrell, 1980; McGinn, Harburg, Julius, & McLeod, 1964; Ostfeld & Shekelle, 1967; Shapiro, Benson, Chobanian, Herd, Julius, Kaplan, Lazarus, Ostfeld, & Syme, 1979; and Weiner, 1977, for comprehensive reviews.)

Several major difficulties have been identified in attempts to identify a so-called "hypertensive personality." The first problem is methodological. Early studies depended primarily upon clinical-psychological descriptions of patients with essential hypertension, rather than upon scores on objective tests. The result of this strategy was imprecise psychological measurement. Many of these studies were also lacking adequate control groups. Moreover, more recent studies, using standardized interviews and psychological assessment techniques, have also produced conflicting results. For example, evidence has been presented that hypertensives exhibit characteristics that may be interpreted as difficulty in expressing hostility (Harburg et al., 1973; Kalis, Harris, Bennett, & Sokolow, 1961). On the other hand, evidence exists that

hypertensives report more enhanced and longer-lasting hostility than normotensives do (Baer, Collins, Bourianoff, & Ketchel, 1979; Mann, 1977). There
are even studies showing no differences between hypertensives and normotensives (Ostfeld & Lebovitz, 1959; Ostfeld & Shekelle, 1967).

Research has also investigated relationships between suppressed hostility
and cardiovascular responses in patients with EH. For example, Sapira *et al.*
(1971) recorded cardiovascular responses in normotensives and hypertensives
during the viewing of two contrasting movies: one in which a physician was
shown as pleasant, and another in which a doctor was depicted as being rude
to a patient. Results indicated greater blood pressure responses to both films
in the hypertensive group. There were also differences in the perceptions
of the two groups. The normotensives reported differences between the
films, but the hypertensives did not. On the other hand, Weiner, Singer,
and Reiser (1962) found that hypertensives showed a *less* reactive pressor
response to Thematic Apperception Test cards. Although increased vascular
reactivity among hypertensives was found in one study and decreased reactivity was found in the other, these diverse findings were given the same
interpretation. Both sets of results were thought to represent efforts by hypertensives to ''screen out'' stimuli to protect themselves from excessive cardiovascular responsiveness. Incidentally, these studies advance an explanation
for trait differences between hypertensives and normotensives that does not
presume that personality plays a direct causal role in the etiology of EH. Instead, the trait of suppressed hostility is viewed as a *result* of the subject's
awareness of his or her physical disorder or predisposition of disease.

Convincing reasons for inconsistencies in the trait and psychophysiological data on EH become apparent when the psychological and biomedical
literature is examined closely. Many clinical studies of hypertension disregard
important subject variables, such as duration and stage of illness, type of
hypertension, age, sex, and socioeconomic status (cf. Weiner, 1977). Furthermore, individuals who consult physicians for their disorder may not be representative of the hypertensive population as a whole, and psychological differences between diagnosed and undiagnosed hypertensives have been
detected (Bergland, Andes, Lindstrom, & Tibblin, 1975; Fahrion, 1981; R.
Haynes, Taylor, & Sackett, 1979).

A second problem with existing research on personality and hypertension derives from a lack of synthesis between biomedical/physiological and
psychosocial results. As we have described, there is substantial evidence that
the physiological mechanisms that initiate EH are quite different from those
that sustain high blood pressure (Julius & Esler, 1975; Obrist, 1981). Therefore, the logic that the personality features evident after disease onset play
an etiological role can be severely questioned (Weiner, 1977).

Future Research on Personality and Hypertension

As we have noted, patients with high blood pressure are not homogeneous
in terms of either physiological or psychological characteristics. This suggests

that it is necessary to differentiate subjects according to type, extent, and duration of hypertension. For example, distinguishing between the types of hypertension associated wtih high or low levels of renin, or between borderline and "established" hypertension, has proven useful. In this regard, a recent study showed convincingly that 30% of a sample of young male patients with EH (namely, those with mild pressure elevations and high plasma renin levels) displayed both elevations in sympathetic nervous system activity *and* higher levels of suppressed hostility (Esler, Julius, Zweifler, Randall, Harburg, Gardiner, & DeQuattro, 1977)—a behavioral trait independently linked to increased nervous system activity.

Investigations of personality and hypertension have defined "suppressed hostility" in many ways (e.g., the tone or style of reporting anger; a lack of expressed anger on self-report scales; higher levels of observer-rated hostility; subjects' not admitting hostility; etc.). Some studies have measured suppressed hostility in a few specific situations (Harburg et al., 1973), whereas other studies have examined habitual patterns expressed in a variety of situations (Gentry, Chesney, Gary, Hall, & Harburg, 1982). Relatively few studies have examined such variables as frequency and amplitude of expressed anger. More careful attention to precise definition of these differences in content, style, and measurement may prove useful in future research.

Some of the more promising work on personality and hypertension has focused on individuals who are at risk of developing the disorder (e.g., people with a family history of EH), and also on the situations and types of circumstances that might activate predispositions to high blood pressure. Thus, in order to understand mechanisms in the *cause* of the disorder, researchers are directing more attention to the beginning stages of the disease, rather than to its culmination. Given that borderline high blood pressure is characterized by heightened responsiveness of the cardiovascular and sympathetic nervous systems to psychological stimuli such as mental stress (Julius & Esler, 1975), recent research has examined the tendency toward large episodic or acute increases in heart rate, blood pressure, and sympathetic nervous system hormonal (catecholamine) activity as possible mechanisms involved in etiology. Several groups of investigators (Manuck & Schaefer, 1978; Obrist, 1981) have found that cardiovascular responsiveness is a stable and persistently evoked response that can be measured reliably in a laboratory situation. Cardiovascular responsiveness to certain psychological stimuli has also been related consistently to a family history of high blood pressure (a hypertension risk factor), even among individuals who have normal resting blood pressure levels and display no overt signs of the disorder (Obrist, 1981). In one representative study (Falkner, Onesti, Angelakos, Fernandes, & Langman, 1979), adolescents with normal blood pressure and at least one parent with EH displayed greater diastolic blood pressure, heart rate, and plasma catecholamine responses to a stressful mental arithmetic task, compared to a control group of adolescents with no family history of EH.

Obrist and coworkers (Obrist, 1981; Obrist, Grignolo, Hastrup, Koepke,

Langer, Light, McCubbin, & Pollak, 1983) report that cardiovascular responsiveness above the level that is efficient for the body's metabolic needs results uniquely from situations where *active coping* or behavioral adjustments are required. In active coping situations, the organism tries to exert some behavioral control over a stimulus. Further research employing sophisticated pharmacological manipulations (such as the administration of drugs that selectively block the responses of certain sympathetic receptors) reveals that active coping with stress can alter regulatory mechanisms involving two physiological processes. In one, the heart pumps excessive amounts of blood; and in the other, the kidney reabsorbs excessive amounts of sodium, with a resultant increase in the volume of blood. Indeed, a recent study by Light (1983) demonstrates that, in humans, stress can facilitate sodium retention among individuals susceptible to EH. The tendency toward "active" versus "passive" coping with stressors may thus prove to be a useful individual-difference variable for future research on EH.

Traits and Cancer Etiology

Cancer is not a single disease; instead, the term is used for more than 100 conditions characterized by unrestrained multiplication of cells and abnormal growth (cf. Ader, 1981; Ader & Cohen, Chapter 5, this volume; Fraumeni, 1975). A number of behavioral scientists have proposed that personality traits precede and are in some way involved in the etiology of human cancer. These psychological characteristics include unconscious conflicts, poor or inappropriate ability to express emotions (especially negative ones), lack of closeness to parents, and depression. As is the case with most of the formulations discussed in this chapter, distinctions between long-lasting traits and more transitory states such as stressful life events are not always clear (Schmale & Iker, 1971). Indeed, it is often suggested that some combination of traits and critical life events predispose the disease (Morrison & Paffenberger, 1981).

We have already reviewed research by Schmale and Iker (1971) on helplessness–hopelessness and its presumed relationship to cervical cancer, and the reader is referred to comprehensive reviews by Fox (1978) and Morrison and Paffenberger (1981) for detailed consideration of the numerous retrospective studies and approaches to personality traits and cancer etiology. However, a prospective study by Thomas and colleagues (Thomas, Duszynski, & Shaffer, 1979) is worthy of note here.

In this research, psychosocial data were obtained from 913 male medical students at Johns Hopkins University long before the clinical appearance of disease. A follow-up showed that 20 of the men developed cancer over the next 10 to 15 years. These men had reported a lack of closeness to parents on a Family Attitude Questionnaire administered at the inception of the study. Scores on this measure distinguished future cancer victims from both subjects who were to remain healthy and those who subsequently developed high blood pressure or myocardial infarctions. However, even this study may be criticized for its statistical methodology. Many variables were measured, and only a few yielded statistically significant differences; thus, these differences may be chance findings. There was also a failure to control for known cancer risk factors, such as smoking; however, recent follow-up study (Shaffer, Duszynski, & Thomas, 1982) found that differences between cancerous and healthy groups persisted after a variety of cancer risk factors were statistically controlled.

Another prospective study has been reviewed earlier in the section on helplessness and illness. This study (Dattore *et al.*, 1980) reported that subjects who developed cancers at a variety of sites scored lower on depression and greater on repression, as measured by the MMPI, than did a group of patients who subsequently developed noncancerous diseases. In this study, no attempt was made to control for other known cancer risk factors. However, the opposite pattern of results—elevated *D* scores among individuals who later developed cancers—was found by Shekelle *et al.* (1981) in a prospective study that *did* control for known cancer risk factors.

Several excellent recent reviews (Barofsky, 1981; Fox, 1978; Morrison & Paffenberger, 1981; Sklar & Anisman, 1981) have considered human research linking stress and personality to the etiology of cancers. The consensus of most of these reviews is that while some associations may exist between the initiation of tumor growth and psychological variables in humans, there is presently little convincing evidence of a causal relation between these variables. Most of the research consists of retrospective studies that are methodologically and empirically deficient (e.g., lacking appropriate control groups).

Results have also been inconsistent and/or lack a theoretical rationale. With the exception of the Shekelle *et al.* (1981) study, most investigations do not control for, or even assess, known risk factors for cancers or carcinogens (e.g., smoking, dietary factors, alcohol consumption, etc.) that could reasonably correlate with the psychological factors of interest (cf. Fox, 1978; Fraumeni, 1975).

Personality research on cancer has also been poorly integrated with the complexities of biomedical knowledge of the disease (cf. Fox, 1978). There are vague references to the possibility that emotional stress may decrease bodily resistance to malignant growth. However, this body of work has, in the past, devoted little systematic attention to pathophysiological mechanisms (including endocrine and immune processes) that might underlie associations between psychosocial variables and the development of cancers. This work is in contrast to recent experimental and clinical work (cf. Ader, 1981; Ader & Cohen, Chapter 5 this volume; Sklar & Anisman, 1981), which is beginning to provide a groundwork for studying such mechanisms. A new interdisciplinary research area, psychoneuroimmunology, examines the interrelationships among central nervous system, endocrine, behavioral, and immunological processes (Ader, 1981). For example, laboratory stressors tend to decrease the responsiveness of the immune system in animals, and stress-responsive hormones, including corticosteroids, can directly and indirectly affect components of the immune response (Ader, 1981; Amkraut & Solomon, 1977; Sklar & Anisman, 1981). Animal and human studies demonstrate that laboratory and naturalistic stressors can reduce the number of lymphocytes (cells important in the immune process), can lower the level of interferon (a substance that may prevent the spread of cancer), and can cause damage in immunologically related tissue. Of particular relevance to cancer are other studies demonstrating that stress can inhibit the body's defenses against malignancy (Sklar & Anisman, 1981).

However, it is risky to conclude from these data alone that personality traits play a role in the etiology of cancer in humans. The processes in cancer etiology are complex, and are believed to involve the transformation and unrestrained multiplication of cells (Levi, 1979). Cancers also have the ability to spread beyond their site of origin. A large number of tumors are therefore slow to appear, sometimes taking many years. Thus, it must be demonstrated that traits are reliable and stable over long time periods, and that they are related to the complex biological mechanisms of tumor development. These many problems do not augur well for future research on cancer etiology. As we have noted, research on progression and growth of diagnosed cancers may hold more promise than attempts to relate personality to etiology.

PERSONALITY AND PROGRESSION OR OUTCOME OF SYMPTOMATIC DISEASE

Instead of considering the role of traits in the early etiology of disease, several approaches propose that personality can affect the clinical course and/or recovery from illness after symptoms are present. Occasionally, if disease is thought to be present but in a preclinical stage, characteristics that cause the disorder to become manifest may be considered under this category. As in the previous section on etiology, some personality traits are thought to have a general influence on clinical outcomes (e.g., recovery) from many disorders, whereas others are linked to specific diseases.

Coping Dispositions: Traits Related to Progression of Many Disorders

The most common framework for conceptualizing psychological differences in disease progression has been in terms of coping styles or dispositions. Illness is viewed as a stressor, and individuals vary in their appraisal of the various physical and psychological threats posed by the disease. "Coping" may be defined as psychological or behavioral actions directed at meeting demands posed by a situation (Coelho, Hamburg, & Adams, 1974; Gatchel *et al.*, 1982; Mechanic, 1968). ''Coping dispositions'' refer to tendencies of an individual to use a particular mode or pattern of coping with some consistency across a variety of stressful encounters (F. Cohen & Lazarus, 1979). The chapter in this volume by Lazarus and Folkman (Chapter 8) provides a detailed discussion of the coping process. We allude only briefly here to several major examples of coping dispositions that have been linked to progression and/or recovery from illness.

Depression and Lowered Psychological Morale

As noted in the section on helplessness, several studies suggest that those who are depressed take longer to recover from illness and/or show higher mortality from serious illness (F. Cohen & Lazarus, 1979). The lowered psychological morale associated with depression is presumed either to alter internal physiological states directly, or to lower the patients' motivation to engage in treatments that are important for recovery (Krantz, 1980; Krantz & Schulz, 1980).

Particularly relevant here is Seligman's (1975) discussion of the psychological state of helplessness that results when individuals encounter aversive events (e.g., serious illness) over which they perceive little control. ''Perceived control'' is defined as the felt ability to escape, avoid, and/or modify threatening stimuli (Averill, 1970; Seligman, 1975). There is little doubt that the onset of serious illness constitutes a stressful and potentially uncontrollable event of major proportions. In addition to physical discomfort and fear of death, patients are confronted with uncertainties about employment, family, and life style. Restrictions of life style and a certain degree of fear and uncertainty may persist for months or even years beyond the acute phase of illness.

Extensive research with both humans and animals has suggested that, in general, the greater the perceived controllability of a stressor, the less harmful its effects on the organism are. The work of Seligman (1975), for example, suggests that a psychological state of helplessness results when individuals encounter aversive events that involve a perceived noncontingency between responses and outcomes. A range of cognitive, emotional, and physiological disturbances have been attributed to this psychological state, including depressive affect and anxiety. As previously noted, several investigators (Engel, 1968; Engel & Schmale, 1972) further propose that severe feelings of helplessness may be a general precursor to physical disease.

Relationships between depression and recovery have been studied in relation to a variety of disorders, including CHD, stroke, cancer, and infectious disease (Cluff, Canter, & Imboden, 1966; F. Cohen & Lazarus, 1979; Krantz, 1980; Krantz & Deckel, 1983). Depression is also frequently studied in conjunction with recovery from surgery (Kimball, 1969; Tufo & Ostfeld, 1968). The *D* scale of the MMPI is the most frequently used measure of this variable. Research has provided some support for associations between heightened D scores and delayed or poorer recovery from a variety of disorders. However, the mechanisms through which depression is linked to poorer recovery are not clear-cut. They appear to vary with the particular disorder, and also to vary from one stage of illness to another.

Studies of heart patients (Kimball, 1969; Pancheri, Bellaterra, Matteoli, Cristofari, Polizzi, & Puletti, 1978) have reported that depressed patients have a more complicated course of recovery in the hospital, presumably because of heightened stress responses. However, it is not always clear that depressed and nondepressed patients are equivalent in medical status at the time of hospital admission. Upon discharge from the hospital, depression is considered to be one of the most formidable problems in cardiac convalescence and rehabilitation (Hackett & Cassem, 1973). The mechanisms active here are not presumed to involve direct effects of mood on physiological functioning. Instead, depressed patients exhibit a maladaptive behavioral response (cf. Garrity, 1973). After the period of hospitalization, many patients are reluctant to resume normal activities or to return to work—often to an extent not justified by their medical disability. One common reaction, termed "cardiac invalidism," is characterized by excessive dependency, helplessness, and restriction of activity. This physical inactivity may, in fact, contribute to a worsening of medical status, due to the physiological effects of physical deconditioning (Garrity, McGill, Becker, Blanchard, Crews, Cullen, Hackett, Taylor, & Valins, 1976).

Critique of Coping Dispositions: The Example of Denial

A dispositional approach to coping with illness makes several assumptions that may not hold up for particular traits, illness situations, or disorders (F. Cohen & Lazarus, 1979). The first concerns consistency in the mode of coping over time or from one situation to another. There is apparently little evidence of such consistency across various illness situations. A number of factors, including severity and stage of illness and prior experience with the disease, have important effects on the coping strategy an individual employs. These factors might also affect the predictive relationships of dispositional measures of coping to illness outcomes (F. Cohen & Lazarus, 1979). The efficacy of personality traits in predicting criterion behaviors in general has been convincingly challenged by Mischel (1968, 1973). Mischel (1968) argues that there is little evidence for the widely held assumption of the consistency of dispositional behavior across a variety of situations.

Secondly, F. Cohen and Lazarus (1979) and others (Hackett & Cassem, 1973; Hofer et al., 1972a, 1972b; Krantz & Deckel, 1983; Mages & Mendelson, 1979) have noted that even with regard to the same major illness, there may be different stages of recovery. At each stage of illness, the mode of coping that is most adaptive may vary. For example, Cassem and Hackett (1971) have developed a model for the time course of emotional reactions of the person who has a myocardial infarction. It is proposed that a patient feels heightened anxiety when first admitted to the coronary care unit. However, denial is soon mobilized, and the patient finds it difficult to believe that he or she really had a heart attack. Anxiety declines; the patient protests detention in the unit, insists on returning to normal activities, and becomes difficult to manage. However, after several days the patient becomes more cognizant of the limitations of his or her true condition, and depression sets in.

In support of the Cassem and Hackett model, several studies have found that patients employing denial tend to be less anxious in early phases of illness than do those not employing denial (Froese, Hackett, Cassem, & Silverberg, 1974; Gentry, Foster, & Haney, 1972). However, long-term follow-up studies suggest that use of denial has been related to long-term resistance to compliance with medical regimens (Croog, Shapiro, & Levine, 1971; Garrity et al., 1976). In sum, use of denial may make for better coping with the early stress of illness in the coronary care unit. But in the long term, patients may endanger their chances of recovery by ignoring medical recommendations that are important for satisfactory rehabilitation.

F. Cohen and Lazarus (1973, 1979) draw a useful distinction between "dispositional" and "process" measures of coping; this distinction may help overcome some of the difficulties of the dispositional approach. Process measures infer the mode of coping from direct observation of the individual's behavior in a particular situation; no assumptions are made about the presumed consistency of coping behavior across a variety of situations. Thus, process measures therefore allow investigators to incorporate the influence of the particular demands of the situation, the coping options available within the setting, and the notion that adaptive coping may involve different stages (cf. F. Cohen & Lazarus, 1979). By incorporating these considerations, the study of coping–disease relationships is enhanced.

Type A Behavior and Progression of Coronary Heart Disease

Research suggests that Type A behavior may be associated with the progression of CHD, as well as with its etiology. This conclusion derives from both epidemiological and clinical data. Findings from the prospective WCGS, reviewed previously, indicate that of those subjects who suffered an initial clinical event, Type A subjects were more than twice as likely to show evidence of a second or recurrent myocardial infarction over the 8½-year duration of the study (Jenkins, Zyzanski, & Rosenman, 1976). Type A behavior, as measured by the JAS, was among the strongest predictors of recurrent heart attack from the array of variables examined; cigarette smoking and serum cholesterol accounted for significant additional variance in predicting recurrence.

There is also some evidence that the magnitude of Type A scores may be related to the progression of atherosclerosis. In a study of patients who underwent repeated coronary angiograms at an average interval of 17 months, Krantz, Sanmarco, Selvester, and Matthews (1979) found that extreme Type A's, as measured by the JAS, were somewhat more likely to show significant progression of coronary artery disease over this period; extreme Type B's were very unlikely to show significant progression.

Increased cardiovascular reactivity among Type A individuals can still be observed in cardiac patients after disease is manifest (Corse *et al.*, 1982; Krantz *et al.*, 1982). Therefore, these responses may possibly influence the course of the disease and subsequent clinical outcomes. In accord with this reasoning, a study of patients undergoing coronary artery bypass surgery found that patients who showed evidence of clinical complications (usually arrhythmias) during or after surgery scored reliably higher in interview-rated intensity of Type A behavior when compared to those patients who displayed no complications (Krantz *et al.*, 1982). A recent retrospective study (Zyzanski, Stanton, Jenkins, & Klein, 1981) also suggests that Type A behavior may be related to poorer posthospital adjustment to coronary bypass surgery. The mechanisms for this latter association are less clear-cut, but the weight of the evidence suggests that Type A behavior is a variable that affects a variety of clinical and social adjustment outcome variables in recovery from CHD. In this regard, A-B differences in styles of coping with heart attack have been observed (Gentry, Oude-Weme, Musch, & Hall, 1981).

Studies of Cancer Prognosis

There is some evidence to suggest that patients' psychological responses to cancer diagnosis and/or treatment may be related to the future course of the disease. The strongest evidence for this assertion derives from two studies of women with cancer of the breast (Derogatis, Abeloff, & Melisaratos, 1979; Greer, Morris, & Pettingale, 1979). These results seem to suggest that those patients who express hostility and anger fare better than either those who do not express negative affect or those who react with helplessness. Additional studies (Rogentine, Van Kammen, Fox, Doherty, Rosenblatt, Boyd, & Bunney, 1979) have examined other cancers, but we confine our discussion to cancer of the breast, since prospective data are available on two independent samples.

Derogatis *et al.* (1979) found that among women with metastatic breast cancer, those who subsequently survived less than 1 year reported less negative affect and were more positively adjusted to illness than were women who later survived longer than 1 year. Greer *et al.* (1979) also studied women with breast cancer, but their subjects had shown no evidence of metastasis at time of initial testing. On the basis of clinical interviews, the Greer *et al.* (1979) patients were classified into four groups: those who denied illness; those who initially reacted optimistically but displayed a "fighting spirit'' and willingness to combat the disease; those who accepted the disease stoically; and those who reacted with helplessness and felt there was little they could do. Results of a 5-year follow-up indicated that both the denial and ''fighting spirit'' groups showed more favorable outcomes than did the groups showing stoic acceptance or helplessness. Although the interview data were related to clinical outcomes, dispositional psychological measures of hostility and anger suppression failed to distinguish the groups. In both studies, clinical data (e.g., measures of medical status taken at intake) did not differentiate those patients with good and poor prognoses.

There are both consistencies and inconsistencies in the results of these two studies. Both suggest that some expression of anger or ''fighting spirit'' is associated with a more favorable prognosis. However, Greer et al. (1979) found that patients who denied their illness also fared well, and that objective test measures of hostility and other affective states did not distinguish the groups.

The apparent discrepancies between the interview and objective test measures in the Greer et al. (1979) study might be reconciled by invoking the distinction between ''process'' and ''dispositional'' measures suggested by F. Cohen and Lazarus (1979). The clinical interview used by Greer et al. (1979) may have measured coping processes utilized by patients in the particular situation, as opposed to the more dispositional characteristics measured by objective tests. The groups in the Derogatis et al. (1979) and Greer et al. (1979) studies also differed according to stage and severity of disease at intake, and these factors may explain apparently discrepant conclusions regarding the relationship of denial and prognosis. However, the inconsistencies in results should be taken seriously. Whereas there is some evidence that psychological factors are predictive of cancer prognosis, inferences about mechanisms of this association must await further replications of these findings. Regarding possible mechanisms involved in these relationships, preliminary data (Pettingale, Greer, & Tee, 1977) suggest relationships between coping responses such as expression or suppression of anger and immunological function. In particular, serum immunoglobulin A was significantly higher among breast cancer patients who suppressed anger.

PERSPECTIVES NOT PRESUMING A CAUSAL EFFECT OF PERSONALITY ON DISEASE

Correlations between psychological variables and illness, especially when derived from cross-sectional data, do not reveal much about direction of causality or mediating mechanisms (cf. McFarland & Cobb, 1967; Steptoe, 1981). Even if associations among traits, behavior patterns, and illness are based on prospective data, a variety of mechanisms or other causal variables may be involved. The perspectives described in this section minimize the causal role of traits or physiological attributes in the etiology or progression of disease. A "somatopsychic" perspective is adopted; instead of noting the effects of psychological processes on disease, the effects of disease on behavior are emphasized. On the one hand, disease might directly affect behavior because of neurological and endocrine changes associated with illness. On the other hand, the patients' experience with symptoms of disease or with the health care system might alter or affect psychological processes.

Effects of Biological Correlates of Disease Processes

The possible effects of mild to moderate disease on psychological attributes have been largely ignored in studies of individual differences and illness. There is some evidence, for example, that certain types of cancers such as leukemia and cancer of the lung can have *direct* effects on brain and behavior, since they often lead to brain metastases (Bunn, Schein, Bankes, & Devita, 1976; Lister, 1977; Mitchell, 1967; Sklar & Anisman, 1981). These metastases are frequently not detected prior to treatment; thus retrospective studies that used patients with similar disorders could have been confounded by this direct effect (cf. Sklar & Anisman, 1981).

Indirect effects of cancers on behavioral and psychological processes have also been suggested; these may result from metabolic, endocrine, and hematological changes occurring before cancer is clinically evident (Sklar & Anisman, 1981; Mitchell, 1967). However, reviewers disagree on the potential importance of these changes in affecting psychological variables assessed just before cancer is clinically diagnosed. For example, it has been suggested that subclinical physiological changes may have altered the affective state of helplessness–hopelessness in a previously discussed study of cervical cancer by Schmale and Iker (1971). There is also some data suggesting that advanced cancer patients with mild neurological deficits survived longer and were less distressed than patients without these impairments (Davies *et al.*, 1973). In this study, patients who felt apathetic or had "given up" died sooner, but the possibility is raised that the psychological state, along with earlier death, may have resulted from the disease process.

The effects of cardiovascular disorders on cognitive functioning have also been examined (Elias & Streeten, 1980); most of this research suggests that hypertension is correlated with very mild impairments on complex tests of speed and intellectual functioning (e.g., Hertzog, Schaie, & Gribbin, 1978; Spieth, 1964). Similar decrements have recently been observed on complex psychomotor tasks for patients with increasing levels of coronary atherosclerosis (Matheson, 1979). The suggestion has therefore been made that hypertension and other cardiovascular disorders might affect personality (Shapiro, 1978; Weiner, 1977). There is at present little evidence that such personality changes can result directly from biological disease processes (see Costa, McCrae, Andres, & Tobin, 1980; Elias & Streeten, 1980). However, as described in the section on hypertension, it is conceivable that an individual diagnosed as hypertensive might inhibit angry responses in order to "protect" himself or herself against an excessive cardiovascular response (Shapiro, 1978; Weiner, 1977).

"Illness Behavior" and the Psychological Correlates of Disease

Many factors unrelated to the biological severity of illness combine to determine who receives care. Persons requiring medical attention do not always seek out medical help, or are otherwise not seen by health care providers. Similarly, individuals who report for medical care frequently display no evidence of physical disease. The process of seeking health care requires that symptoms be perceived, recognized, and acted upon by a prospective patient (Mechanic, 1968). Accordingly, there are strong individual differences in treatment-seeking behavior (Krantz, Baum, & Wideman, 1980; Mechanic, 1968; Zola, 1972). Thus, personality, rather than disease per se, might influence symptom perception or treatment seeking.

For example, many of the psychosocial factors presumed to be general precursors of disease (G. L. Engel, 1968; Schmale, 1972) may have to do with the perception and evaluation of symptoms (F. Cohen, 1979; Haney, 1977). There is evidence that depression, emotional stress, and grief can heighten help seeking (Kasl & Cobb, 1966; Mechanic, 1968). Yet cross-sectional studies of clinical groups often do not contain control groups necessary to determine whether differences between those with and without a particular disorder are attributable to factors that influence the decision to seek medical care.

Even prospective research designs may yield results that stem from the influences of illness behavior. For example, a study of individuals in Maryland who had contracted Asian influenza during 1957–1958 revealed that clinical disease characteristics, such as serological response, height of fever, and symptom severity, failed to distinguish those who recovered quickly from those who retained symptoms for longer periods of time. However, subjects with delayed recovery scored as more "depression-prone" on psychological tests given in advance of the outbreak of illness. This finding was interpreted to indicate that depression-prone individuals exhibit greater concern over illness, and that this concern increased and prolonged their physical complaints and reports of illness. A prospective follow-up study (Cluff et al., 1966) measured actual frequency of infection via assays for rises in serum antibody titers. Among those who were infected, depression scores were not reliably related to antibody measures of infection; thus, increased concern over illness seems the most likely explanation for the relationship between depression and delayed recovery in this sample.

The Cluff et al. (1966) study is notable for its examination of variables allowing for determination of the mechanisms linking psychological variables and illness. Without biological measures of immune processes, one might easily have inferred that trait differences operated via effects on this physiological system. Instead, the study provides a demonstration of the relationship of depression to concern over illness.

Effects of Experience with the Health Care System

Among clinical populations with diagnosed diseases, various experiences encountered during treatment can have major effects on the psychological and behavioral characteristics of patients (Barofsky, 1981; Krantz et al., 1980; Weisman, 1979). Such effects have been described in terms of variables such as doctor–patient interaction (cf. Krantz, Glass, Contrada, & Miller, 1981), effects of the hospital environment (Kornfeld, 1972; Krantz, 1980; Plumb & Holland, 1977), or the effects of undergoing therapeutic treatment (F. Cohen & Lazarus, 1979; Weisman, 1979). Therefore, it has been noted that experiences with the health care system may be an important and often a confounding factor in research examining psychological correlates of progression of disease (Barofsky, 1981).

Consider, for example, a recent critique of research on psychological correlates of cancer progression. The Derogatis et al. (1979) study of patients with metastatic breast cancer indicated that long-term survivors reported more overall symptomatology and higher levels of hostility than did those who survived for shorter periods. Initial measures of biological status did not differentiate the two groups, and the data are interpreted by Derogatis et al. (1979) as suggesting that psychological characteristics contribute to survival. However, Barofsky (1981) notes that the short-term survivors had a somewhat shorter interval between mastectomy and recurrence—the point at which they were tested in the study. The possibility exists, therefore, that short-term survivors were likely to have received up to twice as much chemotherapy prior to psychological testing; the chemotherapy may well have decreased these patients' "fighting spirit" (Barofsky, 1981). Since type and duration of chemotherapy are not described in the Derogatis et al. (1979) study, the influence of this treatment variable may well have accounted for psychological and/or survival differences.

Having cancer and being treated for it can affect both patients and their families. This is illustrated by a finding that cancer patients reported no more depression than their cancer-free families did (Plumb & Holland, 1977). The psychological and biological effects of health care experiences have been largely neglected in research on traits and illness. Such factors must be considered before the influence of coping responses on the progression of disease can be understood.

CONCLUDING COMMENTS AND OBSERVATIONS

This review has described three orientations toward research on behavior patterns, personality, and illness. One approach presumes that traits can play a role in the etiology of disease; a second focuses on individual differences in the progression and course of illness. Both of these orientations assume that personality traits play a causal role in disease. A third orientation presumes an opposite direction of causality (i.e., that illness affects personality), or explains associations between traits and physical illness as a function of other variables, such as the health care system. Many of the studies or models we have reviewed might fit into more than one category, and there are major unresolved research issues that are common to all three approaches. Despite extensive research, clear-cut and consistent associations between personality characteristics and most disorders remain elusive phenomena.

Conceptual and Methodological Issues

Most associations between traits and illness fail to meet stringent epidemiological criteria for acceptance—namely, consistency, specificity, reproducibility, and so forth. Moreover, most of the research has been characterized by a search for correlations, with little emphasis until recently on the exploration of mechanisms linking behavioral processes to disease endpoints. An exception is the Type A behavior pattern, which is arguably not a personality trait, but instead the outcome of a person–situation interaction. This bleak state of affairs has suggested to some (Ostfeld, 1973; Stachnik, 1980) that the study of traits and illness has not led to major scientific advancements in understanding behavior–disease relationships. On the other hand, there are wide individual differences in susceptibility to disease. These differences depend on biological predispositions, such as genetic susceptibility, as well as on situational factors, such as the context in which pathogens or stressful events occur. Individual psychological attributes, including the way in which events are interpreted and the individual's felt ability to cope with conditions of harm or challenge, also appear to account in part for selective susceptibility to disease. Research on Type A behavior and its related components, for example, has contributed to knowledge concerning possible mechanisms in the pathogenesis of CHD.

Biobehavioral Interactions and Measurement Problems

The complex manner in which biological, situational, and dispositional factors interact in determining the relationship between stress and illness suggests that any single predisposing factor ought not to be studied independently of other factors. Yet many dispositional or trait approaches arose from psychodynamic orientations, which focused on traits to the exclusion of situational and biological factors. Where biological predispositions and stressful life events are implicated in theoretical approaches to the behavior–disease relationship (e.g., helplessness–hopelessness), conceptual and operational definitions are vague and difficult to test empirically. Examples of problematic areas for the helplessness–hopelessness model include difficulties in defining concepts such as "symbolic" loss, in arriving at precise criteria for defining "giving up" responses in interviews, and in distinguishing between the onset of symptoms and processes involved in the etiology of disease. Because of the imprecise manner in which variables are defined, it is difficult to determine whether relatively chronic traits or transient "states" are being measured. The possible role of such factors as stressful life events in the precipitation of disorders therefore becomes difficult to disentangle from the effects of personality.

The ability to generalize from study to study has also been impeded by the use of interviews or objective measurements of questionable reliability and validity, and the relationship of pencil-and-paper measures to overt behavior is rarely examined. In addition, research on psychophysiological mechanisms has been impeded by a lack of biomedical sophistication, or by limitations in the state of biomedical knowledge of various disease processes.

Heterogeneity of "Psychosomatic" Disorders

It has been noted (Weiner, 1977) that many diseases frequently studied for their psychophysiological or "psychosomatic" character are heterogeneous; that is, there are different forms or stages of the disease, involving different pathogenic mechanisms. Recall, for example, the physiological distinction between mild or "borderline" and "established" hypertension. Similarly, investigators have often grouped together a variety of heterogeneous disorders and studied them as if they represented a single clinical entity. Examples of such nonhomogeneous diseases include various forms of cancer and different clinical manifestations of CHD. The search for pathogenic mechanisms will be furthered by greater specificity and precision in selection and description of samples.

The Consistency of Traits

Personality traits are usually defined as *consistent* and enduring differences in either style or content of behavior (Willerman, 1979). There is, however, considerable controversy regarding the consistency of personality traits and their ability to predict behavior. Mischel (1968) has argued that trait descriptions have little ability to predict behavior, and that behavior fluctuates widely from situation to situation. He refers to numerous studies that demonstrate little consistency in behavior across different settings. If personality traits are not stable across dissimilar settings and time, it is not reasonable to hypothesize that these dispositions play a role in the etiology and/or progression of chronic disease processes.

However, Mischel's (1968) criticisms have not gone unchallenged. One response of relevance to this chapter emphasizes that it is the interaction between traits and situations—not traits or situations singly—that offers the most comprehensive means of predicting behavior (e.g., Bowers, 1973). For example, Type A behavior is defined in terms of a person–situation interaction (M. Friedman & Rosenman, 1959; Glass, 1977), and is assessed in terms of responses to a challenging interview situation. Other examples of person–situation interactions are what F. Cohen and Lazarus (1979) call "process measures" of the coping strategies used in stressful situations. Increased use of "process" measurement techniques may prove productive for future research. However, reliability and validity of process measures can vary considerably if strategies are assessed with techniques such as interviews. Fox (1978) has provided a more detailed discussion of these issues.

Research on Mechanisms and Future Directions

Critics of the traditional psychosomatic approach have argued that major advances in the understanding of disease have occurred independently of this orientation (Ostfeld, 1973; Stachnik, 1980). This may be because the psychosomatic tradition was descriptively oriented, and, with several notable exceptions, was concerned with establishing correlations between psychological variables and physical disease. In recent years, advances in the behavioral and biomedical sciences have encouraged research that explores underlying mechanisms linking behavioral processes to disease states. A focus on mechanisms is necessary for a precise understanding, rather than a description, of the role of personality traits. Such an emphasis also enables investigators and clinicians to translate such descriptive and epidemiological variables as age, personality, or genetics into pathogenic psychophysiological processes that have the potential to be altered, modified, or prevented. Thus, the identification of potentially modifiable variables in biobehavioral research may determine the extent to which this work will affect medical practice (Stachnik, 1980).

With the exception of research indicating that Type A behavior is related to enhanced sympathetic, cardiovascular, and neuroendocrine responses to challenging or stressful situations, very few person-centered or trait variables have been consistently related to physiological or behavioral processes that play a role in the pathogenesis or progression of disease. Developments in the measurement of cardiovascular, neuroendocrine, and immune processes may encourage further exploration of these physiological processes as they are influenced by behavioral stimuli.

Further research on the psychophysiology of emotion may help clarify relationships between personality and disease. Many psychosomatic theories are based on assumptions about the nature of emotion that either have not received empirical support or remain unsettled issues. In recent years, increasing emphasis has been placed on the role of cognition in emotion (Lang et al., 1972; Schachter & Singer, 1962), and questions have been raised about the physiological specificity of emotional states. Further knowledge is needed about the relationships among experienced affect, cognition, and specific physiological responses if the role of personality in disease is to be understood (see Leventhal, Zimmerman, & Gutmann, Chapter 10, this volume).

Greater care must also be taken to develop precise definitions of conceptual and operational variables in future research on personality and illness. This is true in terms of differentiating biomedical subcategories of diseases, and also in terms of defining and measuring behavioral variables. It is not uncommon to find such emotional constructs as depression, hostility, and anxiety operationalized in a diversity of ways between studies and even within the same study. It is also rare that assessments are made of such parameters as frequency or duration of emotional characteristics.

Instead of relying on intrapsychic variables, which have questionable reliability and show inconsistent relationships with psychophysiological indexes, new dimensions of behavior that affect physiological responses can be examined. For example, we have described the dimension of active versus passive coping with behavioral stressors (Obrist, 1981), which has been shown to influence cardiovascular and neuroendocrine response to stressors. Other investigators (S. Cohen, 1980; Matthews & Brunson, 1979; Williams, 1978) have suggested the relevance for cardiovascular response of the manner in which the individual allocates attention to or focuses attention on the environment. Still other workers (Bulman & Wortman, 1977; Leventhal, Zimmerman, & Gutmann, Chapter 10, this volume) have provided evidence that individual interpretations and beliefs about the nature and causes of disease may be important determinants of the way in which the individual copes with illness. There may also be individual differences in the tendency to seek out stressful life events, or in the ability to establish social support systems that serve as buffers against stressful events.

Many hypotheses concerning personality and physical illness have their roots in the theorizing that preceded current thinking in personality psychology and the psychophysiology of emotion. Further research on factors that predispose individuals to particular disorders must take account of basic research in these areas by examining complex interactions between biological and behavioral characteristics of the individual, as well as features of the situation.

ACKNOWLEDGMENTS

Preparation of this chapter was supported by USUHS Grant Nos. C07214 and RO7233, and by NIH Grant No. HL31514.

REFERENCES

Ader, R. (Ed.). *Psychoneuroimmunology*. New York: Academic Press, 1981.

Alexander, F. Psychoanalytic study of a case of essential hypertension. *Psychosomatic Medicine*, 1939, *1*, 139–152.

Alexander, F. *Psychosomatic medicine*. New York: Norton, 1950.

Amkraut, A. A., & Solomon, G. F. From the symbolic stimulus to the pathophysiologic response: Immune mechanisms. In Z. J. Lipowski, D. R. Lipsitt, & P. C. Whybrow (Eds.), *Psychosomatic medicine: Current trends and clinical applications*. New York: Oxford University Press, 1977.

Averill, J. R. A selective review of cognitive and behavioral factors involved in the regulation of stress. In R. A. Depue (Ed.), *The psychobiology of depressive disorders: Implications for the effects of stress.* New York: Academic Press, 1970.

Baer, P. E., Collins, F. H., Bourianoff, G. G., & Ketchel, M. F. Assessing personality factors in essential hypertension with a brief self-report instrument. *Psychosomatic Medicine*, 1979, *41*, 321–330.

Barofsky, I. Issues and approaches to the psychosocial assessment of the cancer patient. In C. K. Prokop & L. A. Bradley (Eds.), *Medical psychology: Contributions to behavioral medicine.* New York: Academic Press, 1981.

Bergland, G., Andes, S., Lindstrom, B., & Tibblin, G. Personality and reporting of symptoms in normo- and hypertensive 50 year old males. *Journal of Psychosomatic Research*, 1975, *19*, 139–145.

Betz, B. J., & Thomas, C. B. Individual temperament as a predictor of health or premature disease. *John Hopkins Medical Journal*, 1979, *81*, 81–89.

Blumenthal, J. A., Williams, R. B., Kong, Y., Schanberg, S. M., & Thompson, L. W. Type A behavior and angiographically documented coronary disease. *Circulation*, 1978, *58*, 634–639.

Bowers, K. S. Situationism in psychology: An analysis and a critique. *Psychological Review*, 1973, *80*, 307–336.

Brand, R. J., Rosenman, R. H., Jenkins, C. D., Sholtz, R. I., & Zyzanski, S. J. *Comparison of coronary heart disease prediction in the Western Collaborative Group Study using the Structured Interview and the Jenkins Activity Survey assessment of the coronary-prone Type A behavior pattern.* Paper presented at the conference on cardiovascular disease epidemiology of the American Heart Association, Orlando, March 1978.

Bulman, R. J., & Wortman, C. B. Attributions of blame and coping in the "real world": Severe accident victims react to their lot. *Journal of Personality and Social Psychology*, 1977, *35*, 351–363.

Bunn, P. A., Schein, P. S., Bankes, P. M., & Devita, V. T. Central nervous system complications in patients with diffuse histiocytic and undifferentiated lymphoma: Leukemia revisited. *Blood*, 1976, *47*, 3–10.

Buss, A. H. *Psychopathology.* New York: Wiley, 1966.

Cannon, W. B. *Bodily changes in pain, hunger, fear and rage.* New York: Appleton-Century-Crofts, 1929.

Cassem, N. H., & Hackett, T. P. Psychiatric consultation in a coronary care unit. *Annals of Internal Medicine*, 1971, *75*, 9–14.

Chesney, M. A., Black, G. W., Chadwick, J. N., & Rosenman, R. H. Physiological correlates of the Type A behavior pattern. *Journal of Behavioral Medicine*, 1981, *4*, 217–230.

Clayton, P. J. Mortality and morbidity in the first year of widowhood. *Archives of General Psychiatry*, 1974, *30*, 747–750.

Cluff, L. E., Canter, A., & Imboden, J. B. Asian influenza: Infection, disease, and psychological factors. *Archives of Internal Medicine*, 1966, *117*, 159–163.

Coelho, G. V., Hamburg, D. A., & Adams, J. E. (Eds.). *Coping and adaptation.* New York: Basic Books, 1974.

Cohen, F. Personality, stress, and the development of physical illness. In G. C. Stone, F. Cohen, & N. E. Adler (Eds.), *Health psychology: A handbook.* San Francisco: Jossey-Bass, 1979.

Cohen, F., Horowitz, M. J., Lazarus, R. S., Moos, R. H., Robins, L. N., Rose, R. M., & Rutter, M. Panel report on psychosocial assets and modifiers of stress. In G. R. Elliott & C. Eisdorfer (Eds.), *Stress and human health: Analysis and implications of research.* New York: Springer, 1982.

Cohen, F., & Lazarus, R. S. Active coping processes, coping dispositions, and recovery from surgery. *Psychosomatic Medicine*, 1973, *35*, 375–389.

Cohen, F., & Lazarus, R. S. Coping with the stresses of illness. In G. C. Stone, F. Cohen, & N. E. Adler (Eds.), *Health psychology: A handbook.* San Francisco: Jossey-Bass, 1979.

Cohen, J. B., Syme, S. L., Jenkins, C. D., Kagan, A., & Zyzanski, S. J. Cultural context of Type A behavior and risk for CHD: A study of Japanese-American males. *Journal of Behavioral Medicine*, 1979, *2*, 375–384.

Cohen, S. Aftereffects of stress on human performance and social behavior. *Psychological Bulletin*, 1980, *88*, 82–108.

Contrada, R. J., Glass, D. C., Krakoff, L. R., Krantz, D. S., Kehoe, K., Isecke, W., Collins, C., & Elting, E. Effects of control over aversive stimulation and Type A behavior on cardiovascular and plasma catecholamine responses. *Psychophysiology*, 1982, *19*(4), 408–419.

Cooper, T., Detre, T., & Weiss, S. M. (Eds.). Coronary-prone behavior and coronary heart disease: A critical review. *Circulation*, 1981, *63*, 1199–1215.

Corse, C. D., Manuck, S. B., Cantwell, J. D., Giordiani, B., & Matthews, K. A. Coronary prone behavior and cardiovascular response in persons with and without coronary heart disease. *Psychosomatic Medicine*, 1982, *44*, 449–460.

Costa, P. T., McCrae, R. R., Andres, R., & Tobin, J. D. Hypertension, somatic complaints, and personality. In M. F. Elias & D. H. P. Streeten (Eds.), *Hypertension and cognitive processes*. Mount Desert, Maine: Beech Hill, 1980.

Cottington, E. M., Matthews, K. A., Talbott, E., & Kuller, L. H. Environmental events preceding sudden death in women. *Psychosomatic Medicine*, 1980, *42*, 567–574.

Cox, T. *Stress*. Baltimore: University Park Press, 1978.

Croog, S. H., Shapiro, D. S., & Levine, S. Denial among male heart patients: An empirical study. *Psychosomatic Medicine*, 1971, *33*, 385–397.

Dahl, L. K., Heine, M., & Tassinari, L. Role of genetic factors in susceptibility to experimental hypertension due to chronic excess salt ingestion. *Nature*, 1962, *194*, 480–482.

Dattore, P. J., Shontz, F. C., & Coyne, L. Premorbid personality differentiation of cancer and noncancer groups: A test of the hypothesis of cancer proneness. *Journal of Consulting and Clinical Psychology*, 1980, *48*, 388–394.

Davies, R. K., Quinlan, D. M., McKegney, F. P., & Kimball, C. P. Organic factors and psychological adjustment in advanced cancer patients. *Psychosomatic Medicine*, 1973, *35*, 464–471.

Dembroski, T. M., MacDougall, J. M., Herd, J. A., & Shields, J. L. Effects of level of challenge on pressor and heart rate responses in Type A and B subjects. *Journal of Applied Social Psychology*, 1979, *9*, 208–228.

Dembroski, T. M., MacDougall, J. M., & Lushene, R. Interpersonal interaction and cardiovascular response in Type A subjects and coronary patients. *Journal of Human Stress*, 1979, *5*(4), 28–34.

Dembroski, T. M., MacDougall, J. M., Shields, J. L., Petitto, J., & Lushene, R. Components of the Type A coronary-prone behavior pattern and cardiovascular responses to psychomotor performance challenge. *Journal of Behavioral Medicine*, 1978, *1*, 159–176.

Dembroski, T. M., MacDougall, J. M., Williams, R. B., & Haney, T. L. Components of Type A, hostility, and anger in relationship to angiographic findings. Unpublished manuscript, Eckerd College Stress and Cardiovascular Research Center, St. Petersburg, Florida, 1983.

Dembroski, T. M., Weiss, S. M., Shields, J. L., Haynes, S. G., & Feinleib, M. (Eds.). *Coronary-prone behavior*. New York: Springer-Verlag, 1978.

Derogatis, C. R., Abeloff, M. D., & Melisaratos, N. Psychological coping mechanisms and survival time in metastatic breast cancer. *Journal of the American Medical Association*, 1979, *242*, 1504–1508.

Dimsdale, J. E., Hackett, T. P., Hutter, A. M., & Block, P. C. The risk of Type A mediated coronary disease in different populations. *Psychosomatic Medicine*, 1980, *42*, 55–62.

Dunbar, H. F. *Psychosomatic diagnosis*. New York: Hoeber, 1943.

Elias, M. F., & Streeten, D. H. P. (Eds.). *Hypertension and cognitive processes*. Mount Desert, Maine: Beech Hill, 1980.

Engel, B. T., & Bickford, A. F. Response specificity. *Archives of General Psychiatry*, 1961, *5*, 478–489.

Engel, G. L. A life setting conductive to illness: The giving-up-given-up complex. *Bulletin of the Menninger Clinic*, 1968, *32*, 355–365.

Engel, G. L. Sudden and rapid death during psychological stress: Folklore or folk wisdom? *Annals of Internal Medicine*, 1971, *74*, 771–782.

Engel, G. L., & Schmale, A. H. Conservation–withdrawal: A primary regulatory process for organismic homeostasis. In *Physiology, emotion and psychosomatic illness* (Ciba Foundation Symposium, 8). Amsterdam: Elsevier North-Holland, 1972.

Esler, M., Julius, S., Zweifler, A., Randall, O., Harburg, E., Gardiner, H., & DeQuattro, V. Mild high-renin essential hypertension: Neurogenic human hypertension? *New England Journal of Medicine*, 1977, *296*, 405–411.

Fahrion, S. L. *Etiology and intervention in essential hypertension: A behavioral approach.* Unpublished manuscript, The Menninger Foundation, 1981.

Falkner, B., Onesti, G., Angelakos, E. T., Fernandes, M., & Langman, C. Cardiovascular response to mental stress in normal adolescents with hypertensive parents: Hemodynamics and mental stress in adolescents. *Hypertension*, 1979, *1*, 23–30.

Fox, B. H. Premorbid psychological factors as related to cancer incidence. *Journal of Behavioral Medicine*, 1978, *1*, 45–133.

Fraumeni, J. F. *Persons at high risk of cancer: An approach to cancer etiology and control.* New York: Academic Press, 1975.

Friedman, M., Manwaring, J. H., Rosenman, R. H., Donlon, G., Ortega, P., & Grube, S. Instantaneous and sudden death: Clinical and pathological differentiation in coronary artery disease. *Journal of the American Medical Association*, 1973, *225*, 1319–1328.

Friedman, M., & Rosenman, R. H. Association of specific overt behavior pattern with blood and cardiovascular findings: Blood cholesterol level, blood clotting time, incidence of arcus senilis and clinical coronary artery disease. *Journal of the American Medical Association*, 1959, *169*, 1286–1296.

Friedman, M., Rosenman, R. H., & Carroll, V. Changes in the serum cholesterol and blood clotting time in men subjected to cyclic variation of occupational stress. *Circulation*, 1958, *17*, 852–861.

Friedman, R., & Iwai, J. Genetic predisposition and stress-induced hypertension. *Science*, 1976, *193*, 161–162.

Froese, A., Hackett, T. P., Cassem, N. H., & Silverberg, E. L. Trajectories of anxiety and depression in denying and nondenying acute myocardial infarction patients during hospitalization. *Journal of Psychosomatic Research*, 1974, *18*, 413–420.

Garrity, T. F. Social involvement and activeness as predictors of morale six months after myocardial infarction. *Social Science and Medicine*, 1973, *7*, 199–207.

Garrity, T. F., McGill, A., Becker, M., Blanchard, E., Crews, J., Cullen, J., Hackett, T. P., Taylor, J., & Valins, S. Report of the Task Group on Cardiac Rehabilitation. In S. M. Weiss (Ed.), *Proceedings of the National Heart and Lung Institute Working Conference on Health Behavior* (DHEW Publication No. 76-868). Washington, D.C.: U.S. Government Printing Office, 1976.

Gatchel, R. J., Baum, A., & Lang, P. J. Psychosomatic disorders: Basic issues and future research directions. In R. J. Gatchel, A. Baum, & J. E. Singer (Eds.), *Handbook of psychology and health* (Vol. 1). Hillsdale, N.J.: Erlbaum, 1982.

Gentry, W. D., Chesney, A. P., Gary, H. E., Hall, R. P., & Harburg, E. Habitual anger-coping styles: I. Effect on mean blood pressure and risk for essential hypertension. *Psychosomatic Medicine*, 1982, *44*, 195–202.

Gentry, W. D., Foster, S., & Haney, T. Denial as a determinant of an anxiety and perceived health status in the coronary care unit. *Psychosomatic Medicine*, 1972, *34*, 39–44.

Gentry, W. D., Oude-Weme, J. D., Musch, F., & Hall, R. P. Differences in Type A and B behavior in response to myocardial infarction. *Heart and Lung*, 1981, *10*, 1101.

Gesell, A., & Ilg, F. L. *Infant and child in the culture of today.* New York: Harper & Bros., 1943.

Gillum, R., Leon, G. R., Kamp, J., & Becerra-Aldama, J. Prediction of cardiovascular and other disease onset and mortality from 30-year longitudinal MMPI data. *Journal of Consulting and Clinical Psychology*, 1980, *48*, 405–406.

Glass, D. C. *Behavior patterns, stress, and coronary disease.* Hillsdale, N.J.: Erlbaum, 1977.

Glass, D. C., Krakoff, L. R., Contrada, R., Hilton, W. F., Kehoe, K., Mannucci, E. G., Collins,

C., Snow, B., & Elting, E. Effect of harassment and competition upon cardiovascular and plasma catecholamine responses in Type A and Type B individuals. *Psychophysiology*, 1980, *17*, 453–463.

Glass, D. C., Krakoff, L. R., Finkelman, J., Snow, B., Contrada, R., Kehoe, K., Mannucci, E. G., Isecke, W., Collins, C., Hilton, W. F., & Elting, E. Effect of task overload upon cardiovascular and plasma catecholamine responses in Type A and B individuals. *Basic and Applied Social Psychology*, 1980, *1*, 199–218.

Glass, D. C., Ross, D. T., Contrada, R., Isecke, W., & Rosenman, R. H. Relative importance of speech characteristics and content of answers in the assessment of behavior pattern A by the structured interview. *Basic and Applied Social Psychology*, 1982, *3*, 161–168.

Goldstein, I. B. Assessment of hypertension. In C. K. Prokop & L. A. Bradley (Eds.), *Medical psychology: Contributions to behavioral medicine*. New York: Academic Press, 1981.

Grace, W. J., & Graham, D. T. Relationship of specific attitudes and emotions to certain bodily diseases. *Psychosomatic Medicine*, 1952, *14*, 243–251.

Graham, D. T. Psychosomatic medicine. In N. S. Greenfield & R. A. Sternbach (Eds.), *Handbook of psychophysiology*. New York: Holt, Rinehart & Winston, 1972.

Graham, D. T., Kabler, J. D., & Graham, F. K. Physiological response to the suggestion of attitudes specific for hives and hypertension. *Psychosomatic Medicine*, 1962, *24*, 159–168.

Graham, D. T., Lundy, R. M., Benjamin, L. S., Kabler, J. D., Lewis, W. C., Kunish, N. O., & Graham, F. K. Specific attitudes in initial interviews with patients having different "psychosomatic" diseases. *Psychosomatic Medicine*, 1962, *24*, 257–266.

Graham, D. T., Stern, J. A., & Winokur, G. Experimental investigation of the specificity of attitude hypothesis in psychosomatic disease. *Psychosomatic Medicine*, 1958, *20*, 446–457.

Greene, W. A., Goldstein, S., & Moss, A. J. Psychosocial aspects of sudden death. *Archives of Internal Medicine*, 1972, *129*, 725–731.

Greene, W. A., Moss, A. J., & Goldstein, S. Delay, denial, and death in coronary heart disease. In R. S. Eliot (Ed.), *Stress and the heart*. Mount Kisco, N.Y.: Futura, 1974.

Greer, S., Morris, T., & Pettingale, K. W. Psychological response to breast cancer: Effects on outcome. *Lancet*, 1979, *13*, 785–787.

Hackett, T. P., & Cassem, N. H. Psychological adaptation to convalescence in myocardial infarction patients. In J. P. Naughton, H. K. Hellerstein, & I. Mohler (Eds.), *Exercise testing and exercise training in coronary heart disease*. New York: Academic Press, 1973.

Haney, C. A. Illness behavior and psychosocial correlates of cancer. *Social Science and Medicine*, 1977, *11*, 223–228.

Harburg, E., Erfurt, J. C., Hauenstein, L. S., Chape, C., Schull, W. J., & Schork, M. A. Socioecological stress, suppressed hostility, skin color, and black–white male blood pressure: Detroit. *Psychosomatic Medicine*, 1973, *35*, 276–296.

Harrell, J. P. Psychological factors and hypertension: A status report. *Psychological Bulletin*, 1980, *87*, 482–501.

Haynes, R., Taylor, D. W., & Sackett, D. L. *Compliance in health care*. Baltimore: Johns Hopkins University Press, 1979.

Haynes, S. G., & Feinleib, M. Type A behavior and the incidence of coronary heart disease in the Framingham Heart Study. In H. Denolin (Ed.), *Advances in cardiology* (Vol. 29, *Psychological problems before and after myocardial infarction*). Basel: S. Karger, 1982.

Haynes, S. G., Feinleib, M., & Kannel, W. B. The relationship of psychosocial factors to coronary heart disease in the Framingham Study: III. Eight-year incidence of coronary heart disease. *American Journal of Epidemiology*, 1980, *111*, 37–58.

Haynes, S. G., Levine, S., Scotch, N., Feinleib, M., & Kannel, W. B. The relationship of psychosocial factors to coronary heart disease in the Framingham Study: I. Methods and risk factors. *American Journal of Epidemiology*, 1978, *107*, 362–383.

Henry, J. P., & Cassel, J. C. Psychosocial factors in essential hypertension: Recent epidemiologic and animal experimental evidence. *American Journal of Epidemiology*, 1969, *90*, 1971.

Herd, J. A. Physiological correlates of coronary-prone behavior. In T. M. Dembroski, S. M. Weiss,

J. L. Shields, S. G. Haynes, & M. Feinleib (Eds.), *Coronary-prone behavior*. New York: Springer-Verlag, 1978.

Hertzog, C., Schaie, K. W., & Gribbin, K. Cardiovascular diseases and changes in intellectual functioning from middle age to old age. *Journal of Gerontology*, 1978, *33*, 872–883.

Hofer, M. A., Wolff, C. T., Friedman, S. B., & Mason, J. W. A psychoendocrine study of bereavement: Part I. 17-hydroxycorticosteroid excretion rates of parents following death of their children from leukemia. *Psychosomatic Medicine*, 1972, *34*, 481–491. (a)

Hofer, M. A., Wolff, C. T., Friedman, S. B., & Mason, J. W. A psychoendocrine study of bereavement: Part II. Observations on the process of mourning in relation to adrenocortical function. *Psychosomatic Medicine*, 1972, *34*, 492–504. (b)

Hokanson, J. E. The effects of frustration and anxiety on overt aggression. *Journal of Abnormal and Social Psychology*, 1961, *62*, 346–351.

Jacobs, S., & Ostfeld, A. M. An epidemiological review of the mortality of bereavement. *Psychosomatic Medicine*, 1977, *39*, 344–357.

Jenkins, C. D. Psychologic and social precursors of coronary disease. *New England Journal of Medicine*, 1971, *284*, 244–255, 307–317.

Jenkins, C. D. Recent evidence supporting psychologic and social risk factors for coronary disease. *New England Journal of Medicine*, 1976, *294*, 987–994, 1033–1038.

Jenkins, C. D. Behavioral risk factors in coronary artery disease. *Annual Review of Medicine*, 1978, *29*, 543.

Jenkins, C. D., Zyzanski, S. J., & Rosenman, R. H. Progress toward validation of a computer-scored test for the Type A coronary-prone behavior pattern. *Psychosomatic Medicine*, 1971, *33*, 193–202.

Jenkins, C. D., Zyzanski, S. J., & Rosenman, R. H. Prediction of clinical coronary heart disease by a test for the coronary-prone behavior pattern. *New England Journal of Medicine*, 1974, *290*, 1271–1275.

Jenkins, C. D., Zyzanski, S. J., & Rosenman, R. H. Risk of new myocardial infarction in middle aged men with manifest coronary heart disease. *Circulation*, 1976, *53*, 342–347.

Jenkins, C. D., Zyzanski, S. J., & Rosenman, R. H. Coronary-prone behavior: One pattern or several? *Psychosomatic Medicine*, 1978, *40*, 25–43.

Julius, S., & Esler, M. Autonomic nervous cardiovascular regulation in borderline hypertension. *American Journal of Cardiology*, 1975, *36*, 685–696.

Kahn, J. P., Kornfeld, D. S., Frank, K. A., Heller, S. S., & Hoar, P. F. Type A behavior and blood pressure during coronary artery bypass surgery. *Psychosomatic Medicine*, 1980, *42*, 407–414.

Kalis, B. L., Harris, R. E., Bennett, L. F., & Sokolow, M. Personality and life history factors in persons who are potentially hypertensive. *Journal of Nervous and Mental Disorders*, 1961, *132*, 457–468.

Kaplan, N. M. The control of hypertension: A therapeutic breakthrough. *American Scientist*, 1980, *68*, 537–545.

Kasl, S. V., & Cobb, S. Health behavior, illness behavior, and sick role behavior. *Archives of Environmental Health*, 1966, *12*, 246–266, 531–541.

Katz, J. L., Ackman, P., Rothwax, Y., Sachar, E. J., Weiner, H., Hellman, L., & Gallagher, T. F. Psychoendocrine aspects of cancer of the breast. *Psychosomatic Medicine*, 1970, *32*, 1–18.

Kimball, C. P. Psychological responses to the experience of open-heart surgery: I. *American Journal of Psychiatry*, 1969, *126*, 348–359.

Kornfeld, D. S. The hospital environment: Its impact on the patient. *Advances in Psychosomatic Medicine*, 1972, *8*, 252–270.

Krantz, D. S. Cognitive processes and recovery from heart attack: A review and theoretical analysis. *Journal of Human Stress*, 1980, *6*(3), 27–38.

Krantz, D. S., Arabian, J. M., Davia, J. E., & Parker, J. S. Type A behavior and coronary artery bypass surgery: Intraoperative blood pressure and perioperative complications. *Psychosomatic Medicine*, 1982, *44*, 273–284.

Krantz, D. S., Baum, A., & Wideman, M. V. Assessment of preferences for self-treatment and information in health care. *Journal of Personality and Social Psychology*, 1980, *39*, 977–990.

Krantz, D. S., & Deckel, A. W. Coping with coronary heart disease and stroke. In T. Burish & L. A. Bradley (Eds.), *Coping with chronic disease*. New York: Academic Press, 1983.

Krantz, D. S., & Durel, L. A. Psychobiological substrates of the Type A behavior pattern. *Health Psychology*, 1983, *2*, 393–411.

Krantz, D. S., Durel, L. A., Davia, J. E., Shaffer, R. T., Arabian, J. M., Dembroski, T. M., & MacDougall, J. M. Propranolol medication among coronary patients: Relationship to Type A behavior and cardiovascular response. *Journal of Human Stress*, 1982, *8*(3), 4–12.

Krantz, D. S., Glass, D. C., Contrada, R., & Miller, N. E. Behavior and health. In *Five year outlook of science and technology: 1981* (Source materials, Vol. 2). Washington, D.C.: National Science Foundation, 1981.

Krantz, D. S., Glass, D. C., Schaeffer, M. A., & Davia, J. E. Behavior patterns and coronary disease: A critical evaluation. In J. T. Cacioppo & R. E. Petty (Eds.), *Perspectives in cardiovascular psychophysiology*. New York: Guilford Press, 1982.

Krantz, D. S., Sanmarco, M. E., Selvester, R. H., & Matthews, K. A. Psychological correlates of progression of atherosclerosis in men. *Psychosomatic Medicine*, 1979, *41*, 467–475.

Krantz, D. S., Schaeffer, M. A., Davia, J. E., Dembroski, T. M., MacDougall, J. M., & Shaffer, R. T. Extent of coronary atherosclerosis, Type A behavior and cardiovascular response to social interaction. *Psychophysiology*, 1981, *18*, 654–664.

Krantz, D. S., & Schulz, R. A model of life crisis, control, and health outcomes: Cardiac rehabilitation and relocation of the elderly. In A. Baum & J. E. Singer (Eds.), *Advances in environmental psychology* (Vol. 2). Hillsdale, N.J.: Erlbaum, 1980.

Lacey, J. I. Somatic response patterning and stress: Some revision of activation theory. In M. H. Appley & R. Trumbull (Eds.), *Psychological stress*. New York: Appleton-Century-Crofts, 1967.

Lacey, J. I., Kagan, J., Lacey, B. C., & Moss, H. A. The visceral level: Situational determinants and behavioral correlates of autonomic response patterns. In P. H. Knapp (Ed.), *Expression of the emotions in man*. New York: International Universities Press, 1963.

Lacey, J. I., & Lacey, B. C. Verification and extension of the principle of autonomic response stereotypy. *American Journal of Psychology*, 1958, *71*, 50–73.

Lang, P. J. A bio-informational theory of emotional imagery. *Psychophysiology*, 1979, *16*, 495–512.

Lang, P. J., Rice, D. G., & Sternbach, R. A. The psychophysiology of emotion. In N. S. Greenfield & R. A. Sternbach (Eds.), *Handbook of psychophysiology*. New York: Holt, Rinehart & Winston, 1972.

Lawler, J. E., Barker, G. F., Hubbard, J. W., & Allen, M. T. The effects of conflict on tonic levels of blood pressure in the genetically borderline hypertensive rat. *Psychophysiology*, 1980, *17*, 363–370.

Lazarus, R. S. *Psychological stress and the coping process*. New York: McGraw-Hill, 1966.

Lebovitz, B. Z., Shekelle, R. B., Ostfeld, A. M., & Paul, O. Prospectives and retrospective psychological studies of coronary heart disease. *Psychosomatic Medicine*, 1967, *29*, 265–272.

Levi, L. Psychosocial factors in preventive medicine. In *Surgeon General's background papers for healthy people report* (DHEW Publication No. 79-55071A). Washington, D.C.: U.S. Government Printing Office, 1979.

Light, K. Psychological stress induces sodium and fluid retention in men at high risk for hypertension. *Science*, 1983, *220*, 429–431.

Lipowski, Z. J. Psychosomatic medicine in the seventies: An overview. *American Journal of Psychiatry*, 1977, *134*, 233–244.

Lister, T. A. Early central nervous system involvement in adults with acute non-myelogenous leukemia. *British Journal of Cancer*, 1977, *35*, 479–483.

Luborsky, L., Doherty, J. P., & Penick, S. Onset conditions for psychosomatic symptoms: A comparative review of immediate observation with retrospective research. *Psychosomatic Medicine*, 1973, *35*, 187–204.

MacDougall, J. M., Dembroski, T. M., & Musante, L. The structured interview and question-naire methods of assessing coronary-prone behavior in male and female college students. *Journal of Behavioral Medicine*, 1979, *2*, 71–84.

Maddison, D., & Viola, A. The health of widows in the year following bereavement. *Journal of Psychosomatic Research*, 1968, *12*, 297–306.

Mages, N. L., & Mendelson, G. A. Effects of cancer on patients' lives: A personological ap-proach. In G. C. Stone, F. Cohen, & N. E. Adler (Eds.), *Health psychology: A handbook*. San Francisco: Jossey-Bass, 1979.

Mann, G. V. Diet–heart: End of an era. *New England Journal of Medicine*, 1977, *297*, 644–650.

Manuck, S. B., Kaplan, J. R., & Clarkson, T. B. Behaviorally induced heart rate reactivity and atherosclerosis in cynomolgus monkeys. *Psychosomatic Medicine*, 1983, *45*, 95–108.

Manuck, S. B., & Schaefer, D. C. Stability of individual differences in cardiovascular reactiv-ity. *Physiology and Behavior*, 1978, *21*, 675–678.

Matheson, L. H. *Cardiovascular disease, the coronary prone behavior pattern, and central nervous sys-tem function*. Unpublished doctoral dissertation, University of Southern California, 1979.

Matthews, K. A. Psychological perspectives on the Type A behavior pattern. *Psychological Bul-letin*, 1982, *91*, 293–323.

Matthews, K. A., & Brunson, B. I. Allocation of attention and the Type A coronary-prone be-havior pattern. *Journal of Personality and Social Psychology*, 1979, *37*, 2081–2090.

Matthews, K. A., Glass, D. C., Rosenman, R. H., & Bortner, R. W. Competitive drive, Pattern A, and coronary heart disease: A further analysis of some data from the Western Collabora-tive Group Study. *Journal of Chronic Diseases*, 1977, *30*, 489–498.

Matthews, K. A., & Krantz, D. S. Resemblance of twins and their parents in Pattern A behavior. *Psychosomatic Medicine*, 1976, *38*, 140–144.

Matthews, K. A., Krantz, D. S., Dembroski, T. M., & MacDougall, J. M. The unique and common variance in the structured interview and Jenkins Activity Survey measures of the Type A behavior pattern. *Journal of Personality and Social Psychology*, 1982, *42*, 303–313.

Matthews, K. A., Rosenman, R. H., Dembroski, T. M., Harris, E., & MacDougall, J. M. *Familial resemblance in components of the Type A behavior pattern: A reanalysis of the California Type A twin study*. Manuscript submitted for publication, 1983.

McCubbin, J. A., Green, J. H., & Page, I. H. Baroreceptor function in chronic renal hyperten-sion. *Circulation Research*, 1956, *4*, 205–210.

McFarland, D. V., & Cobb, S. Causal interpretations from cross-sectional data: An examina-tion of the stochastic processes involved in the relation between a personal characteristic and coronary heart disease. *Journal of Chronic Disease*, 1967, *20*, 393–406.

McGinn, N. F., Harburg, E., Julius, S., & McLeod, J. M. Psychological correlates of blood pres-sure. *Psychological Bulletin*, 1964, *61*, 209–219.

McMahon, C. E. The role of imagination in the disease process: Pre-Cartesian medical history. *Psychological Medicine*, 1976, *6*, 179–184.

Mears, F. G., & Gatchel, R. J. *Fundamentals of abnormal psychology*. Chicago: Rand McNally, 1979.

Mechanic, D. *Medical sociology*. New York: Free Press, 1968.

Medalie, J. H., Snyder, M., Groen, J. J., Neufeld, H. N., Goldbourt, U., & Riss, E. Angina pec-toris among 10,000 men: Five year incidence and univariate analysis. *American Journal of Medicine*, 1973, *55*, 583–594.

Mischel, W. *Personality and assessment*. New York: Wiley, 1968.

Mischel, W. Toward a cognitive social learning reconceptualization of personality. *Psychological Review*, 1973, *80*, 252–283.

Mitchell, W. M. Etiological factors producing neuropsychiatric syndromes in patients with malignant disease. *International Journal of Neuropsychiatry*, 1967, *3*, 464–468.

Morrison, F. R., & Paffenberger, R. S. Epidemiologic aspects of bio-behavior in the etiology of cancer: A critical review. In S. M. Weiss, J. A. Herd, & B. H. Fox (Eds.), *Perspectives on be-havioral medicine*. New York: Academic Press, 1981.

Nemiah, J. C., Freyberger, H., & Sifneos, P. Alexthymia: A view of the psychosomatic research.

In O. Hill (Ed.), *Modern trends in psychosomatic medicine* (Vol. 3). London: Butterworths, 1976.

Obrist, P. A. *Cardiovascular psychophysiology: A perspective.* New York: Plenum, 1981.

Obrist, P. A., Grignolo, A., Hastrup, J. L., Koepke, J. P., Langer, A. W., Light, K. C., McCubbin, J. A., & Pollak, M. H. Behavioral–cardiac interactions in hypertension. In D. S. Krantz, A. Baum, & J. E. Singer (Eds.), *Handbook of psychology and health* (Vol. 3, *Cardiovascular disorders and behavior*). Hillsdale, N.J.: Erlbaum, 1983.

Osler, W. *Lectures on angina pectoris and allied states.* New York: Appleton-Century-Crofts, 1892.

Ostfeld, A. M. Editorial: What's the payoff in hypertension research? *Psychosomatic Medicine,* 1973, *35,* 1–3.

Ostfeld, A. M., & Lebovits, B. Z. Personality factors and pressor mechanisms in renal and essential hypertension. *Archives of Internal Medicine,* 1959, *104,* 43–52.

Ostfeld, A. M., & Shekelle, R. B. Psychological variables and blood pressure. In J. Stamler, R. Stamler, & T. N. Pullman (Eds.), *The epidemiology of essential hypertension.* New York: Grune & Stratton, 1967.

Page, I. H., & McCubbin, J. A. The physiology of arterial hypertension. In W. F. Hamilton & P. Dow (Eds.), *Handbook of physiology: Circulation* (Vol. 1, Section 2). Washington, D.C.: American Physiological Society, 1966.

Pancheri, P., Bellaterra, M., Matteoli, S., Cristofari, M., Polizzi, C., & Puletti, N. Infarct as a stress agent: Life history and personality characteristics in improved versus non-improved patients after severe heart attack. *Journal of Human Stress,* 1978, *4,* 16–22, 41–42.

Parkes, C. M., Benjamin, B., & Fitzgerald, R. G. Broken heart: A statistical study of increased mortality among widowers. *British Medical Journal,* 1969, *i,* 740–743.

Parkes, C. M., & Brown, R. J. Health after bereavement: A controlled study of young Boston widows and widowers. *Psychosomatic Medicine,* 1972, *34,* 449–461.

Peters, J. E., & Stern, R. M. Specificity of attitude hypothesis in psychosomatic medicine: A reexamination. *Journal of Psychosomatic Research,* 1971, *15,* 129–135.

Pettingale, K. W., Greer, S., & Tee, D. E. H. Serum IGA and emotional expression in breast cancer patients. *Journal of Psychosomatic Research,* 1977, *21,* 395–399.

Pickering, G. W. The inheritance of arterial pressure. In J. Stamler, R. Stamler, & T. N. Pullman (Eds.), *The epidemiology of hypertension.* New York: Grune & Stratton, 1967.

Plumb, M. M., & Holland, J. Comparative studies of psychological function in patients with advanced cancer: 1. Self-reported depressive symptoms. *Psychosomatic Medicine,* 1977, *39,* 264–276.

Rahe, R. H., Hervig, L., & Rosenman, R. H. *Heritability of Type A behavior.* Paper presented at the annual meeting of the American Psychosomatic Society, New Orleans, March 1978.

Reich, P., DeSilva, R. A., Lown, B., & Murawski, B. J. Acute psychological disturbances preceding life-threatening ventricular arrhythmias. *Journal of the American Medical Association,* 1981, *246,* 233–235.

Rogentine, G. N., van Kammen, D. P., Fox, B. H., Doherty, J. P., Rosenblatt, J. E., Boyd, S. C., & Bunney, W. E. Psychological factors in the prognosis of malignant melanoma: A prospective study. *Psychosomatic Medicine,* 1979, *41,* 647–655.

Rosenman, R. H. The interview method of assessment of the coronary-prone behavior pattern. In T. P. Dembroski, S. M. Weiss, J. L. Shields, S. G. Haynes, & M. Feinleib (Eds.), *Coronary-prone behavior.* New York: Springer-Verlag, 1978.

Rosenman, R. H., Brand, R. J., Jenkins, C. D., Friedman, M., Straus, R., & Wurm, M. Coronary heart disease in the Western Collaborative Group Study: Final follow-up experience of 8½ years. *Journal of the American Medical Association,* 1975, *233,* 872—877.

Rowland, K. F. Environmental events predicting death for the elderly. *Psychological Bulletin,* 1977, *84,* 349–372.

Sapira, J. D., Scheib, E. T., Moriarty, R., & Shapiro, A. P. Differences in perception between hypertensive and normotensive populations. *Psychosomatic Medicine,* 1971, *33,* 239–250.

Schachter, S., & Singer, J. E. Cognitive, social, and physiological determinants of emotional state. *Psychological Review,* 1962, *69,* 379–399.

Scherwitz, L., Berton, K., & Leventhal, H. Type A assessment and interaction in the behavior pattern interview. *Psychosomatic Medicine*, 1977, *39*, 229–240.

Schiffer, F., Hartley, L. H., Schulman, C. L., & Abelmann, W. H. The quiz electrocardiogram: A new diagnostic and research technique for evaluating the relation between emotional stress and ischemic heart disease. *American Journal of Cardiology*, 1976, *37*, 41–47.

Schleifer, S. J., Keller, S. E., McKegney, F. P., & Stein, M. *Bereavement and lymphocyte function.* Paper presented at the annual meeting of the American Psychiatric Association, San Francisco, May 1980.

Schmale, A. H., Jr. Relation of separation and depression to disease: I. A report on a hospitalized medical population. *Psychosomatic Medicine*, 1958, *20*, 259–277.

Schmale, A. H., Jr. Giving up as a final common pathway to changes in health. *Advances in Psychosomatic Medicine*, 1972, *8*, 20–40.

Schmale, A. H., Jr., & Iker, H. P. Hopelessness as a predictor of cervical cancer. *Social Science and Medicine*, 1971, *5*, 95–100.

Schucker, B., & Jacobs, D. R. Assessment of behavioral risk of coronary disease by voice characteristics. *Psychosomatic Medicine*, 1977, *39*, 219–228.

Seligman, M. E. *Helplessness: On depression, development, and death.* San Francisco: W. H. Freeman, 1975.

Shaffer, J. W., Duszynski, K. R., & Thomas, C. B. Family attitudes in youth as a possible precursor of cancer among physicians: A search for explanatory mechanisms. *Journal of Behavioral Medicine*, 1982, *5*, 143–164.

Shapiro, A. P. Behavioral and environmental aspects of hypertension. *Journal of Human Stress*, 1978, *4*, 9–17.

Shapiro, A. P., Benson, H., Chobanian, A. V., Herd, J. A., Julius, S., Kaplan, N., Lazarus, R. S., Ostfeld, A. M., & Syme, S. L. The role of stress in hypertension. *Journal of Human Stress*, 1979, *5*, 7–26.

Shekelle, R. B., Raynor, W. J., Ostfeld, A. M., Garron, D. C., Bieliauskas, L. A., Liu, S. C., Maliza, C., & Paul, O. Psychological depression and 17-year risk of death from cancer. *Psychosomatic Medicine*, 1981, *43*, 117–125.

Sklar, L. S., & Anisman, H. Stress and cancer. *Psychological Bulletin*, 1981, *89*, 369–406.

Spieth, W. Cardiovascular health status, age and psychological performance. *Journal of Gerontology*, 1964, *19*, 277–284.

Stachnik, T. Priorities for psychology in medical education and health care delivery. *American Psychologist*, 1980, *35*, 8–15.

Steptoe, A. *Psychological factors in cardiovascular disorders.* London: Academic Press, 1981.

Stroebe, M. S., Stroebe, W., Gergen, K. J., & Gergen, M. The broken heart: Reality or myth? *Omega: Journal of Death and Dying*, 1981, *12*, 87–105.

Thomas, C. B., Duszynski, K. R., & Shaffer, J. W. Family attitudes reported in youth as potential predictors of cancer. *Psychosomatic Medicine*, 1979, *41*, 287–302.

Tufo, H. M., & Ostfeld, A. M. A prospective study of open heart surgery. *Psychosomatic Medicine*, 1968, *30*, 552. (Abstract)

Vaillant, G. E. Natural history of male psychological health: Effects of mental health on physical health. *New England Journal of Medicine*, 1979, *301*, 1249–1254.

Verrier, R. L., DeSilva, R. A., & Lown, B. Psychological factors in cardiac arrhythmias and sudden death. In D. S. Krantz, A. Baum, & J. E. Singer (Eds.), *Handbook of psychology and health* (Vol. 3, *Cardiovascular disorders and behavior*). Hillsdale, N.J.: Erlbaum, 1983.

Weiner, H. *Psychobiology and human disease.* New York: Elsevier, 1977.

Weiner, H., Singer, M. T., & Reiser, M. F. Cardiovascular responses and their psychological correlates: A study in healthy young adults and patients with peptic ulcer and hypertension. *Psychosomatic Medicine*, 1962, *24*, 477–498.

Weiner, H., Thaler, M., Reiser, M. F., & Mirsky, I. A. Etiology of duodenal ulcer: I. Relation of specific psychological characteristics to rate of gastric secretion (serum pepsinogen). *Psychosomatic Medicine*, 1957, *19*, 1–10.

Weisman, A. D. *Coping with cancer.* New York: McGraw-Hill, 1979.

Willerman, L. *The psychology of individual and group differences.* San Francisco: W. H. Freeman, 1979.

Williams, R. B. Psychophysiological processes, the coronary-prone behavior pattern and coronary heart disease. In T. M. Dembroski, S. M. Weiss, J. L. Shields, S. Haynes, & M. Feinleib (Eds.), *Coronary-prone behavior.* New York: Springer-Verlag, 1978.

Williams, R. B., Haney, T. L., Lee, K. L., Kong, V., Blumenthal, J. A., & Whalen, R. E. Type A behavior, hostility, and coronary atherosclerosis. *Psychosomatic Medicine,* 1980, *42,* 529–538.

Zola, I. K. Studying the decision to see a doctor: Review, critique, corrective. *Advances in Psychosomatic Medicine,* 1972, *8,* 216–236.

Zyzanski, S. J., Stanton, B. A., Jenkins, C. D., & Klein, M. D. Medical and psychosocial outcomes in survivors of major heart surgery. *Journal of Psychosomatic Research,* 1981, *25,* 213–221.

CHAPTER 4

Social and Psychological Resources Mediating Stress–Illness Relationships in Humans

W. Doyle Gentry
University of Virginia Medical School

Suzanne C. Ouellette Kobasa
City University of New York

INTRODUCTION

Research in the field of behavioral medicine regarding stress–illness relationships has conveyed a largely pessimistic picture of the linkage between the two. Until very recently, an individual's risk for illness has been solely defined in terms of his or her exposure to stress; the greater the exposure, the greater the likelihood of one's becoming ill. This is true, for example, when one considers the research linking stressful life events (Dohrenwend & Dohrenwend, 1974) and the onset of illnesses such as coronary heart disease (CHD) and childhood leukemia, or the research associating stress with certain personality traits (Jenkins, 1976) or socioecological stress (Harburg, Erfurt, Hauenstein, Chape, Schull, & Schork, 1973).

In the last few years, however, this pessimistic orientation has begun to give way to more optimistic concerns. With the writings of Cassel (1976), Cobb (1976), Wolf (1976), and others, researchers began to realize that stressful life events and other psychosocial stressors do not have an invariant or universal impact on human health status (i.e., do not affect all exposed persons in a similar manner).

We believe, as did these writers before us, that issues of disease causation can no longer be presented in simplistic, unidimensional terms, identifying the presence of a particular stress factor as being illnesss-producing and its absence as not being so. Rather, researchers must recognize the importance of a second set of psychosocial factors—namely, those that serve to buffer or cushion an individual from the untoward psychological and physiological consequences of exposure to stress. By doing so, we may then consider the combined, interactive effects of both susceptibility and resistance factors as they jointly determine the health status of individuals and social groups (Chesney & Gentry, 1982).

This concept of balance or counterbalance (Wolf, 1976) in defining health risk is illustrated in Figure 4.1, which also enumerates some of the major categories of susceptibility (+) and resistance (−) variables that seem to play an active role in determining a person's ultimate risk for stress-induced illness. It should be emphasized from the outset that these variables can and do operate at the individual (personality) and community (social cohesion) level. One should also note that they are not "two sides of the same coin"; that is, susceptibility is not defined merely as the absence of host resistance, or vice versa. On the contrary, each represents a category of related but functionally independent variables that influence the nature and extent of stress–illness relationships.

The main objectives of the present chapter are as follows:

1. To identify some of the major psychosocial factors that operate to protect individuals and social groups from various forms of stress.
2. To consider the methodological strengths and weaknesses of research studies that have thus far addressed the issue of mediators to stress-induced illness.
3. To consider the interplay between resistance factors, where more than one operate in a given instance.
4. To outline some future research objectives in this important topic area.

REVIEW AND CRITIQUE OF THE LITERATURE

In reviewing the existing research on resistance or mediators to stress-induced illness, we concentrate on two categories of studies. The first category covers research done on a social level of analysis, emphasizing the resistance potential of such factors as social cohesion and religious participation. The

FIGURE 4.1. Model of health risk. (From Chesney, A. P., & Gentry, W. D. Psychosocial factors mediating health risk: A balanced perspective. *Preventive Medicine*, 1982, *11*, 612–617. Reprinted by permission.)

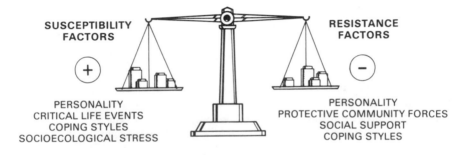

second category deals with psychological or individual-based studies that have focused on the stress mediation of such factors as personality and coping styles. Studies that describe the impact of resistance resources on physical illness are emphasized, in light of the primary concerns expressed by researchers in the field of behavioral medicine with "physical disorders as an end point" (Schwartz & Weiss, 1978).

The studies reviewed here can all be classified as ones that in some way measure the influence of resistance resources on stress–illness relationships, where stress per se is evident; studies investigating the "main effect" relationship of host resistance to illness in the absence of stress are not included. Under consideration are studies that compare illness rates in individuals exposed to stressful circumstances who are high versus low in some resistance factor (e.g., social support), as well as studies that look for differences in resistance resources in stressed individuals and/or communities evidencing high versus low levels of illness (e.g., CHD).

Social Factors

Over 20 years ago, Wolf and coworkers (Stout, Morrow, Brandt, & Wolf, 1964) became intrigued with the unusually low death rate from myocardial infarctions (MIs) found among residents of Roseta, a small Italian-American community established in 1882 in eastern Pennsylvania. Rosetans had a death rate from MIs that was less than half that of comparable neighboring communities or of the United States as a whole. This low incidence of coronary death was particularly noticeable in younger age groups; for example, there were no deaths due to MIs below age 47 during the initial period of study (1955–1961). Ironically, Rosetans enjoyed this remarkable absence of death due to MIs even though, as a group, they (1) had rates of coronary death without evidence of MIs and/or hypertensive disease equal to that of the surrounding towns; (2) were generally overweight and had a total fat consumption substantially greater than that of the average American; (3) had mean serum cholesterol levels comparable to those reported in the Framingham Study; (4) engaged in high rates of cigarette smoking; and (5) led a sedentary life style.

Having concluded that Rosetans' relative immunity from death due to MIs was not a function of dietary, ethnic, or genetic differences (Bruhn, 1965; Bruhn, Chandler, Miller, Wolf, & Lynn, 1966), these researchers began to focus on the social structure (fabric) of this small community as compared to surrounding towns. Here they found what they believed to be the secret to Roseta's success in mediating the stress of everyday life in the larger American society: a pattern of *protective social forces* that uniquely characterized this community. Rosetans were, in fact, distinguished by close family and community ties (social cohesion), and virtually all members of the community engaged in mutually supportive behavior toward one another. Rose tans had strong religious beliefs and regularly participated in religious activities of significance to the community. They had clear, nonoverlapping role expectations for men and women, and they revered their elderly. Unlike other American communities, Roseta allowed older residents to retain their influence on family and community affairs. Rosetans shared a common appreciation of personal and community values and a common sense of what constituted acceptable social behavior. With few exceptions, residents conformed to these values and patterns of behavior. Community members had an extreme sense of group identity, a sense of self-satisfaction for achievement, and perceived purpose in everyday community activities that led to "an unshaken feeling of personal security and continuity" (Benet, 1965, as quoted in Wolf, 1976).

According to Wolf, Grace, Bruhn, and Stout (1973), it was this social interdependence or cohesion that protected the health of Rosetans in the face of premorbid disease (CHD) and the evidence of risk behavior(s) (e.g., smoking, obesity, and sedentary life style). In support of this belief, Wolf and his colleagues predicted that, as Roseta became Americanized (i.e., adopted values and behavior patterns that emphasized individualistic and materialistic pursuits and necessitated increased social mobility), there would be a sharp rise in coronary deaths, to the point where Roseta's mortality figures would no longer differ from those of its neighboring towns or the nation at large. As predicted, beginning in the mid-1960s, Rosetans began to experience a marked increase in fatal MIs, first in older and then in younger age groups. In 1971, the first death due to MI in a man under 45 years of age was reported. Whereas in 1962–1965 Rosetans had experienced only 20% of the coronary deaths seen in towns nearby, by 1970 the coronary death rate from MIs was two-thirds of that found in these comparable communities, Bangor and Nazareth. The increase in MI deaths for Roseta from 1955–1965 to 1966–1975 was 27 times that seen in Bangor during that same time period. As Bruhn and Wolf (1978) noted, this is precisely the period during which "Roseta's traditional closely knit, mutually supportive social structure began to crumble and traditional 'Old World' values began to erode." Subsequent generations of Rosetans not only began to evidence increasing levels of stress and related illness (Bruhn, Philips, & Wolf, 1972); they also apparently had less in the way of resistance resources at their disposal.

Rosetans were in the process of acculturation, and, as such, they were choosing values and behavior patterns that conflicted with a cohesive, well-integrated social structure (Bruhn, Philips, & Wolf, 1982). In the active pursuit of individual advancement and status, they had less time for participation in religious activities, spent less time in community social clubs, and became increasingly dependent on non-Rosetans (persons in other nearby communities) to meet various social and psychological needs. In effect, this change in behavior seen in younger Rosetans reflected a tradeoff of "old for new," "social clubs for country clubs," and "cultural assets for social and material opportunities" (Bruhn et al., 1982; Wolf et al., 1973).

Wolf and colleagues have provided provocative, albeit circumstantial, evidence for the role of protective social forces in mediating stress–illness relationships at the community level. Unfortunately, their data are wholly descriptive in nature and cannot offer substantive conclusions regarding precise, quantitative links among stress, resistance, and health; such links, in turn, might have predictive or prognostic utility for individual Rosetans. The biggest criticism of this line of research has to do with the fact that Wolf's group simultaneously witnessed a rise in stress among Rosetans, along with a decline in resistance resources during the same time period. The former was empirically documented (Bruhn et al., 1972), whereas the latter was chiefly based on anecdotal observations (Bruhn & Wolf, 1978). This, of course, begs the question of whether or not the observed dramatic upsurge in deaths due to MIs was the result of heightened stress, decreased resistance, or both. It is conceivable that those few persons who suffered fatal MIs were simply exposed to more stress than were those who did not suffer this fate. This conclusion is, in fact, suggested by the case studies offered by Wolf et al. (1973, pp. 104–105) to argue the merits of social interdependence as a resistance resource:

> Subject A was born in Roseta, the oldest of four children, three brothers and one sister. In addition, there were three half-brothers and five half-sisters from his mother's previous marriage. His father, a carpenter, had immigrated from Italy and died at age 72 from aplastic anemia. His mother, who [had had] diabetes and hypertension, died at 64 of myocardial infarction.
>
> Mr. A graduated from high school, worked as a carpenter, and at 25 he married a German girl 20 years old, also a high school graduate. He was Roman Catholic, and she converted to Catholicism. He described himself as a tense, nervous person who found it difficult to relax because "I feel I need to get things done and can't waste time."
>
> Two years after the marriage Mr. A started his own construction company in a town about 20 miles away. He worked overtime and smoked three packages of cigarettes a day for 20 years. Neither he nor his wife were members of social and civic organizations in Roseta. The marriage yielded four children. His wife resented the amount of time his work kept him from home. Her interest was in family life. His was in making money. His mother died when he was 28, "the most unhappy time in my life. I tried to lose myself in work." He said he had thought about moving away from Roseta "to get closer to my business."
>
> At age 29, Mr. A was first hospitalized for chest pains when the construction business failed. After bankruptcy he founded a new company. This time the business succeeded financially and Mr. A "lived like a king." He traveled to Puerto Rico, Las Vegas, gambled at the races and bought expen-

sive cars. He spent about $1,000 weekly, gave wrist watches to the children of his relatives and responded generously to others who asked him for money and gifts without concern for repayment. He kept the problems of running the company to himself. His friend said "You would never dream he had pressure on him unless you knew him. He always had it tough, but managed to get out of it." He enjoyed risk-taking. Two months prior to his fatal heart attack, during a trip to Puerto Rico, he lost $9,000 in one night gambling.

He was hospitalized in the intensive care unit for chest pains following his discovery that a bonding company had issued a fake bond in connection with a large contract. Upon being told that his EKG was normal, he signed himself out of the hospital against medical advice, and engaged in a poker game until the early hours of the morning. During the two weeks following his hospitalization, he made ten business trips to adjoining towns in addition to finally reconciling the bonding problem. The day of his death, he engaged in a fist fight with a drunk, was arrested and required to post $1,000 bail in cash. Later that day he attended the wake of a friend in a nearby city and, upon returning home, collapsed and died suddenly at age 39.

Given Mr. A's family history of coronary disease, his pattern of heavy cigarette smoking, his Type A (coronary-prone) personality—time-urgent, hard-driving in relationships with others, and preoccupied with vocational interests (Dembroski, Weiss, Shields, Haynes, & Feinleib, 1978)—and his exposure to a significant number of major critical life events (e.g., marital problems, bankruptcy, financial success, loss of a loved one, fist fight, jail), it is difficult to believe that his untimely death from acute MI was simply a consequence of his not being fully integrated into the social fabric of his home community. One wonders whether any combination of resistance resources could have mediated the unhealthy effects of such a large, ongoing dose of stress.

Despite these criticisms, the Roseta experiment clearly represents a pioneering effort as regards "host resistance" and its role in protecting individuals from stress-induced illness. As a model for longitudinal investigation of resistance resources at the community level, it is unique. It has also served to generate a host of researchable hypotheses regarding the buffering effects of a number of social variables. These include studies that have examined the mediating effects of religious participation on stress–illness relationships, as well as those that have focused on social network and social support.

Studies by Garrity, Somes, and Marx (1977), Comstock and Partridge (1972), and Graham, Kaplan, Cornoni-Huntley, James, Becker, Hames, and Heyden (1978) support the observation by Wolf's group that religious participation and social conformity (i.e., behaving in ways and espousing attitudes strongly endorsed by the social milieu) are both associated with lower health risk. Unfortunately, however, these studies fail to measure stress per se and thus cannot directly address the issue of resistance or mediation to stress.

Psychological Factors

Factors operating at the individual or psychological level to mediate stress–illness relationships include social support, personality traits, and coping styles. In this section, we review the research literature dealing with each of these resources separately, and also examine those studies that have looked at the combined effects of two or more resistance resources in a given sample of stressed individuals.

Social Support

The resistance resource most often cited in the behavioral medicine literature that describes the ability of humans to survive the unhealthy consequences of various types of environmental stress is perceived social support (Cassel, 1976; Cobb, 1976; Dean & Lin, 1977; Kaplan, Cassel, & Gore, 1977). "Social support," as recently pointed out by House (1984), is not a unitary concept. Rather, it is a concept that at a minimum involves "a flow of one or more of four things between people: (1) *emotional concern* (empathy, caring, concern), (2) *instrumental aid* (giving money, assistance), (3) *information* (advice, suggestions, directions), and/or (4) *appraisal* (feedback or social comparison relevant to a person's self-evaluation)." While studies vary considerably in the particular component(s) of support that they measure, all incorporate some aspect of the above definition. The most frequently measured component is that of "emotional concern"—that is, a sense that one is loved and cared for, is esteemed and valued, and belongs to a network of communication and mutual obligation (Cobb, 1976).

Social support can be perceived as coming from a variety of sources: spouse, family, friends, neighbors, supervisors and coworkers, and health care professionals. Because of that, it cannot be defined simply in terms of one's relationship to one other person (e.g., spouse). For this reason, researchers have recently taken greater care in delineating the particular source(s) of support that they suggest play an active role in mediating stress, especially support perceived at work versus at home.

As we have noted, social support is a psychological resource, one that defines the perceptions of an individual as regards the *quality* of his or her interpersonal relationships. "Social network," on the other hand, refers to a "specific set of linkages among a defined set of persons" (Mitchell, 1969). Social network is a social resource, one that defines the actual number or *quantity* of interpersonal relationships (e.g., number of family members, friends, or club memberships). It is relevant to this discussion only insofar as it serves to provide a basis for social support (i.e., defines the number of persons available who can be perceived as supportive in one way or another). As we point out later, social support and social network have independent effects on health outcome in persons exposed to stress.

The question remains: Does social support mediate stress–illness relationships in humans? As Table 4.1 shows, there is now ample evidence that

TABLE 4.1. Summary of Studies Investigating the "Buffer Hypothesis" of Social Support on Stress–Illness Relationships

STUDY	SAMPLE	STRESS	OUTCOME	MAJOR FINDINGS
Caplan (1972)	205 NASA employees	Job	+	Persons under heavy work load show elevated blood pressure, pulse rate, and glucose when support is lacking
Nuckolls, Cassel, & Kaplan (1972)	170 pregnant women	CLE	+	Women high in support had only one-third the birth complications of women low in support
Pinneau (1975)	390 male employees	Job	±	Support for "buffer hypothesis" was weak and inconsistent; depression was psychological outcome most influenced by support; home support appears to be most helpful in reducing stress-induced cholesterol
LaRocco & Jones (1978)	3,725 Navy enlisted men	Job	−	Social support had a main effect on job satisfaction and self-esteem, but not self-reported physical illness
Gore (1978)	100 blue-collar working men	Unemployment	+	Higher levels of support among rural workers; unsupported workers experiencing job loss showed higher levels of serum cholesterol, depression, and self-reported physical illness
House & Wells (1978)	1,809 male employees	Job	+	Support had a differential effect on health outcome(s) (e.g., ulcers vs. angina); wife and supervisor support are more effective than coworker support

Study	Sample	Type	Finding	Description
Andrews, Tennant, Hewson, & Vaillant (1978)	863 community residents	CLE	−	Crisis support had a main effect on psychological impairment
Jenkins (1979)	249 air traffic controllers	CLE	+	Social coping resources mediated high levels of stress on psychological distress (e.g., alcohol abuse, impulse control)
LaRocco, House, & French (1980)	636 working men	Job	+	Support buffers workers from stress-induced depression, irritation, anxiety, and somatic complaints; coworker support was most effective in mediating job-related stress; high levels of stress mobilize support
Schaefer, Coyne, & Lazarus (1981)	100 community residents	CLE	−	Perceived social support, as distinguished from social network, had a main effect on depression and morale; different types of support (emotional vs. tangible vs. informational) had differing effects on outcome measures; no relationships were found for physical health status
Billings & Moos (1981)	294 families	CLE	+	Qualitative social resources mediate stress effects on depression, anxiety, and physical symptoms; social support appears to buffer stress more for women than for men; persons using avoidance coping responses have fewer social support resources

Note. CLE = critical life (stress) events; (+) = positive findings; (−) = negative findings; (±) = partial support for buffer hypothesis.

it does. In the majority of studies listed, support in one form or another did seem to lessen the psychological strain and physical dysfunction (illness) of persons caught in stressful circumstances. The factor of psychological strain includes indexes of neurosis, boredom, job dissatisfaction, anxiety, depression, irritation, diminished self-esteem, and lack of impulse control. The illness factor includes such outcomes as pregnancy complications, elevated serum cholesterol, pulse rate, blood pressure, ulcers, and a variety of other persistent somatic complaints (e.g., headaches; acid stomach or indigestion).

One study that is especially illustrative of the "buffering effect" of social support is that by Nuckolls, Cassel, and Kaplan (1972). These investigators had physicians blindly assess pregnancy complications in 170 women who were classified as (1) being under high, medium, or low levels of critical life stress and (2) having high or low levels of social support. As shown in Table 4.2, the highest proportion of complications (e.g., hospital admission for hyperemesis or preeclampsia, prolonged labor, threatened abortion, stillbirth, or neonatal death within the first three days) was seen in women under conditions of high stress and low support (91%)—a level almost three times that of comparably high-stress/high-support women and twice that of the other two groups.

Other general conclusions that arise from reviewing the studies listed in Table 4.1 include the following:

1. Social support apparently acts as a mediator to stress–illness relationships *only* in circumstances where the individual is exposed to high, chronic levels of stress (see also Boyce, 1981).
2. Support has a differential impact on certain health outcomes as compared to others (e.g., ulcers and neurosis vs. angina pectoris and skin rash) (House & Wells, 1978).
3. Support from a variety of "significant others" comprising one's social network (spouse, work supervisor, coworkers) can mediate the illness-producing effects of stress, and no one category of supportive individuals

TABLE 4.2. Mediating Effects of Social Support on Relationship between Stress and Pregnancy Complications

CRITICAL LIFE STRESS	SOCIAL SUPPORT			
	HIGH		LOW	
	n	%	*n*	%
High	(15)	33.3	(11)	90.9
Medium	(44)	38.6	(44)	45.4
Low	(28)	53.6	(28)	48.2

Note. Adapted from Nuckolls, K. B., Cassel, J., & Kaplan, B. H. Psychosocial assets, life crisis and the prognosis of pregnancy. *American Journal of Epidemiology,* 1972, *95,* 431–441.

is crucial to the health of the stressed individual (House & Wells, 1978; LaRocco, House, & French, 1980).

4. Certain sources of support appear to be more influential in mediating stress-related strain and illness in certain circumstances than are other sources; for example, job-related strains (job dissatisfaction and boredom) are primarily relieved by job-related sources of support (from a supervisor or coworker), whereas more general health outcomes (anxiety, depression, somatic complaints) are affected by a wider range of sources of support (from spouse, family, friends).

5. Support acts as a mediator to stress–illness relationships for individuals from a wide range of sociodemographic and occupational backgrounds: urban versus rural employees, Navy enlisted personnel, pregnant women, air traffic controllers, scientists, administrators, assembly-line workers, and middle-aged community residents.

6. Social support appears to mediate certain types of stress (e.g., that associated with role conflict at work and work overload) more than others (e.g., that associated with job ambiguity, underutilization, and job dissatisfaction).

Methodologically, some of the most sophisticated research on host resistance has been done in this area. The various studies cited typically employed large, well-defined samples from diverse social backgrounds, which makes their findings easily generalizable. The studies have also been both cross-sectional and longitudinal in nature and have looked at self-reports as well as more objective outcome measures (e.g., serum cholesterol levels). More importantly, they have examined increasingly complex, multidimensional relationships between various work and nonwork stressors, sources of support, and strain–illness in an effort to generate a more precise understanding of exactly how, when, and under what circumstances social support serves to buffer the individual from the harmful effects of stress.

However, there are also methodological weaknesses in this work. Foremost among these is a definitional problem (Pearlin & Lieberman, 1977) perpetuated by investigators who overlook the multidimensional nature of social support, and who fail to provide the needed delineation of that aspect of support that they are studying. Related to this problem is the unfortunate tendency of investigators in this area to use rather idiosyncratic and narrow measures of support. This not only leads to the failure of some researchers to take all of the various facets of the interactive processes that constitute social support into account (House, 1984; Schaefer, Coyne, & Lazarus, 1981); it also hampers integrative efforts to draw conclusions from the studies of any more than one investigator at a time. The tendency of some researchers to confuse and/or confound "social support" with "social network" is also a problem, since, as Schaefer et al. (1981) point out, a social network may involve other interpersonal elements (e.g., demands, constraints, interpersonal strife) that dilute or even counteract the otherwise positive effects of support. A final weakness involves the assumption of many researchers that social support is a universally effective moderator of stress. Until recently, this widely held belief about the ameliorative power of social support may have prevented the posing of complex but essential questions about stress resistance. For example, does perceived support have a positive or a negative effect on stress–illness relationships, depending on other factors such as personality traits? A recent study by Kobasa and Puccetti (1983) would suggest that this is indeed the case. They found that high levels of family support were actually detrimental to the health status of some executives under conditions of high work stress. Executives with hardy personalities (see "Personality," below) appeared to use family support to cope effectively with work stress, whereas nonhardy executives actually evidenced a greater amount of reported illness under conditions of high support. In a similar vein, Sandler and Lakey (1982) found that social support moderated the link between negative stressful life events and anxiety and depression for persons with an internal locus of control, but not for those with an external locus.

Personality

In a recent series of experimental studies, Kobasa and coworkers have considered the role of personality as a mediator to the illness-producing effects of stress. Their initial interest in this area was generated by (1) a realization that human beings cannot possibly avoid all stressful circumstances (e.g., serious illness of a spouse or child) encountered in the normal course of everyday life, and (2) their further appreciation of the fact that previous research (Rabkin & Struening, 1976) had failed to demonstrate any strong causal link between one's exposure to stress and subsequent likelihood of illness. The resulting awareness that many, if not most, individuals who experience stress do not in fact become ill made these researchers consider the possibility that some stressed persons' personalities promote the kind of perceptions and handling of stress that minimizes debilitation of the organism.

Kobasa's conceptualization of "hardiness" as the personality style crucial for stress resistance is derived from an existential theory of personality (Kobasa & Maddi, 1977). It is also justified by a variety of empirical studies, including those of positive personality change in adulthood (Neugarten, 1974); effective use of personal control in stressful situations (Rodin & Langer, 1977); "coping" conceived of as threat appraisal influenced by personal belief systems (Lazarus, 1966); and the adaptive function of varied life experience (Fiske & Maddi, 1961). "Hardiness" represents an amalgam of three separate traits: (1) a sense of personal control over external (often stressful) events in one's life; (2) a deep sense of involvement, commitment, and purpose in daily activities; and (3) flexibility in adapting to unexpected changes in one's environment, as though such changes represented exciting challenges to further personal growth. Hardy individuals are easily committed to what they are doing in various areas of their lives (rather than feeling alienated from same); they believe they have some measure of influence or control over the causes and solutions of problems (rather than feeling helpless and powerless); and they see change(s) in life and demands for readjustment as challenges and opportunities (rather than experiencing threat in the face of the unexpected and/or unknown). Kobasa argues that this type of stress appraisal mitigates the potential unhealthy effects of stress and prevents the organismic strain that often leads to illness.

Kobasa's conceptualization of hardiness bears some resemblance to other studies of personality and health status. The "control" component reflects the same type of behavior(s) identified by Averill (1973), Johnson and Sarason (1978), Rodin and Langer (1977), and Schmale and Iker (1966) as correlating with better health and acting as a buffer against stress-induced illness. The "commitment" component resembles key concepts in two major stress and illness models. For example, Moss (1973) has concluded that a person's lack of meaningfulness and integration into the sociocultural setting eventuates in mental and physical debilitation. Similarly, stating the case in positive terms, Antonovsky (1979) argues that the most important single factor in stress resistance is a person's feeling of coherence. According to Antonovsky (1979, p. 123), a "pervasive, enduring though dynamic feeling of confidence that one's internal and external environments are predictable and that there is a high probability that all things will work out well as can reasonably be expected" keeps one healthy. Finally, the emphasis of hardiness on "challenge" finds a parallel in work by Smith, Johnson, and Sarason (1978) and Zuckerman, Kolin, Price, and Zoob (1964) dealing with sensation-seeking tendencies; these, like hardiness, appear to predispose individuals to enjoy change, seek it out actively, and become well practiced at responding to the unexpected.

The first empirical evidence that hardiness plays an active role in protecting individuals from stress comes from a study of highly stressed business executives. Using two conventional stress research instruments—the Holmes and Rahe (1967) Schedule of Recent Life Events, adapted for the population under study, and the Wyler, Masuda, and Holmes (1970) Seriousness of Illness Rating Scale—Kobasa (1979) identified two groups of executives, one showing both high stress and high levels of self-reported illness ($n = 40$), and a second showing similar high stress but little illness ($n = 40$). Kobasa hypothesized that these two groups would differ in terms of hardiness, as well as its various components; the components were measured through a composite questionnaire made up of five individual standardized instruments: the Alienation Test (Maddi, Kobasa, & Hoover, 1979); Internal versus External Locus of Control Scale (Rotter, Seeman, & Liverant, 1962); the Personality Research Form (Jackson, 1974); the California Life Goals Evaluation Schedule (Hahn, 1966); and an adaptation of the Gergen and Morse (1967) Self-Consistency Test.

Discriminant function analysis, along with t tests of mean differences between groups, revealed that high-stress/low-illness executives were indeed hardier in some ways than their high-stress/high-illness counterparts were. That is, albeit under equal stress, low-illness executives reported being more in (internal as opposed to external) control, more committed to (as opposed to alienated from) self, and challenged by (as compared to apathetic about) life circumstances. To test the stability of these differences further, Kobasa conducted a cross-validation study on an additional 80 "holdout" cases originally selected from the same pool of executives. Using only the hardiness data, she was able to classify 78% of the test cases correctly into the low-illness or high-illness groups. For Kobasa, the key protective element attributable to hardiness involved the fact that hardy executives were "not just a victim of a threatening change (e.g., job transfer) but an active determinant of the consequences it brings about" (1979, p. 9). The latter is what Kobasa, Maddi, Donner, Merrick, and White (1984) have more recently referred to as "transformational coping" (see "Coping Styles," below).

The second empirical step in demonstrating a meaningful relationship between hardiness and stress–illness involved a prospective extension of the earlier executive study (Kobasa, Maddi, & Kahn, 1982). In this study, 259 executives identified stressful life events and gave illness report data for each of the 2 years following the Kobasa (1979) project. This provided an analysis of the buffering effects of hardiness over time, as well as an opportunity to adjust for differences in prior illness. These executives were exposed to increasing stress over the period of data collection; this stress, in turn, was modestly $(r = .23)$[1] correlated with self-reported increases in illness. Results of an analysis of covariance, however, indicated that only the high-stress/low-hardiness executives became more ill over time. They reported approximately twice as much illness as their high-stress/high-hardiness colleagues, and over three times as much illness as low-stress executives. Thus, it appeared that (1) hardiness functioned prospectively, as well as retrospectively, as a resistance resource in preserving health; and that (2) it had its greatest effect when stress began to mount.

In yet other studies, Kobasa (1982a, 1982b, 1984) has noted the protective influence of hardiness on both the mental and physical health status of highly stressed career Army officers $(n = 105)$, lawyers $(n = 157)$, and women medically screened for cervical cancer $(n = 100)$. In all three of these studies, the components of commitment and control clearly and consistently played an active role in reducing stress-induced illness; challenge, on the other hand, appeared to lead to both an increase (Army officers) and a decrease (cancer patients) in reported illness.

Moreover, Kobasa has noted the ability of hardiness to interact with other

1. This is the same degree of association found in most studies linking critical life events to illness (Rabkin & Streuning, 1976) and in other studies by Kobasa (e.g., $r = .43$; Kobasa, Maddi, & Puccetti, 1982).

factors to provide additive protection against stress-induced illness. For example, hardy executives who also engage in regular physical exercise are less likely to become ill under stress than are executives who are hardy but do not exercise, those who exercise but are not hardy, or those who are lacking in both types of behavior (Kobasa, Maddi, & Puccetti, 1982). The magnitude of difference in reported illness for persons using both resources versus only one versus neither is approximately 1 : 3 : 6.

In yet another study, Kobasa, Maddi, and Zola (1983) examined the effect of hardiness in reducing the illness risk associated with high levels of work stress and/or Type A behavior; the latter is a coping style (see Chapters 3 and 8, this volume) often seen in executives, which includes excessive job involvement, impatience, and hostility toward others. Hardiness, in fact, did not interact with Type A behavior as such to reduce individuals' likelihood of reporting illness, when this likelihood was examined across conditions of high and low work stress. However, there was a marginally significant three-way interaction among stress, Type A behavior, and hardiness, such that executives high in work stress, high in Type A, and low in hardiness (as compared to all other possible combinations of factors) evidenced by far the greatest degree of self-reported illness. These authors further suggested that the "buffering effect" of hardiness in stressed Type A executives would have been even more pronounced had it not been for the Type A's predilection for underreporting physical symptoms.

Kobasa, Maddi, and Courington (1981) also looked at the interaction between constitutional predisposition for illness (as indicated by parental illness scores) and hardiness in high-stress versus low-stress persons. As with the Type A study, they failed to find any direct mediation effect for hardiness on illness predisposition and/or stressful life events. Rather, the three factors exerted independent main effects on illness report. However, as was noted in the Type A study, persons high in susceptibility (predisposition) and low in resistance (hardiness) had by far the highest amount of illness, whereas those with the reverse situation (low susceptibility, high resistance) had the least.

In general, this is a strong area of research; that is, there are more methodological strengths than weaknesses. For example, Kobasa has conducted both retrospective and prospective studies of the effect of hardiness on stress–illness relationships; the prospective studies provide the most convincing evidence that hardiness is, in fact, an active resistance resource for stressed individuals. She has studied large, well-defined samples of highly stressed persons and has employed consistent measures of stress, hardiness, and health–illness outcome throughout her series of studies. In at least one study (Kobasa et al., 1981), the authors attempted to validate their self-report illness data; in a sample of 48 individuals for whom they had medical records, they found 89% agreement between illness reports provided by the subjects and objective (physicians') diagnoses of some 114 different health problems (e.g., psoriasis, hypertension, and peptic ulcer). Finally, they have investigated the impact of hardiness on stress–illness relationships by (1) taking into consideration additional risk factors such as illness predisposition and the Type A behavior pattern, and (2) looking at the interactive relationships with other potential resistance resources (e.g., regular physical exercise).

On the negative side, Kobasa and her colleagues are not satisfied with the stability (test–retest reliability) of their measure of hardiness ($r = .60$). There is also a potential problem inherent in their strategy of defining various components of hardiness *negatively* (e.g., "commitment" is defined as the absence of alienation, and "challenge" as the absence of vegetativeness). Some critics might simply argue that alienated persons are more at risk for illness, as contrasted to nonalienated persons, and that hardiness is an irrelevant concept. Another objection might be that the authors have focused perhaps too much on white, middle-class business executives and professionals (e.g., lawyers, Army officers), at the expense of investigating hardiness effects in more heterogeneous groups. Finally, and perhaps most importantly, these researchers have only looked to date at the effects of hardiness on health and/or illness. This unidirectional focus fails to take into account the possible reverse effects of health–illness on hardiness. One wonders if, for example, illness experienced early in life can result in a failure to develop hardiness, in that persons experiencing such illnesses learn to perceive themselves as being out of control with respect to their health status or are unable to commit themselves to major tasks of daily living because of disability resulting from the illness. Or, on the contrary, can early illness cause one to become hardy by emphasizing the need to control one's destiny as much as possible (e.g., by maintaining positive health habits) and/or the need to remain flexible in the face of potential life-threatening events, including diagnosed illness?

Coping Styles

By "coping," we refer to those things that people do to avoid being harmed by life strains (Pearlin & Schooler, 1978) or stressors. In this section, we only deal with studies that directly address the issue of coping styles as *mediators* to stress–illness relationships; Lazarus and Folkman deal in more depth with the main effects of coping on health status elsewhere (see Chapter 8, this volume).

Anger-Coping Styles

As Gentry, Chesney, Gary, Hall, and Harburg (1982) have recently noted, anger-coping styles have a direct bearing on an individual's blood pressure status and risk for essential benign hypertension. That is, those persons who *habitually* express anger when provoked by others (e.g., spouse, children, boss, police officer) have on the average lower systolic and diastolic pressures than do similar persons who habitually suppress such feelings. The relative risk ratio for hypertension (i.e., pressure higher than 160 mm Hg systolic and/or 95 mm Hg diastolic) is approximately 1.64 : 1 for "anger-in" versus "anger-out" individuals.

These differences become even more dramatic, however, when one looks at the mediating effects of anger-coping styles on relationships between such factors as job–family strain or chronic hostility and blood pressure. In a study of 431 black and white adult males residing in Detroit, Chesney, Gentry, Gary, Kennedy, and Harburg (1984) found that blood pressure was highest in persons characterized by either high job or family strain *and* a tendency to suppress anger ("anger-in") resulting from same. This interactive effect is seen in Figures 4.2 and 4.3. Persons experiencing these types of strain (stressors) did not have elevated pressure if they openly expressed their anger when provoked; that is, the usual "risk" relationship between strain and illness did not hold in all cases. Here, the magnitude of differences in diastolic blood pressure (DBP) between groups of strained individuals ranged from 9 to 14 mm Hg, depending on their respective anger-coping styles.

Similarly, in a study reported by Kennedy, Chesney, Gentry, Gary, and Harburg (1984), anger-coping styles appeared to mediate the otherwise pathological relationship between chronic (interracial) hostility and DBP observed in 489 adult black males and females. As Figure 4.4 illustrates, those

FIGURE 4.2. Mediating effect of anger-coping style on relationship between job strain and diastolic blood pressure.

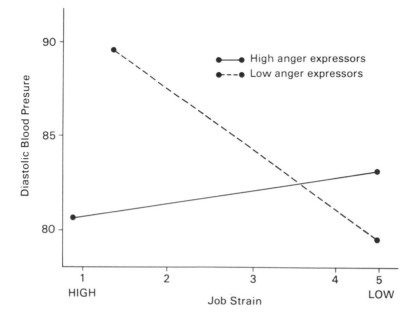

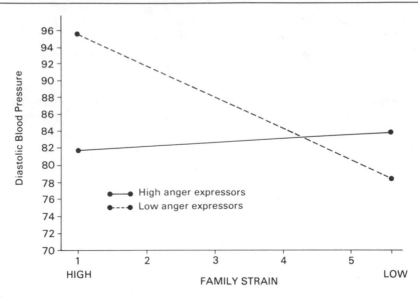

FIGURE 4.3. Mediating effect of anger-coping style on relationship between family strain and diastolic blood pressure.

FIGURE 4.4. Mediating effect of anger-coping style on relationship between hostility and diastolic blood pressure. Numbers in parentheses refer to group size.

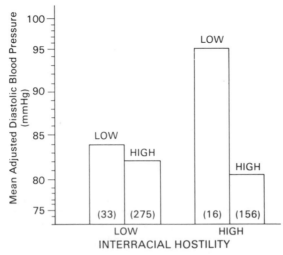

individuals most likely to manifest high DBP were characterized by *both* high levels of hostility (e.g., "When I'm in a place where all of the people are white, I often feel I'm in enemy territory") and low anger expression. Again, this argues that the expected "risk" relationship between hostility and blood pressure (Buss, 1961) holds more or less true, depending on whether one is an "anger-in" or "anger-out" type of individual. The magnitude of difference between persons high versus low in anger expression under conditions of high hostility is approximately 15 mm Hg DBP, comparable to that seen for high versus low anger expressors in the analysis of job–family strain (Chesney *et al.*, 1984). As was true of social support and hardiness, it seems clear that the "buffering" effects of anger expression are evident *only* under conditions of high stress, whether this stress results from external pressures (job and family) or internal concerns (hostility).

Methodologically, this series of studies has many strengths, including (1) the fact that all of the findings from the various investigations are taken from a single, large epidemiological survey of over 1,000 adult residents of Detroit during 1968–1969; (2) the fact that uniform measures of anger expression and hypertension were used throughout; (3) the fact that differences in blood pressure and/or incidence of hypertension were controlled for age and weight, which otherwise have their own independent effect on the dependent measure; and (4) the fact that anger-coping styles reflect a given individual's tendency to express or suppress anger across a range of interpersonal situations (i.e., a trait), rather than classification based on a single situation (e.g., in response to an angry boss; see Harburg *et al.*, 1973). The major limitation of these studies resides in the fact that the data, with the exception of blood pressure measurements, are wholly self-report in nature and cannot be validated in terms of actual observed behavior.

Transformational versus Regressive Coping Styles

Kobasa and coworkers have also argued that certain coping styles are closely linked to hardiness (see "Personality," above) and thus serve to mediate stress–illness relationships. Specifically, they suggest that "transformational coping" (i.e., an attempt to transform a stressful situation into an opportunity for personal growth and societal benefit) is more evident in persons high in hardiness; whereas what they refer to as "regressive coping" (i.e., an attempt to deny, avoid, or escape a stressful situation) is more apt to be seen in low hardiness persons (Kobasa, Maddi, Donner, Merrick, & White, 1984). An example of the behavioral distinction between these two coping styles is provided by Maddi (1980) as regards the stress of losing one's job:

> Transformational coping might involve the optimistic appraisal that you accepted risk when you went into a bureaucratic organization even though you have entrepreneurial leanings, and the decisive actions of interviewing those who fired you with a view toward reassessing whether that kind

of work or some new career best suits your capabilities. In contrast, regressive coping might involve the pessimistic appraisal that the job you lost is irreplaceable and you are unworthy, and the distracting actions of seeking reassurance, drinking heavily, and starting an affair.

Kobasa, Maddi, Donner, Merrick, and White (1984) also liken transformational and regressive coping to what Folkman and Lazarus (1980) have called "problem-focused coping" and "emotion-focused coping," respectively. They further point out that lawyers who are undergoing stressful life events and who avoid regressive coping behaviors (e.g., getting angry, increasing drinking and smoking, taking medication to relax, becoming apathetic or indifferent, and/or physically withdrawing from the stress situation) are much less likely to show signs of physical and mental strain; "strain" is defined in terms of self-reported symptoms of insomnia, heartburn, headaches, diarrhea, shortness of breath, anxiety, and depression.

These two studies obviously do not constitute a direct, robust test of the effect of these two coping styles in mediating stress–strain or stress–illness relationships in the populations under study. Because of this, Kobasa and her colleagues simply argue for having such a study carried out, and they also provide some basis, albeit hypothetical at this point, for defining exactly how personality constructs (mechanisms) such as hardiness affect health outcomes. These researchers thus far have provided a better illustration of what they mean by "regressive coping" than they have for "transformational coping"; more concrete examples of behaviors that might be interpreted as "transformational" obviously appear needed. Also, the investigators might well study the statistical similarity between their coping styles and those of Folkman and Lazarus (1980) to determine to what extent they are measuring the same or different patterns of response on the part of stressed individuals.

Active–Cognitive versus Active–Behavioral versus Avoidance Coping Styles

Billings and Moos (1981) compared the efficacy of three types of coping styles in mediating the effect of stressful life events in an adult community sample of 194 families, comprised primarily of white, middle-class men and women. Table 4.3 illustrates the types of behaviors constituting each of the three styles: active–cognitive, active–behavioral, and avoidance. They used an adaptation of the Holmes and Rahe (1967) Social Readjustment Rating Scale—one that focused particularly on negative life change events (e.g., decreased income, legal problems, the death of a close friend)—to measure stress, and an outcome measure that identified distress in terms of depression, anxiety, and physical symptomatology (e.g., headaches, acid stomach, insomnia, poor appetite). They found that coping styles did, in fact, moderate the event–functioning relationships under study for both men and women. They noted, however, that avoidance coping tends to increase the

TABLE 4.3. Three Types of Coping Styles Mediating Stress

COPING STYLES	BEHAVIORAL RESPONSES
Active–Cognitive	1. Tried to see positive side
	2. Drew on past experiences
	3. Considered several alternatives for handling the problem
Active–Behavioral	1. Talked with professional person (doctor, clergy, lawyer) about the situation
	2. Took some positive action
	3. Tried to find out more about the situation
Avoidance	1. Prepared for the worst
	2. Kept my feelings to myself
	3. Tried to reduce the tension by smoking more

Note. Adapted from Billings, A. G., & Moos, R. H. The role of coping responses and social resources in attenuating the stress of life events. *Journal of Behavioral Medicine*, 1981, *4*, 139–158.

impact of stress on illness, while active–cognitive and active–behavioral coping tends to attenuate this impact. Interestingly, women are more likely to employ the avoidance style than are men.

Billings and Moos (1981) also examined the effects of emotion-focused versus problem-focused coping (Folkman & Lazarus, 1980) and found that these too attenuated the effects of stress on personal functioning: Problem-focused coping led to less stress-induced illness, as compared to emotion-focused coping.

This is a strong piece of research, one that greatly enhances our general understanding of the intricate relationships between various resistance resources (e.g., social support, coping styles; see "Combined Resistance Resources," below) and stress–illness relationships. It is both conceptually and methodologically sound, raising as many important questions as it answers. For example, what constitutes an "effective" coping strategy, and can this be determined without knowing both the prior (coping) history of the individual and the context under which he or she is now handling stress? As Billings and Moos themselves suggest, further research in this area should rely more heavily on observational data regarding coping styles (i.e., less on self-report indexes), should deal with clinical populations (where the range of symptoms is less constrained), and should collect prospective data.

Mature versus Immature Coping Styles

In two studies, Andrews and coworkers (Andrews, Tennant, Hewson, & Schonell, 1978; Andrews, Tennant, Hewson, & Vaillant, 1978) reported negative findings as regards coping resources and stress–illness mediation. In their first study (Andrews, Tennant, Hewson, & Schonell, 1978), these researchers noted that poor (immature) coping had little or no effect on either physical or psychological dysfunction in otherwise stressed persons ($n=863$). "Mature coping" was defined in terms of behaviors such as being charming to people one does not like; cooling one's anger when provoked; and generally avoiding stress by distraction and withdrawal from the stressful situation. "Immature coping," on the other hand, referred to behaviors such as showing anger toward frustrating persons; daydreaming; and various forms of passive–aggressive behavior (e.g., purposely going slowly to thwart someone who has been irritating).

In a second study (Andrews, Tennant, Hewson, & Vaillant, 1978), in which the researchers directly tested the "buffer hypothesis," they noted that neither the mature nor the immature coping style appeared to attenuate the effects of life stress on psychological impairment (as measured by a 20-item general health questionnaire). The percentage of individuals reporting impairment under conditions of high life stress who used mature or immature coping styles was between 30–39% and 29–43%, respectively, depending on whether they were also high or low in social support.

Part of the reason why Andrews and coworkers failed to observe positive mediating effects of coping on stress–illness relationships lies in the fact that they appear to label behaviors as "*mature* coping" that other researchers have included under rubrics such as "avoidance" (Billings & Moos, 1981) and "regressive coping" (Kobasa, Maddi, Donner, Merrick, & White, 1984). For example, Andrews' group suggests that mature coping would include such things as suppressing anger (Gentry et al., 1982), submissive behavior (e.g., taking the blame for someone else in order to avoid further threats from one's boss), burying oneself in activities that avoid direct confrontation with the stress in question (e.g., avoiding dealing with disliked in-laws), and so forth. In short, the definitions of coping styles used by Andrews and coworkers appear inconsistent with those used by other investigators mentioned in this section. Thus, the failure to find a mediation effect here may or may not be of importance in understanding the role of coping in mediating stress–induced illness. It is our opinion that this failure, in fact, does *not* offset the important positive findings of other researchers.

Combined Resistance Resources

Several investigators have examined the combined influence of two or more psychological resistance resources on stress–illness relationships; in general, they have concluded that these resources do indeed result in less illness in persons under stress. For example, Andrews, Tennant, Hewson, and Vaillant (1978) found that the combination of mature coping and social support appeared to mediate psychological impairment to a greater degree in high- and low-stress individuals than did either resource alone. Similarly, Kobasa (1982a) noted that commitment (component of hardiness) and transformational coping (the absence of regressive coping) combined to reduce the impact of stress on illness (strain) in lawyers. Interestingly, Kobasa also noted that social support and/or physical exercise did not add to resistance in lawyers; in fact, support appeared to increase the probability of stress-induced illness slightly. The latter finding was explained in terms of lawyers' supposed idiosyncratic tendency to engage in regressive coping (e.g., becoming angry or drinking) when they perceive others to be supportive; in effect, the perceived support may allow them to avoid dealing with the stress directly.

Billings and Moos (1981) also found that coping skills and social support combined to provide incremental resistance to stress-induced anxiety, depression, and somatic illness. They further observed that these two types of resources have (1) differential degrees of influence on stress–illness relationships for males versus females and (2) a degree of interdependence between them. As regards the latter, Billings and Moos have noted that, for example, persons who engage in avoidance coping behaviors tend to have less in the way of social support, and vice versa. Also, among the women studied, coping and social support added roughly equivalent amounts of resistance to the stress–illness equation; whereas, for the men studied, social support appeared to be less effective than coping in attenuating illness. Because of this, the combination of resistance resources was a more effective mediator of the stress–illness relationship in women than in men. Billings and Moos have suggested that the interdependence between resistance resources may, in fact, lead to an overestimate of the effects of any single resource studied alone. Whether this will prove to be the case hinges on the willingness of researchers in this field to collect data simultaneously on more than one resistance resource at a time for a given sample or population of stressed persons. Elsewhere, Barefoot, Dahlstrom, and Williams (1982) have noted a degree of interdependence between certain factors creating stress/susceptibility (e.g., hostility) and resistance resources (e.g., social support) in persons at risk for CHD ($r = -.25$). Thus, relationships between factors on both sides of the health risk balance (see Figure 4.1) can lead to overestimates or underestimates of the effects of such variables on ultimate health risk. It is important to keep in mind that both Billings and Moos (1981) and Barefoot et al. (1982) found social support, rather than social network (i.e., quantity of social relationships), to be the more influential factor in mediating illness at the individual level.

CONSTRUCTING AN EXPLANATORY MODEL

As noted earlier, we believe that human health risk is influenced by the interplay (balance) between certain factors of psychosocial susceptibility ($+$) and resistance ($-$) that operate at both the social and psychological levels of life experience. This delicate interplay is illustrated in Figure 4.1 in general terms. Figures 4.5 and 4.6 show what happens when the individual expe-

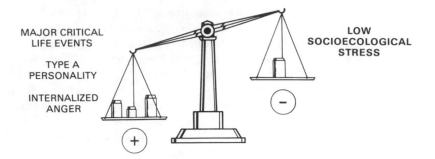

FIGURE 4.5. High health risk. (From Chesney, A. P., & Gentry, W. D. Psychosocial factors mediating health risk: A balanced perspective. *Preventive Medicine*, 1982, *11*, 612–617. Reprinted by permission.)

riences an *imbalance* between the two—that is, a high loading of susceptibility and little in the way of resistance (Figure 4.5) or vice versa (Figure 4.6). To make this model work, we need only to refer to the paper by Kobasa, Maddi, Puccetti, and Zola (1984), which considers the presence or absence of three resistance variables (hardiness, exercise, and work support) in mediating the likelihood of illness in stressed executives. Kobasa, Maddi, Puccetti, and Zola (1984) found that this likelihood increased from 7.69% in persons with all three resources available to 57.69%, 71.87%, and 92.85% in persons with only two, one, or no resistance resources, respectively. We believe that sufficient empirical data is already available at this time to adopt this "balance-sheet model" to predicting and ultimately to treating stress-induced illness (Chesney & Gentry, 1982).

A more precise interplay between individual susceptibility and resistance factors that mediate stress–illness is seen in Figure 4.7. Here, Kobasa, Maddi, Donner, Merrick, and White (1984) illustrate exactly how personality vari-

FIGURE 4.6. Low health risk. (From Chesney, A. P., & Gentry, W. D. Psychosocial factors mediating health risk: A balanced perspective. *Preventive Medicine*, 1982, *11*, 612–617. Reprinted by permission.)

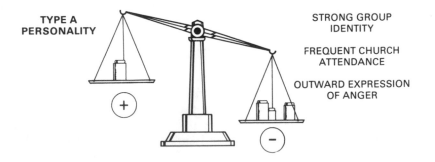

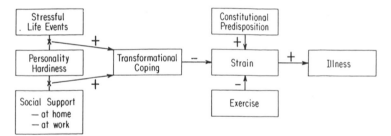

FIGURE 4.7. Model of validation of hardiness as a resistance resource.

ables and social support operate to influence the choice of coping styles, which ultimately affects strain and illness outcomes. This model also takes into account other nonpsychosocial susceptibility and resistance factors that obviously influence outcome in the own right—for example, constitutional predisposition (family history) and regular physical exercise. Persons high in hardiness are, for example, more likely to engage in transformational coping, which in turn lowers their respective risk for strain or illness. Similarly, individuals high in trait hostility are less likely to perceive social support from others in their immediate environment (Barefoot *et al.*, 1982), as are persons who utilize avoidance coping behaviors to deal with stress (Billings & Moos, 1981). Thus, one can easily substitute different personality and coping labels in this model to arrive at the same conceptual and empirical conclusions.

As we have described above, most of the mediation of stress–illness relationships occurs at the individual, psychological level—that is, it has to do with individual perceptions, attitudes, and coping styles. Social factors, in our opinion, operate in the main to promote and facilitate psychological resources; thus their influence is indirect. For example, it seems clear that communities like Roseta serve to promote hardiness (i.e., a sense of purpose and commitment) and perceived social support to an extent greater than that of communities possessing less in the way of social cohesion and social conformity. Regular participation in religious activities (also a big part of life in Roseta) similarly leads to more perceived support, an expanded social network, and exposure to a greater variety of coping models (Graham *et al.*, 1978). This most likely explains, at least in part, why persons residing in high socioecological stress areas (Harburg *et al.*, 1973; James & Kleinbaum, 1976) evidence more stress-related disease and mortality (e.g., deaths due to essential hypertension and coronary artery disease). High socioecological stress involves greater social instability and lower educational opportunities—factors that we believe compete with perceived social support, development of meaningful social networks, and mature/problem-focused coping behaviors.

FUTURE RESEARCH OBJECTIVES

Research investigating the mediating effects of social and psychological factors on stress–illness relationships in humans has become increasingly frequent in the behavioral medicine literature over the past decade. In general, it has been characterized by studies that show ever-increasing conceptual and methodological sophistication, to the point where model building and the prediction of individual health risk is now possible. However, as our review has indicated, a number of prerequisites must be fulfilled if our collective knowledge is to advance from this point on:

1. Investigators must continue to adopt and utilize more conventional and precisely delineated concepts and operational measures in their research (e.g., in defining types and sources of social support). Use of idiosyncratic concepts and measures will, in our estimation, only serve to confuse and confound our appreciation of the links between susceptibility–resistance factors and illness.

2. Researchers must guard against preconceived notions about the positive or negative influence of mediating factors (e.g., social support and/or network) on stress–illness relationships.

3. Investigators should, where possible, include multiple resistance resources in individual studies, in order to increase our understanding of the intricate interdependence among such factors as they combine to mediate stress–illness relationships.

4. Researchers should address issues of stress resistance and mediation in the full range of sociodemographic samples; they should not simply rely on findings from Caucasian male professionals. It would also be of interest to determine base rates of resource behaviors in various subgroups of people (e.g., blacks vs. whites, different cultural groups, etc.).

5. Investigators should rely increasingly on objective, as opposed to self-report, measures of health–illness outcomes; where possible, they should obtain observations of such resource behaviors as anger expression and transformational coping, rather than depending totally on respondents' self-reports of such behaviors.

Moreover, we believe that research efforts should be concentrated on the following empirical questions:

1. *What are the differential, quantitative weights of different susceptibility and resistance factors operating at the individual, psychological level to mediate stress–illness relationships?* Garrity et al. (1977), for example, reported that personality factors influencing resistance to illness contribute much less to health risk than do susceptibility factors such as critical life stress events. Similarly, Billings and Moos (1981) found that, at least for males, social support resulted in less resistance to illness than did active, problem-focused coping behavior. Meanwhile, in the absence of data that argue for certain factors' having more or less influence, we must simply regard their impact on health risk as equivalent in amount or degree.

2. *What are the developmental antecedents of susceptibility and resistance factors that are known or suspected to mediate stress–illness relationships?* Kobasa, Maddi, and Puccetti (1982) have suggested that persons high in hardiness *should* have had differentially positive (as compared to negative) childhood experiences, in contrast to persons low in this personality trait. They speculate that a sense of commitment and purpose in life comes from such positive experiences, whereas alienation is the result of primarily negative childhood exchanges. They further suggest that learning a sense of personal control or mastery (rather than powerlessness) comes from having continuous, regular life experiences that cause the child to stretch to accomplish something (i.e., to cope) and to succeed in the process. The sense of challenge that characterizes hardy persons, they suggest, comes from having a wide range of life experiences early in one's development—experiences in which the child receives encouragement in exercising adaptive imagery, judgment, and social–behavioral skills. Their basic framework for understanding such developmental antecedents is that of social learning theory (Bandura, 1977).

3. *What influences does health or illness have on psychosocial mediators?* That is, does illness itself effect how we perceive others in terms of social support, and/or does it determine the extent to which we appear hardy or engage in mature or immature coping behaviors? As already noted in this chapter, thus far we have only looked at the reverse—that is, the effect of mediation on health or illness.

4. *What are the biomedical correlates of the various susceptibility and/or resistance factors?* As we learn more and more about the physiological, neurogenic, and hormonal correlates and/or consequences of such factors as Type A behavior pattern and suppressed anger (see Chapter 13, this volume), we can better appreciate the direct, albeit often complex, connection between overt behavior and human disease; further study of similar processes accompanying resistance resources would obviously complete such an understanding.

R E F E R E N C E S

Andrews, G., Tennant, C., Hewson, D., & Schonell, M. The relation of social factors to physical and psychiatric illness. *American Journal of Epidemiology*, 1978, *108*, 27–35.

Andrews, G., Tennant, C., Hewson, D., & Vaillant, G. E. Life event stress, social support, coping style, and risk of psychological impairment. *Journal of Nervous and Mental Disease*, 1978, *166*, 307–316.

Antonovsky, A. *Health, stress, and coping.* San Francisco: Jossey-Bass, 1979.

Averill, J. R. Personal control over aversive stimuli and its relationship to stress. *Psychological Bulletin*, 1973, *80*, 286–303.

Bandura, A. Toward a unifying theory of behavioral change. *Psychological Review*, 1977, *84*, 191–215.

Barefoot, J. C., Dahlstrom, W. G., & Williams, R. B. Hostility, CHD incidence, and total mortality: A 25-year follow-up study of 255 physicians. *Psychosomatic Medicine*, 1982, *45*, 59–63.

Billings, A. G., & Moos, R. H. The role of coping resources and social resources in attenuating the stress of life events. *Journal of Behavioral Medicine*, 1981, *4*, 139–158.

Boyce, W. T. Interaction between social variables in stress research. *Journal of Health and Social Behavior*, 1981, *22*, 194–195.

Bruhn, J. G. An epidemiological study of myocardial infarctions in an Italian-American community. *Journal of Chronic Diseases*, 1965, *18*, 353–365.

Bruhn, J. G., Chandler, B., Miller, M. C., Wolf, S., & Lynn, T. N. Social aspects of coronary heart disease in two adjacent, ethnically different communities. *American Journal of Public Health*, 1966, *56*, 1493–1506.

Bruhn, J. G., Philips, B. U., & Wolf, S. Social readjustment and illness patterns: Comparisons between first, second, and third generation Italian-Americans living in the same community. *Journal of Psychosomatic Research*, 1972, *16*, 387–394.

Bruhn, J. G., Philips, B., & Wolf, S. Lessons from Roseta 20 years later: A community study of heart disease. *Southern Medical Journal*, 1982, *75*, 575–580.

Bruhn, J. G., & Wolf, S. Update on Roseta, Pa.: Testing a prediction. *Psychosomatic Medicine*, 1978, *40*, 86.

Buss, A. H. *The psychology of aggression*. New York: Wiley, 1961.

Caplan, R. D. *Organizational stress and individual strain: A social-psychological study of risk factors in coronary heart disease among administrators, engineers, and scientists*. Unpublished doctoral dissertation, University of Michigan, 1972.

Cassel, J. The contribution of the social environment to host resistance. *American Journal of Epidemiology*, 1976, *104*, 107–123.

Chesney, A. P., & Gentry, W. D. Psychosocial factors mediating health risk: A balanced perspective. *Preventive Medicine*, 1982, *11*, 612–617.

Chesney, A. P., Gentry, W. D., Gary, H. E., Kennedy, C., & Harburg, E. *Anger-coping style as a mediator in the relationship between life strain and blood pressure*. Unpublished manuscript, 1984.

Cobb, S. Social support as a moderator of life stress. *Psychosomatic Medicine*, 1976, *38*, 300–314.

Comstock, G. W., & Partridge, K. B. Church attendance and health. *Journal of Chronic Diseases*, 1972, *25*, 665–672.

Dean, A., & Lin, N. The stress-buffering role of social support. *Journal of Nervous and Mental Disease*, 1977, *165*, 403–417.

Dembroski, T., Weiss, S., Shields, J., Haynes, S., & Feinleib, M. (Eds.). *Coronary-prone behavior*. New York: Springer-Verlag, 1978.

Dohrenwend, B. S., & Dohrenwend, B. P. (Eds.). *Stressful life events: Their nature and effects*. New York: Wiley, 1974.

Fiske, D. W., & Maddi, S. R. (Eds.). *Functions of varied experience*. Homewood, Ill.: Dorsey Press, 1961.

Folkman, S., & Lazarus, R. S. An analysis of coping in a middle-aged community sample. *Journal of Health and Social Behavior*, 1980, *21*, 219–239.

Garrity, T. F., Somes, G. W., & Marx, M. B. Personality factors in resistance to illness after recent life changes. *Journal of Psychosomatic Research*, 1977, *21*, 23–32.

Gentry, W. D., Chesney, A. P., Gary, H., Hall, R. P., & Harburg, E. Habitual anger-coping styles: I. Effect on male/female blood pressure and hypertension status. *Psychosomatic Medicine*, 1982, *44*, 195–202.

Gergen, K. J., & Morse, S. J. Self-consistency: Measurement and validation. *Proceedings of the 75th Annual Convention of the American Psychological Association*, 1967, *2*, 207–208.

Gore, S. The effect of social support in moderating the health consequences of unemployment. *Journal of Health and Social Behavior*, 1978, *19*, 157–165.

Graham, T. W., Kaplan, B. H., Cornoni-Huntley, J. C., James, S., Becker, C., Hames, C., & Heyden, S. Frequency of church attendance and blood pressure elevation. *Journal of Behavioral Medicine*, 1978, *1*, 37–44.

Hahn, M. E. *California Life Goals Evaluation Schedule*. Palo Alto, Calif.: Western Psychological Services, 1966.

Harburg, E., Erfurt, J. C., Hauenstein, L. S., Chape, C., Schull, W. J., & Schork, M. A. Socio-ecological stress, suppressed hostility, skin color, and black–white male blood pressure: Detroit. *Psychosomatic Medicine*, 1973, 35, 276–296.

Holmes, T. H., & Rahe, R. H. The Social Readjustment Rating Scale. *Journal of Psychosomatic Research*, 1967, 11, 213–218.

House, J. S. Barriers to work stress: I. Social support. In W. D. Gentry, H. Benson, & C. de Wolff (Eds.), *Behavioral medicine: Work, stress, and health*. The Hague: Martinus Nijhoff, 1984.

House, J. S., & Wells, J. A. Occupational stress, social support and health. In A. McLean, G. Black, & M. Colligan (Eds.), *Reducing occupational stress: Proceedings of a conference* (DHEW Publication No. (NIOSH) 78-140). Washington, D.C.: U.S. Government Printing Office, 1978.

Jackson, D. N. *Personality Research Form manual*. Goshen, N.Y.: Research Psychologists Press, 1974.

James, S. A., & Kleinbaum, D. G. Socioecologic stress and hypertension related mortality rates in North Carolina. *American Journal of Public Health*, 1976, 66, 354–358.

Jenkins, C. D. Recent evidence supporting psychogenic and social risk factors for coronary disease. *New England Journal of Medicine*, 1976, 294, 987–994, 1231–1243.

Jenkins, C. D. Psychosocial modifiers of response to stress. *Journal of Human Stress*, 1979, 5, 3–15.

Johnson, J. H., & Sarason, I. G. Life stress, depression, and anxiety: Internal–external control as a moderator variable. *Journal of Psychosomatic Research*, 1978, 22, 205–208.

Kaplan, B. H., Cassel, J. C., & Gore, S. Social support and health. *Medical Care*, 1977, 25, 47–58.

Kennedy, C. D., Chesney, A. P., Gentry, W. D., Gary, H. E., & Harburg, E. *Anger-coping style as a mediator in the relationship between hostility and blood pressure*. Unpublished manuscript, 1984.

Kobasa, S. C. Stressful life events, personality, and health: An inquiry into hardiness. *Journal of Personality and Social Psychology*, 1979, 37, 1–11.

Kobasa, S. C. Commitment and coping in stress resistance among lawyers. *Journal of Personality and Social Psychology*, 1982, 42, 707–717. (a)

Kobasa, S. C. The hardy personality: Towards a social psychology of stress and health. In J. Suls & G. Sanders (Eds.), *Social psychology of health and illness*. Hillsdale, N.J.: Erlbaum, 1982. (b)

Kobasa, S. C. Barriers to work stress: II. The "hardy" personality. In W. D. Gentry, H. Benson, & C. J. de Wolff (Eds.), *Behavioral medicine: Work, stress and health*. The Hague: Martinus Nijhoff, 1984.

Kobasa, S. C., & Maddi, S. R. Existential personality theory. In R. Corsini (Ed.), *Current personality theories*. Itasca, Ill.: Peacock, 1977.

Kobasa, S. C., Maddi, S. R., & Courington, S. Personality and constitution as mediators in the stress–illness relationship. *Journal of Health and Social Behavior*, 1981, 22, 368–378.

Kobasa, S. C., Maddi, S. R., Donner, E. J., Merrick, W. A., & White, H. *The personality construct of hardiness*. Unpublished manuscript, 1984.

Kobasa, S. C., Maddi, S. R., & Kahn, S. Hardiness and health: A prospective study. *Journal of Personality and Social Psychology*, 1982, 42, 168–177.

Kobasa, S. C., Maddi, S. R., & Puccetti, M. Personality and exercise as buffers in the stress–illness relationship. *Journal of Behavioral Medicine*, 1982, 5, 391–404.

Kobasa, S. C., Maddi, S. R., Puccetti, M. C., & Zola, M. A. *Effectiveness of hardiness, exercise, and social support as resources against illness*. Unpublished manuscript, 1984.

Kobasa, S. C., Maddi, S. R., & Zola, M. A. Type A and hardiness. *Journal of Behavioral Medicine*, 1983, 6, 41–51.

Kobasa, S. C., & Puccetti, M. C. Personality and social resources in stress resistance. *Journal of Personality and Social Psychology*, 1983, 45, 839–850.

Lazarus, R. S. *Psychological stress and the coping process:* New York: McGraw-Hill, 1966.

LaRocco, J. M., & Jones, A. P. Co-worker and leader support as moderators of stress–strain relationships in work situations. *Journal of Applied Psychology*, 1978, 63, 629–634.

LaRocco, J. M., House, J. S., & French, R. P. Social support, occupational stress and health.

Journal of Health and Social Behavior, 1980, *21*, 202–218.

Maddi, S. R. *Personality as a resource in stress-resistance.* Paper presented at the meeting of the American Psychological Association, Montreal, 1980.

Maddi, S. R., Kobasa, S. C., & Hoover, M. An alienation test. *Journal of Humanistic Psychology*, 1979, *19*, 73–76,

Mitchell, J. C. *Social networks in urban situations.* Manchester, England: Manchester University Press, 1969.

Moss, G. E. *Illness, immunity, and social interaction.* New York: Wiley, 1973.

Neugarten, B. L. The middle years. In S. Arieti (Ed.), *American handbook of psychiatry.* New York: Basic Books, 1974.

Nuckolls, K. B., Cassel, J., & Kaplan, B. H. Psychosocial assets, life crisis and the prognosis of pregnancy. *American Journal of Epidemiology*, 1972, *95*, 431–441.

Pearlin, L. I., & Lieberman, M. A. Social sources of emotional distress. In J. Simmons (Ed.), *Research in community and mental health.* Greenwich, Conn.: JAI Press, 1977.

Pearlin, L., & Schooler, C. The structure of coping. *Journal of Health and Social Behavior*, 1978, *19*, 2–21.

Pinneau, S. R. *Effects of social support on psychological and physiological stress.* Unpublished doctoral dissertation, University of Michigan, 1975.

Rabkin, J. G., & Struening, E. L. Life events, stress and illness. *Science*, 1976, *194*, 1013–1020.

Rodin, J., & Langer, E. J. Long-term effects of a controlrelevant intervention with the institutionalized aged. *Journal of Personality and Social Psychology*, 1977, *35*, 897–902.

Rotter, J. B., Seeman, M., & Liverant, S. Internal versus external locus of control of reinforcement: A major variable in behavior theory. In N. F. Washburne (Ed.), *Decisions, values, and groups.* London: Pergamon, 1962.

Sandler, I. N., & Lakey, B. Locus of control as a stress moderator. *American Journal of Community Psychology*, 1982, *10*, 65–80.

Schaefer, C., Coyne, J. C., & Lazarus, R. S. The health-related functions of social support. *Journal of Behavioral Medicine*, 1981, *4*, 381–406.

Schmale, A. H., & Iker, H. P. The effect of hopelessness and the development of cancer. *Psychosomatic Medicine*, 1966, *28*, 714–721.

Schwartz, G. E., & Weiss, S. M. Yale Conference on Behavioral Medicine: A proposed definition and statement of goals. *Journal of Behavioral Medicine*, 1978, *1*, 3–12.

Smith, R. E., Johnson, J. H., & Sarason, I. G. Life change, the sensation seeking motive, and psychological distress. *Journal of Consulting and Clinical Psychology*, 1978, *46*, 348–349.

Stout, C., Morrow, J., Brandt, E., & Wolf, S. Unusually low incidence of death from myocardial infarction: Study of an Italian American community in Pennsylvania. *Journal of American Medical Association*, 1964, *188*, 845–849.

Wolf, S. Protective social forces that counterbalance stress. *Journal of the South Carolina Medical Association*, February 1976 (Suppl.), 57–59.

Wolf, S., Grace, K., Bruhn, J., & Stout, C. Roseta revisited: Further data on the incidence of myocardial infarction in Roseta and neighboring Pennsylvania communities. *Transactions of the American Clinical and Climatological Association*, 1973, *85*, 100–108.

Wyler, A. R., Masuda, M., & Holmes, T. H. Seriousness of Illness Rating Scale: Reproducibility. *Journal of Psychosomatic Research*, 1970, *14*, 59–64.

Zuckerman, M., Kolin, E. A., Price, L. Z., & Zoob, I. Development of a sensation seeking scale. *Journal of Consulting Psychology*, 1964, *26*, 250–260.

CHAPTER 5

Behavior and the Immune System

Robert Ader
University of Rochester School of Medicine and Dentistry
Nicholas Cohen
University of Rochester School of Medicine and Dentistry

INTRODUCTION

As a result of research in psychosomatic and behavioral medicine, it has become clear that there is probably no major organ system or homeostatic defense mechanism that is not subject to the influence of interactions between psychological and physiological events. The complex mechanisms underlying these interactions and their relationship to organic disease, however, are imperfectly understood. Perhaps least understood of all are the interrelations between behavioral and immune processes; nevertheless, these interrelations are what this chapter is all about. We cannot yet clarify the mechanisms involved, but we can provide some documentation of the potential impact of psychosocial factors on immune processes and on pathophysiological processes that involve immune responses.

Despite the emergence and convergence of data from a variety of disciplines derived from studies conducted at different biobehavioral levels of organization, it is not a commonly accepted premise that the central nervous system is capable of exerting some regulatory function over immune processes. On the contrary, the immune system is thought to be an autonomous defense agency. Some authors (e.g., DeWeck & Frey, 1966; Sell, 1972) categorically reject the possibility that the central nervous system is involved in specific immune phenomena; and all one need do is browse through the table of contents or index of almost any immunology textbook to confirm that little or no attention is devoted to the central nervous system, or to psychosocial factors that, operating through the nervous system, could influence immune function. We would contend, however, that like all other physiological systems operating in the interests of homeostasis, immune processes are sensitive to the influence of the central nervous system. As such, the immune system would stand as a mediator of the effects of psychosocial factors on the predisposition to and the precipitation and perpetuation of a variety of diseases.

That the immune system represents a homeostatic defense mechanism that is integrated with other homeostatic processes is not a speculative hypothesis. A great deal of data are available from the fields of neuroendocrinology, neurophysiology, neurochemistry, and pharmacology; from the discipline of immunology itself; and from psychology (Ader, 1981b). The data with respect to behavioral influences include, first, studies documenting the effects of psychosocial factors (or "stress") on susceptibility to disease processes that are presumed to involve immunological mechanisms (e.g., Amkraut & Solomon, 1974; Rogers, Dubey, & Reich, 1979; Solomon, 1981; Weiner, 1977). More directly, there are studies delineating the effects of experiential factors on various *in vitro* and *in vivo* parameters of immunological reactivity per se (e.g., Monjan, 1981). Finally, there are recent studies on the conditioning of immunopharmacological effects (Ader & Cohen, 1981). It is these behavioral influences that are discussed in the present chapter.

PSYCHOSOCIAL FACTORS AND IMMUNOLOGICALLY MEDIATED DISEASE

Studies in Humans

Infectious Diseases

There is a large literature devoted to the relationship between stressful life events and susceptibility to disease (e.g., Gunderson & Rahe, 1974; Rahe, 1974; Rubin, Gunderson, & Arthur, 1972). Insofar as pathogen-mediated disease states are concerned, the role of psychosocial factors is illustrated by the case of infectious diseases where the delicate balance between host and infectious agent is recognized (Friedman & Glasgow, 1966). Admittedly, there is a great deal of accumulated wisdom based on anecdotal evidence, and relatively little experimental data. Nonetheless, infectious disease processes illustrate the ubiquitous observation that, despite a common exposure to pathogenic stimuli, only a relatively small proportion of infected individuals actually manifest disease.

Psychosocial factors appear to be capable of influencing both the likelihood of developing disease and the course of disease. Meyer and Hagerty (1962), for example, followed several families for a period of 1 year and found that chronic "stress" (as reported on a rating scale) was associated with an increased susceptibility to streptococcal disease. M. A. Jacobs, Spilken, Norman, and Anderson (1970) reported that college students who sought medical attention for respiratory illness (as distinct from the total population that may have been experiencing respiratory symptoms) displayed greater problems of adjustment than did a sample of symptom-free students. In terms of recovery, the duration of respiratory illness was prolonged in children scoring high on a scale of life event changes (Boyce, Cassel, Collier, Jensen, Ramey, & Smith, 1977), and there was a relationship between "ego strength" (as measured by the Minnesota Multiphasic Personality Inventory) and recovery from infectious mononucleosis in college students (Greenfield, Roessler, & Crosley, 1959). In addition to the physiological alterations induced by disease states, it would appear that there are psychosocial changes that can alter the course of disease in some of the same ways that they can modify susceptibility (Imboden, Canter, & Cluff, 1961).

As part of a larger study on viral respiratory infections, Jackson, Dowling, Anderson, Riff, Saporta, and Turck (1960) made some observations that are particularly interesting in relation to the data on conditioned immunopharmacological responses described below. A population of control subjects treated with placebo nasal drops showed a linear relationship between their previous susceptibility to natural colds and the development of cold symptoms following inhalation of a small quantity of an isotonic salt solution. Of the subjects who reported having had five or more colds each year, for example, 26% developed the criterion symptoms of a "cold"; of those who reported a history of only one or two colds per year, fewer than 10% developed a "cold." It was also reported that the susceptible individuals were more likely to believe that emotional states could influence physical health, and, in addition, were more likely to report their concern about some personal problem that existed at the time of the experiment. Although personality factors appeared to influence the report of cold symptoms following the placebo treatment, there were no differences between the "susceptible" and "nonsusceptible" groups in response to an inoculation of infectious material.

On the "negative" side, Wilder, Hubble, and Kennedy (1971) found, contrary to their expectations, that college students diagnosed as having infectious mononucleosis reported fewer stressful life experiences than did members of a control population. Also, there appears to be a complex relationship between acute versus chronic disease, on the one hand, and ratings of life changes over an extended period of time in contrast to more rapid fluctuations of mood or feeling states, on the other (Luborsky, Mintz, Brightman, & Katcher, 1976; Wyler, Holmes, & Masuda, 1971).

One of the most extensive studies of psychosocial factors and infectious disease was recently reported by Kasl, Evans, and Neiderman (1979). These authors conducted a long-term prospective study of infectious mononucleosis in more than 1,000 cadets at the West Point Military Academy. Some data are provided on the psychosocial correlates of the initial immunity status at the start of the study, and on seroconversion among susceptible cadets during the course of the study. They concentrated, however, on identifying risk factors predictive of the clinical expression and course of the disease among susceptible students who were known to be infected with Epstein–Barr virus (EBV). At matriculation, approximately two-thirds of the students were found to be immune to infectious mononucleosis (i.e., had EBV antibody). Among the susceptible population, approximately 20% became infected (seroconverted), and a quarter of these seroconverters developed clinical infectious mononucleosis. Psychosocial factors that increased the risk that EBV infection would be expressed as clinical disease included fathers who were "overachievers," high motivation, and relatively poor academic performance. These same risk factors were also predicative of elevated antibody titers among seroconverters with inapparent disease and length of hospitalization among those with clinical infectious mononucleosis.

Autoimmune Diseases

Immunological competence is of particular relevance in autoimmune diseases, a variety of disorders characterized by humoral and/or cell-mediated immune reactions to some component(s) of self (Sampter, 1978). Examples of autoimmune diseases include rheumatoid arthritis (RA), Hashimoto's thyroiditis, hemolytic anemia, and systemic lupus erythematosus.

Early studies of personality factors in RA (Moos, 1963) are essentially anecdotal but nevertheless point up the potential role of psychosocial factors in the onset and course of the disease. The several descriptions of patients with RA, based extensively on interview data, are purported to yield distinctive patterns of personality. Imbedded among the divergent personality profiles described, however, is the frequent notation of the occurrence of and reaction to real or threatened losses (e.g., Ellman & Mitchell, 1936; Ludwig, 1955; Robinson, 1957). More recent and extensive studies of RA patients (Shochet, Lisansky, Schubart, Fiocco, Kurland, & Pope, 1969) provide confirmation of these observations in documenting a temporal relationship between major life changes involving separation and the onset or exacerbation of symptoms. Although Hendrie, Paraskevas, Baragar, and Adamson (1971) did not find any difference in life change scores between RA patients and controls, they did find higher life change scores among those RA patients who had elevated immunoglobulin levels.

The most extensive analyses of the personality characteristics of patients with RA were reported by Moos and Solomon (1964a, 1965a, 1965b). Using a control group of siblings closest in age to the patients with RA, these authors failed to confirm many of the personality profiles previously described (e.g., dependency, athletic participation). There were, however, certain outstanding features in their patient population. In particular, RA patients were more conscientious; they could be characterized as masochistic and self-sacrificing; and they denied hostility. The patients also perceived rejection by their parents to a greater extent than their siblings did. These authors also noted a link between the disease and long-standing stressful circumstances. In attempting to correlate psychological variables with the course of RA, Moos and Solomon (1964b) suggest that those RA patients with the most rapidly progressing disease were experiencing feelings of ego disintegration and concomitant anxiety and depression, which reflected a decrease in their capacity to maintain previously effective modes of coping. This analysis is essentially similar to those derived from observations on other disease states involving immune responses (e.g., Grinker & Robbins, 1954; Wittkower, Durost, & Laing, 1955).

The role of psychosocial factors in rheumatoid arthritis is especially evident in the data collected by Meyerowitz, Jacox, and Hess (1968) on monozygotic twins discordant for RA. They found no consistent developmental differences or differences in health status prior to the onset of RA. However, in four of the five adult twin sets studied in detail, they did find evidence of a common stressful experience that preceded the onset of disease in each of the affected twins.

Henoch, Batson, and Baum (1978) compared 88 children with juvenile RA to members of a random population. Among the RA group, there was a high incidence of divorce or separation of parents or death of one parent, and the prevalence of adoption was much higher in the RA than in the comparison group. Rimon, Belmaker, and Ebstein (1977) were not able to discern any common denominator in the sphere of family interactions among juvenile RA patients, but they did note personality characteristics similar to those observed in adult patients with RA.

A more detailed account of the personality characteristics and participating psychosocial factors that are associated with RA is given by Solomon (1981). Solomon also points out the essential similarity between the data on the personality characteristics of patients with RA and the data on patients with other disorders with autoimmune features, such as ulcerative colitis (Engel, 1955), systemic lupus erythematosus (McClary, Meyer, & Weitzman, 1955; Otto & MacKay, 1967), multiple sclerosis (Grinker & Robbins, 1954), and Graves disease (Mandelbrote & Wittkower, 1955). With respect to the last of these, a recent clinical report (Morillo & Gardner, 1979) described bereavement as an antecedent factor in Graves disease in children. In the four children studied, depression was the common response to a meaningful separation experience or the death of a close relative. It was hypothesized that the neurochemical changes associated with depression could directly or indirectly (via the hypothalamic-pituitary-adrenal axis) suppress immunological surveillance, which, in turn, could permit the formation of thyroid-stimulating immunoglobulins in genetically susceptible individuals.

For a more extensive biopsychosocial analysis of the pathogenesis of RA and Graves disease, the reader is referred to Weiner (1977). It is worth noting that the observation of personality characteristics associated with autoimmune illness in humans is not inconsistent with observations of behavioral changes resulting from interventions involving immune function in animal subjects (Hoffman, Shucard, Harbeck, & Hoffman, 1978; Hotchin & Seegal, 1977; Karpiak, Rapport, & Bowen, 1974; Preachie & Gibson, 1976).

Studies in Animals

Cancer

To the extent that some cancers may have a viral etiology, studies of the effects of psychosocial factors on neoplastic processes constitute one source of data with respect to spontaneous or experimentally induced disease processes involving immunological mechanisms. Only brief mention of these studies is made here. An extensive (and critical) review of studies in humans has been prepared by Fox (1981), and experimental studies in animals have been reviewed by LaBarba (1970) and by Riley, Fitzmaurice, and Spackman (1981).

With few exceptions (e.g., Marchant, 1967), there have been no systematic studies of the *interactions* between stress and genetic factors. Considering that there are marked strain differences in the hormonal responses to environmental stimuli (e.g., Levine & Treiman, 1964), the lack of such studies is conspicuous. Such analyses would undoubtedly yield very complicated results, in light of a recent report (Prehn & Lawler, 1979) that the rank order of sarcoma susceptibility among several strains of mice could be reversed simply by changing the concentration of the carcinogen.

Experientially, the development and/or the response to spontaneously developing or experimentally induced neoplastic disease can be influenced by the manipulation of early life experiences (e.g., Ader & Friedman, 1965a, 1965b; LaBarba, Klein, White, & Lazar, 1970; LaBarba, White, Lazar, & Klein, 1970; Levine & Cohen, 1959; Otis & Scholler, 1967); by the manipulation of social factors (e.g., Ader & Friedman, 1964; Andervont, 1944; DeChambre & Gosse, 1973; Henry, Stephens, & Watson, 1975; Kaliss & Fuller, 1968; LeMonde, 1959; Riley *et al.*, 1981); by other noxious stimulation, such as electric shock and conditioning procedures (e.g., Amkraut & Solomon, 1972; Kalisnik, Vraspir-Porenta, Logonder-Mlinsek, Zorc, & Pajntar, 1979; Plaut, Esterhay, Sutherland, Wareheim, Friedman, Schnaper, & Wiernik, 1981; Rashkis, 1952); or, conversely, by the minimization of environmental disturbances (Riley, 1975). Also, the capacity to cope with stressful environmental circumstances can attenuate tumor growth and mortality (Sklar & Anisman, 1979); "stress" has been reported to increase and/or decrease the incidence of disease, depending upon the pathogenic stimulus and the response measure chosen for analysis; and further consideration of genetic factors, the variety of manipulations that have been imposed, and the variety of pathological processes studied yields, not surprisingly, a contradictory pattern of results that precludes definitive generalization at this time.

Infectious Diseases

Of more direct relevance, perhaps, are the several experimental studies of the effects of experimentally induced stressful conditions on susceptibility to or responses to experimentally induced infectious diseases. It is the recent interest in the influence and mediation of psychosocial factors on immune responses that has refocused attention on these studies, most of which have been in the literature for several years.

The earliest program of research was initiated by Rasmussen and his colleagues (Rasmussen, 1969). Rasmussen, Marsh, and Brill (1957), for example, subjected male mice to a conditioning regimen of electric shock avoidance for 6 hours per day for 1, 14, or 28 days before inoculation with herpes simplex virus. Control mice were exposed to the same conditioned stimuli, but did not receive electric shock. Mortality resulting from the herpes virus (see Figure 5.1) increased from 44% in the controls to 56% in animals stimulated for 14 days, and to 74% in mice stimulated for 28 days before the virus inoculation. Comparable results were also obtained when physical restraint was used intead of avoidance conditioning. Johnson, Lavender, and Marsh (1959) used the same avoidance-conditioning regimen for a period of 4 to 5 weeks before inoculating mice with Coxsackie B virus. The experimental mice showed a significantly greater weight loss than did controls; mortality occurred only within the experimental group; and greater amounts of virus

FIGURE 5.1. Cumulative percentages of mortality in mice subjected to 1, 14, or 28 days of an avoidance-conditioning regimen before inoculation with herpes simplex virus. (Adapted from Rasmussen, A. F., Jr., Marsh, J. T., & Brill, N. Q. Increased susceptibility to herpes simplex in mice subjected to avoidance-learning stress or restraint. *Proceedings of the Society for Experimental Biology and Medicine*, 1957, *96*, 183–189.)

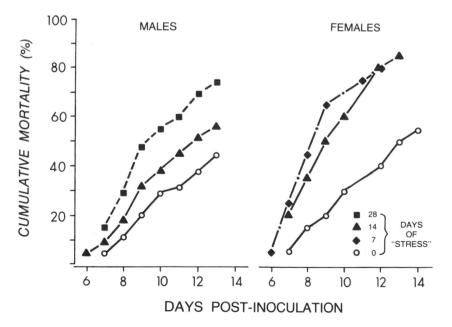

could be detected in the organs of these "stressed" animals, relative to those of controls.

Adult mice are generally resistant to Coxsackie virus, compared to infant animals. However, in an attempt to control for the direct effects of the electric shock used in avoidance-conditioning situations, Friedman, Ader, and Glasgow (1965) subjected individually caged adult mice to a periodic schedule of a light stimulus followed by electric shock; control groups were subjected to either the light or the shock stimulus, alone, on the same periodic schedule, or remained unmanipulated. The experimental conditions were introduced 3 days before and continued for 4 days after inoculation with Coxsackie B virus. Additional groups experienced the same environmental manipulations but were not inoculated with the virus. Neither the "stressful" stimulation nor the virus, alone, was sufficient to cause any weight changes in these adult mice. However, adult mice inoculated with Coxsackie virus *and* subjected to the periodic light–shock stimulation showed a significant reduction in body weight, and all the animals that died came from this experimental group. These results parallel the observations of Holmes, Treuting, and Wolff (1951), who described a situation in which the presence of pollen alone was not sufficient to elicit symptoms in a subject with hay fever, but the combination of pollen and a threatening life situation was.

Rasmussen, Hildemann, and Sellers (1963) inoculated neonatal mice with polyoma virus. When the animals were weaned, they were subjected to stressful stimulation, which did not influence disease susceptibility. The failure to document "stress" effects was attributed to the interval between virus inoculation and the stressful stimulation. When mice that were 2 to 3 weeks old were injected with polyoma virus and immediately thereafter subjected to "sound stress" and then avoidance conditioning, the stimulated animals were found to be more susceptible than controls were (Chang & Rasmussen, 1964).

The critical nature of the temporal relationship between "stress" and infectious challenge is further illustrated by the studies of Jensen and Rasmussen (1963) and Yamada, Jensen, and Rasmussen (1964). In their first experiment, mice were subjected to intense auditory stimulation (123 db) for 3 hours daily and inoculated intranasally with vesicular stomatitis virus (VSV) at different times in relation to the stressful stimulation. Susceptibility to VSV was increased after the first period of stimulation. A biphasic response was seen in animals that were not inoculated until the second "stress" day: Mice inoculated before the auditory stimulation died at a faster rate than controls, while animals inoculated after the stimulation were more resistant than controls. Adrenalectomized mice tested on the second "stress" day responded like intact animals; susceptibility was increased, regardless of the time of VSV inoculation. In their second experiment, mice were subjected to avoidance conditioning for 6 hours each day rather than auditory stimulation, and VSV was introduced intramuscularly. There were no differences between experimental and control animals when VSV was inoculated on the second day of avoidance conditioning. However, when mice were inoculated after 15 days of stressful stimulation, the rate of disappearance of virus was retarded in the experimental animals; the same effect was observed in adrenalectomized mice. These data provide compelling evidence that "a stressful stimulus at a critical time could alter the host's defense mechanisms, allowing an otherwise inconsequential exposure to a pathogenic organism to develop into a clinical disease" (Jensen & Rasmussen, 1963, p. 23).

Parasitic Diseases

A conclusion similar to that of Jensen and Rasmussen was reached by Josephine (1958), based on a study of parasitic infections in kittens. *Entamoeba histolytica* is an important parasitic ameba of the alimentary tract in several animals, but is not especially common in the cat. Littermates infected with *E. histolytica* were separated into groups that were housed in separate cages and maintained on canned cat food, and groups that were housed with other animals in a large outdoor cage and had their diet supplemented with meat and canned milk. The kittens confined to separate cages were described as frightened, nervous animals, whereas the kittens that had the opportunity to engage in normal exercise and association with other animals had placid dispositions and good eating habits. The kittens confined to the individual cages also showed a higher incidence of infection. Despite the confounding of psychosocial and nutritional variables, Josephine's results do suggest that "acute amebiasis in the kitten is probably not the result of infection with the parasite *per se* as usually conceived [but that] the severity of infection . . . may be modified by variable characteristics of the animal, its nutritional status, the presence of intercurrent infection[,] and the psychophysical response to stress[,] resulting in an overwhelming infection in a species of animal which under more normal conditions may be only moderately susceptible to infection with the ameba" (1958, pp. 163–164).

Susceptibility to parasitic infection was also studied by Weinman and Rothman (1967), who observed a decreased resistance to *Hymenolepsis nana*, a tapeworm, when intense fighting occurred among male mice. Hamilton (1974) also observed an increased susceptibility to *H. nana* when mice were exposed to a predator. The mice were infected and then placed into special chambers, where they were exposed to a cat one, two, four, or eight times each day for the next 17 days. Control animals were similarly handled, but were not exposed to a cat. Four days before the final "stress" exposure, all mice were reexposed to the parasite. Rate of infection increased in proportion to the frequency with which immunized mice were subjected to the "predator-induced stress" (see Figure 5.2). Exposure to a cat also increased adrenal gland weight in proportion to the number of daily trials. Plasma corticosterone levels were also elevated, but did not vary with exposure rate.

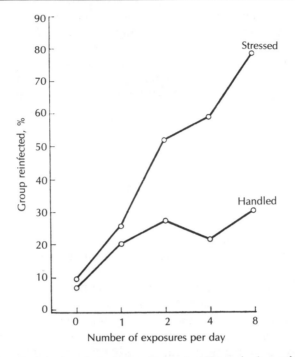

FIGURE 5.2. Rate of reinfection of mice immunized against *Hymenolepsis nana* following exposure to a cat ("stressed") or to an empty chamber ("handled"). (From Hamilton, D. R. Immunosuppressive effects of predator induced stress in mice with acquired immunity to *Hymenolepsisnana*. *Journal of Psychosomatic Research*, 1974, *18*, 143–153. Reprinted by permission of Pergamon Press.)

Although susceptibility to reinfection was greater in the "stressed" than in the "handled" animals, the rate of reinfection also increased with trial frequency in the "handled" group. In the "handled" group, however, there was no corresponding relationship to either adrenal gland weight or the corticosterone levels sampled on the final day of stimulation.

Although the data cited above would seem to indicate that "stress" will increase susceptibility to immunologically mediated disease, this is not always the case. Rogers, Trentham, McCune, Ginsberg, Reich, and David (1979), for example, also used "predator-induced stress" in a study of susceptibility to autoimmune arthritis. Approximately 40% of a population of rats developed arthritis after the intradermal injection of collagen. Exposing the rats to a cat, however, abrogated the development of the collagen-induced arthritis. In contrast, exposing rats to auditory "stress" increased susceptibility to arthritis (Rogers, Trentham, & Reich, 1981).

There are still other studies indicating that "stress" can be without discernable effects or can decrease susceptibility. Subjecting mice to periodic light and/or electric shock stimulation as described above had no effect on susceptibility to encephalomyocarditis virus, but increased resistance to *Plasmodium berghei*, a rodent malaria (Friedman, Ader, & Grota, 1973), and to the spontaneous development of leukemia in AKR mice (Plaut *et al.*, 1981). Prolonged avoidance conditioning increased susceptibility to poliomyelitis virus in mice (Johnsson & Rasmussen, 1965), but decreased susceptibility in monkeys (Marsh, Lavender, Chang, & Rasmussen, 1963). The incidence of tumors induced by murine Moloney sarcoma virus was increased by physical restraint (Seifter, Rettura, Zisblatt, Levenson, Levine, Davidson, & Seifter, 1973), whereas Amkraut and Solomon (1972) reported that fighting and electric shock stimulation decreased tumor size if the stimulation was experienced before the injection of virus (electric shock that was introduced after virus inoculation increased tumor size). In contrast to other data cited above, both avoidance conditioning and auditory stimulation decreased susceptibility of mice to Rauscher leukemia virus (Jensen, 1968), and physical restraint (but not immersion in a cold bath) suppressed development of allergic encephalomyelitis in rats (Levine, Strebel, Wenk, & Harman, 1962).

A further illustration of the multiple effects of "stress" on the development of or responses to disease can be derived from studies in which the social interactions among animals are manipulated, particularly studies of differential housing. Such studies are more often referred to in terms of the effects of "crowding" or "isolation"—inadequately defined terms (Ader, 1976b) that reflect value judgments on the part of the investigator with respect to the deleterious effects of "stress," and, incidentally, bear a striking relationship to the results obtained. To summarize these data, group housing or experimental interventions that increase the social interactions among animals have been found to increase susceptibility to trichinosis (Davis & Read, 1958), rabies virus (Soave, 1964), and arthritic disease (Amkraut, Solomon, & Kraemer, 1971; Ebbesen, 1968). Group housing also increases susceptibility to malaria (Plaut, Ader, Friedman, & Ritterson, 1969), an effect that is determined by the strain of animal infected (Friedman & Glasgow, 1973). In contrast, group housing decreases susceptibility to other pathogenic stimuli, such as encephalomyocarditis virus (Friedman, Glasgow, & Ader, 1969) and *Escherichia coli* (W. B. Gross & Siegel, 1965). In one of the earliest of such studies, Tobach and Bloch (1956) found that susceptibility to tuberculosis was determined by an interaction between gender and the conditions of housing imposed before and/or after the introduction of the infection. Comparable data illustrating the effects of differential housing and other psychosocial influences could be cited in the case of neoplastic and other pathophysiological disorders (Ader, 1970, 1976b).

In demonstrating the effects of environmental manipulations on susceptibility and responses to infectious and autoimmune disease, these are the data that, indirectly at least, indicate that psychosocial factors would be capable of influencing the immune system. While these studies do not clarify the mechanisms that may be involved, they do carry a message with respect to the concepts and strategies that may have to be adopted by immunologists and behavioral scientists alike if this line of interdisciplinary investigation is to be pursued. It is of conceptual as well as methodological importance, for example, to acknowledge that the effects of "stress" are not unitary. The effects of environmental stimulation, whether or not it is labeled as stressful, depend upon several characteristics of the host (e.g., species, strain, gender, age), as well as the psychophysiological state of the particular individual upon whom the stimulation is superimposed. In turn, the effects of stress will contribute to the (experientially determined) state of the organism, upon which potentially pathogenic stimuli may then be superimposed. Also, it seems evident from a detailed analysis of the literature described above that susceptibility to disease will be determined by the temporal relationship between the nature (and/or intensity or chronicity) of the stressful stimulation and the nature (and/or intensity or concentration) of the challenge to the host—not to mention the time and choice of parameters chosen to reflect altered susceptibility.

A variety of presumably noxious stimuli have been used in order to examine the effects of "stress" in altering disease susceptibility. The results, however, have not been uniform; that is, the stimuli used and referred to as being stressful do not necessarily have equivalent effects. In terms of the psychosocial stimulation, then, the labeling of electric shock, avoidance conditioning, restraint, "overcrowding," and so forth as "stressors" contributes little to our understanding of the mechanisms that may mediate alterations in disease susceptibility. Furthermore, such a generalization is likely to impede such understanding because of its implicit assumption that stressors are essentially equivalent in their effects; this fosters the search for simple, one-cause explanations (Ader, 1970, 1980). In terms of the pathophysiological response, it is also clear that psychosocial variables (however imposed or interpreted by the investigator) are neither uniformly detrimental nor uniformly beneficial to the organism. Whether the effects of such "stress" act to increase or decrease susceptibility to disease will depend upon the nature of the disease process under study. That is, the adaptive significance of the psychophysiological response to some natural or experimentally imposed environmental event depends upon the pathogenic agent(s) being harbored by the individual or agent(s) to which the individual may coincidentally or subsequently be exposed. Until we can specify which of the myriad physiological (including immunological) changes accompanying the response to psychosocial events are relevant in modifying the effects of potentially pathogenic stimuli, it will not be possible to predict or control the behavioral influences on disease susceptibility.

If behavioral scientists are going to contribute to an understanding of psychosocial factors in health and disease, and if these contributions are to be accepted in the instigation of collaborative research, we can ill afford to compound the complex relationship between behavior and disease by premature generalizations. It would be much simpler to be able to accept the premise that stress is deleterious and will increase susceptibility to organic disease; it would be more consistent with a multifactorial approach and the available data, however, to ask how different kinds of psychosocial changes influence the predisposition to and the precipitation or perpetuation of which pathological processes in which individual(s).

PSYCHOSOCIAL FACTORS AND IMMUNOLOGICAL REACTIVITY

Studies in Humans

The current interest in psychoneuroimmunological phenomena, and the proposition that the immune system mediates between psychosocial events processed by the central nervous system and pathophysiological processes, are not yet reflected in studies of the effects of psychosocial factors (including "stress") on immunological reactivity in humans. Of course, it is difficult to implement such studies, especially in healthy subjects. The available literature, therefore, is sparse. Investigators are just now beginning to add immunological parameters to the biochemical and endocrinological determinations that have become a part of sophisticated assessments of the physiological concomitants of naturally occurring and experimentally induced alterations of psychosocial circumstances.

One major life event that is generally considered psychologically disruptive or stressful is the death of a spouse, and Bartrop, Lazarus, Luckhurst, Kiloh, and Penny (1977) conducted a prospective study of the impact of bereavement on immune function. Blood samples were obtained approximately 2 and 8 weeks after the death of a spouse from illness or injury. Control subjects were hospital personnel who had experienced no such loss within the past 24 months and were matched for age, sex, and race. Lymphocyte responsivity was measured *in vitro* to mitogenic stimulation with phytohemagglutinin (PHA) and concanavilin A (Con A).[1] Lymphocytes from members of the bereaved group showed a significantly suppressed mitogenic reactivity, particularly on the second of the two tests (see Figure 5.3). Other parameters of immune function (T and B cell numbers, serum protein, electrophophoresis, immunoglobulins, α_2-macroglobulin concentrations, autoantibodies, or delayed hypersensitivity) did not appear to be affected by bereavement. It is especially noteworthy that there were also no changes in

---

1. "Mitogens" are a heterogeneous group of compounds that stimulate proliferation of lymphocytes. Some mitogens (plant lectins such as PHA and Con A) exclusively stimulate thymus-derived lymphocytes, or "T cells"; others stimulate bone-marrow-derived lymphocytes, or "B cells" (e.g., bacterial lipopolysaccharide). Although mitogenic reactivities are not synonymous with immune reactions, they do reflect the availability of normally functioning subpopulations of lymphocytes in the peripheral blood for antigenic stimulation, cell interaction, and antibody production. Thus, mitogenic responses serve as an index of T or B cell presence and function.

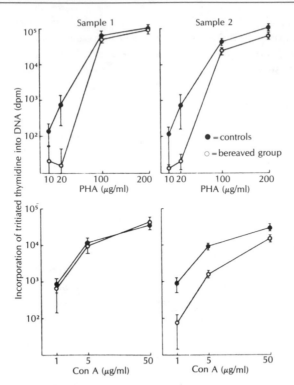

FIGURE 5.3. Geometric mean ($\pm SE$) lymphocyte reactivity to mitogens PHA and Con A in control and bereaved subjects. (From Bartrop, R. W., Lazarus, L., Luckhurst, E., Kiloh, L. G., & Penny, R. Depressed lymphocyte function after bereavement. *Lancet*, 1977, *i*, 834–836. Reprinted by permission.)

serum concentrations of thyroxine, triiodothyronine, cortisol, prolactin, or growth hormone corresponding to the change in immunological reactivity in the bereaved spouses. People who experience radical psychosocial changes, such as the death of a spouse, the loss of a job, and so forth, are prone to the use of alcohol, tranquilizers, or other drugs as a means of coping with such events, and are likely to experience some modification in their eating habits, sleep–wake cycles, and other patterns (Palmblad, 1981). It is therefore necessary to consider the influence of such factors in altering immune function under such circumstances. The report by Bartrop *et al.* is, nonetheless, a dramatic illustration of the impact of psychological factors on immune function that has since been verified (Schleifer, Keller, McKegney, & Stein, 1980).

Other recent reports (Canter, Cluff, & Imboden, 1972; Greene, Betts, Ochitill, Iker, & Douglas, 1978; Locke, Hurst, Heisel, Kraus, & Williams, 1978; Roessler, Cate, Lester, & Couch, 1979) have described preliminary studies undertaken to relate stressful life events and coping styles to humoral and cell-mediated immune competence.[2] In general, high stress or life change scale scores, with low ego strength or presumably unsuccessful coping responses, were associated with depressed immunological defenses.

Another naturally occurring (if currently less common) stressful event is space flight. The observations made on animals during space flight are described below. In astronauts, there is evidence of depressed lymphocyte responses to mitogenic stimulation with PHA and decreased rosette formation[3] on the day of splashdown and a few days following Skylab missions (Kimzey, 1977; Kimzey, Ritzman, Mengel, & Fischer, 1975). It is not clear to what extent the changes are due to the "stress" of splashdown per se, nor how long the depression in immunological reactivity may last, since the depression in reactivity appears to be related to flight duration.

Although more prosaic, such variables as nutritional state and sleep deprivation (and the psychosocial factors that contribute to these conditions) are extremely important considerations in assessing the immunological effects of "stress"; they also constitute events that, in themselves, can alter immunological competence. In people who are overweight, for example, morbidity in infectious disease and the prevalence of infectious disease as a cause of death is increased (Palmblad, 1981).

Undernutrition is frequently associated with high population density, increased exposure to pathogenic agents, and poor health facilities, not to mention psychosocial events (Chandra, 1974; Palmblad, 1981). It is difficult, therefore, to attribute differences in disease susceptibility solely to nutritional factors. On the other hand, there are, for example, alterations in host defense mechanisms associated with anorexia nervosa (Gotch, Spry, Mowat, Beeson, & MacLennon, 1975; Kim & Michael, 1975; Kjosen, Bassoe, & Myking, 1975; Palmblad, Fohlin, & Lundstrom, 1977; Palmblad, Fohlin, & Norberg, 1979), although the clinical significance of such changes is not clear. In experimental studies, normal volunteers subjected to *total* energy deprivation for a period of 10 days showed a depression of some parameters of immunological reactivity (Kjellberg, Levi, Palmblad, Paulsson, Theorell, & Yensen, 1977) and no change in others (Holm & Palmblad, 1976; Palmblad, 1976; Palmblad, Cantell, Holm, Norberg, Strander, & Sunblad, 1977). There was no relationship between changes in host defense measures and measures of endocrine status induced by brief energy deprivation (Palmblad, Levi, Burger,

---

2. Immune responses can be divided into those that are called "cell-mediated" and those that are called "humoral." These terms refer to the effectors of a given immune response. Humoral responses are those mediated by serum antibody; cell-mediated responses are mediated either directly by lymphocytes (usually T cells) or by nonantibody products of lymphocytes, called "lymphokines."

3. The formation of "rosettes" (clusters of erythrocytes bound to lymphocytes) is, in humans, a function of nonimmune thymus-derived T cells.

Melander, Westgren, von Schenck, & Skude, 1977). Further, the effects of restricted feeding depend upon the state of the particular organism upon which it is superimposed (Palmblad, 1981). It would not be surprising, then, to find different effects in normal subjects as compared to obese patients participating in a weight reduction program, patients with existing disease, or even grieving subjects.

In studying sleep deprivation, Palmblad and his colleagues subjected healthy volunteer subjects to 77 hours of sleeplessness, during which the subjects were kept constantly vigilant by a variety of tasks and environmental stimuli. Blood samples were obtained at the same hour of the day before the experimental period, on the second and last days of the vigil, and 5 days after the experiment. The capacity of lymphocytes to produce interferon when Sendai virus was added to blood samples was increased during the vigil and was still elevated 5 days later; leukocyte phagocytic activity decreased during the vigil but was slightly higher than the baseline level 5 days after the "stress" (Palmblad, Cantell, Strander, Froberg, Karlson, Levi, Granstrom, & Unger, 1976). The lymphocyte response to PHA was also reduced during sleep deprivation but returned to normal 5 days later (Palmblad, Petrini, Wasserman, & Akerstedt, 1979). In the first study, the subjects showed increases in cortisol and urinary catecholamine output, but these same responses showed a decrease in the second experiment. Since there was a consistent suppression of granulocyte and lymphocyte function, it is not considered likely that these neuroendocrine responses exerted a major effect on the attenuation of immunological reactivity in this situation (Palmblad, 1981).

In general, these data could be interpreted to indicate that host defenses are compromised during a period of sustained attention and lack of sleep, and, although restoration of normal function occurs fairly rapidly, these changes could signal a period of increased susceptibility to pathogenic stimuli. Should we not also consider the possibility, however, that the total patterning of the immunological changes that occur in response to such stressful circumstances (those that have and have not been simultaneously measured) constitutes, in part, an attempt by the organism to optimize its defensive posture and reflects the changes that occur in the absence of superimposed immunogenic stimulation?

Studies in Animals

On the basis of advances in technology, as well as a recognition of the relevance of the internal milieu in determining immune responses, an increasing number of studies are being initiated to examine the effects of environmental stimulation on immune processes directly. As noted above, one of the "natural" situations that has been studied is space flight. Alterations were observed in the lymphoid organs of rats flown on the Soviet satellite

Kosmos-782 in 1975. The histological changes measured 6 to 10 hours after landing were of two kinds: acute changes due, presumably, to the effects of reentry and landing; and chronic changes (lymphoid hypoplasia) due to effects elicited early in or throughout the flight. Twenty-five days after the flight, the effects could no longer be detected (Portugalov, 1976). In addition to the morphological changes, there was a concomitant depression of DNA synthesis in the spleen, which was also reversible (Tigranyan, 1976). In contrast, Mandel and Balish (1977) found that rats that were aboard Kosmos-782 showed an enhanced cell-mediated response to immunization with a killed culture of *Listeria*.

Back on earth, Gisler, Bussard, Mazie, and Hess (1971) observed a suppression of *in vitro* immunological reactivity 6 to 24 hours after mice were subjected to either acceleration or ether anesthesia. The onset and degree of suppression was a function of the strain of mouse and the particular stimulus used. These *in vitro* results could be reproduced by injection of ACTH (Gisler & Schenkel-Hulliger, 1971), but Solomon, Amkraut, and Rubin (1979) report that neither their laboratory nor Gisler's was able to suppress *in vivo* responses by such hormone administration. Solomon *et al.* (1979) report that the "crowding" of rats (under conditions sufficient to elevate corticosteroid levels) did not influence *in vitro* reactivity, although Joasoo and McKenzie (1976) were able to observe a decrease in the response to human thyroglobulin of splenic lymphocytes obtained from rats maintained under "crowded" living conditions for 5 weeks before the introduction of antigen.

Increases as well as decreases in lymphocyte response have been observed in "stressed" animals (Folch & Waksman, 1974; Monjan & Collector, 1977). In the study by Monjan and Collector, mice were subjected to brief bursts of noise (100 db) for 1 to 3 hours daily. Immunological reactivity was assessed by the *in vitro* responses of lymphoid cells obtained from "stressed" and "nonstressed" animals to mitogenic stimulation with lipopolysaccharide (LPS) to reflect B cell function and with Con A to reflect T cell function. Both assays revealed the same temporal changes in proliferative reactivity (see Figure 5.4). Initially, there was a depression of mitogen-driven lymphocyte proliferation. Comparable results were obtained when an antigenically specific immune reaction was evaluated (i.e., cytotoxic reactions mediated by immune T cells). After approximately 1 month of daily stimulation, however, there was an increase in reactivity. The initial depression in response was accompanied by an increase in circulating corticosteroid levels, but steroid concentrations returned to baseline levels and did not show a change corresponding with the enhanced reactivity that occurred in response to prolonged exposure to the auditory stimulation. While the "stress"-induced changes in reactivity have yet to be explained, the description of a biphasic response reflects, again, the complexity of neuroendocrine–immune interactions and the need to consider temporal factors in the analysis of the effects of psychosocial factors on immune responses.

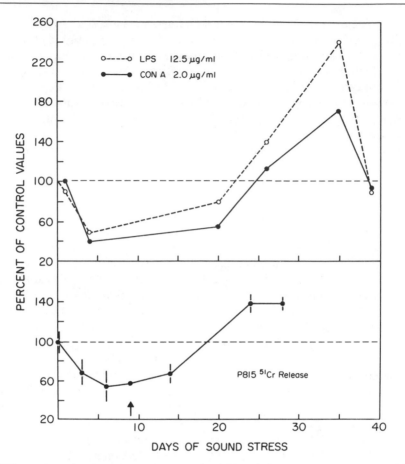

FIGURE 5.4. Lymphocyte reactivity to mitogens LPS and Con A (upper portion) and lymphocyte cytotoxicity (lower portion) in mice subjected to "sound stress" for 1 hour/day for as many as 39 days. (From Monjan, A. A., & Collector, M. I. Stress-induced modulation of the immune response. *Science,* 1977, *196,* 307–308. Copyright 1977 by the American Association for the Advancement of Science. Reprinted by permission.)

In a study by Bonnyne and McKenzie (1979), hypophysectomized, adrenalectomized, thyroidectomized, castrated, or unaltered rats remained unmanipulated or were forced to swim until exhausted, exposed to noise ("rock" music at 92–94 db for 6 hours), or immobilized for 6 hours. A different stimulus was imposed on each of 7 days. Blood samples were obtained at the beginning of the experiment, at the end of the stimulation regimen, and again 7 days later, in order to assess *in vitro* lymphocyte responsiveness to PHA (reflecting T cell activity) and pokeweed mitogen (PWM) (reflecting T and B cell activity). In response to PWM, there were some differences, but the direction of any given difference was determined not only by the nature of the treatment, but by the concentration of PWM and the day of measurement. Intact rats showed an increased response to PWM 1 week after cessation of the stimulation, but did not display an altered response to PHA. Among the surgically altered animals, there was no alteration in the response to PWM, but some differences in responses to PHA: Hypophysectomized rats subjected to "stress" were less reactive when sampled immediately after the "stress" regimen than were hypophysectomized animals that remained unmanipulated; and thyroidectomized rats subjected to "stress" were more reactive when sampled 1 week after the "stress" regimen than were thyroidectomized controls. The relative paucity of differences attributable to either environmental or endocrinological manipulations and the lack of any internal consistency in the data do not provide a persuasive argument for a neuroendocrine modulation of immunological reactivity. However, considering the data on disease susceptibility reviewed earlier and the data described above, these results cannot be interpreted as refutation of the impact of "stress." Such variables as the quality and quantity of stimulation (calculated, in this instance, to obviate adaptation or habituation), duration of stimulation, and time of sampling could have been responsible for some of the variability in these data.

In another recent study (Pavlidis & Chirigos, 1980), the effects of "stress" on the tumoricidal function of macrophages were examined. Nonspecific immunopotentiators, such as interferon or bacterial LPS, will activate resting peritoneal macrophages, rendering them tumoricidal for MBL-2 lymphoblastic leukemia cells. In the absence of "stress," interferon results in an 80% inhibition of tumor growth. Mice were subjected to physical immobilization for varying periods of time, and peritoneal macrophages were then activated *in vitro* with interferon. If more than 18 hours of restraint was imposed, tumoricidal activity was significantly impaired. "Stress" imposed on the day before or the day of an intraperitoneal (ip) injection of interferon also decreased macrophage tumoricidal cytotoxicity. The *in vitro* activation of macrophages by *Salonella typhimurium* LPS was similarly decreased by "stress." That corticosteroids play some role in mediating this effect was indicated by the results of another experiment, in which interferon alone effected a 94% inhibition of tumor cell growth, while the addition of hydrocortisone or prednisone decreased the response (by approximately 52–56%), and dexamethasone almost completely blocked it.

Studies on *in vivo* cellular responses have yielded seemingly disparate results. Using electric shock stimulation, Guy (1952) and Mettrop and Visser (1969) observed an increased reactivity in guinea pigs in response to a topically applied chemical irritant. Using mice, others (Christian & Williamson, 1958; Funk & Jensen, 1967; Smith, Molomut, & Gottfried, 1960) have reported that "crowding" or "auditory stress" reduced the inflammatory response. Pitkin (1965), too, observed a less severe delayed hypersensitivity response in mice exposed to high temperature, and Wistar and Hildemann

(1960) reported prolonged survival of skin allografts[4] in mice subjected to an avoidance-conditioning regimen. In mice placed on a limited feeding schedule, Amkraut, Solomon, Kasper, and Purdue (1973) observed changes in a graft-versus-host response.[5] If limited feeding was imposed before and continued after transplantation of the lymphoid cell graft, the response was suppressed; limited feeding confined to the period before the injection of donor cells did not effect changes in the response. Additional experiments using adrenalectomized or ACTH-treated recipients provided no evidence that the effects of restricted feeding could be attributed to changes in adrenocortical steroid levels.

Mice subjected to a daily avoidance-conditioning regimen are less susceptible to anaphylactic shock[6] than are unstimulated controls. The "stress"-induced resistance to anaphylaxis does not occur in adrenalectomized animals, but can be restored by hydrocortisone treatment (Rasmussen, Spencer, & Marsh, 1959; Treadwell & Rasmussen, 1961). These data, plus the interesting observation that resistance to anaphylaxis occurs within 2 hours of the first exposure to the avoidance conditioning and only lasts for 8 to 10 hours (in contrast to the prolonged exposure required to influence the response to infection with herpes simplex, for example), imply that adrenal activity plays a major role in the effect. As Rasmussen and colleagues have acknowledged, however, it would be premature to attribute such results simply to adrenocortical changes for several reasons, which, incidentally, also apply to much of the literature on "stress" effects cited above. Steroid levels were not actually measured; corticosterone, not hydrocortisone, is the endogenous corticosteroid secreted by the mouse; and the effects of "stress" on resistance on anaphylaxis in hypophysectomized mice were not investigated to evaluate adrenal medullary influences. On the basis of reports that "crowded" animals show increased levels of adrenocortical activity, Treadwell and Rasmussen (1961) also examined the anaphylactic response of group-caged and individually caged mice. Contrary to expectations based on adrenocortical involvement, they found that, under the smaller of two challenge doses, group-housed animals were the more susceptible (see Fig-

4. "Allograft" (homograft) is a transplant from one individual to another of the same species.

5. In the systemic graft-versus-host reaction, a host that is immunologically or immunogenetically incapable of recognizing and rejecting an allograft receives a transplant of immunocompetent lymphocytes. These donor cells mount an immunological attack against the host. This reaction is quite complex in that it involves host as well as donor reactants. Symptomology of this often lethal reaction includes hepatosplenomegaly, diarrhea, loss of hair, a rash, and a general wasting.

6. "Anaphylaxis" is an immediate hypersensitivity shock reaction in which antibody (IgE class in humans) binds to basophils and mast cells, complexes with antigen. This reaction leads to rapid degranulation of the cells and to the release of histamine and other pharmacologically active substances that mediate contraction of smooth muscle and injury to vascular endothelium.

ure 5.5). Instead of questioning the hypothesis of an adrenocortical mediation, however, Treadwell and Rasmussen surmised that individual caging
was more disturbing than group caging and that the results were due to the
"incidental stress of isolation." Again, though, no direct measurements of
steroid levels were made.

There are now several reports documenting the effects of a variety of experiential manipulations on the antibody response to immunogenic stimulation. Monkeys immunized with *Vibrio cholerae* (Felsenfeld, Hill, & Greer,
1966) or bovine serum albumin (Hill, Greer, & Felsenfeld, 1967) and exposed
to a variety of noxious stimuli showed smaller and slower rises in antibody
titer than did controls. In response to immunization with beef serum, Vessey
(1964) observed less precipitating antibody in mice that were moved from
individual to group housing conditions, whereas Glenn and Becker (1969)
found that group-housed mice had the higher antibody levels in response
to a booster injection of the antigen. In response to immunization with
typhoid–paratyphoid vaccine, Edwards and Dean (1977) found a decreased
antibody response among mice housed in high (30 to 60 animals per cage)
as compared to low (2 to 10 animals per cage) density groups. When group
housing was introduced before and continued after immunization, Solomon
(1969) observed a reduced primary and a reduced secondary response to
flagellin, a bacterial antigen (see Figure 5.6).

FIGURE 5.5. Susceptibility to anaphylaxis in group-housed and individually housed mice.
(Adapted from Treadwell, P. E., & Rasmussen, A. F., Jr. Role of the adrenals in stress-induced
resistance to anaphylactic shock. *Journal of Immunology*, 1961, *87*, 492–497.)

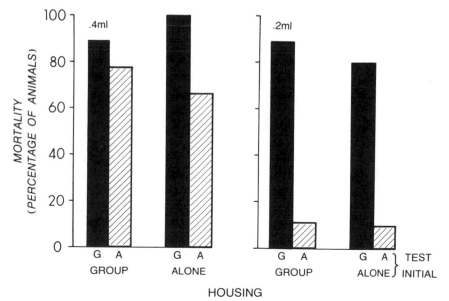

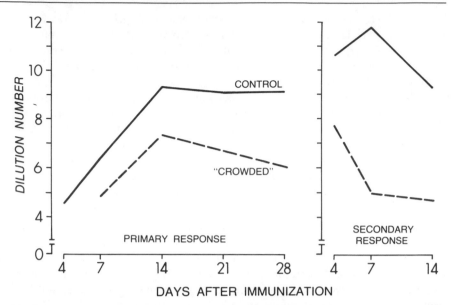

FIGURE 5.6. Primary and secondary antibody responses to a bacterial antigen in group-housed and individually housed rats. (Adapted from Solomon, G. F. Stress and antibody response in rats. *International Archives of Allergy*, 1969, 35, 97–104.)

Finally, there are data to indicate that alterations in the psychophysiological character of the host that result from the experimental manipulation of early life experiences are capable of modifying immunological reactivity. Data collected by Hotchin, Benson, and Gardner (1970) suggest that mortality in mice infected with lymphocytic choriomeningitis virus in infancy is related to the presence of infection in the mother (which does not result in clinical disease) and the nature of mother–young interactions. It has also been found that rats handled daily during the period between birth and weaning have more pronounced primary and secondary responses[7] to inoculation with flagellin than do unstimulated controls when tested as adults (Solomon, Levine, & Kraft, 1968). It is known that nutritional deficiencies can alter immunological competence (e.g., Chandra, 1974; R. L. Gross & Newberne, 1980). It now appears, though, that even in the presence of unlimited food, there is an impairment of primary and secondary antibody responses in the F_1 and F_2 progeny of rats that have been subjected to a calorie-restricted diet for 6 weeks during the period immediately after weaning (Chandra, 1975).

7. As compared with the antibody response to a primary exposure to antigen, the response to a second exposure to the same antigen is associated with a more rapid rise in antibody titer, a higher peak titer, and a more gradual decline in detectable antibody levels. These, plus other changes relating to the class and binding affinities of the antibody, are all indicative of what is known as "anamnesis," or immunological memory.

These studies provide compelling evidence that experiential factors are capable of modifying immune responses (see also Monjan, 1981). Like the data on disease susceptibility described earlier, the effects seem to depend upon the quality and quantity of the environmental stimulation, a variety of host factors, the nature of the immunogenic stimulus, and the parameters of immunological reactivity that are chosen for measurement. As a result, the effects of experiential factors on immunological reactivity are frequently small and, superficially at least, inconsistent. This, we believe, reflects upon our incomplete understanding of the mechanisms involved, rather than upon the phenomenon itself.

CONDITIONED RESPONSES AND THE MODULATION OF IMMUNE RESPONSES

In this section, we describe our own recent studies on conditioned immunopharmacological responses. Historically, the conditioning of physiological responses dates from the work of Pavlov (1928). In the classical (Pavlovian) paradigm, a stimulus (e.g., food) that unconditionally elicits a particular response (salivation) is repeatedly paired with a neutral stimulus (i.e., one that does not unconditionally elicit that particular response). Eventually, the originally neutral stimulus, the conditioned stimulus (CS), will elicit salivation, the conditioned response (CR), in the absence of food, the unconditioned stimulus (US). Similarly, if an external stimulus such as a tone (the CS) is repeatedly associated with an electric shock that unconditionally elicits flexion of the stimulated leg (the US), a conditioned leg flexion will subsequently occur in response to the CS, alone. In contrast, instrumental or operant conditioning involves the reward or reinforcement of some response when it occurs to some specified stimulus or signal. Each reinforcement strengthens or increases the probability of occurrence of the immediately preceding response (the response that was instrumental in procuring the reward).

In addition to altering behavior, classical conditioning and instrumental conditioning have been used to alter physiological responses. The majority of the early research in this area was conducted in physiology laboratories in the Soviet Union (Anokhin, 1974; Razran, 1961). New interest in the field was generated by the studies of Neal Miller and his colleagues (e.g., DiCara, 1970; Miller, 1969), who demonstrated that autonomic responses, previously thought to be involuntary, were subject to instrumental as well as to classical conditioning. For technological and methodological reasons, most of this work has been confined to cardiovascular responses. More recently, visceral and endocrine responses have been studied, and attention has been addressed to the conditioning of a variety of pharmacological responses (e.g., Siegel, 1977a, 1977b).

A relatively new and effective technique for producing a conditioned response has come to be known as "taste aversion learning" (e.g., Garcia, Hankins, & Rusiniak, 1974). In this passive-avoidance paradigm, consumption of a novel, distinctively flavored drinking solution is paired with an injection of a pharmacological agent. For example, water-deprived rats might be provided with a novel drinking solution, such as saccharin, coffee, or tea (the CS), and immediately thereafter injected with a drug such as lithium chloride (LiCl), apomorphine, or cyclophosphamide (CY) that unconditionally produces transient gastrointestinal upset (nausea, diarrhea). The appetitive response to the flavored solution is, in effect, punished by the aversive effects of the drug. An association between the taste of the novel solution and the aversive effects of the drug evidently occurs from the single pairing of these events, since the organism subsequently avoids consumption of that solution on the very next occasion of its presentation—even when the interval between conditioning and testing is as long as 3 months. Given the survival value of being able to form associations between gustatory cues and gastrointestinal consequences, it is not surprising that the effects of this kind of conditioning are so highly reproducible.

The studies described below were derived from observations made during the course of experiments on taste aversion learning in which CY was used as the US (Ader, 1974), and we have continued to use this conditioning paradigm for the study of conditioned immunopharmacological effects. While these studies have yielded new and dramatic results, the application of behavioral conditioning techniques to modify immune responses is probably the oldest of the experimental approaches to the study of central nervous system regulation of immune responses. The first systematic studies of conditioning in the control of host defense mechanisms were initiated in the Soviet Union more than 50 years ago (Metal'nikov & Chorine, 1926, 1928).

Metal'nikov and Chorine attempted to create a CR by repeating injections of foreign material into the peritoneum of guinea pigs and associating the injections with external stimuli. The CS-US pairings occurred once daily for 18 to 25 days. After a rest period to allow the peritoneal exudate to return to normal, the CS was presented without the US. Under normal circumstances, the peritoneal exudate contains mostly mononuclear leukocytes, and the injection of antigen causes an immediate increase in polynucleated cells. In one guinea pig, it was established that polynucleated cells comprised 90% of the exudate 5 hours after the injection of antigen. When, after conditioning trials, the CS was presented alone, polynucleated cells increased from .6% to 62% after 5 hours. Observation of other animals yielded similar results. The reaction to the CS was weaker and more transient than the unconditioned response, but it was clearly demonstrable. Metal'nikov also subjected two guinea pigs to 12 pairings of a CS with the ip injection of a staphlococcus filtrate. Ten days later, the CS was presented alone. On the next day, the experimental animals and an additional animal that had not experienced the CS-US pairings were injected with a lethal dose of a cholera culture. The control animal died, whereas the experimental animals survived. On the basis of these and several additional experiments, it was concluded that CRs can play an important role in immunity.

The early studies on the application of conditioning techniques to the study of immune responses were not very well-controlled experiments. Some controls were added, however, and these studies stimulated a great deal of interest, at least within the Soviet Union. The implications and, indeed, the underlying premise was consistent with the predominant view that all physiological processes were regulated by the central nervous system. The observations of Metal'nikov and Chorine were replicated by several investigators, and the phenomenon was confirmed under a variety of circumstances with a variety of antigenic stimuli in a variety of species (Luk'ianenko, 1961). To place the Soviet literature in perspective, there appears to be data that, taken together with other studies of interoceptive conditioning, provide grounds for optimism regarding the applicability of conditioning techniques in modifying immune responses. A detailed review of this Soviet literature has been provided elsewhere (Ader, 1981a).

Studies of Conditioned Immunosuppression

Initial Studies

The basic design of the studies described below is similar, so the protocol for our initial experiment (Ader & Cohen, 1975) is described here in some detail.

Adult Charles River (CD) male rats were individually housed under a 12-hour light–dark cycle and provided with food and water *ad libitum*. The daily provision of plain tap water was gradually reduced until all animals were provided with and consumed their daily allotment of fluid during a single 15-minute period. Five days under this regimen constituted the initial adaptation period and provided baseline data on fluid consumption. This schedule was maintained throughout the experiments.

On the conditioning day (Day 0), animals were randomly assigned to conditioned, nonconditioned, and placebo groups. During their 15-minute drinking period, conditioned animals were provided with a .1% solution of sodium saccharin in tap water, the CS, and 30 minutes later they were injected ip with CY[8] (50 mg/kg), the US. Nonconditioned animals were provided with plain tap water, and were injected with CY 30 minutes later. Placebo animals received plain water and were injected with an equal volume of vehicle. On the following 2 days, all animals were given plain water during their scheduled 15-minute drinking period.

---

8. The CY was generously supplied by the Mead Johnson Research Center, Evansville, Indiana.

Three days after conditioning, all animals were injected ip with antigen, sheep red blood cells (SRBC; approximately 3×10^8 cells/ml). Thirty minutes later, randomly selected subgroups of conditioned and nonconditioned animals were provided with the saccharin solution or plain water and then received an injection of CY or saline as described below and as schematically illustrated in Table 5.1.

Conditioned animals were divided into three basic subgroups. Group CS, the critical experimental group, received a single drinking bottle containing the saccharin solution, and drinking was followed by an injection of saline. In this first experiment, there were actually three such experimental groups: One was provided with saccharin on Day 3, the day on which antigen was introduced; one received saccharin on Day 6; and one received saccharin on Days 3 and 6. The two additional subgroups of conditioned animals were essentially control groups. One of these, Group US, received plain water followed by an injection of CY; these animals were used to define the unconditioned immunosuppressive effects of CY. The other subgroup, Group CS_0, received plain water followed by an injection of saline, and constituted a control for the prior effects of conditioning per se.

The basic protocol also included nonconditioned animals (Group NC) and animals receiving a placebo (Group P). As described below, NC animals were given plain water and an injection of CY on the conditioning day (Day 0). Subgroups of these animals were subsequently provided with the saccharin drinking solution and injected with saline whenever the corresponding CS groups received saccharin and ip injections, in order to control for the effects of these treatments. P animals remained unmanipulated and received plain water during the 15-minute drinking periods. On Day 9 (6 days after injection with antigen), all animals were sacrificed.

The behavioral results of this initial experiment (see Figure 5.7) reaffirmed that CY is an effective stimulus for inducing a conditioned taste aversion (e.g., Peck & Ader, 1974; Wilcoxon, Dragoin, & Kral, 1971; Wright, Foshee, & McCleary, 1971).

Given the hypothesis that immunosuppression could be influenced by conditioning processes, one should be able to predict the relative difference in antibody titers among the several groups. The hypothesized pattern of results is illustrated in Figure 5.8. Sera from animals in Group P were expected to show relatively high hemagglutinating antibody titers. Sera from animals in Group NC (animals provided with saccharin when injected with antigen) were also expected to have high titers. But Group NC had been treated with CY 3 days before receiving SRBC; as a result, it was anticipated that the titers from NC animals might be somewhat lower than those of P animals because of the residual effects of the drug (Makinodan, Santos, & Quinn, 1970; Santos & Owens, 1964). Conditioned animals that were not reexposed to the conditioned or unconditioned stimuli (Group CS_0) were also expected to show relatively high antibody levels. Like Group NC, how-

TABLE 5.1. Experimental Protocol

		DAYS AFTER CONDITIONING						
		0	3	0		6		9
						DAYS AFTER ANTIGEN		6
GROUP	ADAPTATION	CONDITIONING DAY	SUBGROUP	(ANTIGEN)	1–2	3	4–5	
Conditioned	H_2O (15 min)	SAC+CY	US	H_2O+CY	H_2O	H_2O+–	H_2O	Sample
				H_2O+–	H_2O	H_2O+CY	H_2O	Sample
			CS_0	H_2O+Sal	H_2O	H_2O+–	H_2O	Sample
				H_2O+–	H_2O	H_2O+Sal	H_2O	Sample
			CS_1	SAC+Sal	H_2O	H_2O+–	H_2O	Sample
				H_2O+–	H_2O	SAC+Sal	H_2O	Sample
			CS_2	SAC+Sal	H_2O	SAC+–	H_2O	Sample
Nonconditioned	H_2O (15 min)	H_2O+CY	NC	SAC+Sal	H_2O	H_2O+–	H_2O	Sample
				H_2O+–	H_2O	SAC+Sal	H_2O	Sample
Placebo	H_2O (15 min)	H_2O+Plac	P	H_2O+–	H_2O	H_2O+–	H_2O	Sample

Note. From Ader, R., & Cohen, N. Conditioned immunopharmacologic responses. In R. Ader (Ed.), *Psychoneuroimmunology.* New York: Academic Press, 1981. Reprinted by permission.

Note. Key to abbreviations not appearing in text: SAC, sodium saccharin; Plac, placebo; Sal, saline.

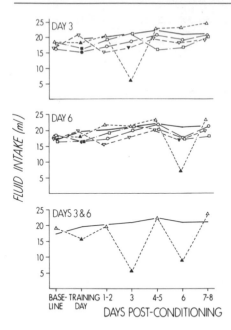

FIGURE 5.7. Mean intake of plain water (open symbols) and saccharin (closed symbols) for placebo (---) and nonconditioned (▲) animals, and for conditioned animals that received saccharin (△), CY (□), or neither (○) on Day 3, Day 6, or Days 3 and 6 after conditioning. As a point of reference, the placebo group is shown in each panel. (From Ader, R., & Cohen, N. Behaviorally conditioned immunosuppression. *Psychosomatic Medicine*, 1975, *37*, 333–340. Reprinted by permission of Elsevier/North-Holland, Inc.)

ever, these animals were injected with CY 3 days before receiving SRBC and were therefore expected to have titers that were lower than those of P animals but equivalent to those of NC animals. Conditioned animals that were injected with CY at the same time that antigen was introduced were expected to show a minimal antibody response to SRBC. The critical experimental groups, those that were reexposed to the CS rather than the US, could show an antibody response that did not differ from Groups NC and CS_0; they could show complete suppression of antibody production, as was expected from Group US; or more reasonably, they could show some diminution of the antibody response.

The actual data are shown in Figure 5.9. Conditioned animals reexposed to saccharin on Day 3 or Day 6 did not differ; these subgroups were collapsed into a single group that received one (CS_1) in contrast to two (CS_2) reexposures to saccharin. The comparable control groups, which also did not differ, were similarly combined. The pattern of observed results was as we had predicted. P animals showed the highest antibody titers, and, as expected, treatment with CY just after injection of antigen (Group US) suppressed antibody production. There were no differences between the NC animals and the conditioned animals that were *not* reexposed to the CS (Group CS_0); both groups had lower titers than those of P animals. It was presumed that this difference reflected the residual effects of CY injected 3 days before antigen was injected. Consequently, the NC and CS_0 groups represented the relevant control conditions against which to assess the effects of condition-

ing (i.e., the antibody response of conditioned animals that were reexposed to the CS). Conditioned animals that experienced either one or two reexposures to saccharin following antigenic stimulation showed an attenuated antibody response that was significantly different from those of both the NC and CS_0 groups. These initial results, then, supported the hypothesis that the association of saccharin with CY would enable saccharin to elicit an immunosuppressive CR.

These rather dramatic findings have been repeated in our laboratory on several occasions, as described below. More to the point, these observations have been independently replicated in three different laboratories. Rogers, Reich, Strom, and Carpenter (1976) followed our procedures quite closely and used a more sensitive assay procedure. Their results are shown in Figure 5.10. A single reexposure to the saccharin drinking solution did not depress

FIGURE 5.8. Conditioned immunosuppression: Predicted pattern of differences in hemagglutinating antibody titer. (From Ader, R., & Cohen, N. Conditioned immunopharmacologic responses. In R. Ader (Ed.), *Psychoneuroimmunology*. New York: Academic Press, 1981. Reprinted by permission.)

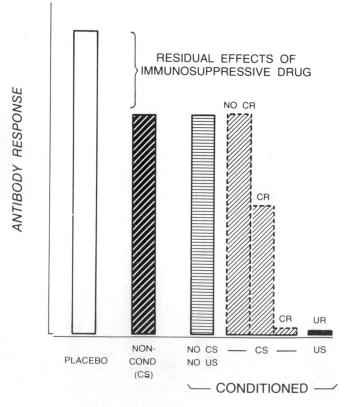

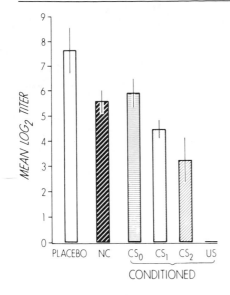

FIGURE 5.9. Hemagglutinating antibody titers (mean ± SE) determined 6 days after injection of SRBC. NC = nonconditioned animals provided with saccharin on Day 0 (day of antigen) or Day 3; CS_0 = conditioned animals that did not receive saccharin after antigen treatment; CS_1 = conditioned animals reexposed to saccharin on Day 0 or Day 3; CS_2 = conditioned animals reexposed to saccharin on Days 0 *and* 3; US = conditioned animals injected with CY following antigenic stimulation. (From Ader, R., & Cohen, N. Behaviorally conditioned immunosuppression. *Psychosomatic Medicine*, 1975, *37*, 333–340. Reprinted by permission of Elsevier/North-Holland, Inc.)

FIGURE 5.10. Effects of conditioning on hemagglutinating antibody titer. Group designations are the same as in Figure 5.9. (Adapted from Rogers, M. P., Reich, P., Strom, T. B., & Carpenter, C. B. Behaviorally conditioned immunosuppression: Replication of a recent study. *Psychosomatic Medicine*, 1976, *38*, 447–452.)

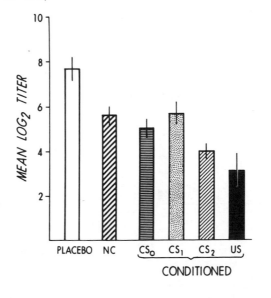

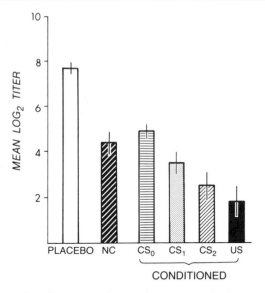

FIGURE 5.11. Effects of conditioning on hemagglutinating antibody titer. Group designations are the same as in Figure 5.9. (Adapted from Wayner, E. A., Flannery, G. R., & Singer, G. The effects of taste aversion conditioning on the primary antibody response to sheep red blood cells and *Brucella abortus* in the albino rat. *Physiology and Behavior*, 1978, *21*, 995–1000. Reprinted by permission.)

antibody titer, but two reexposures to the CS significantly attenuated the antibody response of conditioned animals. Essentially the same results (see Figure 5.11) were reported by Wayner, Flannery, and Singer (1978). Smaller (but statistically significant) differences were also found by King (1979).

In all of these initial studies, hemagglutinating antibody titer was measured 6 days after stimulation with SRBC (we had established that peak production of antibody occurred at about this time with the dose of antigen that was being used). However, this is not necessarily the optimal time for uncovering a conditioned suppression of immunological reactivity. Therefore, in an effort to describe the effects of conditioning more fully, an experiment was conducted in which blood samples were obtained from independent groups of animals at different times.

As can be seen in Figure 5.12, circulating antibody titers were low in all animals 4 days after the injection of SRBC. Six days after antigenic stimulation, the antibody titer in conditioned animals reexposed to the CS was significantly lower than the titers in conditioned rats that were not reexposed to the CS and in nonconditioned animals, confirming the conditioned attenuation of antibody production described above. There were no differences among the groups in antibody titers sampled on Days 8 and 10. Thus, conditioning does not inhibit antibody production; rather, it effects a transient delay in the initiation of those events that culminate in the production of antibody. That is, the production of antibody is delayed by the specific action(s)

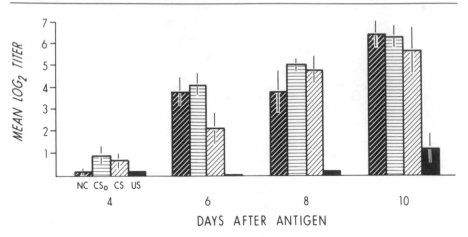

FIGURE 5.12. Effects of conditioning on antibody titers (mean ± SE) measured 4, 6, 8, and 10 days after treatment with SRBC. Group designations are the same as in Figure 5.9. (From Ader, R., & Cohen, N. Conditioned immunopharmacologic responses. In R. Ader (Ed.), *Psychoneuroimmunology*. New York: Academic Press, 1981. Reprinted by permission.)

of the CS introduced at some critical time in the developing response of the conditioned animal.

The kinetics of antibody production will vary as a function of several of the parameters of stimulation, including the degree of immunosuppression induced by CY. For example, in another study (Ader & Cohen, 1981), we increased the dose of CY from 50 to 75 mg/kg. In this instance, there were no differences among the several treatment conditions when antibody titers were sampled 6 days after the injection of SRBC (at a time when all animals had relatively low titers); when antibody titers were sampled 8 days after antigenic stimulation, however, there was again a significant attenuation of the antibody response in conditioned animals reexposed to the CS.

Although we and others have been able to reproduce the phenomenon of conditioned immunosuppression, the magnitude of the conditioned attenuation of a humoral immune response has been relatively small. On theoretical and empirical grounds, however, there may be environmental as well as procedural factors acting to mask or reduce the effects of conditioning.

In our initial studies, for example, one group of conditioned animals, (Group US) was injected with CY at the time that antigen was administered, in order to define the unconditioned effects of the immunosuppressive drug. As a control for this manipulation, animals from all other groups were injected with saline at that same time. Was it necessary or desirable to provide a placebo injection to the remaining animals? It has been recognized (e.g., Dolin, Krylov, Luk'ianenko, & Flerov, 1960; Hutton, Woods, & Makous, 1970; Pavlov, 1928; Siegel, 1975) that the injection procedure can act as a CS in such psychopharmacological research—and in our paradigm, the immunosuppressive effects of CY had been associated with an ip injection for all animals. Therefore, injecting animals in Groups CS_0 and NC with placebo at the time that antigen was introduced may have constituted a CS for immunosuppression.

Another extraneous variable that has existed in all but our most recent studies is the common manner in which the several groups have been housed (i.e., in a single colony room). In other experiments on taste aversion learning, we have noticed that when the CR is assessed under a "preference" or two-bottle testing procedure, conditioned animals drink plain water without necessarily first tasting the fluid in the randomly positioned bottle containing the CS solution. Animals appear to be able to recognize the presence of saccharin in one of the bottles without having to consume any measurable amount. The choice is presumably based on an olfactory discrimination, and it has been shown that a poison-induced avoidance response can be established on the basis of an association involving olfactory cues (Domjan, 1973; Lorden, Kenfield, & Braun, 1970; Lovett, Goodchild, & Booth, 1968; Supak, Macrides, & Chorover, 1971; Taukulis, 1974). Olfactory cues could have influenced our data in several ways: "NC" animals might actually be weakly conditioned animals; the presence of saccharin in the common colony room (e.g., between successive CS presentations after antigen administration) might have promoted extinction of the behavioral and immunosuppressive responses. In one experiment designed to examine the potential influence of olfactory cues in the conditioning of a taste aversion (Ader, 1977), the mere presence of the CS solution (saccharin) in the immediate environment of conditioned animals during the interval between conditioning and testing attenuated the aversion (i.e., facilitated extinction of the CR). In another experiment, it was noted that when conditioned rats that were provided with plain water were tested in the presence of conditioned rats that were provided with the CS solution (saccharin), the consumption of *plain water* was reduced to the level of the consumption of saccharin. As a result of such observations, our routine protocol now dictates that different treatment groups be maintained in separate colony rooms.

Still another critical variable may be the interval between pretreatment with CY and antigenic stimulation. Referring to Figures 5.9–5.11, it can be seen that the difference between Group P and the two control groups (NC animals and conditioned animals that are not reexposed to the CS) is as great as the difference between the control groups and the experimental group (conditioned animals that are reexposed to the CS). The reduced antibody titers in Groups NC and CS_0 can, presumably, be attributed to the residual effects of the CY administered 3 days before the injection of antigen. Residual effects of CY have been reportd (e.g., Mackenzie, Pick, Sibley, & White, 1978; Makinodan *et al.*, 1970; Rollinghoff, Starzinski-Powitz, Pfizenmaier, & Wagner, 1977; Santos & Owens, 1964), and have been confirmed under conditions relevant to our conditioning paradigm (Ader, Cohen, & Grota, 1979).

In animals injected with 50 or 75 mg/kg CY at varying times before inoculation with 3×10^8 SRBC, we observed a dose-related attenuation of antibody production that was inversely related to the interval between immuno-suppressive treatment and antigenic stimulation (see Figure 5.13). It is possi-ble, therefore, that one of the factors contributing to the relatively small differences between experimental and control groups was the mild depres-sion of antibody production that occurred in control relative to P animals—a depression that could have acted to mask the conditioning effect.

Generalizability of Conditioned Immunosuppression

Despite the operation of potentially confounding factors, we and others have been able to repeat the observations of conditioned immunosuppression of a humoral response to sheep erythrocytes, a T-cell-dependent antigen. More-over, it appears that conditioning is capable of modifying immunological reactivity in other models of immune function.

As previously described, Wayner et al. (1978) were able to observe condi-tioned immunosuppression using SRBC in an experimental protocol that was essentially identical to ours. Wayner and her colleagues also examined condi-tioned immunosuppression using Brucella abortus, a T-cell-independent anti-gen.[9] In this case, there were no differences among the treatment groups. It would be premature, however, to conclude that the effects of condition-ing on primary humoral antibody responses are limited to an influence of T lymphocytes. There are too many potentially interacting variables that could influence conditioning (e.g., species and strain, residual effects of CY on T-cell-dependent and T-cell-independent responses, dose of antigen, and particularly the kinetics of antibody production in the two systems and sampling time). We, too, have conducted studies with a T-cell-independent antigen (N. Cohen, Ader, Green, & Bovbjerg, 1979). These studies were carried out in mice stimulated with the hapten[10] 2,4,6-trinitrophenyl (TNP) coupled to the thymus-independent carrier LPS (the combination is known as TNP-LPS); the experiments yielded positive results.

In the first experiment, BDF_1 male mice were treated in a manner essen-tially similar to the rats of previous studies. Nonconditioned mice in these

9. It is well known that antibody production to certain antigens involves a cooperative interac-tion between T cells and B cells. T cells subserve a helper-dependent antigen. Other antigens, such as Brucella abortus and lipopolysaccharide, do not need T cell help to trigger B cells to pro-duce antibody; hence their name, T-cell-independent antigens.

10. A "hapten" is a substance that combines specifically with antibody but does not incite forma-tion of antibody unless attached to a carrier of high molecular weight. If the carrier is a T-cell-dependent antigen (e.g., SRBC), then helper T cells are needed to effect an antihapten response; if the carrier is T-cell-independent (e.g., LPS), then the antibody response to the same hapten is thymus-independent. Regardless of whether the carrier is T-cell-dependent or T-cell-inde-pendent, antibody to the hapten can be measured by passive hemagglutination of erythrocytes to which the hapten has been chemically bound.

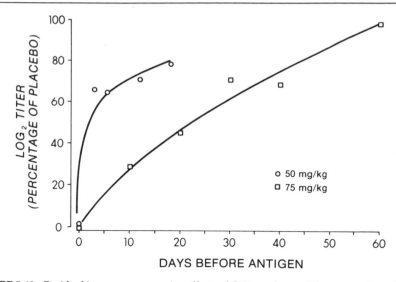

FIGURE 5.13. Residual immunosuppressive effects of CY in male rats. The mean values shown are based on mean hemagglutinating antibody titers obtained 6 days after injection of SRBC from 2 to 17 groups, relative to their respective (same-experiment) placebo-treated control groups. (From Ader, R., Cohen, N., & Grota, L. J. Adrenal involvement in conditioned immunosuppression. *International Journal of Immunopharmacology*, 1979, *1*, 141–145. Reprinted by permission of Pergamon Press.)

experiments were injected with CY after consuming plain water but were exposed to saccharin 5 days later (i.e., a flavored drinking solution that was *not* paired with CY). Also, in consideration of the residual effects of CY, antigen was not introduced until 2 *weeks* after conditioning. Based on a prior analysis of the kinetics of the antibody response to different doses of TNP-LPS, all animals were injected ip with 50 μg TNP-LPS, and blood samples were collected 6 days after antigenic stimulation. In a single-bottle procedure, the CS group was reexposed to saccharin and given an ip injection of saline on the day that antigen was injected, and again 2 days later. In a second experiment, the dose of CY was increased from 200 to 300 mg/kg, and an attempt was made to increase the saliency of the CS; the saccharin solution was introduced by pipette, and mice were immediately thereafter injected with LiCl. When Group CS and Group NC were subsequently reexposed to the CS, both the saccharin drinking solution (in a "preference" testing procedure) and the LiCl were presented.

The results of these two experiments are given in Table 5.2. As expected, antibody titers in the first experiment were higher than in the second; this difference presumably reflects the lower dose of immunosuppressive drug used in the first experiment. The higher dose of CY also appears to have had some residual effects, even after the 2-week interval between conditioning

TABLE 5.2. Effects of Conditioning in BDF_1 Mice on the Antibody Response to a Challenge with TNP-LPS: Mean$\pm$SE (n) Antibody Titer

EXPERIMENT	CONDITIONED STIMULUS	CY (mg/kg)	GROUP				
			P	NC	CS_0	CS	US
1	SAC	200	6.68±.35 (19)	6.78±.16 (23)	6.29±.15 (24)	5.76±.27 (25)	2.53±.30 (15)
2	SAC+LiCl	300	5.00±.17 (15)	4.50±.38 (8)	3.14±.94 (7)	2.28±.84 (7)	0.0 (2)

Note. From Cohen, N., Ader, R., Green, N., & Bovbjerg, D. Conditioned suppression of a thymus independent antibody response. *Psychosomatic Medicine,* 1979, *41,* 487–491. Reprinted by permission of Elsevier/North-Holland, Inc.

and antigenic stimulation (which might also account for the higher variability among animals in Experiment 2).

In the first experiment, the antibody titer in Group CS was significantly lower than in either Group NC or Group CS_0. In Experiment 2, Group CS had the lowest antibody titer, but only the difference between Groups CS and NC was statistically significant. Taken together with the small but significant differences obtained in the first experiment, though, it does appear that a conditioned suppression of the antibody response to a T-cell-independent antigen can be observed.

Antibody production in response to SRBC involves a complex series of interactions among macrophages and subsets of T and B cells (Claman & Chaperon, 1969; Opitz, Lemke, & Hewlett, 1978). Thus, observations of conditioned suppression of the response to xenogeneic erythrocytes described in our initial studies could have resulted from effects on any or all of these cell populations. The observation that conditioning can also result in an attenuation of the antibody response to a T-cell-independent antigen raises the possibility that conditioned immunosuppression might involve a direct effect on B cells. Whatever the mechanism(s), these findings with a T-cell-independent rather than a T-cell-dependent antigen, and with mice rather than rats, replicate and extend previous observations of conditioned immunosuppression.

A further extension of the phenomenon of conditioned immunosuppression is provided by our observation of a conditioned suppression of a cell-mediated immune response (Bovbjerg, Cohen, & Ader, 1981). Whitehouse, Levy, and Beck (1973) had reported that multiple low doses of CY were effective in suppressing a graft-versus-host response[11] if the CY was administered on the day that splenic leukocytes were injected and on the succeeding 2 days. This protocol seemed amenable to a conditioning paradigm that might also enable us to reinforce the previously conditioned response. That is, if *three* successive injections of CY were required to suppress the graft-versus-host response, it might be possible to reinforce the previously conditioned response with a *single* low dose of CY that was not by itself sufficient to depress the graft-versus-host reaction to any significant extent. We could, in effect, introduce a "reminder" of the previous conditioning (cf. Campbell & Jaynes, 1966; Campbell & Spear, 1972).

The design of this experiment required some modification of our basic protocol. Rats were conditioned by pairing consumption of a saccharin solu-

---

11. In the local graft-versus-host response, allogeneic lymphocytes from a parental inbred strain donor (AA) are injected into the footpad of an F_1 hybrid ($A \times B$) host. The F_1 ($A \times B$) recipient sees nothing foreign about the AA lymphocytes, while the AA lymphocytes recognize and react against alloantigens associated with the "B" component of the recipient. This reaction occurs primarily in the popliteal lymph node that drains the injection site. The greater the increase in node weight, the more intense the reaction.

tion with an ip injection of 50 mg/kg CY *48 days* before testing. Recipient females, Lewis×Brown Norwegian hybrids, were initially divided into conditioned, nonconditioned, and placebo groups. On Day 0, all animals were injected subdurally into the plantar surface of a hind footpad with a suspension of splenic leukocytes (2×10^7 spleen cells/footpad) obtained from female Lewis strain donors. The experimental group of conditioned animals (Group CS_r) was treated as follows: On Day 0, they were reexposed to the CS and injected ip with saline; on Day 1, they were reexposed to the CS and injected with 10 mg/kg CY; on Day 2, they were reexposed to the CS and injected with saline. A control group of conditioned rats (Group CS_0) was not reexposed to the CS but was injected with 10 mg/kg CY on Day 1. Conditioned animals in Group US were not reexposed to the CS, but were injected with CY on Days 0, 1, and 2. Nonconditioned animals (Group NC_r) were provided with the saccharin drinking solution on Days 0, 1, and 2, and were injected with 10 mg/kg CY on Day 1 (like the rats in Group CS_r). Placebo animals (Group P) were also provided with saccharin on Days 0, 1, and 2, but received no injections. The animals were tested using the two-bottle, "preference" procedure. Popliteal lymph nodes (which drain the injection site) were harvested and weighed 5 days after inoculation with the cellular graft.

As can be seen in Figure 5.14, the injection of 10 mg/kg CY on Days 0, 1, and 2 (Group US) markedly depressed the graft-versus-host response, relative to the reaction in normal animals (Group P), replicating previous observations (Whitehouse *et al.*, 1973). A *single* injection at this low dose of CY caused a modest attenuation of the response; Group NC_r did not differ from Group P, but Group CS_0 showed less of a node weight response than untreated controls did.

Groups NC_r and CS_0 did not differ; both of these treated control groups that received a *single* injection of CY had a significantly greater GvH response than animals that received three injections of CY (Group US). Conditioned animals that were reexposed to the CS and received a *single* injection of CY, however, did not differ from animals in Group US and showed an attenuation of the graft-versus-host response.

The stimulated lymph nodes harvested from rats in Group CS_r weighed significantly less than those from NC_r and CS_0 animals. In terms of the *change* in node weight (injected node weight – contralateral node weight), CS_r animals differed significantly from Group NC_r but not from Group CS_0. These results, then, provide additional evidence for the effects of conditioning on immune responses.

On the Mediation of Conditioned Immunopharmacological Effects

It is only in recent years that any serious consideration has been given to the possibility that central nervous system processes are capable of modifying immune responses. Considering the complexity of interactions between

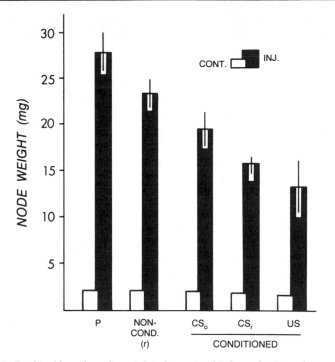

FIGURE 5.14. Popliteal lymph node weights determined 5 days after inoculation with splenic leukocytes. Values for injected and contralateral footpads are given for placebo-treated (P) rats; for nonconditioned (NC_r) animals exposed to a single low dose of CY administered 1 day after the cellular graft; and for conditioned animals given a single low dose of CY and provided with plain water (CS_0), conditioned animals given a single low dose of CY and reexposed to the CS on Days 0, 1, and 2 after the cellular graft (CS_r), and conditioned animals given three low-dose injections of CY (on Days 0, 1, and 2) and provided with plain water (US). (From Ader, R., & Cohen, N. Conditioned immunopharmacologic responses. In R. Ader (Ed.), *Psychoneuroimmunology.* New York: Academic Press, 1981. Reprinted by permission.)

the central nervous system and the immune system, it would be premature and highly speculative to attempt to explain the phenomenon of conditioned immunosuppression on the basis of the data that are currently available to link neuroendocrine and immune responses. We can, however, address certain procedural and general psychophysiological issues that could be advanced to account for the effects of conditioning.

Fluid Deprivation

Conditioned animals that are subsequently provided with a single drinking bottle containing the distinctively flavored (CS) solution that has previously been paired with CY drink very little of the solution; they are well-conditioned animals displaying the taste aversion. Since antigen is introduced on the same day that conditioned animals are reexposed to the CS, it could be hypothesized that the attenuation of antibody titer results from the administration of antigen to animals that are in a relatively water-deprived state or in a peculiar psychophysiological state determined by some interaction between deprivation and the residual immunosuppressive effects of CY.

An alternative means of assessing taste aversion behavior involves a "preference" testing procedure. Instead of providing the animal with a single drinking bottle containing the flavored CS solution, the animal can be provided with two bottles, one containing the CS solution and one containing plain water.

We conducted an experiment in which half the animals of each group were tested under the "forced-choice" or single-bottle procedure and half were tested with a "preference" or two-bottle procedure. Both testing procedures revealed acquisition of an aversion to the saccharin solution that had been paired with CY (see Figure 5.15).

Conditioned animals that were given only a single bottle containing the CS solution consumed relatively small amounts of saccharin, as did animals that were given a choice, but the *total* fluid intake of animals that were provided with plain water in addition to the saccharin solution was not less than that consumed by controls. Both CS groups, however, showed an attenu-

FIGURE 5.15. Mean consumption of saccharin in the one-bottle, "forced-choice" testing procedure, or of saccharin and plain water in the two-bottle, "preference" testing procedure, in conditioned (C) and nonconditioned (NC) rats tested on the day that antigen was injected (Trial 1) and on a test given 3 days later (Trial 2). (From Ader, R., & Cohen, N. Conditioned immunopharmacologic responses. In R. Ader (Ed.), *Psychoneuroimmunology*. New York: Academic Press, 1981. Reprinted by permission.)

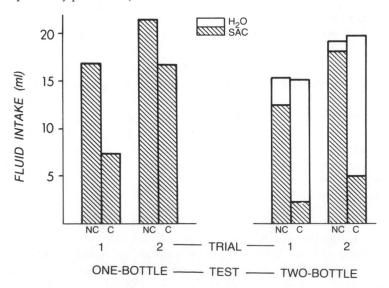

ation of hemagglutinating antibody titer (see Figure 5.16). It should be noted, though, that the experimental animals tested under the single-bottle procedure differed significantly from only one of the two control groups. As described above, we also obtained conditioned suppression in response to a thymus-independent antigen, using a two-bottle testing procedure, in mice (Cohen *et al.*, 1979). Fluid deprivation is not, therefore, an especially critical variable.

Adrenocortical Activation

The relationship between adrenocortical steroids and immune responses is not entirely clear (Parillo & Fauci, 1979). Under certain circumstances, high circulating levels of steroids can exert immunosuppressive effects (e.g., Claman, 1972; Parillo & Fauci, 1979). Since an increase in adrenal activity is associated with "stress," it could be postulated that the depressed antibody response observed in conditioned animals reflects a nonspecific "stress" response induced by the conditioning procedures. Such an hypothesis would be consistent with the prevalent explanation for the effects of emotional states or psychosocial factors on immunological reactivity. However, as may be surmised from the literature reviewed above, all the available data cannot be accounted for by such a hypothesis.

Whatever the explanation, "stress" experiments have entailed more sustained environmental stimulation than the conditioning paradigm does. Nevertheless, the hypothesis that conditioned immunosuppression is an adrenocortically mediated "stress" response is a tenable one. Even if we allow that depressed immune responses can occur in response to stressful stimulation and that these are the result of increases in circulating levels of glucocorticoids, however, it would suggest only that elevations in steroid level *might* account for the phenomenon of conditioned immunosuppression. Besides, if an elevated steroid level can be invoked to account for the observations of conditioned immunopharmacological effects, it is most likely to be the result of a *conditioned* elevation in steroid level. After all, the conditioned animals *that were reexposed to the CS* showed an attenuation in antibody titer. We had speculated (Ader & Cohen, 1975) that the conditioning of a taste aversion might result in a concomitant conditioning of an elevation in steroid level, and it has since been shown possible to condition an adrenocortical response in the taste aversion paradigm (Ader, 1976a; Rigter, 1975).

To evaluate the possibility that an elevation in steroid level might be responsible for the attenuation of antibody titer in conditioned animals, one experiment was conducted in which LiCl, rather than CY, was used as the US (Ader & Cohen, 1975). Like CY, LiCl has noxious gastrointestinal effects, can be used to induce a taste aversion, and is an effective stimulus for conditioning an elevation in steroid level (Ader, 1976a). However, LiCl is not immunosuppressive (Ader, 1976a), and the pairing of saccharin and LiCl did

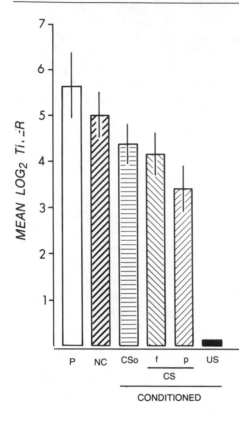

FIGURE 5.16. Mean ($\pm SE$) hemagglutinating antibody titers in placebo (P), nonconditioned (NC), and conditioned animals injected with CY at the time of antigen exposure (US), provided with plain water (CS_0), or provided with the CS solution (CS) under "forced-choice" (f) or "preference" (p) testing procedures. (From Ader, R., & Cohen, N. Conditioned immunopharmacologic responses. In R. Ader (Ed.), *Psychoneuroimmunology*. New York: Academic Press, 1981. Reprinted by permission.)

not result in an attenuated antibody response when conditioned animals were subsequently injected with SRBC and reexposed to the saccharin (see Figure 5.17).

Behaviorally, animals conditioned with LiCl consume no more fluid than do animals conditioned with CY when they are reexposed to the CS, so these observations confirm the findings that a relative state of dehydration coincidental with antigenic stimulation does not appear to be a critical factor. While these results provide no support for the hypothesis of an adrenal mediation of conditioned immunosuppression, the possibility remains that there is some interaction between a conditionally elevated steroid level and the residual immunosuppressive effects of CY. This issue was addressed in two additional experiments (Ader *et al.*, 1979).

In the first experiment, LiCl was used to stimulate an endogenous elevation in steroid level (Ader, 1976a; J. J. Jacobs, 1978). Three days after conditioning, when all rats were injected with SRBC, an additional subgroup of *conditioned* animals was added to the standard protocol. These animals were provided with plain water followed by an ip injection of LiCl. An additional subgroup of nonconditioned animals was also provided with plain water and

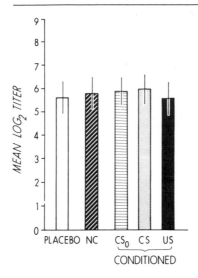

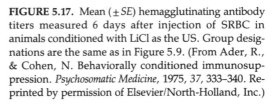

FIGURE 5.17. Mean ($\pm SE$) hemagglutinating antibody titers measured 6 days after injection of SRBC in animals conditioned with LiCl as the US. Group designations are the same as in Figure 5.9. (From Ader, R., & Cohen, N. Behaviorally conditioned immunosuppression. *Psychosomatic Medicine*, 1975, 37, 333–340. Reprinted by permission of Elsevier/North-Holland, Inc.)

injected with LiCl. In the second study, the potential interaction between a high adrenocortical steroid level and the residual effects of CY was tested by examining the effects of an exogenous administration of steroid. An additional subgroup of animals previously conditioned with CY was injected with 1 mg/kg corticosterone instead of being presented with the CS.

Results of the LiCl experiment are shown in Figure 5.18. The antibody response in Group CS was significantly lower than that in Group NC, but

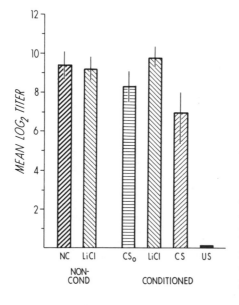

FIGURE 5.18. Hemagglutination titers (mean $\pm$ SE) measured 6 days after injection of SRBC. Nonconditioned rats were injected with saline following consumption of saccharin (NC) or injected with LiCl following consumption of water (LiCl); conditioned animals were provided with water and injected with saline (CS$_0$), LiCl (LiCl), or CY (US), or were provided with saccharin and injected with saline (CS). Treatments occurred on the day animals were injected with antigen. (From Ader, R., Cohen, N., & Grota, L. J. Adrenal involvement in conditioned immunosuppression. *International Journal of Immunopharmacology*, 1979, 1, 141–145. Reprinted by permission of Pergamon Press.)

it was not significantly lower than in Group CS_0. The titer of conditioned animals reexposed to the CS was also significantly lower than the titer of conditioned animals that received an injection of LiCl instead of reexposure to saccharin. These latter animals did not differ from either of the control groups. Similar results (see Figure 5.19) were obtained when conditioned animals were treated with corticosterone rather than the CS. Conditioned animals that were reexposed to the CS had antibody titers that were significantly lower than the titers of both control groups. In contrast, there was only a slight (nonsignificant) attenuation of antibody titer in the conditioned animals treated with steroid. Wayner (1979), too, conducted a study in which conditioned animals were injected with physiological levels of corticosterone and failed to observe an attenuation of antibody titer. None of these studies, then, provided any evidence that high adrenocortical steroid levels superimposed upon the residual immunosuppressive effects of CY were acting to suppress antibody production to any significant extent.

As described above, one can observe a conditioned suppression of antibody production in response to a T-cell-dependent and a T-cell-independent antigen, even when a two-bottle "preference" procedure is used to equate total fluid consumption in the taste aversion paradigm and to obviate differences in levels of circulating steroids. There is a demonstrable taste aversion, but there is no (conditioned) elevation in steroid level when animals are confronted with the preference test (Smotherman, Hennessy, & Levine, 1976; Wayner, 1979). By inference, then, such data indicate that a conditioned suppression of immunological reactivity (as well as a conditioned taste aversion; see Ader, Grota, & Buckland, 1978) is observable in the absence of an elevated steroid level. It should also be noted that the humoral response to T-cell-independent antigens is relatively insensitive to corticosteroids (e.g.,

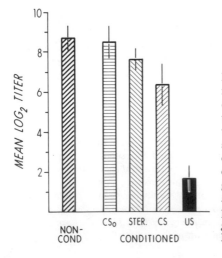

FIGURE 5.19. Hemagglutination titers (mean $\pm$ SE) measured 6 days after injection of SRBC in nonconditioned rats provided with saccharin and injected with saline (NC); conditioned animals provided with water and injected with saline (CS_0), corticosterone (STER), or CY (US), or provided with saccharin and injected with saline (CS). Treatments occurred on the day animals were injected with antigen. (From Ader, R., Cohen, N., & Grota, L. J. Adrenal involvement in conditioned immunosuppression. *International Journal of Immunopharmacology*, 1979, *1*, 141–145. Reprinted by permission of Pergamon Press.)

Mantzouranis & Borel, 1979). The issue with respect to a cell-mediated response, however, is not quite so clear. Although the effects of glucocorticoids on cell-mediated responses has been considered minimal (Ahlqvist, 1981), other data (J. J. Cohen & Claman, 1971) have documented a suppression of splenomegaly when mice were treated with hydrocortisone throughout the graft-versus-host reaction. One must, therefore, entertain the possibility that our data on the conditioned suppression of a *cell-mediated* immune response might be mediated by alterations in circulating steroids. It is necessary to consider, however, that the results obtained by J. J. Cohen and Claman were based on the effects of hydrocortisone rather than endogenous levels of corticosterone, the primary glucocorticoid in the rat and mouse. Furthermore, our data (Bovbjerg *et al.*, 1981) were based on a different model of cellular immunity in a different species, and we used a two-bottle testing procedure that would have reduced or eliminated differences in adrenocortical steroid levels among the several groups.

An elevation in circulating steroid levels may be immunosuppressive under certain therapeutic conditions, and even a transient increase in steroid level may be sufficient to attenuate the antibody response to a minimally effective immunogenic stimulus (Amkraut & Solomon, 1974). This, however, is not the issue. Under the experimental conditions of these experiments, there is no evidence that comparable results can occur simply by elevating steroid level. One could speculate that the defenses of an organism are hierarchically organized so that only those resources needed to combat an existing challenge are initiated in the interest of conserving defensive energies and minimizing homeostatic disturbances. It is possible, then, that an elevation in circulating steroids may be able to attenuate the response to a relatively mild antigenic stimulus, but is incapable of minimizing the immunological reaction to a more potent or threatening challenge. Be that as it may, our several studies, taken together, provide no support for the hypothesis that the attenuation in antibody production seen in conditioned animals reexposed to the CS at the time of antigenic stimulation is mediated by an elevation in adrenocortical steroids.

A Descriptive Reanalysis of Conditioned Immunopharmacological Effects

The phenomenon of conditioned immunosuppression is highly reproducible. As a matter of fact, it is the reliability rather than the magnitude of the effect that is compelling. The basic phenomenon obtains under a variety of experimental circumstances (Ader & Cohen, 1981), but, despite the "improvements" in methodology, we have been unable to magnify the effects of conditioning. The effect is consistent and independently verifiable, but relatively small. While the size of an effect has no necessary bearing on its biological significance, the conditioned immunosuppression is too small to permit us to pose additional questions that relate to conditioning processes (e.g., extinction of the CR) or to the mechanisms mediating the phenomenon. If such issues are to be addressed efficiently, it is necessary, first, to define the conditions that may be optimal for assessing the impact of conditioning in modifying immune responses. An initial question, then, is this: Why are the effects so small?

Hemagglutinating antibody titer measured several days after reexposure to the CS may not be sufficiently sensitive to yield larger differences between conditioned animals and controls. After all, circulating antibody is the result of a complex series of events, and we assume that the effects of conditioning are acting on one or more of these early events. Since CY can differentially influence different populations of lymphocytes and/or can influence them in a differential fashion (e.g., by effecting proliferation, differentiation, etc.— see Hunninghake & Fauci, 1976; Turk & Poulter, 1972), it would be reasonable to suppose that the CS might also have multiple effects, the ultimate combination of which yields an attenuation in antibody titer. An inhibition of suppressor cell activity, for example, could act to dilute the effects of an immunosuppressive CS. This raises the issue of the critical nature of the timing of a CS presentation in relation to its effects, a variable that undoubtedly interacts with parameters of antigenic stimulation. These are relevant considerations and could reasonably account for the small but consistent effects that have been observed so far.

Another approach to the question of why conditioned immunosuppressive effects are small is based, not on the operations of the immune system, but on an analysis of the conditioning paradigm itself. Quite simply, it is proposed that the effects of conditioning in suppressing antibody titer are small because the conditioning paradigm is so effective.

If we consider the entire experimental system in terms of conditioning processes, an antigen is a US for the production of antibody; that is, antibody production is unconditionally elicited by antigenic stimulation. Initially, we pair a neutral stimulus with the immunosuppressive effects of a pharmacological agent, and the neutral stimulus, having been paired with a US for suppression of immunological reactivity, presumably becomes a CS for immunosuppression. When we subsequently present a CS for immunosuppression together with the injection of antigen, we are, in effect, pairing a CS for suppression of immunological reactivity with a US for elicitation of an immune response. By pairing a CS for suppression with a US for activation of some of the same responses, we are presenting stimuli with opposite but unequal effects. There would be no grounds for assuming that the CS would be prepotent—that is, that the effects of the CS would override the effects of a stimulus that, by definition, would unconditionally elicit the response in question.

Our data on conditioned immunosuppression are quite consistent with this descriptive analysis. We see no *inhibition* of antibody production, for example, but a transient *attenuation* of the response. Evidently, there is some interference with the events leading to the production of antibody that may be attributed to the effects of the CS. In a situation in which the failure to mount an antibody response would be teleologically maladaptive and operationally incompatible with the effects of a US, it is still possible to observe a small but consistent effect of conditioning. This, we suggest, attests to the effectiveness of the conditioning paradigm; if this analysis is correct, it may be that a potentiation of immunological reactivity would be more amenable to the effects of conditioning than a suppression of reactivity would be.

SUMMARY

The immune system represents a primary defense mechanism that constantly monitors and mediates the balance between host and pathogen. In this chapter, we have reviewed some of the data indicating that psychosocial influences—that is, experiential events that are processed by the brain—are capable of regulating or modifying host defense mechanisms. The available literature demonstrates that psychosocial factors can influence susceptibility and responses to a variety of pathogen-mediated diseases in much the same way that behavior has been shown to influence other pathophysiological processes. There is, too, a rapidly growing literature indicating that experiential factors can directly influence *in vitro* and *in vivo* immunological reactivity. These effects have been observed in humans and in lower animals.

The effects of psychosocial factors on host defenses are quite variable; they are neither uniformly detrimental nor uniformly beneficial to the organism. The premature labeling of experimental events as stressful (and the consequent emphasis on adrenal function), therefore, has not been especially useful in elucidating the complex neuroendocrine mechanisms that are hypothesized to mediate these immunological changes.

In general, the effect of psychosocial factors on immune competence as reflected by studies of clinical disease or immunological reactivity is determined by several major variables. These include the following:

1. The quality and quantity (and the organism's interpretation) of naturally occurring or experimentally imposed alterations in the psychosocial environment.
2. The quality and quantity of immunogenic or pathogenic stimulation.
3. The myriad host factors upon which the environmental and immunogenic stimuli are superimposed.
4. The temporal relationship between psychosocial and immunological events.
5. Procedural factors, such as the nature of the dependent variables and sampling parameters.
6. The interaction among any or all of the above.

We have also summarized recent research on the conditioning of immuno-pharmacological effects. It has been shown possible to condition suppression of the humoral response to T-cell-dependent and T-cell-independent antigens and to condition suppression of a cell-mediated immune response. The effects of conditioning have not been large, but they have been consistent and independently reproducible. As is the case in studies of "stress," it does not appear that all the observed effects can be accounted for simply on the basis of changes in circulating levels of corticosteroids, and the neuroendocrine processes that are presumed to mediate the phenomenon of conditioned immunosuppression remain to be investigated.

The use of conditioning techniques to study immunological reactivity can be viewed as a major extension of one of the more significant frontiers in the application of principles derived from the behavioral sciences to issues of health and disease—namely, the conditioning of autonomic, visceral, and pharmacological responses. Methodologically, the application of conditioning procedures provides a means for studying the relationship between central nervous system and immune system processes in the intact organism. Clinically, an elaboration of this phenomenon could lead to new regimens of immunopharmacotherapy. Conceptually, the capacity of experiential events, including conditioning, to suppress or enhance immunological reactivity raises new issues with respect to the normal functioning and modifiability of the immune system and the mediation of susceptibility and responses to disease.

Although psychoimmunological research is at its earliest stages, the results obtained thus far reinforce the notion that the immune system is integrated with other physiological systems to form an integrated network of defensive mechanisms that is sensitive to psychosocial events and subject to regulation and modulation by the central nervous system.

A C K N O W L E D G M E N T S

Preparation of this chapter was supported by a USPHS Research Scientist Award (KO5-MH-06318) from the National Institute of Mental Health to Robert Ader. Our research described here was supported by this award and a Research Career Development Award (KO4-AI-70736) from the National Institute of Allergy and Infectious Diseases to Nicholas Cohen and by consecutive research grants from the W. T. Grant Foundation, the National Institute of Child Health and Human Development (HD-09977), and the National Institute of Neurological and Communicative Disease and Stroke (NS-15071). The collaboration of Lee J. Grota, Nicola Green, and Dana Bovbjerg in one or another of these studies, and the able assistance of Sumico Nagai and Wendy Makrides, are gratefully acknowledged.

This chapter was prepared during the Spring of 1980. Although it is a representative introduction to a new field of study, it is not up to date. The interested reader will want to locate the several studies and reviews related to this subject that have since been published.

R E F E R E N C E S

Ader, R. The effects of early life experiences on developmental processes and susceptibility to disease in animals. In J. P. Hill (Ed.), *Minnesota Symposium on Child Psychology*. Minneapolis: University of Minnesota Press, 1970.

Ader, R. Letter to the editor. *Psychosomatic Medicine*, 1974, *36*, 183–184.

Ader, R. Conditioned adrenocortical steroid elevations in the rat. *Journal of Comparative and Physiological Psychology*, 1976, *90*, 1156–1163. (a)

Ader, R. Psychosomatic research in animals. In O. W. Hill (Ed.), *Modern trends in psychosomatic medicine* (Vol. 3). London: Butterworths, 1976. (b)

Ader, R. A note on the role of olfaction in taste aversion learning. *Bulletin of the Psychonomic Society*, 1977, *10*, 402–404.

Ader, R. Animal models in the study of brain, behavior, and bodily disease. *Association for Research in Nervous and Mental Disease*, 1980, *59*, 11–26.

Ader, R. An historical account of conditioned immunobiologic responses. In R. Ader (Ed.), *Psychoneuroimmunology*. New York: Academic Press, 1981. (a)

Ader, R. (Ed.). *Psychoneuroimmunology*. New York: Academic Press, 1981. (b)

Ader, R., & Cohen, N. Behaviorally conditioned immunosuppression. *Psychosomatic Medicine*, 1975, *37*, 333–340.

Ader, R., & Cohen, N. Conditioned immunopharmacologic responses. In R. Ader (Ed.), *Psychoneuroimmunology*. New York: Academic Press, 1981.

Ader, R., Cohen, N., & Grota, L. J. Adrenal involvement in conditioned immunosuppression. *International Journal of Immunopharmacology*, 1979, *1*, 141–145.

Ader, R., & Friedman, S. B. Social factors affecting emotionality and resistance to disease in animals: IV. Differential housing, emotionality, and Walker 256 carcinsarcoma in the rat. *Psychological Reports*, 1964, *15*, 535–541.

Ader, R., & Friedman, S. B. Differential early experiences and susceptibility to transplanted tumor in the rat. *Journal of Comparative and Physiological Psychology*, 1965, *59*, 361–364. (a)

Ader, R., & Friedman, S. B. Social factors affecting emotionality and resistance to disease in animals: V. Early separation from the mother and response to a transplanted tumor in the rat. *Psychosomatic Medicine*, 1965, *27*, 119–122. (b)

Ader, R., Grota, L. J., & Buckland, R. Effects of adrenalectomy on taste aversion learning. *Physiological Psychology*, 1978, *6*, 359–361.

Ahlqvist, J. Hormonal influences on immunological and related phenomena. In R. Ader (Ed.), *Psychoneuroimmunology*. New York: Academic Press, 1981.

Amkraut, A., & Solomon, G. F. Stress and murine sarcoma virus (Maloney)-induced tumors. *Cancer Research*, 1972, *32*, 1428–1443.

Amkraut, A., & Solomon, G. F. From the symbolic stimulus to the pathophysiologic response: Immune mechanisms. *International Journal of Psychiatry in Medicine*, 1974, *5*, 541–563.

Amkraut, A. A., Solomon, G. F., Kasper, P., & Purdue, P. Stress and hormonal intervention in the graft-versus-host response. In B. D. Jankovic & K. Isakovic (Eds.), *Microenvironmental aspects of immunity*. New York: Plenum, 1973.

Amkraut, A. A., Solomon, G. F., & Kraemer, H. C. Stress, early experience and adjuvant-induced arthritis in the rat. *Psychosomatic Medicine*, 1971, *33*, 203–214.

Andervont, H. B. Influence of environment on mammary cancer in mice. *Journal of the National Cancer Institute*, 1944, *4*, 579–581.

Anokhin, P. K. *[Biology and neurophysiology of the conditioned reflex and its role in adaptive behavior]* (S. A. Corson, trans.). Oxford: Pergamon Press, 1974.

Bartrop, R. W., Lazarus, L., Luckhurst, E., Kiloh, L. G., & Penny, R. Depressed lymphocyte function after bereavement. *Lancet*, 1977, *i*, 834–836.

Bonnyne, M., & McKenzie, J. M. Interactions of stress and endocrine status on rat peripheral lymphocyte responsiveness to phytomitogens. *Psychoneuroendocrinology*, 1979, *4*, 67–73.

Bovbjerg, D. H., Cohen, N., & Ader, R. Conditioned suppression of a cell-mediated immune response. *Psychosomatic Medicine*, 1981, *42*, 73. (Abstract)

Boyce, W. T., Cassel, J. C., Collier, A. M., Jensen, E. W., Ramey, C. T., & Smith, A. H. Influence of life events and family routines on childhood respiratory tract illness. *Pediatrics*, 1977, *60*, 609–615.

Campbell, B. A., & Jaynes, J. Reinstatement. *Psychological Review*, 1966, *73*, 478–480.

Campbell, B. A., & Spear, N. E. Ontogeny of memory. *Psychological Review*, 1972, *79*, 215–236.

Canter, A., Cluff, L. E., & Imboden, J. B. Hypersensitive reactions to immunization, inoculations and antecedent psychological vulnerability. *Journal of Psychosomatic Research*, 1972, *16*, 99–101.

Chandra, R. K. Interactions of infection and malnutrition. In L. Brent & J. Holborrow (Eds.), *Progress in immunology* (Vol. 4). New York: Elsevier, 1974.

Chandra, R. K. Antibody formation in first and second generation offspring of nutritionally deprived rats. *Science*, 1975, *190*, 289–290.

Chang, S. S., & Rasmussen, A. F., Jr. Effects of stress on susceptibility of mice to polyoma virus infection. *Bacteriology Proceedings*, 1964, *64*, 134.

Christian, J. J., & Williamson, H. O. Effect of crowding on experimental granuloma formation in mice. *Proceedings of the Society for Experimental Biology and Medicine*, 1958, *99*, 385–387.

Claman, H. N. Corticosteroids and lymphoid cells. *New England Journal of Medicine*, 1972, *287*, 388–397.

Claman, H. N., & Chaperon, E. A. Immunological complementation between thymus and marrow cells: A model for the two cell theory of immunocompetence. *Transplantation Reviews*, 1969, *1*, 92–113.

Cohen, J. J., & Claman, H. N. Hydrocortisone resistance of activated initiator cells in graft versus host reactions. *Nature*, 1971, *229*, 274–275.

Cohen, N., Ader, R., Green, N., & Bovbjerg, D. Conditioned suppression of a thymus independent antibody response. *Psychosomatic Medicine*, 1979, *41*, 487–491.

Davis, D. E., & Read, C. P. Effect of behavior on development of resistance in trichinosis. *Proceedings of the Society for Experimental Biology and Medicine*, 1958, *99*, 269–272.

DeChambre, R. P., & Gosse, C. Individual versus group caging of mice with grafted tumors. *Cancer Research*, 1973, *33*, 140–144.

DeWeck, A. L., & Frey, J. R. *Immunotolerance to simple chemicals*. Basel: S. Karger, 1966.

DiCara, L. V. Learning in the autonomic nervous system. *Scientific American*, 1970, *222*, 31–39.

Dolin, A. O., Krylov, V. N., Luk'ianenko, V. I., & Flerov, B. A. New experimental data on the conditioned reflex production and suppression of immune and allergic reactions. *Zhurnal Vysshei Nervnoi Deiatelnosti Imeni I. P. Pavlova*, 1960, *10*, 832–841.

Domjan, M. Role of ingestion in odor-toxicosis learning in the rat. *Journal of Comparative and Physiological Psychology*, 1973, *84*, 507–521.

Ebbesen, P. Spontaneous amyloidosis in differently grouped and treated DBA/2, BALB/c and CBA mice and thymus fibrosis in estrogen-treated BALB/c males. *Journal of Experimental Medicine*, 1968, *127*, 387–398.

Edwards, E. A., & Dean, L. M. Effects of crowding of mice on humoral antibody formation and protection to lethal antigenic challenge. *Psychosomatic Medicine*, 1977, *39*, 19–24.

Ellman, P., & Mitchell, S. D. The psychological aspects of chronic rheumatoid joint disease. In C. W. Buckley (Ed.), *Reports on chronic rheumatoid disease*. New York: Macmillan, 1936.

Engel, G. Studies of ulcerative colitis: III. The nature of the psychologic process. *American Journal of Medicine*, 1955, *19*, 231–256.

Felsenfeld, O., Hill, C. W., & Greer, W. E. Response of *Cercepitheaus aethiops* to *Cholera vibrio* lipopolysaccharide and psychological stress. *Transactions of the Royal Society of Tropical Medicine and Hygiene*, 1966, *60*, 514–518.

Folch, H., & Waksman, B. H. The splenic suppressor cell. *Journal of Immunology*, 1974, *113*, 127–139.

Fox, B. H. Psychosocial factors and the immune system in human neoplasia. In R. Ader (Ed.), *Psychoneuroimmunology*. New York: Academic Press, 1981.

Friedman, S. B., Ader, R., & Glasgow, L. A. Effects of psychological stress in adult mice inoculated with Coxsackie B viruses. *Psychosomatic Medicine*, 1965, 27, 361–368.

Friedman, S. B., Ader, R., & Grota, L. J. Protective effect of noxious stimulation in mice infected with rodent malaria. *Psychosomatic Medicine*, 1973, 35, 535–537.

Friedman, S. B., & Glasgow, L. A. Psychologic factors and resistance to infectious disease. *Pediatric Clinics of North America*, 1966, 13, 315–335.

Friedman, S. B., & Glasgow, L. A. Interaction of mouse strain and differential housing upon resistance to *Plasmodium berghei*. *Journal of Parasitology*, 1973, 59, 851–854.

Friedman, S. B., Glasgow, L. A., & Ader, R. Psychosocial factors modifying host resistance to experimental infections. *Annals of the New York Academy of Science*, 1969, 164, 381–392.

Funk, G. A., & Jensen, M. M. Influence of stress on granuloma formation. *Proceedings of the Society for Experimental Medicine and Biology*, 1967, 124, 653–655.

Garcia, J., Hankins, W. G., & Rusiniak, K. W. Behavioral regulation of the milieu interne in man and rat. *Science*, 1974, 185, 824–831.

Gisler, R. H., Bussard, A. E., Mazie, J. C., & Hess, R. Hormonal regulation of the immune response: I. Induction of an immune response *in vitro* with lymphoid cells from mice exposed to acute systemic stress. *Cellular Immunology*, 1971, 2, 634–645.

Gisler, R. H., & Schenkel-Hulliger, L. Hormonal regulation of the immune response: II. Influence of pituitary and adrenal activity on immune responsiveness *in vitro*. *Cellular Immunology*, 1971, 2, 646–657.

Glenn, W. G., & Becker, R. E. Individual versus group housing in mice: Immunological response to time-phased injections. *Physiological Zoology*, 1969, 42, 411–416.

Gotch, F. M., Spry, C. J. F., Mowat, A. G., Beeson, P. B., & MacLennon, I. C. M. Reversible granulocyte killing defect in anorexia nervosa. *Clinical and Experimental Immunology*, 1975, 21, 244–249.

Greene, W. A., Betts, R. F., Ochitill, H. N., Iker, H. P., & Douglas, R. G., Jr. Psychosocial factors and immunity: A preliminary report. *Psychosomatic Medicine*, 1978, 40, 87. (Abstract)

Greenfield, N. S., Roessler, R., & Crosley, A. P., Jr. Ego strength and length of recovery from infectious mononucleosis. *Journal of Nervous and Mental Disease*, 1959, 128, 125–128.

Grinker, R. R., Jr., & Robbins, F. P. *Psychosomatic case book*. New York: Blakeston, 1954.

Gross, R. L., & Newberne, P. M. Role of nutrition in immunologic function. *Physiological Reviews*, 1980, 60, 188.

Gross, W. B., & Siegel, H. S. The effect of social stress on resistance to infection with *Escheria coli* or *Mycoplasma gallisepticum*. *Poultry Science*, 1965, 44, 98–1000.

Gunderson, E. K., & Rahe, R. H. (Eds.). *Life stress and illness*. Springfield, Ill.: Charles C Thomas, 1974.

Guy, W. B. Neurogenic factors in contact dermatitis. *Archives für Dermatologie und Syphilis*, 1952, 66, 1–8.

Hamilton, D. R. Immunosuppressive effects of predator induced stress in mice with acquired immunity to *Hymenolepsis nana*. *Journal of Psychosomatic Research*, 1974, 18, 143–153.

Hendrie, H. C., Paraskevas, F., Baragar, F. D., & Adamson, J. D. Stress, immunoglobulin levels and immunological processes. *Journal of Psychosomatic Research*, 1971, 15, 337–342.

Henoch, M. J., Batson, J. W., & Baum, J. Psychosocial factors in juvenile rheumatoid arthritis. *Arthritis and Rheumatism*, 1978, 21, 229–233.

Henry, J. P., Stephens, P. M., & Watson, F. M. C. Force breeding, social disorder and mammary tumor formation in CBA/USC mouse colonies: A pilot study. *Psychosomatic Medicine*, 1975, 37, 277–283.

Hill, C. W., Greer, W. E., & Felsenfeld, O. Psychological stress, early response to foreign protein, and blood cortisol in vervets. *Psychosomatic Medicine*, 1967, 29, 279–283.

Hoffman, S. A., Shucard, W. W., Harbeck, R. J., & Hoffman, A. A. Chronic immune complex disease: Behavioral and immunological correlates. *Journal of Neuropathology and Experimental Neurology*, 1978, 37, 426–436.

Holm, G., & Palmblad, J. Acute energy deprivation in man: Effect on cell-mediated immunological reactions. *Clinical and Experimental Immunology*, 1976, *25*, 207–211.

Holmes, T. H., Treuting, T., & Wolff, H. G. Life situations, emotions and nasal disease: Evidence on summative effects exhibited in patients with "hay fever." *Psychosomatic Medicine*, 1951, *13*, 71–82.

Hotchin, J., Benson, L., & Gardner, J. Mother–infant interaction in lymphocytic choriomeningitis virus infection of the newborn mouse: The effect of maternal health on mortality of offspring. *Pediatric Research*, 1970, *4*, 194–200.

Hotchin, J., & Seegal, R. Virus-induced behavioral alteration of mice. *Science*, 1977, *196*, 671–674.

Hunninghake, G. W., & Fauci, A. S. Divergent effects of cyclophosphamide administration on mononuclear killer cells: Quantitative depletion of cell numbers versus qualitative suppression of functional capabilities. *Journal of Immunology*, 1976, *117*, 337–342.

Hutton, R. A., Woods, S. C., & Makous, W. L. Conditioned hyperglycemia: Pseudoconditioning controls. *Journal of Comparative and Physiological Psychology*, 1970, *71*, 198–201.

Imboden, J. B., Canter, A., & Cluff, L. E. Convalescence from influenza: A study of the psychological and clinical determinants. *Archives of Internal Medicine*, 1961, *108*, 393–399.

Jackson, G. G., Dowling, H. F., Anderson, T. O., Riff, L., Saporta, M. S., & Turck, M. Susceptibility and immunity to common upper respiratory viral infections—the common cold. *Annals of Internal Medicine*, 1960, *53*, 719–738.

Jacobs, J. J. Effects of lithium chloride on adrenocortical function in the rat. *Proceedings of the Society for Experimental Biology and Medicine*, 1978, *157*, 163–167.

Jacobs, M. A., Spilken, A. Z., Norman, M. M., & Anderson, L. S. Life stress and respiratory illness. *Psychosomatic Medicine*, 1970, *32*, 233–242.

Jensen, M. M. The influence of stress on murine leukemia virus infection. *Proceedings of the Society for Experimental Biology and Medicine*, 1968, *127*, 610–614.

Jensen, M. M., & Rasmussen, A. F., Jr. Stress and susceptibility to viral infections: II. Sound stress and susceptibility to vesicular stomatitis virus. *Journal of Immunology*, 1963, *90*, 21–23.

Joasoo, A., & McKenzie, J. M. Stress and the immune response in rats. *International Archives of Allergy and Applied Immunology*, 1976, *50*, 659–663.

Johnson, T., Lavender, J. F., & Marsh, J. T. The influence of avoidance learning stress on resistance to Coxsackie virus in mice. *Federation Proceedings*, 1959, *18*, 575.

Johnsson, T., & Rasmussen, A. F., Jr. Emotional stress and susceptibility to poliomyelitis virus infection in mice. *Archiv für die Gesamte Virusforschung*, 1965, *18*, 392–397.

Josephine, M. A. Experimental studies on *Entamoeba histolytica* in kittens. *American Journal of Tropical Medicine and Hygiene*, 1958, *7*, 158–164.

Kalisnik, M., Vraspir-Porenta, O., Logonder-Mlinsek, M., Zorc, M., & Pajntar, M. Stress and *Ehrlich ascites* tumor in mouse. *Neoplasma*, 1979, *26*, 483–491.

Kaliss, N., & Fuller, J. L. Incidence of lymphatic leukemia and methylcholanthrene-induced cancer in laboratory mice subjected to stress. *Journal of the National Cancer Institute*, 1968, *41*, 967–983.

Karpiak, S. E., Jr., Rapport, M. M., & Bowen, F. P. Immunologically induced behavioral and electrophysiological changes in the rat. *Neuropsychologia*, 1974, *12*, 313–322.

Kasl, S. V., Evans, A. S., & Neiderman, J. C. Psychosocial risk factors in the development of infectious mononucleosis. *Psychosomatic Medicine*, 1979, *41*, 445–466.

Kim, Y., & Michael, A. E. Hypocomplementemia in anorexia nervosa. *Journal of Pediatrics*, 1975, *87*, 582–585.

Kimzey, S. L. Hematology and immunology studies. In R. S. Johnson & L. F. Dietlin (Eds.), *Biochemical results from Skylab*. Washington, D.C.: National Aeronautics and Space Administration, 1977.

Kimzey, S. L., Ritzman, S. E., Mengel, C. E., & Fischer, C. L. Skylab experiment results: Hematology studies. *Acta Astronautica*, 1975, *2*, 141–154.

King, M. G. Personal communication, 1979.

Kjellberg, J., Levi, L., Palmblad, J., Paulsson, L., Theorell, T., & Yensen, R. Energy deprivation in man: Methodological problems and possibilities. *Acta Medica Scandinavica*, 1977, *201*, 9–13.

Kjosen, B., Bassoe, H. H., & Myking, O. The glucose oxidation in isolated leukocytes from female patients suffering from overweight or anorexia nervosa. *Scandinavian Journal of Clinical and Laboratory Investigation*, 1975, *35*, 447–454.

LaBarba, R. C. Experiential and environmental factors in cancer. *Psychosomatic Medicine*, 1970, *32*, 259–276.

LaBarba, R. C., Klein, M. L., White, J. L., & Lazar, J. Effects of early cold stress and handling on the growth of Ehrlich carcinoma in BALB/c mice. *Developmental Psychology*, 1970, *2*, 312–313.

LaBarba, R. C., White, J. L., Lazar, J., & Klein, M. Early maternal separation and the response to Ehrlich carcinoma in BALB/c mice. *Developmental Psychology*, 1970, *3*, 78–80.

LeMonde, P. Influence of fighting on leukemia in mice. *Proceedings of the Society for Experimental Biology and Medicine*, 1959, *102*, 292–295.

Levine, S., & Cohen, C. Differential survival to leukemia as a function of infantile stimulation in DBA/2 mice. *Proceedings of the Soceity for Experimental Biology and Medicine*, 1959, *102*, 53–54.

Levine, S., Strebel, R., Wenk, E. J., & Harman, P. J. Suppression of experimental allergic encephalomyelitis by stress. *Proceedings of the Society for Experimental Biology and Medicine*, 1962, *109*, 294–298.

Levine, S., & Treiman, D. M. Differential plasma corticosterone response to stress in four inbred strains of mice. *Endocrinology*, 1964, *75*, 142–144.

Locke, S. E., Hurst, M. W., Heisel, J., Kraus, L., & Williams, R. M. *The influence of stress on the immune response*. Paper presented at the annual meeting of the American Psychosomatic Society, Washington, D.C., April 1, 1978.

Lorden, J. F., Kenfield, M., & Braun, J. J. Response suppression to odors paired with toxicosis. *Learning and Motivation*, 1970, *1*, 391–400.

Lovett, D., Goodchild, P., & Booth, D. A. Depression of intake of nutrient by association of its odor with effects of insulin. *Psychonomic Science*, 1968, *11*, 27–28.

Luborsky, L., Mintz, J., Brightman, V. J., & Katcher, A. H. Herpes simplex virus and moods: A longitudinal study. *Journal of Psychosomatic Research*, 1976, *20*, 543–548.

Ludwig, A. O. Psychiatric considerations in rheumatoid arthritis. *Arthritis and Rheumatism*, 1955, *6*, 166–171.

Luk'ianenko, V. I. The problem of conditioned reflex regulation of immunobiologic reactions. *Uspekhi Sovremennoi Biologii*, 1961, *51*, 170–187.

McClary, A. R., Meyer, E., & Weitzman, D. J. Observations on role of mechanism of depression in some patients with disseminated lupus erythematosus. *Psychosomatic Medicine*, 1955, *17*, 311–321.

Mackenzie, A. R., Pick, C. R., Sibley, P. R., & White, B. P. Suppression of rat adjuvant disease by cyclophosphamide pretreatment: Evidence for an antibody mediated component in the pathogenesis of the disease. *Clinical and Experimental Immunology*, 1978, *32*, 86–96.

Makinodan, T., Santos, G. W., & Quinn, R. P. Immunosuppressive drugs. *Pharmacological Reviews*, 1970, *22*, 198–247.

Mandel, A. D., & Balish, E. Effect of space flight on cell-mediated immunity. *Aviation and Space Environment Medicine*, 1977, *48*, 1051–1057.

Mandelbrote, B. M., & Wittkower, E. D. Emotional factors in Graves' disease. *Psychosomatic Medicine*, 1955, *17*, 109–117.

Mantzouranis, E., & Borel, Y. Different effects of cortisone on the humoral immune response to T-dependent and T-independent antigens. *Cellular Immunology*, 1979, *43*, 202–208.

Marchant, J. The effects of different social conditions on breast cancer induction in three genetic types of mice by Dibenz(A,H)anthracene and a comparison with breast carcinogenesis by 3-methylcholanthrene. *British Journal of Cancer*, 1967, *21*, 576–585.

Marsh, J. T., Lavender, J. F., Chang, S., & Rasmussen, A. F., Jr. Poliomyelitis in monkeys:

Decreased susceptibility after avoidance stress. *Science*, 1963, *140*, 1415–1416.

Metal'nikov, S., & Chorine, V. Rôle des réflexes conditionnels dans l'immunité. *Annales de l'Institut Pasteur*, 1926, *40*, 893–900.

Metal'nikov, S., & Chorine, V. Rôle des réflexes conditionnels dans la formation des anticorps. *Comptes Rendus de la Société de Biologie*, 1928, *99*, 142–145.

Mettrop, P. J., & Visser, P. Exteroceptive stimulation as a contingent factor in the induction and elicitation of delayed-type hypersensitivity reactions to 1-chloro-2,4-dinitrobenzene in guinea pigs. *Psychophysiology*, 1969, *5*, 385–388.

Meyer, R. J., & Haggerty, R. Streptococcal infections in families: Factors altering individual susceptibility. *Pediatrics*, 1962, *29*, 539–549.

Meyerowitz, S., Jacox, R. F., & Hess, D. W. Monozygotic twins discordant for rheumatoid arthritis: A genetic, clinical and psychological study of 8 sets. *Arthritis and Rheumatism*, 1968, *11*, 1–21.

Miller, N. E. Learning of visceral and glandular responses. *Science*, 1969, *163*, 434–445.

Monjan, A. Stress and immunologic competence: Studies in animals. In R. Ader (Ed.), *Psychoneuroimmunology*. New York: Academic Press, 1981.

Monjan, A. A., & Collector, M. I. Stress-induced modulation of the immune response. *Science*, 1977, *196*, 307–308.

Moos, R. H. Personality factors associated with rheumatoid arthritis: A review. *Journal of Chronic Diseases*, 1963, *17*, 41–55.

Moos, R. H., & Solomon, G. F. Minnesota Multiphasic Personality Inventory response patterns in patients with rheumatoid arthritis. *Journal of Psychosomatic Research*, 1964, *8*, 17–23. (a)

Moos, R. H., & Solomon, G. F. Personality correlates of the rapidity of progression of rheumatoid arthritis. *Annals of the Rheumatic Diseases*, 1964, *23*, 145–151. (b)

Moos, R. H., & Solomon, G. F. Psychologic comparisons between women with rheumatoid arthritis and their non-arthritic sisters: I. Personality test and interview rating data. *Psychosomatic Medicine*, 1965, *27*, 135–149. (a)

Moos, R. H., & Solomon, G. F. Psychologic comparisons between women with rheumatoid arthritis and their non-arthritic sisters: II. Content analysis of interviews. *Psychosomatic Medicine*, 1965, *27*, 150–164. (b)

Morillo, E., & Gardner, L. I. Bereavement as an antecedent factor in thyrotoxicosis of childhood: Four case studies with survey of possible metabolic pathways. *Psychosomatic Medicine*, 1979, *41*, 545–555.

Opitz, H. G., Lemke, H., & Hewlett, G. Activation of T-cells by a macrophage of 2-mercaptoethanol activated serum factor is essential for induction of a primary immune response to heterologous red cells *in vitro*. *Immunological Reviews*, 1978, *40*, 53–77.

Otis, L. S., & Scholler, J. Effects of stress during infancy on tumor development and tumor growth. *Psychological Record*, 1967, *20*, 167–173.

Otto, R., & MacKay, I. Psychosocial and emotional disturbance in systemic lupus erythematosus. *Medical Journal of Australia*, 1967, *2*, 488–493.

Palmblad, J. Fasting in man: Effect on granulocyte function, plasma iron and serum transferring. *Scandinavian Journal of Haematology*, 1976, *17*, 217–226.

Palmblad, J. Stress and immunologic competence: Studies in man. In R. Ader (Ed.), *Psychoneuroimmunology*. New York: Academic Press, 1981.

Palmblad, J., Cantell, K., Holm, G., Norberg, R., Strander, H., & Sunblad, L. Acute energy deprivation in man: Effect on serum immunoglobulin, antibody response, complement factors 3 & 4, acute phase reactants and interferon producing capacity of blood lymphocytes. *Clinical and Experimental Immunology*, 1977, *30*, 50–55.

Palmblad, J., Cantell, K., Strander, H., Froberg, J., Karlson, C.-G., Levi, L., Granstrom, M., & Unger, P. Stressor exposure and immunological response in man: Interferon-producing capacity and phagocytosis. *Journal of Psychosomatic Research*, 1976, *20*, 193–199.

Palmblad, J., Fohlin, L., & Lundstrom, M. Anorexia nervosa and polymorphonuclear (PMN) granulocyte reactions. *Scandinavian Journal of Haematology*, 1977, *19*, 334–342.

Palmblad, J., Fohlin, L., & Norberg, R. Plasma levels of complement factors 3 and 4: Orosmucoid and opsonic functions in anorexia nervosa. *Acta Paediatrica Scandinavica*, 1979, *68*, 617–618.

Palmblad, J., Levi, L., Burger, A., Melander, A., Westgren, U., von Schenck, H., & Skude, G. Effects of total energy withdrawal (fasting) on the levels of growth hormone thyrotropin, cortisol, adrenaline, noradrenaline, T_4, T_3, and rT_3 in healthy males. *Acta Medica Scandinavica*, 1977, *201*, 15–22.

Palmblad, J., Petrini, B., Wasserman, J., & Akerstedt, T. Lymphocyte and granulocyte reactions during sleep deprivation. *Psychosomatic Medicine*, 1979, *41*, 273–278.

Parillo, J. E., & Fauci, A. S. Mechanisms of glucocorticoid action on immune processes. *Annual Review of Pharmacology and Toxicology*, 1979, *19*, 179–201.

Pavlidis, N., & Chirigos, M. Stress-induced impairment of macrophage tumoricidal function. *Psychosomatic Medicine*, 1980, *42*, 47–54.

Pavlov, I. P. *Lectures on conditioned reflexes*. New York: Livewright, 1928.

Peck, J. H., & Ader, R. Illness-induced taste aversion under states of deprivation and satiation. *Animal Learning and Behavior*, 1974, *2*, 6–8.

Pitkin, D. H. Effect of physiological stress on the delayed hypersensitivity reaction. *Proceedings of the Society for Experimental Biology and Medicine*, 1965, *120*, 350–351.

Plaut, S. M., & Ader, R., Friedman, S. B., & Ritterson, A. L. Social factors and resistance to malaria in the mouse: Effects of group versus individual housing on resistance to *Plasmodium berghei* infection. *Psychosomatic Medicine*, 1969, *31*, 536–552.

Plaut, S. M., Esterhay, R. J., Sutherland, J. C., Wareheim, L. E., Friedman, S. B., Schnaper, N., & Wiernik, P. H. Psychological effects on resistance to spontaneous AKR leukemia in mice. *Psychosomatic Medicine*, 1981, *42*, 72. (Abstract)

Portugalov, V. V. *[Morphological and cytochemical study of the organs and tissues of animals on Kosmos-782]* (NASA Technical Translation No. F-17257). Washington, D.C.: National Aeronautics and Space Administration, 1976.

Preachie, M. M., & Gibson, J. E. Effects of cyclophosphamide treatment of newborn mice on the development of swimming and reflex behavior and on adult behavioral performance. *Developmental Psychobiology*, 1976, *9*, 555–567.

Prehn, L. M., & Lawler, E. M. Rank order of sarcoma susceptibility among mouse strains reverses with low concentrations of carcinogen. *Science*, 1979, *204*, 309–310.

Rahe, R. H. Life change and subsequent illness reports. In E. K. E. Gunderson & R. H. Rahe (Eds.), *Life stress and illness*. Springfield, Ill.: Charles C Thomas, 1974.

Rashkis, H. A. Systemic stress as an inhibitor of experimental tumors in Swiss mice. *Science*, 1952, *116*, 169–171.

Rasmussen, A. F., Jr. Emotions and immunity. *Annals of the New York Academy of Science*, 1969, *164*, 458–461.

Rasmussen, A. F., Jr., Hildemann, W. H., & Sellers, M. Malignancy of polyoma virus infection in mice in relation to stress. *Journal of the National Cancer Institute*, 1963, *30*, 101–112.

Rasmussen, A. F., Jr., Marsh, J. T., & Brill, N. Q. Increased susceptibility to herpes simplex in mice subjected to avoidance-learning stress or restraint. *Proceedings of the Society for Experimental Biology and Medicine*, 1957, *96*, 183–189.

Rasmussen, A. F., Jr., Spencer, E. S., & Marsh, J. T. Decrease in susceptibility of mice to passive anaphylaxis following avoidance-learning stress. *Proceedings of the Society for Experimental Biology and Medicine*, 1959, *100*, 878–879.

Razran, G. The observable unconscious and the inferable conscious in current Soviet psychophysiology: Interoceptive conditioning, semantic conditioning, and the orienting reflex. *Psychological Review*, 1961, *68*, 81–147.

Rigter, H. Plasma corticosterone levels as an index of $ACTH_{4-10}$-induced attenuation of amnesia. *Behavioral Biology*, 1975, *15*, 207–211.

Riley, V. Mouse mammary tumors: Alteration of incidence as apparent function of stress. *Science*, 1975, *189*, 465–467.

Riley, V., Fitzmaurice, M. A., & Spackman, D. Psychosocial factors in neoplasia: Studies in animals. In R. Ader (Ed.), *Psychoneuroimmunology*. New York: Academic Press, 1981.

Rimon, R., Belmaker, R. H., & Ebstein, R. Psychosomatic aspects of juvenile rheumatoid arthritis. *Scandinavian Journal of Rheumatology*, 1977, *6*, 1–10.

Robinson, C. E. Emotional factors in rheumatoid arthritis. *Canadian Medical Association Journal*, 1957, *34*, 533–547.

Roessler, R., Cate, T. R., Lester, J. W., & Couch, R. B. *Ego strength, life events, and antibody titers.* Paper presented at the annual meeting of the American Psychosomatic Society, Dallas, March 24, 1979.

Rogers, M. P., Dubey, D., & Reich, P. The influence of the psyche and the brain on immunity and disease susceptibility: A critical review. *Psychosomatic Medicine*, 1979, *41*, 147–164.

Rogers, M. P., Reich, P., Strom, T. B., & Carpenter, C. B. Behaviorally conditioned immunosuppression: Replication of a recent study. *Psychosomatic Medicine*, 1976, *38*, 447–452.

Rogers, M. P., Trentham, D., McCune, J., Ginsberg, B., Reich, P., & David, J. Abrogation of Type II collagen-induced arthritis in rats by psychological stress. *Clinical Research*, 1979, *27*, 513A. (Abstract)

Rogers, M. P., Trentham, D. E., & Reich, P. Modulation of collagen-induced arthritis by different stress protocols. *Psychosomatic Medicine*, 1981, *42*, 72. (Abstract)

Rollinghoff, M., Starzinski-Powitz, A., Pfizenmaier, K., & Wagner, H. Cyclophosphamide-sensitive T lymphocytes suppress the *in vivo* generation of antigen-specific cytotoxic T lymphocytes. *Journal of Experimental Medicine*, 1977, *145*, 455–459.

Rubin, R. T., Gunderson, E. K. E., & Arthur, R. J. Life stress and illness patterns in the U.S. Navy: VI. Environmental, demographic, and prior life change variables in relation to illness onset in naval aviators during a combat cruise. *Psychosomatic Medicine*, 1972, *34*, 533–547.

Sampter, M. (Ed.). *Immunological diseases* (3rd ed.). Boston: Little, Brown, 1978.

Santos, G. W., & Owens, H. A., Jr. A comparison of selected cytotoxic agents on the primary agglutinin response in rats injected with sheep erythrocytes. *Bulletin of the Johns Hopkins Hospital*, 1964, *114*, 384–401.

Schleifer, S., Keller, S., McKegney, F. P., & Stein, M. *Bereavement and lymphocyte function.* Paper presented at the meeting of the American Psychiatric Association, San Francisco, May 1980.

Seifter, E., Rettura, G., Zisblatt, M., Levenson, S. M., Levine, N., Davidson, A., & Seifter, J. Enhancement of tumor development in physically-stressed mice incubated with an oncogenic virus. *Experientia*, 1973, *29*, 1379–1382.

Sell, G. *Immunology, immunopathology and immunity*. Hagerstown, Pa.: Harper, 1972.

Shochet, B. R., Lisansky, E. T., Schubart, A. F., Fiocco, V., Kurland, S., & Pope, M. A medical psychiatric study of patients with rheumatoid arthritis. *Psychosomatics*, 1969, *10*, 271–279.

Siegel, S. Conditioned insulin effects. *Journal of Comparative and Physiological Psychology*, 1975, *89*, 189–199.

Siegel, S. Learning and psychopharmacology. In M. E. Jarvik (Ed.), *Psychopharmacology in the practice of medicine*. New York: Appleton-Century-Crofts, 1977. (a)

Siegel, S. Morphine tolerance acquisition as an associative process. *Journal of Experimental Psychology: Animal Behavioral Processes*, 1977, *3*, 1–13. (b)

Sklar, L. S., & Anisman, H. Stress and coping factors influence tumor growth. *Science*, 1979, *205*, 513–515.

Smith, L. W., Molomut, N., & Gottfried, B. Effect of subconvulsive audiogenic stress in mice on turpentine induced inflammation. *Proceedings of the Society for Experimental Biology and Medicine*, 1960, *103*, 370–372.

Smotherman, W. P., Hennessy, J. W., & Levine, S. Plasma corticosterone levels during recovery from LiCl produced taste aversions. *Behavioral Biology*, 1976, *16*, 401–412.

Soave, O. A. Reactivation of rabies virus infection in the guinea pig due to the stress of crowding. *American Journal of Veterinary Research*, 1964, *25*, 268–269.

Solomon, G. F. Stress and antibody response in rats. *International Archives of Allergy*, 1969, *35*, 97–104.

Solomon, G. F. Emotional and personality factors in the onset and course of autoimmune disease, particularly rheumatoid arthritis. In R. Ader (Ed.), *Psychoneuroimmunology*. New York: Academic Press, 1981.

Solomon, G. F., Amkraut, A. A., & Rubin, R. T. Stress and psychoimmunological response. In B. A. Stoll (Ed.), *Mind and cancer prognosis*. New York: Wiley, 1979.

Solomon, G. F., Levine, S., & Kraft, J. K. Early experience and immunity. *Nature*, 1968, *220*, 821–822.

Supak, T., Macrides, F., & Chorover, S. The baitshyness effect extended to olfactory discrimination. *Communications in Behavioral Biology*, 1971, *5*, 321–324.

Taukulis, H. K. Odor aversions produced over long CS-US delays. *Behavioral Biology*, 1974, *10*, 505–510.

Tigranyan, R. A. *[Kosmos-782 post-flight biochemical studies of various organs and tissues of rats]* (NASA Technical Translation No. F-17237). Washington, D.C.: National Aeronautics and Space Administration, 1976.

Tobach, E., & Bloch, H. Effect of stress by crowding prior to and following tuberculosis infection. *American Journal of Physiology*, 1956, *187*, 399–402.

Treadwell, P. E., & Rasmussen, A. F., Jr. Role of the adrenals in stress-induced resistance to anaphylactic shock. *Journal of Immunology*, 1961, *87*, 492–497.

Turk, J. L., & Poulter, L. W. Selective depletion of lymphoid tissue by cyclophosphamide. *Clinical Experiments in Immunology*, 1972, *10*, 285–296.

Vessey, S. H. Effects of grouping on levels of circulating antibodies in mice. *Proceedings of the Society for Experimental Biology and Medicine*, 1964, *115*, 252–255.

Wayner, E. A. Personal communication, 1979.

Wayner, E. A., Flannery, G. R., & Singer, G. The effects of taste aversion conditioning on the primary antibody response to sheep red blood cells and *Brucella abortus* in the albino rat. *Physiology and Behavior*, 1978, *21*, 995–1000.

Weiner, H. *Psychobiology and human disease*. New York: Elsevier, 1977.

Weinman, C. J., & Rothman, A. H. Effects of stress upon acquired immunity to the dwarf tapeworm *Hymenolepis nana*. *Experimental Parasitology*, 1967, *21*, 61–67.

Whitehouse, M. W., Levy, L., & Beck, F. J. Effect of cyclophosphamide on a local graft-versus-host reaction in the rat: Influence of sex, disease and different dosage regimens. *Agents and Actions*, 1973, *3*, 53–60.

Wilcoxon, H. C., Dragoin, W. B., & Kral, P. A. Illness-induced taste aversions in rats and quail: Relative salience of visual and gustatory cues. *Science*, 1971, *171*, 826–828.

Wilder, R. M., Hubble, J., & Kennedy, C. E. Life change and infectious mononucleosis. *Journal of the American College Health Association*, 1971, *20*, 115–119.

Wistar, R., Jr., & Hildemann, W. H. Effect of stress on skin transplantation immunity in mice. *Science*, 1960, *131*, 159–160.

Wittkower, E. D., Durost, H. B., & Laing, W. A. R. A psychosomatic study of the course of pulmonary tuberculosis. *American Review of Tuberculosis and Pulmonary Diseases*, 1955, *71*, 201–219.

Wright, W. E., Foshee, D. P., & McCleary, G. E. Comparison of taste aversion with various delays and cyclophosphamide dose levels. *Psychonomic Science*, 1971, *22*, 55–56.

Wyler, A. R., Holmes, T. H., & Masuda, M. Magnitude of life events and seriousness of illness. *Psychosomatic Medicine*, 1971, *33*, 115–122.

Yamada, A., Jensen, M. M., & Rasmussen, A. F., Jr. Stress and susceptibility to viral infections: III. Antibody response and viral retention during avoidance learning stress. *Proceedings of the Society for Experimental Biology and Medicine*, 1964, *116*, 677–680.

CHAPTER 6

Behavioral and Psychological Influences on Gastrointestinal Pathology: Experimental Techniques and Findings

Jay M. Weiss

The Rockefeller University

This chapter is concerned with behavioral–psychological research related to gastrointestinal pathology. It is, however, not intended to be a comprehensive summary or review of such research; rather, it is meant to serve as an aid to investigators who wish to carry out future experimental research to examine how behavioral and psychological variables affect gastrointestinal pathology. The chapter thus focuses on the techniques that have been used for conducting experimental studies in this area, and considers some of the theoretical and practical issues related to these techniques.

EXPERIMENTALLY INDUCED GASTROINTESTINAL PATHOLOGY: WHAT IS PRODUCED AND WHAT DOES IT MEAN?

Gastrointestinal Lesions

In studying how behavioral–psychological variables influence gastrointestinal pathology, experimental studies—that is, studies wherein the investigator generates, induces, or manipulates pathology, as contrasted with correlational studies wherein the investigator measures factors associated with normally occurring pathology—have focused on lesions of the gastrointestinal tract. The reason for this is that gastrointestinal lesions can be produced in experimental animals under laboratory conditions. The particular type of lesion most often produced has been the gastric erosion (see Figure 6.1). Erosions are acute, rapidly developing lesions that almost never extend into the muscular region below the mucosa (muscularis mucosa). These lesions apparently heal within a few days without leaving a scar. Such lesions need to be distinguished from ulcers, which also have been produced in experimental animals, but only rarely (see Figure 6.2). Ulcers are chronic lesions

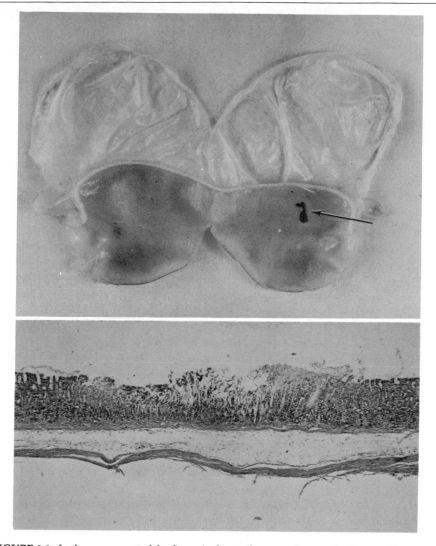

FIGURE 6.1. In the upper part of the figure is shown the opened stomach of a rat with a gastric erosion (indicated by the arrow). Note that the lesion occurs in the lower, glandular portion of the stomach. The rumen of the rat's stomach is seen above the glandular portion. In the lower part of the figure is shown a histological section taken through the lesion shown in the upper part. The lesion is identified by the lack of normal cellular structure seen in the marginal regions of the histological section. (From Weiss, J. M. Effects of coping behavior in different warning-signal conditions on stress pathology in rats. *Journal of Comparative and Physiological Psychology,* 1971, *77,* 1–13. Copyright 1971 by the American Psychological Association. Reprinted by permission of the publisher.)

FIGURE 6.2. In the upper part of the figure is shown the opened stomach of a rat and the duodenum below it. A large perforated duodenal ulcer can be seen in the duodenum. In the lower part of the figure is shown a histological section taken through a duodenal ulcer in a rat. Note how the lesion penetrates completely through the upper mucosa and into the underlying muscularis mucosa. (From Robert, A., Stout, T., & Dale, J. E. Production by secretagogues of duodenal ulcers in the rat. *Gastroenterology*, 1970, *59*, 95–102. Reprinted by permission.)

that extend into the wall of the gastrointestinal tract and may even penetrate through the serosal (outer) surface of the gastrointestinal tract. These lesions often leave a scar upon healing. Ulcers are usually found as single, discrete lesions, while erosions are often multiple and widespread.

Both gastric erosions and ulcers represent serious health problems in humans. Gastric erosions are usually a health hazard because of the bleeding they produce. Erosions are a major complication arising after burns, surgery, and head injury, though the lesions occurring in each of these instances are not identical (Skillman & Silen, 1970; Wangensteen & Golden, 1973). Stress of psychological origin can produce erosions in humans (Wolf & Wolff, 1947; Wolff, Wolf, Grace, Holmes, Stevenson, Straub, Goodell, & Seton, 1948), though the participation of psychological factors in erosions following burns, surgery, and head injury is not clear. Ulcers, like gastric erosions, present a health hazard because of the bleeding that they may produce. In addition, if the lesion perforates the wall of the gastrointestinal tract, the contents of the tract will then enter the peritoneal cavity, causing peritonitis. Finally, chronic lesions, particularly those found in the stomach, have the distinct possibility of being malignant. Blumenthal (1960) estimated that, at that time, one out of every 20 persons in the United States would develop an ulcer during his or her lifetime.

Relevance of Experimentally Induced Lesions to Disease in Humans

Although gastric erosions are an important and frequent health problem for humans, historically it has been ulcers that have been associated with behavioral–psychological factors in medical practice. Thus, when researchers in the laboratory have studied how behavioral and psychological factors influence gastrointestinal pathology, their findings often have been related to ulcers. Since laboratory experiments usually have generated gastric erosions, this raises the question of how experimentally induced erosions are related to ulcers in humans.

Evaluating the relevance of experimentally induced gastric erosions to ulcers in humans is perhaps best begun by describing the stomach of the rat or mouse—the experimental animals used in nearly all behavioral–psychological research on gastric pathology—in comparison with the human stomach. The most striking difference is that the rat or mouse stomach is divided into two distinctly different zones: an upper zone called the "rumen" or "cardiac" region, the cells of which do not secrete acid, and a lower zone called the "fundus" or "glandular" region, containing the parietal cells, which do secrete acid. Although the human stomach also has what is called the cardiac region in the upper portion, this region is not as clearly differentiated morphologically from the rest of the stomach as it is in the rat or mouse.

However, more important than any morphological difference is the possibility that the stomach of the rat or mouse is physiologically different from the human stomach, so that it will not show similar pathology. There is no evidence that this is the case. As indicated above, the human, rat, and mouse stomachs all develop erosions, so that the organs are comparable with respect to this pathological condition. More important is the question of whether rats or mice develop ulcers, particularly the duodenal ulcers that are often found in humans. As stated earlier, virtually all experimental studies with the rat or mouse have shown erosions rather than ulcers, and these have usually appeared in the glandular portion of the stomach rather than the duodenum. However, Andre Robert and his colleagues have shown, in an important series of studies, that duodenal lesions can be produced in the rat by injection of histamine and cholinergic-stimulating agents, which presumably produce high acid secretion (Robert & Stout, 1969; Robert, Stout, & Dale, 1970). Thus, the rat is quite able to develop duodenal ulcers.

Acid Secretion: Role in Ulcers and Erosions

Discussion of duodenal ulcers raises another issue in evaluating the relevance of erosions to ulcers. A major distinction that has been made between ulcers and erosions concerns the role of stomach acid. Certain ulcers, particularly duodenal ulcers, are typically found when acid secretion is high (Baron, 1962; Bockus, Glassmire, & Bank, 1931; Dragstedt, 1967; Vanzant, Alvarez, Berkson, & Eusterman, 1933). In contrast, the appearance of gastric erosions does not necessarily covary with stomach acid in this way. Evidence for this comes, for example, from studies showing that certain stressful conditions that decrease stomach secretion will actually increase gastric erosions (Mikhail, 1971; Paré, 1972; Paré & Livingston, 1973; Polish, Brady, Mason, Thach, & Niemack, 1962). Thus, gastric erosions seem to differ from duodenal ulcers with respect to the role of acid secretion.

However, any distinction between erosions and ulcers that is based on the role of stomach acid is not absolute. First, ulcers in humans occur in the stomach, as well as in the duodenum, and these gastric ulcers have been found in cases where stomach acid is actually lower than normal, or even virtually absent. Consequently, some investigators have suggested that (1) there are different types of gastric ulcers, and (2) gastric ulcers are a disorder different from duodenal ulcers. (An excellent discussion of these issues can be found in Ackerman & Weiner, 1976.) In any case, we can conclude that ulcer disease is not exclusively related to high acid secretion. Second, there are certain erosions in rats that appear to depend quite heavily on acid secretion. These are erosions that occur in the upper portion of the rat's stomach, or rumen. Such erosions appear after long periods of food deprivation (Paré & Temple, 1973) or after ligation of the pylorus (Shay, Komorov, Fels, Moranze, Gruenstein, & Siplet, 1945). These lesions are markedly attenuated by drugs that reduce stomach acidity (e.g., Glavin & Mikhail, 1976). Thus, erosions in rats can depend quite heavily on acid secretion. Third, although the typical erosion in the glandular portion of the rat stomach apparently does not require elevated stomach acid in order for it to develop, there is much evidence that stomach acid increases the severity of gastric erosions. Factors that increase acid secretion, such as steroids (e.g., Robert & Nezamis, 1964), increase erosions, and factors that decrease acid secretion, such as vagotomy (cutting of the vagus nerve; see Bonfils, Rossi, Liefooghe, & Lambling, 1959; Brodie & Hanson, 1960; Hanson, 1963) and administration of acid-depressing drugs (e.g., Dai, Ogle, & Lo, 1975; Levine & Senay, 1970), decrease erosions. Thus, erosions are clearly affected by acid secretion in a manner similar to the manner in which acid affects ulcers. Certain investigators have, in fact, suggested that some acid is essential for certain types of erosions (Skillman & Silen, 1972). In summary, any distinction made between different types of lesions with respect to the role of acid seems best described as a matter of degree. That is, certain lesions—particularly duodenal ulcers, but also erosions in the rumen—depend for their etiology more on high acid secretion than do other lesions, such as erosions in the glandular region of the stomach and some gastric ulcers; however, the evidence indicates that all types of ulcers and erosions are promoted by acid secretion.

Gastrointestinal Lesions: The Importance of Mucosal Impairment

In the final analysis, the usefulness of erosions for telling us about ulcers (or vice versa) will depend on the extent to which the basic causes of these lesions are similar. After all, for behavioral scientists it would matter little which of these lesions they studied if erosions and ulcers proved to be but different endpoints of a similar process. Thus, the most productive approach to the issue of how ulcers and erosions are related is to consider the pathogenesis of these lesions.

In discussing the genesis of gastrointestinal lesions, investigators have repeatedly emphasized that the emergence of gastrointestinal lesions is determined by factors that alter the viability of the gastric mucosa. The gastric mucosa is specialized to coexist with corrosive elements (pepsin, acid) whose function it is to digest food matter, so that the lining of the stomach under normal conditions is prepared to withstand, without the development of pathology, those elements that would otherwise produce pathological changes. Lesions develop when the viability of the mucosa is compromised. Attention has for some time been focused on such factors as changes in blood flow (e.g., Guth & Hall, 1966) and mucosal regeneration rate (e.g., Kim, Kerr, & Lipkin, 1967) as primary in the production of lesions. Such thinking derives from the view that a healthy mucosa will withstand virtually all challenges and that the development of pathology stems primarily from breakdown in the integrity of the mucosa. Even in the case of duodenal ulcer, where high acid secretion seems to be important, mucosal impairment may also be necessary for the lesion to occur, since we know that many persons who also secrete large quantities of acid do not develop lesions.

From this point of view, the key to understanding the production of both erosions and ulcers is seen as the need to discover those basic processes that compromise the viability of the mucosa. Considering how the mucosa becomes compromised in the development of gastric erosions, the evidence points to circulatory changes as being important. Gastrointestinal lesions appear to begin development when the mucosa becomes ischemic—that is, when the mucosa is deprived of normal circulation of blood. In a particularly valuable study, Hase and Moss (1973) found that, as an initial response to stressful conditions, blood flow into the mucosa of rats is restricted by constriction of ascending arterioles. Precisely how the lesion subsequently develops, however, remains a question. An early view (see Ivy, Grossman, & Bachrach, 1950, pp. 184–186, 193–196) was that extreme constriction of blood vessels led to rupture of vessels followed by hemorrhage into the mucosa, and that it was this hemorrhage that impeded normal cell metabolism in the mucosa, leading to the cellular death (necrosis) that marks a lesion. Hase and Moss (1973) observed breakdown of mucosal vasculature in conjunction with the ischemia. The work of Guth and Hall (1966) and Kristt and Freimark (1973) shows the pervasive nature and early development of hemorrhage (also called "engorgement") in conjunction with gastric lesions. Similar phenomena have been noted in humans (see Cushing, 1932, p. 13). On the other hand, it is quite possible that hemorrhage is secondary to lesion development. Both processes, in fact, seem likely. It has also been suggested that stomach acid, acting on an ischemic mucosa, is highly important in the formation of erosions (Skillman & Silen, 1972). These investigators contend that some amount of acid is essential for the lesion to develop. The phenomenon of "back diffusion," referring to acid diffusing back into the mucosa because of an impaired mucosal barrier, is hypothesized to be significant in this regard.

Much less is known about the fundamental processes leading to an ulcer, since, as stated above, an adequate animal model of this lesion has not yet been studied extensively. Nevertheless, it seems very likely that many of the basic processes leading to the development of erosions will be found to participate in the development of ulcers. This statement is supported by both clinical and experimental observations. For example, in the clinical setting, ulcers are often found together with erosions (e.g., de Brito, Montenegro, Leite, Berguo, & Vasconcellos, 1961; Schindler & Baxmeier, 1939; Thompson, 1959). Ulcers and erosions also consistently occur together in an animal model (Manning, Wall, Montgomery, Simmons, & Sessions, 1978). Moreover, conditions that are known to cause erosions, such as burns, can activate ulcer disease (Dragstedt, Ragins, Dragstedt, & Evans, 1956); conversely, factors closely associated with ulcers, such as elevated stomach acid, can produce single, focal erosions (Polish et al., 1962). Also, stressful conditions can generate erosions in regions of the gut, such as the duodenum, that are common sites of ulcer (Natelson, Hoffman, & McKee, 1979). Such findings suggest that an erosion may be a potential ulcer, and that, while almost all erosions heal and disappear, in some instances an erosion may go on to become an ulcer. For those interested in the influence of behavioral and psychological factors on gastric pathology, it seems reasonably clear that much of fundamental significance will be learned about how behavioral and psychological factors affect a wide variety of gastrointestinal disorders, including ulcers, from the study of experimentally induced erosions.

TECHNIQUES FOR STUDYING BEHAVIORAL–PSYCHOLOGICAL INFLUENCES ON DEVELOPMENT OF GASTRIC LESIONS

Under normal laboratory conditions, animals in a colony will not develop lesions of the gastrointestinal tract, so experimental study requires the stimulation of lesion development. A variety of techniques have been discovered for experimental production of gastrointestinal lesions. In choosing from among these techniques for the purpose of studying behavioral and psychological influences on lesion development, the following criteria can be used: The most suitable techniques are those that (1) least disturb the normal physiology of an animal (i.e., use a normal animal), and (2) establish conditions wherein behavioral responses and psychological processes can occur with least constraint.

The techniques for producing experimental lesions can be divided into two general categories: (1) direct physiological manipulations, and (2) stress-environmental manipulations. Direct physiological manipulations, as the term indicates, directly manipulate physiological responses by chemical, surgical, or electrical intervention into the body of the animal. The most widely used techniques of this sort are pharmacological. For example, administrations of reserpine (Lau & Ogle, 1980), ketamine (Cheney, Slogoff, & Allen, 1974), aspirin (Brodie, Tate, & Hooks, 1970; Valman, Parry, & Coghill, 1968), and high doses of steroids (Robert & Nezamis, 1964) all have been used to produce gastric erosions. Also, as mentioned above, administration of carbacol and histamine will produce duodenal ulcers (Robert & Stout, 1969; Robert, Stout, & Dale, 1970). In addition to pharmacological techniques, various surgical methods have been used to induce lesions. Several techniques have been described for use in dogs, but perhaps the most widely used surgical technique was introduced by Shay and his colleagues for use with the rat (Shay et al., 1945); this method produces lesions by ligation of the pylorus. Finally, lesions have also been produced by electrical stimulation of the brain (French, Porter, Cavanaugh, & Longmire, 1957).

Direct physiological manipulations, such as those described in the preceding paragraph, have been used little in behavioral–psychological studies of gastric pathology. Such manipulations violate the first of the two criteria set forth in the last sentence of the opening paragraph of this section. The reason why direct manipulation of physiological responses to induce pathology is undesirable for behavioral–psychological studies is that such physiological manipulations often themselves alter or generate behavioral and psychological responses; consequently, relationships between behavioral-psychological responses and lesion development may be seen that have no relevance to a normal animal. However, such manipulations have been mentioned in this chapter, because in the future investigators may wish to make judicious use of such manipulations in conjunction with behavioral-psychological research in order to predispose animals to gastrointestinal disease.

Stress-environmental manipulations expose animals to environmental stimuli that produce sensory stimulation of sufficient intensity to be stressful. Such stimulation will produce gastrointestinal lesions. To date, virtually all behavioral and psychological studies related to gastrointestinal lesions have utilized such techniques. This is not surprising, since such methods do not violate the first criterion set forth in the opening paragraph, but rather utilize only an animal's normal neural input and physiological responses for lesion development.

Stress-environmental conditions (also called "stressors") to which animals have been exposed in order to produce gastrointestinal lesions include the following: (1) a rotating drum, (2) an oscillating environment with illumination changes, (3) cold, (4) immobilization, (5) prolonged food deprivation, and (6) electric shock. Of these manipulations, the first (Noble & Collip, 1942; Robert, Northam, Nezamis, & Phillips, 1970), which in some instances involves physical trauma (Noble & Collip, 1942), and the second (Levrat & Lambert, 1959) have only been used to a limited extent in behavioral–psychological studies. The third, exposure to cold, has generally been employed as a technique for lesion development in conjunction with other methods, such as immobilization (Brodie & Valitski, 1963; Senay & Levine, 1967), electric shock (Rosenberg, 1967), and alcohol ingestion (Lev, Kawashima, & Glass, 1976); however, in behavioral–psychological studies, cold has been little used, and not at all as the sole stressor in the situation. This leaves the last three stressors, which are now considered in order.

Immobilization

Immobilization (or restraint) of animals is one of the earliest techniques used for developing gastric lesions. Use of this method was first reported by Selye in 1936. In this procedure, the animal is immobilized by having its limbs held in place (usually by tape) or by being placed into a severely restricted space so that it cannot move. The immobilization technique will produce lesions in a physiologically normal, conscious animal. However, immobilization physically restrains the animal severely, so that this procedure obviously restricts behavioral responses; as a result, the technique has pronounced drawbacks with respect to the second criterion described at the outset of this section. Nevertheless, so much research has been carried out using the immobilization technique that a considerable number of studies have been conducted that are of interest to the investigator concerned with behavioral and psychological variables.

In the late 1950s two groups of researchers, one led by Serge Bonfils and the other by David Brodie, defined many of the basic characteristics of gastric lesions induced by immobilization. Bonfils and his coinvestigators generally immobilized animals by placing each one in a wire cylinder with holes cut in the bottom so that the rat's legs protruded through the holes in the cylinder. Brodie and his colleague Harley Hanson initially used this technique, but soon switched to one in which they immobilized animals within wire screens drawn closely around the animals.

The severity of gastric lesions was found to depend upon the closeness and the duration of the restraint. Bonfils and his coworkers (Bonfils, Liefooghe, Gellé, Dubrasquet, & Lambling, 1960) found that as the space within the restraining compartment decreased, the number of animals developing lesions increased. Both groups of researchers (Bonfils, Rossi, Liefooghe, & Lambling, 1959; Brodie & Hanson, 1960) reported that the number of animals developing lesions increased as the duration of exposure to the restraint increased. Both groups also reported that the lesions healed relatively rapidly and without scarring. Whereas 80% to 100% of the animals showed lesions after being restrained for 24 hours, the number of animals having lesions was found to be reduced to 60% 12 hours after they had been removed from restraint. By the third day after restraint, Brodie and Hanson reported that only 20% of the animals showed lesions, and Bonfils, Richir, Potet, Liefooghe, and Lambling (1959) reported a similar reduction by the ninth day.

Other factors found to play a significant role in development of gastric lesions were the age (or weight) of the animals and the degree of food deprivation prior to the immobilization. Both groups of investigators found that the younger (or more lightweight) animals were at the time of immobilization, the more likely they were to develop gastric lesions. Also, food deprivation before the restraining period was found to increase the pathogenic capacity of restraint and/or to prolong the time required for lesions to heal.

Habituation also can apparently occur with respect to lesions induced by immobilization. Bonfils' group reported that repeated immobilization for 24 hours, followed by 24 hours of rest between immobilization periods, resulted in a progressive decline in lesions. Whereas 86% of the animals were found to have lesions after a single 24-hour period of immobilization, only 71% had lesions after two such periods, 51% after three such periods, and 25% after four such periods. Guth and Mendick (1964) reached a similar conclusion, showing that repeated periods of immobilization for 4 hours followed by 20 hours of rest produced a decrease in lesion development, although there was an increase in mortality. On the other hand, Brodie and Hanson (1960) subjected animals to repeated immobilization for 18 hours followed by 6 hours of rest, and found that this regimen resulted in an increase in gastric lesions. Such results suggest that habituation will occur, provided that sufficient recovery time between exposure to immobilization is allowed, but that increased susceptibility will result if only a brief recovery time is allowed between exposures to relatively long immobilization.

Another interesting characteristic of gastric lesions produced by immobilization is the fact that lesions are related to the level of pepsinogen in plasma. Pepsinogen is secreted into the stomach by the chief (or zymogen) cells and is there converted to pepsin (which digests protein) at low pH. Since pepsin is a digestive agent, it is not surprising that very high levels of stomach pepsin, which could attack a compromised mucosa, would dispose an individual to the development of ulcers. Some pepsinogen, presumably a small percentage of that secreted into the stomach, enters the bloodstream. Thus, the level of pepsinogen found in the circulatory system is one predictor of vulnerability to ulcer. In one of the classic studies in psychosomatic medicine, Weiner, Thaler, Reiser, and Mirsky (1957) showed that pepsinogen level in humans was indeed a predictor of duodenal ulcer development. Working with rat subjects, Ader and his associates found that (1) the distribution of plasma pepsinogen in a population of rats was similar to the distribution in humans (Ader, 1963), and (2) rats with high plasma pepsinogen were also more likely to develop lesions as a consequence of immobilization than were animals with low plasma pepsinogen (Ader, Beels, & Tatum, 1960).

Hereditary variables apparently also affect lesions induced by immobilization. This work was primarily conducted by Jacob Sines, who attempted to develop a population of rats that was ulcer-susceptible (e.g., Sines, 1959, 1963). By exposing animals to immobilization and examining them for lesions without sacrificing them, Sines selected animals that developed lesions and inbred them. After inbreeding for six generations, he developed a strain of animals, which, when exposed to 12 hours of restraint, developed lesions in 100% of the cases. Only 20% of animals from normal stock developed lesions in response to this restraint. When Sines mated normal Sprague–Dawley females with sixth-generation "ulcer-susceptible" males, 88% of the offspring from this mating developed lesions in response to this restraint, showing that the ulcer susceptibility could not be explained on the basis of behavior of ulcer-susceptible mothers. A variety of behavioral characteristics were also found in the ulcer-susceptible animals. Most prominently, the rats were more active in novel situations, and they defecated more in an open field (Sines, 1961). They also more readily learned a shuttle avoidance–escape response (Sines, Cleeland, & Adkins, 1963).

Within the last few years, Ackerman and his coworkers (Ackerman, Hofer, & Weiner, 1975) have uncovered an interesting variable affecting immobilization-induced lesions. When animals were separated from their mothers 15 days after birth or earlier (i.e., before weaning), these animals later exhibited a very high vulnerability to gastric lesions in response to 24 hours of restraint. This increased vulnerability was evident until the animals were 100 days of age. On the other hand, animals that were separated from mothers at a slightly later time (21 or 25 days after birth) showed much less vulnerability to gastric lesions when restrained at the same age as the rats separated at 15 days. Further experiments showed that 24-hour food deprivation alone was sufficient to cause marked development of lesions in the early-separated group. As yet there is no adequate explanation for these findings. The fact that profound changes in lesion susceptibility may occur within a very short period of an animal's life makes this observation a potentially valuable one for studying the etiology of gastrointestinal lesions.

Finally, the status of immobilization as a "psychological or emotional" stressor should be commented upon. Selye was of the opinion that immobilization was a psychological or emotional stressor, since the physical assault on the animal appeared to be negligible in comparison with that of other stressors (such as injected toxins, trauma, and surgical operations) that were used in studies of physiological stress reactions. The supposition that immobilization can be used to discern effects of an emotional stressor or psychological stressor is no longer accepted. For example, Feldman, Conforti, Chowers, and Davidson (1970) studied secretion of the pituitary hormone ACTH in animals in which the hypothalamus (and hence the pituitary) was surgically isolated (by knife cuts) from the rest of the brain. The investigators studied the effects of various stressors on such animals. Immobilization, like ether anesthesia, produced an augmented ACTH response despite the lack of neural input from virtually all of the brain. Loud noise, which normally produces an ACTH response, had no such effect in these animals. Consequently, the results indicate that immobilization does not depend on higher nervous integration for some of its "stress" effects, as does a noxious sensory stimulus. Therefore, if one assumes that participation of the brain (other than just the hypothalamus) is necessary for generating what investigators would wish to call emotional or psychological responses, then the immobilization procedure is not adequate as a method for studying the effects of emotional or psychological conditions.

Prolonged Food Deprivation

Prolonged food deprivation has been found to produce gastric lesions (Ogawa, Chiles, & Necheles, 1960; Paré & Temple, 1973; Pfeiffer, Debro, & Muller, 1966; Selye, 1937). In this procedure, animals are totally deprived of food for several days, or their intake is severely restricted for longer periods of time. As a result of these procedures, lesions can appear in the upper, rumenal portion of the stomach, and, less frequently, in the lower, glandular portion of the stomach. The shortcomings of this method for behavioral and psychological study are evident. First, while study of behavioral–psychological variables optimally requires a physiologically normal animal, severe and prolonged food deprivation causes a departure from this optimal condition. Also, when deprivation produces weakness, it will restrict behavioral responses. Finally, manipulation of food intake influences gastric pathology in a way that has not yet been discussed in this chapter. This influence might be called "mechanical." Food in the stomach can, in direct contact with the mucosa, buffer acid or influence gastric contraction (e.g., Mikhail & Hirschberg, 1972). Thus, when altering food intake, an investigator must assess how the presence or absence of material in the alimentary canal directly interacts with the lining of the stomach and intestine.

Despite the drawbacks of prolonged food deprivation, some very interesting behavioral research has been carried out utilizing this method. The studies of greatest interest were primarily conducted by Paré and his colleagues, Vincent and Houser. In this paradigm, animals were fed for 1 hour each day. Paré and his colleagues observed that, when fed on this schedule, animals given access to an activity wheel developed severe gastric erosions and occasionally ulcers, whereas animals fed on the same schedule but not given access to an activity wheel did not develop severe gastric pathology (Paré, 1975, 1976, 1980; Paré & Houser, 1973). The manipulation will produce lesions in hamsters, gerbils, and guinea pigs, in addition to rats (Vincent & Paré, 1976). Clearly, the design of this experiment suggests that the food deprivation per se was not responsible for the severe pathology seen in animals having access to an activity wheel, since comparable pathology was not seen in animals subjected to food deprivation but lacking access to a wheel; rather, running-wheel activity appears to be of critical significance for producing the gastric pathology that was observed.

Paré and his colleagues have verified the importance of activity in several ways. First, when they determined that activity-wheel subjects would, during the course of the experiment, spontaneously eat less than would animals having no wheel at certain stages of the experiment, they matched the food consumption of activity-wheel animals and subjects having no wheel (Paré, 1975); animals having access to the activity wheel still developed far more pathology. In addition, they have found that (1) highly active animals developed more pathology than less active animals (Paré, 1976), and (2) young animals developed more pathology than older animals and were also more active (Paré, 1975). As a result of such findings, Paré and his colleagues have given the name ''activity-stress ulcer'' to the pathology that develops from restricted feeding together with access to an activity wheel.

These investigators have attempted to determine more precisely the cause of activity-stress ulcers. They determined that animals showed a marked fall in body temperature in the later stages of the experiment, coincident with ulcer formation (Paré, 1977a). Since a decrease in body temperature can be a stimulus for acid secretion, they measured gastric acid (Paré, 1977b). However, they determined that acid secretion was low in later stages of the experiment, when severe gastric lesions were present, so that activity-stress ulcers are not caused by hypersecretion of gastric acid. Recently investigators have discovered that gastric pathology is but one aspect of a pervasive and extensive constellation of pathology that develops in animals exposed to the deprivation–activity treatment (Hara & Ogawa, 1981; Lima, Hell, Timo-Iaria, Scivoletto, Dolnikoff, & Pupo, 1981). In fact, many such animals die as a result of the treatment, and death may not be attributable to gastric pathology but to other causes (Natelson, 1982). The hypothesis presently offered by these investigators to explain what occurs is that deprived active animals eventually exhaust themselves metabolically because of the high energy demand of their activity. The gastric pathology may be one expression of this collapse, with lesions developing because the mucosa fails to regenerate, becomes ischemic, and allows back diffusion of acid.

In evaluating the significance of this paradigm from a behavioral and psychological perspective, there is little doubt that motor activity is an important causal ingredient for development of gastric pathology in the experimental paradigm under discussion. However, for the investigator interested in behavioral and psychological influences on gastric pathology, there remains a fundamental question about this phenomenon: Is the influence of behavior (primarily motor activity) on gastric pathology that is seen in this paradigm at all relevant to how such behavior normally affects gastrointestinal disease? For example, if one were to find that motor activity proportionately decreases mucosal blood flow and thereby proportionately increases vulnerability to gastric pathology, then the activity-stress model could well be an extreme expression of a normal process and could be quite valuable for exploring a behavioral influence on gastric pathology that is relevant to normal circumstances. But if, for example, one were to discover that the experimental paradigm somehow generates intense activity, and that this activity eventually produces metabolic exhaustion that leads to gastric pathology, then the activity is merely a part of the manipulation to produce pathology. In this case, motor activity would be little different from a drug or surgical manipulation—a tool to induce pathology—and the link between motor activity and gastric pathology would not describe a behavioral relationship of any validity or relevance to normal development of the disease. Thus, it has yet to be determined whether this intriguing paradigm reveals a behavioral or psychological influence on gastrointestinal disease, or whether it should actually be classified as a direct physiological manipulation that happens to involve behavior as part of the technique.

Electric Shock

The final method for generating gastric pathology to be discussed in this chapter is to subject an animal to electric shock. This method, which can be applied to a conscious, physiologically normal animal, has been used both by itself and in combination with manipulations that predispose the animal to lesion development (such as mild restraint). Electric shock produces little if any constraint on behavioral responses. Also, of all the techniques described thus far, only electric shock can be applied to the animal for very brief, discrete periods of time and then removed relatively completely. This characteristic of shock makes it possible to study the influence of several important behavioral and psychological factors on gastric pathology, including such factors as predictability, coping responses, conflict, and aggressive behavior.

Predictability

Basic Techniques and Findings

Shock can occur randomly, without warning, in an animal's environment, or it can be preceded by some form of signal that will inform the animal that shock is imminent. Several studies have investigated the effects of giving animals unsignaled, or "unpredictable," shock, as opposed to signaled, or "predictable," shock. This chapter now examines such studies to consider their methodology and results.

In an early experiment that reported an effect on gastric lesions, Seligman (1968) was studying the behavior of animals that were pressing a lever for food. He compared the effects of introducing shock into this lever-press situation, contrasting shock that was preceded by a signal (predictable shock) with shock not preceded by a signal (unpredictable shock). The interval between shocks was varied, so that the animals could not learn a temporal discrimination to determine when shocks would occur; the animals thus depended entirely on the signal before shock to predict its occurrence. Animals given predictable (i.e., signaled) shock initially stopped pressing the lever but soon began to press it again, whereas animals given unpredictable shock completely ceased pressing the lever. After 3 weeks in the lever-press situation, the animals were sacrificed and examined for gastric lesions. Eight animals that had received unsignaled shock showed evidence of lesions, whereas no animals that had received signaled shock showed evidence of lesions.

However, because gastric lesions were not the primary focus of Seligman's experiment, factors entered this study that make the lesion results difficult to interpret. For the purpose of this chapter, this experiment enables one to consider possible confounding factors in behavioral–psychological research of gastric pathology. In this study, the animals were pressing a lever for food. Since the animals in the signaled-shock condition began pressing the lever again early in the experiment, they therefore were eating during the test. In contrast, animals receiving unsignaled shock did not press the lever during the session and therefore were not eating at this time. Because gastric lesions are reduced by food intake and food content in the stomach (e.g., Brodie & Hanson, 1960), the conditions may have led to differences in gastric lesions simply because of eating differences that took place during the course of pressing the lever.

A second factor complicating the interpretation has to do with the method by which shock was delivered to the animals. As the result of shock being delivered through a grid floor, lesion differences might have occurred because the groups actually received different amounts of shock. The reason for this is as follows: The signaled-shock group had a warning before the shock, and therefore could have made postural changes on the grid floor to reduce discomfort from the shock. Moreover, the fact that these animals tended to return to pressing the lever meant that shocks would often be received through their tough rear feet. In contrast to this, animals in the unsignaled-shock group had no warning signal to use to adjust their posture just before shock occurred. Because this group ceased pressing the lever completely, these animals were likely to have been standing with all four feet on the grid floor and thereby to have received shock through their more sensitive front feet. Thus, the lesion differences might also have been due simply to the fact that animals in the unsignaled-shock condition received more severe shocks than did the animals in the signaled-shock condition.

It is instructive to consider how these problems can be avoided. At the same time that Seligman was carrying out his study, other studies were underway that were contrasting effects of predictable and unpredictable shock with the express intent of examining pathological changes, including gastric lesions (Weiss, 1968b, 1970). As a result, these experiments were conducted so that the problems listed above would not be encountered. Figure 6.3 shows the apparatus as well as the experimental configuration of subjects used in these studies. These experiments were conducted by exposing triplets of animals (i.e., sets of three animals) to the experimental conditions simultaneously. A triplet consisted of one animal that received a signal before

FIGURE 6.3. In the upper part (A) is shown a rat in the shock chamber used for presenting predictable (signaled) shock and unpredictable (unsignaled) shock. Shock was delivered via tail electrodes. In the lower part (B) is shown a schematic representation of the experimental design. Three animals were used simultaneously, two animals receiving shock (predictable for one and unpredictable for the other) through electrodes wired in series. Reprinted by permission of the publisher from Somatic Effects of Predictable and Unpredictable Shock by J. M. Weiss, *Psychosomatic Medicine*, Vol. 32, pp. 397–408. Copyright 1970 by The American Psychosomatic Society, Inc.

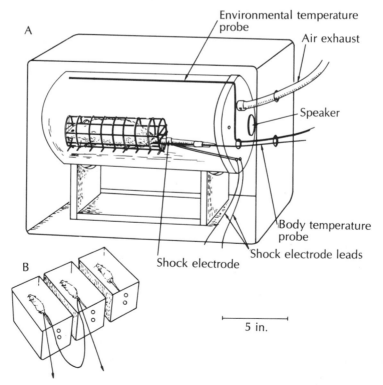

shock, one animal that received the same shocks but with the signal presented randomly with respect to shock, and a third animal that received no shock. Again, the time between shocks was varied (average interval between shocks was 1 minute) so that animals could not learn when shocks would occur, but depended entirely on the signal to predict them. The animals were maintained under these conditions for 19 hours prior to sacrifice.

The problems encountered in Seligman's study were addressed as follows: To eliminate possible differences in intake—the first problem discussed above—all subjects were deprived of food and water throughout the stress session. To eliminate possible differences in shock received by the animals in different conditions—the second problem discussed above—shock was delivered by a method that insured that all animals received the same shock, regardless of what postural changes they made.

The method by which shock was delivered should be explained at this point, because this method has been used not only in the study described here but in many subsequent studies. This technique either uses an electrode assembly (e.g., Weiss, 1967) or directly affixes the electrodes to each animal with tape; nevertheless, the basic operation and principle are the same. With this technique, two shock electrodes are affixed to the surface of the tail, and shock is delivered through these electrodes. When this is done, the bodily movements that an animal makes or the posture it assumes cannot possibly affect the animal's surface contact with the electrodes, since the electrodes are affixed to its body. Moreover, in experiments where multiple animals are shocked simultaneously—such as the study under discussion here—the electrodes of all of these "matched" animals can be wired *in series*. This means that the shock received by the matched animals is necessarily of exactly the same duration, since the animals are wired in series and thus are part of the same circuit. Moreover, because shock intensity apparently derives from the amperage of shock, and because amperage is the same everywhere in a circuit, animals wired in series also receive a shock of identical intensity. As a result, the fixed-electrode technique ensures that animals wired in series receive shocks that are all of exactly the same duration and intensity. In an experiment such as the one being described, where an animal that receives signaled shock is wired in series with an animal that receives unsignaled shock, the two conditions can be perfectly matched with respect to the shock stressor, leaving only the behavioral–psychological component of predictability as the source of difference.

Before the results of this study are discussed, it is worthwhile to note how gastric lesions were quantified. Historically, various methods have been used for the purpose. Initially, investigators noted only whether lesions were present or absent in a subject, but it soon became apparent that the pathological process was a continuum. As a result, more sophisticated methods were developed. Scales for rating pathology were introduced. Also, in an effort to make scoring less subjective than is the case with scales, lesions have been counted, thereby yielding a "number of lesions" score as the quantification of pathology. The method now in wide use is to measure either the length or area of lesions, since this measure can reflect differences that other quantification techniques may not detect (Ganguly, 1969; Sethbhakdi, Pfeiffer, & Roth, 1970). The technique employed in the predictability experiment described here was to measure the length of each lesion in the animal's stomach, add the measurements together, and thereby obtain the "total length of lesioned tissue" for each subject. This method is now in common use (e.g., Lau & Ogle, 1980).

The experiment described above showed that unpredictable shock resulted in much more severe gastric lesions than did predictable shock. Subjects given unpredictable shock showed an average of 8.9 mm of lesions, whereas subjects given predictable shock showed an average of 1.5 mm of lesions. Nonshocked control subjects showed a negligible .5 mm of lesions, on the average. Thus, when confounding factors were controlled, the difference between shock's occurring predictably or unpredictably—a psychological variable—had more influence on the severity of lesions than whether or not the shock occurred or did not occur at all. Other investigators have reported similar results (Mezinskis, Gliner, & Shemberg, 1971; Price, 1972).

The importance of the method used to deliver shock is made clear by comparing these results with those of three earlier studies. These earlier studies had examined the effects of shock predictability on loss of body weight and depression of feeding and drinking (J. P. Brady, Thornton, & de Fisher, 1962; S. B. Friedman & Ader, 1965; Paré, 1964). These studies all showed that predictable shock produced *greater* weight loss and *more* suppression of feeding and drinking than did unpredictable shock—results that seemed opposite to the findings described above, where gastric lesions were measured. The results were indeed opposite, for measurement of weight loss and intake changes in a separate study under conditions used in my experiments showed that predictable shock produced *less* weight loss and *less* suppression of intake than did unpredictable shock (Weiss, 1968b, 1970). How does one explain this difference?

In the earlier studies, shock was delivered through a grid floor, allowing for the possibility that animals could alter shock by changing bodily position. This, of course, was not possible with the use of fixed electrodes. In considering this, it seemed to me that the methodological difference in how shock was delivered might not be a trivial one, but, in fact, might completely reverse the effects of a predictability experiment. Giving shock through a grid floor could enable animals to practice "inefficient coping attempts" (i.e., responses, such as jumping, that momentarily reduced shock but subsequently were punished and/or failed to provide consistent relief from shock), and such inefficient coping attempts could result in more pathology than would occur if an animal made no coping attempts at all. Since animals given predictable shock would be better able to initiate such deleterious behavior because of a warning signal, this could explain why the early studies of weight loss had found predictable shock to be more deleterious.

Tsuda and Hirai (1976) tested this idea. In the same experiment, they compared how predictable shock and unpredictable shock affected gastric lesions when shock was delivered either through fixed electrodes or through a grid floor. When shock was given through a grid floor, predictable shock produced much more gastric pathology than did unpredictable shock, but when the shock electrodes were fixed on the tail, predictable shock produced *less* pathology than did unpredictable shock. These results make clear that the method by which shock is delivered can have important effects on the findings, and investigators should consider possible undesirable factors that may be introduced by a shock technique, particularly by grid shock.

Explaining Results of Predictability Studies

An explanation for why predictable shock produces less severe gastrointestinal lesions than unpredictable shock does can be attempted on different levels. As yet, no one has proposed physiological mechanisms to account for this effect; this is perhaps not surprising, since an explanation on this level may well be premature without a thorough understanding of the physiological mechanisms that underlie development of gastric lesions, which has not yet been achieved. However, an explanation for the effects of predictable and unpredictable shock has been suggested in terms of psychological constructs.

An explanation in terms of psychological constructs makes use of the idea that "fear and arousal" are produced by the shock. Thus, presentation of a warning stimulus prior to each shock causes that stimulus not only to signal the imminence of shock, but simultaneously to become an arousal-inducing, or fear-producing, stimulus. The arousal/fear properties of the warning stimulus develop through classical fear conditioning—that is, through association of the stimulus with the shock, (e.g., Miller, 1951). As a result, animals receiving signaled shock are subjected to a sharply fluctuating level of arousal/fear during the experiment; that is, they experience strong arousal/fear when the warning signal is present, but low to moderate arousal/fear during the majority of time when the warning signal is not present. Animals that receive unsignaled shock undergo a similar fear-conditioning process, but in this case the fear and arousal are not associated with a discrete warning signal; rather, fear and arousal are conditioned to the entire shock situation, since this whole stimulus complex is regularly associated with shock. Thus, animals that receive unsignaled shock experience relatively high arousal/fear during the entire period that they are in the shock situation. From an arousal/fear perspective, it can be said that signaled versus unsignaled shock compares the effect of chronic low to moderate arousal/fear punctuated by brief periods of very high arousal/fear (the sig-

naled-shock condition) with the effect of rather high arousal/fear all of the time (unsignaled-shock conditions).

Differences in gastric lesions produced by predictable versus unpredictable shock have been attributed to the differences in arousal/fear produced by these conditions. Seligman (1968) was the first to articulate the view that predictable (signaled) shock was less stressful, and hence produced less severe lesions, because the net amount of arousal/fear in this condition was lower than when shock was unpredictable (unsignaled). Seligman emphasized that predictable shock produced lower arousal/fear primarily because animals receiving a signal before shock are most of the time aware that shock is *not* imminent, since the warning signal is not present most of the time. He called this the "safety signal" hypothesis.

Despite the obviousness and simplicity of this hypothesis, it is quite difficult to test. This is because the "safety signal" hypothesis has a mirror-image alternative. The alternative says that the ability to predict "danger" (i.e., shock) is what makes predictability effective, rather than the ability to predict "safety" (i.e., shock absent). Virtually all experiments that one can design promise to yield results that are explained equally by both. Seligman presented no experimental tests to support his suggestion. Probably the closest to a test of this hypothesis can be found in data that was gathered for a different purpose (discussed in Weiss, 1970). While studying the effects of coping behavior, I contrasted animals receiving a single, discrete auditory signal before shock with animals receiving a much longer auditory signal that progressively increased in frequency and volume as the shock became closer. Relative to the discrete signal, this latter condition, or progressive-signal condition, supplied the animals with more information about when shock would occur but with less "safety," since the animals received a longer auditory stimulus that had been paired with the shock. Animals that received the discrete warning signal developed less severe lesions than did the animals that received the progressive signal, thus indicating that the beneficial aspect of predictability derived from the amount of safety (i.e., low arousal/fear) that predictability provided, rather than from the ability to predict the aversive event.

Coping Behavior

Basic Techniques and Findings

Another behavioral–psychological variable that has been studied using shock has been coping behavior. Experimenters have compared the effects that result when an animal can control shock (i.e., can avoid and/or escape shock) with the effects that result when an animal is unable to control the same shocks. Again, the nature of the shock stimulus makes such studies possible, because the experimenter can instantaneously remove shock from the stress situation when the animal "in control of shock" makes the appropriate, correct response.

The first study specifically addressed to this question has become one of the most widely known studies in psychosomatic medicine, the "executive-monkey" study. These data were originally published by Porter, Brady, Conrad, Mason, Galambos, and Rioch (1958) and by J. V. Brady, Porter, Conrad, and Mason (1958), and the most well-known exposition of the results appeared in *Scientific American* (J. V. Brady, 1958).

The "executive-monkey" phenomenon is based on results obtained from four pairs of monkeys. A pair of such monkeys is shown in Figure 6.4. In each pair of monkeys, one animal, called the "executive," was able to press a lever that avoided a strong unsignaled shock. Each press of the lever postponed shock onset for 20 seconds, so continued responses within 20 seconds

FIGURE 6.4. An "executive" or avoidance–escape monkey (left) and a yoked monkey (right) in primate chairs during the avoidance procedure. (From Brady, J. V., Porter, R. W., Conrad, D. G., & Mason, J. W. Avoidance behavior and the development of gastroduodenal ulcers. *Journal of the Experimental Analysis of Behavior*, 1958, *1*, 69–72. Copyright 1958 by the Society for the Experimental Analysis of Behavior, Inc. Reprinted by permission.)

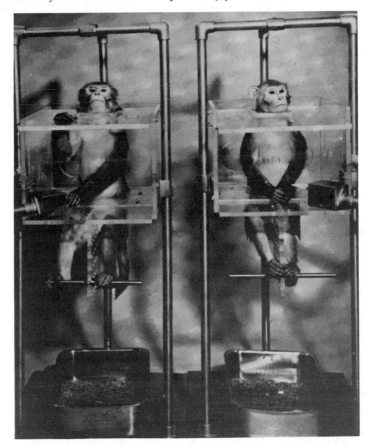

of the last response could postpone shock indefinitely. Any failure to respond within 20 seconds resulted in a shock. This procedure, in which responses postpone shocks that are otherwise presented at regular intervals with no warning signal preceding them, is called an "unsignaled" or "Sidman" avoidance schedule. The other monkey in each pair, called the "yoked monkey," simply received shock whenever the executive monkey failed to postpone the shock. The yoked monkey in each pair therefore received the same shocks as the executive monkey but had no control over them.

In all four pairs, the executive monkeys developed duodenal ulcers and died, whereas the yoked monkeys evidenced no pathology when they were examined. Actually, what occurred was that executive monkeys began dying in the apparatus, and the lesions were subsequently discovered on autopsy; yoked animals were then sacrificed, and no lesions were found in them. It was not until the last two pairs of monkeys were placed into this experiment that the investigators were clearly aware that the shock-avoidance procedure they were using was apt to cause duodenal ulcers. The excitement generated by these results can be sensed from the fact that the production of duodenal lesions by the shock-avoidance method used appeared to represent a genuine discovery.

Unfortunately, subsequent attempts to replicate the executive-monkey experiment failed. When other experimental conditions were attempted, these also did not succeed. A subsequent experiment manipulated the duration of the stress session relative to the rest period but found no duodenal lesions. Other laboratories experienced a similar lack of success. Foltz and Millett (1964) reported that they could not reproduce the original results; in fact, the only pathology that they observed appeared in a yoked animal. For over a decade, the executive-monkey phenomenon seemed to be an anomaly.

In 1968, I published a report that rats able to control shock (avoidance–escape animals) developed less severe gastric erosions than did yoked rats that received the same shocks without having control over them. In this study, (Weiss, 1968a), as in the study of predictability discussed earlier, matched triplets of animals were again exposed to experimental conditions simultaneously. A triplet consisted of one animal that could avoid or escape from shock by performing a selected response; a second animal that had no control over shock, but was simply shocked whenever the first animal received shock; and a third control animal that was not shocked. A signal was presented (to all animals) 10 seconds before the delivery of shock, so that the shock was preceded by a warning signal in this experiment. Figure 6.5 shows the triplet arrangement.

As stated above, this experiment found that avoidance–escape animals developed less severe gastric lesions than did yoked animals. Moreover, the results again showed the importance of behavioral–psychological factors. The animals that could control shock developed an average of only 1.7 mm of lesions, compared with 4.5 mm of lesions in the yoked animals; the non-

Avoidance-escape Yoked Control

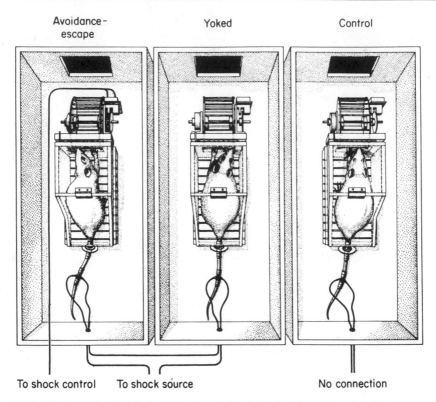

To shock control   To shock source   No connection

FIGURE 6.5. A matched triplet in a study of coping behavior. At left is the avoidance–escape animal, whose wheel is wired in series to the shock control. At center is the yoked animal, whose tail electrodes are wired in series with the avoidance–escape subject but whose wheel turns have no effect on shock. At right is the unshocked control subject.

shocked animals developed a negligible .5 mm of lesions. The avoidance–escape animals were therefore more similar to the nonshocked controls than they were to their yoked, helpless partners, who had received exactly the same shock. Thus, it was seen that control of shock was a more important variable than whether or not shock occurred for the animals.

These results were, of course, opposite to the findings of the executive-monkey study, in which the avoidance–escape, or executive, animal had developed the more severe pathology. Unlike the studies of predictability discussed earlier, differences in the method of shock delivery could not account for these opposite effects, since the monkeys, like the rats, could not alter shock by changing bodily position, and moreover received very few shocks in any event. As a result, a subsequent experiment (Weiss, 1971a) examined another possibility—namely, that differences in the warning given before shock were responsible for these opposite findings. Whereas the avoidance–escape rats (Weiss, 1968a) had been given a warning signal before shock, the executive monkeys had not had any warning signal. Therefore, an experiment was conducted in which some triplets of animals (avoidance–escape, yoked, and nonshocked) were given a warning signal before shock, whereas other triplets received no warning signal before shock. Also, a third tone condition (called the "progressive-signal") condition was included in which triplets received a complex warning signal before shock, which formed a kind of "external clock." Except for the difference in warning signals, the conditions for all triplets were the same. The results of this experiment are shown in Figure 6.6. The idea that the presence or absence of a warning signal before shock might reverse the effects of coping behavior was not supported; it can be seen that the avoidance–escape animals developed less severe gastric lesions than did yoked animals in all warning-signal conditions.

Other studies also appeared at about the same time indicating that rats in control of shock developed less severe lesions than did rats not in control of shock. Gliner (1972) combined coping behavior and predictability differences. He gave all rats uncontrollable shock, but allowed one group to choose for itself whether the shock would be preceded by a signal or not. This group developed the least severe lesions, with progressively more lesions developing in groups that were unable (1) to choose a warning signal or not, and (2) either to choose a signal or to predict shock by a signal. Also, Moot,

FIGURE 6.6. The median total length of gastric lesions for the nonshocked, avoidance–escape, and yoked groups in the various signal conditions. For some triplets, a warning signal preceded shock (signal); for others, a series of signals forming an external clock preceded shock (progressive signal); and for others, no warning signal preceded shock (no signal). (From Weiss, J. M. Effects of coping behavior in different warning-signal conditions on stress pathology in rats. *Journal of Comparative and Physiological Psychology*, 1971, 77, 1–13. Copyright 1971 by the American Psychological Association. Reprinted by permission of the publisher.)

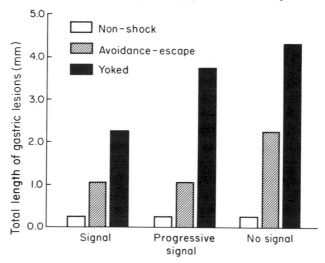

Cebulla, and Crabree (1970) showed that animals that could terminate a shock delivered while they were pressing a lever for food developed significantly fewer gastric lesions than did animals unable to terminate the shock but given shock of the same duration.

Explaining Results of Coping-Behavior Studies

Although the study described above (Weiss, 1971a) failed to show that a warning signal before shock could reverse effects of shock controllability, ultimately it resulted in a formulation that offered an explanation for why the executive monkeys in the 1950s study developed more ulcers than yoked monkeys, whereas avoidance–escape animals usually develop less gastric pathology than yoked animals. Using behavioral and psychological constructs, this formulation attempts to explain what makes coping behavior effective.

Analyzing in detail the relationship between behavior and gastric lesions in his experimental conditions, I found that gastric lesions were a function of two variables. First, gastric lesions were found to increase as the number of responses that animals made increased. On reflection, this was not a surprising observation. When an animal is presented with a stressful stimulus, the animal will make coping attempts. Thus, gastric lesions, or "ulcerogenic stress," was found to be a function of the number of such coping attempts or responses that an animal made in a stressful situation. (This does not mean that the responses themselves *caused* lesions, but simply that responding and lesion severity could be seen to increase together—that they were correlated.) The severity of lesions, however, did not relate to responding alone; it was observed to be equally related to a second variable: the informational feedback that animals received immediately after coping attempts. If responses immediately produced appropriate feedback—that is, if responses immediately brought about stimuli that had no connection with the stressor—then the ulcerogenic condition did not occur. On the other hand, if responses failed to produce such stimuli, then ulcerogenic stress did occur. I referred to the appropriate feedback, which consisted of stress-free stimuli, as "relevant feedback." A nonulcerogenic coping attempt, then, was one that immediately produced relevant feedback. The second functional relationship stated that the greater the amount of relevant feedback that resulted from coping attempts, the fewer the gastric lesions.

It was possible to express these relationships in mathematical form, which is shown in Figure 6.7. This model is generated from the two functional relationships described in the previous paragraph: that is, that gastric lesions increase as the number of responses increases, and that gastric lesions decrease as the amount of relevant feedback increases. The resultant function is a plane; in any condition where the number of responses that an animal makes and the amount of relevant feedback it receives can be determined, the severity of gastric lesions that should develop can be predicted by taking the point of intersection and projecting up to the plane. The height of the plane above the base of the model defines the severity of lesions that can be expected.

This formulation suggests why animals that are in control of stressful situations develop less severe lesions than those of animals that have no control. Because animals that have no control over a stressor cannot, by definition, produce any relevant feedback by responding, the amount of relevant feedback for such animals is necessarily fixed at zero. These animals therefore develop lesions in direct correspondence to the number of responses that

FIGURE 6.7. This three-dimensional figure describes the proposed relationship between responses, feedback, and gastrointestinal lesions (ulceration). The relationship is a plane showing how the two independent variables, responses and feedback, are related to the dependent variable, gastric lesions or "ulceration." The arrows show how this plane is used. Where the number of responses made and the amount of feedback obtained for such responding intersect, the amount of ulceration is determined by the height of the plane above this point. (For ease of reading this figure, responses and feedback are labeled across the axes in the foreground. These labels are customarily placed along the axes in the background, which are parallel to the ones bearing the labels. It therefore should be noted that feedback designations apply to the axis from Point A to the intersection of the three axes, and response designations apply to the axes from Point B to the intersection.) (From Weiss, J. M. Effects of coping behavior in different warning-signal conditions on stress pathology in rats. *Journal of Comparative and Physiological Psychology*, 1971, 77, 1–13. Copyright 1971 by the American Psychological Association. Reprinted by permission of the publisher.)

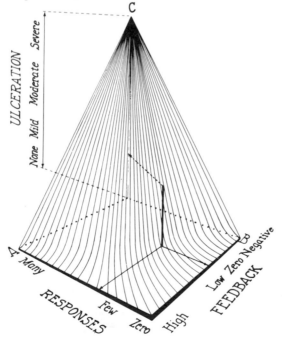

they emit, and since the plane (see Figure 6.7) shows considerable elevation above the zero feedback continuum, these animals develop severe lesions. In contrast, avoidance–escape animals generally produce relevant feedback that is greater than zero; since the elevation of the plane is considerably lower when feedback exceeds zero, these animals therefore develop less severe lesions. The results for avoidance–escape and yoked groups that are shown in Figure 6.6 are presented in Figure 6.8 in relation to this formulation.

The formulation can also explain the executive-monkey results. Since the monkeys developed duodenal ulcers and the rats developed gastric erosions, this explanation obviously rests on the assumption that the psychological and behavioral principles utilized affect both types of lesions similarly. The explanation is as follows: Careful inspection of the conditions used in the executive-monkey experiment revealed that the monkey in each pair that was made the executive was chosen for this group because it showed a higher rate of responding on an initial pretest than did the other subject, which was made its yoked partner (see J. V. Brady *et al.*, 1958). Thus, executive monkeys

FIGURE 6.8. Results from Figure 6.6 presented in relation to the model shown in Figure 6.7. For each group that received shock, the amount of ulceration (height of bar) is shown at the point where responding and feedback for that group intersect. (From Weiss, J. M. Effects of coping behavior in different warning-signal conditions on stress pathology in rats. *Journal of Comparative and Physiological Psychology*, 1971, *77*, 1–13. Copyright 1971 by the American Psychological Association. Reprinted by permission of the publisher.)

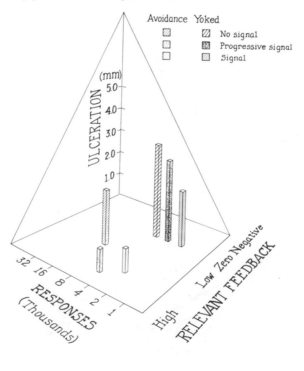

were selected for a higher rate of responding than that of yoked subjects, and therefore, according to the formulation, were more likely to develop lesions than their yoked partners were. Moreover, the Sidman (unsignaled) avoidance schedule provided the executive animals with a relatively low amount of relevant feedback, since there were no external warning signals to be terminated by correct responses. This combination of factors—a high rate of responding and a low amount of relevant feedback—is specified by the formulation to be optimal for development of lesions. Examination of a similar population of avoidance–escape and yoked pairs of rats, in which the avoidance–escape animals were selected for higher rates of responding than those of yoked subjects, revealed that the avoidance–escape animals developed significantly more severe gastric lesions than those of yoked animals in a Sidman-type avoidance condition (Weiss, 1971b). Thus, one can conclude that the executive-monkey study represented an unusual situation in which the normally beneficial effect of having control over a stressor was not obtained, but nevertheless generated a result that was lawful and readily explicable in accordance with the formulation shown in Figure 6.7.

Subsequent Studies
Several subsequent experiments have produced results that are consistent with the formulation described above. Tsuda and Hirai (1975) showed that avoidance–escape animals normally develop less severe lesions than those of yoked animals, but that avoidance–escape animals can be made to develop more severe lesions than those of yoked animals by increasing the amount of avoidance–escape responding and decreasing relevant feedback for responding. Barbaree and Harding (1973) reported that avoidance–escape animals that responded at a very high rate on a Sidman (unsignaled-shock) schedule developed more lesions than did matched yoked animals. Goesling, Buchholz, and Carreira (1974) conversely lowered the activity of avoidance–escape animals by requiring them to be inactive in order to control shock, and found that three of 15 avoidance–escape subjects developed lesions under such conditions, while 13 of 15 yoked subjects did so.

Finally, a note should be added about an ambitious experiment that attempted to develop chronic lesions in monkeys (Natelson, 1977). A major problem in testing any explanation of the executive-monkey phenomenon is that chronic lesions have not been obtainable in monkeys since the original report. Natelson therefore attempted to produce chronic lesions for monkeys by exposing them to conditions designed to be highly stressful. The experiment consisted of three stages beginning with random unavoidable shocks, progressing to unsignaled-shock avoidance–escape (Sidman) sessions, and concluding with the use of several conflict (punishment) paradigms. Stomach pathology was assessed throughout all phases of the experiment by endoscopy carried out twice weekly. Of the eight monkeys studied, one developed no lesions, four developed gastric lesions, and three developed duodenal lesions. In all cases, however, the lesions were short-lived, disappearing in less than a week; in no case was a lesion classifiable as a chronic ulcer. Lesions were seen more frequently during the conflict condition toward the end of the experiment than in the earlier stages. The investigator reported that there was some tendency for animals with higher response rates to show more pathology than animals with low response rates, but this relationship was quite weak. Natelson's study is of importance in that it employed sophisticated behavioral techniques and continual monitoring of gastric pathology. The experiment confirms that, unfortunately, the executive-monkey population was obviously highly susceptible to duodenal ulcers for reasons that are presently unknown, and that such susceptibility does not characterize monkeys now generally used in experimentation. Consequently, a behavioral–psychological model that will reproduce duodenal ulcer remains to be developed.

Conflict

Basic Techniques and Findings
Another behavioral–psychological variable that has been studied has been conflict. Conflict was, in fact, the first behavioral–psychological variable whose influence on gastric pathology was studied experimentally. Interest in studying conflict was probably motivated by the fact that early psychosomatic formulations regarding ulcers, notably the formulations of Alexander (1934), emphasize the importance of conflict. As in the case of other behavioral–psychological variables, the development of studies of conflict illustrates various problems encountered in research, and the progression shows how investigators eventually overcame them.

The initial experimental studies of conflict were carried out principally by Sawrey, Weisz, and Conger, and were published between 1956 and 1958. In these studies, a conflict was established in experimental animals between hunger and an aversive situation. Animals lived in a box, such as the one shown in Figure 6.9, having a food container at one end and a water tube at the other. The floor, made up of a grid of bars, was roughly divided into three sections; the two end sections adjacent to the food and water were electrically charged. Thus, the animal could remain safely in the center section of the box, but if it attempted to procure either food or water, it would receive a shock in doing so. In the usual experimental protocol, the animals were subjected to these conditions for 47 of every 48 hours; during the one remaining hour, the animal could eat or drink without being shocked for doing so. In most studies, animals were maintained in these conditions for 30 days prior to sacrifice.

The first report of this method was made by Sawrey and Weisz (1956). They simply compared a group of animals exposed to this conflict condition with a group of control animals that were deprived of food and water for

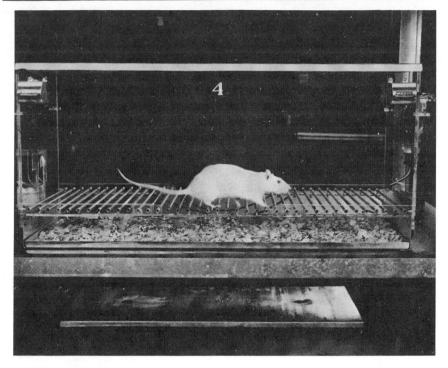

FIGURE 6.9. Apparatus and subject as used in a "conflict" experiment. Food is available at one end of the chamber and water at the other end, but the grid floor in these areas is electrically charged. (From Ader, R. Susceptibility to gastric lesions in the rat. *Journal of Neuropsychiatry*, 1963, 4, 399–408. Reprinted by permission.)

the same periods of time that the conflict condition was in effect. Gastric lesions were found in animals exposed to conflict, but not in those exposed to the control condition. However, because the control condition did not include shock, it was not apparent that conflict was responsible for this difference; the effect might have occurred without conflict simply from exposure to food deprivation and shock or even to shock alone.

Subsequent studies (Sawrey, Conger, & Turrell, 1956; Weisz, 1957) attempted to correct this inadequacy and also to evaluate the importance of the many factors included in this experimental situation. These factors included conflict, shock, hunger, and thirst. Table 6.1 shows the results reported by Sawrey *et al.* (1956) for the various conditions that they examined. They and Weisz (1957) found that animals made hungry and thirsty and exposed to conflict as described by Sawrey and Weisz (1956) developed more gastric lesions than did animals exposed to any other experimental condition. Most important, animals in the conflict condition developed more severe lesions than those of "yoked" animals, which were also made hungry and thirsty and were shocked whenever a matched animal in the conflict sit-

TABLE 6.1. Incidence of Gastric Lesions under Various Experimental Conditions

EXPERIMENTAL CONDITION[a]	NUMBER OF ANIMALS	PERCENT WITH LESIONS	NUMBER OF LESIONS	MEAN WEIGHT LOSS (g)
C H S T	50	76	434	99.5
NC H S T	20	30	44	79.8
NC H S NT	10	40	26	75.1
NC H NS T	10	0	0	54.7
NC NH S T	10	0	0	42.9
NC H NS NT	10	20	4	54.6
NC NH NS T	10	0	0	25.4
NC NH S NT	10	0	0	10.7
NC NH NS NT	10	0	0	29.2[b]

Note. From Sawrey, W. L., Conger, J. J., & Turrell, E. S. An experimental investigation of the role of psychological factors in the production of gastric ulcers in rats. *Journal of Comparative and Physiological Psychology,* 1956, *49,* 457–461. Copyright 1956 by the American Psychological Association. Reprinted by permission of the publisher.)

[a]S—shock; NS—not shocked; T—thirst; NT—not thirsty; H—hunger; NH—not hungry; C—conflict; NC—no conflict.

[b]This group gained weight.

uation received shock. Because these "yoked" animals received similar aversive conditions to those in the conflict situation (deprivation and shock) but did not experience the conflict, the difference between these two groups indicated that conflict could contribute to lesion formation. The other major finding was that groups made hungry (with or without thirst and with or without shock) often developed lesions, which indicated that gastric lesions were highly dependent upon food deprivation.

These studies were quite elegant and thorough for their time; nevertheless, serious questions about the interpretation of these studies have arisen since their completion. First, the type of lesion generally produced in these experiments was not an erosion in the lower, glandular portion of the stomach, such as Selye had observed, but was a lesion that appeared in the upper, rumenal portion of the stomach. This was the type of lesion observed by Shay and his collaborators (1945) following ligation of the pyloric opening at the base of the stomach. Shay's experiments led him to conclude that these rumenal lesions were produced when acid gastric juice came into prolonged contact with the upper, rumenal portion of the stomach, which occurred in his studies when the pylorus was closed. The work of Shay and subsequent researchers has made clear that the development of similar rumenal lesions could also occur as the result of severe and prolonged food deprivation in an unligated stomach; apparently the prolonged absence of food contents from the stomach could also bring acidic gastric juice into sufficient contact with the rumen to cause lesions. Because the type of lesion developed in these early conflict studies is now recognized as highly dependent on food deprivation, it must be considered that the lesions found in these experiments could well have been a secondary consequence of the severe food deprivation that took place during the experiments. Thus, the different experimental conditions might well have had their effects on lesion development because they produced corresponding reductions in food intake. In other words, the various conditions may have caused animals to reduce the food intake by some amount, and the animals in each condition then developed lesions depending upon how little they ate. The correlation between weight loss in each group and lesion development (see Table 6.1) is consistent with this possibility.

The other difficulty with these studies has already been discussed; it pertains to the use of grid shock. Sawrey *et al.* (1956) had been quite ingenious in attempting to equate the shock for each animal in the conflict condition and its yoked partner by wiring the grids for these two animals *in series*. Electronically, the two animals therefore appeared as two resistors in the same circuit, so that the shock they received was of the same duration and intensity. But despite this, the two animals could still receive the shock through very different areas of their bodies, so that the procedure used was not adequate for establishing that both animals received the same shock. For example, a yoked animal might learn to lie on its side so that it hardly felt the shock, whereas the conflict animal would necessarily receive the shock through its sensitive front feet as it moved toward the food. Thus, differences between these groups might have been due to differences in the amount of shock received.

As a result of these criticisms, research on the influence of conflict diminished after publication of the original studies. It was not until 1969 that an experiment appeared that could not be questioned on the same basis as the original conflict experiments. At this time, Lovibond published an account of a study in which he immobilized animals and, while they were immobilized, presented them with stimuli that had been previously paired with food and shock. His results showed that simultaneous presentation of the stimuli for food and for shock resulted in more lesions than did sequential presentation of these stimuli. Lovibond concluded that the presentation of stimuli signaling conflicting drive states could exacerbate gastric lesions. Lovibond's study does not encounter problems of prolonged food deprivation, because the lesions were produced by an acute immobilization procedure, as described previously. Also, the different groups should not have received different amounts of shock, because shock was administered to all animals under similar conditions before the immobilization procedure. On the other hand, because these animals were immobilized and therefore unable actually to perform appropriate approach and avoidance behaviors, the experiment examined only limited aspects of the behavior of normal animals.

A later experiment (Weiss, 1971c) appears to overcome these problems. Rats were first exposed to a situation in which each animal was required to respond (by wheel turning) to avoid or escape a train of shocks to its tail. After 24 hours, the conditions were slightly altered; the animal henceforth was given a pulse of shock whenever it performed the wheel-turning response, so that responses that avoided or escaped from the train of shocks now also resulted in a brief shock to the tail. Thus, the animal now had to accept a small shock in order to avoid or escape a much larger shock. This conflict condition was maintained for 24 more hours, at the end of which time gastric pathology was determined. A yoked animal matched to each "conflict" animal was subjected to all experimental stimuli simultaneously, receiving the same shocks as the conflict subject did throughout all phases of the experiment; however, its behavior had no effect on the occurrence of shocks, so that it was not "in conflict." The problems described above were overcome, because (1) food motivation was not involved, so that all animals were totally deprived throughout the 48-hour experiment; and (2) "conflict" animals (i.e., avoidance–escape) and "nonconflict" animals (i.e., yoked) were shocked through fixed tail electrodes wired in series, so they received identical shocks that could not be altered by changing bodily position.

It was found that animals in the conflict condition developed considerably more severe gastric lesions than those of matched yoked animals. For animals in the conflict condition, the median total length of gastric lesions was twice as large (5.8 mm) as for the matched yoked subjects (2.9 mm). The lesions found were all in the lower, glandular portion of the stomach, as would be expected in a study where prolonged and differential food deprivation was not involved. Some of the animals in the conflict situation developed such severe lesions that they were not likely to have survived for a much longer time had the condition persisted. The results indicated that a conflict condition is one of the most pathogenic of behavioral–psychological circumstances.

Explaining Results of Conflict Studies

Little attention has been devoted to explaining why experimentally induced conflict has the pathogenic effects that it does. The formulation presented earlier (see "Explaining Results of Coping-Behavior Studies," above), however, does generate an explanation (Weiss, 1971c). This explanation attributes the highly pathogenic effects of conflict to the very low relevant feedback for responding that occurs in this condition. As explained earlier, the amount of relevant feedback for a coping attempt (or response) is determined by the amount of nonstress stimuli that occurs following the coping attempt. Since animals in a conflict situation are forced to approach stressful stimuli, many coping attempts actually bring about (i.e., are followed by) stressor-related stimuli, rather than bringing about stimuli not associated with the stressor. In my conflict experiment (Weiss, 1971c), for example, each avoidance-escape response was followed by a pulse of shock. When a coping attempt is followed by stress-related stimuli, the relevant feedback for the coping attempt is even lower than zero, since the coping attempt actually *brings about* stressor stimuli. Thus, conflict conditions are characterized by a negative amount of relevant feedback for responding. Responses in a conflict situation therefore produce even smaller amounts of relevant feedback than do responses in a condition where an animal has no control over the stressor, which produces a zero amount of relevant feedback. As a result, coping attempts in a conflict situation should produce considerable pathology. Consistent with this hypothesis, the severity of pathology that was seen in animals exposed to a conflict situation was directly related to the number of coping attempts that they made (Weiss, 1971c).

Aggression

One study has examined the effects of shock-induced fighting on development of gastric lesions. This study (Weiss, Pohorecky, Salman, & Gruenthal, 1976) showed that administration of tail shock to two animals in the same apparatus, so that they would fight in response to shock, caused these animals to develop less severe gastric lesions than those of animals that received the same shocks while alone.

The design of this experiment is shown in Figure 6.10. The experimental design employed 10 animals used simultaneously. Two of the animals, those in the "fight" condition, were shocked together in a cage of the type used by Weiss (1971a) but of double width. These animals fought vigorously with each other in response to the tail shock. To assess the effects of fighting, these animals were compared with two animals that received identical tail shocks but were each shocked alone ("alone" condition). The average amount of lesioned tissue found in animals that fought was 3.2 mm, whereas the average in animals shocked alone was 8.2 mm. However, although "alone" and "fight" animals received identical shocks, they differed in the amount of stressor stimuli they received because the "fight" animals engaged in physical combat, which did not occur for the "alone" animals; as a result, any differences in gastric lesions between these conditions might be attributable to a difference in physical stressor stimuli, rather than to behavioral-psychological factors involved in aggression. To assess this, we included another pair of animals shocked together in a double-width cage but with a grid of Plexiglas bars between the two animals ("barrier" condition); these animals reared up and made aggressive responses toward each other, but could not make physical contact because of the Plexiglas grid between them. Such animals showed a reduced extent of lesions (3.9 mm) similar to that

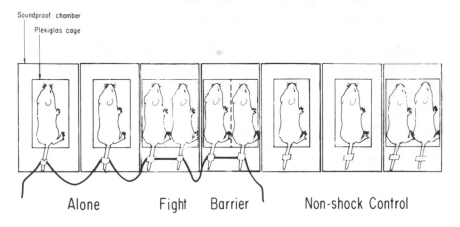

Soundproof chamber

Plexiglas cage

Alone   Fight   Barrier   Non-shock Control

FIGURE 6.10. The experimental configuration used to study effects of aggression on gastric pathology. Six animals received shock simultaneously through fixed electrodes wired in series; two animals received shock in individual cages ("alone" condition), two animals received shock in a double-width cage so that they fought with one another ("fight" condition), and two animals received shock in a double-width cage having a barrier between them that enabled fighting behavior to occur but prevented physical contact between the animals ("barrier" condition). Four nonshocked control animals, two alone and two placed together, were also included in the design. (From Weiss, J. M., Pohorecky, L. A., Salman, S., & Gruenthal, M. Attenuation of gastric lesions by psychological aspects of aggression in rats. *Journal of Comparative and Physiological Psychology*, 1976, 90, 252–259. Copyright 1976 by the American Psychological Association. Reprinted by permission of the publisher.)

of the animals that were allowed to fight; this indicated that the reduction in gastric lesions was not the result of the physical contact that took place during the fight, but of the behavioral responses involved in making the aggressive gestures toward the other animal. As shown in Figure 6.10, the experimental design included four nonshocked control animals, consisting of animals placed in the double-width apparatus and also of animals that were alone; these animals developed no lesions.

Although the results described above point to the importance of fighting behavior in reducing lesions, it remains possible that the foregoing results could be explained simply because shocking two animals in the same location reduces lesions. If true, this would explain why less severe lesions were found both in the "fight" and "barrier" conditions in comparison to the "alone" condition. A second experiment was carried out to evaluate this possibility. This experiment found that if two animals were shocked in the same place, but with a solid, opaque barrier between them so that they did not make aggressive gestures toward one another, they developed gastric lesions as severe as those of animals shocked alone. Animals that fought again showed less severe lesions than "alone" animals. Thus, the presence of two animals receiving shock in the same location was not sufficient to produce the effect; the aggressive response was apparently the significant factor.

COMMENT ON THE NATURE OF ANIMAL MODELS

The preceding section concludes the description of models used in the study of gastric lesions. At this point, a final comment is made on the nature of such models. An investigator newly interested in this field of study will find in his reading many evaluations and criticisms of the various models that have been, and continue to be, used. Examining these evaluations, he will often find that they point out the shortcomings of any model, so that he may become disaffected with this approach. However, if the investigator retains his perspective, he need not develop a negativistic attitude.

It is well to understand the shortcomings of a model, but it is also well to be aware that, by definition, all animal models must have shortcomings. The only model that will totally reproduce the human disorder, particularly when one is concerned with behavioral and psychological influences, is the human disorder itself. Standards that require a model to duplicate the human disorder will, rather than improve the model, essentially make it impossible to construct any suitable model at all.

The purpose of any model is to be useful. An investigator will do well to keep in mind that the value of any model depends upon the use the investigator has for it. In the past, most investigators interested in studying gastrointestinal diseases have been concerned with developing direct interventions to treat gastrointestinal disorders, usually surgical or pharmacological techniques. Consequently, in order to judge the effectiveness of their treatments, these investigators were interested in producing, as nearly as possible, the same pathology as that found in the human gastrointestinal tract. Because these investigators were concerned with reproducing pathology and were not particularly interested in causing disease in a normal manner, many of the techniques they used have definite drawbacks for or are frankly inapplicable to behavioral–psychological study, as has been noted in reviewing techniques in this chapter. This, however, does not make these models poor ones; they were developed for a specific purpose and should be judged with respect to how well they have accomplished that purpose.

This same perspective should be adopted when evaluating models for behavioral–psychological study. Perhaps the most important point one can make in this regard is that, whereas previous investigators often sought to duplicate human pathology by whatever means for the purpose described above, investigators who are interested in behavioral and psychological influences on disease may be less interested in precise reproduction of the pathology seen in humans. Since these investigators are interested in behavioral and psychological influences on disease, they may well learn just as much by studying development of a pathology in experimental animals that differs from the "target" pathology in humans, providing that the pathology seen in the animal model develops through similar physiological processes, or even similar behavioral–psychological processes, to those that underlie the pathology of interest in humans. For the investigators' purpose, what is important is to reproduce the influence of behavioral–psychological factors on those physiological processes involved in generating the human pathology; the particular pathology that results in an animal in the course of such studies is of less consequence.

In summary, it is well to remember that a model that is perfectly suitable for one purpose may not be suitable for another, and that the value of a model must be judged in terms of the purpose for which it is used.

IMPLICATIONS OF EXPERIMENTAL FINDINGS IN GASTROINTESTINAL PATHOLOGY—HIGH ACTIVITY (OR REACTIVITY) AS A BEHAVIORAL MARKER FOR SUSCEPTIBILITY TO DISEASE?

Although the intent of this chapter has been to describe the methodology used to study behavioral–psychological influences on pathology, I conclude by briefly considering some implications of the actual findings from the studies described in this chapter.

One finding in particular emerges persistently from behavioral and psychological studies of gastrointestinal pathology. This finding is that gastrointestinal pathology is related to high levels of motor activity, particularly when the activity is seen in response to a stressful or challenging situation. Each of the stress-environmental techniques discussed in detail in this chapter independently suggests this relationship. When immobilization was used as a lesion-inducing technique, gastric lesions were found to be more severe in highly active than in less active animals (Glavin, 1982). Also, lesions were more severe if animals were immobilized in the dark, when they were usually highly active (Ader, 1964). In addition, in the studies where animals were selectively bred for lesion susceptibility in response to immobilization, susceptible animals were more active than nonsusceptible animals (Sines, 1961; Sines et al., 1963). Similarly, the technique of prolonged food deprivation suggests this same relationship. This technique has produced the "activity-stress ulcer" paradigm. Motor activity has been shown to be critical for development of gastric lesions in this paradigm (Paré, 1975), although, as noted, the issue of whether activity plays a normal role in this context remains to be established. Finally, studies that have used electric shock to induce lesions have similarly found activity (in the form of "amount of responding" or "coping attempts") to be related to the development of gastric lesions (Weiss, 1971a, 1971b, 1971c). In summary, different investigators, often using different experimental situations and working from rather different perspectives, have accumulated evidence that converges to indicate that a high level of motor activity (or, perhaps more accurately, "motor reactivity") is related to a high incidence of or susceptibility to gastric pathology.

One reason that the experimentally observed correlation between activity and gastric pathology is so intriguing is that it may be an analogue of what is observed in many human ulcer patients. For many years, medical practitioners have seen the person who develops an ulcer as likely to be a hard-driving, relentless individual (e.g., Cushing, 1932). If this concept has validity, it seems quite possible that the high-activity, lesion-susceptible animal would be related to this sort of individual. In this regard, I vividly remember my first psychotherapeutic interview with an ulcer patient. This patient, a man in his late 30s, had recently undergone surgery to extirpate an ulcer. In the interview, the patient responded to my rather nondescript opening statement ("Tell me about what brings you to see me") by talking nonstop for 1 hour, precluding any verbal intervention on my part. If verbal output can be considered a measure of response rate or activity, it is hard to imagine how anyone could have scored higher than this man.

This patient was also one of my most salient treatment failures. I was only able to maintain contact with him for a few months, during which he missed the majority of his therapy appointments and finally terminated after missing six consecutive sessions. It is with considerable sadness and frustration that I must report that this young man died 3 years later of a heart attack. Uncomfortable as this incident is to recall, it nevertheless brings to the fore a second point: The high-activity pattern may be related not only to gastrointestinal disease, but also to other diseases, such as cardiovascular pathology. Investigators interested in identifying risk factors for cardiovascular disease have pointed to the Type A personality in humans; such individuals manifest continual activity and lack the ability to relax (e.g., M. Friedman & Rosenman, 1959; Glass, Snyder, & Hollis, 1974; Jenkins, 1971). Thus, what may be seen in the high-activity animal (or individual) is not merely susceptibility to gastrointestinal pathology, but a behavioral manifestation denoting susceptibility to a variety of diseases.

High Activity—Why Is It a Marker
for Susceptibility to Disease?

Why does a high rate of behavioral activity, particularly in an experimental context, correlate with development of gastrointestinal lesions and perhaps with the development of other diseases as well? This question is clearly an important one; the answer to it is likely to tell us a great deal about fundamental mechanisms by which psychological and behavioral variables influence disease. In seeking this answer, it is well to remember that the correlation described above has only recently become evident through the coalescence of years of research; consequently, at present, we have only the most meager insight into the answer. Nevertheless, some basic observations can be made.

Despite the rudimentary state of present knowledge, it is evident that high levels of motor activity are related to development of gastrointestinal lesions and perhaps to other pathology for one of the following two reasons:

Either motor activity itself initiates processes that lead to disease, or there is a common physiological mechanism that, when activated, initiates *both* motor activity and processes leading to disease.

High Activity Causes Disease

The first of the two alternatives—that motor activity itself initiates processes leading to disease—sets forth a causal relationship between motor activity and disease. In this case, feedback from motor activity results in susceptibility to gastric lesions and other diseases. Fortunately, determining the validity of the first alternative is an empirical question that is, at least in principle, relatively easy to answer. If it were true that feedback from motor activity results in susceptibility to disease, then it would be possible to reduce susceptibility by preventing motor activity from occurring. From the experimental perspective, one simply needs to determine whether paralyzed animals are less susceptible to gastrointestinal pathology than nonparalyzed animals are. Of course, what will make the experimental test more difficult to carry out in actual practice is the necessity (1) to paralyze the animal in such a way, or by such an agent, as to have no direct influence on processes involved in producing gastrointestinal pathology, and (2) to verify that the paralyzing manipulation does not interfere with the potential of the lesion-inducing treatment to cause lesions (i.e., to establish that the paralyzing manipulation did not interfere with what might be called "primary afferent inputs"). To illustrate this second concern, suppose that the test experiment is to induce lesions by exposing animals to stressful conditions. In this case, it is necessary to show that the paralyzing manipulation does not interfere with the ability of animals to perceive the stressful stimuli—in other words, to establish that the original stressful stimuli do indeed reach the central nervous system undiminished.

Despite technical barriers to be surmounted, experiments to test the validity of this first alternative ought to be carried out and probably will be, because the potential rewards for success are very large. Clearly, if this first alternative were to prove valid, clinicians would have a powerful manipulation by which to influence the development of pathology; that is, by reducing behavioral activity, they would have the ability to reduce susceptibility to pathology. But it must also be said that this alternative, in stating a causal relationship between motor activity and development of pathology, seems less likely than the second alternative, to which the discussion now turns.

High Activity and Susceptibility to Disease
Caused by a Physiological Mechanism Common to Both—
Possible Involvement of Catecholamines

The second alternative is that there exists a physiological mechanism (or system) that, when activated, produces both motor activity and susceptibility to pathology. In this case, motor activity and pathology are two consequences of the same physiological process. If this is true, then there is no causal relationship between motor activity and pathology; rather, these occur together as manifestations of a common physiological mechanism. In this case, a high level of motor activity serves as a "marker" indicating that a pathology-inducing process is active.

Present knowledge permits one to speculate as to what might be the "common physiological mechanism" that gives rise to motor activity and susceptibility to pathology. In fact, my own laboratory has devoted considerable effort to this issue, having spent much of the last decade studying what appears to be a major biochemical aspect of this mechanism—the catecholamines (dopamine, norepinephrine, epinephrine). (See Weiss, Bailey, Goodman, Hoffman, Ambrose, Salman, & Charry, 1982; Weiss, Glazer, & Pohorecky, 1976; Weiss, Stone, & Harrell, 1970.) Detailed explanation of these studies is not attempted here, nor is it required in the context of this discussion. It is sufficient to state that much evidence indicates that neural release and subsequent biological action of catecholamines could provide a common physiological mediator generating motor activity and various forms of pathology. For instance, increased release of catecholamines from neurons in the brain apparently mediates (brings about) motor activity (e.g., Creese & Iversen, 1975; Geyer, Segal, & Mandell, 1972; Gordon, Spector, Sjoerdsma, & Udenfriend, 1966; Thornburg & Moore, 1973; Weiss, Bailey, Pohorecky, Korzeniowski, & Grillione, 1980), and also increases severity of gastric lesions (e.g., Djanhanguiri, Taubin, & Landsberg, 1973; Osumi, Takaori, & Fujiwara, 1973), while increased release of catecholamines from nerves having access to the circulatory system and the heart is a well-known causal agent in cardiovascular disease (e.g., Bailey & Maclusky, 1978; Chappel, Rona, Balazs, & Gaudry, 1959; B. Friedman, Oester, & Davis, 1955; Haft, 1974; Rosenblum, Wohl, & Stein, 1975). The susceptibility of the Type A individual to cardiovascular disease has, in fact, been related to catecholamines by various investigators (M. Friedman, Byers, Diamant, & Rosenman, 1975; Glass & Contrada, 1982; Williams, Lane, Kuhn, Melosh, White, & Schanberg, 1982). Thus, activation of catecholaminergic systems may be an important part of the common mechanism that causes motor activity to appear while also promoting gastrointestinal and cardiovascular pathology.

Suggestions for Therapy

Pharmacological Interventions

What, then, does the foregoing suggest for therapeutic interventions? A few final comments can be made about such possibilities. To begin with, if one could identify a common physiological (particularly a biochemical) mechanism underlying motor activity and various forms of pathology (such as those alluded to in the preceding paragraph), this would obviously allow the development of pharmacological treatments for dealing with the relevant disease processes. At present, the most effective pharmacological treatments for gastrointestinal disease are those aimed at physiological events in the gastrointestinal tracts (e.g., blockade of H_2 receptors to decrease acid secretion), but someday these treatments may be augmented by approaches that reduce more generalized disease susceptibilities as well.

Reductions of Stressful Conditions

Other possibilities are also apparent. It is likely that the common physiological mechanism involved in the initiation of motor activity and the development of gastric pathology is activated by stressful conditions, since stressful conditions clearly affect both motor activity and gastric pathology (and also cardiovascular pathology). This presents another opportunity for therapeutic intervention. Working from this perspective, the behavior therapist or psychotherapist could conceivably operate to reduce the degree of stress that an individual experiences, and thereby to reduce the activation of the pathology-inducing physiological mechanism. Whereas the techniques utilized by the behavior therapist and psychotherapist may at present be less effective than one would like, it is possible that the influence of stressful stimuli on the relevant physiological mechanism is sufficiently large that stress-reducing interventions would be worthwhile, particularly as biofeedback techniques of stress reduction become more perfected and psychotherapeutic techniques more efficient. The use of these methods should be attempted. Those who doubt that such techniques ought to be used or are "cost-effective" in treating gastrointestinal disease may wish to read an article by Thomas Almy, who advocates these techniques on the basis of decades of experience, and details concrete procedures within the context of medical practice (Almy, 1977).

Increase of "Relevant Feedback"

Finally, there is yet another behavioral approach that may have considerable promise. The methods described in the preceding paragraph seek to prevent the activation of a pathogenic physiological mechanism by reducing stressful conditions, which are an initiator of this mechanism. Another possibility is suggested by experimental findings. These findings indicate that gastric pathology can be prevented not only by procedures that reduce activity (or response rate), but also by manipulations that raise appropriate feedback for behavioral responses. These findings showed that when appropriate feedback (called "relevant feedback") was high enough, gastric pathology did not occur in animals whose response rate was very high (Weiss, 1971c); in fact, high-feedback animals developed very little pathology, despite showing a response rate as high as the rate of animals that developed considerable gastric pathology without such feedback. This result suggests that the common physiological mechanism that gives rise to both activity (i.e., behavioral responding) and gastric pathology may not be a unitary response, but a constellation of reactions; it suggests further that certain stimuli (i.e., large amounts of appropriate feedback) will reduce those aspects of this mechanism that promote pathology without reducing other aspects that promote behavioral responding. In other words, whereas activity-producing and pathology-producing physiological reactions tend to occur together, these reactions are not identical or inseparable, and can be differentially affected by environmental and sensory stimuli.

The importance of the foregoing is as follows: In certain individuals, the mechanism that gives rise to both behavioral responding and pathology may be highly active, either because of genetic influences or because of previously learned patterns of reactivity, so that such individuals are quite resistant to attempts to blunt the initiation of this mechanism. What one observes in such individuals is that their response rate is essentially fixed at a high level. (It should be noted that this is by no means a hypothetical type of person; any psychotherapist can readily describe a percentage of his or her patients who are of this sort.) The tendency to respond in this way would seem to make such individuals continuously likely to develop various types of pathology, but the potential role of relevant feedback offers an escape from this dilemma. As stated above, pathology need not develop even in the presence of a high response rate if the individual is exposed to conditions that contain relevant feedback for responding. Moreover, the experimental findings suggest that the amount of feedback for responding need not be large; a small amount of feedback will suffice, providing that it occurs immediately after responding and often (Weiss, 1971c). In practical terms, feedback may take the form of increasing enjoyable consequences of behavior, and/or of increasing praise and other positive reinforcements following responses. Also, keeping this approach in mind may permit therapists to avoid a common error that is made in dealing with the high-responding individual: A detrimental strategy that is often adopted with such persons is to remove all feedback for their responses in the hope that the rate of responding will fall (e.g., forced retirement), when, in fact, the only successful strategies will be either to increase the reinforcing feedback for responses or to shift the focus of responding toward a different type of feedback. Through the use of these strategies, therapists may find that a highly effective behavioral technique for breaking the correlation between high activity rate and development of pathology is to alter the feedback consequences of behavior; in this event, high rates of responding may no longer be pathogenic.

R E F E R E N C E S

Ackerman, S. H., Hofer, M. A., & Weiner, H. Age at maternal separation and gastric erosion susceptibility in the rat. *Psychosomatic Medicine*, 1975, *37*, 180–184.

Ackerman, S. H., & Weiner, H. Peptic ulcer disease: Some considerations for psychosomatic research. In O. W. Hill (Ed.), *Modern trends in psychosomatic medicine* (Vol. 3). London: Butterworths, 1976.

Ader, R. Susceptibility to gastric lesions in the rat. *Journal of Neuropsychiatry*, 1963, *4*, 399–408.

Ader, R. Gastric erosions in the rat: Effects of immobilization at different points in the activity cycle. *Science*, 1964, *145*, 406–407.

Ader, R., Beels, C. C., & Tatum, R. Social factors affecting emotionality and resistance to disease in animals: II. Susceptibility to gastric ulceration as a function of interruptions in social interactions and the time at which they occur. *Journal of Comparative and Physiological Psychology*, 1960, *53*, 455–458.

Alexander, F. The influence of psychological factors upon gastrointestinal disturbance: General principles, objectives, and preliminary results. *Psychoanalytic Quarterly*, 1934, *3*, 501–539.

Almy, T. P. Therapeutic strategy in stress-related digestive disorders. *Clinics in Gastroenterology*, 1977, *6*, 709–722.

Bailey, W. H., & Maclusky, S. Appearance of creatine kinase isoenzymes in rat plasma following myocardial injury produced by isoproterenol. *Federation Proceedings*, 1978, *37*, 889.

Barbaree, H. E., & Harding, R. K. Free–operant avoidance behavior and gastric ulceration in rats. *Physiology and Behavior*, 1973, *11*, 269–271.

Baron, J. M. Gastric secretion in relation to subsequent duodenal ulcer and family history. *Gut*, 1962, *3*, 158–161.

Blumenthal, I. S. *Research and the ulcer problem*. Santa Monica, Calif.: The Rand Corporation, 1960.

Bockus, H. L., Glassmire, C., & Bank, J. Fractional gastric analysis. *American Journal of Surgery*, 1931, *12*, 6–17,

Bonfils, S., Liefooghe, G., Gellé, Z., Dubrasquet, M., & Lambling, A. "Ulcère" expérimental de contrainte du rat blanc: III. Mise en évidence et analyse du rôle de certains facteurs psychologiques. *Revue Française d'Études Clinques et Biologiques*, 1960, *5*, 571–581.

Bonfils, S., Richir, C., Potet, F., Liefooghe, G., & Lambling, A. "Ulcère" expérimental de contrainte du rat blanc: II. Anatomopathologie des lésions gastriques et de la différentes lésions viscérales. *Revue Française d Etudes Clinques et Biologiques*, 1959, *4*, 888–894.

Bonfils, S., Rossi, G., Liefooghe, G., & Lambling, A. "Ulcère" expérimental du rat blanc: I. Méthodes. Fréquence des lesions. Modifications par certains procédés techniques et pharmacodynamics. *Revue Française d'Études Clinques et Biologiques*, 1959, *4*, 146–150.

Brady, J. P., Thornton, D. R., & deFisher, D. Deleterious effects of anxiety elicited by conditioned pre-aversive stimuli in the rat. *Psychosomatic Medicine*, 1962, *24*, 590–595.

Brady, J. V. Ulcers in "executive" monkeys. *Scientific American*, October 1958, pp. 95–100.

Brady, J. V., Porter, R. W., Conrad, D. G., & Mason, J. W. Avoidance behavior and the development of gastroduodenal ulcers. *Journal of the Experimental Analysis of Behavior*, 1958, *1*, 69–72.

Brodie, D. A., & Hanson, H. M. A study of the factors involved in the production of gastric ulcers by the restraint technique. *Gastroenterology*, 1960, *38*, 353–360.

Brodie, D. A., & Valitski, L. S. Production of gastric hemorrhage in rats by multiple stresses. *Proceedings of the Society for Experimental Biology and Medicine*, 1963, *113*, 998–1001.

Brodie, D. A., Tate, C. L., & Hooks, K. F. Aspirin—intestinal damage in rats. *Science*, 1970, *170*, 183–185.

Chappel, C. I., Rona, G., Balazs, T., & Gaudry, R. N. Comparison of cardiotoxic actions of certain sympathetic amines. *Canadian Journal of Biochemistry and Physiology*, 1959, *37*, 37–42.

Cheney, D. H., Slogoff, S., & Allen, G. W. Ketamine-induced stress ulcers in the rat. *Anesthesiology*, 1974, *10*, 531–534.

Creese, I., & Iversen, S. The pharmacological and anatomical substrates of the amphetamine response in the rat. *Brain Research*, 1975, *83*, 419–436.

Cushing, H. Peptic ulcers and the interbrain. *Surgery, Gynecology, and Obstetrics*, 1932, *55*, 1–34.

Dai, S., Ogle, C. W., & Lo, C. H. The effects of metiamide on gastric secretion and stress ulceration in rats. *European Journal of Pharmacology*, 1975, *33*, 277–282.

de Brito, T., Montenegro, M. R., Leite, O. C., Berquo, E., & Vasconcellos, E. The relations between gastritis, peptic ulcers, and gastric carcinoma in surgically resected stomachs. *Gastroenterologia*, 1961, *95*, 341–351.

Djanhanguiri, B., Taubin, H. L., & Landsberg, L. Increased sympathetic activity in the pathogenesis of restraint ulcer in the rat. *Journal of Pharmacology and Experimental Therapeutics*, 1973, *184*, 163–168.

Dragstedt, L. R. Gastric secretion and duodenal ulcer. In T. K. Shnitka, J. Gilbert, & R. C. Harrison (Eds.), *Gastric secretion: Mechanisms and control*. New York: Pergamon Press, 1967.

Dragstedt, L. R., Ragins, H., Dragstedt, L. R., III, & Evans, S. O. Stress and duodenal ulcer. *Annals of Surgery*, 1956, *144*, 450–463.

Feldman, S., Conforti, N., Chowers, I., & Davidson, J. Pituitary–adrenal activation in rats with medial basal hypothalamic islands. *Acta Endocrinologica*, 1970, *63*, 405–414.

Foltz, E. L., & Millett, F. E. Experimental psychosomatic disease states in monkeys: I. Peptic "ulcer-executive" monkeys. *Journal of Surgical Research*, 1964, *4*, 445–463.

French, J. D., Porter, R. W., Cavanaugh, E. D., & Longmire, R. L. Experimental gastroduodenal lesions induced by stimulation of the brain. *Psychosomatic Medicine*, 1957, *19*, 209–220.

Friedman, B., Oester, Y. T., & Davis, D. F. The effect of epinephrine on experimental arteriopathy. *Archives of International Pharmacodynamics*, 1955, *102*, 226–234.

Friedman, M., & Rosenman, R. H. Association of specific overt behavior patterns with blood and cardiovascular findings. *Journal of the American Medical Association*, 1959, *169*, 1286–1296.

Friedman, M., Byers, S. O., Diamant, J., & Rosenman, R. H. Plasma catecholamine response of coronary-prone subjects (Type A) to a specific challenge. *Metabolism*, 1975, *24*, 205–210.

Friedman, S. B., & Ader, R. Parameters relevant to the experimental production of stress in the mouse. *Psychosomatic Medicine*, 1965, *27*, 27–30.

Ganguly, A. K. A method for quantitative assessment of experimentally produced ulcers in the stomach of albino rats. *Experientia*, 1969, *25*, 1224.

Geyer, M. A., Segal, D. S., & Mandell, A. J. Effect of intraventricular dopamine and norepinephrine on motor activity. *Physiology and Behavior*, 1972, *8*, 653–658.

Glass, D. C., & Contrada, R. J. Type A behavior and catecholamines. In C. R. Lake & M. Zigmond (Eds.), *Norepinephrine: Clinical aspects*. Baltimore: Williams & Wilkins, 1982.

Glass, D. C., Snyder, M. L., & Hollis, J. F. Time urgency and the type A coronary-prone behavior pattern. *Journal of Applied and Social Psychology*, 1974, *4*, 125–140.

Glavin, G. B. Subject emotionality and coping responses as predisposing and precipitating factors in restraint ulcer in rats. In S. Umehara & H. Ito (Eds.), *Advances in experimental ulcer*. Tokyo: Tokyo Medical College Press, 1982.

Glavin, G. B., & Mikhail, A. A. Role of gastric acid in restraint-induced ulceration in the rat. *Physiology and Behavior*, 1976, *17*, 777–780.

Gliner, J. A. Predictable versus unpredictable shock: Preference behavior and stomach ulceration. *Physiology and Behavior*, 1972, *9*, 693–698.

Goesling, W. J., Buchholz, A. R., & Carreira, C. J. Conditioned immobility and ulcer development in rats. *Journal of General Psychology*, 1974, *91*, 231–236.

Gordon, R., Spector, S., Sjoerdsma, A., & Udenfriend, S. Increased synthesis of norepinephrine and epinephrine in the intact rat during exercise and exposure to cold. *Journal of Pharmacology and Experimental Therapeutics*, 1966, *153*, 440–447.

Guth, P. H., & Hall, P. Microcirculatory and mast cell changes in restraint-induced gastric ulcer. *Gastroenterology*, 1966, *50*, 562–570.

Guth, P. H., & Mendick, R. The effect of chronic restraint stress on gastric ulceration in the rat. *Gastroenterology*, 1964, *46*, 285–286.

Haft, J. I. Cardiovascular injury produced by sympathetic catecholamines. *Progress in Cardiovascular Disease*, 1974, *17*, 73–86.

Hanson, H. M. Restraint and gastric ulcers. *Journal of Neuropsychiatry*, 1963, *4*, 390–396.

Hara, C., & Ogawa, N. The activity-stress ulcer and antibody production in rats. *Physiology and Behavior*, 1981, *27*, 609–613.

Hase, T., & Moss, B. Microvascular changes of gastric mucosa in the development of stress ulcer in rats. *Gastroenterology*, 1973, *65*, 224–234.

Ivy, A. C., Grossman, M. I., & Bachrach, W. H. *Peptic ulcer*. Philadelphia: Blakiston, 1950.

Jenkins, C. D. Psychologic and social precursors of coronary disease. *New England Journal of Medicine*, 1971, *284*, 244–255, 307–317.

Kim, Y. S., Kerr, R., & Lipkin, M. Cell proliferation during the development of stress erosions in mouse stomach. *Nature*, 1967, *215*, 1180–1181.

Kristt, D. A., & Freimark, S. J. Histopathology and pathogenesis of behaviorally induced gastric lesions in rats. *American Journal of Pathology*, 1973, *73*, 411–420.

Lau, H. K., & Ogle, C. W. A comparative study of the gastric ulcerogenic effects of stress and reserpine in rats with decreased stomach wall mast cell populations. *Experientia*, 1980, *36*, 995–996.

Lev, R., Kawashima, F., & Glass, G. B. Morphological features and healing of stress ulcers induced by alcohol and restraint. *Archives of Pathology and Laboratory Medicine*, 1976, *100*, 554–588.

Levine, R. J., & Senay, E. C. Histamine in the pathogenesis of stress ulcers in the rat. *Psychosomatic Medicine*, 1970, *43*, 61–65.

Levrat, M., & Lambert, R. Experimental ulcers produced in rats by modification of environment. *Gastroenterology*, 1959, *37*, 421–426.

Lima, F. B., Hell, N. S., Timo-Iaria, C., Scivoletto, R., Dolnikoff, M. S., & Pupo, A. A. Metabolic consequences of food restriction in rats. *Physiology and Behavior*, 1981, *27*, 115–123.

Lovibond, S. H. Effect of patterns of aversive and appetitive conditioned stimuli on the incidence of gastric lesions in the immobilized rat. *Journal of Comparative and Physiological Psychology*, 1969, *69*, 636–639.

Manning, F. J., Wall, H. G., Montgomery, Jr., C. A., Simmons, C. J., & Sessions, G. R. Microscopic examination of the activity-stress ulcer in the rat. *Physiology and Behavior*, 1978, *21*, 269–274.

Mezinskis, J., Gliner, J., & Shemberg, K. Somatic response as a function of no signal, random signal, or signalled shock with variable or constant durations of shock. *Psychonomic Science*, 1971, *25*, 271–272.

Mikhail, A. A. Effects of acute and chronic stress situations on stomach acidity in rats. *Journal of Comparative and Physiological Psychology*, 1971, *74*, 23–27.

Mikhail, A., & Hirschberg, J. Ulceration in the rat's forestomach: Its reduction by non-nutritive bulky substances. *Physiology and Behavior*, 1972, *8*, 769–770.

Miller, N. E. Learnable drives and rewards. In S. S. Stevens (Ed.), *Handbook of experimental psychology*. New York: Wiley, 1951.

Moot, S. A., Cebulla, R. P., & Crabtree, J. M. Instrumental control and ulceration in rat. *Journal of Comparative and Physiological Psychology*, 1970, *71*, 405–410.

Natelson, B. H. The executive monkey revisited. In F. P. Brooks & P. W. Evers (Eds.), *Nerves and the gut*. Thorofare, N.J.: C. B. Slack, 1977.

Natelson, B. H. Personal communication, 1982.

Natelson, B. H., Hoffman, S. L., & McKee, C. N. Duodenal pathology in rats following cold–restraint stress. *Physiology and Behavior*. 1979, *23*, 963–966.

Noble, R. L., & Collip, J. B. A quantitative method for the production of experimental traumatic shock without haemorrhage in unanaesthetized animals. *Quarterly Journal of Experimental Physiology*, 1942, *31*, 187.

Ogawa, T., Chiles, T., & Necheles, H. Starvation ulcer in the mouse. *American Journal of Physiology*, 1960, *198*, 619–620.

Osumi, Y., Takaori, S., & Fujiwara, M. Preventive effect of fusaric acid, a dopamine hydroxylase inhibitor, on the gastric ulceration induced by water-immersion in rats. *Japanese Journal of Pharmacology*, 1973, *23*, 904–906.

Paré, W. P. The effect of chronic environmental stress on stomach ulceration, adrenal function, and consummatory behavior in the rat. *Journal of Psychology*, 1964, *57*, 143–151.

Paré, W. P. Conditioning and avoidance-responding effects on gastric secretion in the rat with chronic fistula. *Journal of Comparative and Physiological Psychology*, 1972, *80*, 150–162.

Paré, W. P. The influence of food consumption and running activity on the activity-stress ulcer in the rat. *American Journal of Digestive Diseases*, 1975, *20*(3), 262–273.

Paré, W. P. The activity-stress ulcer: Frequency and chronicity. *Physiology and Behavior*, 1976, *16*, 699–704.

Paré, W. P. Body temperature and the activity-stress ulcer in the rat. *Physiology and Behavior*, 1977, *18*, 219–223. (a)

Paré, W. P. Gastric secretion and activity-stress lesions in the rat. *Journal of Comparative and Physiological Psychology*, 1977, *91*(4), 778–783. (b)

Paré, W. P. Psychological studies of stress ulcer in the rat. *Brain Research Bulletin*, 1980, *5*(Suppl. 1), 73–79.

Paré, W. P., & Houser, V. P. Activity and food-restriction effects on gastric glandular lesions in the rat: The activity-stress ulcer. *Bulletin of the Psychonomic Society*, 1973, *2*, 213–214.

Paré, W. P., & Livingston, A., Jr. Shock predictability and gastric secretion in the chronic gastric fistula rat. *Physiology and Behavior*, 1973, *11*, 521–526.

Paré, W. P., & Temple, L. J. Food deprivation, shock stress and stomach lesions in the rat. *Physiology and Behavior*, 1973, *11*, 371–375.

Pfeiffer, C. J., Debro, F. R., & Muller, P. J. Gastric pathologic and biochemical changes induced by starvation of weaning rats. *Life Sciences* (Part 1), 1966, *5*, 509–519.

Polish, E., Brady, J. V., Mason, J. W., Thach, J. F., & Niemack, W. Gastric contents and the occurrence of duodenal lesions in the rhesus monkey during avoidance behavior. *Gastroenterology*, 1962, *43*, 193–201.

Porter, R. W., Brady, J. V., Conrad, D., Mason, J. W., Galambos, R., & Rioch, D. Some experimental observations on gastrointestinal lesions in behaviorally conditioned monkeys. *Psychosomatic Medicine*, 1958, *20*, 379–394.

Price, K. P. Predictable and unpredictable shock: Their pathological effects on restrained and unrestrained rats. *Psychological Reports*, 1972, *30*, 419–426.

Robert, A., & Nezamis, J. Histopathology of steroid-induced ulcers. *Archives of Pathology*, 1964, *77*, 407–423.

Robert, A., Northam, J. I., Nezamis, J. E., & Phillips, J. P. Exertion ulcers in the rat. *American Journal of Digestive Diseases*, 1970, *15*, 497–507.

Robert, A., & Stout, T. Production of duodenal ulcers in rats. *Federation Proceedings*, 1969, *28*, 323.

Robert, A., Stout, T., & Dale, J. E. Production by secretagogues of duodenal ulcers in the rat. *Gastroenterology*, 1970, *59*, 95–102.

Rosenberg, A. Production of gastric lesions in rats by combined cold and electrostress. *American Journal of Digestive Diseases*, 1967, *12*, 1140–1148.

Rosenblum, I., Wohl, M. A., & Stein, A. A. Studies in cardiac necrosis: I. Production of cardiac lesions with sympathomimetic amines. *Toxicology and Applied Pharmacology*, 1975, *7*, 1–8.

Sawrey, W. L., Conger, J. J., & Turrell, E. S. An experimental investigation of the role of psychological factors in the production of gastric ulcers in rats. *Journal of Comparative and Physiological Psychology*, 1956, *49*, 457–461.

Sawrey, W. L., & Weisz, J. D. An experimental method of producing gastric ulcers. *Journal of Comparative and Physiological Psychology*, 1956, *49*, 269–270.

Schindler, R., & Baxmeier, R. I. Mucosal changes accompanying gastric ulcer: A gastroscopic study. *Annals of Internal Medicine*, 1939, *13*, 693–699.

Seligman, M. E. P. Chronic fear produced by unpredictable shock. *Journal of Comparative and Physiological Psychology*, 1968, *66*, 402–411.

Selye, H. A syndrome produced by diverse nocuous agents. *Nature*, 1936, *138*, 32.

Selye, H. Studies on adaptation. *Endocrinology*, 1937, *21*, 169–188.

Senay, E. C., & Levine, R. J. Synergism between cold and restraint for rapid production of stress ulcers in rats. *Proceedings of the Society for Experimental Biology and Medicine*, 1967, *124*, 1221–1228.

Sethbhakdi, S., Pfeiffer, C. J., & Roth, J. L. A. Gastric mucosal ulceration following vasoactive agents: A new experimental approach. *American Journal of Digestive Diseases*, 1970, *15*, 261–270.

Shay, H., Komorov, S. A., Fels, F. F., Moranze, D., Gruenstein, M., & Siplet, H. A. A simple method for the uniform production of gastric ulceration in the rat. *Gastroenterology*, 1945, *5*, 43–61.

Sines, J. O. Selective breeding for development of stomach lesions following stress in the rat. *Journal of Comparative and Physiological Psychology*, 1959, *52*, 615–617.

Sines, J. O. Behavioral correlates of genetically enhanced susceptibility to stomach lesion development. *Journal of Psychosomatic Research*, 1961, *5*, 120–126.

Sines, J. O. Physiological and behavioral characteristics of rats selectively bred for susceptibility to stomach lesion development. *Journal of Neuropsychiatry*, 1963, *4*, 396–398.

Sines, J. O., Cleeland, C., & Adkins, J. The behavior of normal and stomach lesion susceptible rats in several learning situations. *Journal of Genetic Psychology*, 1963, *102*, 91–94.

Skillman, J. J., & Silen, W. Acute gastroduodenal "stress" ulceration. Barrier disruption of varied pathogenesis. *Gastroenterology*, 1970, *59*, 479–482.

Skillman, J. J., & Silen, W. Stress ulcers. *Lancet*, 1972, *ii*, 1303–1306.

Thompson, H. Gastritis in partial gastrectomy specimens. *Gastroenterology*, 1959, *36*, 861.

Thornburg, J. E., & Moore, K. E. The relative importance of dopaminergic and noradrenergic neuronal systems for the stimulation of locomotor activity induced by amphetamine and other drugs. *Neuropharmacology*, 1973, *12*, 853–866.

Tsuda, A., & Hirai, H. Effects of the amount of required coping response tasks on gastrointestinal lesions in rats. *Japanese Psychological Research*, 1975, *17*, 119–132.

Tsuda, A., & Hirai, H. Effects of signal-shock contingency probability on gastric lesions in rats as a function of shock region. *Japanese Journal of Psychology*, 1976, *47*, 258–267.

Valman, H. B., Parry, D. J., & Coghill, N. F. Lesions associated with gastroduodenal haemorrhage in relation to aspirin intake. *British Medical Journal*, 1968, *iv*, 661–663.

Vanzant, F. R., Alvarez, W. C., Berkson, J., & Eusterman, C. B. Changes in gastric acidity in peptic ulcer, cholecystitis, and other diseases. *Archives of Internal Medicine*, 1933, *52*, 616–631.

Vincent, G. P., & Paré, W. P. Activity-stress ulcer in the rat, hamster, gerbil and guinea pig. *Physiology and Behavior*, 1976, *16*, 557–560.

Wangensteen, S. C., & Golden, G. T. Acute "stress" ulcers of the stomach: A review. *American Surgeon*, 1973, *39*, 562–567.

Weiner, H., Thaler, M., Reiser, M. F., & Mirsky, I. A. Etiology of duodenal ulcer: I. Relation of specific psychological characteristics to rate of gastric secretion (serum pepsinogen). *Psychosomatic Medicine*, 1957, *19*, 1–10.

Weiss, J. M. A tail electrode for unrestrained rats. *Journal of the Experimental Analysis of Behavior*, 1967, *10*, 85–86.

Weiss, J. M. Effects of coping responses on stress. *Journal of Comparative and Physiological Psychology*, 1968, *65*, 251–260.

Weiss, J. M. Effects of predictable and unpredictable shock on development of gastrointestinal lesions in rats. *Proceedings of the 76th Annual Convention of the American Psychological Association*, 1968, *3*, 263–264. (b)

Weiss, J. M. Somatic effects of predictable and unpredictable shock. *Psychosomatic Medicine*, 1970, *32*, 397–408.

Weiss, J. M. Effects of coping behavior in different warning-signal conditions on stress pathology in rats. *Journal of Comparative and Physiological Psychology*, 1971, *77*, 1–13. (a)

Weiss, J. M. Effects of coping behavior with and without a feedback signal on stress pathology in rats. *Journal of Comparative and Physiological Psychology*, 1971, *77*, 22–30. (b)

Weiss, J. M. Effects of punishing the coping response (conflict) on stress pathology in rats. *Journal of Comparative and Physiological Psychology*, 1971, 77, 14–21. (c)

Weiss, J. M., Bailey, W. H., Goodman, P. A., Hoffman, L. J., Ambrose, M. J., Salman, S., & Charry, J. M. A model for neurochemical study of depression. In M. Y. Spiegelstein & A. Levy (Eds.), *Behavioral models and the analysis of drug action*. Amsterdam: Elsevier, 1982.

Weiss, J. M., Bailey, W. H., Pohorecky, L. A., Korzeniowski, D., & Grillione, G. Stress-induced depression of motor activity correlates with regional changes in brain norepinephrine but not in dopamine. *Neurochemical Research*, 1980, 5, 9–22.

Weiss, J. M., Glazer, H. I., & Pohorecky, L. A. Coping behavior and neurochemical changes: An alternative explanation for the original "learned helplessness" experiments. In G. Serban & A. Kling (Eds.), *Animal models in human psychobiology*. New York: Plenum, 1976.

Weiss, J. M., Pohorecky, L. A., Salman, S., & Gruenthal, M. Attenuation of gastric lesions by psychological aspects of aggression in rats. *Journal of Comparative and Physiological Psychology*, 1976, 90, 252–259.

Weiss, J. M., Stone, E. A., & Harrell, N. Coping behavior and brain norepinephrine level of rats. *Journal of Comparative and Physiological Psychology*, 1970, 72, 153–160.

Weisz, J. D. The etiology of experimental gastric ulceration. *Psychosomatic Medicine*, 1957, 19, 61–73.

Williams, R. B., Lane, J. D., Kuhn, C. M., Melosh, W., White, A. D., & Schanberg, S. M. Type A behavior and elevated physiological neuroendocrine responses to cognitive tasks. *Science*, 1982, 218, 483–485.

Wolf, S., & Wolff, H. G. *Human gastric function*. New York: Oxford University Press, 1947.

Wolff, H. G., Wolf, S., Grace, W. J., Holmes, T. E., Stevenson, I., Straub, L., Goodell, H., & Seton, P. Changes in form and function of mucous membranes occurring as part of protective reaction patterns in man during periods of life stress and emotional conflict. *Transactions of the Association of American Physicians*, 1948, 61, 313–334.

C H A P T E R   7

Cardiovascular Disease and Hypertension

J. Alan Herd
Baylor College of Medicine

INTRODUCTION

The pathophysiological links between behavioral factors and cardiovascular disease explain how behavioral–ecological factors influence health and illness, indicate what interventions might be successful in treatment, and suggest promising avenues for behavioral medicine research. The objective of this chapter is to assess the impact of social, psychological, and behavioral factors on the physiological and biochemical processes that are known to influence the pathogenesis of cardiovascular disease.

Many lines of evidence already suggest that behavioral factors are related to cardiovascular disease and hypertension. Epidemiological studies have demonstrated associations between the Type A behavior pattern and heart disease, manifested as myocardial infarction and sudden cardiac death. Analysis of social support systems in population studies have shown an association between weak social supports and coronary heart disease (CHD) as well as between weak supports and death from all causes. A recent history of profound life changes has been associated with the onset of myocardial infarction and sudden cardiac death. Finally, mental illness in the form of severe depression has been found to be associated with angina pectoris, myocardial infarction, and sudden cardiac death. Although epidemiological studies do not provide information about mechanisms linking behavior to disease, associations suggest promising avenues of research in clinical studies and laboratory experiments.

Many clinical studies have suggested links between neuroendocrine factors and cardiovascular disease. In particular, the severity of coronary arteriosclerosis in asymptomatic subjects has been found to be related to levels of cortisol and the rate of its disappearance from serum during late morning hours (Troxler, Sprague, Albanese, Fuchs, & Thompson, 1977). Arterial hypertension in patients with elevated levels of plasma renin activity and high plasma levels of norepinephrine is frequently found in association with hostility (Esler, Julius, Zweifler, Randall, Harburg, Gardiner, & DeQuattro, 1977). Psychological factors are frequently found in association with cardiac arrhythmias and sudden cardiac death, particularly in patients with electrocardiographic abnormalities (Lown, DeSilva, Reich, & Murawski, 1980), suggesting an imbalance of adrenergic influence on cardiac function (Schwartz & Stone, 1978). Although clinical studies do not provide definitive proof concerning the effects of behavioral factors on cardiovascular disease, the experience of many investigators is consistent with such pathophysiological links.

More convincing evidence is available from laboratory studies with human subjects, nonhuman primates, and other laboratory animals. Administration of cortisol, along with a diet high in saturated fat and cholesterol, enhances the severity of aortic atherosclerosis in cynomolgus monkeys (Sprague, Troxler, Peterson, Schmidt, & Young, 1980). Behavioral procedures in human subjects, nonhuman primates, and dogs cause elevations of arterial pressure that may persist for hours, weeks, or months. Experiments with dogs have shown that stellate ganglion stimulation and behavioral procedures cause ventricular tachycardia and fibrillation (Lown & Verrier, 1978). Although laboratory studies seldom replicate human disease states exactly, results obtained by many different investigators in several different laboratories are consistent with the conclusion that the sympathoadrenomedullary activity and pituitary adrenocortical activity elicited by social, psychological, and behavioral factors contribute to the pathogenesis of cardiovascular disease.

All of these studies suggest that neuroendocrine factors are involved in the pathophysiology of cardiovascular disease and hypertension. The rationale for studying physiological mechanisms is to direct our research toward possible etiological agents and pathophysiological processes that are compatible with our concepts of the pathogenesis underlying arteriosclerosis, arterial hypertension, and sudden cardiac death. The study of cardiovascular diseases and hypertension has proceeded vigorously along many different lines of investigation. Since the study of pathophysiological links between behavioral factors and cardiovascular disease is relatively recent in comparison to other approaches, it is possible to take advantage of progress made in the study of fundamental pathophysiological mechanisms. The lesions of atherosclerosis develop principally in the innermost layer of the arterial wall and consist of intimal smooth muscle cell proliferation, formation of large amounts of connective tissue, and accumulation of lipids both within the cells and in the connective tissues surrounding them. Arterial hypertension is associated with increased resistance to blood flow through arterioles, or elevation of cardiac output, or combinations of these two processes, in association with decreased renal excretion of sodium and water at elevated levels of arterial blood pressure. Sudden cardiac death occurs most frequently in association with myocardial disease, especially coronary atherosclerosis, but is influenced by neurogenic, endocrine, metabolic, pharmacological, and toxic factors under the influence of central nervous system processes, which link behavioral factors to cardiac dysfunction.

Our working hypothesis is that sympathoadrenomedullary activity and pituitary adrenocortical activity enhance lipoprotein metabolism, release free fatty acids (FFAs), elevate plasma glucose, reduce insulin sensitivity, increase circulating levels of insulin, reduce renal excretion of salt and water, and increase arteriolar and venous tone. It is proposed that these effects alter arterial permeability, promote platelet aggregation, enhance proliferation of vascular smooth muscle, and increase lipid accumulation in arterial lesions, as well as enhancing renal reabsorption of sodium, increasing vascular constriction, and increasing cardiac irritability.

LIPIDS AND LIPOPROTEIN METABOLISM

Association with Atherosclerosis

The concept that lipid metabolism, particularly as it affects blood cholesterol level, is a central factor in the production of atherosclerosis arose from population studies and analyses of risk factors (J. L. Goldstein, Hazzard, & Schrott, 1973; Johnson, Epstein, & Kjelsberg, 1965). A relation to dietary lipids arose from studies of experimental atherosclerosis in rats, rabbits, and nonhuman primates. In these laboratory studies, continued feeding of a cholesterol-rich diet, particularly one high in saturated fat, produced atherosclerosis that could be reversed by reducing the intake of cholesterol and fat (Kokatnur, Malcolm, Eggen, & Strong, 1975). Although the nutritional contribution to atherosclerosis remains a focus of research, recent studies indicate that a common origin of atherosclerosis is likely to be endothelial injury followed by platelet deposition and subintimal cellular proliferation, in addition to incorporation of lipid into the wall (Ross, 1979). Thus, the effects of hemodynamics, platelet aggregation, hormonal effects, and metabolic influences are not fully understood, but many new avenues of research have developed. In experimental animals, the intima can be injured by many physical (R. J. Friedman, Moore, & Singal, 1975; Moore, 1973) and chemical factors (Harker, Ross, Slichter, & Scott, 1976; Harker, Slichter, Scott, & Ross, 1974), including high levels of arterial blood pressure, blood turbulence, toxic substances, and carbon monoxide. When intimal injury occurs, a repair process begins, in which smooth muscle cells penetrate into the subendothelial space and new connective tissue forms (Ross & Glomset, 1973). When hypercholesterolemia is present, lipid accumulation occurs selectively at injured sites and causes an exaggerated repair process (Ross & Harker, 1976). Incorporation of platelet elements into the wall also leads to atherogenesis, and microthrombi are deposited in animals with increased dietary fat in the absence of significant hypercholesterolemia. Also, low-density lipoproteins, which may enter the arterial wall in injured areas, stimulate the rate of smooth muscle cell migration and proliferation in the subintimal layers. Chronic hypercholesterolemia itself has been noted to cause endothelial cell desquamation and decreased platelet survival, as well as lipid accumulation within the arterial wall (Ross & Harker, 1976). Finally, there is evidence that a proportion of subjects who have atherosclerosis have elevated circulating insulin levels (Tzagournis, Chiles, Ryan, & Skillman, 1968). These high insulin levels may be secondary to metabolic abnormalities such as obesity and adult-onset diabetes mellitus, or may be of exogenous origin in insulin-treated diabetics. The association of abnormal lipid metabolism, reduced insulin sensitivity, and glucose intolerance suggests an association among FFA metabolism, high circulating levels of insulin, and atherosclerosis.

Neuroendocrines and Lipid Metabolism

Administration of such neuroendocrines as epinephrine (Soman, Shamoon, & Sherwin, 1980) and cortisol (Shamoon, Soman, & Sherwin, 1980) in physiological amounts has effects on glucose utilization and lipid metabolism. Soman and colleagues have reported results of laboratory studies in which normal humans received an infusion of epinephrine for 4 hours, which increased plasma epinephrine levels to approximately 400 pg/ml, a level within the range of normal physiological variation. During the experiment, glucose clearance decreased by 25% and remained suppressed for 4 hours. In addition, epinephrine blocked the rise in glucose uptake that normally accompanies hyperglycemia, and it produced a sustained decline in glucose clearance. No significant effect was observed on plasma insulin or glucagon levels. However, the effects of epinephrine on hepatic glucose output and plasma FFA levels were transient. A prompt rise of 45% in glucose output and a rise in FFA level of 120% both declined to basal levels within 60–90 minutes. Thus, although epinephrine had a persistent effect in decreasing glucose clearance, it only transiently increased hepatic glucose output and FFA levels. These data provide evidence in humans for disparate effects of physiological elevations of epinephrine on hepatic glucose output and lipolysis, on the one hand, and peripheral glucose utilization, on the other.

Similar effects on glucose metabolism were observed by Shamoon et al. (1980) during a 5-hour primed-continuous infusion of cortisol, which raised plasma cortisol levels to 40 μg/dl. As shown in Figure 7.1, plasma glucose gradually increased during cortisol infusion. In addition, glucose output tended to decline, and glucose uptake fell significantly below preinfusion values. Similarly, glucose clearance progressively decreased by 30% during cortisol administration. However, the cortisol infusion had no significant effect on plasma FFA concentrations. These effects of cortisol on glucose metabolism occurred in the absence of significant changes in the plasma insulin or glucagon concentrations. Furthermore, cortisol infusion had no effect on insulin binding to circulating monocytes, suggesting that acute elevations of plasma cortisol may have antiinsulin effects in humans that occur independently of alterations in insulin receptors.

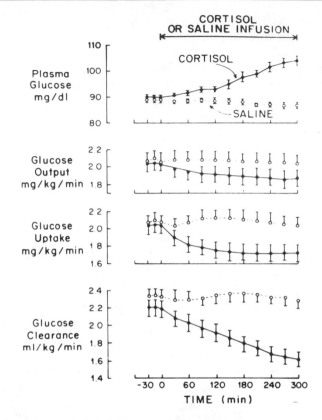

FIGURE 7.1. Glucose metabolism in human subjects during cortisol administration. Abscissa indicates time in minutes before and during continuous intravenous infusion of cortisol. The top panel indicates concentration of glucose in plasma in subjects receiving cortisol compared to subjects receiving saline. The panel second from the top indicates the amount of glucose entering the circulation per minute, and the panel third from the top indicates the amount removed from the circulation during the same time. The bottom panel indicates the volume of plasma that would be completely cleared of glucose each minute if all the glucose were removed from a few milliliters, rather than a small amount removed from many milliliters. The closed and open circles represent mean values for each group, and the lines and bars represent 1 standard error of the mean. Note that administration of cortisol reduced the rate at which glucose was removed from plasma, even though the plasma levels were continuously increased. (From Shamoon, H., Samon, V., & Sherwin, R. S. The influence of acute physiological increments on fuel metabolism and insulin binding to monocytes in normal humans. *Journal of Clinical Endocrinology and Metabolism*, 1980, *50*, 294–297. Reprinted by permission.)

In contrast to the lack of effect of acute glucocorticoid administration on insulin receptors, results from other investigators indicate that chronic glucocorticoid administration results in a decrease in insulin binding to liver and adipose tissue. However, chronic glucocorticoid administration results in increased levels of plasma insulin, which may have an adverse effect on insulin receptors (Olefsky, Johnson, Liu, Jen, & Reaven, 1975). Thus, chronic administration of glucocorticoids results in increased FFA levels in humans (Baxter, 1976) and has an inhibitory effect on lipolysis in isolated human adipocytes (Cigolini & Smith, 1979). However, acute elevations of plasma cortisol levels have their greatest effects on glucose utilization and insulin sensitivity.

Under natural conditions, mobilization of FFAs occurs more by release of norepinephrine from sympathetic nerve endings than by release of epinephrine from the adrenal medulla. Exposure of human subjects to a cold environment causes an increase in oxygen utilization, an increase in plasma concentrations of norepinephrine, and an increase in plasma FFA concentrations. Jessen (1980a) reported that exposure of adult men to cold air after administration of chlorpromazine to block cutaneous vasoconstriction increased oxygen consumption by 30% to 41%, increased plasma norepinephrine concentration by 300%, and increased plasma FFA concentration by 96%, with no effect on plasma epinephrine concentration. Plasma glucose concentration actually fell slightly. Thus, it is apparent that sympathetic nervous system activity causing release of norepinephrine from nerve endings elevates plasma levels of FFAs with no elevation in plasma glucose levels, whereas infusions of epinephrine cause elevations of glucose without elevating plasma levels of FFAs.

The utilization of FFAs produced by sympathetic nervous system activity occurs through several mechanisms. Some FFAs may be metabolized in muscular activity and heat production; some may be reesterified and stored as triglycerides in adipose tissue; and some may be utilized for the production of very low-density lipoprotein triglyceride by the liver. Schonfield and Pfleger (1971) showed that livers of rats fed a high-carbohydrate diet extracted FFAs from plasma in proportion to their plasma concentrations. In turn, the rate of secretion of triglycerides was directly related to uptake of FFAs. The triglycerides secreted were predominantly in the form of very low-density lipoproteins. Thus, the hepatic output of very low-density lipoprotein triglycerides was influenced by the concentration of FFAs in plasma.

The proportion of FFAs oxidized is influenced by the plasma levels of glucose. In the fasting state, plasma levels of glucose are low, levels of FFA are high, and the majority of FFAs are removed from plasma through oxidation and formation of ketone bodies. In the fed state, esterification and triglyceride synthesis predominate. Elevated levels of plasma triglycerides and occurrence of ischemic heart disease are known to be associated. In addition, men with electrocardiographic evidence of ischemic heart disease have been found to have less of a relationship between FFAs and beta-hydroxybutyrate than men with normal electrocardiograms have been (D. J. A. Jenkins, Welborn, & Goff, 1970). Thus, men with ischemic heart disease may divert FFAs from ketogenesis to triglyceride synthesis in such a way as to elevate plasma levels of triglycerides. This metabolic pathway would be accentuated by high plasma levels of glucose and therefore may occur more readily in subjects with a relative glucose intolerance.

Plasma levels of FFA, triglycerides, and catecholamines also may be induced by psychological factors. Taggart and Carruthers (1971) sampled blood from automobile race drivers before and after a race. The results are shown in Figure 7.2. The total catecholamine levels were elevated at the time of the race and returned to baseline values within 60 minutes following the race. The FFA levels were elevated both before and immediately after the race, with values approaching baseline levels 1 or 2 hours following the race. Triglyceride levels were slightly raised immediately after the race, and peak values were obtained after 1 hour. Cholesterol levels did not increase throughout the period studied. A strong positive correlation was present between total catecholamine levels and FFA levels in plasma. The results suggested that psychological factors causing sympathetic nervous system stimulation mobilized FFAs in excess of amounts required for muscular activity. The time course of observed increases in levels of FFAs and triglycerides suggested that conversion of FFAs to triglycerides had occurred through hepatic synthesis.

Circulating levels of FFAs have other influences. Studies in perfused hearts (Challoner & Steinberg, 1966) and in human subjects during cardiac catheterization (Simonsen & Kjekshus, 1978) have shown that FFAs increased myocardial oxygen consumption. Simonsen and Kjekshus (1978) studied the effect of FFA on myocardial oxygen consumption in relation to mechanical work of the heart in patients with coronary artery disease. Catecholamine stimulation was achieved through infusions of isoproterenol, a beta-adrenergic catecholamine. In some experiments, levels of FFAs were increased through administration of heparin and intralipid, a fat emulsion administered intravenously. In other experiments, levels of FFAs were reduced by administering beta-pyridyl carbinol, an analogue of nicotinic acid that inhibits lipolysis. Increased heart rate contributed 47% and FFAs 50% of the increase in myocardial oxygen consumption during catecholamine stimulation. Inhibition of lipolysis lowered plasma levels of FFAs and reduced myocardial oxygen consumption significantly. Because catecholamines increased myocardial oxygen consumption in several ways, the effects of FFAs could be demonstrated by controlling heart rate and measuring aortic systolic blood pressure while altering plasma levels of FFAs. When changes in heart rate were accounted for, the inhibition of lipolysis almost abolished the effect of isoproterenol on myocardial oxygen utilization. This indicates that myocardial uptake of FFAs is a major determinant of myocardial oxygen requirement during concomitant catecholamine stimulation.

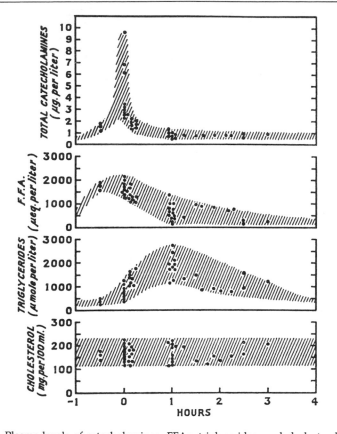

FIGURE 7.2. Plasma levels of catecholamines, FFAs, triglycerides, and cholesterol in racing car drivers. Abscissa indicates time in hours before and after a race. The top panel indicates the rise in plasma catecholamines observed before, during, and after the race, with the panel second from the top indicating the rise in FFAs during the same time. The panel third from the top indicates the rise in triglycerides seen during and after the race, with the bottom panel indicating a constant level of cholesterol throughout the same time. The closed circles represent individual values and the shaded areas represent the range for each variable. Note the sequential elevations in plasma catecholamines, FFAs, and triglycerides, with elevations in triglycerides persisting several hours after the race. (From Taggart, P., & Carruthers, M. Endogenous hyperlipidemia induced by emotional stress of racing driving. *Lancet*, 1971, *i*, 363–366. Reprinted by permission.)

Increases in FFA concentrations in plasma also influence platelet aggregation. Burstein, Berns, Heldenberg, Kahn, Werbin, and Tamir (1978) studied platelet aggregation following intravenous injection of heparin in healthy adult human subjects. Since injection of small amounts of heparin is followed by an immediate rise in FFA concentration, it was possible to show an increase in the rate of platelet aggregation that was directly correlated with changes in plasma FFA concentration. Interpretation of these results suggests that the increase in platelet aggregation is due to an alteration in the platelet membrane as a result of an increased level of plasma FFAs.

ARTERIAL BLOOD PRESSURE REGULATION

Analysis of Cardiovascular and Renal Function

Cardiovascular function and renal function are regulated to maintain a constant arterial blood pressure. Although there are neurogenic mechanisms such as arterial baroreceptor reflexes that influence cardiac function, arteriolar resistance, and venous tone in a way that tends to keep arterial pressure within a narrow range, the ultimate control of arterial blood pressure resides more in cardiac function, tissue metabolic requirements, and renal function than in neurogenic mechanisms. An increase in arteriolar resistance, which increases arterial pressure, causes greater work for the heart and a reduction in cardiac output. Reduced tissue blood flow reduces arteriolar resistance, and arterial pressure returns toward original values. In addition, an elevation in arterial pressure causes an increase in renal excretion of salt and water, with a consequent reduction in blood volume and a decrease in venous return to the heart. When less blood is returned to the heart, less is pumped to the periphery, and arterial blood pressure returns toward original values. Other control systems are equally complex. In some organs, such as skin and kidneys, blood circulates far in excess of metabolic requirements. The myocardium is at the other extreme, in that coronary blood circulates at a rate closer to myocardial metabolic requirements. Although much is known about local regulation of blood flow and systemic regulation of arterial blood pressure, it is still not known entirely which variables are regulated by what mechanism under normal conditions. The pathophysiology of cardiovascular disease and arterial hypertension is still more complex.

An engineering approach to the heart and circulation has been taken in an effort to determine the interrelationships among cardiac output, arterial blood pressure, total peripheral resistance, blood volume, and extracellular fluid volume. Guyton has developed a complex analysis of circulatory function, cardiac output regulation, arterial blood pressure regulation, and renal function (Guyton, Jones, & Coleman, 1973). Figure 7.3 depicts a simplified analysis in which the heart, circulation, kidneys, and fluid volumes are depicted as a negative feedback-control system. Block 1 of the simplified analysis shows that as arterial blood pressure increases, renal excretion of salt and water increases. Block 2 balances the intake of water and salt by mouth against the output of salt and water by the kidneys. Block 3 integrates the rate of change of extracellular fluid volume. Block 4 shows that as extracellular fluid volume increases, blood volume also increases. Block 5 illustrates that as blood volume increases, the pressure throughout the circulation also

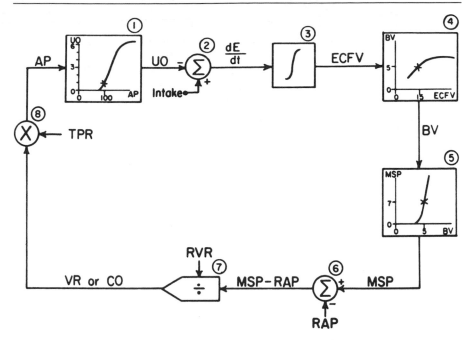

FIGURE 7.3. Simplified systems analysis of cardiac output, circulation, and fluid volumes. Each block represents functional relations between physiological variables influencing regulation of arterial blood pressure. Note that the negative feedback-control system depicted in this figure emphasizes the dependence of arterial blood pressure regulation on cardiac function, arteriolar and venous tone, and fluid volumes regulated by renal function. (From Guyton, A. C., Jones, C. E., & Coleman, T. G. (Eds.). *Circulatory physiology: Cardiac output and its regulation.* Philadelphia: W. B. Saunders, 1973. Reprinted by permission.)

increases. Block 6 is the gradient for flow of blood from the peripheral circulation back to the right atrium. Block 7 is the ratio of pressure gradient for venous return to resistance against venous return and represents venous return to the heart. Since the heart pumps whatever amount of blood flows into the right atrium, an increase or decrease in venous return causes a similar increase or decrease in cardiac output. Block 8 is the product of cardiac output and total peripheral vascular resistance, which determines systemic arterial blood pressure. Thus, if the arterial pressure increases, the output of kidneys also increases, extracellular fluid volume decreases, blood volume decreases, pressure gradient for flow of blood back to the heart decreases, venous return and cardiac output decrease, and arterial blood pressure returns toward original values. This analysis of the heart and circulation developed by Guyton and his colleagues emphasizes the dependence of arterial blood pressure on renal function. Any effects of cardiac, neurogenic, hormonal, psychological, behavioral, nutritional, or other influences must be examined ultimately for effects on renal function.

In any discussion of behavioral influences on arterial blood pressure, the effects of the autonomic nervous system and endocrine function on the cardiovascular system must be considered. Both neurogenic and endocrine factors are known to influence the following factors in the following blocks: Block 1, the relationship between arterial pressure and urinary output; Block 2, the intake of salt and water; Block 4, the relationship between extracellular fluid volume and blood volume; Block 5, venous tone, which influences the relationship between blood volume and circulatory pressures; Block 7, the relationship between cardiac function and right atrial pressure; and Block 8, the relationship between total peripheral vascular resistance, which includes arteriolar tone under the influence of neurogenic and hormonal factors. Ultimately, neurogenic and hormonal factors influence renal excretion of salt and water through several mechanisms, but the relationship to extracellular fluid volume, blood volume, venous tone, arteriolar tone, and cardiac function may be substantially different under various normal and pathological conditions.

Behavioral Influences on Blood Pressure Regulation

Although there have been many reports indicating a relationship between behavioral factors and elevations in arterial blood pressure, the physiological mechanisms have been difficult to demonstrate. In particular, little attention has been paid to the relationship among behavioral factors, arterial blood pressure, and renal function. Some of the earliest demonstrations of a relationship between behavioral factors and renal function were reported by Homer Smith (1940). He reported that strong emotional states such as fear were associated with reductions in renal clearance of inulin and para-aminohippurate. These changes in renal function were interpreted as evidence of increased sympathetic nervous system function's causing a reduction in renal blood flow.

More detailed studies of cardiovascular and renal function were performed by Brod and his colleagues (Brod, Fencl, Hejl, & Jirka, 1959). They used mental arithmetic as a psychological stimulus, administered in a way that caused subjects to become tense and nervous, to make frequent mistakes, and to blush with embarrassment. Both normotensive and hypertensive subjects were measured for blood pressure, using direct arterial puncture; cardiac output, using the dye dilution technique; renal plasma flow, estimated from para-aminohippurate clearance; forearm blood flow, using occlusion plethysmography; and skin temperature, using a thermocouple. Results of a typical experiment are shown in Figure 7.4. During the stimulus of mental arithmetic, the systolic, diastolic, and mean blood pressures rose in association with an increase in cardiac output and a reduction in total peripheral vascular resistance. Renal clearance of para-aminohippurate decreased, indicating an increase in renal vascular resistance; forearm skin tem-

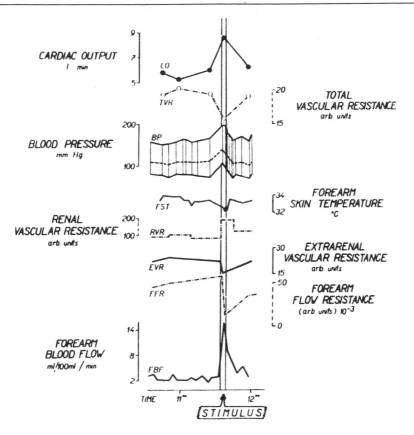

FIGURE 7.4. Blood pressure and cardiac output during mental arithmetic. Abscissa indicates time before, during, and following mental arithmetic by a human subject. The top two sections indicate increases in cardiac output and blood pressure during the stimulus. The section labeled "renal vascular resistance" indicates an increase in association with reduction in extrarenal vascular resistance. The bottom section indicates a marked increase in forearm blood flow during the stimulus. Note that an elevation in blood pressure occurred in this subject through an increase in cardiac output that was proportionately greater than the fall that occurred in total peripheral vascular resistance. Note also that renal vascular resistance increased in contrast to vascular resistance in other regions. (From Brod, J., Fencl, V., Hejl, Z., & Jirka, J. Circulatory changes underlying blood pressure elevation during acute emotional stress (mental arithmetic) in normotensive and hypertensive subjects. *Clinical Science*, 1959, *18*, 269–279. Reprinted by permission.)

perature fell, indicating skin vasoconstriction; and blood flow through skeletal muscle in the forearm rose to more than six times its original value. Cardiovascular and renal function returned to original values within a few minutes after the mental arithmetic was stopped. In general, the cardiovascular and renal responses to mental arithmetic between normotensive and hypertensive subjects were similar. Patients with arterial hypertension had higher resting levels of blood pressure, greater renal vasoconstriction, less vasodilation in skeletal muscles, and a prolongation of hemodynamic response to mental arithmetic, compared to the normotensive subjects. However, only the differences in resting levels of arterial blood pressure reached statistical significance.

The behavioral stimulus of mental arithmetic had several pathophysiological effects necessary to produce sustained elevations of arterial blood pressure. The behavioral state produced by mental arithmetic caused both a rise in arterial blood pressure and a reduction in renal blood flow. Brod and his colleagues recognized the significance of cardiovascular and renal responses in hypertensive subjects, in that greater renal vasoconstriction was noted in the hypertensive than in the normotensive subjects. Also, they noted the persistence of the cardiovascular and renal responses for a longer period of time in the hypertensive subjects than in those with normal levels of blood pressure. However, the similarity of the cardiovascular responses during behavioral stimuli to those occurring during exercise drew attention to vasodilation in forearm skeletal muscle. Subsequent studies by other investigators have also focused attention on skeletal muscle blood flow as part of the defense reaction, and effects of behavioral stimuli on renal function have been less thoroughly studied.

CARDIAC EXCITABILITY AND VENTRICULAR ARRHYTHMIAS

Ventricular Vulnerability to Fibrillation

The concern with cardiac excitability and ventricular arrhythmia arises from the realization that the mechanism of sudden cardiac death in human subjects is usually ventricular fibrillation. Although sudden cardiac death occurs most frequently in the presence of severe ischemic heart disease (Kuller, Cooper, & Perper, 1972), the coronary pathology evident in victims of sudden cardiac death is seldom incompatible with survival (Baba, Bushe, Keller, Geer, & Anthony, 1975). Consequently, if ventricular fibrillation can be prevented or reversed, sudden cardiac death need not occur. Increasingly, it has become evident that sudden cardiac death is an electrical accident that follows a fortuitous combination of risk factors, which includes myocardial ischemia, discrepancies of refractory periods in adjacent regions of the left ventricle, nonuniformity of stimulation by cardiac nerves, circulating hormonal and toxic factors, and metabolic factors. In particular, nonuniformity of cardiac excitability during the relative refractory period is known to be an important factor in the induction of ventricular fibrillation. The compelling association between behavioral factors and sudden cardiac death has focused attention on the influence of cardiac sympathetic nerves on ventricular vulnerability to fibrillation.

Studies by Han, Garcia de Jalon, and Moe (1964) in anesthetized dogs have illustrated the adrenergic affect on ventricular vulnerability. Figure 7.5

shows the experimental arrangement involved in stimulating the cardiac sympathetic nerves while stimulating ventricular myocardium through bipolar electrodes near the pulmonary conus. To determine the vulnerability of the ventricle, a 10-msec test stimulus was delivered during the vulnerable period of the cardiac cycle. The strength of the test stimulus was increased progressively in order to determine the threshold for either multiple responses or fibrillation. During experiments, the lowest threshold for multiple responses was chosen as the measure of ventricular vulnerability. The effects of stimulation of the cardiac sympathetic nerves and intravenous administration of sympathomimetic amines on ventricular vulnerability were compared.

Stimulation of the cardiac sympathetic nerves and intravenous administration of sympathomimetic amines had different effects on ventricular vulnerability to fibrillation. Figure 7.6 shows the results obtained during stimulation of cardiac nerves from the left stellate ganglion and infusions of epinephrine and norepinephrine. Stimulation of cardiac nerves from the left stellate ganglion increased vulnerability throughout the 15-minute period of stimulation. In contrast, both norepinephrine and epinephrine administered intravenously produced an initial increase in vulnerability, followed by a decrease which lasted until the infusion was stopped. Further experiments showed the effects of sympathetic nerve stimulation on diastolic excitabili-

FIGURE 7.5. Experimental arrangement for testing ventricular vulnerability to electrical stimulation. The heart in the open chest of an anesthetized dog was attached to Pulse Generator A, which controlled heart rate, and Pulse Generator B, which delivered electrical stimuli of controlled intensity. CRO Channel A recorded surface electrocardiograms, and Channel B was used to control the temporal delivery of test stimulations. (From Han, J., Garcia de Jalon, P., & Moe, G. K. Adrenergic effects on ventricular vulnerability. *Circulation Research*, 1964, *14*, 516–524. Reprinted by permission.)

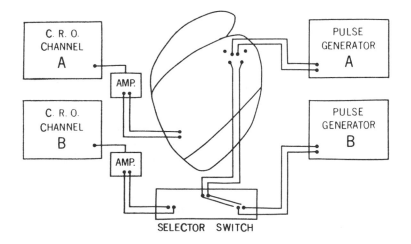

EXP. 1·16·63 (A)

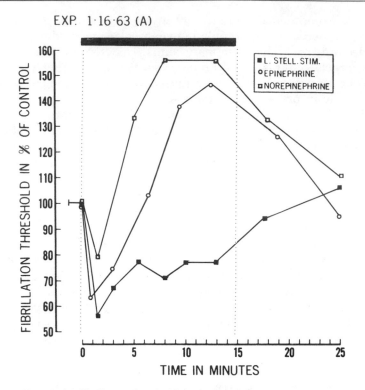

FIGURE 7.6. Ventricular fibrillation threshold during left stellate ganglion stimulation and infusions of epinephrine and norepinephrine. Abscissa indicates time in minutes during experimental conditions (0–15 minutes, indicated by solid bar) and during recovery in an anesthetized dog with controlled heart rate and controlled electrical stimulations to the right ventricle. Closed squares represent data during stimulation of the left stellate ganglion, and open circles and squares represent data obtained during infusion of catecholamines. Note that left stellate ganglion stimulation reduced the threshold for ventricular fibrillation, whereas the predominant effect of catecholamine infusions was an increase in threshold. (From Han, J., Garcia de Jalon, P., & Moe, G. K. Adrenergic effects on ventricular vulnerability. *Circulation Research*, 1964, *14*, 516–524. Reprinted by permission of the American Heart Association, Inc.)

ty, duration and temporal dispersion of the refractory period, and intraventricular conduction times. In general, stimulation of cardiac nerves from the left stellate ganglion shortened the ventricular refractory period, increased the temporal dispersion of refractory periods, and increased ventricular vulnerability to fibrillation. During the intravenous administration of epinephrine and norepinephrine, ventricular vulnerability to fibrillation was increased initially at a time when temporal dispersion of refractory periods was also increased. As intravenous infusions were continued, ventricular vulnerability decreased, and the temporal dispersion of refractory periods was also decreased.

In all experiments, the temporal dispersion of recovery of excitability and the degree of ventricular vulnerability were closely related; the ventricle was more vulnerable to fibrillation when the dispersion was increased. Results of previous investigators had been interpreted as demonstrating adrenergic facilitation of fibrillation by increased automaticity, decreased diastolic threshold, and decreased duration of refractory periods. The results of the studies by Han et al. (1964) indicated that the critical effect of adrenergic facilitation was the nonuniformity of recovery of excitability during stimulation of cardiac sympathetic nerves, rather than during infusion of sympathomimetic amines.

Similar studies performed by Schwartz, Snebold, and Brown (1976) demonstrated differences between right and left cardiac sympathetic nerve stimulation. Control fibrillation threshold measurements were determined during reversible blockade of the right or left stellate ganglion and after surgical removal of one or both ganglia. The results of these experiments are shown in Figure 7.7. In all animals, ablation or cooling of the left stellate ganglion increased the ventricular fibrillation threshold and decreased ventricular vulnerability. In contrast, ablation or cooling of the right stellate ganglion lowered the threshold and increased ventricular vulnerability. These results were interpreted as showing that right and left cardiac sympathetic nerves had different effects on cardiac excitability. In addition, they provided an experimental basis for the treatment of patients with recurrent ventricular fibrillation by excision of the left stellate ganglion.

Adrenergic Effects on Electrocardiogram and Q-T Interval

Prediction and prevention of sudden cardiac death would be greatly enhanced if noninvasive techniques were available to assess the risks for ventricular fibrillation. The electrocardiogram of human subjects does provide one means for evaluating risk of ventricular fibrillation and cardiac death. In particular, prolongation of the Q-T interval on the electrocardiogram is associated with a high risk for cardiac arrhythmias and sudden cardiac death (Schwartz & Wolf, 1978). Causes for prolonged Q-T intervals include drug intoxication, electrolyte imbalance, lesions of the central nervous system, and a familial type of long Q-T syndrome (Abildskov, 1979). However, Abildskov (1976) has shown that the relationship between Q-T interval and ventricular recovery time is complex. For example, left stellate ganglion stimulation in dogs frequently caused prolongation of the Q-T interval, in association with reductions in refractory period in the innervated area. Rapid intravenous injection of epinephrine or norepinephrine or brief stimulation of cardiac sympathetic nerves resulted in prolongation of the Q-T interval in anesthetized dogs. Slow infusions of the catecholamines or prolonged sympathetic nerve stimulation reduced the duration of the Q-T interval. These results suggested to Abildskov that Q-T prolongation is the result of localized influences, while

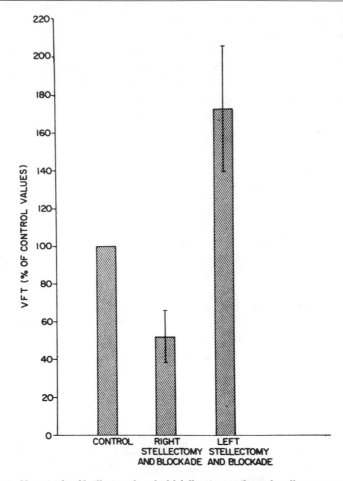

FIGURE 7.7. Ventricular fibrillation threshold following unilateral stellectomy and blockade. Ventricular vulnerability to fibrillation was tested using recording and stimulating electrodes attached to the heart in the open chest of anesthetized dogs. The threshold to ventricular fibrillation was tested in each subject before excising or blocking either stellate ganglion, and observations were repeated following blockade by cooling or surgical excision of the right or the left stellate ganglion. Note that ablation or cooling of the left stellate ganglion decreased ventricular vulnerability to ventricular fibrillation by raising the fibrillation threshold, whereas ablation or cooling of the right stellate ganglion increased ventricular vulnerability. (From Schwartz, P. J., Snebold, N. G., & Brown, A. M. Effects of unilateral cardiac sympathetic denervation on the ventricular fibrillation threshold. *American Journal of Cardiology*, 1976, 37, 1034–1040. Reprinted by permission.)

Q-T reduction is the effect of more widespread influences on ventricular recovery. If the actual time required for ventricular electrical repolarization exceeds the duration of the Q-T interval in the body-surface electrocardiogram, then portions of late recovery cancel each other. Reduction of recovery time in one of these portions exposes the electrocardiographic effects of others, which prolongs the Q-T interval (Abildskov & Klein, 1962). In experimental studies on anesthetized dogs, evidence was obtained that the duration of the ventricular repolarization exceeds the duration of the Q-T interval following normal ventricular excitation (Abildskov & Klein, 1962; Burgess, Millar, & Abildskov, 1969). This suggests that late portions of recovery were not evident in the Q-T interval until localized regions of the ventricular myocardium had reductions in recovery time. Conditions displaying a paradoxical Q-T prolongation would therefore be ones in which the normal disparity of recovery times was increased and would increase the risk of ventricular fibrillation. Any condition that reduced ventricular recovery time but prolonged the Q-T interval, and any condition that prolonged recovery time but reduced the Q-T interval, should theoretically increase the risk of ventricular fibrillation.

Another electrocardiographic phenomenon that may be associated with increased risk for ventricular fibrillation is alternation of the T wave without any concomitant change in the QRS complex (Schwartz & Malliani, 1975). In animal experiments, T wave alternans has been observed following occlusion of a coronary artery, increases in circulating catecholamines, and hypocalcemia. It also has been noted in patients affected by the long Q-T syndrome. The occurrence of a long Q-T interval in families is associated with a high familial incidence of syncopal attacks due to ventricular fibrillation and of sudden cardiac death. In patients with this syndrome, the prolongation of the Q-T interval represents a stable feature, while T wave alternans is related to the occurrence of intense physical or psychological stimuli. Thus, both clinical observations and results of animal experiments suggest that regional disparities of ventricular repolarization in response to sympathetic nerve stimulation can elicit not only a prolongation of the Q-T interval, but also T wave alternans. Presumably, sustained alteration of T wave vectors, as may be seen in some forms of intracranial disease, may be caused by disparities of stimulation through cardiac nerves from the left and right stellate ganglia.

Mechanisms of Ventricular Arrhythmias

Clinical experience with patients who have suffered acute myocardial infarctions indicates that severe ventricular arrhythmias, such as ventricular tachycardia and ventricular fibrillation, occur under special circumstances involving neurogenic factors, hormonal influences, and metabolic causes. Although coronary arteriosclerosis and myocardial ischemia favor the occurrence of ventricular premature beats, which may trigger ventricular fibrillation, the severity of ventricular arrhythmias is not necessarily proportional to the severity of coronary artery or myocardial disease. Other risk factors apparently contribute to occurrence of severe ventricular arrhythmias. These include elevated circulating levels of FFAs (Kurien & Oliver, 1966), increased sympathetic nervous system activity, elevated circulating levels of catecholamines (Ceremuzynski, Staszewska-Barczak, & Herbacynska-Cedro, 1969), and potassium loss from myocardial cells (Regan, Harman, Lehan, Burke, & Oldewurtel, 1967).

Effects of circulating levels of FFAs on cardiac arrhythmias has been demonstrated both in patients with acute myocardial infarctions caused by coronary arteriosclerosis (Kurien & Oliver, 1966) and in experimental animals with myocardial infarctions caused by experimental occlusion of the left circumflex artery (Kurien, Yates, & Oliver, 1969). In both human patients and experimental animals, subjects with high levels of FFAs were more likely to develop serious ventricular arrhythmias, culminating in sudden cardiac death than were subjects with low levels. In human patients, high levels of FFAs are probably caused by increased adipose tissue lipolysis, which is in turn caused by sympathetic nervous system activity and high circulating levels of catecholamines. In experimental animals, high levels of FFAs were induced by administering Intralipid, a lipid emulsion containing triglyceride, then activating the plasma lipolytic system with heparin (Kurien et al., 1969). The association between high plasma FFA levels and disorders of cardiac rhythm during myocardial ischemia can be related to the effects of FFAs on myocardial cellular metabolism and function. The FFAs increase myocardial oxygen requirements (Simonsen & Kjekshus, 1978) and interfere with mitochondrial oxygen transport.

Sympathetic nervous system activity may also influence ventricular electrical stability through direct actions on the heart. The regions of the brain most likely to influence cardiac rhythm are located in the hypothalamus. Stimulation in regions that influence cardiac rhythm also elicits sympathetic nervous system activity. In normal hearts, hypothalamic stimulation does not provoke ventricular fibrillation (Lown & Verrier, 1978). However, following acute myocardial ischemia caused by occlusion of the left anterior descending coronary artery, hypothalamic stimulation caused ventricular fibrillation in a majority of experimental animals (Lown & Verrier, 1978). Electrical stimulation of stellate ganglia, eliciting increased sympathetic nervous system stimulation of the heart, also produced ventricular fibrillation in a majority of animal subjects (Lown & Verrier, 1976). Tonic vagal efferent activity also exerts a significant influence on cardiac rhythm in animals following acute myocardial infarction. Blockade of vagal efferent activity with atropine produced a significant increase in ventricular vulnerability (Rabinowitz, Verrier, & Lown, 1976). Administration of propranolol, which produces beta-adrenergic blockade, reduced the likelihood of ventricular fibrillation (Brooks,

rved with the same
vulnerability to ar-
d by administration
that sympathetic
o ventricular fib-
of the effects of
adipose tissue
ay be induced
olamines lib-
Myocardial
ction poten-
ion of myo-
ion, stim-
FAs from
rdial tis-
a dele-
to con-

athetic and parasympa-
illation.

en studied in experi-
ced by occlusion of the
ation of electrical current
es (Matta, Verrier, & Lown,
ses to a single electrical stim-
of ventricular fibrillation cur-
sity of stimuli delivered during
e and then multiple extrasystoles,
ar fibrillation.

e used to demonstrate the effects of
arrhythmias. Dogs were exposed to a
e electrical stimuli were administered on
Verrier, & Corbalan, 1973). Following this
terior descending coronary artery was occlud-
ecovered from the coronary occlusion and were
they were reexposed to the Pavlovian sling. As
threshold for repetitive ventricular extrasystoles was

ar vulnerability to arrhythmia during classical conditioning. Threshold
dlar extrasystoles was tested in an unanesthetized dog with electrodes
art, following conditioning to aversive electrical stimuli administered in a
nd following occlusion of the left anterior descending coronary artery. Note
old for ventricular arrhythmia was lower with the animal in the aversive sling
than with the animal in a cage where aversive stimuli had never been administered.
n, B., & Verrier, R. Neural factors in sudden death. In A. M. Brown, A. Malliani,
vartz, & A. Zanchetti (Eds.), *Neural mechanisms in cardiac arrhythmias*. New York: Raven
1978. Reprinted by permission.)

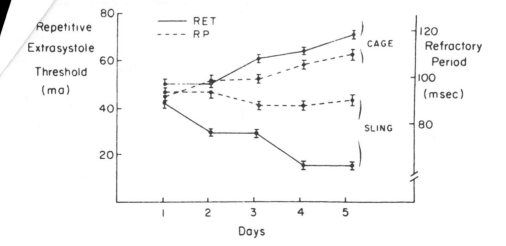

lowered markedly in comparison to the threshold obs[...]
animals in their home cages. This increase in ventricular
rhythmia induced by the Pavlovian sling could be prevente[...]
of beta-adrenergic-blocking drugs. These results suggest[...]
nervous system activity increases ventricular vulnerability [...]
rillation in the presence of an ischemic myocardium. Part[...]
sympathetic nervous system activity may be mediated throug[...]
lipolysis with elevated circulating levels of FFAs, and part m[...]
by direct effects of catecholamines in circulating blood or catec[...]
erated from cardiac nerves on the ventricular repolarization[...]
ischemia is known to shorten the duration of ventricular muscle a[...]
tials, and adrenergic stimulation reduces the repolarization durat[...]
cardial cells that have been spared the ischemic insult. In addi[...]
ulation of cardiac sympathetic nerves would result in release of F[...]
triglycerides stored in the myocardium, through activation of myoc[...]
sue lipase by catecholamines. These FFAs would be expected to hav[...]
terious effect on both myocardial oxygen requirements and the ability
vert glucose to energy.

PATHOGENESIS OF ATHEROSCLEROSIS

The Response-to-Injury Hypothesis

The lesions of atherosclerosis are limited principally to the innermost laye[...]
of the artery wall and consist of intimal smooth muscle cell proliferation, for[...]
mation of large amounts of connective tissue matrix by the proliferated
smooth muscle, and deposition of lipids both within the cells and in the connective tissues surrounding them (Ross & Glomset, 1976). Although the accumulation of lipid and calcium gives the appearance of a degenerative process
to lesions of atherosclerosis, the earlier phases of alterations in the intimal
endothelial cells and proliferation of vascular smooth muscle cells suggest
that injury may be more important as an initiating mechanism than degen-
eration may be (Ross, 1979). The "response-to-injury hypothesis" arose because of the similarity in appearance between the early lesions of atherosclerosis and the response of artery walls to experimentally induced injury. The
hypothesis suggests that endothelial cells become detached from the lining
of the artery, platelets adhere to the exposed subendothelial connective
tissue, and material released from the platelets enters into the artery wall
(Stemerman & Ross, 1972). Furthermore, the hypothesis suggests that the
interaction between plasma components and platelet constituents upon the
smooth muscle cells of the artery wall causes migration of smooth muscle
cells from the media into the intima. These smooth muscle cells produce relatively large amounts of connective tissue matrix macromolecules. Experiments in animal models have shown that platelet adherence, aggregation,
and release of platelet substances occur after mechanical injury (R. J. Fried-

man *et al.*, 1975; Moore, 1973), as well as after several forms of chemical injury (Harker *et al.*, 1974, 1976). Examination of sites where platelets have adhered shows that smooth muscle cells have migrated from the media into the intima and have begun to proliferate. In monkeys with hyperlipidemia caused by a high-fat diet, smooth muscle proliferation, new connective tissue formation, and lipid deposition were all apparent (Ross & Harker, 1976). The intimal smooth muscle proliferative response appears to be reversible, but endothelial regeneration appears to be defective in experimental animals with hypercholesterolemia. The sequence of events postulated by this hypothesis is illustrated in Figure 7.9 (Ross & Harker, 1976).

FIGURE 7.9. The response-to-injury hypothesis. The outer cycle represents a sequence of events following endothelial injury. Starting at the top of the figure and moving in a clockwise direction, note the sequence of injury (the first section) leading to desquamation in the second section, which leads in turn to platelet adherence, aggregation, and release of platelet factors in the third section; this is followed by intimal smooth muscle proliferation and connective tissue formation in the fourth section. The fifth section in the outer cycle represents a phase of healing and regression, restoring the artery wall to its original condition. The inner cycle represents effects of repeated or chronic injury, in which lipid deposition and continued smooth muscle proliferation occur, with progression to complicated lesions that calcify. (From Ross, R. The arterial wall and atherosclerosis. *Annual Review of Medicine*, 1979, *30*, 1–15. Reproduced, with permission, from the *Annual Review of Medicine*, Vol. 30 © 1979 by Annual Reviews, Inc.)

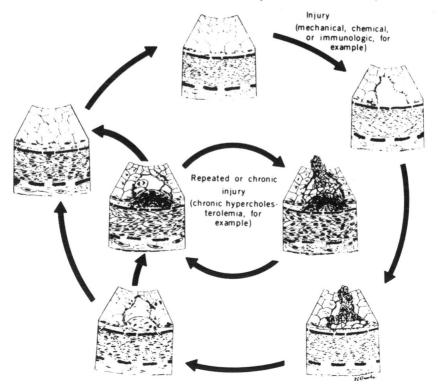

The outer cycle in this figure illustrates the sequence of endothelial injury leading to desquamation, platelet adherence, aggregation, and release, followed by intimal smooth muscle proliferation and connective tissue formation. The outer cycle also shows regression and healing, whereas the inner cycle demonstrates the consequences of repeated endothelial injury or delayed endothelial regeneration. In the inner cycle, lipid deposition, as well as continued smooth muscle proliferation, leads to complex lesions that calcify.

The formation of atherosclerotic lesions in response to continued intimal injury of the aorta first was demonstrated in normolipemic rabbits (Moore, 1973). The insertion of a plastic catheter through the femoral artery into the aorta induced lesions in the aorta at points where continuous wall contact occurred between aorta and catheter. Lipid was deposited in regions that were not repaired by endothelial cell regeneration, suggesting that continuous or repeated injury enhanced platelet adherence, thrombosis, and deposition of lipid in intimal cells.

A number of different serum factors have been shown to stimulate both vascular smooth muscle cell proliferation and cell migration. Arterial smooth muscle cells growing in tissue culture increase in number at a fairly constant rate in the presence of 1% blood serum. Figure 7.10 shows the rate of increase of three different cell cultures incubated in 1% pooled serum for 7 days and then incubated in either 5% blood serum, 5% plasma serum, or 0% serum (Ross, Glomset, Kariya, & Harker, 1974). Further experiments in which intact platelets were removed and then replaced in plasma serum indicated that the growth-promoting activity of blood serum is derived from platelets. A number of other experiments have demonstrated that cell proliferation is stimulated by lipoproteins, insulin, and several other hormones.

Endocrine Influences

The influence of endocrines on atherogenesis might occur through accentuation of endothelial cell loss, platelet aggregation, and vascular smooth muscle cell proliferation. Causes of endothelial cell loss have not been studied extensively. However, neuroendocrine factors may cause intimal injury through effects of sympathetic nervous system activity; in turn, this injury may cause elevations in blood pressure, increases in cardiac output, turbulence at bifurcations, and direct chemical effects of catecholamines on endothelial cells. Endocrine influences on platelet aggregation may occur through elevated levels of circulating catecholamines, which enhance platelet aggregation and promote vascular thrombosis. Although these influences are plausible, no experimental evidence has been obtained that demonstrates effects of neuroendocrine factors on atherogenesis through these mechanisms.

More experimental evidence is available concerning the influence of hormones on vascular smooth muscle cell proliferation. For example, exposure of arterial tissue to insulin results in proliferation of smooth muscle cells; inhi-

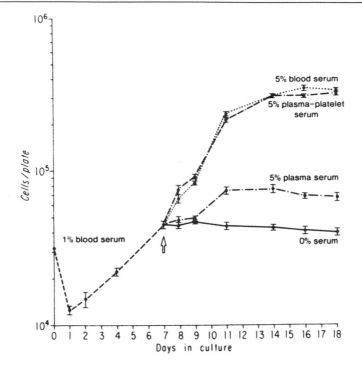

FIGURE 7.10. Platelet factors and arterial smooth muscle proliferation. Abscissa indicates time for culture of arterial smooth muscle cells from nonhuman primates, in culture dishes incubated in medium containing 1% blood serum. After 7 days (see arrow) the cells were incubated either in serum-free medium, a medium containing 5% dialyzed serum from whole blood containing platelets, a medium containing 5% dialyzed serum from plasma containing platelet factors, and a medium containing 5% dialyzed serum from plasma with no platelets. Closed circles represent the number of smooth muscle cells in each of several cultures, and the lines and bars represent 1 standard error of the mean for each value. Note that the 5% dialyzed serum from plasma had little or no proliferative effect unless platelets or platelet factors were present. (From Ross, R., Glomset, J., Kariya, B., & Harker, L. A platelet-dependent serum factor that stimulates the proliferation of arterial smooth muscle cells "in vitro." *Proceedings of the National Academy of Sciences USA*, 1974, 71, 1207–1210. Reprinted by permission.)

bition of lipolysis; and synthesis of cholesterol, phospholipid, and triglyceride. Insulin in small concentrations stimulates proliferation of cultured smooth muscle cells (Stout, Bierman, & Ross, 1975). When serum from which insulin has been removed is added to cell cultures, smooth muscle growth is reduced. Thus, insulin has the ability to promote changes in the artery that may progress to atherosclerosis. Other hormones tested for their effects on fibroblasts in cell culture have demonstrated enhanced growth. Thus, evidence suggests that hormonal factors that gain access to the subintimal region of the artery wall may enhance smooth muscle cell proliferation more readily than may hormones that are separated from subintimal tissues by an intact layer of endothelial cells.

Plasma Cortisol and Atherosclerosis

The association of elevated plasma cortisol and early atherosclerosis has been demonstrated by coronary angiography in human subjects (Troxler *et al.*, 1977) and in nonhuman primates fed a high-cholesterol diet (Sprague *et al.*, 1980). Significant correlations were found between elevated serial-morning plasma cortisol levels and moderate to severe coronary atherosclerosis in men who had coronary angiography (Troxler *et al.*, 1977). These men were U.S. Air Force air crew members with medical conditions or electrocardiographic signs that could preclude performance of flying duties. A complete medical evaluation, including coronary angiography, was performed to determine risk for coronary heart disease. Plasma cortisol, serum cholesterol, triglycerides, percentage of body fat, blood pressure, age, smoking habits, and coronary angiograms were the variables measured on 71 patients. Figure 7.11 shows the group mean cortisol levels across time for three groups of subjects: one group with no evidence of coronary artery disease, one with mild coronary disease, and one with moderate to severe disease. These results indicate that patients with fewer coronary lesions had a more rapid decline in plasma cortisol levels with time than did patients with greater numbers of lesions. A significant correlation was found between plasma cortisol and cholesterol, blood pressure, and smoking. Furthermore, a patient with a cholesterol level above the sample median had a 6.56 times greater chance of having lesions on angiography than a patient with a cholesterol level below or equal to the sample median. In comparison, a patient with a high 2-hour level of cortisol had a 5.17 times greater chance of having lesions on angiography than a patient with a cortisol level below or equal to the median. Although the mechanism whereby cortisol influences atherosclerosis may be found in the correlation of cortisol and cholesterol levels, it also is possible that cortisol causes either vascular endothelial cell injury, increased platelet aggregation, or enhanced proliferation of vascular smooth muscle.

Experiments designed to evaluate the possible relationship between cortisol and atherosclerosis were carried out with cynomolgus monkeys fed a high-cholesterol diet (Sprague *et al.*, 1980). Male monkeys were given one of four treatments: a controlled diet, an administration of hydrocortisone cypionate orally in orange juice, a .25% cholesterol diet, and cortisol plus a high-cholesterol diet. Cortisol was administered orally each day in the early afternoon. Although all animals fed a high-cholesterol diet developed hypercholesterolemia, cortisol had no significant effect on serum cholesterol levels in the presence of either diet. However, a significant increase in the percentage of aortic intimal surface involved with atherosclerotic lesions was observed in monkeys receiving both cortisol and a high-cholesterol diet, compared to monkeys receiving the high-cholesterol diet only. Cortisol alone did not significantly increase lesion development, compared to the control diet alone. These results suggest that the atherogeneic effect occurred independ-

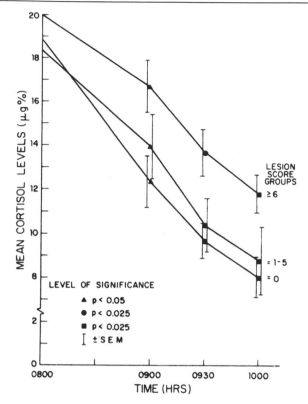

FIGURE 7.11. Plasma concentrations of cortisol in men with and without coronary arteriosclerosis. Abscissa is time during a glucose tolerance test conducted during late morning hours in air crew members subjected to coronary angiography. The upper line represents data collected from men with the greatest severity of arteriosclerotic lesions; the middle and lower lines represent data collected from men with less severe lesions or with no signs of arteriosclerosis. The closed symbols represent mean values, and lines and bars represent 1 standard error of the mean. Note that men with the greatest severity of lesions had higher levels of plasma cortisol and a slower rate of decline in plasma cortisol levels than did subjects with fewer lesions. (From Troxler, R. G., Sprague, E. A., Albanese, R. A., Fuchs, R., & Thompson, A. J. The association of elevated plasma cortisol and early atherosclerosis as demonstrated by coronary angiography. *Atherosclerosis,* 1977, 26, 151–162. Reprinted by permission.)

ently of any effect of cortisol on serum or lipoprotein cholesterol concentrations. Thus, cortisol may have direct effects on the artery wall or on platelet aggregation.

Further evidence suggesting a connection between abnormal ACTH–cortisol rhythms and atherosclerosis arises from the association between myocardial infarction and symptoms of anxiety and depression (Bianchi, Ferguson, & Walsh, 1978). Endogenously depressed psychiatric patients show a loss of circadian rhythmicity in cortisol values, similar to that seen in patients with Cushing's disease (Sachar, Asnis, Halbreich, & Halpern, 1980). Elevations of the urinary free cortisol levels and corticosteroid metabolites in endogenously depressed patients have also been described, as has the reversion to normal rhythm patterns in urinary and cerebral spinal fluid levels after clinical remission of the depression (Carroll, 1976). Stressful life events, anxiety, and depression may modify adrenocortical activity, and psychological factors may influence the atherogenic process and precipitate complications of coronary heart disease.

ARTERIAL HYPERTENSION

Plasma Norepinephrine Levels in Essential Hypertension

Interpretation of results from studies in patients with essential hypertension is complicated by the realization that many pathophysiological mechanisms contribute to elevation of arterial blood pressure. These mechanisms include renal, cardiac, vascular, endocrine, metabolic, and neurogenic factors and are influenced by diet, exercise, and psychological state, as well as by genetic factors. Since there are different combinations of these pathophysiological characteristics evident in patients, it has become apparent that essential hypertension is caused by different pathogenic mechanisms. Although it is too soon to make definite statements about types of essential hypertension, evidence suggests that renal, cardiac, vascular, endocrine, metabolic, or neurogenic factors each contribute the major effect in causation of essential hypertension in certain subgroups of patients. However, evidence also suggests that neurogenic and renal factors contribute to the maintenance of essential hypertension in all patients. Using this approach to prevention and treatment of essential hypertension, controlling the neurogenic and renal factors maintaining essential hypertension should be somewhat effective for all patients. However, the relative effectiveness of controlling renal and neurogenic factors should be greatest in patients with renal or neurogenic causes of elevated blood pressure. Special attention has been focused on neurogenic factors, since renal, cardiac, and vascular mechanisms are influenced by sympathetic nervous system activity.

Many comparative studies of sympathetic nervous system activity have been carried out in patients with essential hypertension and human subjects with average levels of blood pressure. Although many indicators have been used to estimate relative sympathetic nervous system activity, plasma norepinephrine levels are the physiological variable accepted by most investigators as the most valid measure available in human subjects. Many comparative studies of plasma norepinephrine levels in patients with essential hypertension have reported higher levels of norepinephrine in hypertensive groups than in normotensive controls, but the differences have been small when blood has been sampled under resting conditions. However, results of several studies suggest that patients with essential hypertension show exaggerated norepinephrine responses to physiological stimuli associated with orthostasis, isotonic and isometric exercise, exposure to cold, hypoglycemia, hypoxia, or pain, and psychological stimuli eliciting such emotional responses as anxiety or anger. D. S. Goldstein (1981) has reviewed the medical literature to determine the hypertensive–normotensive differences in norepinephrine responses to physiological and psychological stimuli. Of the several physiological stimuli known to affect the sympathetic nervous system, only orthostasis and exercise have been extensively studied. Among 24 studies involving orthostasis, the increment in plasma norepinephrine levels with standing was similar for hypertensives and normotensives. In contrast, among eight studies involving exercise, the increment in plasma levels of norepinephrine was significantly greater in hypertensives (834 vs. 450 pg/ml). During both standing and isotonic exercises, absolute increments in plasma levels of norepinephrine correlated with basal levels in hypertensive subjects but not in control subjects. D. S. Goldstein interprets these results as indicating that there is a subgroup of patients among the hypertensive population with elevated plasma levels of norepinephrine at rest and increased sympathetic nervous system responsiveness to standing and isotonic exercise. He also concludes that there is insufficent evidence available to determine whether other types of physiological stimuli or psychological stimuli elicit abnormal increases in sympathetic nervous system activity.

Many studies of sympathetic nervous system activity in association with psychological stimuli have been reported in which blood pressure and heart rate have been the independent variables measured. The associations among blood pressure, heart rate, and plasma norepinephrine levels have been studied during physical activity in hypertensive men. Watson, Hamilton, Reid, and Littler (1979) investigated these variables during a range of physical activity in eight hypertensive subjects to determine the quantitative relationship between plasma levels of norepinephrine and other physiological variables. Blood pressure was recorded over 24 hours from an intraarterial cannula. Venous blood specimens were obtained for measurements of norepinephrine from a forearm venous cannula. Blood samples were obtained during sleeping, lying quietly while awake, sitting, standing, walking, and following 8 minutes of upright exercise on a bicycle ergometer. Figure 7.12 shows the mean level of plasma norepinephrine level plotted against mean systolic blood pressure during each activity. In each subject, a statistically significant linear relationship was observed between the logarithm of plasma norepinephrine and systolic blood pressure. A similar relationship was observed between the logarithm of plasma norepinephrine and heart rate in most subjects. Analysis of variance showed that there was a strong association between the logarithm of plasma norepinephrine and systolic blood pressure ($r = .59$) and between the logarithm of norepinephrine and heart rate ($r = .69$), with a weaker relationship between the logarithm of norepinephrine and dia-

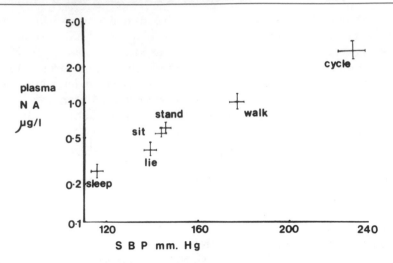

FIGURE 7.12. Systolic blood pressure and plasma norepinephrine levels during various physical activities. Abscissa is systolic blood pressure recorded from an intraarterial cannula in eight hypertensive subjects during a range of physical activities. Ordinate is plasma concentration of norepinephrine plotted on a logarithmic scale. Values are expressed as means obtained from eight subjects, and lines and bars represent 1 standard error of the mean. Note that a linear relationship was observed between the logarithm of plasma norepinephrine concentration and systolic blood pressure. (From Watson, R. D. S., Hamilton, C. A., Reid, J. L., & Littler, W. A. Changes in plasma norepinephrine, blood pressure and heart rate during physical activity in hypertensive man. *Hypertension*, 1979, *1*, 342–346. Reprinted by permission.)

stolic blood pressure ($r = .36$) when the patients were considered as a group. Since heart rate, systolic blood pressure, and diastolic blood pressure are not independent variables, a multiple-correlation coefficient was determined, which indicated that 66% of the variance of plasma norepinephrine was associated with changes in blood pressure and heart rate. These observations suggest that plasma norepinephrine levels reflect short-term changes in sympathetic nervous system activity. However, evidence from experiments in which norepinephrine was infused intravenously (Dargie, Davies, Dean, Dollery, Maling, & Reid, 1977) indicates that distribution volume and norepinephrine clearance rates may vary widely among individuals. Therefore, plasma levels may vary among individuals for reasons other than changes in sympathetic nervous system activity. Further refinements in the study of sympathetic nervous system activity during the administration of physiological and psychological stimuli should include measurements of norepinephrine clearance rate, as well as absolute levels of norepinephrine during various experimental states.

Studies have also been made of plasma epinephrine concentrations in patients with essential hypertension, and the results have been compared to plasma concentrations in human subjects with average levels of blood pressure. Franco-Morselli, Elghozi, Joly, DiGiuilio, and Meyer (1977) reported that plasma levels of epinephrine in normotensive subjects showed little increase between lying and standing. In patients with essential hypertension, plasma epinephrine concentrations were considerably higher while lying and increased remarkably during standing. The highest levels of plasma epinephrine were observed in hypertensive subjects over the age of 35 years. Although an increase in mean heart rate was observed in hypertensive patients, no significant correlation was found between heart rate and plasma levels of epinephrine. No differences were observed in plasma levels of norepinephrine, dopamine, or plasma renin activity in hypertensive subjects lying in a supine position or after standing for 10 minutes. These results suggest that plasma levels of epinephrine in hypertensive patients may be a useful index of sympathetic nervous system activity.

High-Renin Essential Hypertension

An association between sympathetic nervous system activity and renal function has been observed in the control of renin release by the kidneys. Experiments in laboratory animals have shown that adrenergic stimuli through infusions of catecholamines and stimulation of renal nerves increases renal secretion of renin (Vander, 1965). Also, hypertensive patients with low levels of plasma renin activity have physiological signs of low sympathetic nervous system activity (Esler, Randall, Bennett, Zweifler, Julius, Rydelek, Cohen, & DeQuattro, 1976). Therefore, it has been suggested that patients with mild essential hypertension and elevated levels of plasma renin activity have abnormal levels of sympathetic nervous system activity, which may contribute to the maintenance of elevated blood pressure levels (Esler & Nestel, 1973).

Esler et al. (1977) have compared indexes of sympathetic nervous system activity in patients with mild high-renin essential hypertension, hypertensive patients with normal plasma renin activity, and normal human subjects. Figure 7.13 shows the levels of plasma norepinephrine concentrations in normal subjects and patients with essential hypertension. Plasma norepinephrine concentration was elevated in patients with high-renin hypertension, as compared to normal subjects and the hypertensive patients with normal plasma renin activity. However, plasma epinephrine concentration was similar in all three groups. Evidence for increased sympathetic nervous system function in high-renin hypertension was obtained following administration of propranolol given intravenously to block the cardiac beta-adrenergic influences of the sympathetic nervous system. Blockade of the peripheral effects of sympathetic nervous system activity on vascular resistance was achieved by administration of phentolamine, an alpha-adrenergic blocking agent. As shown in Figure 7.14, total peripheral vascular resistance fell significantly only in the group with high-renin hypertension. Studies of heart

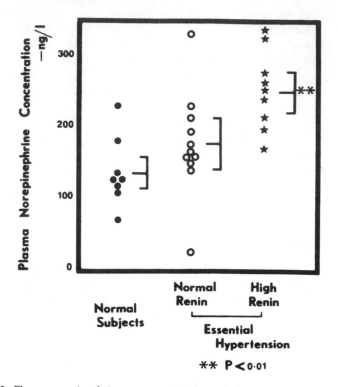

FIGURE 7.13. Plasma norepinephrine concentrations in normal subjects and patients with essential hypertension having normal and high plasma renin activities. Closed circles represent plasma norepinephrine concentrations in normal subjects; open circles represent values from patients with essential hypertension having normal plasma renin activity; and closed stars are concentrations measured in patients with essential hypertension in association with high plasma renin activity. The horizontal lines and brackets represent mean values and 1 standard deviation of the mean for each group. Note that patients with essential hypertension in association with high plasma renin activity as a group had a significantly higher mean plasma norepinephrine concentration than did patients with normal plasma renin activity or normal subjects. (From Esler, M., Randall, O., Bennett, J., Zweifler, A., Julius, S., Rydelek, P., Cohen, E., & DeQuattro, V. Suppression of sympathetic nervous function in low-renin and normal-renin essential hypertension. *Lancet*, 1976, *ii*, 115–118. Reprinted by permission.)

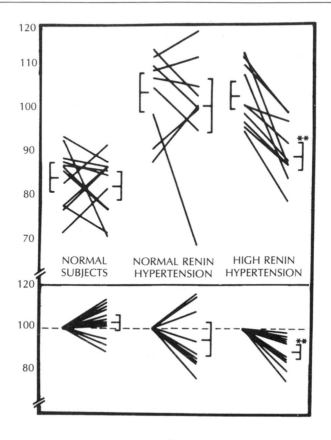

**P<0.01

FIGURE 7.14. Arterial blood pressure and peripheral vascular resistance before and during autonomic blockade with atropine, propranolol, and phentolamine. The top panel shows mean arterial blood pressure (in mm Hg) before and after intravenous administration of atropine, .4 mg per kg; propranolol, .2 mg per kg; and phentolamine, 15 mg. The bottom panel shows the percentage of change in total peripheral vascular resistance before and after administration of phentolamine intravenously, after prior administration of atropine and propranolol. The horizontal lines and brackets indicate mean values for each group with 1 standard deviation of the mean. Note that patients with essential hypertension associated with high plasma renin activity had significant reductions in arterial blood pressure following autonomic blockade with atropine, propranolol, and phentolamine, whereas changes in blood pressure were not significant in the other groups. Note also that administration of phentolamine to patients with essential hypertension associated with high plasma renin activity caused a reduction in peripheral vascular resistance, whereas subjects in the other two groups did not show consistent changes. (From Esler, M., Randall, O., Bennett, J., Zweifler, A., Julius, S., Rydelek, P., Cohen, E., & DeQuattro, V. Suppression of sympathetic nervous function in low-renin and normal-renin essential hypertension. *Lancet*, 1976, *ii*, 115–118. Reprinted by permission.)

rate and cardiac output before and after beta-adrenergic blockade alone revealed a greater reduction in heart rate and cardiac output in patients with high-renin hypertension than in the other two groups. Results of these studies suggest there was increased sympathetic nervous system activity in patients with mild high-renin essential hypertension. They presented a picture of adrenergic cardiovascular excitation with sympathetic stimulation of the heart and resistance vessels.

Possible origins of the increased sympathetic nervous system activity also were investigated, which included measurements of psychological factors. Anxiety levels were estimated with the Institute for Personality and Ability Testing (IPAT) Anxiety Scale Questionnaire. The level of suppressed hostility was estimated from the response to the Buss–Durkee Personality Inventory, the "Anger in–Anger out" scale of Harburg, and the IPAT 16 Personality Factor Questionnaire. Hypertensive patients were found to have normal anxiety levels as assessed by psychometric instruments. Suppressed hostility was prominent in the hypertensive patients but only in those with elevated plasma renin activity. The patients with high-renin essential hypertension as a group were controlled, guilt prone, and submissive, with a high level of unexpressed anger. Esler *et al.* (1977) suggest that hypertension in these patients with high-renin activity was neurogenic and possibly caused by psychological factors.

An association between sympathetic nervous system activity and plasma renin activity has also been demonstrated during sodium deprivation. Human subjects on a low-sodium diet might be expected to have low arterial pressure, except that increased sympathetic nervous system activity and renin release occur as feedback-control mechanisms to maintain arterial pressure (Tarazi, Dustan, Frohlich, Gifford, & Hoffman, 1970). Thus, the response to sodium deprivation can be used to estimate the adrenergic and renin responses to a physiological stimulus. Robertson and his colleagues (Robertson, Shand, Hollifield, Nies, Frolich, & Oates, 1979) studied the effect of sodium deprivation in normal subjects and patients with mild or borderline hypertension in the supine posture, upright posture, and during exercise on a treadmill. While the subjects were in sodium balance on a normal-sodium diet, there was no difference between the normal and hypertensive groups in levels of plasma norepinephrine or plasma renin activity in either the supine or standing position. The concentration of norepinephrine in plasma rose in both groups after exercise on a treadmill, and levels of norepinephrine were significantly greater in the hypertensive group. The concentration of epinephrine in plasma immediately after exercise was not significantly different between the two groups, but the level of epinephrine in the period just before stepping on to the treadmill was greater in the hypertensive group. After the subjects came into balance on a low-sodium diet, the average plasma concentration of norepinephrine was significantly higher in the hypertensive group in the supine position and after upright posture.

Plasma renin activity during sodium deprivation also rose to a higher level in the hypertensive group than in the normotensive subjects. Neither plasma epinephrine levels nor urinary levels of metanephrine increased significantly with sodium deprivation. No differences were observed in hemodynamic responses to the cold-pressor test or hand-grip exercise. The results of these investigations suggest that hypertensive subjects have an abnormal response of sympathetic nervous system activity and renin secretion during exercise and sodium deprivation, which may indicate a neurogenic mechanism maintaining high levels of blood pressure in patients with essential hypertension.

Prediction of Essential Hypertension

A challenge for clinical investigators concerned with the pathogenesis of essential hypertension is the prediction of sustained levels of high blood pressure in normotensive subjects with certain cardiovascular characteristics. Although initial blood pressure levels are the strongest known predictor of future hypertension (Julius & Schork, 1978), other predictors have been sought. Predictor characteristics that have been evaluated include family history, resting blood pressure, resting heart rate, body weight, and hemodynamic response to physiological and psychological stimuli. Falkner and his colleagues (Falkner, Kushner, Gaddo, & Angelakos, 1981) have evaluated a group of adolescents with systolic or diastolic blood pressures between the 90th and 95th percentiles. In a follow-up period of 5 to 41 months (median of 17 months), 28 of the total group of 50 adolescents developed sustained hypertension. At the time of initial evaluation, these 28 hypertensive adolescents had greater body weight, higher systolic blood pressure, and higher diastolic blood pressure; females also had higher resting heart rates than those adolescents who were normotensive. Measurements of blood pressure and heart rate also were made before and during a 10-minute behavioral task involving mental arithmetic (sequential subtraction). The group of subjects that later became hypertensive demonstrated an increase in blood pressure during mental arithmetic, with the greatest differences observed in levels of diastolic blood pressure before and during the behavioral task. The normotensive controls demonstrated an initial increase of heart rate and blood pressure at the onset of mental arithmetic, with a progressive reduction in heart rate and systolic pressure during the behavioral task. In the subjects who became hypertensive, the initial increases of blood pressure and heart rate were sustained throughout mental arithmetic and may indicate the presence of a dysregulatory neurogenic component in the mechanisms regulating their blood pressure. Thus, subjects with high normal levels of blood pressure and with increased and prolonged responses to psychological stimuli may be at increased risk for developing essential hypertension in the future.

SUDDEN CARDIAC DEATH

Repetitive Ventricular Response

Complications of coronary arteriosclerosis may take many forms, but the most dramatic and most common is sudden cardiac death. Although the definition of sudden cardiac death is changeable, most investigators utilize the 1-hour definition, in which death is due to cardiac causes either instantaneously or up to 1 hour after the onset of symptoms in an individual who may or may not have known preexisting heart disease, but in whom the time and mode of death occurred unexpectedly. The most common cause of sudden cardiac death is CHD, even though the incidence of sudden death is more common in patients with other forms of heart disease. Despite the diffuse nature of coronary atherosclerosis in sudden cardiac death, only one-third of such patients have occlusive coronary artery thrombi (Baba *et al.*, 1975). In patients dying within 30 seconds after onset of any symptoms, almost no evidence of an acute pathological lesion has been found (M. Friedman, Manwaring, Rosenman, Donlon, Ortega, & Grube, 1973). These findings suggest that sudden cardiac death in many cases may be an electrical event that is not the result of acute coronary thrombosis and myocardial infarction.

The largest group of patients at greatest risk for sudden cardiac death are those who have survived recent acute myocardial infarctions. Patients who have been resuscitated from sudden cardiac death who do not have acute myocardial infarctions are the most likely of all to have sudden cardiac death in the future, but their numbers are much fewer than those who have recovered from recent myocardial infarctions. Greene and his colleagues (Greene, Reid, & Schaeffer, 1978) studied 48 survivors of acute myocardial infarctions. During a 1-year follow-up period, 19 of those patients (40%) had symptomatic ventricular tachycardia or sudden death. In an effort to find a predictor of sudden death in this group, these investigators used a ventricular pacing technique to assess ventricular electrical instability. Following the insertion of electrode catheters high in the right atrium and at the apex of the right ventricle, pacing stimuli were administered to the right atrium, while a single ventricular stimulus was introduced every eight beats. These ventricular stimuli were first introduced at the QRS complex and progressively moved toward the preceding T wave until ventricular refractoriness was reached, or until repetitive ventricular responses were produced. These were defined as two or more ventricular premature beats in response to a single electrical stimulus. Of the 48 survivors of myocardial infarctions, 19 had repetitive ventricular responses. During the next 12 months, 15 of those patients (79%) had symptomatic ventricular tachycardia or sudden death, as compared with four of 29 patients (14%) who did not have repetitive ventricular responses. The greatest risk for ventricular tachycardia or sudden death occurred in patients with poor left ventricular function in addition to repetitive ventricular responses. Also, ventricular tachycardia revealed during a 34-hour ambulatory monitoring was highly predictive of ventricular tachycardia or sudden death in patients surviving myocardial infarctions. These results indicate that patients with increased cardiac excitability and ventricular arrhythmias may be the ones most liable to sudden cardiac death in response to physiological or psychological stimuli.

Prolonged Q-T Interval

Patients who have survived acute myocardial infarction also have been studied for their vulnerability to sudden cardiac death in relation to prolonged Q-T intervals in their electrocardiograms. Studies with experimental animals have shown that imbalance in the sympathetic nervous system stimulation of the heart, which prolongs the Q-T interval, increases vulnerability to ventricular arrhythmias following coronary artery occlusion (Schulze, Humphrie, Griffith, Ducci, Achuff, Baird, Mettits, & Pitt, 1977). The possibility that prolongation of the Q-T interval might be associated with increased risk of sudden cardiac death was suggested by a number of clinical conditions associated with long Q-T intervals that frequently result in ventricular fibrillation or sudden death (Han & Goel, 1972). Congenital prolongation of the Q-T interval (long Q-T syndrome) is also associated with an extremely high incidence of ventricular fibrillation and sudden death (Schwartz, Periti, & Malliani, 1975). To test the prognostic significance of a consistently prolonged Q-T interval, Schwartz and Wolf (1978) made a 10-year study of a group of patients with previous myocardial infarctions. A total of 55 patients with recent myocardial infarctions and 55 healthy controls matched for age, sex, race, height, weight, education, and job had electrocardiograms taken every 2 months for 7 years. At the end of 7 years of repeated observation and 3 additional years of follow-up study, 28 of the 55 patients had died suddenly. Among the 55 subjects in the control group, the subject with the longest Q-T interval had died suddenly, while the other 54 control subjects were still alive. Figure 7.15 illustrates a comparison of the Q-T values (corrected for heart rate) among control subjects, all patients who had previously suffered acute myocardial infarctions, patients who survived the follow-up period of 10 years, and those patients who died during the follow-up study. The Q-T interval among the deceased patients was significantly longer than the value for the surviving patients. The increase in risk of sudden cardiac death associated with a prolonged Q-T interval was more than twice the risk for those with a normal Q-T interval. These results suggest that local myocardial changes responsible for prolongation of the Q-T interval may increase vulnerability to physiological and psychological stimuli. In particular, the greater the variability of Q-T interval from month to month, the greater was the risk of sudden cardiac death. Although many factors other than sympathetic nerv-

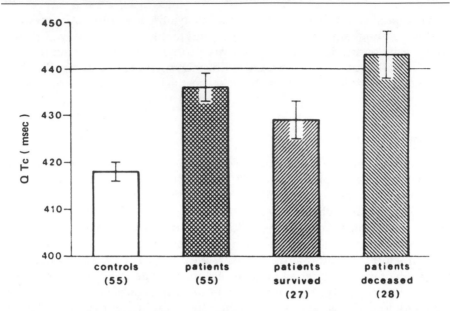

FIGURE 7.15. Electrocardiographic data for Q-T intervals among normal subjects and patients with histories of myocardial infarctions. The Q-T interval (corrected for R-R interval) is represented for normal subjects in the first (open) bar, and for patients who previously suffered acute myocardial infarctions in the second (cross-hatched) bar. The third vertical bar indicates the Q-T values for patients who survived a follow-up period of 10 years, and the fourth vertical bar represents the remaining patients who died during the follow-up study. The vertical and horizontal lines indicate 1 standard deviation of the mean. Note that the Q-T interval among the deceased patients was significantly longer than the value among the surviving patients. (From Schwartz, P. J., & Wolf, S. Q-T interval prolongation as predictor of sudden death in patients with myocardial infarction. *Circulation*, 1978, *57*, 107–110. Reprinted by permission of the American Heart Association, Inc.)

ous system activity may cause the variability in Q-T interval, it also is possible that patients destined for sudden cardiac death had greater imbalances in cardiac sympathetic stimulation.

The increase in vulnerability to ventricular fibrillation in patients with the long Q-T syndrome indicates a need for effective treatment. These patients have frequent episodes of ventricular fibrillation that are almost always triggered by physical or psychological stimuli and lead to the sudden death of most of these patients (Schwartz *et al.*, 1975). Schwartz and Stone (1978) have proposed that these patients have a specific imbalance between the right and left components of cardiac sympathetic innervation, with an increased stimulation of the heart through the left sympathetic cardiac nerves and a reduced stimulation through the right sympathetic cardiac nerves. Accordingly, treatment was attempted using left stellectomy or beta-adrenergic blockade. Out of a total group of 357 patients, 128 were treated with beta-adrenergic blockers and 15 with left stellectomy. In a group of 102 patients who received no treatment, mortality was 78%. In those treated with beta-adrenergic blockers, the mortality was 6%, and in those treated with left stellectomy, no deaths and no syncopal episodes were recorded. Perhaps the effectiveness of treatment with beta-adrenergic blockade in survivors of acute myocardial infarction may be attributed to suppression of an imbalance in sympathetic nervous system stimulation to the heart.

The Electrocardiogram in Central Nervous System Disease

Cardiac rhythm disturbances and abnormalities of the electrocardiogram have been noted in association with acute disturbances of the central nervous system in experimental animals and humans. In experimental animals, the effects of central nervous system stimulation on cardiac rate and rhythm (Mauck & Hockman, 1967) and electrocardiographic wave forms (Weinberg & Foster, 1960) have been demonstrated by localized hypothalamic stimulations. The effects of stimulating subcortical areas on the electrocardiogram and on sympathetic nervous system activity suggested that the sympathetic nervous system might mediate these abnormalities (Korteweg, Boeles, & Ten Cate, 1957). Observations in patients with central nervous system disease have also suggested that electrocardiographic wave-form abnormalities and cardiac arrhythmias in acute central nervous system disease may be caused by abnormal sympathetic nervous system stimulation. This evidence has led to treatments of patients by left stellate ganglion block in an effort to reduce the risk of sudden cardiac death.

One of the first descriptions of electrocardiographic abnormalities in patients with acute central nervous system disease was reported by Burch, Meyers, and Abildskov (1954). They described a pattern encountered in patients with cerebrovascular accidents, which consisted of T waves of considerable amplitude and width and a long Q-T interval. These patterns, described in 17 patients with cerebrovascular accidents, lasted for several days in many of the patients. More recently, Grossman (1976) described treatment of cardiac arrhythmia in a patient with acute subarachnoid hemorrhage. This patient had a prolonged Q-T interval, broad symmetrical T waves, and gradual development of multifocal ventricular tachycardia. When response to treatment with antiarrhythmic drugs failed to control the arrhythmia, a left stellate ganglion block was produced by injecting 1% lidocaine into the region of the left stellate ganglion. Grossman reported that the rhythm disturbance was abolished within 15 minutes, and the abnormalities in the Q-T interval improved over a matter of hours. Unfortunately, the patient died of the cerebrovascular accident when attempts to ligate an aneurysm at the bifurcation of the basilar artery into posterior cerebral arteries failed. However, the improvement of cardiac rhythm and electrocardiogram in this patient illustrated the potential deleterious effects of imbalance in sympathetic nervous system stimulation of the heart.

NEUROENDOCRINE CONTROL MECHANISMS

Physical Factors

Neuroendocrine responses to physiological stimuli have been reported to include sympathetic adrenomedullary and pituitary adrenocortical responses, as well as increases in growth hormone, prolactin, testosterone, thyroid hormone, insulin, angiotensin, and aldosterone. Difficulties in interpretation of these results arise from the realization that many experimental situations have included psychological as well as physiological stimuli. When experimental interventions include novel, strange, or unfamiliar stimuli, neuroendocrine responses to these psychological stimuli are added to the responses to physiological stimuli (Rose, 1980). Similarly, neuroendocrine responses to such physiological stimuli as sodium deprivation (Nicholls, Kiowski, Zweifler, Julius, Schork, & Greenhouse, 1980), upright posture (Henry, Luft, Weinberger, Fineberg, & Grim, 1980), exercise (Watson *et al.*, 1979), and exposure to cold ambient temperature (Jessen, 1980a) all influence plasma levels of norepinephrine, and extremes of these physiological stimuli may increase plasma concentrations of cortisol. Consequently, careful attention must be given to controlling both physiological and psychological factors in measurements of neuroendocrine response mechanisms. A comparison of neuroendocrine responses to physiological and psychological factors has been presented by LeBlanc, Cote, Jobin, and Labrie (1979) in studies with normal human subjects. Physiological stimuli consisted of immersion of one hand in cold water; psychological stimuli consisted of an arithmetic test, in which randomized numbers were given verbally to subjects, who were told to add them mentally. Plasma epinephrine and norepinephrine concentrations as well as blood pressure were measured in 12 male subjects before, during, and after a cold-hand test, the mental arithmetic test, and a combination of both of these tests. As shown in Figure 7.16, systolic blood pressure increased during immersion of one hand in water at 5°C for 2 minutes, during the mental arithmetic test (also lasting 2 minutes), and during both tests when these were given simultaneously. However, the response of plasma epinephrine levels was different during physiological and psychological test conditions. Figure 7.17 illustrates the plasma levels of epinephrine during the cold-hand test, the mental arithmetic test, and a combination of both tests. As illustrated in Figures 7.16 and 7.17, the physiological and psychological stimuli caused by the cold-hand and mental tests had comparable effects on blood pressure, whereas the psychological stimuli produced by the mental test produced a greater increase in plasma concentrations of epinephrine than was observed during the physiological stimuli caused by the cold-hand test. Plasma levels of norepinephrine, illustrated in Figure 7.18, were more affected by the cold-hand test than by the mental test. Results of these experiments indicate that the neuroendocrine responses to physiological stimuli include greater plasma levels of norepinephrine,

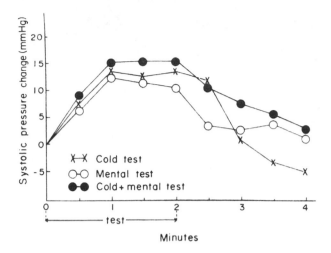

FIGURE 7.16. Systolic blood pressure during cold-pressor and mental arithmetic tests. Abscissa indicates time of exposure to the cold-pressor test, the mental arithmetic test, or the combination of cold-pressor and mental arithmetic tests during the first 2 minutes and the 2 minutes following these tests in 12 normal human subjects. Note that systolic blood pressure increased between 10 and 15 mm Hg for these subjects during all test procedures. (From LeBlanc, J., Cote, J., Jobin, M., & Labrie, A. Plasma catecholamines and cardiovascular responses to cold and mental activity. *Journal of Applied Physiology*, 1979, 47, 1207–1211. Reprinted by permission.)

FIGURE 7.17. Increase in plasma epinephrine concentration during cold-pressor and mental arithmetic tests. Open circles indicate increases in concentration during mental arithmetic, and closed circles indicate increases when both tests were given simultaneously. Crosses indicate increases in concentration during cold-pressor test alone. Note that increases in plasma concentrations of epinephrine were greatest during the mental arithmetic test, both alone and in combination with the cold-pressor test. Increases were significantly lower during administration of the cold-pressor test alone. (From LeBlanc, J., Cote, J., Jobin, M., & Labrie, A. Plasma catecholamines and cardiovascular responses to cold and mental activity. *Journal of Applied Physiology*, 1979, 47, 1207–1211. Reprinted by permission.)

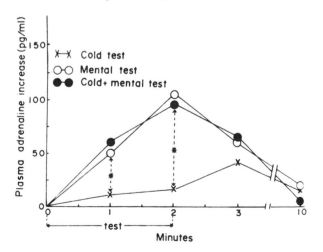

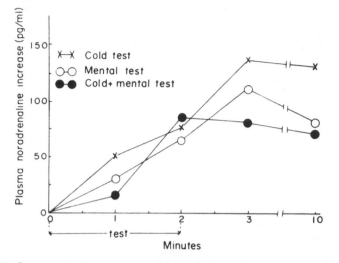

FIGURE 7.18. Increases in plasma norepinephrine during cold-pressor and mental arithmetic tests. Open and closed circles indicate increases during trials in which mental arithmetic tests were administered, and crosses indicate increases during the cold-pressor test alone. Note that increases in plasma norepinephrine were similar during the cold-pressor and mental arithmetic tests, both alone and when given simultaneously. (From LeBlanc, J., Cote, J., & Labrie, A. Plasma catecholamines and cardiovascular responses to cold and mental activity. *Journal of Applied Physiology*, 1979, 47, 1207–1211. Reprinted by permission.)

whereas responses to psychological stimuli include greater plasma levels of epinephrine.

Differential effects of physiological and psychological stimuli on plasma levels of epinephrine also were reported by Dimsdale and Moss (1980). These investigators used a portable blood-withdrawal pump to collect samples continuously from nine young male physicians during physical exercise and public speaking. They observed a disparity between plasma norepinephrine and epinephrine levels in these two different situations. During public speaking, epinephrine levels increased twofold, whereas during physical exercise, norepinephrine levels increased threefold. They suggested that psychological stimuli induced primarily an epinephrine response.

Concentrations of cortisol in plasma also are affected more by psychological than by physiological stimuli. Physical factors have little effect on cortisol concentrations except in extreme conditions. Hartley, Mason, Hogan, Jones, Kotchen, Mougey, Wherry, Pennington, and Ricketts (1972) reported that plasma cortisol concentrations during exercise showed little increase until exercise approached maximal intensities. Jessen (1980b) showed that exposure of human subjects to low ambient temperature had no effect on plasma cortisol concentrations. These results suggest that plasma cortisol levels are little affected by physiological stimuli under normal conditions.

Psychological Factors

Neuroendocrine responses to psychological stimuli have been studied in nonhuman primates by Mason (1968a, 1968b). When rhesus monkeys were exposed to unpredictable stimuli with a noxious quality, epinephrine and norepinephrine were found to increase (Mason, 1968b). However, when stimuli were merely noxious, repetitive, or stereotyped, epinephrine did not increase, and norepinephrine alone was elevated. Elevations of plasma cortisol concentrations in response to psychological stimuli show rapid returns to baseline values, and a chronic exposure to psychological stimuli may actually suppress values below baseline (Mason, Brady, & Tolliver, 1968).

Although studies of neuroendocrine responses to psychological stimuli under laboratory conditions suggest that subjects adapt rapidly, studies of human subjects under field conditions suggest that adrenomedullary and adrenocortical responses may remain elevated over long periods of exposure to psychological stimuli. Timio and Gentili (1976) made serial measurements of urinary epinephrine, norepinephrine, and 11-hydroxycorticosteroid excretion on 32 healthy men under these conditions: piecework with payment by results; work on an assembly line; and performance of work under ordinary conditions (for salary and away from an assembly line). A statistically significant increase in epinephrine, norepinephrine, and 11-hydroxycorticosteroids was observed for piecework and assembly-line workers, compared to salaried workers under ordinary conditions. In a further study, Timio, Gentili, and Pede (1979) made measurements on industrial workers doing piecework with payment by results and working on assembly lines. An increase in the urinary level of free epinephrine and norepinephrine was observed; this increase persisted throughout 4 days of observation, with low levels observed during fixed-wage days away from the assembly line. These differences persisted on retesting after 6 months of alternating work regimens. Thus, the effect of prolonged exposure and habituation did not decrease the urinary excretion of catecholamines in normal subjects under conditions of piecework and of work on an assembly line.

A study of the relationship between plasma levels of cortisol and ordinary occupational tasks was reported by Caplan, Cobb, and French (1979). A total of 200 NASA employees in administration, engineering, and science completed self-report questionnaires and gave blood samples. Respondents were put into groups according to the time of day when their blood was sampled and into groups of high, medium, and low levels on an index of subjectively assessed quantitative workload. Employees who reported low workloads showed the expected high values in the early morning hours and low values in the afternoon. Employees reporting high workloads showed lower than normal levels of plasma cortisol in the morning, with no difference in values from morning to afternoon. These results suggest that loss of circadian rhythmicity may be more characteristic of intense psychological stimuli under occupational conditions than high or low levels of cortisol in relation to workload may be.

Other correlates of psychological stimuli have also been reported in subjects studied over long periods of time. Francis (1979) measured serum levels of cortisol, high-density lipoprotein cholesterol, low-density lipoprotein cholesterol, and psychometric indexes of anxiety, hostility, and depression. These psychological variables were evaluated, using the State–Trait Anxiety Inventory and the Multiple Affect Adjective Check List. Subjects were 20 physical therapy students studied over a 2½-month academic quarter that included midterm and final exams. The observed changes in serum cortisol were highly correlated with changes in anxiety and depression. Serum cholesterol and the low-density lipoprotein cholesterol subfraction were significantly elevated above control levels and remained elevated throughout the quarter. Absolute levels of high-density lipoprotein cholesterol varied little throughout the quarter. Thus, the psychological variables apparently influenced not only the levels of serum cortisol, but also levels of serum cholesterol. Studies by Cooper and Aygen (1979) indicated that a relaxation technique caused a significant reduction in serum cholesterol levels in 12 hypercholesterolemic subjects who regularly practiced meditation over an 11-month period of time. Apparently psychological stimuli may influence neuroendocrine and metabolic responses over prolonged periods of time.

Coping Mechanisms

The psychological processes eliciting neuroendocrine responses appear to adapt as subjects are exposed repeatedly to a set of conditions. Studies of the training of parachute jumpers illustrated this process of adaptation (Ursin, Baade, & Levine, 1978). Subjects were 44 men who were initiated into the Norwegian Army Parachute School. Samples of blood and urine were collected before and after training in basic jump techniques from a tower. Instructors kept records of performances during jumps, and subjects were asked to fill in self-ratings of fear before and after each jump. Figure 7.19 shows performances in the tower for each jump day, with the percentages of jumps that reached the acceptance criterion. Figure 7.20 shows the self-ratings of fear recorded by men who went through tower training. There was a gradual reduction in the fear levels reported for the whole group, which showed an inverse correlation with performances rated by instructors. Neuroendocrine responses also showed an inverse relation with performance ratings. Blood samples were obtained immediately after each jump and 20 minutes later. As illustrated in Figure 7.21, there was a significant decrease in cortisol levels following the first jump until the fifth day of jumps, when the levels seemed to reach a plateau. Thus, the neuroendocrine responses were lessened as each parachutist gained experience. How individuals become adapted to psychological stimuli is not known. Apparently each individual's

Performance
(% accepted jumps)

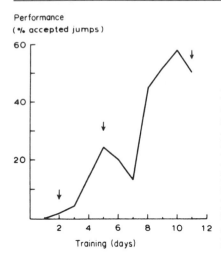

Training (days)

FIGURE 7.19. Performance of parachute jumpers during training. Abscissa is time during training of men in the Norwegian Army Parachute School to jump from a tower, with percentage of accepted jumps for the whole group judged by instructors. Arrows indicate days on which measurements of physiological and psychological variables were performed. Note that performance of the group improved during the period of observations. (From Ursin, H., Baade, E., & Levine, S. (Eds.). *Psychobiology of stress: A study of coping men.* New York: Academic Press, 1978. Reprinted by permission.)

Fear score

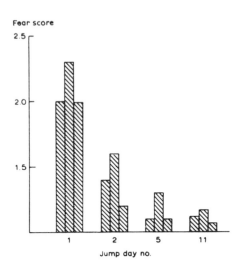

Jump day no.

FIGURE 7.20. Self-rating of fear reported by parachute jumpers during tower training. The three columns in the first set of vertical bars represent the average scores reported at the bottom of the tower, average scores reported just before jumping from the platform, and average scores following the jump. The second, third, and fourth sets of vertical bars represent scores on self-reports during observations recorded on the second, fifth, and eleventh jump days. (From Ursin, H., Baade, E., & Levine, S. (Eds.). *Psychobiology of stress: A study of coping men.* New York: Academic Press, 1978. Reprinted by permission.)

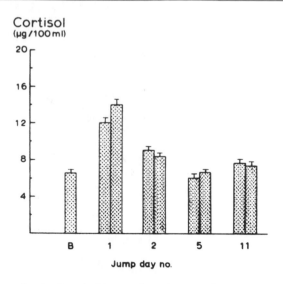

FIGURE 7.21. Plasma levels of cortisol in parachute jumpers during tower training. The first vertical bar (labeled B) represents concentrations of cortisol in plasma of parachute jumpers under basal conditions, before training began. The following four pairs of vertical bars, representing the first, second, fifth, and eleventh jump days indicate concentrations of cortisol in plasma; these were sampled immediately after each subject jumped from the tower and 20 minutes after each jump was completed. The vertical and horizontal lines on the top of each bar indicate 1 standard error of the mean. Note that plasma levels of cortisol were greatest on the first 2 days of training, with a rapid return to baseline values as performances improved and self-ratings of fear decreased. (From Ursin, H., Baade, E., & Levine, S. (Eds.). *Psychobiology of stress: A study of coping men.* New York: Academic Press, 1978. Reprinted by permission.)

perception of psychological stimuli is the major determinant of neuroendo-crine responses (Rose, 1980).

Abnormal neuroendocrine responses and abnormal coping mechanisms may be observed in patients with severe mental illness (Sachar, 1970). Elevations of plasma cortisol levels have been seen in patients with major depressive disorders and patients with schizophrenia. However, it appears as if the elevated levels of cortisol in patients with schizophrenia are a response to disordered perceptions of psychological stimuli, whereas elevations in patients with severe depression apparently reflect altered levels of neurotransmitters in hypothalamic neuroendocrine cells (Sachar *et al.*, 1980). Recent studies in the neuroendocrinology of major depressive disorders by Sachar *et al.* (1980) have shown that about 50% of patients with major depression have substantially increased levels of cortisol secretion, which remit in association with clinical recovery. This hypersecretion is caused by increased secretion of ACTH and is not associated with any change in peripheral metabolism of cortisol. In addition, the 24-hour plasma cortisol levels show less than normal variation. In particular, depressive patients show disproportionately high levels of cortisol secretion in the afternoon, evening, and early morning hours, when cortisol secretion is minimal in normal subjects. Figure 7.22 shows mean hourly plasma cortisol levels in seven unmedicated depressed patients and 54 normal subjects. A flattened circadian pattern is apparent in the hypersecretors, suggesting a disturbance in the diurnal regulation of ACTH secretion. Thus, it can be seen that disordered psychological states may be associated with a central neuroendocrine abnormality. Although the relationship between psychological mechanisms and neuroendocrine response is unknown, evidence suggests that sympathetic adrenomedullary and pituitary adrenocortical activity may be influenced by psychological mechanisms. These, in turn, are influenced by adaptation to psychological stimuli, as well as by psychiatric disorders.

CENTRAL NERVOUS SYSTEM CONTROL MECHANISMS

Adrenergic Mechanisms

The observation that plasma norepinephrine concentrations are increased in many patients with essential hypertension has directed attention to the central sympathetic nervous system. Norepinephrine is present throughout the brain and the gray matter of the spinal cord, with concentrations apparent in areas involved in blood pressure regulation, such as the brain stem and hypothalamus. The role of brain catecholamines in hypertension has been studied by a depletion of catecholamines with 6-hydroxydopamine and by measurement of catecholamines in brain nuclei. Depletion of norepinephrine from brain and spinal cord prevents experimental hypertension in rats (Kubo & Hashimoto, 1978; Lamprecht, St. Richardson, Williams, & Kopin, 1977). These results indicate that catecholamines in the brain and spinal cord are important for the development of experimental hypertension. However, administration of epinephrine and norepinephrine into one lateral ventricle of the brain causes a reduction in arterial blood pressure (Struyker Boudier, Smeets, Brouwer, & VanRossum, 1974). Since intraventricular catecholamines reach many cells lining the cerebral ventricles and aqueduct, it seems likely that administering catecholamines in this way does not stimulate release from catecholamine-containing cells.

Since hyperactivity of the central sympathetic nervous system might raise concentrations of norepinephrine in cerebrospinal fluid, Eide, Kolloch, DeQuattro, Miano, Dugger, and Van der Meulen (1979) measured concentrations of norepinephrine, epinephrine, and dopamine-beta-hydroxylase in cerebrospinal fluid in patients with essential hypertension, and compared these values with concentrations measured in normotensive patients. They

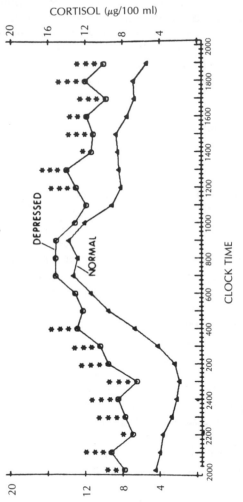

FIGURE 7.22 Plasma cortisol concentrations during 24 hours of observation in normal subjects and patients with major depressive disorders. The abscissa represents time in hours during 24 hours of 1 day. The open circles represent plasma levels of cortisol in seven unmedicated depressed patients, and the closed triangles represent levels in 54 normal subjects. Note that plasma levels of cortisol in the depressed patients did not fall to the low levels measured in normal subjects during late evening and early morning hours (From Sachar, E. J., Asnis, G., Halbreich, U., & Halpern, F. Recent studies in the neuroendocrinology of major depressive disorders. *Psychiatric Clinics of North America*, 1980, 3, 313–326. Reprinted by permission.)

also measured concentrations of norepinephrine, epinephrine, dopamine-beta-hydroxylase, and plasma renin activity in plasma. The levels of dopamine-beta-hydroxylase were used to estimate rate of release of catecholamines from synaptic vesicles, since this substance is not taken back into nerve terminals after release. Norepinephrine concentrations in plasma and cerebrospinal fluid were increased in patients with essential hypertension, as compared to patients with normal levels of blood pressure. Norepinephrine in cerebrospinal fluid was related to diastolic blood pressure and correlated with the natural logarithm of plasma renin activity. These observations were interpreted as evidence that the central sympathetic nervous system contributes to the pathogenesis of essential hypertension. The influence of central dopaminergic regions in the development of essential hypertension also has been studied. Kolloch, Kobayashi, and DeQuattro (1980) administered bromocriptine, a centrally acting dopaminergic agonist, to patients with essential hypertension. As illustrated in Figure 7.23, administration of this drug for 1 week reduced blood pressure in supine, sitting, and standing positions. Plasma norepinephrine concentration was reduced, and urinary excretion rates of norepinephrine were lowered. Since bromocriptine has been shown to reduce the concentration of norepinephrine in cerebrospinal fluid (Ziegler, Lake, Williams, Teychenne, Shoulson, & Steinsland, 1979), results of this study suggest that stimulation of central dopaminergic mechanisms reduces the activity of central noradrenergic neurons. Further studies will be necessary to demonstrate functional relationships among various central adrenergic mechanisms.

Catecholamine neurons also have an influence on mood and emotion. Tranquilizing drugs, such as phenothiazines, butyrophenones, and thiothixenes, act by blocking dopamine receptors. Tricyclic antidepressant drugs, which include dibenzazepines (such as imipramine) and dibenzocycloheptadines (such as amitriptyline), inhibit the uptake of norepinephrine, prolonging its action in the brain and elevating mood. Amphetamines, which are primarily dopamine releasers, are relatively ineffective in treatment for depressive illnesses. Tricyclic antidepressants, which primarily enhance noradrenergic or serotonergic action, are often effective. Thus, some forms of depression seem to be correlated with reduced norepinephrine activity, because many antidepressant drugs are characterized by enhancing norepinephrine action (McGeer & McGeer, 1980).

Abnormalities of central adrenergic mechanisms may also cause cortisol hypersecretion in depression. Sachar et al. (1980) administered dextroamphetamine intravenously to patients with major depressive disorders. Their cortisol responses were compared to those of 10 other depressives, matched in all respects, who received no amphetamine. The group receiving amphetamine showed a significant drop to normal plasma cortisol levels within 90 minutes, while the group without amphetamine maintained elevated cor-

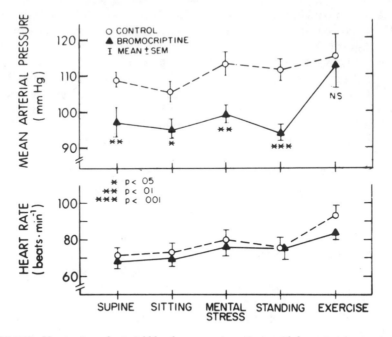

FIGURE 7.23. Heart rate and arterial blood pressure in patients with hypertension treated with bromocriptine. The closed triangles represent values for mean arterial blood pressure (mm Hg) and heart rate in patients with essential hypertension treated for 7 days with bromocriptine. Observations were made during various physical activities and during a cognitive task. The open circles represent values obtained during placebo treatment. Note that bromocriptine treatment reduced blood pressure during basal conditions, sitting, standing, and the cognitive task without influencing heart rate during any condition. Blood pressure during exercise was not reduced. Vertical and horizontal lines indicate 1 standard error of the mean for each value. (From Kolloch, R., Kobayashi, K., & DeQuattro, V. Dopaminergic control of sympathetic tone and blood pressure: Evidence in primary hypertension. *Hypertension*, 1980, 2, 390–394. Reprinted by permission.)

tisol levels. These results were interpreted as evidence that dextroamphetamine's norepinephrine effect temporarily corrected the catecholamine deficit underlying the cortisol hypersecretion. In addition, there is evidence for a normal daily rhythm in norepinephrine levels in cerebrospinal fluid (Guyton, Coleman, Cowley, Manning, Norman, & Ferguson, 1974). It is possible that cortisol-hypersecreting depressives also have a flattened daily rhythm of brain norepinephrine, with a deficient rise in norepinephrine in the afternoon and evening.

Relationships among psychological stimuli, mood, and cardiovascular function will require further study. At the present time, it is evident that antihypertensive drugs (such as propranolol) that affect noradrenergic mechanisms also influence mood, and drugs (such as reserpine) that have a tranquilizing effect also influence the regulation of blood pressure.

Neuropeptides

Radioactively labeled opiate compounds injected intravenously into experimental animals bind to opiate receptors concentrated in areas of the brain that are involved in the perception of pain and in the integration of behavior. The anatomical proximity of regions with opiate receptors and catecholamines is remarkable. Studies by many investigators have indicated that endorphins are released from the pituitary gland in response to physical and psychological stimuli that cause secretion of ACTH. The relationship between ACTH and endorphins has been shown by neurochemical studies. Mains, Eipper, and Lin (1977) have shown that ACTH and beta-endorphin are products of a much larger precursor glycoprotein molecule. Stimuli known to activate the pituitary adrenocortical system have been reported to decrease anterior pituitary endorphin content and to produce a parallel increase in plasma endorphin and ACTH levels (Guillemin, Vargo, Rossier, Minick, Ling, Rivier, Vale, & Bloom, 1977; Wiedenann, Satio, Linfoot, & Li, 1979). However, other studies have demonstrated that increased plasma levels of beta-endorphin may not be accompanied by increase in concentrations of beta-endorphin in the brain (Rossier, Grench, Rivier, Ling, Guillemin, & Bloom, 1977).

In the brain, endorphins apparently function to modulate neural systems that play a role in behavioral responses to physical and psychological stimuli. For example, stimuli that produce an increase in blood or brain levels of endorphins also produce analgesia (Grau, Hyson, & Maier, 1981). Administration of naltrexone, a specific narcotic receptor antagonist, blocks a form of analgesia elicited by 20 minutes of noxious stimuli, but does not block analgesia elicited by 3 minutes of noxious stimuli. These results suggest that nonopiate pathways may be involved as well. Results of other experiments (Fanselow, 1979) demonstrate that administration of naloxone has behavioral effects consistent with the hypothesis that painful stimuli cause the release of endorphins within the brain, which attenuate the physiological and behavioral responses to those stimuli.

Although the neurobiological links between psychological stimuli and cardiovascular disease are still unknown, a general concept is emerging. Physiological and psychological stimuli that are aversive modify both adrenomedullary activity and adrenocortical activity through central secretion of catecholamines and neuropeptides. These neurochemicals also modify behavior and may be conditioned by environmental stimuli to be secreted even in the absence of aversive stimuli. Adrenomedullary and adrenocortical secretions appear to influence the development of cardiovascular disease and hypertension, but the pathophysiological mechanisms are still unknown.

PRACTICAL APPLICATIONS

Evaluation of Neuroendocrine Influences

Many physiological and behavioral indexes have been used to estimate the effects of psychological stimuli on cardiovascular function. Although many of these, such as blood pressure, heart rate, and self-reports of anxiety and tension, have the advantage of being easily obtained, their usefulness is limited. At present, it seems that measures of neuroendocrine activity show the greatest promise of predicting relationships between behavioral influences and cardiovascular disease. Measurements of central neurobiological processes would be valuable, but are essentially unobtainable in human subjects. At present, it seems that plasma levels of norepinephrine, epinephrine, and cortisol provide useful estimates of neuroendocrine activity, provided that they can be supplemented with timed urinary excretion of free cortisol and plasma turnover rates for norepinephrine and epinephrine. Measurements of catecholamines in cerebrospinal fluid show promise of indicating central sympathetic nervous system activity, but the difficulties in obtaining samples preclude extensive use of this technique.

Evaluation of neuroendocrine influences can also be extended to assessing effects of treatment. Although it is attractive to use simple measurements, such as heart rate and blood pressure or behavioral indexes, to assess effects of treatment for lowering neuroendocrine activity, there are no good substitutes for repeated measures of plasma concentrations of these substances, along with measurements of their secretion rates or turnover rates.

Clinical Diagnosis and Treatment

Although high levels of neuroendocrine activity may have deleterious effects in normal subjects, clinical experience suggests that deleterious effects of behavioral influences are most likely to occur in patients at high risk for cardiovascular disease for other reasons. For example, patients most at risk for sudden cardiac death are those with abnormal Q-T intervals on electrocardiograms or with previous histories of acute myocardial infarctions. Those at greatest risk for hypertensive cardiovascular disease are those with high resting levels of blood pressure, family histories of hypertension, and increased sensitivity to dietary intake of sodium chloride. Those at greatest risk for acute myocardial infarctions are patients with high serum levels of cholesterol, high levels of arterial blood pressure, and recent histories of cigarette smoking. Even though behavioral influences may have a deleterious effect in others, our attention inevitably must be focused on patients at high risk for cardiovascular disease and hypertension.

BEHAVIORAL MEDICINE RESEARCH

Physiological Issues

A major effort should be made to determine the effects of neurobiological processes on cardiovascular disease and hypertension. From numerous epidemiological studies, considerable evidence indicates that many disorders, including adverse coronary events, are precipitated by such environmental stressors as moving, unemployment, and bereavement (C. D. Jenkins, 1971, 1976; Kaplan, Cassel, Tyroler, Cornoni, Kleinbaum, & Hames, 1971; Rahe, 1972; Syme, Hyman, & Enterline, 1964). The extent of community disintegration, a family's lack of social supports, and the number of stressful events in the life of an individual have been found to affect the occurrence and severity of illness, and indeed life expectancy.

The strongest evidence of a relationship between any psychosocial factor and CHD is that from two prospective studies, showing an association between the Type A behavior pattern and increased risk of CHD events. Type A persons are characterized by high levels of achievement striving, speed and impatience, and aggressive, hostile behavior. In a prospective study of over 3,000 middle-aged men who were healthy at intake, the Western Collaborative Group Study found that those who were Type A experienced about twice as many clinical CHD events over an 8½-year follow-up as did their counterparts who were Type B (Rosenman, Brand, Jenkins, Friedman, Straus, & Wurm, 1975; Rosenman, Brand, Sholtz, & Friedman, 1976). This prospective association between Type A behavior pattern and increased CHD rates has also been confirmed in the Framingham Study (Haynes, Feinleib, Levine, Scotch, & Kannel, 1978).

An important extension of this epidemiological research lies in the identification of pathophysiological mechanisms that may translate behaviorally related risk factors into CHD. From such research has developed an expanding body of circumstantial evidence suggesting that exaggerated cardiovascular reaction to situational or behavioral stressors is linked to the incidence and prevalence of CHD, hypertension, and sudden cardiac death (Keys, Taylor, Blackburn, Brozek, Anderson, & Simonson, 1971; Solomon, Delores, & Dews, 1981). In addition, a number of studies have been undertaken in attempts to identify psychophysiological and neuroendocrine mechanisms that might account for the increased CHD rates observed among Type A persons. When challenged to perform a variety of behavioral tasks, Type A's were observed to show greater increases in heart rate, blood pressure, and catecholamine secretion (Dembroski, MacDougall, Shields, Petitto, & Lushene,

1978; Glass, Krakoff, Contrada, Hilton, Kehoe, Mannucci, Collins, Snow, & Elting, 1980). Among those psychological characteristics that have been implicated in the tendency to display overt Type A behavior under challenge are increased need for control (Glass, 1977), increased self-involvement (Scherwitz, Berton, & Leventhal, 1978), and increased levels of hostility (Glass, 1977). Similarly, stress-induced physiological reactivity has also been associated with a familial history of hypertension (Falkner et al., 1981; Falkner, Onesti, Angelakos, Fernandes, & Langmann, 1979), borderline hypertension (Brod et al., 1959), the male sex (Dembroski et al., 1978), and the black race (Alpert, Dover, Booker, Martin, & Strong, 1981), all of which are risk factors for CHD.

In addition to studies of cardiovascular reactivity, studies are needed concerning the influence of such neuroendocrines as cortisol and the effects of sympathetic nervous system stimulation on arteriosclerosis. Similar efforts should be made to discover the influence of sympathetic nervous system activity on subgroups of patients with a neurogenic component for systemic arterial hypertension. Finally, explanations for the vulnerability of subgroups of patients with arteriosclerotic heart disease for sudden cardiac death should be sought through studies of pathophysiological mechanisms involving sympathetic nervous system activity in high-risk patients. Thus, it is apparent that much remains to be discovered concerning the mechanisms that influence neuroendocrine secretion, and a great deal must be learned concerning the pathophysiological mechanisms of cardiovascular disease and hypertension.

Behavioral Issues

The interrelationships between neurobiological processes and behavior remain to be determined. Although a great deal of information is available concerning neuroanatomic and neurochemical details, surprisingly little is known about how regional alterations in brain function influence behavior. For example, a variety of dietary, pharmacological, and physiological states influence regional concentrations of neurochemicals, but little is known about the behavioral effects. Similarly, little is known about the influences of behavior on neurochemical and neuroendocrine processes. Even such simple behavioral states as waking and sleeping are poorly understood in terms of their effects on neurobiological processes. Since several clinical studies with human subjects suggest that psychological stimuli influence neuroendocrine activity, it follows that similar psychological stimuli may influence neurobiological processes. Therefore, information must be obtained concerning behavior and central nervous system function before progress can be made in the study of behavioral influences on cardiovascular disease and hypertension.

Psychological Issues

The process of adaptation or accommodation to psychological stimuli needs more study. Certain psychological stimuli are provocative of neuroendocrine responses that eventually cease as the individual becomes familiar with the stimuli. However, some individuals maintain a high level of neuroendocrine activity, even though behavioral measures indicate that the individual has become familiar with the task. The process whereby coping mechanisms and neuroendocrine responses evolve is still obscure. In particular, individual differences in response to psychological stimuli require further study.

Psychological research must also be undertaken to demonstrate the influence of affective state on neuroendocrine function. The major psychotic disorders, including depression and schizophrenia, are characterized by increased levels of cortisol secretion and increased levels of plasma catecholamines. These neuroendocrine effects may also be seen in patients who do not have psychiatric disease as such, but who display disturbances of mood, behavior, and cardiovascular function. The psychological mechanisms involved in these processes must be known before the transition from behavior to disease can be understood.

SUMMARY AND CONCLUSIONS

The influence of behavior on cardiovascular disease and hypertension is evident in the pathogenesis of basic processes, the management of clinical disease, and the prevention of cardiovascular disease and hypertension. Recent progress in all these areas has come from interdisciplinary research in which the interactions among physiological, psychological, and behavioral processes have been explored. In addition, basic neurobiological studies have indicated mechanisms whereby behavioral processes influence metabolic, endocrine, and hemodynamic processes.

Associations between neuroendocrine functions and behavior have been known for some time. Results of recent research have demonstrated the neurochemical processes involved in the interaction of behavior and neuroendocrine function, and it now seems possible to demonstrate relations to cardiovascular disease and hypertension. Although the neurobiological links are still unknown, a general concept is emerging: Physiological and psychological stimuli that are aversive modify both adrenomedullary and adrenocortical activity through secretion of catecholamines and neuropeptides. These neurochemicals also modify behavior and may be conditioned by psychological, behavioral, environmental, and physiological stimuli to be secreted in the presence of stimuli that have no direct aversive effects. The neuroendocrine activities appear to influence the development of cardiovascular disease and hypertension, but much more must be discovered before specific treatments and preventive measures can be adopted.

REFERENCES

Abildskov, J. A. Adrenergic effects on the QT interval of the electrocardiogram. *American Heart Journal*, 1976, *92*, 201–216.

Abildskov, J. A. The prolonged QT interval. *Annual Review of Medicine*, 1979, *30*, 171–179.

Abildskov, J. A., & Klein, R. M. Cancellation of electrocardiographic effects during ventricular excitation. *Circulation Research*, 1962, *11*, 247–251.

Alpert, B., Dover, E. V., Booker, B., Martin, B., & Strong, W. Blood pressure response to dynamic exercise in healthy children: Black and white. *Journal of Pediatrics*, 1981, *99*, 556–560.

Baba, N., Bushe, W. J., Keller, M. D., Geer, J. C., & Anthony, J. R. Pathology of atherosclerotic heart disease in sudden death: Organizing thrombosis and acute coronary vessel lesions. *Circulation*, 1975, *51–52*, 53–59.

Baxter, J. D. Glucocorticoid hormone action. *Pharmacology and Therapeutics*, 1976, *2*, 605–659.

Bianchi, G., Ferguson, D., & Walshe, M. A. Psychiatric antecedents of myocardial infarction. *Medical Journal of Australia*, 1978, *1*, 297–301.

Brod, J., Fencl, V., Hejl, Z., & Jirka, J. Circulatory changes underlying blood pressure elevation during acute emotional stress (mental arithmetic) in normotensive and hypertensive subjects. *Clinical Science*, 1959, *18*, 269–279.

Brooks, W. W., Verrier, R. L., & Lown, B. Influence of vagal tone on stellectomy-induced changes in ventricular electrical stability. *American Journal of Physiology: Heart Circulatory Physiology*, 1978, *3*, 503–507.

Burch, G. E., Meyers, R., & Abildskov, J. A. A new electrocardiographic pattern observed in cerebrovascular accidents. *Circulation*, 1954, *9*, 719–723.

Burgess, M. J., Millar, K., & Abildskov, J. A. Cancellation of electrocardiographic effects during ventricular recovery. *Journal of Electrocardiology*, 1969, *2*, 101–108.

Burstein, Y., Berns, L., Heldenberg, D., Kahn, Y., Werbin, B. Z., & Tamir, I. Increase in platelet aggregation following a rise in plasma free fatty acids. *American Journal of Hematology*, 1978, *4*, 17–22.

Caplan, R. D., Cobb, S., & French, R. P., Jr. White collar work load and cortisol: Disruption of a circadian rhythm by job stress? *Journal of Psychosomatic Research*, 1979, *23*, 181–192.

Carroll, B. J. Limbic-system–adrenal cortex regulation in depression and schizophrenia. *Psychosomatic Medicine*, 1976, *38*, 106–121.

Ceremuzynski, L., Staszewska-Barczak, J., & Herbaczynska-Cedro, K. Cardiac rhythm disturbances and the release of catecholamines after acute coronary occlusion in dogs. *Cardiovascular Research*, 1969, *3*, 190–197.

Challoner, D. R., & Steinberg, D. Oxidative metabolism of myocardium as influenced by fatty acids and epinephrine. *American Journal of Physiology*, 1966, *211*, 897–902.

Cigolini, M., & Smith, V. Human adipose tissue in culture: VIII. Studies on the insulin-antagonistic effect of glucocorticoids. *Metabolism*, 1979, *28*, 502–510.

Cooper, M. J., & Aygen, M. M. A relaxation technique in the management of hypercholesterolemia. *Journal of Human Stress*, 1979, *5*, 24–27.

Dargie, H., Davies, D., Dean, C., Dollery, C., Maling, T., & Reid, J. The effect of noradrenaline infusion on blood pressure and plasma noradrenaline following clonidine administration in man. *British Journal of Clinical Pharmacology*, 1977, *4*, 389–390.

Dembroski, T. M., MacDougall, J. M., Shields, J. L., Petitto, J., & Lushene, R. Components of the Type A coronary-prone behavior pattern and cardiovascular responses to psychomotor performance challenge. *Journal of Behavioral Medicine*, 1978, *1*, 159–176.

Dimsdale, J. E., & Moss, J. Plasma catecholamines in stress and exercise. *Journal of the American Medical Association*, 1980, *243*, 340–342.

Eide, I., Kolloch, R., DeQuattro, V., Miano, L., Dugger, R., & Van der Meulen, J. Raised cerebrospinal fluid norepinephrine in some patients with primary hypertension. *Hypertension*, 1979, *1*, 255–260.

Esler, M., Julius, S., Zweifler, A., Randall, O., Harburg, E., Gardiner, H., & DeQuattro, V. Mild high-renin essential hypertension. *New England Journal of Medicine*, 1977, *296*, 405–411.

Esler, M. D., & Nestel, P. J. Renin and sympathetic nervous system responsiveness to adrenergic stimuli in essential hypertension. *American Journal of Cardiology*, 1973, *32*, 643–649.

Esler, M., Randall, O., Bennett, J., Zweifler, A., Julius, S., Rydelek, P., Cohen, E., & DeQuattro, V. Suppression of sympathetic nervous function in low-renin and normal-renin essential hypertension. *Lancet*, 1976, *ii*, 115–118.

Falkner, B., Kushner, H., Gaddo, O., & Angelakos, E. Cardiovascular characteristics in adolescents who develop essential hypertension. *Hypertension*, 1981, *3*, 521–527.

Falkner, B., Onesti, G., Angelakos, E., Fernandes, M., & Langmann, D. Cardiovascular responses to mental stress in normal adolescents with hypertensive parents. *Hypertension*, 1979, *1*, 23–33.

Fanselow, M. Naloxone attenuates rat's preference for signaled shock. *Physiological Psychology*, 1979, *7*, 70–74.

Francis, K. T. Psychologic correlates of serum indicators of stress in man: A longitudinal study. *Psychosomatic Medicine*, 1979, *41*, 617–628.

Franco-Morselli, R., Elghozi, J. L., Joly, E., DiGiuilio, S., & Meyer, P. Increased plasma adrenaline concentrations in benign essential hypertension. *British Medical Journal*, 1977, *ii*, 1251–1254.

Friedman, M., Manwaring, J. H., Rosenman, R. H., Donlon, G., Ortega, P., & Grube, S. M. Instantaneous and sudden deaths: Clinical and pathological differentiation in coronary artery disease. *Journal of the American Medical Association*, 1973, *225*, 1319–1328.

Friedman, R. J., Moore, S., & Singal, D. P. Repeated endothelial injury and induction of atherosclerosis in normolipemic rabbits by human serum. *Laboratory Investigator*, 1975, *32*, 404–415.

Glass, D. C. *Behavior patterns, stress and coronary disease*. Hillsdale, N.J.: Erlbaum, 1977.

Glass, D. C., Krakoff, L. R., Contrada, R., Hilton, W. F., Kehoe, K., Mannucci, E. G., Collins, C., Snow, B., & Elting, E. Effects of harassment and competition upon cardiovascular and catecholamine responses in Type A and Type B individuals. *Psychophysiology*, 1980, *17*, 453–463.

Goldstein, D. S. Plasma norepinephrine during stress in essential hypertension. *Hypertension*, 1981, *3*, 551–556.

Goldstein, J. L., Hazzard, W. R., & Schrott, H. G. Hyperlipidemia in coronary heart disease: I. Lipid levels in 500 survivors of myocardial infarction. *Journal of Clinical Investigation*, 1973, *52*, 1533–1543.

Grau, J., Hyson, R., & Maier, S. E. Long-term stress-induced analgesia and activation of the opiate system. *Science*, 1981, *213*, 1409–1411.

Greene, H. L., Reid, P. R., & Schaeffer, A. H. The repetitive ventricular response in man: A predictor of sudden death. *New England Journal of Medicine*, 1978, *299*, 725–731.

Grossman, M. A. Cardiac arrhythmias in acute central nervous system disease: Successful management with stellate ganglion block. *Archives of Internal Medicine*, 1976, *136*, 203–209.

Guillemin, R., Vargo, T., Rossier, J., Minick, S., Ling, N., Rivier, C., Vale, W., & Bloom, F. B-endorphin and adrenocorticotropin are secreted concomitantly by the pituitary gland. *Science*, 1977, *74*, 1367–1369.

Guyton, A. C., Coleman, T. G., Cowley, A. W., Manning, R. D., Norman, R. A., & Ferguson, J. D. A systems analysis approach to understanding long range arterial blood pressure control and hypertension. *Circulation Research*, 1974, *35*, 159–176.

Guyton, A. C., Jones, C. E., & Coleman, T. G. (Eds.). *Circulatory physiology: Cardiac output and its regulation*. Philadelphia: W. B. Saunders, 1973.

Han, J., Garcia de Jalon, P., & Moe, G. K. Adrenergic effects on ventricular vulnerability. *Circulation Research*, 1964, *14*, 516–524.

Han, J., & Goel, B. G. Electrophysiologic precursors of ventricular tachyarrhythmias. *Archives of Internal Medicine*, 1972, *129*, 749–755.

Harker, L., Ross, R., Slichter, S., & Scott, C. Homocystine-induced arteriosclerosis: The role of endothelial cell injury and platelet response in its genesis. *Journal of Clinical Investigation*, 1976, *58*, 731–741.

Harker, L. A., Slichter, S. J., Scott, C. R., & Ross, R. Homocysteinemia-vascular injury and arterial thrombosis. *New England Journal of Medicine*, 1974, *291*, 537–543.

Hartley, H., Mason, J. W., Hogan, R. P., Jones, L. G., Kotchen, T. A., Mougey, E. H., Wherry, L. L., Pennington, L. L., & Ricketts, P. T. Multiple hormonal responses to graded exercise in relation to physical training. *Journal of Applied Physiology*, 1972, *33*, 602–606.

Haynes, S. G., Feinleib, M., Levine, S., Scotch, N., & Kannel, W. B. The relationship of psychosocial factors to coronary heart disease in the Framingham Study: II. Prevalence of coronary heart disease. *American Journal of Epidemiology*, 1978, *107*, 384–402.

Henry, D. P., Luft, F. C., Weinberger, M. H., Fineberg, N. S., & Grim, C. E. Norepinephrine in urine and plasma following provocative maneuvers in normal and hypertensive subjects. *Hypertension*, 1980, *2*, 20–28.

Jenkins, C. D. Psychologic and social precursors of coronary disease. *New England Journal of Medicine*, 1971, *284*, 244–255, 307–317.

Jenkins, C. D. Recent evidence supporting psychologic and social risk factors for coronary heart disease. *New England Journal of Medicine*, 1976, *294*, 987–994, 1033–1038.

Jenkins, D. J. A., Welborn, T. A., & Goff, D. V. Free fatty acids, beta-hydroxybutyrate, and ischemic heart disease. *Lancet*, 1970, *i*, 865–866.

Jessen, K. An assessment of human regulatory nonshivering thermogenesis. *Scandinavian Society of Anaesthesiologists*, 1980, *24*, 138–143. (a)

Jessen, K. The cortisol fluctuations in plasma in relation to human regulatory nonshivering thermogenesis. *Scandinavian Society of Anaesthesiologists*, 1980, *24*, 151–154. (b)

Johnson, B. V., Epstein, F. H., & Kjelsberg, M. O. Distributions and familial studies of blood pressure and serum cholesterol levels in a total community—Tecumseh, Michigan. *Journal of Chronic Disease*, 1965, *18*, 147–160.

Julius, S., & Schork, M. A. Predictors of hypertension. In H. M. Perry, Jr., & W. M. Smith (Eds.), *Mild hypertension: To treat or not to treat*. New York: New York Academy of Sciences, 1978.

Kaplan, B. H., Cassel, J. C., Tyroler, H. A., Cornoni, J. C., Kleinbaum, D. G., & Hames, C. G. Occupational mobility and coronary heart disease. *Archives of Internal Medicine*, 1971, *128*, 938–942.

Keys, A., Taylor, H. L., Blackburn, H., Brozek, J., Anderson, J. T., & Simonson, E. Mortality and coronary heart disease among men studied for 23 years. *Archives of Internal Medicine*, 1971, *128*, 201–214.

Kokatnur, M. G., Malcolm, G. T., Eggen, D. A., & Strong, J. P. Depletion of aortic free and ester cholesterol by dietary means in rhesus monkeys with fatty streaks. *Atherosclerosis*, 1975, *21*, 195–203.

Kolloch, R., Kobayashi, K., & DeQuattro, V. Dopaminergic control of sympathetic tone and blood pressure: Evidence in primary hypertension. *Hypertension*, 1980, *2*, 390–394.

Korteweg, G. C. J., Boeles, J. T. F., & Ten Cate, J. Influence of stimulation of some subcortical areas on electrocardiogram. *Journal of Neurophysiology*, 1957, *20*, 100–107.

Kubo, T., & Hashimoto, M. Effects of intraventricular and introspinal 6-hydroxydopamine on blood pressure of renal hypertensive rats. *Archives of Internal Pharmacology*, 1978, *232*, 166–176.

Kuller, L., Cooper, M., & Perper, J. Epidemiology and sudden death. *Archives of Internal Medicine*, 1972, *129*, 714–719.

Kurien, V. A., & Oliver, M. F. Serum-free fatty acids after acute myocardial infarction and cerebral vascular occlusion. *Lancet*, 1966, *ii*, 122–133.

Kurien, V. A., Yates, P. A., & Oliver, M. F. Free fatty acids, heparin, and arrhythmias during experimental myocardial infarction. *Lancet*, 1969, *ii*, 185–187.

Lamprecht, R., St. Richardson, J., Williams, R. B., & Kopin, I. J. 6-Hydroxydopamine destruction of central adrenergic neurons prevents or reverses developing DOCA-salt hypertension in rats. *Journal of Neural Transmission, 1977, 40,* 149–158.

LeBlanc, J., Cote, J., Jobin, M., & Labrie, A. Plasma catecholamines and cardiovascular responses to cold and mental activity. *Journal of Applied Physiology, 1979, 47,* 1207–1211.

Lown, B., DeSilva, R. A., Reich, P., & Murawski, B. J. Psychophysiologic factors in sudden cardiac death. *American Journal of Psychiatry, 1980, 137,* 1325–1335.

Lown, B., & Verrier, R. L. Neural activity and ventricular fibrillation. *New England Journal of Medicine, 1976, 294,* 1165–1170.

Lown, B., & Verrier, R. Neural factors in sudden death. In A. M. Brown, A. Malliani, P. J. Schwartz, & A. Zanchetti (Eds.), *Neural mechanisms in cardiac arrhythmias.* New York: Raven Press, 1978.

Lown, B., Verrier, R., & Corbalan, R. Psychologic stress and threshold for repetitive ventricular response. *Science, 1973, 182,* 834–836.

Mains, R. E., Eipper, B. A., & Lin, N. Common precursor to corticotropins and endorphins. *Proceedings of the National Academy of Sciences USA, 1977, 74,* 3014–3018.

Mason, J. W. A review of psychoendocrine research on the pituitary–adrenal cortical system. *Psychosomatic Medicine, 1968, 30,* 576–607. (a)

Mason, J. W. A review of psychoendocrine research on the sympathetic–adrenal medullary system. *Psychosomatic Medicine, 1968, 30,* 631–653. (b)

Mason, J. W., Brady, J. V., & Tolliver, G. A. Plasma and urinary 17-hydroxycorticosteroid responses to 72-hour avoidance sessions in the monkey. *Psychosomatic Medicine, 1968, 30,* 608–630.

Matta, R. J., Verrier, R. L., & Lown, B. The repetitive extrasystole as an index of vulnerability to ventricular fibrillation. *American Journal of Physiology, 1976, 230,* 1469–1473.

Mauck, H. P., Jr., & Hockman, C. H. Central nervous system mechanisms mediating cardiac rate and rhythm. *American Heart Journal, 1967, 74,* 96–109.

McGeer, P. L., & McGeer, E. G. Chemistry of mood and emotion. *Annual Review of Psychology, 1980, 31,* 273–307.

Moore, S. Thromboatherosclerosis in normolipemic rabbits: A result of continued endothelial damage. *Laboratory Investigator, 1973, 29,* 478–487.

Nicholls, M. G., Kiowski, W., Zweifler, A. J., Julius, S., Schork, M. A., & Greenhouse, J. Plasma norepinephrine variations with dietary sodium intake. *Hypertension, 1980, 2,* 29–32.

Olefsky, J. M., Johnson, F., Liu, F., Jen, P., & Reaven, G. M. The effects of acute chronic dexamethasone treatment on insulin binding to isolated rat hepatocytes and adipocytes. *Metabolism, 1975, 24,* 517–527.

Rabinowitz, S. H., Verrier, R. L., & Lown, B. Muscarinic effects of vagosympathetic trunk stimulation on the repetitive extrasystole threshold. *Circulation, 1976, 53,* 622–627.

Rahe, R. H. Subjects' recent life changes and their near-future illness reports: A review. *Annals of Clinical Research, 1972, 4,* 250–265.

Regan, T. J., Harman, M. A., Lehan, P. H., Burke, W. M., & Oldewurtel, H. A. Ventricular arrhythmias and K^+ transfer during myocardial ischemia and intervention with procaine amide, insulin, or glucose solution. *Journal of Clinical Investigation, 1967, 46,* 1657–1668.

Robertson, D., Shand, D. G., Hollifield, J. W., Nies, A. S., Frolich, J. C., & Oates, J. A. Alterations in the responses of the sympathetic nervous system and renin in borderline hypertension. *Hypertension, 1979, 1,* 118–124.

Rose, R. M. Endocrine responses to stressful psychological events. *Psychiatric Clinics of North America, 1980, 3,* 251–276.

Rosenman, R. H., Brand, R. J., Jenkins, C. D., Friedman, M., Straus, R., & Wurm, M. Coronary heart disease in the Western Collaborative Group Study. *Journal of the American Medical Association, 1975, 233,* 872–877.

Rosenman, R. H., Brand, R. J., Sholtz, R. E., & Friedman, M. Multivariate prediction of coronary heart disease during 8.5 year follow-up in the Western Collaborative Group Study. *American Journal of Cardiology*, 1976, *37*, 903–910.

Ross, R. The arterial wall and atherosclerosis. *Annual Review of Medicine*, 1979, *30*, 1–15.

Ross, R., & Glomset, J. Atherosclerosis and the arterial smooth muscle cell. *Science*, 1973, *180*, 1332–1339.

Ross, R. M., & Glomset, J. A. The pathogenesis of atherosclerosis. *New England Journal of Medicine*, 1976, *295*, 369–377, 420–425.

Ross, R., Glomset, J., Kariya, B., & Harker, L. A platelet-dependent serum factor that stimulates the proliferation of arterial smooth muscle cells "in vitro." *Proceedings of the National Academy of Sciences USA*, 1974, *71*, 1207–1210.

Ross, R., & Harker, L. Hyperlipidemia and atherosclerosis. *Science*, 1976, *193*, 1094–1100.

Rossier, J., Grench, E. D., Rivier, C., Ling, N., Guillemin, R., & Bloom, F. E. Footshock induced stress increases B-endorphin levels in blood but not brain. *Nature*, 1977, *270*, 618–620.

Sachar, E. J. Psychological factors relating to activation and inhibition of the adrenocortical stress response in man: A review. *Progressive Brain Research*, 1970, *32*, 316–324.

Sachar, E. J., Asnis, G., Halbreich, U., & Halpern F. Recent studies in the neuroendocrinology of major depressive disorders. *Psychiatric Clinics of North America*, 1980, *3*, 313–326.

Scherwitz, L., Berton, K., & Leventhal, H. Type A behavior, self-involvement, and cardiovascular response. *Psychosomatic Medicine*, 1978, *40*, 593–609.

Schonfeld, G., & Pfleger, B. Utilization of exogenous free fatty acids for the production of very low density lipoprotein triglyceride by livers of carbohydrate fed rats. *Journal of Lipid Research*, 1971, *12*, 614–621.

Schulze, R. A., Humphrie, J. O., Griffith, L. S. C., Ducci, H., Achuff, S., Baird, M. D., Mettits, E. D., & Pitt, B. Left ventricular and coronary angiographic anatomy: Relationship to ventricular irritability in the late hospital phase of acute myocardial infarction. *Circulation*, 1977, *55*, 839–843.

Schwartz, P. J., Periti, M., & Malliani, A. The long Q-T syndrome. *American Heart Journal*, 1975, *89*, 378–390.

Schwartz, P. J., & Malliani, A. Electrical alternation of the T-wave: Clinical and experimental evidence of its relationship with the sympathetic nervous system and with the long Q-T syndrome. *American Heart Journal*, 1975, *89*, 45–50.

Schwartz, P. J., Snebold, N. G., & Brown, A. M. Effects of unilateral cardiac sympathetic denervation on the ventricular fibrillation threshold. *American Journal of Cardiology*, 1976, *37*, 1034–1040.

Schwartz, P. J., & Stone, H. L. Unilateral stellectomy and sudden death. In A. M. Brown, A. Malliani, P. J. Schwartz, & A. Zanchetti (Eds.), *Neural mechanisms in cardiac arrhythmias*. New York: Raven Press, 1978.

Schwartz, P. J., & Wolf, S. Q-T interval prolongation as predictor of sudden death in patients with myocardial infarction. *Circulation*, 1978, *57*, 107–110.

Shamoon, H., Soman, V., & Sherwin, R. S. The influence of acute physiological increments of cortisol on fuel metabolism and insulin binding to monocytes in normal humans. *Journal of Clinical Endocrinology and Metabolism*, 1980, *50*, 495–501.

Simonsen, S., & Kjekshus, J. D. The effect of free fatty acids on myocardial oxygen consumption during atrial pacing and catecholamine infusion in man. *Circulation*, 1978, *58*, 484–491.

Smith, H. W. Physiology of the renal circulation. *Harvey Lectures*, 1940, *35*, 166–220.

Solomon, F., Delores, L., & Dews, P. *Biobehavioral factors in sudden cardiac death*. Washington, D.C.: National Academy of Sciences, 1981.

Soman, V. R., Shamoon, H., & Sherwin, R. S. Effects of physiological infusion of epinephrine in normal humans: Relationship between the metabolic response and β-adrenergic binding. *Journal of Clinical Endocrinology and Metabolism*, 1980, *50*, 294–297.

Sprague, E. A., Troxler, R. G., Peterson, D. F., Schmidt, R. E., & Young, J. T. Effect of cortisol on the development of atherosclerosis in cynomolgus monkeys. In S. S. Kalter (Ed.), *The use of nonhuman primates in cardiovascular diseases.* Austin: University of Texas Press, 1980.

Stemerman, M. B., & Ross, R. Experimental arteriosclerosis: I. Fibrous plaque formation in primates, an electron microscope study. *Journal of Experimental Medicine,* 1972, *136,* 769–789.

Stout, R. W., Bierman, E. L., & Ross, R. The effect of insulin on the proliferation of cultured primate arterial smooth muscle cells. *Circulation Research,* 1975, *36,* 319–327.

Struyker Boudier, H. A. J., Smeets, G. W. M., Brower, G. M., & VanRossum, J. M. Hypothalmic alpha adrenergic receptors in cardiovascular regulation. *Neuropharmacology,* 1974, *13,* 837–846.

Syme, S. L., Hyman, M. M., & Enterline, P. E. Some social and cultural factors associated with the occurrence of coronary heart disease. *Journal of Chronic Diseases,* 1964, *17,* 277–289.

Taggart, P., & Carruthers, M. Endogenous hyperlipidemia induced by emotional stress of racing driving. *Lancet,* 1971, i, 363–366.

Tarazi, R. C., Dustan, H. P., Frohlich, E. D., Gifford, R. W., Jr., & Hoffman, G. C. Plasma volume and chronic hypertension. *Archives of Internal Medicine,* 1970, *125,* 835–842.

Timio, M., & Gentili, S. Adrenosympathetic overactivity under conditions of work stress. *British Journal of Preventive Social Medicine,* 1976, *30,* 262–265.

Timio, M., Gentili, S., & Pede, S. Free adrenaline and noradrenaline excretion related to occupational stress. *British Heart Journal,* 1979, *42,* 471–474.

Troxler, R. G., Sprague, E. A., Albanese, R. A., Fuchs, R., & Thompson, A. J. The association of elevated plasma cortisol and early atherosclerosis as demonstrated by coronary angiography. *Atherosclerosis,* 1977, *26,* 151–162.

Tzagournis, M., Chiles, R., Ryan, J. M., & Skillman, T. G. Interrelationships of hyperinsulinism and hypertriglyceridemia in young patients in coronary heart disease. *Circulation,* 1968, *38,* 1156–1163.

Ursin, H., Baade, E., & Levine, S. (Eds.). *Psychobiology of stress: A study of coping men.* New York: Academic Press, 1978.

Vander, A. J. Effect of catecholamines and the renal nerves on renin secretion in anesthetized dogs. *American Journal of Physiology,* 1965, *209,* 659–662.

Watson, R. D. S., Hamilton, C. A., Reid, J. L., & Littler, W. A. Changes in plasma norepinephrine, blood pressure and heart rate during physical activity in hypertensive man. *Hypertension,* 1979, *1,* 342–346.

Weinberg, S. J., & Foster, J. M. Electrocardiographic changes produced by localized hypothalmic situations. *Annals of Internal Medicine,* 1960, *53,* 332–341.

Wiedenann, E., Satio, T., Linfoot, J. A., & Li, C. H. Specific radioimmunoassay of human beta-endorphin in unextracted plasma. *Journal of Clinical Endocrinal Metabolism,* 1979, *49,* 478–480.

Ziegler, M. G., Lake, C. R., Williams, A. C., Teychenne, P. F., Shoulson, I., & Steinsland, O. Bromocriptine inhibits norepinephrine release. *Clinical Pharmacology and Therapeutics,* 1979, *25,* 137–142.

CHAPTER 8

Coping and Adaptation

Richard S. Lazarus
University of California, Berkeley

Susan Folkman
University of California, Berkeley

Coping has long been ascribed a central role in human adaptation. In the heyday of psychodiagnosis during the 1940s and 1950s, the concept of coping was a major theme in clinical description and evaluation, and psychotherapy is often conceptualized as an effort to change counterproductive ways of coping into more serviceable ones (e.g., Goldfried, 1980), whether or not the word "coping" is actually employed. "Coping" is also as much a colloquial term as a scientific one. It is part of the vernacular, and is the subject of numerous self-help books as well as a variation on the name of an over-the-counter medication. Yet coping as a theoretical concept has not lived up to its promise in research. There is confusion as to what coping means, and there is a dearth of effective measurement approaches.

It is time to struggle with the difficult task of systematizing the concept and to raise important issues that are touched on by the small but increasing flow of books and articles that give coping a dominant place in research (e.g., Coelho, Hamburg, & Adams, 1974; Cohen & Lazarus, 1979; Folkman & Lazarus, 1980; Haan, 1977; Lazarus, 1966, 1981; Lazarus & Launier, 1978; Murphy, 1974; Pearlin & Schooler, 1978). This chapter attempts to examine the concept of coping as it has evolved in recent years; to address issues of definition, function, and assessment; and to assess the role of coping in somatic and mental health.

THE CONCEPT OF COPING

There are analogues of coping in numerous disciplines. Sociologists, for example, refer to the ways in which a social order adjusts to a crisis, and biologists speak of the adjustment of a tissue system or the body to noxious agents, as in Selye's (1956, 1976) "general adaptation syndrome." However, coping is primarily a psychological concept. In psychological usage there are many definitions of "coping," but all share a central theme—namely, the struggle with external and internal demands, conflicts, and distressing emotions.

Some definitions, such as those of Menninger (1963), Haan (1977), and Vaillant (1977), imply a hierarchy of adaptationally focused efforts, with "coping" representing mature ego processes and "defenses" representing immature and less serviceable variations of the same essential cognitive processes. Whenever coping is conceptualized within a hierarchical scheme, an *a priori* value judgment is being made as to the inherent goodness or adaptiveness of internal processes. This judgment is context-free, because it judges goodness and badness without taking the demands and possibilities of the situation into account.

The psychoanalytic (or ego-psychological) tendency to assign positive and negative value to various internal processes or modes of defense, without evidence about their effects on the total psychological economy of the person and without reference to context, has led to an unwise equation of "defense" with "pathology" (Lazarus, 1981). For example, denial and avoidance are widely regarded as poor ways of dealing with stress. We argue that good coping should not be distinguished from poor coping solely on the basis of the type of process a person employs, since we presently know little about the adaptational outcomes of diverse patterns of coping (see also Lazarus, 1966). We have more to say about this later in the chapter; for now, it is important merely to recognize the value-laden nature of certain traditional ways in which "coping" has been defined.

For these and other reasons, we prefer to define "coping" at the psychological level of analysis as *the process of managing demands (external or internal) that are appraised as taxing or exceeding the resources of the person.* This definition has several important functions. First, it emphasizes "process," as distinguished from trait or style; we elaborate on this below. Second, it speaks of "management" rather than mastery; since many human problems (e.g., terminal illness, incapacitation, aging) cannot be mastered, they must be redefined, tolerated, endured, or accepted for optimal adaptation. Third, the term "appraisal" indicates the central role of psychological mediation. Finally, we view coping as entailing the mobilization of effort. Many of the things we do to get along become automatic and therefore fail to satisfy this criterion. For example, when we drive an automobile in most routine situations, we are often not particularly conscious of using the clutch and brake, steering, or stopping for traffic signals, nor is there much special effort involved. If we are experienced, we do these things automatically, so much so that we can even think about a problem at work while engaging in all the complex acts needed to get us where we are going. Are these acts to be considered coping? If so, then coping would consist of almost everything we do.

There is an emerging consensus that "coping" and "adaptation" should be distinguished. Several recent writers (e.g., Lazarus, Averill, & Opton,

1974; Murphy, 1974; White, 1974) have taken the position that adaptation is a broader concept that includes routine, even automatic, modes of getting along, whereas coping always involves some sort of stress. White, for example, speaks of coping as a subcategory of adaptation that occurs only under relatively difficult conditions, and Murphy emphasizes newness and drawing upon normally unused resources. What distinguishes coping from adaptation, then, is mobilization of effort. Coping occurs only when the person cannot routinely handle the demands or requirements of living, but must draw upon something extra. This distinction allows us to narrow the definition of "coping" to include only nonroutine acts and to keep "adaptation" as the generic term for processes affecting how well the person gets along.

FUNCTIONS OF COPING

If we are ultimately to evaluate the quality or effectiveness of coping for practical purposes, we must also have some notion about its functions. White (1974, p. 55) cites three: to "keep securing adequate information about the environment," to "maintain satisfactory internal conditions both for action and for processing information," and to maintain "autonomy or freedom of movement, freedom to use [one's] repertoire in a flexible fashion." Mechanic (1974) also cites three functions: dealing with social and environmental demands, having the motivation to meet such demands, and maintaining a state of psychological equilibrium in order to direct energy and skill toward meeting external demands. Pearlin and Schooler (1978) likewise identify three functions, which include changing the situation out of which strainful (stressful) experiences arise, controlling the meaning of such experiences before they become stressful, and controlling stress itself after it has been generated. Cohen and Lazarus (1979), in a synthesis of the contributions of many writers (e.g., Hamburg & Adams, 1967; Lipowski, 1970, 1975; Mages & Mendelsohn, 1979) who have discussed the coping requirements imposed by illness, describe five main coping tasks:

> (1) to reduce harmful environmental conditions and enhance prospects of recovery, (2) to tolerate or adjust to negative events and realities, (3) to maintain a positive self-image, (4) to maintain emotional equilibrium, and (5) to continue satisfying relationships with others. (p. 232)

Common to all of these coping tasks is a distinction we believe is of overriding importance—namely, that between "problem-focused" and "emotion-focused" coping (Cohen & Lazarus, 1979; Folkman & Lazarus, 1980). "Problem-focused" coping refers to efforts directed at doing something constructive about the conditions that harm, threaten, or challenge. "Emotion-focused" coping refers to efforts directed at regulating the emotion itself, whether the focus of such regulation is behavior and expression, physiological disturbance, subjective distress, or all three (see also Folkman & Lazarus,

1980; Lazarus, 1975, 1981; Lazarus & Launier, 1978). This distinction has been made by Mechanic (1974), Kahn, Wolfe, Quinn, and Snoek (1964), and White (1974).

The same coping strategy can serve both coping functions on different occasions, and sometimes even simultaneously. For example, one can use information search as an emotion-focused strategy to bolster a decision already made and so to sustain morale (see Janis, 1974) on one occasion, and as a problem-focused strategy to find out what has to be done on another occasion. Similarly, tangible social support that has a problem-focused function, as when a friend arranges for a funeral, cooks for the guests, or takes care of the children in an emergency, can simultaneously be of emotional value by making the person feel protected, wanted, and cared for.

Our research group, the Berkeley Stress and Coping Project, has been obtaining clear evidence that most people use both emotion-focused *and* problem-focused modes of coping in daily stressful encounters (e.g., Folkman & Lazarus, 1980). This evidence comes from a study of 100 men and women, aged 45 to 64, interviewed and assessed monthly over a period of 1 year. Special attention was paid to how they coped, using a 68-item checklist of both problem-focused and emotion-focused acts and thoughts that they used to cope in a given encounter. In less than 2% of the 1,332 coping episodes studied, only one or the other type of coping was used; this figure points up dramatically that most commonly people use both. This also means that approaches to coping that overemphasize emotion regulation or defense (e.g., Haan, 1977; Menninger, 1963; Vaillant, 1977) are dealing with only a limited aspect of the coping process; likewise, systems that center mainly on problem-focused coping (e.g., the decision-making approach of Janis & Mann, 1977) are also incomplete.

The importance of both emotion- and problem-focused coping can be illustrated in the case of serious illness. The person must be alert to danger signals and active in the prevention of complications, while at the same time maintaining morale. Quite obviously, such patients must use a suitable mix of emotion-regulating and problem-solving forms of coping. That this is a reasonable hypothesis about the interactive roles of emotion- and problem-focused coping in illness is supported by analyses and reviews of research on uncooperative patients by Farberow (1980) and A. M. Goldstein (1980). A. M. Goldstein, for example, writes about dialysis patients:

> I see the "uncooperative" patient as a person who is frightened, over-whelmed, and reaching out for any and all evidence that his condition is not critical and that he will recover, continue to survive, and lead a normal happy life. Like the rest of us, the chronically ill or terminally ill patient employs a variety of coping strategies designed to make life more bearable by avoiding realities which might prove to be overwhelming if directly confronted. Thus, "uncooperative" behaviors employed by such patients are viewed as attempts to minimize or avoid the recognition of one's tenuous

hold on life by "proving" to themselves and to others that life-threatening treatments are not required and, therefore, that they are not as critically ill as others might fear. However, by denying the severity of their condition and the need for treatment, such patients risk their lives through noncompliance with the treatment regimen. They engage in forms of indirect self-destructive behavior. . . . (p. 90)

Although this example concerns a matter of life or death, such combinations of problem- and emotion-focused coping must also be part of everyday living if people are to function effectively and to maintain high morale. We all use a complex mix of these strategies; what is needed is information about how their various combinations affect adaptational outcomes, including somatic health, and how they vary from person to person and across situational contexts.

COPING AS PROCESS, TRAIT, OR STYLE

In recent years much attention has been paid to the distinction between trait and state variables. "Trait" refers to a stable property of a person—a disposition to respond—that affects actions and reactions under a variety of circumstances. To a greater or lesser degree, therefore, the concept of trait transcends situations or classes of situations. "State," on the other hand, is a transient reaction pattern, changing with circumstances (see Averill & Opton, 1968).

Anxiety as a trait, for example, is the disposition to react to numerous situations with anxiety (see Lazarus, 1966; Spielberger, 1966, 1972). Such a disposition may be undefined as to its psychological properties, in which case one simply speaks of an anxious person. On the other hand, the disposing psychological variable may be specified, as, for example, when frequent or chronic anxiety is said to be the result of feelings of inadequacy or low self-esteem. For a person who suffers from these feelings, any new situation may seem threatening (Lazarus, 1966); the reaction pattern is stable across situations, and is therefore to some degree predictable. A state, on the other hand, can fluctuate. Thus, a reaction of anxiety in one situation says nothing about whether it will occur in another situation; even a few occurrences do not make an "anxious person."

In an analogous fashion, a "coping trait" means that a person is disposed to engage in given coping behaviors under certain eliciting conditions. The more general the trait, the less it is limited to any particular situational context. Thus, a coping trait is a stable tendency from which a prediction is made about how the person will cope in some or all types of stressful encounters. Trait and style are fundamentally similar ideas, and we often speak of "coping style" to refer to a characteristic way of handling situations. The term "style," as in Alfred Adler's "style of life," tends to imply a very broad and encompassing disposition, whereas a "trait" can be very limited and narrow. There is something about the connotation of "style" that suggests sustained, complex strategies for relating to the world.

Consider, for example, the observations and clinical inferences made by Weiner, Singer, and Reiser (1962) with hypertensive and normotensive subjects. In clinical interviews dealing with threatening topics, it was noted that the hypertensives engaged in a coping strategy of insulating or distancing themselves, a process that served to control their blood pressure in this particular stress situation. The process of insulating or distancing can also be an overriding style with which a person relates to almost everyone and everything, especially in emotional contexts. Psychoanalytically oriented writers have used the terms "isolation," "undoing," and "intellectualization" to refer to this style of coping, which is said to characterize the obsessive–compulsive neurotic (see also the "cognitive style" concept; e.g., Gardner, Holzman, Klein, Linton, & Spence, 1959). Other styles characterize hysteria and paranoia (Shapiro, 1965).

One problem with many of our concepts of coping style is that they are derived from one particular theoretical formulation—namely, psychoanalytic ego psychology; adopting this formulation carries additional theoretical freight. Moreover, as noted in our comments about the work of Menninger, Vaillant, and Haan, the system of ideas from which it springs centers on pathology and on intrapsychic processes and defenses. These are only part of the larger concept of coping, which includes attention to environmental demands, opportunities, and constraints.

There are potentially a large number of coping styles, and any given scheme for describing and classifying them raises a confusing welter of complex theoretically and empirically derived alternatives (Folkman & Lazarus, 1981). Researchers on coping and adaptation have only begun to address the question of how to describe and assess coping styles.

In contrast to a coping trait or style, a "coping process" refers to (1) what the person *actually does in a particular encounter*, and (2) *how what is done changes* as the encounter unfolds, or from encounter to encounter when they are united by some common theme. "Process" is analogous to "state" because it refers to what actually happens in a specific context, and to how it changes. By definition, process means change. State is evanescent; so is process. A state such as anxiety comes and goes with the circumstances, varies in degree, and has diverse qualities. So it is with process. Instead of looking at a still photo, as it were, of a single act or thought embedded in a discrete time frame, process is a motion picture portraying the flow of events.

The nature of coping as process can be illustrated with loss of a loved one and grieving. Grief is a process that changes from the moment of the loss to its ultimate resolution. Although there are apt to be great individual differences in the pattern of grieving, there may also be a common core of processes, widely shared, that leads to the clinical impression of predictable stages. The first reaction may be shock and disbelief, coupled with (coping) efforts to deny the loss or to restore the image of the person who has died. There may be frantic activity, agitated depression, tearfulness, or valiant efforts to carry on. This pattern is far different from later stages of the grief process, when the loss is acknowledged and a degree of disengagement occurs, followed ultimately by acceptance of the loss, reengagement, and attachment to other persons. The entire process may take as long as several years and may be characterized by complex and changing patterns of emotion and coping.

Bereavement and grief work highlight the importance of temporal factors in the coping process. For example, denial may be useful early in a crisis, but, continued too long, it may prevent a person from coming to terms with reality and doing what must be done to cope effectively. The research of Wolff, Friedman, Hofer, and Mason (1964) and Hofer, Wolff, Friedman, and Mason (1972) on the stress of having a child with a terminal illness is a case in point. Their findings suggest that parents who were well defended while their children were dying showed less evidence of physiological stress; but later, after the death of the children, these parents seemed worse off. It is tempting to suggest that the "well-defended" parents had to pay for their denial-like coping, which protected them during their children's illness but left them vulnerable to distress later (see also Lindemann, 1944). At the very least, this example should alert us to the possibility not only that coping changes over time and with changes in the context, but also that a coping strategy that serves a positive function at one stage of a stressful episode might have negative consequences at other times (see also Lazarus, 1983).

Our emphasis on process distinguishes our approach from most others, which are trait-oriented. If the assessment of coping traits really allowed us to predict what a person would actually do to cope in any stressful encounter, research would be a simple matter. For all intents and purposes, traits could then stand for process; for example, if a person coped with threat by avoidance, we would expect avoidance to occur whenever he or she felt threatened. However, the assessment of coping traits actually has had very modest predictive value with respect to coping processes.

The problem with traits as predictors is well illustrated by Cohen and Lazarus' (1973) research on coping with the threat of surgery. Patients were interviewed in the hospital the evening before surgery; an assessment was made of how much they knew about their illness, the surgical procedure, and the postsurgical course, and how much interest they showed in finding out about these. They were then arrayed on a dimension ranging from avoidance (they knew little and clearly did not want to know) to the other extreme of vigilance (they had much information and sought even more). In addition, a standard trait measure of this dimension, called repression–sensitization (Byrne, 1964), was administered; some people fell on the repression end and others on the sensitization end of the continuum. However, no correlation was found between the standard trait measure and what people did in the actual situation of surgical threat. The trait measure did not predict the process of coping with the specific threat.

Findings such as those of Cohen and Lazarus (1973) do not mean that coping traits do not exist; rather, they mean that existing measures of what we call coping traits do not represent the complexity and variability that characterize actual coping processes. Much of this variability can be ascribed to the demands of the specific situation. The Berkeley Project study (Folkman & Lazarus, 1980) cited earlier illustrates the influence of the context on coping. We found that a number of contextual variables influenced the relative emphasis on problem-solving versus emotion-focused coping activities. Stressful episodes connected with work, for example, favored problem-solving modes of coping, while those connected with health favored emotion-focused coping. Furthermore, despite the stereotype that women are more emotion-focused than men, there were no important gender differences, and where they seemed to occur, this was because men reported more work episodes than women; in short, it was the situational context rather than gender that influenced the coping pattern. To determine whether and how coping (as a trait or style) transcends the demands of specific situations requires seeking a level of abstraction in the assessment of coping that is not situation-specific. (For discussion of these issues, see Folkman & Lazarus, 1980, 1981.)

COGNITIVE PROCESSES IN STRESS AND COPING

Coping is, in part, a reaction to being in a stressful relationship with the environment. To experience psychological stress requires that the person sense that this relationship has damaged his or her well-being, threatens it, or offers the possibility of gain (challenge). If, on the other hand, nothing of value is judged to be at stake in the encounter, psychological stress does not occur. The difference between psychological stress and stress at the social and physiological levels is that the psychological variant is determined by a thinking being who makes interpretations of ongoing relationships with the environment.

In other writings (e.g., Coyne & Lazarus, 1980; Folkman, Schaefer, & Lazarus, 1979; Lazarus, 1966, 1981; Lazarus, Averill, & Opton, 1970), we have used the term "cognitive appraisal" to refer to this evaluative process. Three kinds of appraisal are encompassed by psychological stress—namely, harm, threat, and challenge. The differences among these are important, because they affect how a person copes. "Harm" (including loss) represents damage already done; "threat" involves the potential for harm; and "challenge" means the potential for some significant gain under difficult odds.

Without some cognitive mediational concept, we could never account for individual differences in the levels of stress response displayed to common environmental conditions—differences that are manifest even in extreme conditions, such as those in a concentration camp (Benner, Roskies, & Lazarus, 1980). Considering that no one today is surprised that plants have protein discrimination mechanisms to prevent self-fertilization, or that fowl can distinguish dangerous predators such as the hawk from benign birds (Tinbergen, 1951), why should it be surprising that humans have developed a highly symbolic mechanism for differentiating among experiences that harm, threaten, challenge, or nurture? Whether one calls this mechanism "cognitive appraisal" or "evaluative perception," without it our actions and feelings would frequently fail to accord with the values, needs, and commitments on which our actual and subjective sense of well-being depends.

Broadly speaking, degree of stress depends mainly on the appraisal of how much appears to be at stake in the transaction (in terms, for example, of values, motives, or commitments) and the relative power of the environmental demand to do harm, compared with the power of the person to prevent or manage such harm. There probably is an interactive relationship between how much is at stake and the person's appraisal of his or her ability to produce a positive outcome. When much is at stake, threat seems to be disproportionately high, even in a situation in which the person assumes that he or she has much control, because a small error of judgment or a bit of bad luck could be very costly; when there is little at stake, failure to control the situation is not likely to cause distress.

"Harm" is damaged well-being as defined by a person's values and commitments. The harm can be temporary, as perhaps in a social insult, a poor school or job evaluation, an acute but not serious illness, or a temporary loss in social support. Sometimes harm is long-term or permanent, as in life-threatening or incapacitating illness, and requires redefinition or a change in values and commitments in order for a person to manage successfully. In any case, coping is required to overcome the damage or loss, to prevent things from getting worse, to come to terms with the situation as it is, or to reinterpret what has happened. Consider the example of a negative evaluation by another that damages the person's social esteem and perhaps even self-esteem. In the instance of damage to social esteem, one coping strategy is to convince important others (e.g., those affecting the potential for advancement) that the effort being evaluated is not representative of one's worth. Another is to resolve to undo the damage in the future by working harder or by changing one's approach. With respect to damage to self-esteem, the person can generate acceptable excuses or can recognize and accept his or her limitations.

Notice that coping with harm usually contains a heavy weighting of undoing or reinterpreting what is already past, although there is also usually some anticipatory coping as well—for example, in making resolutions and plans to do differently in the future. The past always weighs heavily in coping with harm; the extent to which it is the primary focus seems to depend on the type and degree of harm that has been sustained and its implications for the future (see Lazarus & Launier, 1978).

In the case of "threat," the dynamics of coping are almost always heavily weighted by future considerations, and we can speak of "anticipatory coping." A threatened person must prepare for the harm that may come. This requires an evaluation of what will happen, when it will happen, and how bad it will be; the possibilities for preventing, surviving, or tolerating it; and the chances for recouping in the event that it actually occurs. Often the information needed for these evaluations is missing or incomplete, in which case the person must deal with a high degree of ambiguity and uncertainty. Vigilance (see, e.g., Janis, 1974; Janis & Mann, 1977)—that is, the attentive search for information about a danger and factors relevant to it—is particularly important in conditions of threat, especially when there is ambiguity and uncertainty. In life one rarely engages solely in anticipatory coping, but, instead, in coping that is oriented to the past and the present as well; how one handles future dangers is likely to depend on one's past experience, which can provide clues about what to expect and do.

"Challenge," like threat, is also oriented toward the future, with attention and expectations directed more at what can be gained than at what might be lost. We know little about a person's state of mind in challenge as opposed to threat, or about the modes of coping that characterize this state of mind. Perhaps the most important elements in coping with challenge are a positive outlook and the enthusiasm with which encounters are addressed.

We have suggested elsewhere (Lazarus, Cohen, Folkman, Kanner, & Schaefer, 1980) that people may cope better when challenged than when threatened, because they are less conflicted and suffer less from such emotions as anxiety, anger, guilt, or jealousy. Their whole being is attuned to pursuing their commitment. Consider, for example, performing artists who feel strongly and positively about their encounters with the audience. Challenged and threatened performers may be equally "stressed," but the former seem to enjoy the process, their minds working smoothly and freely, while the latter, preoccupied with possible audience rejection, may be generally ill at ease and anxious for the encounter to end. In sum, how coping is carried out depends not only on whether the focus is on the past, present, or future, but also on whether the encounter is approached with a sense of challenge or threat.

Central to the above discussion is the idea that coping is to a large extent sensitive to the requirements, constraints, and available resources characterizing a stressful encounter, as these are appraised by the person. The process of cognitive appraisal can be exemplified by a set of questions a person asks about the encounter—namely, "What is happening or going to happen?," "How bad (or good) could it be?," "What can I do about it?," and "What might the consequences of my actions be?" Such questions are not necessarily conscious or deliberate; they may be implicit, automatic, and virtually instantaneous. Nevertheless, cognitive processes about what is at stake and what the options for action are shape coping decisions in every stressful encounter. Such processes are influenced jointly by the actual situational context and by personality factors.

Findings from the Berkeley Project's field study of middle-aged men and women, cited earlier (Folkman & Lazarus, 1980), suggest how appraisal can influence coping. For each stressful encounter, subjects had to choose among statements describing how they appraised it. The statements described the situation as either one that had to be accepted because nothing could be done or as one in which action was possible. Appraisals that nothing could be done favored the use of emotion-focused modes of coping, whereas encounters in which action was possible favored problem-solving modes. In other words, the appraisal of options influenced how people coped with stressful encounters.

One of the difficulties inherent in a cognitive approach to coping is that appraisal and coping are often interdependent and difficult to distinguish. An important class of coping consists of cognitive or intrapsychic strategies (Lazarus & Launier, 1978) that we call "reappraisal." Some reappraisals are products of changes in the environment. We may, for example, at first view another person as malevolent until his or her behavior informs us to the contrary, in which case the threat is reappraised as benign. Other reappraisals are self-generated, as when we use defenses such as denial or reaction formation. Even when faced with evidence to the contrary, we convince ourselves that we are not ill, dying, likely to fail, disliked, or in jeopardy in some other way. Such reappraisals must be thought of as cognitive coping efforts clearly directed at managing the demands or the distress. There is no simple way to differentiate an initial benign appraisal—for example, that there is no danger or that we have not been harmed—from a cognitive coping strategy. Coping and appraisal are interdependent, because many coping strategies can have an appraisal function in that they shape the meaning of an event, and, conversely, many forms of appraisal can have a coping function in that they help regulate distress.

DETERMINANTS OF COPING

We have said that coping is sensitive to situational requirements, constraints, and available resources, and that it is affected also by person factors. Such influences interact in shaping the mediating process of appraisal, which, in turn, influences the choice of coping activity. Because of their importance in coping, and because they are highly relevant to behavioral medicine, we now separately examine a few situation and person factors that shape coping through cognitive appraisal. (For an earlier account of research on the influence of these factors, the reader should consult Lazarus, 1966.)

Situation Factors

Situation factors can be either formal or substantive. There are many potential formal factors—for example, imminence and degree of harm; ambiguity about whether there will be harm and about coping options; and the frequency, duration, and chronicity of the harmful encounter. Substantive factors include the nature of the harm (e.g., physical and psychological); personal resources such as skills, energy, and stamina; and environmental resources such as social networks and support systems, money, and institutional supports. We use ambiguity to illustrate formal factors and social resources to illustrate substantive factors.

Ambiguity

Ambiguity is particularly interesting, since it is ubiquitous and plays a major role in appraisal and coping. We use the term "ambiguity" to refer to environmental conditions, and call its subjective counterpart "uncertainty." In other words, ambiguity refers to lack of clarity in the environment, and uncertainty refers to lack of clarity in the person's mind. They are by no means perfectly correlated. For example, one can be certain in what most others would consider an ambiguous situation, and one can be uncertain in a consensually clear context. Only if humans were perfect information-processing machines would the two be highly related. In such an instance, personal agendas—patterns of commitment and assumptions about oneself and the world—would be ruled out as affecting the processing of information (see Folkman et al., 1979).

Ambiguity plays a major role in appraisal and coping, because it makes it difficult to evaluate (appraise) whether there will be harm and how severe it will be. Ambiguity is also important because it makes it difficult to decide whether anything can be done to evade, master, or even tolerate the harm, or to decide on the forms of action that are likely to have a felicitous outcome.

Most of the social contexts in which people operate are ambiguous. This ambiguity leads to widespread variations in the ways these social encounters are appraised and managed, in that it increases the role of person factors in interpreting and dealing with the environment. In the absence of clear information, the situation is like a projective test, and the person makes inferences based on personality dispositions, beliefs, and general experience in order to create understanding as to what is happening. The greater the ambiguity, the more inference is required, and consequently the more influence person factors (such as beliefs and dispositions) have in determining the meaning of the environmental configuration (cf. Lazarus, Eriksen, & Fonda, 1951; Schank & Abelson, 1977). When the situation is unambiguous, situation factors are major determinants of appraisal and coping.

Archer (1979) observed this interplay between ambiguity and person and environment variables. Persons with low trait anxiety reported a significantly greater expectancy of avoiding shocks than did those high in trait anxiety, but only in the experimental condition in which the possibility of control was ambiguous. On the other hand, the personality variable "trait anxiety" played a negligible role when the possibility of control was unambiguous. This finding points up the circumstances under which it may be more fruitful to study person factors versus environmental factors as influences on stress and coping.

The traditional psychological view is that ambiguity is always threatening, on the assumption that people always need to know what is happening and that not to know is to feel helpless, hence also anxious and depressed. This assumption led Frenkel-Brunswik (1949) to speak of intolerance of ambiguity as a condition of psychological vulnerability, and Loevinger (1976) to regard it as characteristic of immature ego development.

However, there appear to be conditions in which ambiguity is a balm, in that it allows the person to construct a hopeful or even a benign interpretation of the situation. Surely, feelings of hope are encouraged when the information given to a terminally ill patient omits details about the chances for recovery or estimates of how much time is left. In the usual case, hope wanes as the symptoms of a terminal illness become more extreme, and as loved ones and professionals reveal through their reactions just how desperate the situation really is. This example illustrates the simplistic nature of the assertion that ambiguity is always threatening.

Despite the importance of ambiguity, there has been surprisingly little research on its various forms and effects. Laboratory studies have examined primarily one kind of ambiguity—that is, lack of clarity about whether a (harmful) event will happen. Breznitz's (1976) research on false alarms has shown that uncertainty increases when warnings about military attacks or destructive storms prove false; with such experiences, people become less willing to believe in the reality of the danger and more often fail to take protective action, such as evacuating their homes in advance of predicted hurricanes. This issue is important for the field of behavioral medicine with respect to compliance. It seems likely that problems with compliance to medical regimens will be greater in conditions when the consequences of the regimen are ambiguous, either because of false alarms or because the information itself is unclear. A substantial body of cognitively oriented research and theory that pertains to this issue already exists (e.g., Becker, 1974a, 1974b, 1976; Becker & Maiman, 1975). An earlier series of studies was directed at the effects of threatening information about dental care and related problems (see, e.g., Janis & Feshbach, 1953; Leventhal, 1965, 1970).

Gaines, Smith, and Skolnick (1977) have shown that the effect of ambiguity about an event's occurrence (whether or not an electric shock would occur) depended on person factors—namely, the cognitive style of field dependence–independence. Monat, Averill, and Lazarus (1972) compared the effects of this same type of ambiguity on stress and coping with another kind of ambiguity—that is, not knowing *when* shock would occur. They found that although what they called "temporal uncertainty" produced greater stress than did "event uncertainty," it was also associated with avoidant forms of cognitive coping as the wait was extended, with a corresponding reduction of autonomic and subjective stress. In other words, stress and coping processes differed with the type of ambiguity. Ambiguity about when an aversive stimulus would occur favored avoidant modes of coping over time, which, if a cause-and-effect interpretation were offered, could be said to have lowered stress. This means that in speaking of ambiguity, one must consider its type and not assume that all forms affect stress and coping in the same way.

Shalit (1977) has maintained that ambiguity is one of the most important factors in appraisal and coping, and that coping effectiveness depends on the ability to resolve ambiguity. Shalit views ambiguity as dependent on the structural complexity of the situation, which is defined by three factors: the number of perceived possibilities for interpretation, the ease with which these possibilities can be rank-ordered, and their positive or negative emotional loading. Reviewing a number of studies involving these variables, Shalit concluded that the person's ability to rank-order the possibilities is the most essential of the factors for effective coping.

In sum, the environmental factor of ambiguity seems logically and empirically important in threat appraisal and coping. Moreover, there will be a greater role for person factors in appraisal and coping as ambiguity increases. Finally, the factor of ambiguity is itself more complex than is ordinarily acknowledged, varying with respect to kind of ambiguity as well as with respect to its consequences for different persons. The concept of ambiguity offers an important and rich area of theory and research, which could further our understanding of situation and person factors in appraisal and coping.

Social Resources

Social networks and supports are receiving much attention in behavioral medicine. "Social network" describes the number and kinds of people with whom a person associates, from intimates to casual contacts (see, e.g., Mitchell, 1969). "Social supports," on the other hand, can be regarded from within either a social or a psychological framework. The term itself implies not merely a social structure of which a person is a part, but the presence of different types of support—including, for example, tangible help, information, and emotional support, such as that provided when another's actions or presence provides comfort. It may also be important to distinguish between the well-intended efforts of others to provide such support and the ways in which such efforts are actually appraised. For example, having a spouse may be taken as normatively socially supportive (e.g., Berkman & Syme, 1979);

however, some spouses may generate rather than relieve stress. In short, "social support" has many different meanings and is typically inferred from the social characteristics of a person's life, rather than from the psychological effects of social relationships.

Most current work on social support assumes that its role in relation to outcome is to buffer stress (Dean & Lin, 1977; Nuckolls, Cassel, & Kaplan, 1972), or, in some instances, that social support has a direct and protective effect on health (Berkman & Syme, 1979; Henderson, 1977). However, these effects have thus far received only limited research support, and the mechanisms through which these effects might occur are far from being clearly spelled out. There are also a number of possible spurious bases for the association between social support and health outcome, as well as alternative hypotheses about such an association. We mention some of the most obvious below.

First, it is possible, as Bloom (1979) suggests, that social support is at least partly a correlate of other variables that affect health outcome—for example, coping competence. Weisman and Worden (1975) suggest from their findings with terminal cancer patients that people who remain in good touch with others and can accept their help without alienating them live longer than do those who withdraw and become depressed. This implies that maintaining effective social supports could be regarded as a coping skill. Put differently, social support may be available to and useful for some people in crisis not simply adventitiously, but as a result of careful cultivation and use.

Second, few investigators seem alert to the possibility—or perhaps they simply do not have the data with which to examine it—that social support can easily be confounded with earlier illness status. That is, people with few members in their social networks, or with low social support, may be isolated due to illness or impairment of either psychological or physiological origin. Such people are at higher risk for poor adaptational outcome of all types. In other words, it is not that social support necessarily produces positive outcomes, but that negative outcomes produce stress and poor social support, thus reversing the direction of cause and effect. In the case of depression, for example, Coyne (1976) has provided evidence and argued effectively that the behavior (psychological symptoms) of the depressed person can alienate needed sources of social support, or can produce well-meaning but counterproductive support behavior (Watzlawick & Coyne, 1980), thus intensifying symptoms in a downward spiral of negative events. Confusion about the basis of the relationship between social support and adaptational outcomes is especially likely in research in which the prior health of the subjects is unknown (e.g., Henderson, Byrne, Duncan-Jones, Adcock, Scott, & Steele, 1978; Lin, Simeone, Ensel, & Kuo, 1979). The possibility that the causal relationship can work both ways—from social support to health outcome and from health outcome to social support—must be taken quite seriously.

Third, a negative correlation between stressful life events scores and social support scores can reflect the presence on most life events lists of losses from the social network as a result of death, divorce, job loss, and change in place of residence. To the extent that this is so, investigators may be studying the effects of stress due to recent losses of social ties, rather than the effects of low social support per se. The two variables, loss of support and stress, are apt to be confounded, and only their separation in research can determine whether it is the loss itself or the absence of social support that influences adaptational outcome.

Fourth, from a psychological standpoint, variables such as social networks and supports engender a varied assortment of psychologically relevant processes that are seldom examined, as we have noted. Without identifying these processes in more detail, we cannot know whether the social behavior of an intimate is supportive, neutral, or even negative in its consequences. It may be that quality of support is far more important than quantity of relationships, though at present we have little to guide us on this. Two published anecdotal examples come to mind. Mechanic (1962) describes the ''supportive'' behavior of two wives of very anxious doctoral students facing a crucial examination. On hearing of the husband's distress, one responds that she is not worried and knows he will do well. The other woman acknowledges her own concern and adds that he should do the best he can, but that whatever happens they will manage.

The latter comment is probably more effective as emotional support than the former, in that the wife acknowledges the problem and gives reassurance that a bad outcome would not be disastrous. In contrast, the former wife belittles her husband's concern by denying that there is anything to worry about, and adds herself to the list of those who would be disappointed if he performs poorly. Another example is that of the grandparents and parents of children dying of leukemia (Friedman, Chodoff, Mason, & Hamburg, 1963), in which the parents who succeeded in controlling their distress were criticized by the grandparents as being callous and indifferent.

These examples of the negative consequences of well-intended social supports can be counterbalanced, of course, with highly positive ones. However, they raise an issue little considered in the present social support literature—namely, that efforts at support can have negative as well as positive effects, and that we know little about which actions and statements are positive or negative, or about the conditions that make a difference. Knowledge of the mediating psychological processes having to do with what makes a social network or a social support variable a resource or liability (e.g., Mechanic, 1974) would greatly add to our understanding of the effects of social relationships on stress and coping, the role of social competence in obtaining and using support, and the impact of all this on health. Needless to say, such a view is particularly compatible with a cognitive approach to stress, coping, and adaptation.

Person Factors

The personality traits on which appraisal and coping processes depend can be drawn from a seemingly endless list of motivational, cognitive, and emotional factors that are said to affect human behavior and experience. Those particularly relevant to stress theory and behavioral medicine include motive pattern (e.g., Vogel, Raymond, & Lazarus, 1959), belief systems such as those concerning self-esteem and locus of control (e.g., Averill, 1973; Bandura, 1977; Epstein, 1973), cognitive styles (Klein, 1970; Shapiro, 1965; Witkin, Goodenough, & Oltman, 1979) ego development (Loevinger, 1976), intelligence and knowledge (Lazarus, 1966), and social competence (Wrubel, Benner, & Lazarus, 1981). There is growing interest in person factors in behavioral medicine research and theory, and we have chosen two of these factors as illustrations: pattern of motivation (or commitment), and beliefs (or assumptions) about personal control.

Pattern of Motivation

"Pattern of motivation," or "commitment," as we prefer to speak of it, defines a person's stakes in any given encounter. That is, it conceptualizes what is important and unimportant to a person, and hence it identifies that person's vulnerability to harm or threat and the potential for being challenged. In short, a person is more likely to appraise a situation as harmful, threatening, or challenging when the situation engages a strong commitment than when what is at stake is minor or unimportant. Since people differ in their patterns of commitment, they will also differ in what harms, threatens, or challenges them and to what degree.

Motivational interpretations have sometimes been made, explicitly or implicitly, of the Type A life style and its effect on the risk of heart attacks. Type A's seem more heavily committed to achievement and are more aggressive and time-pressured than Type B's; these values are sometimes supported by occupational, social or cultural settings. The term "life style" should not obscure the point that the Type A pattern includes an intense motive or commitment, with the expectation of high energy and persistence. Even before the current interest in the health implications of such personality characteristics, Vogel et al. (1959) suggested that people oriented mainly toward achievement, as compared with those oriented toward maintaining warm and friendly social relationships, displayed greater stress reactions in a situation threatening successful achievement than in one threatening rejection by others; the opposite was found for persons oriented mainly toward affiliation.

One of the interesting arenas in which commitment seems to be important, in terms of appraisal and coping, is that of life-threatening or incapacitating illness. Clinicians dealing with people in health crises often use the expression "will to live" to refer to what we call a commitment. Some patients struggle to function despite handicapping illness, take toxic drugs to stay alive, or accept a demanding regimen of self-treatments; others give up easily and decline rapidly. Weisman and Worden (1975) have provided evidence that terminal cancer patients survive longer if they maintain active social networks and draw on them for help instead of withdrawing and becoming depressed. Effective coping in chronic life-threatening situations seems dependent on the commitment to live, and effectiveness diminishes when the commitment founders.

In recent years there has been a notable absence of research on individual differences in motive or commitment patterns as factors in coping. Research and theory on the related concept of "compliance," for instance, tends to center more on cognitive processes—that is, on what the person believes about the possibilities of correcting a medical problem by treatment of preventive efforts—than on motivational factors. Becker's (1976) health belief model, for example, appears to omit motivational traits or to subsume them under such cognitive concepts as perceived threat of disease and the perceived benefits of preventive action. Current thinking in this and related areas tends to be concerned with beliefs or assumptions about causality that operate as personality traits or dispositions (Rodin, 1978; Wortman, 1976). Thus, we can readily make a transition here from the topic of motivation to current work on beliefs or assumptions about oneself and the world. The central theme, as most readers will recognize, is the personal control a person has, or believes he or she has, over events.

Personal Control

The idea that people vary in the extent to which they believe they can control their fate, and that this in turn affects their appraisal of threat and their efforts to cope, got its major impetus from social learning theory and the work of Rotter (1966) on locus of control (see also Lefcourt, 1973, 1976). The basic concept was that as a result of experience and socialization, some people believe that they can control desired or undesired outcomes (internal locus of control), whereas others believe that such outcomes are the result of fate, luck, or other forces (external locus of control). With the development by Rotter of a scale measuring beliefs about locus of control, there has been an enormous volume of studies on the validity of the basic thesis.

This thesis has begun to penetrate behavioral medicine research, as is evident in a review by Strickland (1978) of research on locus of control and health-related behaviors. The dependent variables include health knowledge, precautionary health practices, psychological reactions to physical disorders, and the effects of various treatment strategies. The locus of control variable is a person factor having to do with beliefs about the world. Strickland notes that the magnitude of the observed effects of the person factor tends to be rather small, which raises the issue of the practical implications of locus of control. On the importance of locus of control, Strickland (1978) writes as follows:

In spite of the problems, research on the I-E (internal–external) dimension in relation to health appears to have opened significant avenues of investigation that should be pursued. Although results are not altogether clear, convincing, and as free of conflict as one might hope, the bulk of the research is consistent in implying that when faced with health problems, internal individuals do appear to engage in more generally adaptive responses than do externals. These range from engagement in preventive and precautionary health measures through appropriate remedial strategies when disease or disorder occurs. Findings suggest that the development of an internal orientation could lead to improved health practices for some individuals who have been inclined to believe that life events are beyond their responsiblity and more a function of external control. One must be quite cautious, however, in assuming that internal beliefs are always facilitative. The continued alertness of internals and their attempts at mastery behavior is most appropriate when events are actually controllable. When individuals persist in efforts that bring no relief, then they may find themselves to be actually exacerbating the undesirable characteristics of the situation in which they find themselves. Perhaps the wisest course is that people learn to specify the reality of their life situations, their possible responses, and the potentiality of forthcoming reinforcement. (pp. 1204–1205)

The latter point relates well to Glass' (1977) observation that as compared with Type B persons, Type A's, who are presumably internal in locus of control, engage in exaggerated struggles to control encounters and feel considerably more helpless and distressed when their efforts at control are unsuccessful; this makes them vulnerable in many situations. Glass suggests that this pattern of coping contributes to increased risk of heart attack, due to the major changes in catecholamine secretions (adrenaline and noradrenaline) that accompany this activity.

Strickland's point also draws attention to the positive value of emotion-focused or palliative modes of coping, which is often overlooked because of our cultural and professional bias in favor of problem-focused modes, and against coping solutions that merely make us feel better. In the last sentence of the above quotation, Strickland opts for a conception of psychological health that is similar to the Alcoholics Anonymous "serenity prayer," to wit: "God grant me the serenity to accept the things I cannot change, the courage to change the things I can, and the wisdom to know the difference." Perhaps internals have the advantage in some situations whereas externals have it in others.

Averill (1973) has distinguished a number of types of control, each having different implications for stress and coping. These include "cognitive control," which refers to the interpretation of events, as in the concept of appraisal; "decisional control," which involves a choice among alternative courses of action; and "behavioral control," in which one engages in direct action on the environment. Particularly important from the perspective of a cognitive approach to stress and coping is Averill's analysis, which we interpret liberally, that the stress-enhancing and stress-reducing properties of personal control depend mainly on the meaning of the control response for the individual—a meaning that is always embedded in a particular context of commitments and situational demands, resources and constraints.

Numerous intriguing issues regarding the relationship among personal control, appraisal, and coping need to be addressed. Some examples include the following:

1. Under what conditions does control lead to increases in stress? (For reviews, see Averill, 1973; Thompson, 1981.)
2. In the laboratory the aversive stimulus that is to be controlled is usually quite clear, whereas in real-life situations the object of control is often unclear. For instance, it can be an aspect of the environment or an aspect of the person's response to the environment. Further, a single stressful event often contains multiple outcomes. The ambiguity and complexity that characterize outcomes in real-life person–environment relationships affect how control is defined in specific contexts.
3. How do beliefs about control shift, both within an encounter as it unfolds and across successive encounters, and how do such shifts affect appraisal and coping?

For related discussions of these and other relevant issues, see Folkman (in press) and Silver and Wortman (1980). In view of the importance of the concept of personal control for health-related behavior in both prevention and treatment, and its obvious explanatory and potentially predictive power, we expect that it will continue to play a large and growing role in stress and coping research and in behavioral medicine.

ASSESSMENT OF COPING

The assessment of coping is plagued with definitional and conceptual difficulties. We first discuss the definitional problems and then take up the main conceptual paradigms, with illustrations from coping research.

Definitional Confusions

We do not speak here of the definition of coping in general, but of definitions of various coping strategies that fall under its heading. Lists of coping strategies are common, but none is complete or accurate, and most derive from psychoanalytic formulations. Elsewhere we too have presented a classificatory scheme (Lazarus & Launier, 1978), but it is rudimentary in that it does not adequately specify details and assessment methods for the many varieties of coping that are found in descriptive accounts. Categories for searching for and handling information, inhibiting action, and using social support should be added. Our scheme does, however, take into account both emotion-focused and problem-focused strategies.

Given the weaknesses of existing schemes for ordering and describing the extensive variety of coping strategies, we are left with considerable confusion when trying to assess the coping process. The process of denial provides one of the clearest illustrations (see Lazarus, 1983). The core difficulty is that there are many varieties of what is called "denial," and not only are their borders hard to draw, but their diverse characteristics lead to distortion when they are subsumed under the generic heading of "denial."

"Denial" means the negation of something in word or act. The original Freudian position (A. Freud, 1946; S. Freud, 1966) was that denial applies to external facts ("I am not sick or dying"), whereas repression applies to dangerous inner impulses ("I am not angry"). Others have tried to extend the concept to include both external and internal sources of threat, thus adding further to the definitional confusion. Moreover, there is a distinction between denial, as in the statement "I am not sick," and what Lipowski (1970) calls "minimization," as in "My illness is not so very serious," or "My handicap is not so severe and I can learn to overcome it."

In this connection, it is useful to distinguish between denial of *fact* and denial of *implication*. In dealing with cancer patients, Weisman (1972) has noted that as the illness progresses, denial of the fact of illness ultimately becomes untenable; it is, however, still possible to deny the implications— for example, that the disease is not terminal, that death is not imminent, or that one can function well despite the disease. Freud regarded denial as a psychotic process, a disavowal of reality. However, under conditions of great ambiguity, the denying of implications can have considerable utility, in that it allows the person reason for functioning.

One cannot deny what is not known, and this raises the question of whether we can properly use the word "denial" to refer to a benign or even a positive appraisal of ambiguous evidence. Is denial the same as the maintenance of hope or optimism, or the attempt to see things in the most positive light possible? Or are these latter processes, though perhaps akin to denial, distinctively different strategies of coping that are subject to different causal conditions and with different correlates and consequences?

Definitional and, by implication, measurement confusions can also be illustrated in the common tendency to identify a denial process on the basis of evidence of avoidance. When Anna Freud spoke of denial in word or act, "act" could easily mean the refusal to *talk* about a particular threat—for example, a terminal illness. However, many people studiously avoid thinking about such a threat, and censor the thought from their speech without necessarily denying the fact that they are dying. Avoidance is different from denial, and to assume that the absence of a topic in conversation is tantamount to denial is to compound the confusion between the two processes and to court an erroneous assessment.

The definitional problems cited above, including the distinctions between denial and minimization and between denial and avoidance, are evident in attempts to develop scales of denial in the settings of illness. Writing of their own efforts in constructing such scales, Hackett and Cassem (1974) note the distinction between explicit verbal denial and implicit denial, "in which the patient avoids talking about the disability." These researchers, from their work with patients who suffered myocardial infarctions, observe that denial was the most common defense, as well as the most effective in reducing anxiety. Yet examination of the scale shows that it includes items reflecting minimization, delay in seeking help, avoidance, nonchalance, and a host of other behavior patterns; taken together, these items broaden the concept of denial far beyond its original definition. Although such breadth of definition is consistent with the theme stated by Hackett and Cassem and implied by Anna Freud that denial can be achieved by many diverse strategies, it is quite possible that by broadening the definition, we weaken our ability to distinguish among the many coping strategies people use under different stressful circumstances. We might learn more by separating instances of explicit denial from those, for example, in which there is merely avoidance or minimization. Perhaps, too, denial of fact should be differentiated from denial of implications. As of now, different investigators use "denial" to refer to different phenomena, so that it is difficult to compare one study with another. Similar difficulties can be found with respect to any cognitive coping strategy, and in the case of coping styles that combine several strategies, the difficulties are compounded. Ultimately, to evaluate cognitive coping strategies as factors in adaptational outcomes requires careful attention to definitional boundaries.

Conceptual Paradigms

Current approaches to measurement are based on three common theoretical perspectives about coping, each quite different from our own predilections, which have been summarized earlier under the general headings of coping as process and coping as cognitive mediation. The three common perspectives are these: ego process, trait, and situation. It is instructive to examine each of them briefly, since they dominate research. We also review some of the most influential current work (see also Folkman & Lazarus, 1980).

Coping as Ego Process

Haan (1977), Vaillant (1977), and Menninger (1963) conceive of coping from a psychoanalytic ego-psychological point of view, emphasizing coping as a hierarchically organized set of ego processes. For Menninger and Vaillant, the emphasis is on defenses, some of which are positively valued and reflect a strong ego, and others of which are pathogenic. Haan (1969, 1977) treats the former type as "coping" as distinguished from "defense," which is rigid and neurotic, thus reflecting the standard psychoanalytic notion of a hierarchy progressing from healthy to neurotic to psychotic. Research on coping by each of these three writers reflects this type of conceptualization and value judgment about the inherent maturity or healthiness of the ego processes seen in the management of stress.

There are three main difficulties with this formulation with respect to assessment. First, process and outcome seem always to be confounded, in that certain processes are, by definition, considered neurotic or immature. Moreover, when researchers operating within this perspective report empirical observations, they sometimes further confound process and adaptational outcome by allowing the latter to influence measurement of the former. For example, Vaillant (1977) allows information about the subjects' overall functioning to enter into the assignment of defense scores. Therefore, when functioning is explained by reference to type of defense, there is an unknown degree of confounding. Another example is the well-known study by Wolff *et al.* (1964), who were able to predict stress hormone levels (serum hydrocortisone) from clinical ratings of how "well defended" parents were in handling the stressful experiences of having a child who was dying of leukemia. Since the scores for well-defendedness included behavioral evidence of emotional distress or its absence, it is no great surprise that well-defendedness correlated highly with stress hormone level, which is, in part, another measure of emotional distress. As with Vaillant's approach, the defense process was confounded with an index of adaptational outcome—namely, how well emotional distress was regulated.

Second, when coping is viewed as a system of defenses, the emphasis tends to be more on tension reduction than on problem solving, which is acknowledged only as reality testing. Reality testing is a cognitive (ego) function that communicates nothing directly about the patterns of action and expression capable of altering (managing, solving) a troubled person–environment relationship. That is, a person can perceive and appraise reality accurately without necessarily doing anything about it. Acting on oneself or the environment is a crucial aspect of coping that depends on but is not the same as reality testing. Moreover, as we have already observed, some of the processes useful in the toleration or acceptance of inevitable harms, such as denial, intellectualization, and avoidance, would be treated as immature, pathological, or pathogenic from the ego-psychological perspective. Healthy coping must strike a balance between problem solving and emotion regulation.

The third difficulty—namely, that interrater reliability of judgments of ego processes is low—is probably less important than the others, since it is possible that such reliability might ultimately be improved. This problem is cited as a serious one by Vaillant (1971), as well as by Morrissey (1977) in a review of studies using Haan's system. The reason for rater disagreement is probably that too much inference is often required to identify an ego process, as is illustrated by Vaillant's (1977) struggle to distinguish reaction formation from altruism.

Coping as Trait and Style

The most common approach to coping and its assessment is as a personality trait or style. This perspective heavily overlaps coping as ego process, because most often the content of the coping traits or styles used in research is a defense polarity. The most notable example in psychological research had its origin in the Freudian defenses of repression and isolation (or intellectualization), which are tackled in three assessment measures—namely, repression–isolation (e.g., Gardner *et al.*, 1959; Levine & Spivack, 1964; Luborsky, Blinder, & Schimek, 1965; see also Schafer, 1954), repression–sensitization (e.g., Byrne, 1964; Welsh, 1956), and coping–avoidance (M. J. Goldstein, 1959, 1973). A newer assessment approach that draws upon these and other Freudian mechanisms is that of Gleser and Ihilevich (1969). Moos (1974) has reviewed a considerable number of such scales.

All three of these approaches are trait measures, in that they are worded in terms of what the person says he or she *usually* does in certain types of stressful encounters. However, there is no direct evidence for consistency across situational contexts, because the measures are never used repeatedly to assess coping in different stressful encounters. Thus, they are trait or style measures only in the sense that they are so defined by the scale developer.

As we have said earlier, trait measures are poor predictors of coping processes. First, actual consistency across stressful encounters may be moderate or even low, as we have found in our research (Folkman & Lazarus, 1980). Moreover, we do not have rules for identifying the situational contexts under which a common or variable defense process would occur. In short, we cannot specify the trait × situation interaction (cf. Bowers, 1973; Ekehammar, 1974; Magnusson & Endler, 1977; Pervin & Lewis, 1978). As yet, studies of such interaction do not seem greatly to improve the capacity of trait measures to predict actual behavior.

Second, existing trait measures, such as those cited above, are unidimensional and do not reflect the multidimensional quality of actual coping. Coping is a complex amalgam of thoughts and actions, and as most observers of coping with illness recognize (e.g., Cohen & Lazarus, 1979; Hamburg & Adams, 1967; Lipowski, 1970; Moos & Tsu, 1977), many sources of stress must be managed, including pain, incapacitation, hospitalization, treatment regimens, the maintenance of working relationships with family and friends, and the preservation of a satisfactory self-image. These are multiple and complex tasks that no single coping act can successfully handle.

Third, coping is a process that changes over time, not a well-established and fixed behavior pattern. At some times a person must rely on one form of coping—say, an emotion-focused strategy—while at others he or she must shift to problem-solving strategies. It is difficult to see how the unfolding nature of most stressful encounters, and the concomitant changes in coping, could be adequately described by a presumably *static* measure of a general trait or personality disposition (Folkman & Lazarus, 1980).

Coping as a Response to Situational Demands

Along with a recent clinical shift away from strictly intrapsychic processes has come a shift toward the opposite extreme of environmentalism and a focus on environmental stressors (consider, for example, life events research) and coping with specific environmental demands. Situational approaches to the assessment of coping define the problem by referring to specific types of situations, such as life-threatening or incapacitating illness, doctoral examinations, natural disasters, the threat of speaking in public, bereavement, divorce, military combat or terrorist attack, and so on through the wide panoply of stressful situations to which people can be exposed (see, e.g., Brim & Ryff, 1980; Lazarus & Cohen, 1977).

The most serious shortcoming of the study of coping as a response to particular situational demands is that in most cases we cannot compare coping across diverse stressors. To the extent that coping patterns are specific to particular circumstances generating special demands, we are not likely to learn about coping with one kind of stressful circumstances from a study of another. Such stressors are also in some sense unusual; this does not mean that they do not happen to many people at some time in their lives, but they are not the usual variety of stressors that comprise our everyday lives. The research findings, therefore, tend not to be generalizable to other contexts. We have already cited a few instances of process measures with a strong situational focus—namely, the measurement of coping with terminal cancer (Weisman & Worden, 1976–1977), and the rating scale of denial offered by Hackett and Cassem (1974) and used mainly for postcoronary patients. Still another example is a diabetes adjustment rating scale (Sullivan, 1979), which includes items such as whether the patient administers his or her own insulin, clearly a matter of great interest and potential value in the management of the specific situation of diabetes.

An exception to the ungeneralizability of situationally focused studies of coping is the research of Pearlin and Schooler (1978). These researchers were concerned with the ordinary stresses in living that arise from continuing social roles, such as being a marriage partner, the economic manager of a household, a parent, and a coworker. Pearlin and Schooler found that people used a wide range of coping strategies, some of which were consistent across all four social roles, while others were specific to one given role context. This is an extremely important finding in an area about which we have little knowledge as yet.

Although the Pearlin and Schooler (1978) study is one of the few extensive examinations of coping in several situational contexts, and is rare in its attention to the ordinary and daily role stresses of living, it has a few limitations from our perspective. The first is that survey questions reflected a trait definition of coping; the respondents were asked how they *usually* coped with general sources of stress, rather than how they actually coped with specific situations. An example is the question, "How strongly do you agree or disagree that I cannot be myself around my spouse?" When a person is asked how he or she usually reacts, information is being sought about a personality trait or disposition. Moreover, the source of stress is defined in terms of a social atmosphere, rather than as a specific encounter. Different information might have been received if the respondent had been asked how he or she reacted to and dealt with a specific episode of a "cold shoulder," a deflating statement, a criticism, a moralizing comment, a plea for consideration, or any of a wide range of interpersonal acts that comprise a generally constraining social atmosphere. The best way to learn about how a person copes with specific situational demands may be to define situations more concretely, such as in the approach to assessment of coping found in the study of terminal cancer patients by Weisman and Worden (1976–1977).

A second limitation of Pearlin and Schooler's study is its emphasis on *persistent* life strains, since these must, by definition, be those that respondents have *not* been successful in resolving. This emphasis deprives us of viewing a large domain of coping responses that are effective in management of the situation generating the "strainful" reaction. It might explain why Pearlin and Schooler found that coping directed at problem solving in the work setting represented only three out of the 17 types of coping factors identified, whereas we (Folkman & Lazarus, 1980) found problem-focused coping strategies to be as frequent in stressful work encounters as emotion-focused strategies were.

Quite clearly, we need to identify the situational context of the coping process if we are to make advances in our understanding. However, if our efforts are to be fruitful, we must also compare coping across situational contexts, and must determine its stability and variability. This means that we should be centering our assessments of coping, at least some of the time, on actual, specific encounters; if possible, we should also focus on how coping changes as an encounter unfolds, and how well it generalizes across comparable situational contexts. In short, we need to study coping as a *process*.

OUTCOMES OF COPING

Now we reach the bottom line of the argument, which is that coping undoubtedly affects adaptational outcomes over the course of our lives. Before we consider how this might be, however, we must give some attention to such outcomes themselves.

Types of Adaptational Outcomes

Research on coping must consider at least three kinds of outcomes—namely, morale, social functioning, and somatic health, either singly or in combination. "Morale" can be said to consist of how we feel about ourselves and the condition of our lives, and the extent to which we feel satisfaction or unhappiness. It is closely tied to our emotions, though the ties are by no means clear. For example, to what extent are the kinds and intensities of emotions experienced (or expressed), or the balance between negatively toned and positively toned emotions, relevant to morale? In noting the most significant components of morale, a host of theoretical and methodological problems become apparent. For example, to what extent is felt or avowed happiness or satisfaction the best criterion of morale? Can positive statements by the respondent be taken at face value, or are they defensive? Since terms such as "satisfaction," "happiness," and "positive feeling" have many meanings and connotations, and are viewed differently among various ideological and religious groups, what terms should be employed in assessing morale? Should positive and negative feelings be assessed separately or combined in some fashion? Widely used current assessment procedures seldom deal systematically with this difficult array of issues. Examinations of these and related problems appear in three useful analytic reviews (Campbell, 1976; Wilson, 1967; Zautra & Goodhart, 1979).

"Social functioning" is no less a complex and ephemeral outcome than morale. An approach to the measurement of social functioning has been developed by Renne (1974); it illustrates some of the difficult definitional, conceptual, and methodological issues that surround this outcome. Using survey data, Renne evaluated employability (using different standards for men and women), marital satisfaction, community involvement, and sociability, and combined them into a single index, which she termed "social health." She found that this index was associated strongly with family income, race, and area of residence, and that it correlated positively with physical and psychological health (or well-being).

Renne's approach illustrates a problem that seems to characterize work in the definition and assessment of social functioning. She defines social functioning or social health in terms of satisfaction, a psychological variable, and role behavior (e.g., employability, community involvement), a social variable. These perspectives generate very different definitions of social functioning, and their juxtaposition leads us to ask whether satisfaction (morale) and role behavior are really components of what we should regard as the same quality. In other words, are social functioning and morale two sides of the same coin, and are both these variables partly or wholly the same as mental health? For example, if one rates marital satisfaction as Renne did, and uses the rating as part of an index of social health, how then do we treat the concept of morale, which is in some sense comprised of feelings about one's life situation, including marriage? In addition, where do the several widely used measures of symptoms of psychological malaise, such as the Hopkins Symptom Checklist (Derogatis, Lipman, Rickels, Uhlenhuth, & Covi, 1974) and the Horowitz (1976) measure of "stress response syndromes," fit in? Are these to be regarded as separate categories of social health, or merely as variants of the same basic concepts? Without detailed information about relationships among the diverse measures, there is no way to disentangle the various components of what we mean by "social functioning." (For reviews of the assessment of social functioning, see Platt, 1981; Weissman, 1975; Weissman, Sholomskas, & John, 1981.) In addition, there are numerous problems involved in the sociological or role approach to functioning. For example, there is little consensus as to how any role should be defined and what constitutes "good" or "bad," "appropriate" or "inappropriate" role behavior. The issues involved are complex, and their discussion is beyond the scope of this chapter (for a review of these issues see Platt, 1981); nevertheless, interest in social functioning appears to be increasing.

"Somatic health" also generates difficult assessment issues. For example, we cannot identify disease in its early stages, and it will be missed on both laboratory and clinical examinations. Lack of agreement between subjective (clinical) criteria and laboratory test criteria is also common. The latter problem is finessed, in some degree, by health status questionnaire approaches, and strong correlations have been demonstrated between such questionnaire data and the use of medical records (Meltzer & Hochstim, 1970). The questionnaire used by Meltzer and Hochstim and converted into ratings has also been shown to predict mortality 9 years after it was administered (Berkman & Syme, 1979)—a finding that bodes well for questionnaire approaches to health status.

Finally, in assessing adaptational outcomes we should not use a purely individual standard that compares one person with another; an *intra*individual standard should be used as well. Interindividual standards force us to compare people on outcome variables under conditions that may vary from optimal to nonoptimal for any given person, thereby yielding an exaggeratedly high or low rating and adding error variance. Stress, for example, occurs in different kinds and degrees to the same individual at different times or periods of life, and there are also apt to be ups and downs in functioning. Moreover, it is often more useful to know that a given individual (or group) is doing well or badly in comparison with his or her own norm or ideal than it is to know that one individual or group is more or less effective in functioning as compared with others.

Despite the unresolved problems of assessing adaptational outcomes, the existence of workable procedures for assessing the three main forms— morale, social functioning, and somatic health—makes it at least possible to determine the impact of various modes of coping. At present we have little evidence as to impact, largely as a result of the lack of adequate measures of coping. Nevertheless, it is still possible to address the role of coping theoretically.

How Coping Affects Adaptational Outcomes

It may strike some readers as odd that there is any doubt that coping affects morale, social functioning, and somatic health. Thus far, theory in this area is limited and fragmentary. Moreover, aside from scattered studies, the empirical case is not clear. Research on the problem has been reviewed by Cohen (1979), Cohen and Lazarus (1979), and Silver and Wortman (1980). We restrict ourselves here to theoretical principles in an effort to provide some rational order.

The impact of coping depends on the particular adaptational outcome of concern. Although behavioral medicine centers mainly on somatic health– illness, it is equally important to consider morale and the quality of functioning in the world, because we sometimes pay for positive outcomes in one arena with negative outcomes in another. The Type A behavior pattern is an example, since it seems to increase the risk of heart disease in vulnerable persons, while at the same time providing great personal and social value.

In the discussions that follow, we try to examine some of the ways in which appraisal and coping processes could affect each major type of adaptational outcome. To tie this discussion to earlier ones, we also draw upon some of the theoretical distinctions already made—for example, between process and trait, between types of appraisal and the person and environment variables that shape them, and among variants of the coping process itself.

Morale

We have argued that an assessment of coping requires that we distinguish between a stable coping trait or style and a coping process. A coping trait implies that the process observed in one environmental setting is in whole or in part repeated in other contexts. A coping process, on the other hand, may be unique to a given context and may occur in its particular form once or only rarely. How is this relevant to morale? The answer is that although it may for the moment feel good to master harm or threat, to handle a demanding task effectively, or to overcome an adversity, any particular encounter by itself cannot automatically reveal much about the long-term effects of coping on morale unless effective coping is a *consistent* property of a given person's transactions.

If a person manages many or most difficulties with effectiveness, stress is less likely to be an oppressive factor in that person's life. There also should be less drain on energy (because the frequency and intensity of mobilization are less) and more satisfaction in realizing goals. In sum, there should be a minimum of negative and a maximum of positive experiences in the life of a person who copes effectively. Coping skills (or competence) prevent stress where it might arise, or permit extrication from or management of inevitable stressful encounters. For sustained good morale, one would assume a reasonably close fit between the person's coping resources and the environmental demands that must be faced (e.g., French, Rodgers, & Cobb, 1974; Van Harrison, 1978). There is little research on the stability of coping effectiveness, although studies by Andreason, Noyes, and Hartford (1972) with severely burned patients, and by Phillips (1953, 1968) with hospitalized mental patients, suggest that coping effectiveness might be stable over an extended period of life. On the other hand, even those people we might regard as quite competent much of the time can be exposed to conditions that severely tax or exceed their coping resources (see Benner *et al.*, 1980; Wrubel *et al.*, 1981), which can lead to temporary incapacity.

Appraisal-related processes and their determinants seem also to be relevant to both short- and long-term morale. It is quite possible that people differ generally in their tendency to be challenged, or to minimize or deny harm or threat even when their actual life circumstances are quite negative. Thus, over and above coping effectiveness, we should consider people's tendency to appraise or reappraise harsh life circumstances in a positive light and hence to maintain positive morale over a long time. What is sometimes called ''the power of positive thinking''—or, if one wishes to put it in more pejorative terms, defense or self-deception—may be far more important in the lives of many people than has been acknowledged by professional workers. Religious beliefs and commitments should also be accorded due attention as factors that can influence morale over the long run.

The issue of ''positive thinking'' raises many unresolved questions, some of which have been touched on earlier. For example, is positive morale that is derived from denial-like processes substantial, or is it merely a brittle shell or surface presentation of self? Do the numerous measures employed to get at a given defense assess the same or a different process? There is some evidence, for example, that the trait of denial–avoidance, or ''repression'' in Byrne's (1961, 1964) terminology, is associated with a more positive frame of mind (morale) than is its contrasting trait of ''sensitization.'' However, the case is still weak that such a coping style contributes to overall morale.

Appraisal-related processes depend on a host of person and environment variables that can readily interact to produce a general tendency for a person to evaluate his or her transactions in particular ways. Therefore, each of these variables has a potential for study, individually and in combination, as a short- and long-run source of morale. This is the premise, not always explicit, underlying the use of the two popular person variables we discussed earlier (sense of personal control and pattern of commitment) and the two environment variables (ambiguity and social resources) as factors in adaptational outcome. Morale, however, has not been a favorite outcome variable in such research.

Finally, it is worth speculating on how the emotion-focused and problem-focused functions of coping might be linked to morale. Those who conceive of coping as an ego process evaluated on a hierarchy of health–pathology or maturity–immaturity tend to assume that emotion-focused coping, especially those forms that involve reality distortion, should yield high distress and low morale. It is reasoned that emotion-focused coping traps the person in a vicious circle of increased and sustained vulnerability to threat, or requires enervating intrapsychic efforts that eventuate in a state sometimes referred to as "asthenia" and involve chronic anxiety, depression, and fatigue (e.g., Andrews, Kiloh, & Kehoe, 1978). However, we are inclined to think that the nature or context of an encounter is of major importance in understanding the relationship between emotion-focused coping and morale. Elsewhere (Lazarus, 1983), for example, we have attempted to suggest principles for distinguishing the costs and benefits of denial-like forms of coping. Despite our traditional prejudices, we must take seriously that emotion-focused coping is often beneficial and could contribute to the maintenance of positive morale.

The relationship between problem-focused coping and morale seems less complex. We would anticipate that effective problem-focused coping should be associated with positive morale, in that its outcome has a good possibility of being satisfying to the coper. Even in circumstances in which a favorable outcome is not possible, people are often heard to say, "Just doing everything I could made me feel better." As noted above, problem-focused coping was associated with morale in our study of 45- to 64-year-olds, regardless of whether the situation was one that could or could not be changed.

Social Functioning

Social functioning is determined by many factors, including on the one hand the person's history, with its attendant implications regarding dependency, autonomy, trust, intimacy, and so on, and on the other hand, cultural values and expectations regarding social roles and how they should be enacted. These factors are enduring characteristics of the person and the person's environment that play a major role in determining the individuals with whom the person will have relationships, the functions of these relationships, and the ways in which they will be subjectively experienced and expressed in behavior. However, although these personal and cultural factors impel a person toward a particular constellation of social roles and relationships, these roles and relationships are developed, altered, and maintained through the ongoing mediation of appraisal and coping. The question of interest here, then, is how appraisal and coping might affect social functioning.

Appraisals must match or at least approximate the flow of events if a person is to be effective in identifying interpersonal problems. Whether a relationship has to do with work, parenting, or marriage, a problem that is inaccurately appraised can lead to poor problem-focused coping and thus to hurt feelings and misunderstandings. Many relationships can withstand occasional errors of appraisal, but any relationship will be put to a severe test if inappropriate appraisals are frequent. To the extent that appraisal errors are frequent over the range of a person's relationships, his or her general social functioning is likely to be poor. This outcome is evident in the extreme case of paranoid persons, who are virtually unable to establish and maintain relationships because of the suspicion and fear that infuse their appraisals of other people's intentions and behaviors.

Similarly, in fulfilling the tasks associated with various roles, there needs to be a shared understanding between the person and relevant others as to the nature of the task and what needs to be done. Such shared understanding can be achieved only if the people involved evaluate the nature of the task in similar ways.

The evaluation of the nature of the task is, however, only a part of appraisal. The meaning of the task, or its significance to the person, is the other aspect of appraisal, and is responsible for individual differences in stress and emotion. The person who tends to be consistently threatened more than challenged is likely to have problems with social functioning, even when his or her appraisals do a relatively good job of matching the flow of events. Threat can encourage withdrawal or defensive operations that turn the person inward, or it can encourage hostile, aggressive behavior. In either case, the person's behavior is likely to generate negative social reactions, which, as Coyne (1976) has noted in the case of depression, are sensed by the person, reinforce his or her negative self-appraisals, and promote a vicious downward spiral. Threat can also interfere with efficient cognitive operations and effective problem-focused coping (see, e.g., Easterbrook, 1959; Janis & Mann, 1977; Lazarus, 1966; Lazarus, Deese, & Osler, 1952), and in this way it hinders effective social functioning. Challenge, on the other hand, encourages venture and openness, and thus increases the possibilities of good communication and effective problem solving. These processes are apt to be facilitated by the positive emotions and optimal arousal that accompany challenge.

Finally, it goes almost without saying that good social functioning depends also on possessing good social and problem-solving skills. These skills are necessary if the inevitable conflicts and misunderstandings that characterize human relationships are to be managed or resolved, and if the tasks associated with role expectations are to be satisfactorily carried out. Such skills are a part of coping competence, which underlies the relationships between coping and all adaptational outcomes.

Somatic Health

Of the mechanisms through which appraisal and coping affect adaptational outcomes, nowhere are the possibilities more intriguing or complex than with respect to those pertaining to somatic outcomes. The mechanism that has received the most attention in the literature is mobilization, which is involved in both appraisal (through emotion) and coping (through effort).

Two models dominate thinking about the relationship between mobilization and somatic illness: the generality model and the specificity model (see Cohen, 1979; Lazarus, 1978; Lazarus, Cohen, Folkman, Kanner, & Schaefer, 1980; Lazarus, Kanner, & Folkman, 1980). In the generality model, physiological stress responses are seen as resulting from the mobilization associated with any noxious stimulus, regardless of its nature. Mobilization precipitates tissue damage or increased vulnerability to illness through direct effects on tissues (e.g., gastrointestinal ulceration) and indirect effects of associated neuroendocrine activity (e.g., shrinkage of the thymus gland). Selye's (1976) general adaptation syndrome triad exemplifies this approach. In the specificity model, each illness (e.g., hypertension, gastric ulcers, colitis, etc.) is said to have its own distinctive pattern of emotion, mobilization, and physiological response (cf. Alexander & Selesnick, 1966; Lipowski, 1977). (For a discussion of variants of the specificity model, see Cohen, 1979.) Although the generality model has been the more popular of the two over the last several decades, there is growing evidence in support of the specificity model (e.g., Engel, 1960; Engel & Bickford, 1961; Graham, 1962; Lacey, 1967; Mason, 1975; Mason, Maher, Hartley, Mougey, Perlow, & Jones, 1976). The corollary of the specificity model that is relevant here states that particular stressors may be linked through specific patterns of appraisal and coping to specific patterns of physiological response and hence to specific illness outcomes (see also Averill & Opton, 1968; Lazarus, 1966). For example, recent research suggests that the mobilization accompanying threat is different from that accompanying challenge (Holroyd & Lazarus, 1982). Threat is associated with elevations in catecholamine and cortisol levels; challenge is associated only with elevations in catecholamine levels, while cortisol levels remain normal or even become depressed (Frankenhaeuser, 1980; Rose, 1980).

Generally, the theme of the bodily costs of stress and coping centers on negative emotions. As the findings regarding challenge suggest, attention might also be fruitfully given to the bodily consequences of positive emotions, such as joy, love, and exhilaration, or to challenge-related emotions as distinguished from threat-related ones. It has been suggested, for example, that just as negative emotions can result in damaging hormonal secretion patterns, positive ones might produce biochemical substances having protective tissue effects, perhaps warding off disease or even facilitating recovery and health (see Lazarus, Cohen, Folkman, Kanner, & Schaefer, 1980, and Lazarus, Kanner, & Folkman, 1980, for a more elaborate discussion). A major protagonist of this position is Norman Cousins (1976), who writes engagingly about his own bout with a normally fatal collagen disease and the possible role of positive emotions:

> The inevitable question arose in my mind: What about the positive emotions? If negative emotions produce negative chemical changes in the body, wouldn't the positive emotions produce positive chemical changes? Is it possible that love, hope, faith, laughter, confidence and the will to live have therapeutic value? Do chemical changes occur only on the downside? (p. 1459)

To our knowledge, there is no dependable evidence that this intriguing hypothesis, valued especially in "holistic" medicine, is true, nor does it seem to be taken very seriously by researchers. If Mason (1975) and others are correct that the hormonal correlates of emotion vary with emotion quality, then Cousins' hypothesis makes sense. Consider also the discovery that the pituitary gland secretes beta-endorphin (see Rossier, Bloom, & Guillemin, 1980) along with ACTH; the latter activates the adrenal cortex to produce stress-related corticosteroids. While the former acts perhaps as a stress-induced psychedelic and analgesic or a morphine-like drug. This suggests that our concept of stress-related hormones is much too narrow, and that substances in the brain could serve as a physiological analogue of palliative forms of cognitive coping. Moreover, Selye's (1974) distinction between "eustress" and "distress," and our own between "threat" and "challenge," also imply the existence of different biochemical patterns for each, and these surely make Cousins' questions more trenchant. Thus, despite the absence of adequate evidence, it might be fruitful to keep the issue alive through further research.

Mobilization and physiological response due to appraisal and emotion are, however, not sufficient to explain how mobilization ultimately affects somatic outcomes. After all, to mobilize is adaptive, not maladaptive, when we are faced with a harm, threat, or challenge. It is only when mobilization is continual or uninterrupted that it results in direct tissue damage, as in ulcers, or in indirect damage, as when it depresses the effectiveness of the immune response. This brings us to the critical question: What are the mechanisms that account for continual or uninterrupted mobilization? Here is where coping assumes importance.

Problem-focused coping can be used to prevent a stressful event from occurring, or it can enable a person to avoid or resolve difficulties that do occur. When problem-focused coping is effective in these ways, it can lead to reduced mobilization by eliminating environmental demands that would otherwise lead the person to remain mobilized for action. In contrast, when problem-focused coping is not effective, the situation can be aggravated, leading to sustained and even increased mobilization (cf. Holroyd & Lazarus, 1982). Perseveration in problem-focused coping in situations that cannot be changed can also lead to sustained and potentially damaging mobilization.

Changes in mobilization can be brought about also by emotion-focused coping. Denial or avoidant strategies are likely to lead to reduced mobilization (e.g., Wolff et al., 1964). Similar reductions can be expected when the significance of a threat is diminished or minimized, or when the person uses such palliatives as drugs or alcohol. Emotion-focused coping can lead to increased arousal, as when people take out their feelings on others, engage in self-blame, or express their feelings openly. The patterns of mobilization that accompany these strategies may differ from those that accompany parallel shifts in mobilization through problem-focused coping, and thus shifts in similar directions may have different consequences in physiological response patterns.

When patterns of appraisal and coping are repeated across a wide variety of encounters, we can speak of an appraisal and coping "style." Styles that lead to sustained or increased mobilization are likely to be maladaptive in the long run. An example of such a style is suggested by Linden and Feuerstein (1981), who describe a tendency of hypertensives to be disposed toward threat appraisals and aggressive or angry behavior in social situations. They conceptualize this style as a deficit in social competence. Glass (Glass, 1977; Glass, Krakoff, Contrada, Hilton, Kehoe, Mannucci, Collins, Snow, & Elting, 1980) has argued that a style that alternates between intense efforts to control stressful transactions and helplessness when coping efforts fail is associated with fluctuations in catecholamines sufficiently dramatic to influence the pathogenesis of coronary heart disease (Holroyd & Lazarus, 1982).

The Type A style, for example, which greatly increases the risk of heart disease, can be viewed both as a form of self-sustaining chronic stress and as a way of coping. In effect, the person responds to (copes with) external pressures and incentives to be effective, ambitious, competitive, and successful by cultivating an appropriate life style and internalizing it. The risk of heart attack is increased (e.g., Haynes, Feinleib, & Kannel, 1980) through particular mediating physiological mechanisms such as increased blood pressure (now more controversial in light of new findings by Rose, Jenkins, & Hurst, 1978), increases in serum cholesterol and other lipids, and changes in platelets and fibrinogen that result in more rapid blood clotting. Although such bodily changes might also increase the risk of other illnesses, they seem particularly important in heart disease.

Another important mechanism through which coping can affect somatic outcomes, although conceptually less complex than mobilization or style, is the mechanism of specific coping behaviors. A person may smoke, drink, or take drugs to reduce stress, but in so doing may increase the risk of illness. For example, men at risk for coronary heart disease may initiate or aggravate disease processes if they increase their smoking in response to stress (Horowitz, Hulley, Alvarez, Reynolds, Benfari, Blair, Borhani, & Simon, 1979). Similarly, people with peptic duodenal ulcers are likely to exacerbate their disease if they increase their consumption of alcohol as a response to work stress (Weisman, 1956). Conversely, patients can use behaviors to reduce stress that do not exacerbate illness (e.g., judicious exercise); in such instances coping should not increase somatic problems, and might even reduce them.

As most social scientists recognize, what have been called "health-related behaviors" can also mask illness, exaggerate its severity, or mimic it. For example, in discussing the possible mechanisms whereby life events might affect the measurement of illness, Cleghorn and Streiner (1979) suggest that life events might encourage a "propensity to seek medical care in response to distress," or "produce a heightened awareness of symptoms." In addition, tendencies exist in some individuals and groups to complain excessively of symptoms and illness (as in "sick role" behavior, or modes of appraisal and coping based on individual or cultural conditioning), or, conversely, to minimize symptoms or avoid medical care (see Mechanic, 1966; Zborowski, 1969). A colorful language has emerged for describing such patterns—for example, "the worried well" and "health-rejecting complainers."

When the behavioral and physiological (mobilization) levels of analysis are viewed in tandem, it becomes immediately evident that no clear relationship exists between the two. A "positive" effect at the physiological level can have a "negative" effect at the behavioral level, and vice versa. In other words, the denial or avoidant strategies that can lead to a reduction in mobilization can at the same time interfere with needed problem-focused coping. This pattern is described in a study by Katz, Weiner, Gallagher, and Hellman (1970). Through the use of denial-like processes, women in this study were able to minimize the significance of breast lumps and thus to reduce their psychological distress; however, these very processes delayed their seeking important medical attention. (For further discussion of the positive and negative consequences of denial, see Lazarus, 1983.) On the other hand, one can imagine a situation where heightened awareness and vigilance allow the person to consider numerous alternatives and to reflect before acting. These characteristics, in fact, are associated with high-quality decision making (Janis & Mann, 1977). In this case, increased mobilization can be associated with an absence of behavioral activity, at least during the period of reflection. In short, susceptibility to illness due to heightened mobilization depends primarily on the effectiveness of coping.

FINAL THOUGHTS

The central theme of this chapter is that coping is an important concept for behavioral medicine because it affects adaptational outcomes. In the past, clinical workers attributed a major role in health outcomes to coping, often just implicitly. Today, it is no longer unusual for clinicians to view treatment as training in coping skills and an opportunity to help the person substitute effective forms of coping for counterproductive ones. This view is particularly widespread among cognitive-behavior therapists (see Roskies & Lazarus, 1980; see also Bowers & Kelly, 1979). For example, Goldfried (1980) entitled a recent article "Psychotherapy as Coping Skills Training"; Gotlib and Asarnow (1979) teach problem-solving skills to mildly depressed university students; Ellis (1962) instructs his troubled patients that their difficulties in living stem from faulty assumptions about themselves, which he tries to get them to give up; Meichenbaum (1975, 1976, 1977) and Novaco (1976, 1977, 1979) describe procedures that they call "stress inoculation," which is a term for cognitive preparation for inevitable stressful encounters; Novaco has used the procedure in the control of both anger (in police officers) and depression; and Holroyd (1979) has reviewed many efforts to provide training in coping, in the management of emotional states such as anger, depression, and anxiety, and in the treatment of such stress-related disorders as tension headaches, migraine, peptic ulcers, and essential hypertension.

Behavioral medicine is concerned with prevention as well as with treatment, but the same issues apply to both. The wide audiences for a series of conferences on prevention (see Albee & Joffe, 1977) reflect growing interest; these conferences give some attention to the teaching of coping as a tool of prevention. Similar issues are also being dealt with under the rubric of education, particularly as expressed in the concept of social competence (see Wine & Smye, 1981). Education for social competence is parallel in scope to prevention of psychopathology and promotion of psychological and somatic health. Moreover, the issues tackled here extend beyond childhood development to the life course, and this extension of concern requires attention to coping and adaptational processes at various stages of life (e.g., Lieberman, 1975).

Coping is always a major focus in these efforts, whether it is labeled as such or not. Indeed, a moment's thought confirms that the concept of "prevention" parallels that of "anticipatory coping." Whatever terms one uses to talk about health maintenance and restoration, coping processes are always involved. We have tried to show here that principles comparable to those involved in maintaining or improving morale and social functioning also apply to somatic health and illness. Building knowledge about coping, including information about the conditions that shape it, the variety of coping processes and how they combine in stressful encounters, and above all the adaptational outcomes of coping, should ultimately contribute significantly to prevention and treatment and to the general field of behavioral medicine.

ACKNOWLEDGMENT

We want to thank Carol Carr for her valuable editorial suggestions during the development of this chapter.

REFERENCES

Albee, G. W., & Joffe, J. M. (Eds.). *Primary prevention of psychopathology* (Vol. 1, *The issues*). Hanover, N.H.: University Press of New England, 1977.

Alexander, F. G., & Selesnick, S. T. *The history of psychiatry*. New York: Harper & Row, 1966.

Andreason, N. J. C., Noyes, R., & Hartford, C. E. Factors influencing adjustment of burn patients during hospitalization. *Psychosomatic Medicine*, 1972, *34*, 517–525.

Andrews, G., Kiloh, L. G., & Kehoe, L. Asthenic personality, myth or reality. *Australian and New Zealand Journal of Psychiatry*, 1978, *12*, 95–98.

Archer, R. P. Relationships between locus of control, trait anxiety, and state anxiety: An interactionist perspective. *Journal of Personality*, 1979, *47*, 305–316.

Averill, J. R. Personal control over aversive stimuli and its relationship to stress. *Psychological Bulletin*, 1973, *80*, 286–303.

Averill, J. R., & Opton, E. M., Jr. Psychophysiological assessment: Rationale and problems. In P. McReynolds (Ed.), *Advances in psychological assessment* (Vol. 1). Palo Alto, Calif.: Science and Behavior Books, 1968.

Bandura, A. *Social learning theory*. Englewood Cliffs, N.J.: Prentice-Hall, 1977.

Becker, M. H. The health belief model and sick role behavior. *Health Education Monographs*, 1974, *2* (Whole No. 4), 409–419. (a)

Becker, M. H. (Ed.). The health belief model and person health behavior. *Health Education Monographs*, 1974, *2* (Whole No. 4). (b)

Becker, M. H. Sociobehavioral determinants of compliance. In D. L. Sackett & R. B. Haynes (Eds.), *Compliance with therapeutic regimens*. Baltimore: Johns Hopkins University Press, 1976.

Becker, M. H., & Maiman, L. A. Sociobehavioral determinants of compliance with health and medical care recommendations. *Medical Care*, 1975, *13*, 10–24.

Benner, P., Roskies, E., & Lazarus, R. S. Stress and coping under extreme conditions. In J. E. Dimsdale (Ed.), *Survivors, victims, and perpetrators: Essays on the Nazi Holocaust*. Washington, D.C.: Hemisphere, 1980.

Berkman, L. F., & Syme, S. L. Social networks, host resistance, and mortality: A nine-year follow-up study of Alameda County residents. *American Journal of Epidemiology*, 1979, *109*, 186–204.

Bloom, J. R. Psychosocial measurement and specific hypotheses: A research note. *Journal of Consulting and Clinical Psychology*, 1979, *47*, 637–639.

Bowers, K. S. Situationism in psychology: An analysis and critique. *Psychological Review*, 1973, *80*, 307–336.

Bowers, K. S., & Kelly, P. Stress, disease, psychotherapy, and hypnosis. *Journal of Abnormal Psychology*, 1979, *88*, 490–505.

Breznitz, S. False alarms: Their effect on fear and adjustment. In I. G. Sarason & C. D. Spielberger (Eds.), *Stress and anxiety* (Vol. 3). New York: Academic Press, 1976.

Brim, O. G., Jr., & Ryff, C. D. On the properties of life events. In P. B. Baltes & O. G. Brim, Jr. (Eds.), *Life-span development and behavior* (Vol. 3). New York: Academic Press, 1980.

Byrne, D. The Repression–Sensitization Scale: Rationale, reliability and validity. *Journal of Personality*, 1961, *29*, 334–349.

Byrne, D. Repression–sensitization as a dimension of personality. In B. A. Maher (Ed.), *Progress in experimental personality research* (Vol. 1). New York: Academic Press, 1964.

Campbell, A. Subjective measures of well-being. *American Psychologist*, 1976, *31*, 117–124.

Cleghorn, J. M., & Streiner, B. J. Prediction of symptoms and illness behavior from measures of life change and verbalized depressive themes. *Journal of Human Stress*, 1979, *5*, 16–23.

Coelho, G. V., Hamburg, D. A., & Adams, J. E. (Eds.). *Coping and adaptation*. New York: Basic Books, 1974.

Cohen, F. Personality, stress, and the development of physical illness. In G. C. Stone, F. Cohen, & N. E. Adler (Eds.), *Health psychology*. San Francisco: Jossey-Bass, 1979.

Cohen, F., & Lazarus, R. S. Active coping processes, coping dispositions, and recovery from surgery. *Psychosomatic Medicine*, 1973, *35*, 375–389.

Cohen, F., & Lazarus, R. S. Coping with the stresses of illness. In G. C. Stone, F. Cohen, & N. E. Adler (Eds.), *Health psychology*. San Francisco: Jossey-Bass, 1979.

Cousins, N. Anatomy of an illness (as perceived by the patient). *New England Journal of Medicine*, 1976, *295*, 1458–1463.

Coyne, J. C. Toward an interactional description of depression. *Psychiatry*, 1976, *39*, 28–40.

Coyne, J. C., & Lazarus, R. S. Cognitive style, stress perception, and coping. In I. L. Kutash &

L. B. Schlesinger (Eds.), *Handbook on stress and anxiety: Contemporary knowledge, theory, and treatment.* San Francisco: Jossey-Bass, 1980.

Dean, A., & Lin, N. The stress-buffering role of social support. *Journal of Nervous and Mental Disease,* 1977, *169,* 403–417.

Derogatis, L. R., Lipman, R. S., Rickels, K., Uhlenhuth, E. H., & Covi, L. The Hopkins Symptom Checklist (HSCL): A measure of primary symptom dimensions. In P. Pichot (Ed.), *Modern problems in pharmacopsychiatry* (Vol. 7, *Psychological measurements in psychopharmacology*). Basel: Karger, 1974.

Easterbrook, J. A. The effect of emotion on cue utilization and the organization of behavior. *Psychological Review,* 1959, *66,* 183–201.

Ekehammar, B. Interactionism in personality from a historical perspective. *Psychological Bulletin,* 1974, *81,* 1026–1048.

Ellis, A. *Reason and emotion in psychotherapy.* New York: Lyle Stuart, 1962.

Engel, B. T. Stimulus–response and individual response specificity. *Archives of General Psychiatry,* 1960, *2,* 305–313.

Engel, B. T., & Bickford, A. F. Response specificity. *Archives of General Psychiatry,* 1961, *3,* 478–489.

Epstein, S. The self-concept revisited: Or a theory of a theory. *American Psychologist,* 1973, *28,* 404–416.

Farberow, N. L. Indirect self-destructive behavior in diabetics and Buerger's disease patients. In N. L. Farberow (Ed.), *The many faces of suicide: Indirect self-destructive behavior.* New York: McGraw-Hill, 1980.

Folkman, S. Personal control from the perspective of a cognitive theory of stress and coping. *Journal of Personality and Social Psychology,* in press.

Folkman, S., & Lazarus, R. S. An analysis of coping in a middle-aged community sample. *Journal of Health and Social Behavior,* 1980, *21,* 219–239.

Folkman, S., & Lazarus, R. S. Reply to Shinn & Krantz. *Journal of Health and Social Behavior,* 1981, *22,* 457–459.

Folkman, S., Schaefer, C., & Lazarus, R. S. Cognitive processes as mediators of stress and coping. In V. Hamilton & D. M. Warburton (Eds.), *Human stress and cognition: An information-processing approach.* London: Wiley, 1979.

Frankenhaeuser, M. Psychobiological aspects of life stress. In S. Levine & H. Ursin (Eds.), *Coping and health.* New York: Plenum, 1980.

French, J .R. P., Jr., Rodgers, W., & Cobb, S. Adjustment and person–environment fit. In G. V. Coelho, D. A. Hamburg, & J. E. Adams (Eds.), *Coping and adaptation.* New York: Basic Books, 1974.

Frenkel-Brunswik, E. Intolerance of ambiguity as an emotional and perceptual variable. *Journal of Personality,* 1949, *18,* 108–143.

Freud, A. *The ego and the mechanisms of defence.* New York: International Universities Press, 1946.

Freud, S. *The standard edition of the complete psychological works.* London: Hogarth, 1966.

Friedman, S. B., Chodoff, P., Mason, J. W., & Hamburg, D. A. Behavioral observations on parents anticipating the death of a child. *Pediatrics,* 1963, *32,* 610–625.

Gaines, L. S., Smith, B. D., & Skolnick, B. E. Psychological differentiation, event uncertainty, and heart rate. *Journal of Human Stress,* 1977, *3,* 11–25.

Gardner, R. W., Holzman, P. S., Klein, G. S., Linton, H. B., & Spence, D. P. Cognitive control: A study of individual consistencies in cognitive behavior. *Psychological Issues,* 1959, *1*(4). (Monograph)

Glass, D. C. *Behavior patterns, stress and coronary disease.* Hillsdale, N.J.: Erlbaum, 1977.

Glass, D. C., Krakoff, L. R., Contrada, R., Hilton, W. F., Kehoe, K., Mannucci, E. G., Collins, C., Snow, B., & Elting, E. Effect of harassment and competition upon cardiovascular and plasma catecholamine responses in Type A and Type B individuals. *Psychophysiology,* 1980, *17,* 453–463.

Gleser, G. C., & Ihilevich, D. An objective instrument for measuring defense mechanisms. *Journal of Consulting and Clinical Psychology,* 1969, *33,* 51–60.

Goldfried, M. R. Psychotherapy as coping skills training. In M. J. Mahoney (Ed.), *Psychotherapy process: Current issues and future directions*. New York: Plenum, 1980.

Goldstein, A. M. The "uncooperative" patient: Self-destructive behavior in hemodialysis patients. In N. L. Farberow (Ed.), *The many faces of suicide: Indirect self-destructive behavior*. New York· McGraw-Hill, 1980.

Goldstein, M. J. The relationship between coping and avoiding behavior and response to fear-arousing propaganda. *Journal of Abnormal and Social Psychology*, 1959, *58*, 247–252.

Goldstein, M. J. Individual differences in response to stress. *American Journal of Community Psychology*, 1973, *1*, 113–137.

Gotlib, I. H., & Asarnow, R. F. Interpersonal and impersonal problem-solving skills in mildly and clinically depressed university students. *Journal of Consulting and Clinical Psychology*, 1979, *47*, 86–95.

Graham, D. T. Some research on psychophysiologic specificity and its relation to psychosomatic disease. In R. Roessier & N. S. Greenfield (Eds.), *Physiological correlates of psychological disorder*. Madison: University of Wisconsin Press, 1962.

Haan, N. A tripartite model of ego functioning: Values and clinical research applications. *Journal of Nervous and Mental Disease*, 1969, *148*, 14–30.

Haan, N. *Coping and defending*. New York: Academic Press, 1977.

Hackett T. P., & Cassem, N. H. Development of a quantitative rating scale to assess denial. *Journal of Psychosomatic Research*, 1974, *18*, 93–100.

Hamburg, D. A., & Adams, J. E. A perspective on coping behavior: Seeking and utilizing information in major transitions. *Archives of General Psychiatry*, 1967, *17*, 227–284.

Haynes, S. G., Feinleib, M., & Kannel, W. B. The relationship of psychosocial factors to coronary heart disease in the Framingham Study: III. Eight-year incidence of coronary heart disease. *American Journal of Epidemiology*, 1980, *3*, 37–58.

Henderson, S. The social network, support and neurosis: The functions of attachment in adult life. *British Journal of Psychiatry*, 1977, *131*, 185–191.

Henderson, S. K., Byrne, D. G., Duncan-Jones, P., Adcock, S., Scott, R., & Steele, G. P. Social bonds in the epidemiology of neurosis: A preliminary communication. *British Journal of Psychiatry*, 1978, *132*, 463–466.

Hofer, M. A., Wolff, E. T., Friedman, S. B., & Mason, J. W. A psychoendocrine study of bereavement, Parts I and II. *Psychosomatic Medicine*, 1972, *34*, 481–504.

Holroyd, K. A. Stress, coping, and the treatment of stress-related illnesses. In J. R. McNamara (Ed.), *Behavioral approaches to medicine*. New York: Plenum, 1979.

Holroyd, K. A., & Lazarus, R. S. Stress, coping and somatic adaptation. In L. Goldberger & S. Breznitz (Eds.), *Handbook of stress*. New York: Free Press, 1982.

Horowitz, M. *Stress response syndromes*. New York: Jason Aronson, 1976.

Horowitz, M., Hulley, S., Alvarez, W., Reynolds, A. M., Benfari, R., Blair, S., Borhani, N., & Simon, N. Life events, risk factors, and coronary disease. *Psychosomatics*, 1979, *20*, 586–592.

Janis, I. L. Vigilance and decision-making in personal crises. In G. V. Coelho, D. A. Hamburg, & J. E. Adams (Eds.), *Coping and adaptation*. New York: Basic Books, 1974.

Janis, I. L., & Feshbach, S. Effects of fear-arousing communications. *Journal of Abnormal and Social Psychology*, 1953, *48*, 78–92.

Janis, I. L., & Mann, L. *Decision making*. New York: Free Press, 1977.

Kahn, R. L., Wolfe, D. M., Quinn, R. P., & Snoek, J. D. *Organizational stress: Studies in role conflict and ambiguity*. New York: Wiley, 1964.

Katz, J. L., Weiner, H., Gallagher, T. G., & Hellman, L. Stress, distress, and ego defenses. *Archives of General Psychiatry*, 1970, *23*, 131–142.

Klein, G. S. *Perception, motives and personality*. New York: Knopf, 1970.

Lacey, J. I. Somatic response patterning and stress: Some revisions of activation theory in psychological stress. In M. H. Appley & R. Trumbull (Eds.), *Psychological stress*. New York: Appleton-Century-Crofts, 1967.

Lazarus, R. S. *Psychological stress and the coping process*. New York: McGraw-Hill, 1966.

Lazarus, R. S. The self-regulation of emotion. In L. Levi (Ed.), *Emotions: Their parameters and measurement.* New York: Raven Press, 1975.

Lazarus, R. S. A strategy for research on psychological and social factors in hypertension. *Journal of Human Stress,* 1978, *4,* 35–40.

Lazarus, R. S. The stress and coping paradigm. In C. Eisdorfer, D. Cohen, A. Kleinman, & P. Maxim (Eds.), *Models for clinical psychopathology.* New York: Spectrum, 1981.

Lazarus, R. S. The costs and benefits of denial. In S. Breznitz (Ed.), *Denial of stress.* New York: International Universities Press, 1983.

Lazarus, R. S., Averill, J. R., & Opton, E. M., Jr. Toward a cognitive theory of emotions. In M. Arnold (Ed.), *Feelings and emotions.* New York: Academic Press, 1970.

Lazarus, R. S., Averill, J. R., & Opton, E. M., Jr. The psychology of coping: Issues of research and assessment. In G. V. Coelho, D. A. Hamburg, & J. E. Adams (Eds.), *Coping and adaptation.* New York: Basic Books, 1974.

Lazarus, R. S., & Cohen, J. B. Environmental stress. In I. Altman & J. F. Wohlwill (Eds.), *Human behavior and the environment: Current theory and research.* New York: Plenum, 1977.

Lazarus, R. S., Cohen, J. B., Folkman, S., Kanner, A., & Schaefer, C. Psychological stress and adaptation: Some unresolved issues. In H. Selye (Ed.), *Selye's guide to stress research* (Vol. 1). New York: Van Nostrand Reinhold, 1980.

Lazarus, R. S., Deese, J., & Osler, S. F. The effects of psychological stress upon performance. *Psychological Bulletin,* 1952, *49,* 293–317.

Lazarus, R. S., Eriksen, C. W., & Fonda, C. P. Personality dynamics and auditory perceptual recognition. *Journal of Personality,* 1951, *19,* 471–482.

Lazarus, R. S., Kanner, A., & Folkman, S. Emotions: A cognitive–phenomenological analysis. In R. Plutchik & H. Kellerman (Eds.), *Theories of emotion.* New York: Academic Press, 1980.

Lazarus, R. S., & Launier, R. Stress-related transactions between person and environment. In L. A. Pervin & M. Lewis (Eds.), *Perspectives in interactional psychology.* New York: Plenum, 1978.

Lefcourt, H. M. The function of the illusions of control and freedom. *American Psychologist,* 1973, *28,* 417–425.

Lefcourt, H. M. *Locus of control: Current trends in theory and research.* New York: Halstead, 1976.

Leventhal, H. Fear communications in the acceptance of preventive health practice. *Bulletin of the New York Academy of Medicine,* 1965, *41,* 1144.

Leventhal, H. Findings and theory in the study of fear communications. *Advances in Experimental Social Psychology,* 1970, *5,* 119–186.

Levine, M., & Spivack, G. *The Rorschach index of repressive style.* Springfield, Ill.: Charles C Thomas, 1964.

Lieberman, M. A. Adaptive processes in late life. In N. Datan & L. H. Ginsberg (Eds.), *Life-span developmental psychology.* New York: Academic Press, 1975.

Lin, N., Simeone, R., Ensel, W. M., & Kuo, W. Social support, stressful life events and illness: A model and empirical test. *Journal of Health and Social Behavior,* 1979, *20,* 108–119.

Lindemann, E. Symptomatology and management of acute grief. *American Journal of Psychiatry,* 1944, *101,* 141–148.

Linden, W., & Feuerstein, M. Essential hypertension and social coping behavior. *Journal of Human Stress,* 1981, *7,* 28–34.

Lipowski, Z. J. Physical illness, the individual and the coping process. *International Journal of Psychiatry in Medicine,* 1970, *1,* 91–102.

Lipowski, Z. J. Physical illness, the patient, and his environment: Psychosocial foundations of medicine. In S. Arieti (Ed.), *American handbook of psychiatry* (2nd ed., Vol. 4). New York: Basic Books, 1975.

Lipowski, Z. J. Psychosomatic medicine in the seventies: An overview. *American Journal of Psychiatry,* 1977, *134,* 233–244.

Loevinger, J. *Ego development.* San Francisco: Jossey-Bass, 1976.

Luborsky, L., Blinder, M., & Schimek, J. Looking, recalling, and the GSR as a function of defense. *Journal of Abnormal Psychology*, 1965, *70*, 270–280.

Mages, N. L., & Mendelsohn, G. A. Effects of cancer on patients' lives: A personological approach. In G. C. Stone, F. Cohen, & N. E. Adler (Eds.), *Health psychology*. San Francisco: Jossey-Bass, 1979.

Magnusson, D., & Endler, N. S. (Eds.). *Personality at the crossroads*. Hillsdale, N.J.: Erlbaum, 1977.

Mason, J.W. Emotion as reflected in patterns of endocrine integration. In L. Levi (Ed.), *Emotions: Their parameters and measurement*. New York: Raven Press, 1975.

Mason, J. W., Maher, J. T., Hartley, L. H., Mougey, E., Perlow, M. J., & Jones, L. G. Selectivity of corticosteroid and catecholamine response to various natural stimuli. In G. Serban (Ed.), *Psychopathology of human adaptation*. New York: Plenum, 1976.

Mechanic, D. *Students under stress*. New York: Free Press, 1962.

Mechanic, D. Response factors in illness: The study of illness behavior. *Social Psychiatry*, 1966, *1*, 11–20.

Mechanic, D. Social structure and personality adaptation: Some neglected dimensions. In G. V. Coelho, D. A. Hamburg, & J. E. Adams (Eds.), *Coping and adaptation*. New York: Basic Books, 1974.

Meichenbaum, D. A self-instructional approach to stress management: A proposal for stress inoculation training. In C. D. Spielberger & I. Sarason (Eds.), *Stress and anxiety* (Vol. 2). New York: Wiley, 1975.

Meichenbaum, D. Toward a cognitive theory of self-control. In G. Schwartz & D. Shapiro (Eds.), *Consciousness and self-regulation: Advances in research*. New York: Plenum, 1976.

Meichenbaum, D. *Cognitive-behavior modification: An integrative approach*. New York: Plenum, 1977.

Meltzer, J., & Hochstim, J. Reliability and validity of survey data on physical health. *Public Health Reports*, 1970, *85*, 1075–1086.

Menninger, K. *The vital balance: The life process in mental health and illness*. New York: Viking, 1963.

Mitchell, J. C. (Ed.). *Social networks in urban situations*. Manchester, England: Manchester University Press, 1969.

Monat, A., Averill, J. R., & Lazarus, R. S. Anticipatory stress and coping reactions under various conditions of uncertainty. *Journal of Personality and Social Psychology*, 1972, *24*, 237–253.

Moos, R. H. Psychological techniques in the assessment of adaptive behavior. In G. V. Coelho, D. A. Hamburg, & J. E. Adams (Eds.), *Coping and adaptation*. New York: Basic Books, 1974.

Moos, R. H., & Tsu, V. D. The crisis of physical illness: An overview. In R. H. Moos (Ed.), *Coping with physical illness*. New York: Plenum, 1977.

Morrissey, R. F. The Haan model of ego functioning: An assessment of empirical research. In N. Haan (Ed.), *Coping and defending*. New York: Academic Press, 1977.

Murphy, L. B. Coping, vulnerability and resilience in childhood. In G. V. Coelho, D. A. Hamburg, & J. E. Adams (Eds.), *Coping and adaptation*. New York: Basic Books, 1974.

Novaco, R. W. The treatment of anger through cognitive and relaxation controls. *Journal of Consulting and Clinical Psychology*, 1976, *44*, 681.

Novaco, R. W. Stress inoculation: A cognitive therapy for anger and its application to a case of depression. *Journal of Consulting and Clinical Psychology*, 1977, *45*, 600–608.

Novaco, R. W. The cognitive regulation of anger and stress. In P. C. Kendall & S. D. Hollon (Eds.), *Cognitive-behavioral interventions: Theory, research, and procedures*. New York: Academic Press, 1979.

Nuckolls, K. B., Cassel, J., & Kaplan, B. H. Psychosocial assets, life crisis, and the prognosis of pregnancy. *American Journal of Epidemiology*, 1972, *95*, 431–441.

Pearlin, L. I., & Schooler, C. The structure of coping. *Journal of Health and Social Behavior*, 1978, *19*, 2–21.

Pervin, L. A., & Lewis, M. (Eds.). *Perspectives in interactional psychology*. New York: Plenum, 1978.

Phillips, L. Case history data and prognosis in schizophrenia. *Journal of Nervous and Mental Disease,* 1953, *117,* 515–525.

Phillips, L. *Human adaptation and its failures.* New York: Academic Press, 1968.

Platt, S. Social adjustment as a criterion of treatment success: Just what are we measuring? *Psychiatry,* 1981, *44,* 95–112.

Renne, K. S. Measurement of social health in a general population survey. *Social Science Research,* 1974, *3,* 25–44.

Rodin, J. Somatopsychics and attribution. *Personality and Social Psychology Bulletin,* 1978, *4,* 531–540.

Rose, R. M. Endocrine responses to stressful psychological events. *Psychiatric Clinics of North America,* 1980, *3,* 1–15.

Rose, R. M., Jenkins, C. D., & Hurst, M. W. Air traffic controller health change study (Report prepared for Federal Aviation Administration), M. A. Levin (Ed.). Boston: Boston University School of Medicine, 1978.

Roskies, E., & Lazarus, R. S. Coping theory and the teaching of coping skils. In P. Davidson & S. Davidson (Eds.), *Behavioral medicine: Changing health life styles.* New York: Brunner/ Mazel, 1980.

Rossier, J., Bloom, F. E., & Guillemin, R. Endorphins and stress. In H. Selye (Ed.), *Selye's guide to stress research* (Vol. 1). New York: Van Nostrand Reinhold, 1980.

Rotter, J. B. Generalized expectancies for internal versus external control of reinforcement. *Psychological Monographs: General and Applied,* 1966, *80* (1, Whole No. 609).

Schafer, R. *Psychoanalytic interpretation in Rorschach testing.* New York: Grune & Stratton, 1954.

Schank, R., & Abelson, R. *Scripts, plans, goals and understanding.* New York: Wiley, 1977.

Selye, H. *The stress of life.* New York: McGraw-Hill, 1956.

Selye, H. *Stress without distress.* Philadelphia: J. B. Lippincott, 1974.

Selye, H. *The stress of life* (Rev. ed.). New York: McGraw-Hill, 1976.

Shalit, B. Structural ambiguity and limits to coping. *Journal of Human Stress,* 1977, *3,* 32–45.

Shapiro, D. *Neurotic styles.* New York: Basic Books, 1965.

Silver, R. L., & Wortman, C. B. Coping with undesirable life events. In J. Garber & M. E. P. Seligman (Eds.), *Human helplessness: Theory and application.* New York: Academic Press, 1980.

Spielberger, C. D. Theory and research on anxiety. In C. D. Spielberger (Ed.), *Anxiety and behavior.* New York: Academic Press, 1966.

Spielberger, C. D. Anxiety as an emotional state. In C. D. Spielberger (Ed.), *Anxiety: Current trends in theory and research* (Vol. 1). New York: Academic Press, 1972.

Strickland, B. R. Internal–external expectancies and health-related behaviors. *Journal of Consulting and Clinical Psychology,* 1978, *46,* 1192–1211.

Sullivan, B. J. Adjustment in diabetic adolescent girls: I. Development of the Diabetic Adjustment Scale. *Psychosomatic Medicine,* 1979, *41,* 119–216.

Thompson, S. C. Will it hurt less if I can control it?: A complex answer to a simple question. *Psychological Bulletin,* 1981, *90,* 89–101.

Tinbergen, N. *The study of instincts.* London: Oxford University Press, 1951.

Vaillant, G. E. Theoretical hierarchy of adaptive ego mechanisms. *Archives of General Psychiatry,* 1971, *24,* 107–118.

Vaillant, G. E. *Adaptation to life.* Boston: Little, Brown, 1977.

Van Harrison, R. Person–environment fit and job stress. In C. L. Cooper & R. Payne (Eds.), *Stress at work.* New York: Wiley, 1978.

Vogel, W., Raymond, S., & Lazarus, R. S. Intrinsic motivation and psychological stress. *Journal of Abnormal and Social Psychology,* 1959, *58,* 225–233.

Watzlawick, P., & Coyne, J. C. Depression following stroke: Brief, problem-focused family treatment. *Family Process,* 1980, *19,* 13–18.

Weiner, H., Singer, M. T., & Reiser, M. F. Cardiovascular responses and their psychological correlates: I. A study in healthy young adults and patients with peptic ulcer and hypertension. *Psychosomatic Medicine,* 1962, *24,* 477–498.

Weisman, A. D. A study of the psychodynamics of duodenal ulcer exacerbation with special reference to treatment and the problem of specificity. *Psychosomatic Medicine,* 1956, *18,* 2–42.

Weisman, A. D. *On dying and denying: A psychiatric study of terminality.* New York: Behavioral Publications, 1972.

Weisman, A. D., & Worden, J. W. Psychosocial analysis of cancer deaths. *Omega: Journal of Death and Dying,* 1975, *6,* 61–75.

Weisman, A. D., & Worden, J. W. The existential plight in cancer: Significance of the first 100 days. *International Journal of Psychiatry in Medicine,* 1976–1977, *7,* 1–15.

Weissman, M. M. The assessment of social adjustment: A review of techniques. *Archives of General Psychiatry,* 1975, *32,* 357–365.

Weissman, M. M., Sholomskas, D., & John, K. The assessment of social adjustment: An update. *Archives of General Psychiatry,* 1981, *38,* 1250–1258.

Welsh, G. S. Factor dimensions A and R. In G. S. Welsh & W. G. Dahlstrom (Eds.), *Basic readings on the MMPI in psychology and medicine.* Minneapolis: University of Minnesota Press, 1956.

White, R. Strategies of adaptation: An attempt at systematic description. In G. V. Coelho, D. A. Hamburg, & J. E. Adams (Eds.), *Coping and adaptation.* New York: Basic Books, 1974.

Wilson, W. Correlates of avowed happiness. *Psychological Bulletin,* 1967, *67,* 294–306.

Wine, J. D., & Smye, M. D. (Eds.). *Social competence.* New York: Guilford Press, 1981.

Witkin, H. A., Goodenough, D. R., & Oltman, P. K. Psychological differentiation: Current status. *Journal of Personality and Social Psychology,* 1979, *37,* 1127–1145.

Wolff, C. T., Friedman, S. B., Hofer, M. A., & Mason, J. W. Relationship between psychological defenses and mean urinary 17-hydroxycorticosteroid excretion rates, Parts I & II. *Psychosomatic Medicine,* 1964, *26,* 576–609.

Wortman, C. B. Causal attributions and personal control. In J. H. Harvey, W. J. Ickes, & R. F. Kidd (Eds.), *New directions in attribution research* (Vol. 1). Hillsdale, N.J.: Erlbaum, 1976.

Wrubel, J., Benner, P., & Lazarus, R. S. Social competence from the perspective of stress and coping. In J. D. Wine & M. D. Smye (Eds.), *Social competence.* New York: Guilford Press, 1981.

Zautra, A., & Goodhart, D. Quality of life indicators: A review of the literature. *Community Mental Health Review,* 1979, *4,* 1–10.

Zborowski, M. *People in pain.* San Francisco: Jossey-Bass, 1969.

CHAPTER 9

The Patient as Decision Maker

Irving L. Janis
Yale University

During recent decades there has been a marked change in the way people in our society, including health experts, view the role of the patient. No longer are patients seen as passive recipients of health care who are expected to do willingly whatever the doctor says. Rather, they are increasingly regarded as active decision makers, making a series of crucial choices that can markedly affect the kind of treatments they receive and the outcome. Those choices include whether or not to seek medical aid and from whom, whether or not to undergo whichever of the available treatments is recommended by the physician, and subsequently whether to stop or to continue following the prescribed medical regimen. Such decisions are generally recognized as being among the most vital ones a person ever has to make, sometimes being literally a matter of life and death. Even when people are healthy, they have to make comparable decisions with regard to taking preventive measures recommended by health experts, which can affect both the duration and the quality of their lives.

This chapter focuses primarily on *sources of error* in personal decision making that pertain to matters of health. Erroneous decisions in this sphere not only decrease a person's chances of optimal health and survival, but also result in intense reactions of regret when avoidable setbacks occur. Regret is characterized by marked increases in emotional arousal—anxiety, guilt, and reactive depression. Such reactions frequently entail loss of sleep, along with physiological stress reactions. Although the relationships between reactions of postdecisional regret and the onset of psychosomatic disorders have not yet been adequately investigated, it seems quite possible that when ill people make unsound decisions, they not only reduce their chances of rapid, uncomplicated, and full recovery, but also increase their chances of developing new illnesses.

In reviewing the literature on personal decision making, I concentrate on recent developments in theory and empirical research that look most promising. I also call attention to major methodological problems in order to highlight the need for new approaches for improving theory and research in this area.

THEORIES OF DECISION MAKING

Models of Rational Choice

The theoretical concepts that have been dominant in the literature on decision making for over 25 years are based on cognitive theories, such as "game theory" and "subjective expected utility" (SEU) theory, which assume that people make deliberate choices on a rational basis, taking account of the values and the probabilities of the consequences to be expected from choosing each of the available alternatives. (See, e.g., Edwards, 1954; Miller & Star, 1967; Raiffa, 1968.) In recent years such theories have been called seriously into question as *descriptive* models that explain how people actually do make decisions (e.g., Broadhurst, 1976; Kahneman & Tversky, 1979; Lee, 1971; Simon, 1976; Slovic, Fishhoff, & Lichtenstein, 1977). Nevertheless, they have led to new developments of formal methods for decision analysis, which provide *prescriptive* (normative) models specifying how people should make sound decisions when they have to make risky choices.

The prescriptive methods that follow from these models are sometimes used in the business world, where cost–benefit analysis can be quantified in terms of money. The prescriptive methods are also occasionally applied to professional decisions made by physicians and other practitioners (see Elstein & Bordage, 1979). But they are difficult to apply to personal decisions made by individual patients, because they require quantitative estimates of the desirability of each of the outcomes and of their corresponding probabilities in order to choose the course of action that maximizes expected utility.

In *A Practical Guide for Making Decisions* (Wheeler & Janis, 1980), we point out that even though the specific quantitative techniques may be inapplicable, the two central ideas of prescriptive methods based on rational models of decision making can be applied whenever anyone has to make a vital decision, such as what to do about a serious physical defect or illness:

> The first central idea is that in order to make a sound decision it is necessary to make the best estimates of the probability that each of the expected consequences will occur. The second is that a sound decision requires taking into consideration the relative importance of each of the anticipated favorable and unfavorable consequences—their expected utility value from your own standpoint. If you keep in mind these two ideas you are more likely to arrive at a choice that you will not regret even though you do not use any of the mathematics. . . . You will be less likely to overlook serious drawbacks or to give undue weight to vivid considerations that are really not essential to you or that are unlikely to materialize. You will be in a better position to make a choice that meets your main objectives, gives you the best chance of overall gains, and keeps unnecessary costs and risks to a minimum. (Wheeler & Janis, 1980, p. 81)

In applying these two central ideas, indirect side effects need to be assessed in addition to the more obvious direct effects of the course of action under consideration, as McGuire (1980) has emphasized. For example, when considering the potential value of jogging for a middle-aged executive, "one should evaluate not only the efficacy of the procedure for weight control, coronary blood supply, etc., but also its costs in knee injuries, automobile accidents, dog bites, etc." (McGuire, 1980, p. 21).

The most extensively investigated of the rational models in psychological research is the SEU model developed by Edwards (1954). It is regarded as a better candidate for describing how choices are made than the classical variants of rational decision theory because it replaces objective or scientific valuation of outcomes with subjective estimates in terms of the value system of the decision maker. For example, salient health risks of dangerous driving and drug use, which from an objective standpoint would be expected to be deterrents, might have a positive rather than a negative appeal to many youths (McGuire, 1980). The SEU model assumes that a decision maker arrives at an overall utility estimate for each alternative by multiplying his or her subjective estimate of the utility values for each outcome by his or her subjective estimate of the probability that it will occur. The decision maker then selects the outcome with the highest positive value. This approach is compatible with Lewin's (1951) concept of valences as determinants of action and Fishbein's (1967) theoretical analysis of attitudes and intentions.

In the area of health behavior, the most cogent test of the SEU model as a descriptive theory was made by Mausner and Platt (1971) in a series of studies on the decision to stop smoking. These investigators asked subjects to make ratings on a variety of potential outcomes that might occur as a result of smoking and as a result of not smoking. For each of the possible outcomes (e.g., the risk of getting bronchitis), subjects were asked to make three ratings—one concerning its subjective utility ("How much do you care about _____?"), and the other two pertaining to its expected probability of occurrence ("if you continued to smoke" and "if you stopped smoking").

Mausner and Platt (1971) initially validated the SEU ratings to some extent by obtaining the expected differences between smokers and nonsmokers. Then they went on to investigate changes in SEU scores induced in smokers who were given behavioral change treatments. Their results partially confirmed predictions from the model. Smokers who subsequently cut down on cigarette consumption did not differ in SEU ratings for smoking from those who remained unchanged; however, the two groups did differ as expected in SEU ratings for *not* smoking, which resulted in a difference in overall utility ratings in the expected direction. The serendipitous findings suggest that for some smokers special rewards and other benefits from abstinence are the crucial incentives for stopping smoking, rather than fear of health hazards from continuing to smoke.

Unfortunately, in other decision-making studies, predictions from the

SEU descriptive model have fared much worse (see Rapoport & Wallsten, 1972; Slovic *et al.*, 1977). A number of studies do not support one of the fundamental assumptions of the SEU model—namely, that people's estimates of the probability of an outcome are independent of their estimates of the desirability or utility of that outcome (Elstein & Bordage, 1979; Walsten, 1978). Elstein and Bordage (1979) call attention to another dubious assumption in SEU theory and in all other theories of rational choice, which is that preferences will remain sufficiently stable so that the person will regard any given outcome as having essentially the same utility shortly after making a decision as he or she did at the time the decision was made. This assumption is especially questionable when people are ill:

> . . . radical changes in preference . . . may be induced when a patient is in severe pain or perceives the situation to be life threatening. A patient in severe pain or grave distress may evaluate a variety of outcomes quite differently than when pain and distress are absent. Consequently, a set of utility estimates obtained under one condition may not apply when conditions are altered. (Elstein & Bordage, 1979, p. 363)

These and other sources of error can make for gross deviations from the decision-making behavior predicted by the SEU descriptive model for certain types of decisions, such as those made by patients who need medical treatments or surgery. Nevertheless, it is quite possible that for other types of health-related decisions, such as those pertaining to preventive measures, the model may predict behavior fairly well. Proponents of the SEU or other rational-choice models might profitably direct subsequent research to specifying in what circumstances and for which types of persons the theoretical analysis is valid. A more comprehensive theory might then be evolved to predict and explain when rational choices will be made and when not.

Most of the criticisms of SEU theory as a descriptive account of how people actually do make decisions also apply to the well-known variants of the "health belief model," which incorporate essentially the same assumptions about rational choices. This model was originally developed by Hochbaum (1958) to account for preventive actions. The model contains three basic components as determinants of the decision to adopt a new health practice. All three components can be readily translated into the key terms of the SEU model: (1) subjective beliefs about the severity of the threat of suffering ill health and personal susceptibility to that threat; (2) subjective beliefs that the recommended course of action will protect one against the threat; and (3) subjective beliefs about the barriers or costs to be expected if one takes the recommended course of action. Evidence in support of the model has been obtained in many studies, which show that the three components are related to preventive actions, such as having medical checkups and obtaining immunizations (see Becker, Kaback, Rosenstock, & Ruth, 1975; Kirscht & Rosenstock, 1979).

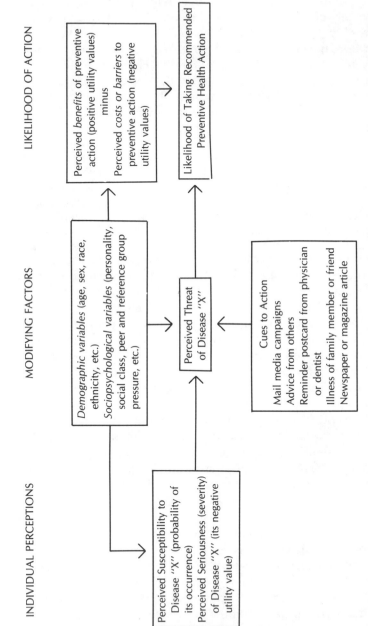

INDIVIDUAL PERCEPTIONS

MODIFYING FACTORS

LIKELIHOOD OF ACTION

Demographic variables (age, sex, race, ethnicity, etc.)
Sociopsychological variables (personality, social class, peer and reference group pressure, etc.)

Perceived Susceptibility to Disease "X" (probability of its occurrence)
Perceived Seriousness (severity) of Disease "X" (its negative utility value)

Perceived Threat of Disease "X"

Cues to Action

Mail media campaigns
Advice from others
Reminder postcard from physician or dentist
Illness of family member or friend
Newspaper or magazine article

Perceived benefits of preventive action (positive utility values)
minus
Perceived costs or barriers to preventive action (negative utility values)

Likelihood of Taking Recommended Preventive Health Action

FIGURE 9.1. Basic components of the health belief model. (Adapted from Becker, M. H., & Maiman, L. A. Sociobehavioral determinants of compliance with health and medical care recommendations. *Medical Care,* 1975, *13,* 10–24.)

Additional variables were added to the model by Becker and Maiman (1975) in order to apply it to patients' adherence to medical regimens. The basic components of their version of the model are shown in Figure 9.1. In their review of the literature on patients' acceptance of physicians' recommendations, Becker and Maiman (1975) find considerable support for the model from studies of acute illnesses. Subsequently, Becker, Maiman, Kirscht, Haefner, and Drachman (1977) expanded the model to include positive health incentives, faith in doctors, perceived control over health matters, and a number of other factors that have been found to be predictive of adherence. In a study of the mothers of obese children, they found that each of the major components in their expanded model, as expected, was correlated with the children's loss of weight over a 2-month period and with the mothers' keeping of appointments with the physician. Their findings from a multiple-regression analysis were confirmatory of the model as a whole.

Stone (1979) points out that even though the health belief model has been expanded to include a large number of independent variables, it is still incomplete, because it does not take sufficient account of certain determinants that arise from the transactions that go on between the patients and health care experts. The omitted variables pertain to task-relevant habits, beliefs, and expectations ''of both expert and client concerning the roles, responsibilities and credentials of each and beliefs of each party concerning the goals of the other'' (Stone, 1979, p. 46). To fill in this gap it would be necessary to increase the number of independent variables greatly, since these would include such considerations as the patient's suspicions (both justified and unjustified) that the physician is trying to ''look good,'' avoid blame, or elicit gratitude, and the physician's expectations (both correct and incorrect) that the patient is worried about invasion of privacy, is seeking assurance that nothing is seriously wrong, or wants to satisfy neurotic dependency needs.

The beginnings of a transactional approach are to be found in a theoretical paper by Szasz and Hollender (1956) and in more recent studies on expectations of patients and physicians (e.g., Hayes-Bautista, 1976; Kirscht, 1977; Parsons, 1975; Quesada, 1976; Stone, 1979; Veatch, 1972; Waitzkin & Stoeckle, 1976). But as yet no comprehensive theory has been formulated integrating the components of the health belief model and the transactional concepts. In order to reduce the number of independent variables to a manageable number for purposes of arriving at a testable comprehensive theory, future analysis might profitably be devoted to efforts at ''chunking'' those that can be treated as functionally equivalent determinants (i.e., sharing common antecedent conditions and common consequences).

Even with the proliferation of variables in the expanded health belief model, it is still so incomplete that many important aspects of patients' decisions fall between the cracks. For example, the model does not provide an adequate explanation for the widespread tendency of patients who have painful heart attacks to delay obtaining medical aid. According to Hackett and Cassem (1975), the vast majority of patients with acute myocardial infarctions delay calling a physician for 4 or 5 hours. Typically, when the afflicted person thinks of the possibility that it might be a heart attack, he or she assumes that "it couldn't be happening to me." The patients' delay of treatment is not attributable to unavailability of medical aid or transportation delays; approximately 75% of the delay time elapses before a patient decides to contact a physician. As Hackett and Cassem (1975) put it, "the decision making process gets jammed by the patient's inability to admit that he is mortally sick" (p. 27). A sizeable number of patients even take active steps to demonstrate to themselves that their acute chest pains could not be signs of a heart attack by running up stairs or engaging in other vigorous actions that can augment heart damage. The delay phenomenon, which significantly increases a patient's chances of dying, has been found among patients in both sexes and in all socioeconomic, age, and educational levels. Patients who have had a prior heart attack show just as much delay as do those who have not (Hackett & Cassem, 1975).

Similar maladaptive delays have been frequently observed among patients suffering from symptoms of cancer (e.g., Blackwell, 1963; Kasl & Cobb, 1966). One study found that over 30% of a sizeable sample of cancer patients postponed seeing a physician for 3 months or longer after the onset of symptoms that they knew were ominous danger signs (Goldsen, Gerhardt, & Handy, 1957). Ignorance does not seem to account for the majority of instances of procrastination, because it has been found that patients who had decided to postpone having a medical examination were even more familiar with the danger signs of cancer than were patients who had decided to seek medical aid promptly (Goldsen et al., 1957; Kutner, Makover, & Oppenheim, 1958). The most plausible explanation seems to be that those patients try to ward off anxiety by avoiding exposure to threat cues, including distressing communications from a medical expert.

Proponents of the health belief model could argue on an ad hoc basis that the model can account for these maladaptive delays by postulating that in such instances the patients give overriding weight to avoidance of the subjective discomfort of being authoritatively informed that they do, in fact, have the life-threatening disease they suspect they might have. But, again, the important point is that the health belief model, like other models of rational choice, fails to specify under what conditions people will give priority to avoiding subjective discomfort at the cost of endangering their lives, and under what conditions they will make a more rational decision by seeking for and taking into account the available medical information about the real consequences of alternative courses of action so as to maximize their chances of survival.

The conflict theory model of personal decision making, to which I turn next, attempts to specify the crucial conditions that determine when patients will use sound decision-making procedures to arrive at a rational choice and when they will display maladaptive patterns of coping with threat.

The Conflict Theory Model

The conflict theory model, as formulated elsewhere (Janis & Mann, 1977), takes account of the stresses of making major decisions and the various ways people deal with those stresses, which frequently result in defective forms of problem solving that fail to meet the standards of rational decision making. We have attempted to give a very broad descriptive account of decision-making behavior, both effective and ineffective, starting with an initial stage of appraising whatever threat (or opportunity) instigates the decision-making process to a final stage of adherence despite setbacks after decision makers have committed themselves to a chosen course of action. According to our theoretical view, none of the models of rational choice, such as the SEU theory or the health belief model, is necessarily incorrect as descriptive theory. Rather, those models apply only to a limited aspect of the decision-making activities that occur during the five stages of decision making, and only when people are displaying a vigilant mode of coping with stress, not when they are displaying other coping patterns.

The five main stages in arriving at a *stable* decision, and the major concerns associated with each, as described in our account of conflict theory, are shown in Table 9.1. These stages were originally delineated on the basis of observations of people who made health decisions that they subsequently carried out successfully—giving up smoking, losing weight on a low-calorie diet, or contemplating a series of recommended medical treatments. Tak-

TABLE 9.1. Stages in Arriving at a Stable Decision

STAGE	KEY QUESTIONS
1. Appraising the challenge	Are the risks serious if I don't change?
2. Surveying alternatives	Is this (salient) alternative an acceptable means for dealing with the challenge?
	Have I sufficiently surveyed the available alternatives?
3. Weighing alternatives	Which alternative is best?
	Could the best alternative meet the essential requirements?
4. Deliberating about commitment	Shall I implement the best alternative and allow others to know?
5. Adhering despite negative feedback	Are the risks serious if I *don't* change? Are the risks serious if I *do* change?

Note. Adapted from Janis, I. L., & Mann, L. *Decision making: A psychological analysis of conflict, choice, and commitment.* New York: Free Press, 1977.

ing account of comparative observations of people who commit themselves to the same decisions but *fail* to adhere to them, we postulated that if any of the five stages are omitted or carried out in a perfunctory manner, the decision maker is likely to react with postdecisional regret and to reverse the decision when difficulties arise. This assumption appears to be plausible for a wide variety of personal decisions (see Janis & Mann, 1977, Chapter 7).

Decision making is assumed to begin when people are confronted with a challenge to their current course of action. The challenges can be either events or communications that convey threats or opportunities. The central question facing decision makers during Stage 1 is whether the threat or opportunity is important enough to warrant the effort of making an active decision about it. Ignoring or rejecting the challenge leads to complacently pursuing the original course of action without any change, simply continuing business as usual. Accepting the challenge, or deciding to decide, leads to the next stage of active decision making.

When a current course of action is challenged, effective decision makers begin searching for alternatives (Stage 2). They thoroughly consider their goals (or values) relevant to the decision, and they search carefully for available alternatives that have some promise of achieving those goals.

During Stage 3, the advantages and disadvantages of each alternative are carefully considered. This stage usually involves considerable effort in searching for dependable information relevant to the expected utilities of the outcomes and the likelihood that each of the possible outcomes will occur. The decision makers seek facts and forecasts from a wide variety of sources about all the various consequences of the alternatives they are considering. They carefully weigh new evidence that may go against their initial preference. At the end of Stage 3, the cautious decision maker usually reaches a tentative decision, based on all the information he or she has gathered.

In Stage 4 decision makers arrive at their final choice and become more and more committed to the new course of action as they inform interested parties about their decision. During this stage, they reexamine all the information they have gathered, figure out how to implement the decision, and make contingency plans for losses that are likely to materialize.

In Stage 5, decision makers discount any minor challenges in the form of new threats or opportunities. They tend to give a negative response to the initial key question for this stage ("Are the risks serious if I *don't* change?"). When major setbacks or losses occur, however, they may give a positive response to this key question, in which case Stage 5 becomes equivalent to Stage 1 of a new decision. Nevertheless, Stage 5 is different from Stage 1 when the person has carefully gone through all the preceding stages in arriving at a stable decision: Even though the challenge may be a strong one, the decision maker tends to be only temporarily shaken and tends to end up deciding not to give up implementing the decision.

The major determinants of effective decision making in each stage, according to our assumptions, are those that influence the decision maker's pattern of coping with decisional conflict. All major decisions, especially those pertaining to health, entail considerable stress arising from conflict about what to do. People realize that whichever course of action or inaction they choose could lead to serious material or social losses, such as becoming physically incapacitated or losing the esteem of loved ones. The decisions made by seriously ill patients often require acceptance of short-term losses, such as the physical discomforts of nauseating medicines or painful surgery, in order to attain the long-term goals of counteracting the disease. The more severe the anticipated losses for each of the available alternatives, the greater the stress engendered by the decisional conflict. Studies of the psychological and physiological concomitants of decision making have found that there are increases in anxiety symptoms, sleeplessness, and psychosomatic symptoms, as well as marked changes in heart rate, finger pulse amplitude, and galvanic skin response, when a person is required to make a difficult choice (Gerard, 1967; Jones & Johnson, 1973; Mann, Janis, & Chaplin, 1969).

The conflict theory model is based on the assumption that the stress itself is frequently a major cause of errors in decision making. This assumption does not deny the influence of other common causes of misjudgments, such as information overload and the limitations of human information processing, group pressures, blinding prejudice, ignorance, and organizational constraints (see Janis, 1974, 1982a; Simon, 1976). It maintains, however, that a major reason for many ill-conceived and poorly implemented decisions has to do with the motivational consequences of decisional conflict, particularly attempts to ward off the stresses generated by agonizingly difficult choices.

Linked with the initial assumption is a set of postulates that describes five basic patterns of coping with a realistic challenge, each of which is associated with a specific set of antecedent conditions and a characteristic level of stress. These patterns were derived from an analysis of the research literature on how people react to disaster warnings and fear-arousing messages about health hazards that urge protective action. The five coping patterns and their determinants are shown in Figure 9.2.

According to the conflict theory model, the decision maker's coping pattern is determined by the presence or absence of three conditions: (1) awareness of serious risks for whichever alternative is chosen (i.e., arousal of conflict); (2) hope of finding a better alternative; and (3) belief that there is adequate time to search and deliberate before a decision is required. The model specifies that the vigilance pattern occurs only when all three of these conditions are met. It specifies further that if the first condition (conflict) is not met, unconflicted adherence or unconflicted change is to be expected; if the second condition (hope) is not met, defensive avoidance will be the dominant coping pattern; if the third condition (adequate time) is the only one that is not met, hypervigilance will be the dominant coping pattern.

Antecedent Conditions   Mediating

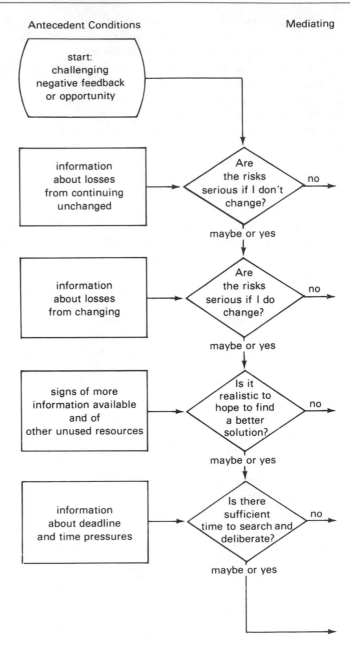

Processes   Consequences

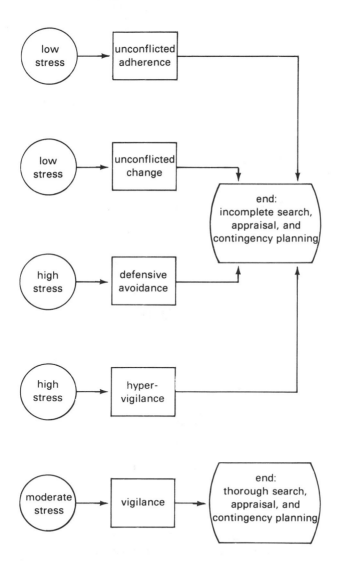

FIGURE 9.2. The conflict theory model of coping patterns. (Adapted from Janis, I. L., & Mann, L. *Decision making: A psychological analysis of conflict, choice, and commitment.* New York: Free Press, 1977.)

The four defective coping patterns are characterized by different forms of behavior that are highly maladaptive when the challenge consists of symptoms of a serious disease or a warning by a trustworthy physician that an illness or physical defect will worsen without remedial medical treatment. These patterns are as follows:

1. *Unconflicted adherence.* The decision maker complacently decides to continue whatever he or she has been doing, ignoring available information about the risks.
2. *Unconflicted change.* The decision maker uncritically adopts whichever new course of action is most salient or most strongly recommended, without making any contingency plans and without preparing psychologically for setbacks.
3. *Defensive avoidance.* The decision maker evades the conflict by procrastinating, shifting responsibility to someone else, or constructing wishful rationalizations that minimize expected unfavorable consequences in order to bolster the least objectionable alternative.
4. *Hypervigilance.* The decision maker searches frantically for a way out of the dilemma, rapidly shifts back and forth between alternatives, and impulsively seizes upon a hastily contrived solution that seems to promise immediate relief; he or she thus overlooks the full range of consequences of his or her choice because of emotional excitement, repetitive thinking, and cognitive constriction (manifested by reduction in immediate memory span and simplistic ideas). In its most extreme form, hypervigilance is referred to as "panic."

The conflict theory model differs from the SEU and health belief models with regard to the way people arrive at decisions when the conditions making for any one of the four defective coping patterns is present. Our model postulates that people will weigh the benefits of a recommended course of action against the perceived costs or barriers to taking that action, as is assumed by rational-choice models, *only when their coping pattern is vigilance.* When any of the four defective coping patterns is dominant, the decision maker will *fail* to carry out the essential tasks of the four stages necessary for arriving at stable decisions. Then when they experience undesirable consequences, such as the usual unpleasant side effects of a standard medical treatment, they are likely to overreact to the minor challenge. They suffer not just from the distressing setback itself, but also from strong feelings of regret, which may interfere with their ability to curtail the losses and to make a sound new decision that will enable them to recover rapidly from the setback. Postdecisional regret often entails the arousal of such intense emotions as anxiety and rage, which can contribute to an exacerbation of a patient's illness. Little is known at present about the psychosomatic effects of postdecisional regret following patients' decisions to undergo surgery or medical treatments, but this topic obviously warrants intensive investigation.

According to the conflict theory model, all four defective coping patterns, as well as the vigilance pattern of coping, are in the repertoire of every adult person, although there may be marked individual differences in the readiness with which different people display one or another of the five patterns. The model specifies that the five coping patterns have distinctive behavioral consequences, which are summarized in Table 9.2. The columns of the table represent the major criteria that can be used to judge whether a decision is of high quality with regard to the problem-solving procedures that lead up to the act of commitment. These criteria were extracted from the extensive literature on effective decision making (Janis & Mann, 1977). It seems plausible to assume that when personal decisions satisfy these procedural criteria, they have the best chance of attaining the decision maker's objectives and of being adhered to in the long run. It follows from this analysis that patients with life-threatening diseases are more likely to make rational decisions to accept and adhere to the best available medical regimens prescribed by medical experts if their dominant coping pattern is vigilance, rather than one of the other four coping patterns.

A distinctive feature of the model is the specification of conditions relating to conflict, hope, and time pressure that mediate vigilance as against the other coping patterns. It is not assumed that the five patterns occur only as a result of the conditions specified in Figure 9.2. The claim is that the patterns are linked dependably with those conditions. The model thus has testable implications about the effects of environmental circumstances and interventions that could counteract the beliefs responsible for defective coping patterns.

One of the values of the conflict theory model is that it suggests a number of ways in which health care advisors can help people make more vigilant decisions (see Janis & Mann, 1977, pp. 376–392). Later in this chapter I describe a ''balance-sheet'' procedure and a number of other predecisional interventions we have developed to promote the vigilant coping pattern by requiring decision makers to confront and answer questions about potential risks and gains, some of which they may not have previously contemplated. Preliminary evidence of the effectiveness of these interventions is consistent with a major assumption of conflict theory: When the vigilance pattern becomes the dominant one and persists, the decision maker is more likely to go through all the essential stages of decision making in a thorough fashion before implementing a new course of action, and thereafter to remain relatively unshaken by setbacks that challenge the decision.

On the basis of the conflict theory model, we have presented a set of general prescriptive hypotheses, which state what physicians, nurses, and other practitioners can do to help their patients to function more effectively as decision makers:

> 1. If the counselor ascertains that the client sees no serious risks in persisting in his present course of action and he surmises that this is an unrealistic assessment, he can attempt to prevent unconflicted adherence to whatever course of action or inaction the person has been pursuing. He can raise questions about the potential significance of the negative feedback the

TABLE 9.2. Predecisional Behavior Characteristic of the Five Basic Patterns of Decision Making

CRITERIA FOR HIGH-QUALITY DECISION MAKING

PATTERN OF COPING WITH CHALLENGE	(1) THOROUGH SURVEYING OF ALTERNATIVES	(2) THOROUGH CANVASSING OF OBJECTIVES	(3) CAREFUL EVALUATION OF CONSEQUENCES OF — A. CURRENT COURSE OF ACTION	B. NEW COURSES OF ACTION	(4) THOROUGH SEARCH FOR INFORMATION	(5) UNBIASED ASSIMILATION OF NEW INFORMATION	(6) CAREFUL RE-EVALUATION OF CONSEQUENCES	(7) THOROUGH PLANNING FOR IMPLEMENTATION AND CONTINGENCIES
Unconflicted adherence	–	–	–	–	–	+	–	–
Unconflicted change	–	–	+	–	–	+	–	–
Defensive avoidance	–	–	–	–	–	–	–	–
Hypervigilance	–	–	±	±	±	–	–	–
Vigilance	+	+	+	+	+	+	+	+

Note. Adapted from Janis, I. L., & Mann, L. *Decision making: A psychological analysis of conflict, choice, and commitment.* New York: Free Press, 1977.

Note. + = the decision maker meets the criterion to the best of his or her ability; – = the decision maker fails to meet the criterion; ± = the decision maker's performance fluctuates, sometimes meeting the criterion to the best of his or her ability and sometimes not. All evaluative terms such as *thorough* and *unbiased* are to be understood as intrapersonal comparative assessments, relative to the person's highest possible level of cognitive performance.

client has already encountered, induce the client to consider possible un-favorable outcomes in the future, and encourage him to obtain objective in-formation and expert opinion about the costs and risks of not changing.

2. If the counselor ascertains that the client sees no serious risks in adopt-ing an attractive new course of action and he surmises that this is an un-realistic assessment, he can attempt to prevent unconflicted change. This requires encouraging the client to obtain objective information and expert opinion about the risks of making the intended change and inducing him to consider the unfavorable outcomes he may be overlooking, including po-tential losses from failing to live up to prior commitments.

3. If the counselor ascertains that the client is in a state of acute con-flict and believes that there is no realistic basis for hoping to resolve the con-flict, he can try to counteract this pessimistic expectation in order to pre-vent defensive avoidance. The counselor might encourage the client to discuss his dilemma with respected individuals in his personal network of relatives, friends, or mentors who might give him new perspectives and help him to maintain hope. He can also suggest that more information is available and tell the client where he might find it by mentioning pertinent books, pamphlets, and articles or by recommending professional experts who could be consulted. Above all, the decision counselor can himself convey a sense of optimism about the client's chances of finding a good solution to the problem.

4. If the counselor ascertains that the client is in a state of acute con-flict and believes that there is insufficient time to find a good solution, he can try to counteract the panicky vacillation and premature choice that char-acterizes hypervigilance. He might give realistic reassurances about what can be accomplished before the final deadline is at hand. Or he might en-courage the client to find out if the deadline is negotiable, to see if he can obtain an extension without serious costs or risks.

All four prescriptive hypotheses are also applicable as "self-help" sug-gestions for anyone who is striving to attain a vigilant approach, provided that he can somehow take on the role of an objective self-interrogator, which is not easy to do. (Janis & Mann, 1977, p. 374).

These four hypotheses and other implications of the conflict theory model have not yet been fully tested. In a review of social-psychological stud-ies bearing on premature closure, postdecisional regret, and a number of other aspects of decisional behavior, we have called attention to scattered findings consistent with predictions about the behavioral consequences of vigilant versus nonvigilant coping patterns, from which we have concluded that our theoretical analysis is plausible. (See Janis & Mann, 1977, Chapters 4–12.) One experiment, for example, dealt with threats of the type that be-set many patients who have to make decisions about taking medications or undergoing treatments that create nausea and other temporary side effects that are harmless but unpleasant. The experiment was designed to test a complicated hypothesis derived from the conflict theory model, concerning the conditions under which defensive avoidance rather than vigilance will tend to be dominant. The hypothesis is that at any time prior to commitment when decision makers are led to believe that they have already received all the relevant information available about the consequences of the alternative choices open to them, their loss of hope of finding a better solution will increase the chances that defensive avoidance will become the dominant coping pattern; this pattern will be manifested by *bolstering* of the least objectionable alternative (i.e., playing down its disadvantages and playing up its alleged advantages over the other alternatives). The experiment to test this hypothesis was carried out with female students at the University of Melbourne, Australia (Mann *et al.*, 1969). The women were told that the experiment dealt with the effect of unpleasant physiological stimulation on ability to carry out intellectual tasks. To create the conditions for conflict, subjects were given a choice between noxious taste or noise and were told that each could produce temporary side effects such as nausea, dizziness, headaches, and other disagreeable symptoms. To maintain the hope of obtaining additional information that could lead to a better solution, the experimenter told one group of subjects that some estimates about the percentages of people suffering side effects from the different stimulations would be provided later on. In contrast, a second group was told that nothing was definitely known about the percentages of people suffering side effects from the two alternatives.

As predicted by the conflict theory model, when subjects were led to believe that no additional information could be expected, they tended to bolster the alternative they had originally preferred; this bolstering was evidenced by a spread in the relative attractiveness of the two alternatives. But when subjects expected more information, there was virtually no tendency to bolster—a finding that is also consistent with the conflict theory model, which specifies that vigilance will be the dominant coping pattern under these circumstances. This experiment not only bore out the theoretical assumptions about the conditions under which defensive avoidance rather than vigilance will be the dominant pattern, but also put to the test a different theoretical position held by Leon Festinger (1964) and his coworkers, which predicts that bolstering, which is a manifestation of cognitive dissonance reduction, will never occur before a decision maker announces his or her choice to others. The results indicate that bolstering does occur before overt commitment if the conditions that foster defensive avoidance are present.

None of the studies carried out so far can be regarded as "crucial" experiments that definitively test the conflict theory model or enable one to decide whether this model is "better" in general than other social-psychological theories that have something to say about information seeking, errors in estimating probabilities, or other aspects of decision making. Efforts to design so-called crucial experiments to test rival theories will continue to be premature, in my opinion, until more precise techniques are developed for investigating the mediating processes that occur when people make consequential choices. In the present early stage of research on decision making, the conflict theory model may at least have some heuristic value, in that it calls attention to neglected research problems that might be systematically explored to advance our understanding of the determinants of postdecisional regret.

RESEARCH FINDINGS

The recent research literature on the ways in which people make personal decisions to improve or maintain their health contains many partially confirmed conclusions about how and why patients accept or fail to accept recommendations by their physicians or other health experts (see Janis, 1982b, 1983a, 1983b; Janis & Mann, 1977; Janis & Rodin, 1979). Unfortunately, many of the earlier studies in the literature on behavioral medicine are methodologically deficient because they used inadequate controls, confounded the independent variables under investigation with extraneous variables, obtained unreliable or unvalidated measures of the dependent behavioral variables, and/or failed to use appropriate tests of statistical significance. Nevertheless, a substantial number of studies can now be drawn upon to provide promising leads for explaining health-related behavior and for developing practical applications that might help to prevent patients from choosing maladaptive courses of action (such as delay in seeking medical aid for ominous symptoms of heart disease or cancer) and to improve the quality of their decision-making procedures in general. Some of the most valuable studies deal with the effects of warnings by physicians or public health authorities, which pertain primarily to the first stage of decision making (accepting the challenge); other noteworthy studies pertain to one or another of the later stages—generating alternatives, evaluating consequences, becoming committed after making a final choice, and adhering to the decision despite setbacks. In the sections that follow, I use the five stages (discussed on pages 333–334) as a set of descriptive categories for sorting out the pertinent evidence bearing on empirical generalizations, explanatory hypotheses, and practical applications extracted from the research literature.

Effective and Ineffective Warnings

Throughout their entire lives, people are exposed to an unending stream of challenging warnings that call attention to the risks of suffering serious losses unless they adopt a new course of protective action. The challenging information is sometimes conveyed by disturbing *events*, as when a heavy smoker develops a chronic cough. Fairly often, the challenging information that initiates the decision-making process is contained in impressive communications, such as warnings from one's physician after a physical checkup has revealed high blood pressure, or authoritative messages in the mass media about contaminated foods that should be avoided.

Numerous studies indicate that physician's communications often are ineffective in influencing patients to accept their recommendations for diminishing or preventing health hazards. (See reviews of the literature on adherence by Kasl, 1975; Kirscht & Rosenstock, 1979; Sackett, 1976; Stone, 1979.) But the findings tell us relatively little about why the physicians' recommendations so frequently go unheeded. We have no clear indications as to how often physicians' lack of success is primarily attributable to defective communication on their part. Health care practitioners may fail to convey their warnings and recommendations clearly enough to avoid being misunderstood by their patients. Or they may fail to motivate their patients sufficiently to overcome resistances arising from the unpleasantness and other costs of taking the warnings seriously and carrying out the recommendations. Obviously, if for any reason the patients do not follow the medical advice they are given, the physicians' skills in diagnosing the illness and in prescribing appropriate treatments or regimens are of no use whatsoever.

Physicians, nurses, and other health care personnel frequently try to induce patients to change their behavior by deliberately highlighting the suffering and disabilities that can be expected if they continue to disregard medical recommendations. Sometimes they feel it is necessary to "scare the hell out of the patient." Elsewhere (Janis & Rodin, 1979), we describe the extreme example of a specialist in the treatment of liver diseases who felt that he had to do something drastic to get his patients in the early stages of cirrhosis to stop imbibing alcohol. He was especially concerned about those who felt that moderate drinking was essential for business contacts or for relaxation and believed that it was not very harmful. He hospitalized them for medical tests and deliberately arranged for them to be in rooms where they would see the agony of other patients dying of the same disease. The physician told them that this was what would happen to them before very long unless they stopped drinking completely. He reported that he continues to use this tactic because it is very successful. Often, however, the physicians who resort to any such scare tactic have no way of knowing when it succeeds in inducing patients to accept their recommendations and when it results in demoralization or has other boomerang effects.

Even when physicians do not want to scare their patients, they often find it necessary to give disturbing information in order to obtain informed consent or to explain why they are prescribing a particular medical treatment or regimen. Just as with scare propaganda, authentic warnings that arouse intense emotional reactions can make for misattributions, erroneous judgments, and defective decisions, sometimes as a result of provoking panic or extreme reactions of defensive avoidance. What can be done to prevent such adverse reactions? Under what conditions are fear-arousing warnings most likely to be effective?

Some tentative answers can be inferred from the extensive investigations on the effects of warnings and emotional appeals by social psychologists (see

Janis, 1967, 1971; Leventhal, 1973; McGuire, 1969; Rogers & Mewborn, 1976). Dozens of controlled attitude change experiments have been carried out to determine whether acceptance of precautionary health recommendations increases or decreases when strong fear appeals are used in warning messages as compared with milder ones. One set of such experiments, dealing with real-life threats of illness or physical disability, indicates that there can be diminishing returns as the level of fear arousal is increased. These experiments support the conclusion that when fear is strongly aroused by a communication but is not fully relieved by reassurances, the recipients will be motivated to ignore, minimize, or deny the importance of the threat (e.g., Janis & Feshbach, 1953; Janis & Terwilliger, 1962; Rogers & Thistlethwaite, 1970). But another set of experiments dealing with similar threats shows that strong threat appeals can be more effective than milder ones; these experiments point to the facilitating effects of fear arousal (e.g., Insko, Arkoff, & Insko, 1965; Leventhal, Singer, & Jones, 1965).

Taken together, the two sets of results suggest that changes in feelings of vulnerability to a threat and subsequent adoption of a recommended course of action depend upon the relative strength of facilitating and interfering reactions, both of which are likely to be evoked whenever a warning by an authority arouses fear. If this is so, we cannot expect to discover any simple generalization applicable to warnings given by authoritative sources—one that will tell us whether strong fear-arousing presentations that vividly depict the expected dangers or milder versions that merely allude to the threats will be more effective in general. Rather, we must expect the optimal level of fear arousal to vary for different types of threat, for different types of recommended action, and for different personalities.

There is general agreement among social-psychological investigators that the effectiveness of any fear-arousing communication depends partly upon three content variables that interact in complex ways (see Hovland, Janis, & Kelley, 1953; McGuire, 1969; Rogers & Mewborn, 1976):

1. Magnitude of the threat (if it were to materialize).
2. Probability of the threat materializing (if no protective action is taken).
3. Probable effectiveness of the recommended protective action or other reassurances about averting or minimizing the threat.

These three components are among the key components of the SEU model and the health belief model, discussed earlier. According to those rational-choice models, people suffering from an illness can be expected to accept their physicians' recommendations if they believe that the probable consequences of doing what is recommended, despite all the costs in terms of money, time, effort, and discomfort, are preferable to the consequences of the illness. But, as I have indicated in the discussion of the conflict theory model, this model is expected to hold only when conditions are present that make for a vigilant pattern of coping with threat. Some of the findings cited earlier on delay of treatment and other maladaptive responses among patients suffering from heart disease or cancer appear to bear out this assumption.

For anyone who comes to a clinic or hospital, the third component listed above (i.e., efficacy) would include not only the anticipated effectiveness of whatever treatments are prescribed, but also the person's general level of confidence in the staff (see Howard & Strauss, 1975). The crucial role of statements about the efficacy of the recommended means for averting or minimizing the threat is repeatedly borne out by social-psychological studies of the effects of public health messages that contain fear-arousing warnings (see Chu, 1966; Leventhal, 1973; Leventhal, Singer, & Jones, 1965; Rogers & Deckner, 1975; Rogers & Thistlethwaite, 1970). A study by Rogers and Mewborn (1976), for example, found that assertions about the efficacy of recommended protective actions had a significant effect on college students' intentions to adopt the practices recommended in three different public health communications dealing with well-known hazards that produce preventable human suffering—lung cancer, automobile accident injuries, and venereal disease.

The findings just cited appear to be consistent with the following hypothesis derived from the conflict theory model: When a warning message presents realistic information about the unfavorable consequences of alternative courses of action—including consent forms that describe the risks and suffering that could arise from undergoing surgery or painful medical treatments—it is more likely to induce vigilance and to instigate sound decision-making procedures if it is accompanied by impressive information about the expected efficacy of the recommended course of action, which instills hope about dealing effectively with the anticipated threats. This hypothesis is in line with the intuitive practices of some, but not all, physicians.

Perceived efficacy of the recommended protective action is a major determinant of the optimal level of fear arousal, according to my theoretical analysis of effective warnings (Janis, 1967, 1971). There are two main assumptions in this analysis: (1) As fear increases from a low level to a moderate level, the arousal of vigilance will motivate attention, learning, and acceptance of the information contained in realistic warnings; and (2) as fear mounts to higher and higher levels, the probability that the person will accept and act upon the protective recommendations decreases because of the disruptive effects of strong arousal, which result in hypervigilance or defensive avoidance. Taken together, these two assumptions lead one to expect that the relation between the intensity of fear aroused by a warning and the adequacy of decision making will be curvilinear (an inverted U-shaped function), as has been found in studies of the effects of emotional arousal on a variety of cognitive performances. Thus, when a sound medical recommendation is given to a patient in an authentic warning communication, it will be rejected if the level of fear evoked by the warning exceeds an optimal level, beyond which the interfering effects of emotional arousal outweigh the facilitating effects. For anyone exposed to information about a particular threat, the optimal level is not expected to be at a fixed point on the fear-arousal continuum; it can be at a relatively high or low level of arousal, depending on such factors as the perceived trustworthiness of the communicator, which influence the degree of resistance to assimilating a distressing message.

Some evidence suggesting that perceived efficacy of the recommendations is a major determinant of the optimal level of fear arousal is provided in a study by Leventhal and Watts (1966). Their experiment, which involved showing an antismoking film at a state fair, compared a strong-fear version of the film (which showed the gory details of surgery for lung cancer) with a moderate-fear version and a mild-fear version. Follow-up results on adherence obtained 5 months later showed that the most effective version was not the same for the two different recommendations presented in the film. For the recommendation to stop smoking, the strong-fear version was most effective, but for the recommendation to have a chest X-ray, that same version was least effective. From various additional findings, Leventhal and Watts inferred that having an X-ray was regarded by the subjects as an action that could lead to painful surgery, like the horrible operation shown in the strong-fear version of the movie, and at best could merely prevent a serious danger (lung cancer) from getting worse; whereas cutting down on smoking was perceived as an efficacious course of action for preventing the threat of lung cancer from materializing.

The concept of optimal level of fear arousal carries the implication that whenever an expert recommends a sound course of protective action, as when a physician tells a hypertensive patient that he or she should take a prescribed medication every day, the likelihood of acceptance will depend not only on the person's judgment as to how efficacious that action will prove to be, but also on whether the person's level of induced fear is below, at, or above the optimal level. The predicted decrease in effectiveness of a warning at very high levels of fear is highly controversial, because, as I have mentioned, some studies appear to have found it and others have not.

A related controversial point pertains to the source of fear. According to the analysis of optimal level of fear, the detrimental effects of a very high level of fear will occur even when it is not induced by relevant threat information. In the case of the hypertensive patient for whom medication is being recommended, the level of fear aroused by relevant threat information (pertaining to the danger of having a heart attack or stroke if the patient's blood pressure continues to be chronically elevated) would be increased if the patient has just read a news story about a serious threat of financial losses in his or her business, or if he or she has just seen a mutilated victim of an auto accident being carried in for emergency treatment. The prediction is that when an authoritative warning evokes a moderate or fairly high degree of fear, any additional source of fear—whether relevant or irrelevant to the threat described in the warning—is likely to raise fear to such a high degree that it exceeds the optimal level, with the result that the authoritative recommendations are less likely to be accepted than if that additional source of fear were not present.

Evidence bearing on this prediction was obtained in a well-designed experiment by Krisher, Darley, and Darley (1973). These investigators presented two equivalent groups of male college students with the same warning message concerning the dangers of becoming sterile and suffering other distressing consequences from catching mumps, which concluded with the strong recommendation to go to the university health service to be vaccinated against mumps. One of the two groups was given bogus heart rate feedback (a huge increase from about 70 to 140 beats per minute) during exposure to the warning message, and the other group was not. Prior research has shown that this type of false physiological feedback heightens fear arousal (Darley, 1969; Harris & Jellison, 1971; Valins, 1966). A third experimental group, which was given the same recommendation, received only a low-fear-arousing message. Behavioral data indicating whether or not each subject came in for the mumps vaccination were obtained from medical records in the university health service. The results showed that behavioral adherence to the medical recommendation was curvilinearly related to level of induced fear, just as predicted by the optimal level analysis. Students in the moderate-fear condition were more likely to get the vaccination than were those in the low-fear condition or in the high-fear condition.

The authors interpret their findings in terms of defensive avoidance:

> The subjects in the heart rate condition felt considerable fear which they associated with mumps. As Janis (1967) suggested, this high fear may have been unpleasant enough so that defensive reactions and avoidance responses became dominant. Since subjects in the present study were run in the evening, it was impossible for them to go immediately to the Health Service for the vaccine. This created a situation in which it would be necessary for the subject to think again about mumps in order to decide to go to take the shot. Subjects in the heart rate condition may simply have avoided the topic, since this would have led to the rearousal of their fear; in doing so, they may have inadvertently decided not to receive the vaccine. (Krisher et al., 1973, p. 307)

The investigators emphasize that the decline in adherence to the recommendation among the subjects in the high-fear condition is particularly noteworthy because their fear was increased solely by a physiological feedback procedure and not by any change in the content of the warning message, which was identical for the high-fear and the moderate-fear groups. Consequently, the decline in preventive action cannot be attributed to any informational inputs about the consequences of the disease, the efficacy of the recommendations, or any other relevant component of a rational-choice model of decision making.

This evidence does not bear out the implications of Fishbein's (1977) critique of research on emotional appeals, which lead one to expect that any differential behavioral effects of different levels of fear arousal can be accounted for in terms of content differences pertaining to the nature of the threat or the consequences of alternative courses of action. Fishbein is quite correct in emphasizing that most of the studies on emotional appeals have confounded level of emotional arousal with differential content of the messages employed to induce arousal; but, as is indicated by the findings of the Krisher et al. (1973) experiment, differential effects can be obtained when fear arousal is varied independently of any content changes. Those findings, if replicated, will be particularly important in indicating that the purely cognitive theoretical approach of Fishbein and other advocates of rational-choice models needs to be supplemented by considerations of emotional dynamics, such as those postulated by advocates of the optimal-level concept. Of course an ad hoc cognitive explanation could be offered in terms of changes in attributions based on self-observation, using Bem's (1972) model to account for the increased fear evoked by the false physiological feedback: Subjects might think to themselves, "If I am so aroused by this message, I must feel that the danger of mumps is very great." But it is not at all easy to explain how this change in attributions would lead to a *decrease* in adherence to the protective recommendation, nor would the ad hoc explanation be compatible with the basic assumptions of any rational-choice model of decision making. Obviously, the controversial issues posed by the contrasting predictions from theoretical models of rational choice and those that take account of emotional as well as cognitive processes will require further research along the lines of the experiment by Krisher et al. (1973). Such experiments are needed to determine the effects of fear stimuli that augment the level of emotional arousal accompanying warning messages, without introducing any new information about the external threat or about protective measures.

Screening of Warnings

Vigilant as well as hypervigilant reactions to warnings may have high costs in time and energy, and perhaps also in the form of psychosomatic disorders (see Jenkins, 1979). Executives who are constantly exposed to large numbers of challenging threats and opportunities that require daily decisions have about three times as many fatal heart attacks as do persons working in other occupations (Rummel & Rader, 1978). Studies of the physiological concomitants of decisional conflict indicate marked increases in heart rate, finger pulse amplitude, and galvanic skin response when a person who is given the responsibility to make a choice is trying to decide what to do. (See Gerard, 1967; Jones & Johnson, 1973; Mann, et al., 1969.)

In order for executives, professionals, and others with decision-making responsibilities to avoid the undesirable effects of decisional overloads on their efficiency and health, it is probably essential for them to be highly discriminating about the potential challenges they accept and those they reject. They need to use sound criteria to screen information about potential losses and about opportunities for gains that they might fail to realize if they do not change to a new course of action. Similarly, seriously ill patients who undergo all sorts of annoying changes in bodily functions that may or may not be alarming symptoms cannot be responsive to all potential challenges without becoming emotionally distressed, which could exacerbate their physical disorders. Even when they are not ill, people cannot think about and be responsive to the large number of apparent challenges they encounter daily in news stories, advertisements, and word-of-mouth rumors about health hazards. If they did, they would undergo constant psychological stress and would have little time or energy to think about anything else. Nevertheless, if executives, patients, or anyone else were to ignore all warnings until there was clear and present danger, they would undergo one avoidable crisis after another. By the time they realize that a new decision is urgently needed, it is usually too late to find an optimal or even a barely satisfactory solution.

Although no definitive generalizations have as yet been validated as effective rules for screening challenges, there are a few key questions that might be useful as guidelines (Wheeler & Janis, 1980). These could prove to be especially valuable for hospitalized patients who cannot help noticing their own bodily discomforts at a time when they are being exposed to a steady flow of challenging messages, ranging from authoritative diagnostic statements by well-qualified physicians to vague hints and rumors from uninformed aides or visitors. The key questions and related guidelines we have proposed, which fall into three main categories, could probably be taught to large numbers of people in training programs on health self-care:

Appraising credibility of information
- Is my source in a position to know the truth?
- If so, is my source likely to be honest or dishonest? (For example, is he trying to sell something or to make scare propaganda for his own purposes?)
- Is any evidence given that makes the predicted threat seem plausible and, if so, how good is the evidence?
- If there are serious doubts about the credibility of the information, is there a trustworthy source who could easily be consulted—someone who is an impartial expert or someone who would be willing to give inside information? . . .

Importance of the threat
- If there is some real danger, how likely is it to materialize?
- How likely is it to affect me or people I care about?
- How severe might the losses be?

Urgency
- If the danger is likely to materialize and lead to serious losses, might it happen soon or is it unlikely to occur for a long time to come?
- Even if it is likely to occur soon, will the danger develop gradually so that there would be ample time to plan protective actions if I wait to see what happens? Or is the danger likely to come on so suddenly that I will be caught short and be unable to protect myself if I postpone doing anything about it?

- If some immediate planning of protective action is urgent, could I do just a part of it now and safely postpone the rest until the first signs of danger appear?

. . . Sometimes asking yourself only one or two of the questions is sufficient to dismiss a warning as just so much hot air or as too trivial to bother with. It is worthwhile to ask all the above questions only when a warning is very impressive and is starting to get through to you. . . .

If you deliberately train yourself to make use of these questions, especially for the most impressive warnings about possible losses and the most impressive promises of possible gains, you may be able to cut down on the number of errors you make in screening challenges. You may still make serious errors, sometimes ignoring a really serious challenge that should have been taken seriously and sometimes overreacting to an inauthentic, unimportant, or nonurgent challenge that should have been ignored. The value of asking yourself these questions can be completely undermined if you give biased answers that express what you would like to believe rather than what you really think is true. At times you may have to be somewhat skeptical about whether you are being honest with yourself and perhaps suspect yourself of giving rationalizations if you see signs that you might be indulging in wishful thinking rather than making an objective appraisal. Nevertheless, you can probably do a somewhat better job at screening challenges than you have been doing if you conscientiously attempt to give honest answers to the three sets of questions about the credibility, importance, and urgency of the potential threats and opportunities that momentarily capture your attention. (Wheeler & Janis, 1980, pp. 34–36)

In order to help people to improve their effectiveness in screening potential challenges concerning the threats of ill health and physical disabilities, it might be beneficial to develop a training program that explains the rationale for the key questions listed above and teaches ways to answer them as conscientiously and as knowledgeably as possible. The appropriate training could probably be included in high-school courses on personal hygiene, in community courses and executive workshops on health problems, and in a variety of educational settings for people who are concerned about maintaining their physical well-being. So far as I know, however, no such program for screening potential challenges pertaining to health problems has as yet been tried out and evaluated in pilot studies with an eye to large-scale application. This gap in the field of health education might not be difficult to eliminate if it is given sufficient priority by well-qualified specialists in educational research and development.

Generating Viable Alternatives

After effective decision makers accept a challenge in the first stage of decision making, they search in the next stage for viable alternatives available to them for meeting the challenge. Unfortunately, medical patients often miss the best available alternatives, because when they are in this stage of decision making they do not know how to make full use of physicians and other health practitioners upon whose expert knowledge they must rely. One well-known source of error is a patient's failure to understand exactly what is being recommended. This situation may arise either because the physician communicates badly or because the patient is too emotionally aroused to comprehend a perfectly clear message (see Stone, 1979). Here are a few typical findings from research on patients' compliance: One study revealed that over 60% of the patients misunderstood what their physicians said about taking medications (Boyd, Covington, Stanaszek, & Coussons, 1974). Another reported very similar misunderstandings in an outpatient clinic in Liverpool, England: More than half of the medical instructions given by the physicians could not be recalled accurately by the patients immediately after they left the consulting room (Ley & Spelman, 1965). Inui, Yourtee, and Williamson (1976) found that giving physicians a 1- to 2-hour tutorial on communicating clearly and on inducing compliance was followed by a marked improvement in the behavior of their hypertensive patients; over 30% more of the patients responded satisfactorily to the physicians' recommendations.

Although considerable research has been carried out on the deficiencies that physicians need to overcome in order to function as effective transmitters of communications about their medical recommendations, relatively little research has been done on the deficiencies that patients need to overcome in order to elicit adequate information concerning alternatives. Even when a patient adequately comprehends the medical recommendation being given, he or she may still fail to function as an effective decision maker with regard to exploring the full range of viable alternatives. Especially for minor illnesses, a patient may miss out on finding a course of action that is far better than the particular one selected by the physician. Since most people lack medical knowledge, they do not attempt to ferret out possible alternatives by reading medical books, and do not even seek further information about the ones mentioned in the consent forms that they are asked to sign.

When patients expect the recommended treatment to be risky or painful, and also expect that allowing the illness to go untreated will be dangerous, they will be strongly motivated to search for a better alternative. And, of course, for any serious illness that may require a life-threatening form of treatment, such as major surgery, there is a well-established route that a patient can follow, which now seems to be in the process of becoming institutionalized as a standard procedure by health insurance firms in the United States—obtaining a second expert opinion about the best available course of action. Recent books and articles by lay persons who have been through the mill themselves as patients suffering from cancer or other dire diseases emphasize the need for obtaining an *independent* recommendation from another expert, whether the first physician likes the idea or not. (See, e.g., Kushner, 1975.)

But what about the vast majority of medical recommendations that most people receive from their physicians most of the time—for low back pain, gastritis, ringworm, edema, hay fever, and hundreds of other ills that do not entail such potentially dangerous consequences as to warrant the special efforts and added expense of obtaining a second expert opinion? What can a patient do to avoid being limited from the outset to a simplistic binary choice—either do the one thing the physician recommends, or do nothing at all? Elsewhere, we (Wheeler & Janis, 1980) indicate how patients can take an active role in inducing their physician to generate a more complete set of viable alternatives and to clarify whichever alternative they mention. The main suggestion is that before the medical consultation is over, the patient should tactfully reverse the roles of interviewer and interviewee, with the patient interviewing the medical expert on those dilemmas about which more information, more clarification, or more alternatives are needed.

One of the main obstacles to the proposed type of interchange is that many physicians are reluctant to answer their patients' questions and some may even resent having to "waste time" doing so. Many years ago, Szasz and Hollender (1956) described the "mutual participation" model of physician–patient interaction as "essentially foreign to medicine." The winds of change in medical practice have not yet become very brisk, although there are some hopeful signs (see Veatch, 1972). Another major difficulty is that when physicians are willing to answer questions, patients are so ineffective at interviewing that they might elicit little more than reassuring answers biased in the direction that the physicians think the patients want to hear. A third is that even when useful information is elicited, the patients may fail to remember it accurately. In order to overcome these obstacles, we propose that patients take account of what is known about the art and science of interviewing as developed by behavioral scientists by learning the standard rules that are "tricks of the trade" (Wheeler & Janis, 1980). Patients require some form of preparation to improve their ability to ask the right questions in the right way at the right time. They must also treat the expert with respect, as someone with superior knowledge and skill in his or her own specialty, and with due regard for the physician's discontent if he or she is one of those who does not welcome the reversal of roles even for just a few minutes. We outline and explain the standard rules for building rapport, avoiding biased questions, preventing ambiguities and misunderstandings, overcoming evasiveness, encouraging full answers, and relying on notes rather than memory.

Applied research is needed to find out whether we are correct in our surmise that the majority of people with just a high-school education could learn to use those rules sufficiently well to elicit valuable information from the medical experts they consult, including clarification of the course of action being recommended and additional viable alternatives that might otherwise remain unmentioned. If a training program on effective interviewing for the general public is developed along these lines, it could also contain useful tips about how to select a well-qualified physician who warrants confidence not only with regard to making accurate diagnoses and giving adequate treatment, but also with regard to referring their patients to the best available specialists when needed. Unfortunately, few research workers in applied behavioral science have the technical background necessary for devising and evaluating any such educational program for the general public. But by working in collaboration with experts who are knowledgeable about present-day medical practices, a number of behavioral scientists can undoubtedly use their methodological expertise to help solve the problems just discussed.

Some health-related decisions do not require medical expertise, but require, instead, personal problem solving to work out ways of living up to well-established public health recommendations, such as cutting down on cigarette smoking, without giving in to temptations to backslide or becoming demoralized. There are many other important examples of personal deficiencies that require alterations in life style in order to reduce risks to health —overeating, neglect of sexual hygiene, insufficient sleep, lack of exercise, careless auto driving, excessive use of alcohol or other drugs, and so forth. Similar personal decisions are often required when patients have to figure out ways of living up to the daily demands of the medical regimens prescribed for diabetes, heart disease, or other chronic illnesses.

From the research literature on decision making, a few useful rules for generating alternatives can be extracted; these rules may be applicable to personal "life style" decisions intended to improve or maintain physical health, and to any other consequential choice. Most of the rules come from studies of "brainstorming" methods that were designed to foster creative problem solving by groups of people working together on executive decisions in business or government. Individuals working alone on personal problems may also benefit from using some of those same rules. Seven main rules have been extracted from the decision-making literature:

> Rule 1. Don't evaluate at the beginning. Think of possible choices and write them down without worrying about what is wrong with them. . . .
> Rule 2. Generate as many alternatives as possible. The more alternatives you consider, the less likely you are to miss the ones that are best. It is always possible later to cut down the choices to a smaller, more manageable set that contains the most promising choices. . . .
> Rule 3. Try to be original. Deliberately try to think up a few far-out choices to include on your list. The choices you find when you are looking for unusual possibilities will frequently turn out to be more practical than they seem at first. . . . One method that some people find helpful in stimulating their imagination is to indulge in frankly wishful daydreams about an ideal outcome. . . .
> Rule 4. Modify flawed alternatives. Use the alternatives that you have already generated as springboards for new ideas. The old ideas can be combined, broken apart, or shifted around to avoid their flaws. . . .
> Rule 5. Ask other people. Everyone looks at the world in a different way.

Combining the ideas from several people produces a wider variety than any one person could have produced. . . .

Rule 6. Use contemplation as a source of ideas. If you set aside some time to engage in free-floating contemplation of a decision you are facing, practically any train of thought or external stimulus can serve as the source of an idea. There is no need to try to be transcendental in these meditations. . . .

Rule 7. Avoid dichotomies. . . . Whenever you are faced with an either-or choice, you should try to take a broader view of the situation and consider alternative ways of solving the main problem confronting you. This could change the yes–no choice into a problem for which there may be other acceptable solutions. (Wheeler & Janis, 1980, pp. 43–48)

Here again, applied research is needed to determine whether it is worthwhile to encourage people to use the rules developed for generating alternatives in making executive decisions when they are making personal decisions to reduce health risks. It should be possible to carry out the research in such settings as weight reduction clinics, where people could be taught the rules for generating viable alternatives and encouraged to use them to arrive at personal solutions to the problems of overeating, and of avoiding temptations to backslide. Criterion measures could include blind ratings of the quality and number of viable alternatives generated, and also behavioral assessments of long-term weight loss. Similar studies could be made on the effectiveness of the rules for generating alternatives among those patients with respiratory disorders, diabetes, heart disease, or other illnesses who have repeatedly tried but failed to work out some way of changing their daily life routines so as to carry out the essential medical regimens prescribed by their physicians.

Evaluating Consequences

Evaluating the consequences of each viable alternative, which is the main cognitive activity during the third stage of effective decision making, is of crucial importance for arriving at a choice that has the best chance of being successful. During this stage, the questions that decision makers ask themselves are "What might happen if I choose this alternative? How will I be affected? How will others be affected? How will I feel about myself? How will others who are important persons in my life feel about me?" A vigilant decision maker not only seeks information to answer these questions, but also uses his or her imagination to construct plausible scenarios about the best, the most probable, and the worst of the likely outcomes for each reasonable alternative.

One of the major difficulties during this stage is that the amount of information about the ramifications and consequences may be so enormous that people cannot keep all the relevant considerations in mind at one time.

The decision makers are likely to fluctuate in their preference first for one alternative and then for another as different consequences come into the focus of their attention. Another major problem is that decision makers often remain unaware of the gaps in their information about drawbacks at the time they commit themselves to a new course of action, such as agreeing to their physicians' recommendation to undergo risky medical treatments. The more gaps there are at the time people become committed, the more likely they will be shaken by setbacks and regret their decisions. When it is too late to reverse the decision without exorbitant costs, people may realize that they have made a bad mistake because they were unaware of crippling objections to what seemed the best thing to do at the time.

A systematic decisional "balance-sheet" procedure (described in Janis & Mann, 1977) has been designed to help people to surmount some of these difficulties by organizing the information they have collected in a useful array, which may enable them to keep in mind the full range of consequences and also make them aware of gaps that need to be filled. The balance sheet for each alternative is divided into the following categories so that none of the important areas will be omitted: (1) utilitarian gains and losses for the decision maker; (2) utilitarian gains and losses for the decision maker's family, friends, or associates who will be affected by the decision; (3) self-approval or self-disapproval, including ethical considerations; and (4) approval or disapproval from others whose opinions are important to the decision maker. Decision makers are instructed to do the best they can to fill out a balance-sheet grid for each alternative, describing the favorable and unfavorable consequences expected in each of the four categories.

Originally developed and found to be fairly effective as an aid for making career decisions, the balance-sheet procedure has also been found to be of value for health-related decisions. (See Janis & Mann, 1977, pp. 149–155.) For example, evidence has been obtained of its effectiveness in a field experiment with women who had signed up for an early-morning exercise class (Hoyt & Janis, 1975). Twenty of the women were assigned on a random basis to a balance-sheet condition in which they were induced to consider carefully all the advantages and disadvantages of regular participation in the exercise class. Twenty others, randomly assigned to the control condition, were given an irrelevant balance-sheet procedure; they were asked to consider all the pros and cons involved in a completely different health-oriented decision—abstaining from cigarette smoking. Records of attendance in the exercise class for a 7-week period were used to obtain an unobtrusive behavioral measure of the effect of these treatments. As predicted, the women given the relevant balance-sheet procedure attended significantly more classes over a 7-week period than did those in the comparison group. Similar results were obtained from a field experiment (Colten & Janis, 1982) conducted in a diet clinic. On a random basis, 80 overweight women were given an interview that elicited either a moderate or low level of self-disclosure, and then either a balance-sheet procedure dealing with the pros and cons of going on a recommended 1,200-calorie diet or a control interview that gave the clients essentially the same information but did not induce them to consider the pros and cons of the alternative courses of action. The women who underwent both the moderate self-disclosure interview and the balance-sheet procedure showed significantly more adherence to the recommended plan than the others did. They sent in more weekly reports concerning their dieting and were found to be more successful in losing weight when they returned for a follow-up session 1 month later.

Observations made in these and other studies on the effectiveness of the balance-sheet procedure indicate that vague feelings of uneasiness, as well as concerns about specific unfavorable consequences, often occur while people are writing down their entries on the balance-sheet grid. Sometimes they become aware of discrepancies between their gut feelings and the rosy picture that emerges from the written entries, which make them realize that they must be leaving out something. When this happens, the procedure can lead to self-insights that go far beyond what is to be expected from a mere bookkeeping operation requiring people to write down what they already know. After filling out a balance sheet, decision makers are likely to ask themselves constructive questions about their remaining uncertainties, such as "Is this desirable outcome really likely to occur?" "Can I really count on it?" Such questioning can lead to a further search for information that could improve their probability estimates of crucial consequences.

Other systematic procedures for structuring the consequences of a set of alternatives are recommended by decision theorists who favor rational-choice models. (See Elstein & Bordage, 1979.) The central feature of these procedures is that the decision maker is required to give ratings of the subjective utility values and probabilities for expected outcomes of each alternative, as illustrated earlier in this chapter by the ratings of SEU obtained in the research by Mausner and Platt (1971) with smokers. But although a number of systematic studies have been carried out to see how well SEU ratings predict actual behavior, such as stopping smoking, little research has been done to see whether the procedure itself has beneficial effects in decreasing postdecisional regret and increasing long-term adherence. Such research would seem to be well worthwhile, because, like the decisional balance-sheet procedure, the methods used to calculate SEUs might help people keep in mind a large number of relevant considerations when they are making their choices, and might also help them to identify gaps requiring a further search for information that could improve their probability estimates.

There is another major source of difficulty when people have to evaluate the uncertain consequences of alternative courses of action. Recent research has repeatedly called attention to a variety of errors that most people make in judging the probabilities that potential events, whether desirable or undesirable, will occur. (See Nisbett & Ross, 1980; Tversky & Kahneman, 1974;

Wheeler & Janis, 1980.) Most people seem to rely on very simple rules of thumb (heuristics) that are sometimes valid for making probability estimates but often lead to gross underestimates or overestimates. According to evidence from psychological research carefully reviewed by Nisbett and Ross (1980), all sorts of people, including medical scientists and statisticians, often make five main types of errors in estimating probabilities: (1) overestimating the likelihood of events that can be easily and vividly imagined; (2) giving too much weight to information about representativeness; (3) ignoring information about base rates; (4) relying too much on evidence from small samples; and (5) failing to discount evidence from biased samples.

The first of these errors, which is perhaps among the most pervasive of all sources of judgmental error, involves the *availability* heuristic—estimating that the probability of an event is high if a vivid image of that event is immediately available when the decision maker starts to think about it.

> Availability is often poorly correlated with actual frequency or probability and thus leads to systematic errors. For example, in our daily lives, we seldom encounter persons suffering from severe respiratory diseases such as emphysema or lung cancer and, consequently, vivid images of those diseases are not available to our imagination when we hear about the health consequences of smoking. We are likely, therefore, to underestimate the likelihood that those illnesses could befall us and to ignore the recommended preventive action of cutting down on smoking. But when an illness is close to home or publicized by the mass media—as when both Mrs. Ford and Mrs. Rockefeller had mastectomies because of breast cancer—the tendency is to increase one's estimate of the likelihood of becoming a victim of such a disease. According to the availability hypothesis, judgments about the probability of being afflicted by any disease depend partly on the extent to which vivid images of that disease are available when people think about it. An implication of this hypothesis is that public health communications could sometimes prove to be more effective if, instead of being restricted to solely verbal warnings and information, they provide, along with factual evidence, a series of concrete images that increase the "availability" of the unfavorable consequences that the warnings are intended to prevent (. . . [provided that account is taken of problems] of excessive fear arousal). (Janis & Rodin, 1979, pp. 494–495)

As yet, little educational research has been done on training people to avoid the common sources of error arising from the widespread use of availability and other heuristics that make for miscalculations about the probable outcome of any type of personal decision, including those pertaining to physical health. Can people be taught in high-school or college courses to be aware of these sources of error? Can such instruction improve their estimates about such matters as the likelihood of contracting certain diseases if one does not take certain precautions and the likelihood of being cured of a given disease by a new medical treatment? Is it worthwhile to try to make people aware of their own tendency to draw general conclusions from a single vivid case, or their tendencies to commit the four other major types of error made in drawing inferences? Perhaps many people would benefit from being given a more accurate conception of what kind of evidence is needed to make sound inferences by teaching them the implications of the following technical definition of probability, which requires evidence from a large number of cases:

$$\text{Probability of an outcome} = \frac{\text{Number of times that outcome occurred}}{\text{Total number of all relevant cases}}$$

The faulty heuristics that many individuals spontaneously rely upon might be at least partially counteracted if people were taught rules embodying this formula in a set of easy-to-remember heuristics—for instance, that little weight should be given to evidence from a single case, no matter how vividly dramatic it may be; or that more weight should be given to large than to small samples, to random than to selected samples, and to unbiased than to biased samples. The development and assessment of a training program on how to make sound probability estimates should, in my opinion, have high priority on the research agenda of educational psychologists who want to improve the decision-making capabilities of the consumers of health services.

At the end of the third stage, a vigilant decision maker arrives at a tentative decision, which occurs when he or she feels satisfied with the answers to the two key questions, "Which alternative is best?" and "Is the best alternative good enough?" In answering these questions, people adopt many different methods for using the information they have acquired about positive and negative consequences. The methods range from deliberate use of the SEU formula (which is rarely adopted) to a purely intuitive use of gut feelings, without conscious employment of any particular decision rule. (See the review of decision rules in Janis & Mann, 1977, Chapter 2.) Little research has been carried out so far on ways of helping people to improve their methods of selecting the best choice, probably in part because there are so many disagreements among decision theorists as to what are the best methods.

Becoming Committed and Adhering to the Decision

Once they arrive at their tentative choice, irrespective of the method they use to get there, vigilant decision makers go on to the next stage, in which they ask two additional key questions: "What implementation and contingency plans do I need to make?" and "Am I really ready to make a commitment?" Sometimes, when decision makers try to answer these questions, they realize that the best alternative is not adequate; in this case, they go back to the earlier stage of generating new alternatives, which may involve modifying the best available alternative in some way that appears to enable it to work better.

We have surmised from numerous case study observations that the decisions most likely to be adhered to in the long run are those for which the decision makers have carried out a careful information search to answer all the key questions from Stage 1 to Stage 4, and with which they feel well satisfied at the time of commitment (Janis & Mann, 1977). This sense of satisfaction pertains not only to whatever choice is made, but also to the steps taken to arrive at it (e.g., ''I feel good about having done everything that could be done to make the right decision'').

It happens fairly often that a decision maker gets ''cold feet'' just after making a tentative choice. One major source of hesitation and vacillation at that point is concern about unknown consequences (e.g., ''What if this brand-new medical treatment turns out to have bad side effects that have not yet been discovered?''). Sometimes this type of concern is a maladaptive anxiety reaction that unnecessarily delays an essential decision, such as undergoing surgery for an operable cancer. But concern about the unknown risks can also be constructive. It may impel the decision maker to consult additional experts who could supply new information that either is reassuring and helps resolve the debatable issues or is unsettling and redirects the choice toward a more satisfactory course of action. A patient who is on the verge of accepting a get-cured-quick remedy promoted by a fast-talking quack or offered by a careless medical practitioner may start wondering about the possibility of a hidden ''catch,'' become constructively worried about the unknown consequences, and seek out additional information that reveals unacceptable risks. In some instances of ''constructive procrastination,'' the decision makers obtain new information that transforms the balance sheet so drastically that they refuse to commit themselves to the unwise course of action they were almost ready to begin pursuing. In other instances, the additional information may be reassuring and may make them feel more confident about committing themselves, so that they carry out the new course of action more conscientiously than they would have without it.

Psychological research has shown that if people can be induced to go through a series of small steps involving minor commitments, they are likely to end up acting in a new way that they would have rejected if the decision to take the new action had been made outright. The best-known example is the ''foot-in-the-door'' technique used by clever salespeople (see Freedman & Fraser, 1966; Janis & Mann, 1977, Chapter 11). Schwartz (1970) found a similar step-by-step commitment sequence in a study of 144 bone-marrow donors. Many of them displayed a ''momentum of compliance'' after they first volunteered to donate blood, then complied with the request to talk with a recruiter, then agreed to have their blood tested for compatability in case they might decide to donate bone marrow, and finally agreed to join the bone-marrow donor pool. Unfortunately, this study did not have a control group that was given only the final request, so we cannot be certain that Schwartz is correct in surmising that the percentage who agreed to donate bone marrow was higher as a result of having gone through the earlier steps in the commitment sequence. His surmise, however, is in line with findings from controlled experiments conducted in psychological laboratories (see Milgram, 1974).

Similar stepwise commitment sequences appear to be by no means rare in medical practice, especially with cancer patients showing signs of metastasis, for whom drastic surgery or massive doses of radiation and chemotherapy are last resorts that their physicians believe are worth trying, despite the high risks and undesirable side effects. Is it justifiable to use a stepwise sequence of commitments, even with extreme cases? From a psychological as well as an ethical standpoint, there are serious objections to using it with the majority of patients who feel somewhat reluctant to undergo standard medical treatments that are unpleasant. A number of studies indicate that patients feel resentful and become uncooperative when the unpleasantness is experienced if they feel that the physician maneuvered them into the disagreeable treatment, or that they had not been given sufficient opportunity to make their own decision about undergoing the treatment (see Janis & Rodin, 1979).

When patients have a sense of personal responsibility for the decision and feel that they went into it with their eyes wide open, they are more likely to tolerate the painful consequences and whatever medical complications or setbacks arise (see Janis, 1983a, 1983b). Under these conditions, a strong sense of commitment keeps postdecisional regret to a minimum. Research on commitment indicates that if a person is given the opportunity to consider the alternatives and then announces his or her intention to an esteemed other, such as a physician or a health counselor in a weight reduction clinic, the person is anchored to the decision not just by anticipated social disapproval, but also by anticipated self-disapproval (Janis & Mann, 1977, Chapter 11; Kiesler, 1971; McFall & Hammen, 1971).

The stabilizing effect of commitment, according to Kiesler's (1971) research, is enhanced by exposure to a mild challenging attack, such as opposing arguments that are easy to refute. The information about risks contained in informed-consent forms and in stress inoculation procedures might serve the function of providing a mild challenging attack by calling attention to the obstacles and drawbacks to be expected, provided that impressive information is also given about how those obstacles and drawbacks can be overcome or minimized.

A study by McFall and Hammen (1971) indicates that three very simple maneuvers by a counselor are successful in helping heavy smokers to reduce their smoking—eliciting a statement of commitment; giving reminders of the commitment; and instructing clients to engage in self-monitoring, which frequently makes the commitment salient. This relatively simple combination was found to be just as effective as several more elaborate therapeutic procedures commonly used in antismoking clinics.

Findings on the positive effects of eliciting commitment have changed the conception of self-control in contemporary psychology. Earlier psychologists thought of self-control, as exemplified by adherence to a no-smoking or dieting regimen, almost exclusively in terms of such predispositional attributes as ego strength and impulse control, just as laymen think that it is all a matter of having "will power." But as Kanfer and Karoly (1972) emphasize, the research evidence on the phenomena of self-control can best be conceptualized in terms of the joint action of situational variables and predispositional variables. Among the situational or environmental determinants are those that influence the degree of *explicitness* of commitment elicited by an interested party and the degree of *volition* (freedom of choice) perceived by the decision maker, both of which influence subsequent self-control in adhering to a difficult course of action such as stopping smoking or sticking to a prescribed diet (see Kiesler, 1971, Chapter 2).

A number of studies have shown that inducing a person to sign a formal agreement as a contract increases the probability that the person will live up to the agreement. For example, an experiment by Kanfer, Cox, Greiner, and Karoly (1974) compared the pain tolerance on the cold-pressor test of two groups. One was a randomly assigned experimental group of female college students who were asked to sign a contract (after having signed the standard informed-consent form). The other was an equivalent group of women randomly assigned to a control condition, in which they were given the same information but were asked to sign only the informed-consent form. The cold-pressor test used by these investigators, which requires subjects to keep one hand immersed in ice water as long as they can despite the increasing pain, is similar to certain kinds of medical treatments that require patients to tolerate pain for as long a time as possible.

Similar positive results are reported by Stekel and Swain (1977) for hypertensive patients. A marked increase in compliance with the medical regimen was observed when the patients were given assistance in working out manageable steps to take for each component of the regimen (such as changing their diet) and then writing it all down in the form of a contract. Other studies show that related external factors, such as the subsequent presence of reminders that make an earlier commitment salient, also influence adherence (see Kiesler, 1971).

When patients arrive at the stage where they are ready to decide whether to undergo whatever treatment is prescribed by the physician, how much help are they likely to get as they consider the key questions of Stage 4? Not very much, according to numerous pertinent studies reviewed by Stone (1979). Nevertheless, as I mention at the beginning of this chapter, there appears to be a growing trend among physicians away from encouraging mature patients to remain exclusively in a passive role, and toward treating patients as clients who are retaining them as expert medical consultants. A change in the direction of an expert–client model is also fostered by grassroots consumer movements. If this trend continues, we can expect that physicians will take on increasingly more responsibility than they have in the past for helping patients to anticipate the difficulties they are likely to encounter in carrying out prescribed medical regimens, and for suggesting how those difficulties might be overcome.

In accordance with the expert–client model, the health care practitioner would take it for granted that he or she needs to fulfill three important functions after making a recommendation: (1) to familiarize the patient with the main drawbacks of the prescribed regimen, as well as the hazards of failing to adhere to that regimen; (2) to explore with the patient any goals that might be incompatible with the prescribed regimen and any foreseeable obstacles that might prevent the patient from carrying it out, with a view to finding a workable compromise and making contingency plans for overcoming the obstacles; and (3) to induce commitment to the prescribed regimen through either a formal contract or an implicit contract, with some provisions for monitoring that will make the commitment salient and provide opportunities for social reinforcement from the expert. All three of these functions would be expected to increase the probability that patients will adhere to the recommendations made by physicians, nurses, counselors in weight reduction clinics, and other health care personnel (Janis, 1982b).

A number of special procedures to foster adherence, in addition to the ones already mentioned, have been developed and at least partially tested. These include such psychological interventions as stress inoculation, teaching positive self-talk as a coping device, focusing attention on short-term goals, and providing social support by means of the "buddy" system (see Janis, 1982b, 1983a; Meichenbaum, 1977; Melamed, 1977).

My own research on effective counseling in health clinics suggests that the here-and-now reward value of maintaining contact with a respected helper can tip the balance in favor of good intentions when the client is tempted to avoid the here-and-now costs and suffering. The new social incentives arising from a positive relationship with a health care professional may be able to compensate for the relative weakness of anticipated long-term gains when the client is reluctant to be committed wholeheartedly to a new course of action requiring short-term deprivations. The hypotheses that my collaborators and I have been investigating derive from analysis of critical phases in an effective helping relationship. These involve (1) acquiring motivational power as a significant "reference person" by becoming a dependable enhancer of the client's self-esteem, (2) avoiding impairment of the supportive relationship when making recommendations that the client may perceive as demands entailing contingent acceptance and rejection, and (3) counteracting the client's disappointment and resentment when direct contact with the supportive helper is terminated. So far our studies have focused mainly on the first phase of a successful supportive relationship. In a series of field experiments conducted in weight reduction clinics and other health-related clinical settings, we have found that adherence to a counselor's recommendations is significantly increased if the counselor (1) elicits a moderate level of self-disclosure rather than a very low or a very high level and (2) gives consistently positive feedback conveying acceptance (Janis, 1982b, 1983b). Our preliminary results for certain of the variables in the second and third phase, such as giving communications that build confidence about succeeding without the continued aid of the counselor, appear to be promising with regard to increasing the long-term effectiveness of supportive health care providers.

IMPROVEMENTS IN THE QUALITY OF RESEARCH ON ADHERENCE

In the past, research studies on psychological interventions that can affect adherence to medical recommendations have been plagued by methodological deficiencies, which have precluded drawing any definitive conclusions. In most of the early studies during the 1950s and 1960s, inadequate controls were used, and the interventions consisted of complex packages of psychological treatments that confounded a number of potentially potent variables. There was no way to draw dependable inferences from such data as to which variables in isolation or in interaction were responsible for whatever allegedly positive effects were found. Another deficiency was that the dependent variables used to judge the effectiveness of the treatments often relied upon verbal reports by patients (which were influenced by demand characteristics and other sources of distortion) or subjective judgments by the investigators (which were contaminated by their knowledge of which patients received the special treatments).

Fortunately, in recent years there has been a marked improvement in the quality of research on psychological interventions. Many investigators in behavioral medicine, like those in the biomedical sciences, are now ready to admit that nothing improves the observed effectiveness of a new intervention so much as the lack of controls. More and more investigators have come to realize the need for using factorial designs to investigate the main effects and interactions of the independent variables and to hold constant all other potentially pertinent factors, such as the type of patient being treated, duration of the illness, prognosis, amount and quality of contact with health care practitioners, and the like.

With regard to the dependent measures used to assess the effectiveness of the psychological interventions, investigators nowadays are likely to arrange for blind ratings, which eliminate the problem of contaminated judgments. Above all, they are likely to rely less on verbal reports and more on objective behavioral data, such as weight loss, to assess adherence to a recommended regimen. As a result of these essential improvements in methodology, we can expect not only an increase in basic understanding of the psychological determinants of adherence to medical regimens, but also more dependable information about effective interventions that can be used by practitioners to help patients carry out sound decisions to improve or maintain their health.

R E F E R E N C E S

Becker, M. H., Kaback, M., Rosenstock, I. M., & Ruth, M. Some influences on public participation in a genetic screening program. *Journal of Community Health*, 1975, *1*, 3–14.
Becker, M. H., & Maiman, L. A. Sociobehavioral determinants of compliance with health and medical care recommendations. *Medical Care*, 1975, *13*, 10–24.
Becker, M. H., Maiman, L. A., Kirscht, J. P., Haefner, D. P., & Drachman, R. H. The health belief model and dietary compliance: A field experiment. *Journal of Health and Social Behavior*, 1977, *18*, 348–366.
Bem, D. J. Self-perception theory. In L. Berkowitz (Ed.), *Advances in experimental social psychology*. New York: Academic Press, 1972.
Blackwell, B. The literature of delay in seeking medical care for chronic illnesses. *Health Education Monographs*, 3(Whole No. 16), 1963.
Boyd, J. R., Covington, T. R., Stanaszek, W. F., & Coussons, R. T. Drug-defaulting: II. Analysis of noncompliance patterns. *American Journal of Hospital Pharmacy*, 1974, *31*, 485–491.
Broadhurst, A. Applications of the psychology of decisions. In M. P. Feldman & A. Broadhurst (Eds.), *Theoretical and experimental bases of the behavior therapies*. London: Wiley, 1976.
Chu, C. C. Fear arousal, efficacy, and imminency. *Journal of Personality and Social Psychology*, 1966, *4*, 517–524.
Colton, M. E., & Janis, I. L. Effects of moderate self-disclosure interviews and the balance-sheet procedure. In I. L. Janis (Ed.), *Counseling on personal decisions: Theory and research on short-term helping relationships*. New Haven: Yale University Press, 1982.
Darley, S. *Cognitive and personality factors in emotional expression under conditions of false heart-rate feedback*. Unpublished doctoral dissertation, New York University, 1969.
Edwards, W. The theory of decision making. *Psychological Bulletin*, 1954, *51*, 380–417.
Elstein, A. A., & Bordage, G. Psychology of clinical reasoning. In G. C. Stone, F. Cohen, & N. E. Adler, (Eds.), *Health psychology*. San Francisco: Jossey-Bass, 1979.
Festinger, L. *Conflict, decision and dissonance*. Stanford, Calif.: Stanford University Press, 1964.
Fishbein, M. Attitude and the prediction of behavior. In M. Fishbein (Ed.), *Readings in attitude theory and measurement*. New York: Wiley, 1967.
Fishbein, M. Consumer beliefs and behavior with respect to cigarette smoking: A critical analysis of the public literature. In *Federal Trade Commission report to Congress pursuant to the Public Health Cigarette Smoking Act for the year 1976*. Washington, D.C.: U.S. Government Printing Office, 1977.
Freedman, J. L., & Fraser, S. C. Compliance without pressure: The foot-in-the-door technique. *Journal of Personality and Social Psychology*, 1966, *4*, 195–202.
Gerard, H. B. Choice difficulty, dissonance, and the decision sequence. *Journal of Personality*, 1967, *35*, 91–108.
Goldsen, R. K., Gerhardt, P. T., & Handy, V. H. Some factors related to patient delay in seeking diagnosis for cancer symptoms. *Cancer*, 1957, *10*, 1–7.
Hackett, T. P., & Cassem, N. H. Psychological management of the myocardial infarction patient. *Journal of Human Stress*, 1975, *1*, 25–38.

Harris, V. A., & Jellison, J. M. Fear-arousing communications, false physiological feedback and the acceptance of recommendations. *Journal of Experimental Social Psychology*, 1971, *7*, 269–279.

Hayes-Bautista, D. E. Modifying the treatment: Patient compliance, patient control and medical care. *Social Science and Medicine*, 1976, *10*, 233–238.

Hochbaum, G. *Public participation in medical screening programs: A sociopsychological study* (DHEW Publication No. (PHS) 572). Washington, D.C.: U.S. Government Printing Office, 1958.

Hovland, C. I., Janis, I. L., & Kelley, H. H. *Communication and persuasion.* New Haven: Yale University Press, 1953.

Howard, J., & Strauss, A. (Eds.). *Humanizing health care.* New York: Wiley, 1975.

Hoyt, M. F., & Janis, I. L. Increasing adherence to a stressful decision via a motivational balance-sheet procedure: A field experiment. *Journal of Personality and Social Psychology*, 1975, *31*, 833–839.

Insko, C. A., Arkoff, A., & Insko, U. M. Effects of high and low fear arousing communications upon opinions toward smoking. *Journal of Experimental Social Psychology*, 1965, *1*, 256–266.

Inui, J. F., Yourtee, E. L., & Williamson, J. W. Improved outcomes in hypertension after physician tutorials. *Annals of Internal Medicine*, 1976, *84*, 646–651.

Janis, I. L. Effects of fear arousal on attitude change: Recent developments in theory and research. In L. Berkowitz (Ed.), *Advances in experimental social psychology* (Vol. 3). New York: Academic Press, 1967.

Janis, I. L. *Stress and frustration.* New York: Harcourt Brace Jovanovich, 1971.

Janis, I. L. Vigilance and decision-making in personal crises. In C. V. Coelho, D. A. Hamburg, & J. E. Adams (Eds.), *Coping and adaptation.* New York: Academic Press, 1974.

Janis, I. L. *Groupthink: Psychological studies of policy decisions and fiascos.* Boston: Houghton Mifflin, 1982. (a)

Janis, I. L. (Ed.). *Counseling on personal decisions: Theory and research on short-term helping relationships.* New Haven: Yale University Press, 1982. (b)

Janis, I. L. Stress inoculation in health care: Theory and research. In D. Meichenbaum & M. Jaremko (Eds.), *Stress prevention and management: A cognitive–behavioral approach.* New York: Plenum, 1983. (a)

Janis, I. L. The role of social support in adherence to stressful decisions. *American Psychologist*, 1983, *38*, 143–160. (b)

Janis, I. L., & Feshbach, S. Effects of fear-arousing communications. *Journal of Abnormal and Social Psychology*, 1953, *48*, 78–92.

Janis, I. L., & Mann, L. *Decision making: A psychological analysis of conflict, choice, and commitment.* New York: Free Press, 1977.

Janis, I. L., & Rodin, J. Attribution, control and decision-making: Social psychology in health care. In G. C. Stone, F. Cohen, & N. E. Adler (Eds.), *Health psychology.* San Francisco: Jossey-Bass, 1979.

Janis, I. L., & Terwilliger, R. An experimental study of psychological resistance to fear-arousing communications. *Journal of Abnormal and Social Psychology*, 1962, *65*, 403–410.

Jenkins, C. D. Psychosocial modifiers of response to stress. *Journal of Human Stress*, 1979, *5*, 3–15.

Jones, E. E., & Johnson, C. A. Delay of consequences and the riskiness of decisions. *Journal of Personality*, 1973, *42*, 613–637.

Kahneman, D., & Tversky, A. Prospect theory: An analysis of decision under risk. *Econometrica*, 1979, *47*, 263–292.

Kanfer, F. H., Cox, L. E., Greiner, J. M., & Karoly, P. Contracts, demand characteristics and self-control. *Journal of Personality and Social Psychology*, 1974, *30*, 605–619.

Kanfer, F. H., & Karoly, P. Self-control: A behavioristic excursion into the lion's den. *Behavior Therapy*, 1972, *3*, 398–416.

Kasl, S. V. Issues in patient adherence to health care regimens. *Journal of Human Stress*, 1975, *1*, 5–18.

Kasl, S. V., & Cobb, S. Health behavior, illness behavior, and sick role behavior. *Archives of Environmental Health*, 1966, *12*, 246–266, 531–541.

Kiesler, C. A. (Ed.). *The psychology of commitment*. New York: Academic Press, 1971.

Kirscht, J. P. Communication between patients and physicians. *Annals of Internal Medicine*, 1977, *86*, 499–500.

Kirscht, J. P., & Rosenstock, I. M. Patients' problems in following recommendations of health experts. In G. C. Stone, F. Cohen, & N. E. Adler (Eds.), *Health psychology*. San Francisco: Jossey-Bass, 1979.

Krisher, H. P., Darley, S. A., & Darley, J. M. Fear provoking recommendations, intentions to take preventive actions, and actual preventive action. *Journal of Personality and Social Psychology*, 1973, *26*, 301–308.

Kushner, R. *Breast cancer: A personal history and an investigative report*. New York: Harcourt Brace Jovanovich, 1975.

Kutner, B., Makover, H. B., & Oppenheim, A. Delay in the diagnosis and treatment of cancer: A critical analysis of the literature. *Journal of Chronic Diseases*, 1958, *7*, 95–120.

Lee, W. *Decision theory and human behavior*. New York: Wiley, 1971.

Leventhal, H. Changing attitudes and habits to reduce risk factors in chronic disease. *American Journal of Cardiology*, 1973, *31*, 571–580.

Leventhal, H., Singer, R. E., & Jones, S. Effects of fear and specificity of recommendations. *Journal of Personality and Social Psychology*, 1965, *2*, 20–29.

Leventhal, H., & Watts, J. C. Sources of resistance to fear-arousing communications on smoking and lung cancer. *Journal of Personality*, 1966, *34*, 155–175.

Lewin, K. *Field theory in social science*. New York: Harper, 1951.

Ley, P., & Spelman, M. S. Communications in an out-patient setting. *British Journal of Social and Clinical Psychology*, 1965, *4*, 114–116.

Mann, L., Janis, I. L., & Chaplin, R. The effects of anticipation of forthcoming information on predecisional processes. *Journal of Personality and Social Psychology*, 1969, *11*, 10–16.

Mausner, B., & Platt, E. S. *Smoking: A behavioral analysis*. Elmsford, N.Y.: Pergamon Press, 1971.

McFall, R. M., & Hammen, L. Motivation, structure, and self-monitoring: Role of nonspecific factors in smoking reduction. *Journal of Consulting and Clinical Psychology*, 1971, *37*, 80–86.

McGuire, W. J. The nature of attitudes and attitude change. In G. Lindzey & E. Aronson (Eds.), *The handbook of social psychology* (Vol. 3). Reading, Mass.: Addison-Wesley, 1969.

McGuire, W. J. Behavioral medicine, public health, and communication theories. *National Forum*, 1980, 18–31.

Meichenbaum, D. *Cognitive-behavior modification: An integrative approach*. New York: Plenum, 1977.

Melamed, B. G. Psychological preparation for hospitalization. In S. Rachman (Ed.), *Contributions to medical psychology* (Vol. 1). New York: Pergamon Press, 1977.

Milgram, S. *Obedience to authority*. New York: Harper & Row, 1974.

Miller, D. W., & Star, M. K. *The structure of human decisions*. Englewood Cliffs, N.J.: Prentice-Hall, 1967.

Nisbett, R., & Ross, L. *Human inference*. Englewood Cliffs, N.J.: Prentice-Hall, 1980.

Parsons, T. The sick role and the role of the physician reconsidered. *Milbank Memorial Fund Quarterly*, 1975, *53*, 257–278.

Quesada, G. M. Language and communication barriers for health delivery to a minority group. *Social Science and Medicine*, 1976, *10*, 323–327.

Raiffa, H. *Decision analysis*. Reading, Mass.: Addison-Wesley, 1968.

Rapoport, A., & Wallsten, T. S. Individual decision behavior. *Annual Review of Psychology*, 1972, *23*, 131–175.

Rogers, R. W., & Deckner, C. W. Effects of fear appeals and physiological arousal upon emotion, attitudes, and cigarette smoking. *Journal of Personality and Social Psychology*, 1975, *32*, 220–230.

Rogers, R. W., & Mewborn, C. R. Fear appeals and attitude change: Effects of a threat's noxious-ness, probability of occurrence and the efficacy of coping responses. *Journal of Personality and Social Psychology*, 1976, *34*, 54–61.

Rogers, R. W., & Thistlethwaite, D. L. Effects of fear arousal and reassurance upon attitude change. *Journal of Personality and Social Psychology*, 1970, *15*, 227–233.

Rummel, R. M., & Radar, J. W. Coping with executive stress. *Personnel Journal*, 1978, *55*, 305–332.

Sackett, D. L. The magnitude of compliance and noncompliance. In D. L. Sackett & R. B. Hayes (Eds.), *Compliance with therapeutic regimens*. Baltimore: Johns Hopkins University Press, 1976.

Schwartz, S. Elicitation of moral obligation and self-sacrificing behavior: An experimental study of volunteering to be a bone marrow donor. *Journal of Personality and Social Psychology*, 1970, *15*, 283–293.

Simon, H. A. *Administrative behavior: A study of decision-making processes in administrative organi-zation* (3rd ed.). New York: Free Press, 1976.

Slovic, P., Fishhoff, B., & Lichtenstein, S. Behavioral decision theory. *Annual Review of Psychology*, 1977, *28*, 1–39.

Stekel, S., & Swain, M. The use of written contracts to increase adherence. *Hospitals*, 1977, *51*, 81–84.

Stone, G. C. Patient compliance and the role of the expert. *Journal of Social Issues*, 1979, *35*, 34–59.

Szasz, T. S., & Hollender, M. H. A contribution to the philosophy of medicine: The basic models of the doctor–patient relationship. *Archives of Internal Medicine*, 1956, *97*, 585–592.

Tversky, A., & Kahneman, D. Judgment under uncertainty: Heuristics and biases. *Science*, 1974, *185*, 1124–1131.

Valins, S. Cognitive effects of false heart-rate feedback. *Journal of Personality and Social Psychology*, 1966, *4*, 400–408.

Veatch, R. Updating the Hippocratic oath. *Medical Opinion*, 1972, *8*, 56–61.

Waitzkin, H., & Stoeckle, J. D. Information control and the micropolitics of health care: Sum-mary of an ongoing research project. *Social Science and Medicine*, 1976, *10*, 263–276.

Walsten, T. S. *Three biases in the cognitive processing of diagnostic information*. Unpublished manu-script, Psychometric Laboratory, University of North Carolina at Chapel Hill, 1978.

Wheeler, D., & Janis, I. L. *A practical guide for making decisions*. New York: Free Press, 1980.

CHAPTER 10

Compliance: A Self-Regulation Perspective

Howard Leventhal
University of Wisconsin–Madison

Rick Zimmerman
University of Miami

Mary Gutmann
University of Wisconsin School of Medicine
Mount Sinai Hospital, Milwaukee

Improvements in biomedical knowledge no longer seem to translate into marked improvements in morbidity and mortality; as a nation, we are "doing better and feeling worse" (Knowles, 1977). Two reasons for disappointment immediately come to mind. First, the very high level of our health status may preclude dramatic improvement. Rates for many major killers are at or approaching zero (Dingle, 1973; Lerner & Anderson, 1963). Second, our current ills are different from those we faced at the turn of the century, when such infectious diseases as pneumonia, tuberculosis, and gastrointestinal enteritis were the top three causes of mortality, and coronary disease and malignancies ranked fourth and eighth. By 1970, the top three infectious diseases of 1900 were no longer among the top 10 causes of mortality, and diseases of the heart ranked first and cancers ranked second (Dingle, 1973). These last illnesses have proven refractory to technological solution: There are no "cures" for cancer or heart disease. The best medical science can offer are halfway technologies, which slow disease progression or allow the individual to achieve a reasonable level of comfort and involvement in life while moving inexorably toward early death (Thomas, 1977).

There are two less obvious reasons for our disappointment. First, we have come to believe that biomedicine was responsible for the disappearance of the killer diseases of the 19th century, and, therefore, we expect sharp reductions in morbidity and mortality with each widely heralded biomedical advance. This belief is incorrect, however; improvements in diet and hygiene, due to an improved standard of living, were the major factors in eliminating infectious disease (Dingle, 1973; Dubos, 1968; McKeown, 1976; McKinlay & McKinlay, 1981).

The second of the less obvious factors is that we have been slow to recognize barriers to the application of existing technology. The level of inoculation for polio, diphtheria, tetanus, and other preventable disorders is dangerously low. Mortimer (1978) estimates that only 64.8% of 1- to 4-year-old children had received three or more doses of poliomyelitis vaccine in 1975, as compared to 73.9% in 1965; only 75.2% of 1- to 4-year-olds had received three or more doses of diphtheria, tetanus, and pertussis vaccine in 1975. In too many areas, too many are unprotected (Center for Disease Control, 1976).

The picture is even less favorable for other medical problems. Hypertension is a known and alterable risk factor, and reductions in pressure reduce morbidity and mortality (Veterans Administration Cooperative Study Group on Antihypertensive Agents, 1967, 1970). Yet in 1970, follow-up for treatment was sought by only half of those detected with high blood pressure at screening sites, and only half of those who followed up remained in treatment. And of those that remained, only half achieved adequate levels of blood pressure control (Schoenberger, Stamler, Shekelle, & Shekelle, 1972). This means that no more than 12.5% of the known hypertensives in the population under study were under control. Recent statistics (Ward, 1977) suggest an improvement over the "half" rule, and we can now expect one-third of the detected cases to fail to seek treatment, one-third to drop out, and one-third to be uncontrolled. This means that 30% of the known hypertensives are controlled, while 70% are at risk for the consequences of high blood pressure. The best of inoculants cannot work their magic if they go unused.

"Noncompliance" to a wide range of preventive as well as curative actions appears, therefore, to be a clear barrier to the further decline of morbidity and mortality. The data are similar over a wide range of actions: People are about as likely to quit cigarettes or to stick with their diets as they are to adhere to blood pressure treatment. Noncompliance is nearly equally likely for simple as for complex preventive actions and for prescribed treatments.

THREE PERSPECTIVES ON THE COMPLIANCE TOPIC

The substantial level of noncompliance across a variety of prescribed behaviors has suggested that the personality characteristics of the participants might be the cause of noncompliance in medical treatment and prevention programs. This perspective reflects in part a biomedical view of the compliance problem. This personal responsibility view has been supplanted in part by that of behavioral modification, where investigators avoid blaming the individuals for noncompliance and focus instead on the environmental conditions promoting adherence to a behavioral program (Stunkard, 1979). Most recently, investigators have taken yet another step away from focusing on the prescribed action and have attempted to understand the point of view of the participant by using theories of self-regulation. We discuss each of these perspectives briefly here (for a more extended treatment, see Leventhal, Meyer, & Gutmann, 1980).

The Medical Model and Compliance

Stimson (1974) has suggested that labeling patients as "noncompliant" helps define a relationship in which the practitioner is viewed as an expert acting to benefit an uninformed help seeker. The uninformed patient presents a complaint that reflects an underlying disease process, and the expert practitioner diagnoses the process and prescribes a chemical corrective. If the patient is following his or her "best interests," he or she must comply with the prescribed treatment. Not adhering to treatment suggests ignorance, laziness, or willful neglect. The medical model encourages labeling the patient as "noncompliant" and searching for characteristics that differentiate the noncompliant person from the compliant person. Personality labeling is abetted because practitioners are already focused on attaching a disease label to the patient. The brevity of the medical encounter and its focus on specific diagnostic procedures also screens the practitioner from the type of information that might work against labeling. For example, the practitioner is usually ignorant of the many environmental conditions associated with the onset of symptoms, the decision to seek care, and failure to comply with treatment. Hence, the practitioner may fail to recognize that symptoms are as prevalent in those who are not seeking help as in those who are, and he or she may misperceive the basis for the patient's visit and draw erroneous conclusions about the likelihood and the determinants of noncompliance.

Stunkard (1979) suggests that the term "noncompliance" has focused investigators on the patient and produced a body of null findings. Compliers and noncompliers have been compared on personality characteristics, demographic factors such as income and education, and variables such as ethnicity (M. Marston, 1970; J. H. Mitchell, 1974), all to no avail. These studies have produced a body of insignificant findings, in which no factor is consistently associated with following or not following medical prescriptions. Stunkard (1979) concludes that the search to define the characteristics of the noncomplier has failed.

The Behavioral Viewpoint: Compliance as Adherence

The redefinition of the compliance problem as one of adherence may seem of little significance, but slight changes in perspective can lead to major changes in theory and research. When we talk about "compliers" and "noncompliers," we are talking about individuals and their characteristics. When we talk about adherence, we are talking about what people *do*. This shift of perspective led investigators of diet and weight control to move away from studies of the attributes or character structure and childhood experiences of obese persons (Bruch, 1973) to studies of how obese persons ate (Stunkard, 1975). When, where, how often, and how much did such individuals eat? What cues preceded eating? What did the eating response pattern look like? Was it fast or slow? Was the food savored or gulped? What were the consequences (i.e., how did the individuals feel about themselves after eating)?

The focus on the behavior of obese persons led to the development and rigorous testing of behavioral procedures for monitoring food intake, eating in the same situation at all times, eating small portions, eating slowly, savoring the food, rewarding oneself for adhering to proper eating behavior, and paying less attention to the readings on the scale (Stunkard, 1975, 1979). These techniques were designed and first used in single-case or single-condition studies (Stuart, 1967, 1971), and then evaluated against increasingly complex controls and applied to real-world eating programs (Garb & Stunkard, 1974; Levitz & Stunkard, 1974). A similar evolution took place in antismoking therapies; attention gradually shifted from concern with the personality dispositions and motives underlying smoking to smoking behavior itself (Bernstein & McAlister, 1976; Leventhal & Cleary, 1980; Lichtenstein, 1971; Lichtenstein & Danaher, 1975; Mausner & Platt, 1971; Yates, 1975).

There is little reason to dispute the dramatic impact of the behavioral approach. Behavioral regimens typically produced high (60–90%) success rates in weight control, quitting smoking, and other such targets; they worked better than anything that had been tried before. Unfortunately, immediate posttreatment success was seldom followed by the maintenance of change over the long term. Hunt and his associates (Hunt & Bespalec, 1974; Hunt & Matarazzo, 1971) plotted therapeutic outcomes for three target behaviors: withdrawal from smoking, heroin, and alcohol. For all three, 60% of those "successfully" treated had reverted to prior behavior patterns 3 months after therapy, increasing to 70% at 6 months and 75% at 12 months.

The failure to achieve long-term adherence stimulated the addition of new components to behavior therapy packages (e.g., Delahunt & Curran, 1976; Marlatt & Gordon, 1980). Some have attempted to add a variety of posttreatment environmental supports, supplying clients with booster sessions (Levine, Green, Deeds, Chwalow, Russell, & Finlay, 1979) and social support systems (Levy, 1980). Others have focused on increasing the intensity of patients' motivation and enlarging on their understanding of their illness or risk problem (Leventhal, Singer, & Jones, 1965; Taylor, Sackett, & Haynes, 1978). As we point out, none of these uniformly enhanced long-term success. While these outcomes are typically regarded as failures of technology (Zifferblatt, 1975), we believe they are failures of theory. Behavioral approaches treat behavior as a product of antecedent environmental conditions. They do not conceptualize behavior as "future-oriented" or goal-directed. Hence, most behavioral attempts at resolving the problem of long-term compliance have focused on the treatment itself—adding more stimuli, introducing more environmental constraints, or generating better matches between subjects and particular therapies (Leventhal & Cleary, 1979, 1980)—and have not examined how best to integrate behavioral change into an individual's long-term life patterns.

Control Theory: Adherence as Self-Regulation

Investigators are now introducing control or systems concepts into contemporary behavioral medical research (e.g., Carver, 1979; Carver & Scheier, 1982; Leventhal, 1970, 1982a, 1982b; Miller, Galanter, & Pribram, 1960; Nerenz & Leventhal, 1983; G. E. Schwartz, 1979a). Control theory views behavior as pulled toward goals rather than pushed by stimuli (Arbib, 1972; Powers, 1973). When applied to health and illness behavior, control theory has emphasized that people generate their own representations of health threats, and plan and act in relation to their representations (Hayes-Bautista, 1976; Lazarus, 1966; Leventhal, Meyer, & Gutmann, 1980; Leventhal, Meyer, & Nerenz, 1980). The representation of a health problem is built up from information from media, friends, health practitioners and family members, as well as from symptoms and sensations from the body. Information from all of these sources is integrated into a representation of a current illness episode or a future illness threat. The representation then guides planning and action.

Planning and action, or coping, is directed by the representation. But acting upon the representation depends on at least three other types of factors: (1) the individual's self-esteem or sense of effectance (Bandura, 1977); (2) the individual's strategies for relating himself or herself to problem situations and for testing the effectiveness of response alternatives; and (3) the individual's repertoire of specific coping responses or coping tactics and beliefs in the effectiveness of these responses (M. H. Becker & Maiman, 1975; Mischel, 1973). "Effectance," or self-esteem, appears to combine beliefs that one can manage the environment and one's own behaviors, including one's own emotional reactions (T. J. Rosen, Terry, & Leventhal, 1982). These coping factors appear to play an important role in stimulating the individual to view a situation or problem as manageable; in combination with the individual's view or representation of the problem, they will lead to specific coping reactions that are appraised for their effectiveness in meeting specified goals (Folkman & Lazarus, 1980; Lazarus, 1966; Lazarus & Launier, 1978; Leventhal, Meyer, & Nerenz, 1980; Leventhal & Nerenz, 1983). If the response meets expectations, the behavior can be stopped or maintained at the same level of output. If it does not meet expectations, a new behavior will be tried, or the amplitude of the old behavior will be altered.

Finally, strategies for appraising outcomes determine the way an outcome is interpreted—that is, whether the response, the representation of the problem, or the self (effectance) is seen as effective or as ineffective (Kanfer, 1977; Marlatt & Gordon, 1980). An example of a strategy would be the individual's view of himself or herself as an observer or experimenter whose goal is to test and accept or reject specific acts, in contrast to a view of the self as responsible for success or failure. The former strategy can preserve the sense of effectance when specific responses fail, as it allows the individual to see the response failure as a sign of ability to discover and reject ineffective coping tactics, and not as a sign of self-inadequacy.

The basic components we have reviewed—the representation, coping, and appraisal of outcomes—comprise the basic constituents of a self-regulative or self-control mechanism. Control theory would predict that long-term self-regulative action will take place if a behavioral treatment constructs such a system in the mind of the patient—that is, if it is learned, seen as one's own and makes sense in the individual's total life context (Antonovsky, 1979).

Comparison of the Three Perspectives

The medical, behavioral, and self-regulation models can be compared on both theoretical and methodological grounds. We do this to illustrate the important ways in which the models differ with respect to generating procedures for enhancing compliance and selecting measures for its assessment.

Conceptual Comparisons

The most important difference among the models concerns their perspective on the behavior of a patient. The medical model clearly adopts an external or observer frame of reference, while the self-regulation model takes an internal or actor frame of reference (Jones & Nisbett, 1971). Thus, the medical viewpoint defines a medical goal (destruction of a disease agent and correction of specific pathology) and prescribes a medical action. The patient's viewpoint—his or her understanding of the disease process or the means to cure it—is irrelevant (Engel, 1977; Fabrega, 1975; Stimson, 1974). The self-regulation model, on the other hand, requires that we define the patient's construction or representation of the problem—that is, what he or she views as the nature or identity of the illness; its cause, consequences, and duration; and appropriate steps for intervention. Hence, the definition of the illness, the goals of treatment, and the means of reaching them may differ from those defined by the medical model.

For example, the medical perspective is indifferent to a patient's *beliefs* that a symptom (e.g., headache) indicates the presence of a disease (e.g., high blood pressure), and it is typically unconcerned as to whether a patient has the specific skills needed to perform a recommended coping response. The self-regulation model, on the other hand, is concerned with individuals' projection of goals for their behavior—for example, whether they expect treatment to eliminate their symptoms, how quickly they expect this to happen, and how they evaluate treatments that fail to meet their criteria (Leventhal & Nerenz, 1983).

Behavioral models fall in between the medical and self-regulation perspectives and differ among themselves in the degree to which they adopt an observer or actor perspective on the compliance problem. Operant approaches, in many instances, focus on regulating rewards for behavior, with little regard for how they are perceived by the actor. Not all operant approaches ignore these factors, and some investigators conduct empirical investigation to determine which rewards are in fact rewarding and which cues are guides for behavior.

Wooley, Blackwell, and Winget's (1978) effort to construct an operant environment to control pain behaviors provides an excellent example of the more actor-oriented perspective. To identify rewards, patients were instructed to give tokens whenever someone interacted with them in the way they liked. The results showed that patients gave tokens for (and were presumably rewarded by) other people's behaviors that expressed interest in pain (e.g., statements of sympathy), but did not give tokens for expressions of interest in work or other outgoing forms of social behavior. These investigators then created an operant environment that ignored pain behaviors and rewarded problem-solving activity. The selection of rewards and actions was guided in part by the data from the prior study of token disbursement, which was obviously a means of obtaining information on the patients' view of their environment.

Still more attention is paid to the patient's perspective in other behavioral frames of reference. The health belief model (M. H. Becker, 1974, 1976; M. H. Becker & Maiman, 1975; Rosenstock, 1975) is one of a class of so-called "social learning models" (see Leventhal, Meyer, & Gutmann, 1980), in which behavior is viewed as the product of such internal, cognitive mediators as perceived goals, perceived instrumentalities, and the perception of the probability that particular actions will lead to particular goals in a specific environment (Bandura, 1977; Mischel, 1973; Rotter, 1954). But these models encase the actor's view of his or her environment in the conceptual framework of decision theory (i.e., in probabilities of actions reaching outcomes), when we have no assurance that people make use of probability and value notions, and if they do, when and how they do so. These approaches have also tended to ignore precisely how the actor views the problem and the actions needed to solve it—that is, how illness or an illness threat are experienced, and how the required responses are viewed and understood.

Methodological Comparison

The differences among the models become more clear and more salient if we try to use them to develop interventions and to select measures for research or practice. We discuss interventions first.

Interventions: The Independent Variables in Compliance Research

A major failing of the medical model is its inadequacy for educational intervention. The medical model provides content about disease threat and disease process, but no clues as to how to educate other than the suggestion that the practitioner instruct, exhort, and demand. None of these approaches has been demonstrated to be effective (Haynes, 1979b).

The behavioral perspective offers a far broader and more potent array of tools for intervention in both medical treatment and prevention. One important disadvantage, however, of the behavioral approach is that it is usually dependent upon a costly, therapeutic relationship, though the advent of computer-controlled (Lang, Melamed, & Hart, 1970; McFall & Lillesand, 1971; Muehlenhard, 1981) and self-instructional manuals represents a major advance and perhaps a departure from traditional behavioral therapies (Glasgow & Rosen, 1978; Lando, 1975; G. M. Rosen, 1976). Second, as we have already mentioned, behavioral therapies have yet to solve the problem of long-term adherence. When the environmental supports introduced by therapy are withdrawn, the control of the behavior reverts to pretherapy regulatory systems, and most therapeutic gains are lost (Hunt & Matarazzo, 1971; Kirschenbaum & Tomarkin, 1982; Leventhal & Cleary, 1980). The environmental focus of behavioral theory has failed to suggest a procedure for stabilizing or internalizing new control systems.

Self-regulation theory brings two key sets of factors into focus: (1) the components underlying the regulation of the behavior (Leventhal & Nerenz, 1983; Leventhal & Cleary, 1980), and (2) concern for the match between the factors regulating behavior and the individual's perception of these factors (if there is a discrepancy between the determinants of the actor's behavior and his or her perception of these determinants, the outlook for long-term adherence is substantially lessened; see also Nerenz & Leventhal, 1983). While self-regulatory notions are less well evaluated, they have been incorporated into behavioral models, and empirical tests suggest great promise for long-term success (e.g., Kanfer, 1977; Marlatt & Gordon, 1980).

Endpoints: The Dependent Measures in Compliance Research

The medical model focuses first on mortality and morbidity and on the physiological changes that precede them. While these are important endpoints, changes in medical indicators do not provide evidence on the effectiveness of a compliance-inducing technology (Leventhal, Safer, Cleary, & Gutmann, 1980; Levine et al., 1979). One must demonstrate that the compliance intervention has changed behavior and show that the change has been responsible for reductions in the epidemiological indicators. A program may change behavior and fail to alter these indicators if there is no relationship between behavior and medical endpoints or if the relationship between them is not reversible; for example, smoking may cause lung disease, but stopping smoking may not reverse established disease. Medical indicators can also change for reasons other than changes in behavior. In any case, medical indicators cannot be used by themselves to assess the effectiveness of a behaviorally oriented compliance intervention.

Behavioral approaches focus on actions; that is, the target of the compliance intervention trial is the target of evaluation. If the goal is to have patients comply with use of penicillin for rheumatic fever (Heinzelmann, 1962), take a tetanus inoculation (Leventhal *et al.*, 1965; Leventhal, Jones, & Trembly, 1966), adhere to diet, exercise, and pill taking for diabetes (Lowe & Lutzker, 1979), or take medication for hypertension control (Haynes, Sackett, Gibson, Hackett, Taylor, Roberts, & Johnson, 1976; Sackett, Haynes, Gibson, Hackett, Taylor, Roberts, & Johnson, 1975), the performance of the behavior is the key dependent measure. Some behavioral approaches focus on actions leading up to the specified dependent measure—that is, on details of the act and on important actions that may immediately precede and follow the primary behavioral criterion. For example, weight control programs specify a host of specific actions for reducing caloric intake, ranging from eating smaller portions, substituting low- for high-calorie foods, eating slowly and chewing food deliberately, always eating in the same place, and eating at similar times each day (Stunkard, 1979). Each of these behaviors may be preceded by a variety of actions, such as changes in food purchases, food preparation, and the selection of a method to signal eating; both the specific acts and their antecedents would be important outcome criteria for a behavioral weight control program. One critical shortcoming of behavioral models is that they often fail to specify this chain of behavioral events, either from the perspective of the investigator or from that of the actor.

Studies of compliance to antihypertensive medication can be used to illustrate how biomedical and behavioral approaches differ in selective dependent variables from systems or self-regulation models. The medically oriented investigations of compliance with regimens of antihypertension medication usually define compliance categorically: If 80% or more of the prescribed medication is taken, the patient is judged compliant (Haynes, 1979a; Sackett, 1978). If the research is conducted from the perspective of a behavioral model, a continuous, quantitative measure is likely to be taken (e.g., pill counts or percentage of medication taken) (Dunbar, 1980; Haynes, 1979a). Both approaches, however, tend to ignore the pattern of use. By contrast, a self-regulation perspective focuses on the cues patients use to regulate their performance and asks when and how patients use medication to validate these hypotheses (Meyer, 1981). Thus, self-regulation perspectives would ask whether patients are taking all of their medication the few days before visiting the clinic and none at other times, or taking double or triple doses when they are symptomatic and none when they are asymptomatic.

Behavioral models may also focus on the pattern of the behavior, as in studies of diet and smoking control. The behavioral models seldom ask, however, about other responses that patients adopt to protect themselves against illness. Hayes-Bautista (1976) reports that patients supplement their treatment regimens with a wide range of responses, such as exercise (to strengthen the body), diet change (to remove risk-inducing substances), and relaxation (e.g., cutting back on work), as insurance against danger. In some instances, these responses are used as substitutes for the recommended practice. Tradeoffs of this kind can only be understood from a patient's view of the illness (see also Chrisman, 1977; Nerenz, 1979; Ringler, 1981).

The self-regulation model makes a third important suggestion for measurement, in pointing to the need to assess the perceived links between the compliance response and the actors' goals, attitudes, and self-concepts. If the actors link compliance to their attitudes and self-concepts, it is likely that they will make a variety of attributions about their ability to generate healthful behaviors and their interest in generating such behaviors. This can help them to build a coherent behavioral regulatory system and to insure long-term involvement in health action. To date, few such assessments have been undertaken, although some investigators have looked at the degree to which participation in treatment strengthens the attitudes specified by the health belief model (M. H. Becker, Drachman, & Kirscht, 1972), and some have examined whether taking action has strengthened beliefs in self-control (Bandura, 1977).

The Value of Multiple Perspectives

Though we are partial to the systems or self-regulation approach, we are also strong advocates of the need to examine problems of compliance from an interdisciplinary perspective. Each of the three perspectives we have reviewed raises different questions, and all three are dynamic and changing. Indeed, our characterization of the medical model is highly stereotyped (Engel, 1977), as multifactorial and systems approaches are found in medical epidemiology (Lilienfeld & Lilienfeld, 1980), cardiology (Guyton, Coleman, Cowley, Scheel, Manning, & Norman, 1972), and immunology and endocrinology (Ader, 1981; Ganong, 1980). Examining behavioral problems from a complex medical perspective can suggest both a variety of medical endpoints and ways in which physiological responses might constrain behavior and generate changes in body sensations and moods that would alter self-regulation. Similarly, the behavioral perspective, particularly the growth of cognitive models in experimental psychology (e.g., Bower, 1981; Massaro, 1975; Neisser, 1967; Nilsson, 1979; Posner, 1973) and social learning theory (Bandura, 1977; Kanfer, 1977; Mischel, 1973; Rotter, 1954), will provide a rich set of heuristics for generating interventions and outcome measures. Attribution theory (Kelley, 1972), developmental cognitive theory, and the growing literature on internalization of motives (Deci & Ryan, 1980; Lepper & Greene, 1978) hold out the promise of making important contributions to self-regulation theory (see Leventhal, 1983; Leventhal, Meyer, & Gutmann, 1980; Leventhal & Nerenz, 1983). It is our belief, however, that the self-regulation or systems approach offers the most comprehensive theoretical framework for research in behavioral medicine.

APPLICATIONS OF THE MODELS TO EMPIRICAL RESEARCH

We cover compliance research in three areas: (1) adherence to medical regimens, (2) adherence to programs for reduction of risk factors, and (3) doctor–patient interaction and adherence. In each area, we review key findings and hypotheses; we also examine how the medical, behavioral, and self-regulation perspectives have influenced existing research, and how they can further alter future research if applied more systematically.

Adherence to Medical Regimens

Research on adherence to medical regimens looks at the treatment setting and views compliance problems within the economic and organizational system structured by the biomedical framework. Treatments are given by a practitioner to a person who has adopted the sick role, the patient (Parsons, 1951), and the threat of illness is assumed to create shared objectives for practitioner and patient (M. S. Davis, 1966; Dimsdale, Klerman, & Shershow, 1979; Kadushin, 1968). Patients typically come with a specifiable set of complaints that are expected to lead to diagnosis and treatment, and physicians are expected to help them reach this goal.

Medical Focus on Compliance

The stereotyped view of the medical encounter described above is what most people generate when asked to write a paragraph about going to the doctor (Bower, Black, & Turner, 1979). It is a view that has conditioned most compliance research, despite the demonstration by sociologists that medical encounters can and do satisfy many other needs than the cure of illness, such as the management of stressful life events (Bennett, 1977) and the quest for social support and human contact (Mechanic, 1972; Shuval, 1970).

The medical view on compliance is presented most clearly by Haynes, Taylor, and Sackett (1979), in a review of the results of 537 studies (Sackett & Snow, 1979, p. 11) of compliance with medical regimens; this review updates an earlier volume by Sackett and Haynes (1976). The studies were selected according to a set of six methodological rules with respect to study design, sample selection and specification, description of the illness, description of the therapeutic regimen, completeness of the definition of compliance, and the adequacy of the compliance measure. Haynes (1979a) summarizes the results of these studies under the following four headings: (1) the features of the disease, (2) the features of the referral process, (3) the features of the clinical setting, and (4) the features of the regimen. The last category divides into (*a*) alternative treatments (e.g., use of oral vs. injected medication), (*b*) classes of medications, (*c*) duration of treatment, (*d*) complexity of treatment, (e) dose effects, (f) side effects, (g) cost, and (h) method of dispensing.

It is interesting to examine Haynes' procedure for synthesizing the findings and his conclusions for two of these categories: features of disease and features of the regimens. Haynes suggests that the features of the disease are unimportant, as "less than half of the reports found any significant correlations" with compliance, and for those that did, no factor was consistently related to compliance (Haynes, 1979a, p. 51). Five of the eight studies reporting a link between diagnosis and compliance were of psychiatric patients; schizophrenic patients were less compliant with medications than were other patients. And "counter to common wisdom, not a single study has found that increasing severity of symptoms encourages compliance" (Haynes, 1979a, p. 51): Four studies showed reduced compliance with more severe symptoms, and these were balanced by three studies that showed a positive relationship between degree of disability and compliance. Finally, clinical improvement also appears unrelated to compliance in a systematic manner. It was followed by reduced compliance in some instances and bore no relationship to compliance in others, and patients reported it as a reason for stopping medication in 13 studies. Haynes suggests that the very same reason might be given by some people for complying with medication as by others for not complying. He then concludes: "Since none of these factors offers much of an opportunity for the detection or improvement of compliance, future research in this area must have a relatively low priority" (Haynes, 1979a, p. 53).

Haynes' review of studies on the treatment regimen proceeds along similar lines. He makes the important point that manufacturers and clinicians generally attribute noncompliance to side effects, though research has provided little or no evidence for such claims (see M. S. Davis, 1966). In discussing "classes of medication," he finds more compliance for cardiac and antidiabetic drugs than for tranquilizers, sedatives, antituberculin drugs, and analgesics (Closson & Kikugawa, 1975; Hemminki & Heikkila, 1975; Hulka, Kupper, Cassel, Efird, & Burdette, 1975). Haynes suggests that these differences relate to differences in management associated with treatment. He does not suggest, however, that the findings may be inconsistent with his prior conclusion that the type of disease is unimportant for compliance behaviors.

Haynes offers a far more encouraging picture when reviewing the impact on compliance of treatment duration and regimen complexity. In this instance, 12 studies showed higher levels of compliance for short-term than for long-term treatment regimens, and another 13 found higher levels of adherence to less complex than to more complex treatment regimens. Exceptions to these "rules" were rare. He is also favorable to research on the process of referral to treatment sites (Haynes, 1979a, p. 53), as studies consistently found higher levels of compliance when referral delays were short rather than long (Glogow, 1973; Hoenig & Ragg, 1966). The differences in this area were sometimes dramatic: F. A. Finnerty, Shaw, and Himmelsbach (1973) found an increase from 50% to 95% when referral appointment delays for hypertensives were reduced from 1 to 2 weeks to 1 or 2 days. Data also suggest that self-referrals were less likely to lead to no-shows than practitioner referrals were (Hertroijs, 1974), and referrals to a psychiatric clinic were less likely to result in no-shows if the patient was directed to a specific psychiatrist (Hoenig & Ragg, 1966). Haynes concludes: "Further research into the effect of the referral process on compliance should have high priority, since the findings presented here suggest that rather simple logistical changes can substantially improve compliance with follow-up appointments" (1979a, p. 55).

Comments on the Medical Approach to Compliance

We have referred to the Sackett and Haynes volumes (Haynes *et al.*, 1979; Sackett & Haynes, 1976) at length, both because they are essential tools for the investigator of compliance, and because they make clear the major features of a biomedical, medical-practice orientation. We can list at least four features of the approach that are highlighted in these volumes. First, the authors acknowledge the lack of methodological sophistication that pervades medical research on compliance. Much of the research on the factors that affect the onset and response to illness is based on case reports culled from medical records, with inadequate attention to the population served by the catchment area, the sampling procedure used for selecting cases, the definition of the independent and dependent variables, and the method of data analysis. The few "experimental" studies also suffer from a lack of definition of both independent and dependent variables, questionable procedures for assignment to conditions, and the use of inappropriate control groups. Clear warnings are also posted in the 1979 volume about the risks of drawing conclusions from cross-sectional data rather than studying specific cohorts from the inception of treatment (Sackett & Snow, 1979). Many of these issues are second nature to the well-trained social researcher (see, e.g., Campbell, & Stanley, 1966; Ostrom, 1978). Hence, Sackett and Haynes' efforts at rigor and their use of a specific set of criteria for accepting studies for review serve as a valuable tool for educating investigators who lack training in epidemiology and social research.

Second, Sackett and Haynes provide a useful prescriptive summary for the practitioner. The major headings in both volumes are practice-oriented, and the specific variables under each can usually be translated into simple operations. It is important for the social scientist to recognize the practice orientation of the consumers of his or her findings: The typical practitioner wants to know *what* to do.

Third, Sackett and Haynes raise the issue of cost-effectiveness by comparing a technical approach to compliance to complex behavioral approaches. The intent of both policy makers and practitioners is to arrive at a reasonable solution to a problem in the least time at the lowest cost. The decision-making process does not always favor complex behavioral interventions (Etzioni & Remp, 1972).

Finally, Sackett and Haynes make it clear that the practice approach is atheoretical. Practitioners of biomedicine seldom ask how particular compliance effects do (or do not) occur, and practically never raise such questions from a coherent theoretical frame of reference.

The absence of theory is the basic reason why these authors run into the three specific problems we now wish to emphasize. First, they sometimes fail to recognize the difference between questions for investigative research and questions for practice or evaluation research. For example, there is virtually no justification for conducting randomized trials on factors such as appointment times and individualized appointments. These are simple variables with obvious outcomes; they are factors that can be manipulated at a discrete point in time, and their impact can be assessed on measures (e.g., appointment no-shows) that can be monitored continually in the practice setting. Techniques for such analysis are discussed by Cook and Campbell (1979) and Ostrom (1978). Experimental research should be dedicated to more substantial questions—for example, to questions for which theory suggests nonintuitive outcomes or competing theories suggest contrasting outcomes. Experimentation is also critical in areas where it is important to demonstrate the relative merits of competing practices that are costly in money and pain (Kloster, Kremkau, Ritzmann, Rahimtoola, Rosch, & Kanarek, 1979). But where a simple factor, such as arranging specific appointment times, can raise compliance to levels of 90% or even higher, there may be little reason to concern ourselves with the determinants of the remaining variance. There will be no shortage of problems for which simple, technical solutions fail, and to which we can address questions yielding rich rewards about the determinants of behavior.

Our two remaining criticisms of the medical approach are that it focuses on main effects and fails to consider that different compliance behaviors may depend on different processes. Both of the Sackett and Haynes volumes examine each compliance issue (e.g., complexity of regimens, specific illness features or symptoms, and delays in appointments), factor by factor. They seldom ask whether the variables that predict or alter compliance interact in different ways within each of these problem domains. If the same variable predicts and alters compliance while other factors vary, it is safe to make a prescriptive rule, which one hopes practitioners will follow. Simplifying rules to insure practitioners' compliance is not a trivial problem (Inui, Yourtee, & Williamson, 1976; Svarstad, 1976). But this approach ignores issues that are significant for long-term adherence and for understanding the "compliance process." We can illustrate our point with two concrete examples.

First, Haynes (1979a) argues that the presence or absence of symptoms is of no importance for compliance across diseases and of no significance for noncompliance with particular medications. We do not dispute Haynes' contention that there are no main effects in these areas, though we suspect they would be detected if severity of symptoms, as defined by the patient, were related to reduced delay in seeking medical care (Safer, Tharps, Jackson, & Leventhal, 1979; Suchman, 1965). It would also be unwise to ignore Haynes' admonitions about the risks of relying on conflicting post hoc verbal reports to explain behavioral outcomes. On the other hand, it is reasonable to believe that different illnesses generate different symptoms, and that patients may have different expectations about the ways in which treatment ought to affect these symptoms and about whether the disappearance or nondisappearance of symptoms means the treatment is working or failing and should be continued or stopped. These interactions may only be visible when patient populations are carefully divided by disease type, severity of illness, and expectation and knowledge factors (Romm, Hulka, & Mayo, 1976). But we are unlikely to search for or comprehend interactions such as these in the absence of a model of the ways in which patients construe disease episodes. We present such a model of illness cognition later, in discussing self-regulation and compliance to medication.

Second, Haynes rejects the value of health education and knowledge as significant determinants of compliance, since educational factors seem to influence the individual's entry into the medical care system but to have little or no effect on compliance to treatment (Sackett et al., 1975; Tagliacozzo, Luskin, Lashof, & Ima, 1974). This conclusion may be premature, however, as the literature also shows complex interactions of knowledge with other factors. For example, Hulka et al. (1975) report that patients with complete knowledge about their medication make fewer errors in drug use than their less well-informed peers do when they all have been prescribed fewer than four medications a day. It is clear that findings of this sort are too complex to generate simple rules for the practitioner. Indeed, if we stay at the level of describing relationships between operationally defined variables, we cannot possibly offer the practitioner an educational method for improving compliance. But if research is conducted to develop our understanding of underlying theoretical relationships, we may be able to provide the practitioner with a model for the analysis of compliance problems and with usable, stepwise procedures for their correction.

The Behavioral Science Perspective on Medication Adherence

Three important classes of behavioral theory have served as guides to the development of compliance interventions: (1) operant behaviorism, (2) cognitive (social learning) behaviorism, and (3) communication or attitude change theory (see Leventhal & Cleary, 1980; Leventhal, Meyer, & Gutmann, 1980).

Operant Behaviorism

Operant behaviorism is a skill-learning model in which the environment is designed to deliver rewards or reinforcements to shape the desired behavior. Two recently published case studies provide good examples of the operant approach. In one (Dapcich-Miura & Hovell, 1979), an elderly heart patient was trained to adhere to a complex regimen involving exercise, a high-potassium diet, and medication taking. In the other (Lowe & Lutzker, 1979), a juvenile diabetic patient was trained to adhere to a regimen involving diet, urine testing, and skin care. In both instances, concrete rewards (poker chips or points) were earned for performing specific actions. These reinforcements were exchanged for gifts (e.g., a weekly meal at a restaurant) according to predetermined schedules. The results are easy to describe: When the reinforcements were given, behavior rapidly climbed to 90–100% adherence. When rewards were withdrawn, it returned nearly as quickly to baseline levels (20–50% adherence). Reinforcements effectively shape or alter response probabilities, but the probabilities return to baseline with the removal of reinforcement.

Most of the studies using operant procedures in the clinical setting focus on the withdrawal from medication and the elimination of pain behaviors in chronic pain patients (Fordyce, 1974; Sternbach, 1974). We have already presented an example of this type of research in our description of the study by Wooley et al. (1978). The results for the pain studies are similar to those already described: Operant procedures have good success in reducing pain medication and decreasing pain behaviors in a substantial number of cases. Success is contingent on a patient's commitment to the procedure and the absence of secondary gain for pain behavior. Once again, however, we find problems with maintaining change. Patients maintain their treatment gains if they return to intact families that sustain the goals of operant therapy. Patients who return to solitary living or to families uncooperative with therapy soon revert to their pretreatment condition.

Cognitive–Behavioral Models

The health belief model is the cognitive model most frequently used in studies of health behavior and compliance (M. H. Becker, 1974; M. H. Becker & Maiman, 1975; Hochbaum, 1958; Kirscht & Rosenstock, 1979; Rosenstock, 1974a, 1974b, 1975). The model views health behavior as the product of beliefs in susceptibility to an illness threat, concerns about the severity of the threat, beliefs about the effectiveness and potential harms and benefits of protective action, and cues making the threat salient. It has been used in a large number of studies designed to predict compliance to a variety of health recommendations (see M. H. Becker, Haefner, Kasl, Kirscht, Maiman, & Rosenstock, 1977).

The health belief model has generated little research, however, on ways of modifying compliance behaviors. This is a curious state of affairs, given the implication of the model that different types of information are needed to alter the various factors mediating compliance. The few studies that have examined the impact of interventions on health beliefs have used either practice-oriented procedures, such as enhanced continuity of care (M. H. Becker, Drachman, & Kirscht, 1974), or procedures already existing in the experimental literature, such as fear-arousing messages (M. H. Becker, Maiman, Kirscht, Haefner, & Drachman, 1977), and contracting and social support (Cummings, Becker, Kirscht, & Levin, 1981). The study of continuity of care found that enhanced continuity led to more favorable health beliefs and better adherence to both appointments and treatment regimens; the study of fear-arousing messages found that the more threatening messages increased mothers' concern with obesity in their children and also increased adherence to diet and weight loss, particularly for the children of those mothers initially low in health concern. But it remains to be demonstrated that the health belief model can serve by itself as a guide for the development of educational techniques, and that changes in these mediators alter compliance in a systematic manner.

The cognitive–behavioral models use such procedures as modeling (Bandura, 1971, 1977), inducements to engage in a behavior that is expected to change goals or attitude (Festinger, 1954), education and persuasion to change health attitudes and action (Hovland, Janis, & Kelley, 1953; Leventhal, 1970; McGuire, 1968), guided participation (Bandura, 1977; Bandura, Blanchard, & Ritter, 1969), rehearsal (Meichenbaum, 1977), and altered goal setting (Goldfried, 1979; Kanfer, 1977; Kanfer, Cox, Gruner, & Karoly, 1974) to change the processes assumed to mediate between stimulus and response. Whatever the technique, information is passed from a source to a recipient in order to modify action. These theories begin to correct one of the major shortcomings of prior cognitive approaches—the failure to deal with behavior and behavioral change.

Communication and Attitude Change for Compliance

Models of communication (Hovland, 1954; Weiss, 1969) and attitude change (Bem, 1972; Fishbein & Ajzen, 1975; Hovland et al., 1953; Leventhal, 1973; McGuire, 1968) have played a significant role in compliance research aimed at both adherence to treatment and risk reduction (see Jaccard, 1974; Janis & Leventhal, 1967; Janis & Rodin, 1979; Leventhal, 1970, 1973; Rogers, 1975). Research on communication and attitude change focuses on one or more of the steps that lead from sending a message to action. We discuss selected findings on each of the following six steps: (1) generating the message, (2) reception of the message, (3) comprehension of the message, (4) retention of the message, (5) acceptance of the message, and (6) taking action on the message.

Generating the Message. Before initiating formal data collection on her important study of physician–patient interaction, Svarstad (1974) made the critical decision to observe physician–patient interactions informally in the clinic setting. Three factors stood out from these observations: (1) the practitioners failed to state the regimen 17% of the time; (2) Svarstad often could not make sense of the prescribed regimen when it was given; (3) when the regimen was both stated and written (e.g., when the physician would indicate how antihypertension medication was to be taken and the pharmacist wrote this on the prescription label), the two statements proved contradictory 20% of the time. We are unlikely to obtain robust findings on the relationship between compliance and psychologically "interesting" variables, such as a physician's autocratic style or his or her monitoring of a patient's behavior, when the patient is uninformed of the regimen.

We do not wish to imply that all nonadherence can be accounted for by the failure of practitioners to state the treatment regimen clearly. In a well-designed field study, Hulka and her associates examined practitioner–patient pairs for 68% ($n=46$) of the practitioners listed in the Fort Wayne–Allen County Medical Society Directory (Romm et al., 1976). They found that communication contributed to adherence only in those cases where patients were relatively asymptomatic, and only for medications whose major impact was on the central nervous system or on gastric distress: medications for control of critical medical conditions, such as cardiac and antidiabetic agents, were more likely to be taken as prescribed (Hulka et al., 1975). Thus, Svarstad's results, obtained with a small sample of practitioners, may not apply to larger practitioner populations. It is important to note, however, that Hulka's and other studies used indirect indicators, not direct observation, of the communication process.

Reception. Presenting information does not assure its reception. This is particularly true when the mass media are used to educate the public about illness threats (Hovland, 1959; Weiss, 1969). Health information typically filters down from the media to "opinion leaders" who serve as sources of information for those not using the media (E. Katz, 1957). Unfortunately, there is little assurance that these messages will be received by those most in need of the information, since those in need (i.e., people at high risk) may be less likely to use the media and may be most resistant to participation in intensive intervention programs. Heavy smokers are a good example, as they are often the least likely to participate in antismoking treatments (Leventhal & Cleary, 1980; Leventhal, Safer, Cleary, & Gutmann, 1980).

Message reception may seem less of a problem in the clinic setting. But even when a message is appropriately assembled and presented to a patient, there is no assurance that it will be attended to. Ley and his colleagues (see Ley, 1977) review a number of studies that illustrate the importance of timing and order of information presentation for both reception and recall. For example, practitioners tend to present the diagnosis of a condition prior to spelling out the treatment regimen. This may be "logical" from the perspective of medical practice, but it is not necessarily good for reception, recall, acceptance, and behavioral adherence, because patients may recall their diagnoses and fail to retain their treatment regimen. This "primacy" effect may occur because the diagnosis stimulates a good deal of imagining and thinking about the impact of the illness on future activities, so that information on treatment is unattended to and/or forgotten.

Comprehension. There are at least two distinct types of comprehension. The first, which we call "text comprehension," depends on the patient's ability to understand the words in the communication. The second, "structural comprehension," depends on the way in which the patient interprets and relates the information to his or her self-concept system. One might think of structural comprehension as reflecting the individual's coding of the information in relation to past experiences that affect his or her perception of vulnerability to an illness threat, and the ways in which he or she will experience the magnitude of the threat and assess his or her ability to cope with it.

Ley and his colleagues have conducted a number of simple but important studies on text comprehension (Ley, 1977; Ley & Spelman, 1967) and have shown that the difficult terms used in health communications often exceed the reading level of the clients served by their readers. This lack of understanding can translate into misunderstanding rather than simple nonunderstanding. For example, the technical term for high blood pressure, "hypertension," is regularly misunderstood to mean "high levels of nervous tension" (National Institutes of Health, 1981). A misunderstanding of this sort can influence the patient's perception of the cause of high blood pressure and can lead him or her to drop out of treatment when life stresses have abated (Hayes-Bautista, 1976; D. Meyer, 1981).

Retention. While repetition undoubtedly plays a role in learning and memory, its importance has been greatly exaggerated (see Jenkins, 1974). Both organization and active rehearsal of the material by the recipient appear to be far more important to insure retention (Nilsson, 1979; Norman, 1969). Ley (1977) suggests that practitioners first present their organization (e.g., "I am going to describe the medication you are to take, then I will describe the changes needed in your daily habit patterns," etc.) and repeat each category label as they present their information. This procedure can enhance comprehension, retention, and compliance with treatment. In one instance, recall enhanced through organization of material led to 8 pounds more being lost (Ley, Bradshaw, Eaves, & Walker, 1973) in experimental than in control groups—a surprising result, given the difficulty of achieving weight loss by anything other than intensive behavioral management.

Acceptance. Knowing a fact is not equivalent to its acceptance. Subjects can acquire information without changing their beliefs or values (Kelly, Kegeles, Lund, & Weisenberg, 1976). This outcome has been seen in a substantial number of studies that have examined the effectiveness of fear-arousing messages in altering attitudes and behavior to reduce the risks of tetanus, automotive injury, lung cancer, and tooth decay. Although arguments persist about the mechanism underlying the effects of fear communications (Janis, 1967; Leventhal, 1970; Rogers, 1983), there is little evidence that people learn more about a threat after exposure to a high-fear than to a low-fear message. It is clear, however, that stimulating higher levels of fear typically leads to more favorable attitudes toward the communicators' position—for example, toward less favorable views of smoking (Leventhal & Watts, 1966; Leventhal, Watts, & Pagano, 1967; Niles, 1964; T. J. Rosen et al., 1982; Watts, 1972) and more favorable attitudes toward tetanus inoculations (Leventhal et al., 1965; Leventhal et al., 1967), regular dental hygiene practices (Haefner, 1965; Leventhal & Singer, 1966; Singer, 1965), participation in weight loss programs (Lund, Kegeles, & Weisenberg, 1977), and so forth. (See also Rogers, 1975; Rogers & Deckner, 1975; Rogers, Deckner, & Mewborn, 1978; Rogers & Mewborn, 1976.)

The acceptance (change in attitude) stimulated by the arousal of emotional states such as fear has stronger effects for the short than for the long term, and most of the movement toward the communication position fades as the fear dissipates. In some instances, the return to baseline occurs within 24 hours (Leventhal & Niles, 1965). More permanent acceptance may occur when a communication links the object with attitudes already held by the participant. For example, in a recent study subjects were asked to list their most cherished values and then to examine whether or not a risk behavior such as smoking helped or hindered reaching these values. This technique has generated surprisingly stable changes in behavior in the few instances in which it has been applied (Conroy, 1979). It is also clear that communication acceptance depends on the type of information, or elaboration, the recipient brings to mind while thinking about the message topic (Cacioppo & Petty, 1981; Genest & Turk, 1981; Greenwald, 1968). Thus, while there is clearly a step from retention to acceptance, we do not have as clear a view of the acceptance process as we might hope to have.

Action. The final step in the sequence is acting on the recommendations of the message. Three factors seem crucial for moving from belief to action. First, the person's belief must be formulated as or must strongly suggest an intention to act (Fishbein & Ajzen, 1975; Jaccard, 1974). Second, environmental factors must be favorable toward action (Fishbein & Ajzen, 1975). Finally, the individual must generate a plan for action; that is, he or she must know what to do, how to do it, and believe him or herself capable of acting (Bandura, 1977; Leventhal, 1970).

Seeing action as a necessary outcome of beliefs means that the individual represents or formulates specific situations as requiring action (Leventhal & Nerenz, 1983). The relationship of definitions of problems to action is made clear in our discussion of systems views of self-regulation processes. Environmental factors that encourage action are either interpersonal communication or group norms. Congruence between a person's own beliefs and messages from relevant sources can have powerful effects on action.

Mazen and Leventhal (1972) found mothers most likely to "room in" and to breast-feed their newborn infants if they tended to favor these actions prior to giving birth and were told to room in or to breast-feed by women who were also pregnant and similar in race.

Interpersonal communication, however, does not always produce simple and/or expected effects. For example, Suchman (1965) compared face-to-face communication through community groups with booklets and printed media that urged sugar cane cutters to wear a special safety glove. Because the community was in a state of disarray, with traditional groups disintegrating under the pressures of urbanization, the impersonal media proved superior for modifying this safety practice. Social communication may also appear to produce contrasting findings until closer examination reveals the complexity of the social process. For example, people are less likely to delay seeking medical care for specific symptoms if they have discussed the symptoms with friends or acquaintances. On the other hand, delay may be greater if a person has had such a discussion with a family member. Reduced delay with people outside the family occurs because such persons are more likely to communicate cosmopolitan norms favoring the use of technical medical services, while information within the family is more likely to reflect traditional values, mutual comparison of symptoms, and the use of self-treatment (Berkanovic & Telesky, 1982; Freidson, 1961). These findings should serve as another warning against expecting simple main effects. The mechanisms controlling individual and social behavior are complex, and interact in a complex manner in generating response outcomes.

Generating a plan for action seems to involve integrating the behavior into daily routines by locating the occasions most suitable for action, identifying cues for action, and rehearsing the specific components of the action so that they can be performed smoothly in the real world. Miller and Dworkin (1980) discuss an unusual example of integrating a treatment behavior into everyday activities, in which patients were taught a variety of behavioral strategies to control cardiac reflexes and avoid sinus arrhythmias and sudden drops in blood pressure. The patients learned all of these strategies, but adopted and used only those that were unobtrusive and not socially embarrassing.

A key point in each of these examples is that the information needed to perform an action is different from that needed to form an attitude.

Comments on the Behavioral Perspective

The operant, cognitive, and communication models all focus on the transfer of information from an environmental source to a patient/participant. From this perspective, the operant model can be regarded as a theory to guide the communication behavior of the investigator and the practitioner. Operant theory tells the practitioner to deliver rewards whenever he or she views a behavior that corresponds to a desired criterion. But, as we have said earlier, the operant model does not specify what type of communication will be "rewarding"; that is, it does not say what message components are needed to move through the steps that lead from reception to action.

The step model, on the other hand, defines a frame of reference or a set of steps that are presumed to be necessary to move from reception to action. But the model fails to specify the processes or variables operating at each step. The health belief model, and the cognitive–behavioral and decision models, are designed to describe the internal cognitive processes operating between communication and action. The data generated by studies using these models in the communication framework provide some clues as to the types of information needed to move from reception through comprehension, retention, and acceptance to action. It is clear, for example, that at least two different types of information are needed to complete this step sequence —one defining the illness threat, the second formulating the action. Both the health belief model and the cognitive–behavioral models specify factors important for taking action: The health belief model points to the importance of action expectations, or beliefs about the effectiveness of particular actions for reaching goals (Kirscht, Becker, & Eveland, 1976), and the cognitive–behavioral models point to the importance of self-effectance, or the individual's belief in his or her competence or ability to perform illness-controlling or risk-reducing actions. The fear communication studies suggest a third type of process—that of developing specific response plans and embedding these in the individual's daily routines.

The behavioral studies and models give little insight, however, into the ways in which respondents perceive or define health problems. These processes need to be specified and related to the factors involved in the control of responding. This is best done, in our opinion, by systems models of self-regulation. In the following section, we illustrate a systems approach to self-regulation of medication use in treatment settings. After elaborating this model of what we presume to be the essential mediators of compliance behaviors, we contrast medical, behavioral, and self-regulation models by addressing the controversial issue of the effectiveness or ineffectiveness of education for achieving compliance in the treatment setting. The aim of this comparison is twofold: first, to show that education can alter compliance when it is directed toward the processes underlying the perception or representation of the health problem, as well as toward the processes controlling planning and action; second, to compare the three types of models and to show their respective strengths and weaknesses for designing messages to intervene in and enhance compliance.

The Role of Self-Regulation in Adherence

To encourage successful long-term performance of treatment regimens, we need a different orientation from that provided either by the medical or by the behavioral and communication models. These models view the recipient as an empty tablet to be written on by communicators and dispensers of rewards, who must be skillful in bypassing the recipient's defenses and able, therefore, to insert new beliefs and actions into the recipient's repertoire (Janis, 1967).

The self-regulation or control perspective views patients as active agents choosing their own goals, which are determined by their perceptions or representations of their illness and the treatment setting, their selection of responses to reach these goals, and their evaluation of their progress in goal attainment (Schulman, 1979). Self-regulation also makes clear that when patients take in information, they assimilate it to preexisting meaning and action structures and assemble their own representations of their illness problems and their own plans for action. This way of formulating the communication process requires that we take into account the deeper structures used to decode and encode information. It sees common processes underlying comprehension and acceptance—processes we have called "structural comprehension" above—and suggests that information is not understood by the recipient as it is understood by the communicator. How are illnesses construed by patients, and how do these constructions affect self-regulation (compliance)?

Symptoms and Labels: How Patients Represent Illness

People appear to define or represent illness at two levels: a concrete level of symptom experience, and an abstract level of disease labels. The process is symmetrical, as the mind operates simultaneously at concrete and abstract levels (Posner, 1973; Powers, 1973), and illnesses are represented at both levels.

The process of labeling and symptom finding involves both deliberate search and automatic decoding by perceptual memory codes. Deliberate search is seen in talking to others to compare symptoms, reading about symptoms and illness experiences, and so on (Safer *et al.*, 1979). Automatic search is seen in instantaneous emotional reactions and intuitive feelings that one is ill in response to labels and, primarily, to symptoms (Leventhal, 1970, 1980; Leventhal, Nerenz, & Straus, 1980; Pennebaker, 1980; Pennebaker & Skelton, 1981). As a consequence, when they experience body sensations or symptoms, they seek labels or diagnoses. And when people are diagnosed or labeled, they seek and find symptoms (Leventhal, Meyer, & Nerenz, 1980). The multilevel representation of illness is seen in Meyer's study of hypertensive patients. When asked, "Can people tell when their blood pressure is high?" 80% of these patients gave the normative, medically acceptable answer: They disagreed. But when this question was followed by the probe, "Can *you* tell?" 90% believed they could tell when their blood pressure was elevated; they did so by monitoring such symptoms as headaches and face flushing. The data show that this belief develops over time (Meyer, Leventhal, & Gutmann, in press). Thus, high blood pressure is asymptomatic (as such patients have been told) for *other* people, but it is both labeled and identified by its symptoms in themselves.

Illness Representations and Coping

If symptoms are reliable indicators of high blood pressure, patients can use them to decide whether to remain in treatment and when to take medication (Meyer et al., in press). For example, 61% of the 23 newly treated patients who had reported symptoms to their physician when they came for treatment had dropped out by the 6-month follow-up. By contrast, only 24% of the 42 newly treated patients who had not reported symptoms (many had come to the clinic for unrelated complaints) had dropped out of treatment by the 6-month follow-up. Among the 50 patients who had been in active treatment for 3 months to 15 years, those with symptoms were very much more likely to be compliant if they believed treatment had a positive effect rather than no effect on their symptoms (70% compliant vs. 31% compliant). Blood pressure control was significantly better among the compliant than among the non-compliant patients.

Representations of illness also include beliefs about the cause of the illness, expectations about its duration (acute, cyclic, or chronic), and beliefs about its consequences and susceptibility to treatment. These attributes also affect "treatment" and therefore compliance. Hayes-Bautista (1976), Chrisman (1977), A. Kleinman (1980), and others have found that patients adopt a variety of self-treatment regimens, from over-the-counter medications and vitamins to special diets, exercise, and stress reduction regimens (cutbacks in work, etc.), in order to cope with the perceived causes of disease. Hulka and her colleagues reported a finding related to this type of "compliance" problem: They found errors of commission (i.e., patients' taking unprescribed medication) to be the major source of "noncompliance" in their Indianapolis sample (Hulka, Cassel, Kupper, & Burdette, 1976).

It is clear that conflict is possible between practitioner and patient if the patient develops a private, common-sense representation of a health problem and regulates his or her coping on the basis of this representation. This possibility is illustrated by chronic pain patients—that is, patients manifesting the "illness behavior" syndrome (Wooley et al., 1978). These patients have their own agenda (Sternbach, 1974): They use pain to manipulate others for monetary gain or for drugs, and to challenge the competence of their practitioner. They insist that their pain is physical and amenable to medical treatment in order to maintain their self-esteem. As a consequence, they challenge the therapist to cure their pain and reject behavioral treatments, because such treatments imply that the pain is not "organic." In short, the pain patient's representation or goals call for coping strategies quite different from those prescribed at a pain clinic.

Differences between practitioner and patient in the representation of health and illness problems and in the perceived need for coping seem to be involved in many studies reporting noncompliance with medications. For example, some mothers stop treating children who have otitis media when the children's symptoms clear up; other mothers believe the prescribed medication is so powerful that it should only be used for brief periods of time (M. H. Becker, 1976; M. H. Becker et al., 1972; Elling, Whittemore, & Green, 1960). Similar effects are found with psychiatric patients (Dimsdale et al., 1979) and patients in treatment for hypertension (Garrity, 1980), and diabetes (Espenshade, 1982). We believe that the failure to explore patients' representations of their illnesses and to reconcile these representations to ongoing treatment regimens is a major factor underlying patients' dissatisfaction with communication and their noncompliance with treatment.

The Organization of Self-Regulation Systems

Much of the self-regulated behavior we have observed appears to reflect the influence of a small number of underlying implicit models. The most important of these is the one we have termed the "acute disease schema" (Leventhal, Meyer, & Gutmann, 1980; Leventhal, Meyer, & Nerenz, 1980). This schema has the following four features: (1) The illness is symptomatic and can be labeled (and different illnesses have different symptoms); (2) the illness is caused by external disease agents; (3) the illness is short-term; (4) treatment can eliminate symptoms and cure the underlying disease process.

The acute disease schema appears to be a powerful guide to coping among patients with cardiovascular disease (Gutmann, Pollock, Schmidt, & Dudek, 1981; Meyer, 1981) and cancer (Nerenz, 1979; Ringler, 1981). Because they expect diseases to be symptomatic and treatment to eliminate symptoms, hypertensives drop out of treatment; coronary bypass patients who were presurgically asymptomatic have difficulty adjusting when the pain from surgery disappears, as their bodies now feel the same as they did when ill (Gutmann et al., 1981); and cancer patients have difficulty with long-term chemotherapy that produces symptoms, if the symptoms of their disease (tumors) are in remission (Nerenz, 1979). Acute disease thinking may also be responsible for the finding by Sackett and his colleagues that intensive education about hypertension increased the proportion of foundry workers entering treatment (both at the worksite and with local practitioners), but did not increase adherence to blood pressure treatment (Sackett et al., 1975). We suspect that the educational program persuaded these men of the need for continual monitoring by the medical care system, given the assumption that practitioners could detect and "cure" short-term rises in pressure. If an educational program focuses on the nature, risks, and treatment of hypertension, but fails to identify, combat, and/or inoculate against such acute disease thinking, the program can easily produce such "unexpected" outcomes.

The Education Controversy

Haynes (1976, 1979b) suggests that health education has little or no effect on compliance with treatment regimens, and supports his conclusion by citing a long list of studies showing no effect of education on medication adherence. One of the studies on which he relies is the well-controlled study of adherence to antihypertension medication among employees at a large Canadian foundry, conducted by the McMaster University group (Sackett *et al.*, 1975). Half of the 230 participants in that study were given mastery learning, which was designed to provide them with a high level of information about the determinants, risks, and means of treatment for hypertension. This program had no effect whatsoever on compliance behavior. Haynes (1979b) and his associates (Sackett *et al.*, 1975) distinguish between the type of education used in their study and strategies for behavioral management, arguing that the latter, but not the former, can generate useful compliance strategies. Green (1977) takes issue with this argument and states that educational and behavioral strategies cannot be distinguished as readily as Sackett and Haynes would have us believe. Green defines health education as ''any combination of learning opportunities designed to facilitate voluntary adaptations of behavior conducive to health'' (p. 160).

These authors clearly disagree as to the substance (i.e., the content, medium, and form) of health education, as well as to whether health messages should be labeled ''educational messages'' or ''behavior change messages.'' If the contesting parties were asked to choose the one message from a set of messages that was most likely to be effective, we suspect they would probably make a common choice. But we are not sure! Our uncertainty would be increased if we admit yet a third party to the controversy, S. G. Rosenberg (1976), who sides with Green. S. G. Rosenberg's defense of educational approaches rests on a set of studies in which information was used to reduce reports of distress, amount of analgesic used, and duration of hospitalization for adults undergoing abdominal surgery (Egbert, Battit, Welch, & Bartlett, 1964). He also reviews studies in which education given to parents reduced their children's postoperative emesis, sleep disturbance, temperature, pulse rate, blood pressure, and time for recovery following tonsillectomies and adenoidectomies (Skipper & Leonard, 1968). However, S. G. Rosenberg fails to address the relationship, if any, between preparation for surgery and education for treatment adherence.

Two issues are intertwined in the argument about the effects of education. The first concerns the definition of education or the type of information content that should be labeled ''educational.'' The second is the behavioral effects that we can and should expect from these programs. At a practical level, the two issues point to the need for a clear notion of objectives prior to constructing educational messages, and the need to tailor the content of these messages to their objectives (see Ajzen & Fishbein, 1973). But success in practice implies mastery of important theoretical issues in message construction. To achieve our adherence objectives, we must understand the cognitive processes underlying the behavior and present the type of information needed to achieve them. It is simpler to say that we need such understanding than it is to acquire and to apply it. For example, Blackwell (1979) suggests that adherence to drug regimens is affected by their complexity, which is in turn a composite of two factors: the number of medications, and the number of doses of any specific medication. Data show that an increased number of medications is related to decreased adherence to the regimen, while increased dosage is not. What is it that underlies subtle behavioral differences of this type? The answer to this question requires the development of a theory of information that conceptualizes differences in information content and in the steps of information processing (e.g., storage and retrieval).

One barrier to developing a theory of information is that educational packages are complex and their effective ingredients are unknown. To isolate these ingredients inductively (i.e., by systematic analysis of components in randomized trials) would be expensive and time-consuming, and we are unlikely to reach meaningful conclusions unless we are guided by some notions as to how information is organized and used. The preparation packages cited by M. Rosenberg (1979) have been analyzed into two specific components: (1) how the stressful setting will be represented in concrete experience; and (2) information about coping—that is, how to act in response to specific cues, and how to appraise or recognize effective from ineffective outcomes (Leventhal & Johnson, 1980). Control theory defines the areas for education. When it is combined with empirical work exploring the attributes of representations, the responses perceived as relevant for coping, and criteria and strategies for appraisal, it provides a powerful heuristic for message construction.

An early example is a study by Johnson and Leventhal (1974). They prepared four groups of patients for an endoscopic examination; one group received information about the sensations they would experience during the swallowing of the endoscopic tube and instructions on how to breathe and swallow during the procedure. A control group was uninformed about these facts, and two other experimental groups were given either the sensory information alone or the action instructions alone. The results suggested that sensation information played the major role in reducing indicators of emotional distress (heart rate, etc.), while the action instructions were essential for altering swallowing time. However, the action instructions for breathing and swallowing were ineffective in the absence of the sensation information. The combined package, which included both of the key elements specified by control theory (i.e., concrete sensations defining the representation of the stressor and the action instructions for coping), was needed to influence both emotional responding (heart rate and gagging) and performance (time to swallow the camera tube). The results of this and a large number of subsequent studies in a variety of laboratory settings (Leventhal, Brown, Shacham, & Engquist, 1979; Reinhardt, 1979; Shacham, 1979) and field settings (Johnson, 1975; Johnson, Rice, Fuller, & Endress, 1978) provide a convincing demonstration of the value of sensory information for reducing emotional stress responses and increasing the possibility of problem-solving or compliance behaviors (Leventhal & Johnson, 1980).

The research on stress reduction that has used information on sensations of stressors combined with information on coping illustrates the value of a cognitive, systems theory approach to health education. Instructional messages can influence behavior if they contain the necessary informational components. These components are partly, but not completely, specified by control theory. The specification is partial, because control theory points only to the need to include information about problem representation, coping, and appraisal, and does not say precisely what the information content should be. This was resolved by careful observation and pilot interviewing and "common sense" (i.e., by the simple observations that such specific tasks as swabbing the throat with anesthetic and swallowing a fiber optic tube would necessarily result in specific sensations). The studies of self-regulation discussed earlier have also helped define specific attributes of representations, such as their identity (labels and concrete symptoms), cause (genetic, externally caused infection or injury, own behavior, etc.), time line (acute, cyclic, or chronic), and consequences (varying degrees of disability and life disruption). At this point in time, however, it is clear that specifying essential informational contents to enhance adherence to any specific treatment regimen is very much an empirical task. One must discover the common-sense representations of the illness process (i.e., the sensations or symptoms used to identify it), check the validity of these indicators (the causal perceptions of the problem, etc.), and determine how these representational attributes influence reception, understanding, retention, acceptance, and action on treatment prescriptions.

In summary, the education controversy contrasts the biomedical, behavioral, and self-regulation approaches to using information to influence patients' behavior. The biomedical investigator conceptualizes information giving from the perspective of the expert, who tells the uninformed patient about the nature of disease risks, the recommended treatment, and its benefits. From a biomedical perspective, this information is a prescription for action, and failure to follow it implies inadequacy of the recipient or the educational procedure. The behavioral perspective, as advocated by Green, emphasizes information that can reward and control behavior and separates information about the biomedical problem from information needed to regulate action. The behavioral approach tries different types of "rewards" until one is found that works. The reward concept also determines the sequence for presenting information; that is, rewards are contingent upon or follow the desired behavior.

To inform from the perspective of self-regulation, one must first identify those attributes of the representation that define the goals toward which the patient is moving, and then alter or redefine incorrect goals and increase the salience of environmental cues related to the corrected goals. The second task is to teach the skills needed to reach defined goals. Identifying the type of information that will alter goals and coping reactions is both an empirical and theoretical issue when the communication is guided by models of the substance and structure of information such as those described above—that is, when illness is represented as a set of attributes including cause, identity, duration, and consequences, and when information is regarded as both abstract (labels) and concrete (symptoms and sensations that stimulate fear). The differentiated view of information is both theoretically sophisticated and useful for practice. As we point out later, however, the self-regulation perspective does not provide as clear a definition of this information when we move from compliance with a treatment regimen to adherence to behaviors for the prevention of future illness. Compliance with treatment clearly falls within the framework of illness representations. But what does it mean to represent hypothetical risk? Is risk a label? Where are the symptoms to remind us of it? Are there other types of representations (e.g., looking sexually attractive, gaining strength to engage in rough athletics, etc.) that play a role in setting and maintaining goals for risk behaviors equal to or stronger than the role they play for treatment behaviors? And do people adopt these risk-inducing and risk-reducing behaviors without perceiving or caring about their relationship to health? We address these issues in the following section.

Compliance in Risk Reduction

The changes in patterns of morbidity and mortality from acute to chronic causes require a variety of changes in our concepts of disease and our concepts of risk. Ideas about disease and/or about risk derive from cultural beliefs and institutions, from a wealth of medical information in the public domain, and from personal experiences with symptoms and illness episodes. Risk states differ from illness states in several respects, however, and these differences are of great importance for our conception of risk of chronic illness (Leventhal, 1973; Leventhal & Cleary, 1980). First, most illness episodes are acute; they are time-limited and accompanied by concrete symptoms. Recovery has occurred when symptoms disappear, and treatment is said to be effective if it removes symptoms. Frequent experience with the risks of minor, acute disease may even follow this pattern, with low-level symptoms stimulating secondary preventive measures (e.g., sleep, diet change, etc.) that may prevent a full-blown acute episode. In contrast, risk of chronic illness usually has an indefinite time span and exists in the absence of visible signs or symptoms (Baric, 1969). Fluctuations in risk status are not readily monitored by the onset and disappearance of concrete symptoms. Hence, risk remains an abstract concept.

Second, a diagnosis of disease brings with it a right to treatment, exemption from a variety of daily social responsibilities, and the obligation to comply with treatment recommendations. By contrast, a person labeled "at risk" not only fails to receive exemptions from social responsibilities; he or she may assume the added burden of being seen as responsible for his or her condition and being expected to take responsible action to change it (Baric,

1969). Hence, the person at risk for chronic illness must initiate and maintain change over an indefinite period of time toward an uncertain reward, with only signs of failure (i.e., disease symptoms) and without clear objective evidence of progress. Given the relative lack of clarity of the risk concept and risk role, and the important differences of these from the illness concept and sick role, it may prove inappropriate to apply acute models of disease and treatment to risk reduction for chronic disease prevention, since the latter requires long-term self-maintenance rather than compliance with prescribed regimens over a short and defined time period.

In the section that follows, we review both the basic models (medical and behavioral) underlying risk reduction research and the data produced by this research, and then critique this body of work. We believe that research in this area has provided important insights into the processes underlying change in knowledge, attitude, intentions, and behavior. We also believe that the existing work has specific shortcomings. First, it has failed to conceptualize or describe how the individual at risk (not the health expert) represents (experiences and stores in memory) health threats. As suggested before, the deficits are most apparent with respect to how people represent the concrete (symptoms) and the temporal (acute–chronic) aspects of illness threats. Second, the research has not yet enlarged our understanding as to how the acquisition of specific response skills affects and relates to the individual's belief in his or her personal, long-term competency at risk reduction and the individual's representation of long-term threats. These conceptual deficits lead to methodological errors, which arise out of a medical definition of risk and a narrow focus on behavioral outcomes.

Following the critique, we present a self-regulation model of risk reduction, which offers a new perspective and corrects for some of the deficits of prior models. The major feature of the self-regulation model is that it views health-related behaviors as arising out of the individual's own representation of risk (or health threat), skills learned in coping with the threat, strategies for appraisal and self-regulation, and integration of new behaviors into a personal life style. As we see it, health actions based on this self-regulatory process are more likely to persist for the long term than are prescribed regimens presented strictly from a medical or behavioral perspective.

Medical and Behavioral Approaches to Risk Reduction

Medical and Behavioral Models
Within current medical practice, "risk" is defined as the probability of future illness consequences (Ansel & Roncari, 1978; Breslow, 1978; Goetz, Duff, & Bernstein, 1980; Hulley, Rosenman, Bawol, & Brand, 1980; Thorsen, Jacobs, Grimm, Keys, Taylor, & Blackburn, 1979). These probabilities are based on such epidemiological studies as the Framingham (Dawber, Meadors, & Moore, 1951), Minnesota (Keys, Taylor, Blackburn, Brozek, & Anderson,

1963), and Western Collaborative (Rosenman, Friedman, Straus, Jenkins, Zyzanski, & Wurm, 1970) studies. The final probability product is a quantitative risk index or multiple logistic function (Truett, Cornfield, & Kannel, 1967), which can be computed with such screening tools as the Health Hazard Appraisal (Hall & Zwemer, 1979; Robbins & Hall, 1970; Safer, 1982). It is assumed that the identification of high-risk individuals and the reduction in their identified risk factors would result in a reduction in their morbidity and mortality.

Behavioral models accept the medical definition of risk but focus specifically on the behavioral antecedents of disease as targets of change (Foreyt & Gotto, 1979; Leon, 1976; A. R. Marston & McFall, 1971; Stuart, 1977). The primary objective of the behaviorist is to change risk-inducing behaviors through the application of behavioral rather than biomedical technology. Both the medical and behavior models take a prescriptive approach to risk reduction: A patient (client) is identified as "at risk" and is expected to follow a prescribed regimen. For instance, physicians will focus on and treat the condition of "obesity," while behaviorists will focus on and treat such "obese behaviors" as speed of chewing, portion size, and place of eating (Cooke & Meyers, 1980). The patient's compliance with the prescribed regimens is seen as essential for success.

Evidence for Behavioral Approaches to Risk Reduction

By far the most substantial literature in prevention is that generated by behavioral investigators concerned with the development of skills for the management of such risk behaviors as eating and smoking. For smoking, the methods of development range from conditioned aversion and relaxation therapies on the one hand, through operant methods to psychotherapy and hypnotherapy on the other. Several excellent reviews of behavioral methods in the treatment of obesity have been published (Coates & Thoreson, 1978; B. A. Davis & Roncari, 1978; Kingsley & Wilson, 1977; Leon, 1976; Loro, Levenkron, & Fisher, 1979; Stunkard & Penick, 1979; Wing & Jeffery, 1979) and smoking (Best & Bloch, 1979; Leventhal & Cleary, 1980; J. L. Schwartz, 1969; Wynder & Hoffmann, 1979). The results from these interventions have been remarkably similar in showing a good initial response. For example, 69–90% of smokers who complete a treatment program have quit smoking by the end of treatment (Harrup, Hansen, & Soghikian, 1979; Wynder & Hoffmann, 1979). Unfortunately, there is a high dropout rate from treatment (Abraham & Johnson, 1980; Stunkard & Mahoney, 1976; Wynder & Hoffmann, 1979), with attrition rates of 50% being reported for both smoking and obesity programs. The exclusion of these treatment dropouts from the final outcome figures clearly inflates the success rates reported. In addition, there is rapid relapse after termination of treatment, such that only 25–30% are still abstaining from smoking by the end of 1 year (Harrup *et al.*, 1979; Leventhal & Cleary, 1980; Wynder & Hoffmann, 1979). Relapse after weight loss programs is equally problematic, although there is considerable variation in the results reported by different studies (Currey, Malcolm, Riddle, & Schacthe, 1977; B. A. Davis & Roncari, 1978; Foreyt & Gotto, 1979; Stunkard & Penick, 1979). Use of booster sessions during follow-up has improved maintenance in some studies (Kingsley & Wilson, 1977; Wollersheim, 1970), but not in others (Ashby & Wilson, 1977; Currey et al., 1977; Stunkard & Penick, 1979).

In addition to the high attrition and relapse rates, there is a dearth of evidence for differential outcome for different therapeutic methods. For example, weight loss from a variety of medical (drugs and diet) and behavioral methods has averaged around 12 pounds (5.4 kg) after 8 to 10 weeks of active treatment (Currey et al., 1977; Stunkard & Penick, 1979; Wing & Jeffery, 1979), regardless of the type of treatment used (Foreyt & Gotto, 1979). In fact, patients in attention control groups or placebo treatments have been reported to lose as much weight as or more weight than patients in active treatment have (Wing & Jeffery, 1979). Success rates for different approaches to smoking cessation have also not differed markedly, implying that "it is simply better to do something than nothing" (Leventhal & Cleary, 1980).

Critique of Medical and Behavioral Approaches

Conceptual Problems. The summary of experimental outcomes reviewed above makes clear some of the major strengths and weaknesses of current approaches to risk reduction. These methods focus on the management of the risk behavior. By doing so, they provide little insight into how individuals perceive risk and become motivated to initiate and participate in risk reduction, either alone or with others (for an exception, see Mausner, 1973). The studies fail to conceptualize adequately the dropout process, and have little to offer in terms of innovative approaches to sustain their impressively high posttreatment success rates. Behavioral research, therefore, has largely ignored the way people think about (represent) risk. It does not explain the gap between public notions of risk and personal representations of risk and coping with risk. What accounts for this gap? How are behaviors effective in dealing with acute stresses, or threats transformed into long-term changes in life style? And how do individuals evaluate the effectiveness of their risk reduction strategies and gain a sense of competence in dealing with health threats?

As we have indicated earlier, the medical model defines "risk" as the probability of future illness consequences and a "risk factor" as a predictor of such consequences; behavioral researchers accept these epidemiological definitions or representations of risk and risk factors in selecting targets for behavioral intervention. There are two difficulties with this approach to identifying risk. First, the probabilities are computed from population data. The translation of population statistics into predictions for an individual is both theoretically and clinically questionable (Leventhal, Nerenz, & Straus, 1980): "Risk estimation is not the prediction of a person's future medical history"

(Goetz et al., 1980). Second, the multiple logistical predictions do not define causation, even though a causal relationship is often assumed in intervention strategies (Goetz et al., 1980). Because the causal links between given risk factors and disease are often unclear, questions have been raised about the ethics of widespread screening and intervention with asymptomatic populations (Hulley et al., 1980; Louria, Kidwell, Lavenhar, Thind, & Naje, 1976).

It has been especially difficult to validate causal links between behavioral risk factors and disease states. Behavioral factors are typically the first of a sequence of steps leading to illness; for example, smoking may alter blood pressure, which in turn affects atherosclerosis and increases the likelihood of a stroke and/or a heart attack. Each of the steps is linked probabilistically, making it difficult to detect the impact of behavioral change on illness. It is also frequently the case that significant change in behavior produces clinically insignificant change at the next step in the sequence (e.g., the measure of blood pressure or blood lipids) (Ahrens, 1976; Stunkard & Mahoney, 1976), and changes in clinical measures may be due to factors other than changes in target behaviors (J. C. Kleinman, Feldman, & Monk, 1979; Nichols, Ravenscroft, Lamphiear, & Ostrander, 1976). The epidemiological representation of risk (i.e., the multiple logistical function) identifies factors associated with disease, but it does not define how these factors are related to disease, whether change in the factors can alter morbidity and mortality, or how individuals perceive these links. For example, although there is a widespread belief that smoking is harmful (Wynder & Hoffmann, 1979), one-third of the population of the United States continues to smoke (U.S. Public Health Service, 1979). Why does this discrepancy exist? Through the communication of epidemiological data and medical influence, the public has developed a set of beliefs about what ought to be done to control risk. However, a personal representation of risk depends on factors other than morbidity–mortality statistics.

In a survey conducted for the American Cancer Society in 1975 (U.S. Public Health Service, 1979), teenage smoking was perceived to be more prevalent than it actually is—a perception that speaks to its social visibility and potential acceptability. Although most teenagers see smoking as potentially habit-forming, two-thirds consider experimental smoking to be harmless. There is a prevailing belief that people could stop smoking if they wanted to, without any awareness of the problems of addiction and dependence. Both the benign interpretation of noxious sensations during initial trials and later adaptation contribute further to the perception of smoking as safe (Leventhal & Cleary, 1980). Thus, individuals may accept the general notion of risk, but their personal representation of risk may contrast with abstract, publicly statable formulations of the risk problems.

Similar patterns are found in beliefs about obesity. Approximately 13% of adult males and 23% of adult females in the United States are obese, and one-third of these might be considered severely obese. However, twice as many rate themselves as obese, and two-thirds of these are attempting to lose weight (Abraham & Johnson, 1980; Foreyt & Gotto, 1979). That is, over 58 million people perceive themselves as having a weight problem, and 37 million are trying to do something about it.

In a recent survey of adolescent views on obesity, the definition of obesity was more dependent on subjective or personal criteria (e.g., "feeling fat") than on shared, public criteria such as weight and weight norms (Worsley, 1979). Of particular interest was the heavy reliance on sensory cues such as "feeling tired" or "looking fat" as signs of obesity. These concrete cues may play a critical role in the decision to lose weight. Although there was awareness of the long-term medical problems of obesity, only 21% of healthy persons wanting to lose weight cited health as their reason for doing so. Physical appearance and social acceptance were far more common as motives for weight reduction (Knapp, 1978). Again, perceived risk may be in contrast to general notions of risk, and though being overweight may be seen as a risk factor for illness, behavioral change may be motivated by goals other than that of reduced illness risk.

These findings suggest several potential barriers to the appropriate formation of a concept of risk. First, there is a dissociation between the acceptance of an abstract notion of risk and the belief that one's health is actually jeopardized by certain habits. The sense of being "at risk" may depend on concrete sensory "symptoms" that are interpreted as precursors of disease. This could lead to faulty monitoring of risk status if immediate sensory feedback is expected to reflect actual or anticipated physical damage. Preliminary results from interviews with cardiac patients revealed that patients who did not perceive themselves at risk prior to diagnosis, particularly patients who were asymptomatic, were more distressed by the diagnosis and treatment and had less compliance with recommendations for risk control (Gutmann et al., 1981). Lacking concrete signs to represent risk, these patients were more likely to view surgical treatment as curative rather than protective. No matter how well we develop people's skills in exercising, resisting social influence to smoke, and so forth, there is no reason to believe that people will engage in risk reduction efforts over the *long term* if they represent their health problems and evaluate their efforts in relation to an acute, symptomatic representation of risk.

Second, health motives may not be important for long-term behavior change. Health motives may be important in initiating behavior change, but the development of secondary positive goals (e.g., improved self-image) may be essential for long-term maintenance. Health habits that are associated with positive affect (e.g., "runner's high") or reduction of negative affect (e.g., depression, anxiety) can themselves be "addicting" (Dishman, 1982; Glasser, 1976; Leventhal & Hirschman, 1982; Solomon & Corbit, 1974). Thus, maintenance of long-term health habits may require not only the learning of behavioral skills, but also an "emotional hooker" that makes the action personally reinforcing and meaningful (Gutmann & Meyer, 1981). The problems mentioned above—particularly those involved in translations of epidemiological data into personal representations of risk, limited individual experience with chronic illnesses (hence low visibility of risk in relation to illness outcomes), and the questionable link between perceived benefits of behavioral change and actual risk reduction—probably account for the gap between epidemiological and everyday or common-sense representations of illness risk (Leventhal, Nerenz, & Straus, 1980) and reinforce the acute model of risk reduction rather than the development of long-term self-regulatory skills.

Methodological Problems. The conceptual deficits discussed above have led to several methodological problems in behavioral research. First, the rigid adherence to public notions of risk and the prescriptive approach to behavioral change have led naturally to an emphasis on outcomes rather than on process. Furthermore, medical and behavioral models assume that adherence to treatment is directly related to treatment outcome; that patients who adhere to recommended actions will be more successful; and that success is evidence of greater adherence (Dunbar & Stunkard, 1979; Loro *et al.*, 1979). It is valid to ask, however, whether people actually adhere to prescribed behaviors when they succeed in altering risk factors.

Unfortunately, few studies have actually assessed or reported adherence to treatment recommendations (Cooke & Meyers, 1980; Feinstein & Ransohoff, 1976; Loro *et al.*, 1979; Wilson, 1978); among those that have, documented behavior change has not always correlated significantly with such objective outcome criteria as weight loss (Brownell & Stunkard, 1978; Foreyt & Gotto, 1979; Jeffery, Wing, & Stunkard, 1978; Stalonas, Johnson, & Christ, 1978). For example, one study (Stalonas *et al.*, 1978) reported a fairly high level of adherence to 10 program behaviors, but only one of the 10 (i.e., uncontrolled eating) was significantly related to weight change. After reviewing several studies on weight loss programs, Brownell and Stunkard (1978) concluded that there were insufficient data to support the assumed relationship between adherence and outcome. However, several methodological issues need to be considered before any final conclusions can be drawn. These issues highlight the difficulties of an orientation that focuses on outcome and neglects individual change processes.

Second, outcome measures are usually reported as group means, which obscure the large individual variations found in both weight loss programs (Stunkard, 1977; Stunkard & Mahoney, 1976) and smoking cessation programs (Harrup *et al.*, 1979; Hunt & Matarazzo, 1971; Leventhal & Cleary, 1980; Schlesel & Kunetsky, 1977). The great variability among individuals in their responses to treatment would inevitably negate any significant correlation between adherence measures and group outcomes. Few studies have examined the impact of specific interventions on subgroups of smokers (Leventhal & Cleary, 1980) or obese persons (Cooke & Meyers, 1980). When changes in target behaviors have been measured separately for individuals and correlated with their weight loss, significant relationships have been found (Lansky, 1981). These relationships and patterns are lost when individual differences are ignored and the focus is only on mean outcome.

Third, adherence to treatment protocol is important only if a prescription is appropriate for a given individual. Since the mechanisms and functions of smoking or obesity differ for each individual, different strategies are needed for intervention. For example, desensitization techniques might be most effective with people who smoke to control anxiety, while aversive conditioning methods would be more appropriate for smokers who enjoy the taste of cigarettes or who smoke for positive affect (Leventhal & Cleary, 1980). As Lansky (1981) and Yates (1975) have pointed out, different individuals manifest different problem behaviors and thus require changes in different habits to achieve common goals.

Fourth, an overriding concern with main effects obscures the potential impact of interactions. For example, adherence measures may not correlate significantly with outcome measures if the types of adherence errors are not differentiated (Dunbar & Stunkard, 1979). Errors of omission are functionally different from errors of commission, yet may have the same devastating effect on outcome.

The critical issue is not blind adherence to total treatment packages, but adherence to behavioral techniques useful for both short- and long-term behavioral change and for maintaining the individual's sense of control of a perceptible threat. Unless the prescribed treatment is relevant and effective for the individual's unique pattern of behavior, adherence is a moot point. Indeed, it is sometimes difficult to know just what contributes to success. Mahoney and Mahoney (1976), for example, maintain that reinforcement of appropriate behavior change is more effective than rewarding weight loss itself is. It has been suggested that initial weight loss may be dependent on changing eating behaviors, but that long-term change involves a broader social perspective, with alterations in other personal habits, attitudes, and coping styles (Cooke & Meyers, 1980; Kingsley & Wilson, 1977). Thus, modification of behaviors that alter self-concept, such as assertiveness and social skills, have also been effective in producing sustained weight loss (Wilson, 1976). Short- and long-term objectives require changes in different behaviors, each with its own mechanisms for maintaining change. External rewards may work well for rapid weight reduction, but a permanent change in eating patterns requires a multitude of other changes (e.g., activity patterns), as well as a change in self-perception (e.g., "I am a jogger").

Self-perceptions, particularly those related to perceiving the self as competent (Bandura, 1977; T. J. Rosen et al., 1982), also seem important in accounting for a number of unanticipated "nonspecific" effects observed in behavioral studies. "Nonspecific" effects have been difficult to evaluate because of the absence of adequate control groups (Bernstein & McAlister, 1976;

Evans, Henderson, Hill, & Raines, 1979; Leon, 1976; A. R. Marston & McFall, 1971; Wilson, 1978). When no-treatment control groups have been included in the design, the results have sometimes been surprising. For example, Schlesel and Kunetsky (1977) found a greater percentage of abstinence among participants in a "Five-Day Plan to Stop Smoking" program than in a control group, but the control group also experienced a decline in percentage of smokers and number of cigarettes smoked. Furthermore, the treatment group showed an increase in cigarette consumption during follow-up, while the control group continued to decrease slightly. It has been suggested that behavioral change in treatment control groups represents the effects of "unaided effort" (Paul, 1969), which may have better long-term results. People do manage to quit smoking or change behaviors on their own. Surveys showed a marked decrease in current smokers from 52% to 40% of the general population, and an increase in former smokers from 22% to 29% in a 10-year period from 1964 to 1975 (U.S. Public Health Service, 1979). Yet, only 33% of current smokers who want to quit are willing to attend formal treatment programs (Paul, 1969). A. R. Marston and McFall (1971) have suggested that urging smokers to quit on their own may be as effective as applying formal intervention—a conclusion supported by data collected by Schachter (1982), which suggest that two-thirds of those who wish to quit smoking on their own succeed and do so for a period of years! Simple advice from a physician has also been found to be effective in reducing smoking, and has resulted in 3–5% still abstaining at the end of 1 year (Russell, Wilson, Taylor, & Becker, 1979). Thus, formal behavioral skills training may be unnecessary for some individuals and insufficient for others in producing long-term change for risk reduction.

In weight reduction, poor long-term results are compounded by a paradoxical negative correlation between initial response during active treatment and subsequent weight loss during follow-up (Kingsley & Wilson, 1977; Stunkard, 1977; Stunkard & Penick, 1979). Few patients lose additional weight after termination of active treatment, but those who are more successful in treatment show greater relapse during follow-up (Stunkard, 1977). This suggests different mechanisms in treatment and follow-up for maintaining weight loss. The negative correlation is paradoxical only if we fail to recognize that therapists' activities may be critical for weight loss during treatment, and that unaided effort and self-regulation may be critical for maintaining weight loss during follow-up. Patients who respond well to therapists' interventions may show high recidivism, because they have not learned adequate self-regulatory skills. In fact, the ability to monitor and reinforce one's own behaviors has been found to be predictive of outcome in weight reduction programs (Cooke & Meyers, 1980; McFall & Hammen, 1971), and programs aimed at self-control rather than therapist control have been shown to improve outcome (Rozensky & Bellack, 1976). Recidivism could conceivably result from overly strict adherence to treatment protocol, which may prevent the development of self-regulatory skills necessary for long-term maintenance.

If we were to state what appears to be the fundamental problem underlying medical and behavioral approaches to risk reduction, it would be that they tend to be too narrow in their definition of the problem and to focus only on target behaviors or specific outcomes. Hence, they adopt a prescriptive approach that seems inconsistent with their stated objective of developing "self-control" (Kanfer, 1977; Kanfer et al., 1974). This leads them to ignore both the process of change and the functional differences in health habits for given individuals. There is no attention to self-concept (M. Rosenberg, 1979), associative learning (Hunt, Matarazzo, Weiss, & Gentry, 1979), development of secondary positive goals and life style changes (Leventhal & Cleary, 1980; Leventhal & Hirschman, 1982) or learning of self-regulatory skills needed for long-term changes of complex behavior patterns or life styles. Adherence is relevant only to the change process that is dependent on therapists' activity and prescription. A self-regulation model allows the individual to move from short- to long-term goals, and to integrate the change into a personal life style.

The Self-Regulation Model of Risk Reduction

The primary focus in a self-regulation model is the process of change and stabilization, not adherence to a prescribed regimen. Compliance is an evaluative concept, and refers to the overlap between the patient's self-selected pattern of regulatory behaviors and the prescription. In a self-regulation model, the "gold standard" is not the prescribed treatment, but the pattern of behaviors that would follow, given the individual's representation (abstract and concrete) of the problem, coping skills (for the problem and for emotion), and appraisal of outcomes. Thus, in self-regulation for risk reduction, there are four key components: (1) the representation of risk as developed by the individual, (2) the acquisition of self-regulatory skills for behavioral change and maintenance, (3) the appraisal of outcomes and the attribution of change to one's own efforts in generating effective responses, and (4) the integration of new habits into a personal life style.

First, risk is defined from the perspective of the individual and represents an integration of abstract information (i.e., statistical probabilities) and concrete sensory input from the body. What does it mean to be at "20% risk for heart disease"? It could mean that one out of five brothers will develop heart disease; or it could be a firm conviction that one has heart disease every time one experiences chest discomfort—a conviction that is forgotten when one feels well. If concepts of risk are based on past experiences with acute illness episodes, accompanied by symptoms that disappear on recovery, then the lack of concrete cues may serve as a barrier to risk reduction for health reasons. Other concrete cues may be used to assess risk status, and secondary positive goals (e.g., weight loss, increased energy level, emotional well-being) might be more effective than negative health goals in maintaining behavior change (Leventhal & Hirschman, 1982). The transition from short-term, concrete goals (e.g., "lose 10 pounds") to more abstract, long-term motives (e.g., "be lean and healthy") implies a gradual change in risk representation, as well as a change in self-definition. Up to this point in time, investigators have conceptualized representations in *their* frames of reference rather than that of the patients! For example, the health belief model (M. H. Becker, 1976) incorporates patients' perceptions of disease susceptibility, severity, and treatment efficacy as predictors of compliance; however, these variables are inventions of the investigator and may tell us little about the individuals' representations.

Second, self-regulation in risk reduction depends on the acquisition and development of requisite skills. Behavioral approaches have provided the technology for skills training, but the degree of structure and supervision required puts the therapist, not the patient or client, in charge of change and limits the long-term effectiveness of such approaches. Just as short-term concrete goals require specific behavior interventions, long-term behavioral change requires increasing automaticity for speed and stability, as well as independence from external reinforcement, in order to generalize across situations (Hunt *et al.*, 1979). Thus, intervention strategies that employ a problem-solving format and focus on self-management outside of treatment settings may be more appropriate for long-term maintenance (Coates & Thoreson, 1978).

Third, the extent to which risk reduction efforts are made will depend on an individual's perceived ability to alter risk status. "Self-attribution of behavior change increases the likelihood of maintaining that change" (Kopel & Arkowitz, 1975), and successful self-control in one area (e.g., smoking) leads to a belief in self-efficacy in other areas (e.g., weight control) (C. Mitchell & Stuart, 1979). Expectation of success has also been associated with better long-term maintenance in smoking cessation (Schlesel & Kunetsky, 1977). The salient question is not simply how to teach self-management skills, but how individuals develop a perception of themselves as effective self-managers. Bem's (1972) self-perception theory suggests that observation of one's own behavior may affect subsequent behavior, attitudes, and beliefs. This implies a feedback system that allows continuous appraisal and adjustment of strategies. Little is known about this process of appraisal and feedback for behavioral change and maintenance.

Finally, health behaviors do not occur in isolation. They are interrelated to form a cohesive pattern or "life style" (Breslow & Enstrom, 1980; Criqui, Barrett-Connor, Holdbrook, Austin, & Turner, 1980; Leventhal, Safer, Cleary, & Gutmann, 1980). Positive health habits could be viewed as constituting an effective life style that reflects an ability to anticipate problems and to meet and cope with them actively (Mechanic & Cleary, 1980). The individual's personal concept of risk, its concrete and abstract representations, and its perceived links to specific behaviors affect both decisions to modify habits and strategies adopted to regulate and monitor risk status. The evolution of risk representation and transition from short- to long-term objectives, the development of requisite self-management skills and associated changes in self-concept, all culminate in a life style change that has much broader implications for the individual than a reduction in specific risks does. In summary, the self-regulation model views risk reduction as a process of redefinition or change, rather than as an end product achieved through prescriptive therapy.

Compliance and the Practitioner–Patient Relationship

How the practitioner and the patient interact with each other, what they say and think, and how they feel about each other affect the way in which the patient formulates or defines illness problems, develops coping responses, and appraises outcomes. Many previous treatments of the compliance problem deal with patients as isolated entities and attempt to explain compliance by describing an individual, an individual's behavior, or a specific treatment regimen. But people do not live in a vacuum; they behave in a social context, and the practitioner–patient relationship within the larger medical and social systems plays an important role in adherence to medical and behavioral regimens. Until now, we have addressed these concerns only implicitly. In this section, they become the focus as we probe the dynamics of the practitioner–patient relationship and their impact on compliance.

Though research in both areas—that of the practitioner–patient relationship and that of compliance—has grown rapidly over the last 10 to 15 years, the two sets of literature have rarely overlapped. A complaint lodged by M. S. Davis in 1968 would apply nearly as well today: "Few empirical investigations have dealt with the way in which interaction between patient and practitioner influences patient compliance. Those who have studied this factor empirically have . . . not considered *how* this might influence the patient's decision regarding compliance" (M. S. Davis, 1968, p. 276).

Socioscientific Perspective

The focus of research on the practitioner–patient interaction has been on understanding features of the interaction itself and how they correlate with outcomes, rather than on how they generate outcomes. Researchers have, by and large, used the practitioner–patient interaction to pursue their own research interests (e.g., power relationships, organization of talk as it relates to memory, communication of interpersonal feelings, the communication process between two individuals, etc.). "Patient satisfaction" has served as the criterion variable to measure the impact of these interaction factors. A link is also suggested, but seldom examined, between patients' satisfaction and patients' compliance.

Expectations

Both patient and physician have specific expectations of and preferences for the type of relationship they will enjoy and the outcomes they anticipate from their interaction. The expectations held by each party may differ considerably (Dimsdale *et al.*, 1979; Zimmerman, 1982), and these differences may go unrecognized (Korsch, Freemon, & Negrete, 1971; Meyer *et al.*, in press). Since the role relationship places the physician in general control of the interaction (West, 1982; Wolinsky, 1980), the substance of the appointment is likely to conform more closely to his or her expectations. Thus, to the extent that the patient's and the physician's expectations differ, the patient may ultimately be unhappy with the care and may be less likely to remain in and comply with treatment.

The classic study of the effect of the match of patients' expectations about appointments and actual care received during the appointment was conducted by Korsch and her associates (Korsch, Gozzi, & Francis, 1968). The research group studied tape recordings of 800 interactions of physicians with pediatric patients and their mothers. Additional data were provided by interviews with mothers immediately after the appointment and 1 week later. Mothers for whom any of a variety of (retrospectively reported) expectations were unmet during the appointment were less satisfied. Furthermore, the greater the number of unmet expectations, the less compliant the mothers reported themselves to be (Francis, Korsch, & Morris, 1969).

The importance of mutuality of expectations was demonstrated in a recent study of interaction between dental students and patients, conducted in a preventive dental clinic (Zimmerman, 1982). This study was a significant advance beyond that of Korsch's group in two ways. First, practitioners' expectations were assessed independently of the patients'. Second, patients were asked *before* the appointment about their expectations, and *after* the appointment about their satisfaction, instead of being questioned about both after the appointment. A few days before their first appointment in the clinic, each of 54 patients completed a 15-item appointment preference scale, on which they rated the importance to them of various aspects of practitioners' behavior. Items rated included friendliness, thoroughness, care in explaining treatment, sense of humor, time taken with them as patients, and questions answered. Each of the 44 dental-student practitioners involved also completed the appointment preference scale. In the first appointment, each dental student collected data on two criterion measures (gum inflammation and plaque accumulation) and conducted an education session on toothbrushing and flossing. After the appointment, patients rated their satisfaction with the dental students' performance and indicated their intentions to improve a number of their oral hygiene habits. At the second appointment, about 1 week later, the criterion measures were assessed again for each patient, the educational material was reviewed, and the patient's teeth were cleaned. After this appointment, patients reported changes in their oral hygiene habits. To measure patient–practitioner differences in expectations, the absolute values of differences in importance were summed over all 15 items completed prior to the first visit for each of the 54 practitioner–patient pairs. The more discrepant the preferences (expectations), the less satisfied the patient was after the visit; the less likely he or she was to report compliance with the dental student's recommendations; and the less his or her plaque and gum inflammation scores improved (all relationships were statistically significant). The evidence is consistent, therefore, in suggesting that congruence of patients' and practitioners' expectations, and of patients' expectations and the course of the appointment, lead to greater patient satisfaction and to greater compliance.

Cognition

If the role of the practitioner is to do his or her best to *get the patient to do something*, then exactly what is communicated and how it is received, understood, and retained are of great importance. As mentioned in the earlier discussion of the communication steps, the physician often fails to state the precise regimen to be followed, or states it in an unclear or too technical fashion (McKinlay, 1975; Svarstad, 1974, 1976). When the physician's instructions are clear, the patient is more likely to comply (Svarstad, 1976). Not only does the information often go unmentioned or uncomprehended, but if it is understood, it is frequently forgotten. Across five studies summarized by Ley (1977), 141 patients remembered, on average, only 57% of the statements made by their physicians within 2 hours of their appointments. Ley and associates (Bradshaw, Ley, Kincey, & Bradshaw, 1975; Ley, 1972; Ley, Bradshaw, Eaves, & Walker, 1973; Ley & Spelman, 1967; Ley, Whitworth, Skilbeck, Woodward, Pinset, Pike, Clarkson, & Clark, 1976) make six suggestions for increasing patients' recall:

1. Whenever possible, present information about the course of action to be followed near the beginning of the interaction.
2. When providing patients with the course of action to be adhered to, stress how important it is.
3. Use short words and short sentences.
4. Use explicit categorization of topics where possible.
5. Repeat things where feasible.
6. When giving advice, make it as specific, detailed, and concrete as possible.

In two studies (Ley *et al.*, 1973; Ley *et al.*, 1976) testing these principles, patients remembered more after their general practitioners had been instructed to follow Ley's six suggestions, and lost more weight when they received a pamphlet prepared according to these procedures than did patients in control groups.

Affect

Investigators have increasingly focused on the hypothesis that a positively toned interaction or an emotionally satisfying practitioner–patient relationship correlates with patients' satisfaction and compliance. Two assumptions have been made by most researchers in this area: first, that patients who are satisfied with their appointments comply; and, second, that asking patients about the extent to which they comply is the same as measuring compliance. Ignoring for now the validity of these assumptions, we report on the research using satisfaction and reported compliance as outcome measures, along with studies that employed more "objective" compliance measures.

In an exploratory study, M. S. Davis (1968) studied 154 patients and their general practitioners and found compliance to be lower when the communication between practitioner and patient departed from the norm. The deviant patterns included the following: a patient's disagreeing with a physician, resulting in tension and antagonism; the combination of a permissive physician and an active patient; and a physician's asking a lot of questions while giving little information, with the patient simply giving answers. In another study, Freemon, Negrete, Davis, and Korsch (1971) found that a low proportion of negative statements and a high proportion of positive statements by a physician were related to increased patient satisfaction and greater reported compliance. These investigators also found a result congruent with Svarstad's (1974, 1976), showing that physicians' "approachability" and perceived friendliness were positively related to compliance.

Studies conducted during the past few years have replicated and extended our understanding of the association between positive affect in the practitioner–patient relationship and improved outcomes. Ben-Sira (1976, 1980) found patients' satisfaction with care to be more strongly related to the patients' evaluation of the affective, as compared to the technical, component of the appointment. Stiles and his associates, using his "verbal response modes" taxonomy of interaction categories (Stiles, 1978), analyzed 52 taped physician–patient visits at a general medical screening clinic and found that patients were more likely to be satisfied with affective aspects of the appointment if they were allowed to tell their own story in the first part of the appointment, and that they were more likely to be satisfied with cognitive features of the interaction if their physicians gave feedback in the final, instructional segment (Stiles, Putnam, Wolf, & James, 1979). In a study of 164 ambulatory patients and 178 medical inpatients of a community teaching hospital, Friedman (1979) found a relationship between a patient's evaluation of a physician and commitment to continuing the treatment relationship. Patients were more likely to want to see a particular practitioner again if they were satisfied that he or she listened, took enough time, explained their medical condition, was available by phone, and cared about them as persons.

Research on the communication of affect through nonverbal cues suggests that physicians' ability to communicate accurately and understand others' nonverbal cues is related to patients' satisfaction with care. Studies by Friedman and DiMatteo indicate that physicians who were judged to be more accurate in identifying the affective meaning of others' body movements were rated by patients as more caring and sensitive than were physicians who lacked this skill. The number of inaccurate emotional messages sent by the physicians (statements intended as positive, but judged as negative) was negatively related to patients' perceptions of the physicians as caring and sensitive (DiMatteo, Taranta, Friedman, & Prince, 1980).

In a more recent study, Hall, Roter, and Rand (1981) examined the link between affect in an interaction and later keeping of appointments. Naive judges rated samples of physicians' and patients' speech on seven affective dimensions and judged the probability of the patients' returning for their next appointment. In addition, scales on attitudes toward physicians and contentment with the appointment were administered to patients. Two measures of patients' compliance—previous and subsequent percentages of appointments that were kept—were also collected. A patient whose voice was rated as satisfied was more likely to have kept past appointments, and was also more likely to keep future appointments. In addition, when physicians simultaneously expressed positive affect verbally (e.g., ''I like what you're doing'') and negative affect in tone of voice, patients interpreted the physician's behavior in an overall *positive* sense, as reflective of sincerity, concern, and a task orientation (Hall *et al.*, 1981, p. 28).

Social Roles

Our social system can be conceptualized as a large set of roles that we move into and out of in our daily lives. For each role, there are rules that guide expectations of our and others' role-appropriate behavior. This makes it easier for us to act without constantly having to worry about what to do in a particular situation. From the outset, we know how patients and physicians should act. Hence, when we enter a new physician–patient relationship, we have guidelines for our behavior. Szasz and Hollender (1956) described three physician–patient role structures in their important ''contribution to the philosophy of medicine.'' One type of relationship is that of the active doctor and the passive patient. This role is typified by the relationship in cases of acute trauma and coma, in which the patient is essentially unable to respond. The second type of relationship is that of the guiding physician and the cooperative patient, applied in much of general medicine and the postoperative care of surgical patients; the physician tells the patient what to do and expects the patient to cooperate. The third type of relationship is characterized by mutual participation. Here, the physician helps the patient to participate in helping himself or herself. The authors conclude not that one or the other type of relationship is fundamentally better, but that the best relationship depends on the patient's and the physician's preferences, the disease itself, the stage of the disease, and the past history of that relationship.

The conclusion that different types of role relationships are best for different patients and diseases has, unfortunately, been largely ignored. For example, Stimson (1974) has suggested that instead of viewing the patient from the medical perspective (i.e., as passive, obedient, and unquestioning), that the patient's perspective be adopted by viewing the interaction as an endeavor in mutual participation. From this perspective, the patient is an active human being who has expectations of the practitioner, evaluates the practitioner's actions, and is able to make his or her own treatment decisions. Four specific advantages of greater patient participation have been suggested: (1) more complete communication, (2) more realistic expectations of care, (3) improvement in the quality of clinical decision making, and (4) greater patient compliance (Brody, 1980; Eisenberg, 1979; Schulman, 1979).

Unfortunately, the few empirical studies in this area have produced inconsistent findings, and the published material on this topic consists of politically motivated rhetoric and sheer speculation. Two correlational studies are exceptions. Eisenthal, Lazare, and their colleagues (Eisenthal & Lazare, 1977; Eisenthal, Emery, Lazare, & Udin, 1979) have found that patient–psychiatrist interviews lead to greater patient satisfaction and better adherence to medical regimens if the patients report a high level of negotiation, especially if they indicate that they participated in the decision making and that their clinicians understood their requests for help. In addition, patients given the treatment plan they desire are more likely to be satisfied and to adhere to it. In a study of the "active patient orientation" of hypertensive patients, Schulman (1979) similarly found a positive effect of the active patient role on outcomes. The more active the patient's orientation (as measured on an 11-item questionnaire), the lower a patient's blood pressure. Self-reports of adherence were also greater for the active patient group.

While there are alternative explanations for these findings, they do at least suggest the beneficial nature of providing the patient with an active role in treatment. A specific procedure that expands the traditional role, contracting, has also been shown to be effective in improving patient outcomes. In a study exemplary for its use of random assignment, Steckel and Swain (1977) assigned hypertensives to one of three groups—routine care, educational intervention, and contracting. The contracting group experienced the greatest increase in knowledge about high blood pressure, the lowest dropout rate, the best blood pressure control, and the greatest weight loss.

The Self-Regulation Approach: Tying the Interaction to Adherence

As we have seen, research on the practitioner–patient interaction has suggested links among expectations, cognitions, affect, social roles, satisfaction, and compliance. But the processes by which the practitioner–patient interaction is connected to adherence (i.e., the situations, events, feelings, and ideas of the patient) have not been systematically studied. The self-regulation approach can make a significant contribution to our understanding of this process. From this perspective, the patient is seen as formulating an illness representation and coping plans and as repeatedly reappraising outcomes before, during, and after interactions with the physician. Thus the entire form and substance of the practitioner–patient interaction, and its relationship to behavioral events both between interactions and in subsequent interactions, are all important parts of the adherence process. Self-regulation theory substitutes interest in the long-term adherence process for the attention to isolated interaction episodes that is seen in most research. The practitioner–patient relationship affects the self-regulation process and the patient's cognitive, affective, social, and self-concept systems at three points in time: before, during, and after an appointment.

The preappointment phase is composed of three important elements—illness experience, the decision to seek care, and appointment expectations. The illness experience consists of both previous and current symptom experience (internal) and previous sick role experience (external). The symptoms the person has experienced before play a large part in how the individual labels his or her present condition and ultimately decides that something is wrong and care is needed. The decision to seek care is itself based on many facets of the patient's psychological, physical, and emotional condition, both past and present (see McKinlay, 1981; Safer *et al.*, 1979).

Having made the decision to seek care, the patient develops expectations and preferences for the upcoming appointment. They include anticipations and preferences about the tone and style of the coming interaction, beliefs about what are reasonable and unreasonable questions and answers for the interaction, questions about how much control to give the physician, what the physician will probably say and how to react or act, and so forth. These expectations and the prior experiences that have shaped them affect how information is processed and stored during the interaction and retrieved and acted upon afterward.

The second phase of the self-regulation process is the appointment itself. How does self-regulation theory alter our view of these processes? The patient is seen as active at every moment of the interaction—integrating elements from affective, cognitive, and social spheres into his or her representation of the illness problem, feelings, repertoire of behavioral skills, and images of self. Even a "passive" patient is processing information, encoding it, and fitting it into such existing schemas as those for health, illness, and the self. In a recent study (Zimmerman, Linz, Leventhal, & Penrod, 1982), we found that within 10 minutes of being labeled as hypertensive, individuals' schemas of health and illness and of self-identity had altered significantly.

The typical visit to a physician opens with the patient's presenting the history of the present complaint, sometimes adding his or her explicit "lay diagnosis." Prior sick role experience shapes the patient's approach to the appointment. This experience may have generated feelings of trust (for physicians in general and this one in particular), attitudes about talking with physicians ("Are they straight with me? Are they helpful?"), a general liking or disliking for physicians, notions about appropriate roles, feelings about appropriate delays in seeking care and appropriate length of treatment plans, and a "compliance history" of following or not following health and illness plans in the past. This last factor (e.g., previous experience and experimentation with dosage, side effects, and efficacy of prescribed regimens for this or other previous problems) may have a profound impact on how the practitioner–patient interaction affects adherence to treatment for the current illness episode. The assumption that the patient has new ideas, feelings, and action plans only at the end of the appointment is not accurate. These elements of the patient's world may have changed many times during the appointment. One implication of this, as suggested earlier, is that physicians should pay more careful attention to the sequence in which they present medical concepts, since poor temporal placement may lead patients to forget important material or to see connections between unrelated ideas. For example, if a physician asks questions about potential symptoms of hypertension and does not explain that he or she is interested in these as side effects, the patient may link the symptoms to his or her high blood pressure and may generate a plausible but medically incorrect theory of the disease (Steele & Leventhal, 1982). Finally, if the patient actively participates with the physician in clarifying his or her experience (representation) and interpretation of the illness, in generating coping strategies, and in setting up criteria for appraising treatment outcome, he or she may develop a sense of effectance and control and may follow a pattern of positive self-care after the particular therapeutic relationship has ended.

The third phase is the postappointment period. It is in this period that "compliance" research usually obtains its dependent measures. This is the time when the emotional and cognitive representations of the illness are solidified, plans for coping are developed, behavior is carried out, and the emotional and cognitive outcomes are evaluated (leading to further coping behavior, if necessary). Environmental cues, social support and influence, the emotional and cognitive experience of the past appointment, and anticipation of future appointments all feed into this self-regulating process.

A Self-Regulation Critique of the Literature
on Doctor–Patient Interactions

As illustrated in the preceding section on the three phases of the practitioner-patient interaction, the self-regulation model can stimulate research on the link between the interaction and adherence along a variety of paths. We examine three specific areas: expanding our repertoire of independent variables, improving our assessment of dependent variables, and broadening our scope.

Independent Variables

Though a number of interaction variables have been studied, including difficulty of the dicussion, amount of questioning and answering by physician and patient, and interpersonal affect communicated between the two, it is still unclear exactly what aspects of the interaction should relate to compliance outcomes. We also believe that the real substance of the interaction, the verbal exchange between practitioner and patient, has been slighted.

Most of the studies that have examined the pattern of communication between practitioner and patient have used categories that were designed for other contexts, and have ignored the medical content of the interaction. The Davis and Korsch groups (M. S. Davis, 1968; Freemon et al., 1971) used Bales' (1950) Interaction Process Analysis, which had been designed for use in task-oriented small groups. Stiles et al. (1979) constructed a coding scheme (Stiles, 1978) for analyzing psychiatrist–client interactions that comes closer to capturing the interaction content than the Bales scheme does, but it still ignores much of the information exchanged about the patient's disease and the medical setting, while focusing on extraneous linguistic information. Studies by Svarstad (1974) and Dervin, Harlock, Atwood, and Garzona (1980) are rare examples of investigators' use of more detailed health- and disease-specific content categories for coding the interaction as perceived by the patient. Thus, while Bales' and Stiles' schemes have accounted in two instances for as much as 25% and 40%, respectively, of the variance of patients' satisfaction or reported compliance (Carter, Inui, Kukull, & Haigh, 1982; Inui, Carter, Kukull, & Haigh, 1982), it is unlikely that they will ever help us fully understand the compliance process, since they ignore the medical content of the interaction (i.e., information that helps define the patient's representation of the disease, coping strategies, and evaluation criteria).

In addition, most studies obtain summary frequency counts of practitioner–patient behavior and fail to capture the pattern of the interaction. At a minimum, we must study complete interaction sequences, or "interacts," in which a physician's statement is paired with its prior or subsequent patient's statement. As we examine and even diagram the interaction pattern of the entire encounter, we can begin to comprehend its meaning for the participants.

Still more microanalytic views of the interaction can be adopted. Conversational analysis (Psathas, 1979; Schenkein, 1979) has focused on interaction as a multitude of simultaneous activities. Pauses, interruptions, overlapping talk, sequences of utterances, opening and closing statements, and talking about the interaction itself are all aspects of the interaction that may have meaning for the participants. For example, West (1982) studied physician–patient talk and showed that the difference in status of practitioners' and patients' roles was visible in the practitioners' interruptions of patients' statements. We need to understand how patients process information both affectively and cognitively at this level, and to examine its relationship to later cognitions, affect, and behavior. Microanalysis may be of special importance if we expect to develop educational programs to alter practitioners' behavior in ways that enhance liking, satisfaction, and compliance.

Not only can we study the substance of the practitioner–patient interaction in ways that are more meaningful to patients, but we can also ask patients about important aspects of the substance of the interaction. Questions used in most research focus on global reactions (e.g., ''Did the practitioner care enough?'' ''Did he or she give you enough information?''). But vague questions yield vague answers. Patients can be asked about specific elements of the interaction (e.g., ''Did you feel the instructions about medication taking were clear?'' ''Did the physician allow you to ask everything you wanted to know about the cause of your illness?''). And these questions can address specific aspects and points in the interaction.

In summary, the practitioner–patient interaction should be examined with respect to the type of information presented by both practitioner and patient and the understanding each has of the other's communications. And the medical content of the interaction (i.e., representations of the illness, coping recommendations, and ways of appraising treatment outcomes) cannot be ignored. We must explore specific events in the interaction at the microcommunicative level of conversation, and determine how these are perceived by the participants, in order to understand the interpersonal affect communicated in the encounter and the ways in which processed information feeds into preexisting schemas. In short, we need to develop coding schemes that capture the meaning of the medical content and the meaning of the interpersonal behaviors for both participants, and to compare these to their expectations for the interaction and for the course of treatment.

Dependent Variables

Patients' satisfaction has been the major dependent variable employed in research on the practitioner–patient interaction. It is entirely possible, however, that patients do not immediately formulate attitudes or feelings about certain specific or even global features of the appointment. Researchers may be creating these attitudes by asking the questions (cf. Bem, 1972). In addition, questions about satisfaction are often asked along with questions about

patients' reports of events in the appointment. It is likely that one set of answers will affect the other, and that the relatively high correlation (in the .4–.6
range) between patients' satisfaction and reports of events in the interaction
may be due to their proximity in time when reporting; in other words, the
method effect may be great. And it is not always clear whether patients' reports on the interaction (independent variables) are truly separate from patients' satisfaction with the interaction (dependent variables). In short, we
need better evidence of the independent existence and meaningfulness of
the variable of patients' satisfaction. As suggested earlier, it may be that "satisfaction" is simply a catchall word for the variables that mediate the interaction–adherence relationship—that is, for variables such as liking the practitioner, feelings about what he or she is saying, thoughts of self, notions
of the practitioner's competence, desire for continued care, and feelings
about the health care setting.

In order to understand more fully the meaning of patients' satisfaction,
it is essential for us to understand more fully the relationship between patients' satisfaction and compliance. In general, satisfaction and compliance
have been found to be positively correlated, and the magnitude of the correlation has been moderate (Korsch et al., 1971). An intuitive notion that "if
you're satisfied with the appointment and the doctor, you'll go home and
do what the doctor said" is at the heart of much of the past research. On
occasion, however, patients' satisfaction and adherence have been unrelated
(Hulka et al., 1976), or related to separate sets of independent variables (Francis et al., 1969). We have proposed more specific hypothetical links for study:
for example, that satisfaction leads to increased communication during the
interaction, which then leads to greater compliance; or that satisfaction leads
to greater retention of the material presented in the interaction and thus to
greater compliance. The self-regulation perspective suggests ways of specifying mediating variables and linking them to outcome measures such as
compliance. But more research is necessary before the relationship of the two
variables—satisfaction and adherence—can be understood.

The weakness of many compliance measures, a criticism raised earlier in
this chapter, is perhaps nowhere more apparent than in research on practitioner–patient interaction. Single-patient reports are often the only compliance measures used. While important, they are not sufficient for a thorough
study of patient adherence, for they may tell us more about the patient's
beliefs and needs than about his or her behavior.

Scope

A final shortcoming, the narrow scope of research on the practitioner–patient
interaction, is highlighted by the self-regulation model. Our prior discussion
of the phases of adherence has illustrated how the self-regulation view can
expand our awareness of this process. One important extension suggested
by the self-regulation model is the development of concepts to connect mo-

ment-by-moment adjustment to longer-term behavior patterns. One possible way of doing this is to examine how self-regulation develops into an "adherence career." Sociologists use the term "career" (cf. H. S. Becker & Strauss, 1956) to refer to behavior patterns that both have some stability and emerge in accordance with self-defined and socially defined rules governing the career role. This concept seems useful in capturing the patient's perspective, for two reasons. First, it recognizes that compliance with a regimen for a particular disease or risk factor often takes place over a series of episodes extended over long periods of time. Second, it suggests that compliance attempts and successes should be examined for multiple illnesses or risk factors. Each individual has a compliance history that extends over a multitude of regimens for different purposes; how this history is structured, and how it affects self-regulatory processes and adherence to regimens for a current illness episode, are important areas for study. The representation of a previous problem and the effects of various coping patterns are both important factors in the development of an individual's present representation and coping style.

In sum, a self-regulation or systems perspective expands research on practitioner–patient interaction across interaction episodes, events between episodes, and a history of disease experiences. The relationship of the practitioner–patient interaction to adherence begins with individuals' first bouts with illness and ends only with their last.

CONCLUSION

We have summarized three perspectives on the compliance problem: the biomedical, the behavioral, and the self-regulation models. The biomedical model is designed to define disease and disease risks and to suggest treatment and prevention regimens. It does not focus on the dynamics of behavioral change, and its orientation is to demand compliance to prescribed behaviors in order to reduce disease rates. Behavioral models, operant and cognitive, focus on the participant's action. Their aim is to develop procedures to shape individual action to facilitate cure, control, or prevention of disease. For these models, the performance of specific actions is the criterion for success. Finally, we have proposed a systems view, in which the organism regulates itself by developing a representation of an illness threat, either current or future; behavioral plans for curing, controlling, or preventing disease; and criteria for appraising the outcomes of coping efforts.

We have exmained the way in which each perspective generates research and contributes to our understanding of the processes involved in adherence to medical treatments, prevention or risk reduction, and the interaction between practitioner and patient. We have suggested that each of the three models makes important contributions to understanding how patients use the medical care system and act to reduce risk. The biomedical framework provides an objective definition of disease threats and future disease risks, and points to avenues for action. Unfortunately, this framework appears to make investigators overly attentive to single causes and cures, leading them to ignore the multivariate aspect of disease causation and prevention and to disregard the contribution of behavioral factors to each (Leventhal & Hirschman, 1982). Despite this weakness, the biomedical framework and the disease focus are intrinsic to all compliance investigations. Indeed, it may be necessary to use the term "compliance" to capture the interest of medical practitioners and to maintain communication between them and behavioral investigators. There is clearly a consensus that we cannot dispense with any of the three theoretical frameworks—biomedical, behavioral, or self-regulation. We would prefer, however, to use all three perspectives at every temporal phase of the practitioner–patient encounter, and not to restrict any one to a particular time period (e.g., self-regulation to the postencounter period), though we agree that different time periods may be more readily characterized in one of the frameworks for some patients.

Behavioral studies have taught us a great deal about ways to shape specific responses and to develop the skills needed for both controlling and reducing risk. It is also clear that the behavioral approach is insufficient to achieve long-term behavioral compliance for either the control of current illness or the prevention of future illness. To sustain treatment and/or preventive behaviors, people need something in addition to behavioral skills.

The self-regulation view suggests several sets of factors that may sustain health and illness behaviors. One such set consists of the attributes that define the individual's representation or view of a health problem or health threat. Another is the acquisition of strategies for coping—in particular, learning to view oneself as a problem solver, actively monitoring outcomes, and searching for new tactics to deal with behavioral setbacks (D'Zurilla & Goldfried, 1971). Specific behavioral skills or action plans are nested within or at the service of these broader strategies. Finally, a third type of factor—self-effectance (Bandura, 1977), self-esteem, or self-competence (Leventhal & Nerenz, 1983)—can be defined as an overarching sense of self, or a representation of and sense of confidence in one's own behavioral system, that may help to sustain the use of strategies and specific skills. Awareness of the processes underlying one's action (from representation through coping to appraisal) and experimentation with those processes are crucial parts of self-regulation. This "experimenter" aspect of the self-regulation perspective also helps us to understand how people adopt a very wide range of actions both to treat and prevent illness without medical advice. This seems particularly valuable for understanding preventive action, as many preventive practices lie outside the realm of biomedical rationality.

The systems aspect of self-regulation approaches also provides the conceptual tools needed to connect individual cognition to the social environment (Leventhal & Hirschman, 1982; Steele & Leventhal, 1982). This is explicit in our review of practitioner–patient interaction. In this review, we have raised questions about the impact of the institutional and social context of the medical encounter on the patient's representation of a current illness or a future illness risk, as well as on his or her coping tactics, skills, strategies, and perceived self-competence; we have also questioned how the medical encounter is affected by prior illness history and will affect postencounter thought and behavior. We have not, however, emphasized enough that the encounter needs to be viewed within a larger social context. Thus, social institutions—including such diverse examples as organization of the practice setting, third-party payers, and cultural values regarding the worth of practitioners, treatment, and prevention—shape the encounter as do the beliefs and behaviors of the individual participants. Theoretical elaborations in this area can be viewed as an extension of Ajzen and Fishbein's (1973) model of reasoned action, which emphasizes beliefs about the evaluation of behavior (i.e., the values placed on specific actions, such as smoking) as a critical factor in moving from intentions to performance.

Leventhal and Cleary (1979, 1980) have emphasized the importance of cultural values in evaluating programs for prevention and individual risk reduction. They have suggested that individual behavioral change may be incorrectly attributed to specific intervention programs when the success of the program reflects change in either the perception or the content of cultural norms respecting preventive actions. Thus, an intervention program that is ineffective at one point in history may prove effective at another, because of changes in the context in which it is applied. As a result, interventions must always be compared to control conditions, since it is entirely possible that cultural changes are producing equally large behavioral effects in the population at large. A good example of this phenomenon has recently been seen in the evaluation of the Multiple Risk Factor Intervention Trials: Change in risk behaviors was as substantial in the control conditions as in the experimental intervention groups (Multiple Risk Factor Intervention Trial Research Group, 1982).

Each of the theoretical models also suggests a specific type or set of interventions and measurements, and places more or less importance on different endpoints or criteria for evaluating the success of risk reduction programs. Taken as a whole, these suggestions can help formulate effective public health policies. Used singly to generate programs, they can lead to outcomes that are problematic and discouraging from a public health perspective. For example, health belief theorists may develop and test interventions that succeed in changing perceptions of illness and illness behavior without necessarily leading to improvement in disease indicators. On the other hand, the biomedical practitioner may construct a trial to lower morbidity and mortality rates; may ignore perceptual, attitudinal, and behavioral measures; and may blame the absence of positive outcomes on failures of compliance, when the true culprit is an ineffective treatment. Similarly, both behavioral and biomedical investigators may be overly ready to accept success in lowering morbidity and mortality as evidence of the success of a compliance intervention when the morbidity and mortality reductions are unrelated to the specific intervention. A comprehensive approach to the compliance problem requires that we use each of the perspectives in generating and evaluating compliance programs. It is our conviction, however, that a systems approach emphasizing self-regulation offers the most comprehensive approach to the behavioral aspect of the compliance problem, and that it incorporates the best of the theoretical and empirical suggestions of the behavioral models. Rather than ignoring the many important methods and findings of prior behavioral approaches, the systems/self-regulation model places them in a more comprehensive context, one that connects them more effectively to one another and to social and cultural factors. This may prove to be an important step toward solving the problem of maintenance of behavioral change. Moreover, the homeostatic feature of the self-regulation model is compatible with contemporary biomedical models of disease. Hence, it permits the linking of psychological and biological languages in a common, comprehensive frame of reference (Leventhal, 1983; G. E. Schwartz, 1979b).

Finally, following Szasz and Hollender's (1956) lead, we can see that each of the three models suggests a particular social-psychological or cultural role perspective. The biomedical model, for example, suggests the sick role as the appropriate cultural definition of individual behavior for biomedically defined disease. Behavioral models suggest the role relationship of teacher to student, with the student/patient learning by instruction, imitation, and rehearsal to engage in behaviors prescribed for risk reduction. The self-regulation model expands this role relationship to one of shared problem solving, where participants share information to develop a common view of both present and potential illness threats, and decide upon individual participants' responsibilities and rights and upon the skills needed to engage in curative, controlling, or preventive action. Roles defined by the systems self-regulation approach might be best labeled a type of collaborative health maintenance.

The problems of collaborative health maintenance not only make clear the need for sharing information about the representation, coping, and appraisal processes for disease avoidance; they also make clear the need for alteration in individual decision making and individual responsibility for specific outcomes. This implies that patients must seek and be given control and must seek assistance and yield control as tasks change. The collaborative role model also points to the interrelation of the practitioner to the patient's social environment. Linking the patient to his or her environment system is a responsibility of both the patient and the practitioner. The patient must inform the practitioner of anticipated difficulties in carrying out curative and preventive routines within his or her social and economic context, and must seek the assistance that the practitioner is uniquely qualified to give. This is not, of course, a novel role relationship. Every student has probably requested from his or her physician an excuse for absence from school; this is clearly a case where the patient uses the practitioner to control the external, social environment. The practitioner, however, also has a role in seeking information about and making suggestions for the control of the patient–environment system. This model needs to be extended to diet, smoking, sleeping, and working behaviors that impinge upon the individual's health. Self-regulation theory offers the challenge, therefore, of connecting individual cognition to the immediate and larger social context, both in research and in defining more complete roles and intervention models for maintaining health.

While many of these suggestions have been couched in the language of health practice or public health programs, they are also suggestions for research. Can we investigate the links of individual cognition to social systems? Can we determine how the professional's perception of his or her role facilitate or limits patients' acquisition of preventive health actions? Is it possible to alter the professional's role perceptions? And what elements are most important in the change of these perceptions: the behavior of the patient, the payment system, professional socialization, or other factors? When the compliance problem is viewed within an expanded systems self-regulation framework, it raises a host of new questions regarding the ways in which normative and idiosyncratic representations and coping strategies affect the use of medical services, medications, foods, and other health nostrums, and how these uses affect health, illness, morbidity, and mortality. Our hope is that we can develop the interdisciplinary spirit and inquisitiveness needed to investigate these issues; to test, develop further, and invigorate our theories; and to make a positive contribution to people's health.

R E F E R E N C E S

Abraham, S., & Johnson, C. Prevalence of severe obesity in adults in the United States. *American Journal of Clinical Nutrition*, 1980, *33*, 364–369.

Ader, R. *Psychoneuroimmunology*. New York: Academic Press, 1981.

Ahrens, E. H. The management of hyperlipidemia: Whether, rather than how. *Annals of Internal Medicine*, 1976, *85*, 87–93.

Ajzen, I., & Fishbein, M. Attitudinal and normative variables as predictors of specific behaviors. *Journal of Personality and Social Psychology*, 1973, *27*, 41–57.

Ansel, A., & Roncari, D. A. K. Medical complication of obesity. *Journal of the Canadian Medical Association*, 1978, *119*, 1408–1411.

Antonovsky, A. *Health, stress, and coping*. San Francisco: Jossey-Bass, 1979.

Arbib, M. A. *The metaphorical brain*. New York: Wiley-Interscience, 1972.

Ashby, W. A., & Wilson, G. T. Behavior therapy for obesity: Booster sessions and long-term maintenance of weight loss. *Behaviour Research and Therapy*, 1977, *15*, 451–464.

Bales, R. F. *Interaction process analysis: A method for the study of small groups*. Reading, Mass. Addison-Wesley, 1950.

Bandura, A. *Social learning theory*. New York: General Learning Press, 1971.

Bandura, A. Self-efficacy: Toward a unifying theory of behavioral change. *Psychological Review*, 1977, *84*, 191–215.

Bandura, A., Blanchard, E., & Ritter, R. Relative efficacy of desensitization and modeling approaches for inducing behavioral, affective, and attitudinal changes. *Journal of Personality and Social Psychology*, 1969, *13*, 173–199.

Baric, L. Recognition of the "at-risk" role: A means to influence health behaviour. *International Journal of Health Education*, 1969, *12*, 24–34.

Becker, H. S., & Strauss, A. Careers, personality and adult socialization. *American Journal of Sociology*, 1956, *62*, 253–263.

Becker, M. H. (Ed.). The health belief model and personal health behavior. *Health Education Monographs*, 1974, *2* (Whole No. 4).

Becker, M. H. Sociobehavioral determinants of compliance. In D. L. Sackett & R. B. Haynes (Eds.), *Compliance with therapeutic regimens*. Baltimore: Johns Hopkins University Press, 1976.

Becker, M. H., Drachman, R. H., & Kirscht, J. P. Predicting mothers' compliance with pediatric medical regimens. *Journal of Pediatrics*, 1972, *81*, 843–845.

Becker, M. H., Drachman, R. H., & Kirscht, J. P. A field experiment to evaluate various outcomes of continuity of physician care. *American Journal of Public Health*, 1974, *64*, 1062–1070.

Becker, M. H., Haefner, D. P., Kasl, S. V., Kirscht, J. P., Maiman, L. A., & Rosenstock, I. M. Selected psychosocial models and correlates of individual health-related behaviors. *Medical Care*, 1977, *15* (Suppl.), 27–46.

Becker, M. H., & Maiman, L. A. Sociobehavioral determinants of compliance with health and medical care recommendations. *Medical Care*, 1975, *13*, 10–24.

Becker, M. H., Maiman, L. A., Kirscht, J., Haefner, P., & Drachman, R. The health belief model and prediction of dietary compliance: A field experiment. *Journal of Health and Social Behavior*, 1977, *18*, 348–365.

Bem, D. J. Self-perception theory. In L. Berkowitz (Ed.), *Advances in experimental social psychology* (Vol. 6). New York: Academic Press, 1972.

Bennett, A. E. *Communication between doctors and patients*. New York: Oxford University Press, 1977.

Ben-Sira, Z. The function of the professional's affective behavior in client satisfaction: A revised approach to social interaction theory. *Journal of Health and Social Behavior*, 1976, *17*, 3–11.

Ben-Sira, Z. Affective and instrumental components in the physician–patient relationship: An additional dimension of interaction theory. *Journal of Health and Social Behavior*, 1980, *21*, 170–180.

Berkanovic, E., & Telesky, C. Social networks, beliefs, and the decision to seek medical care: An analysis of congruent and incongruent patterns. *Medical Care*, 1982, *20*, 1018–1026.

Bernstein, D. A., & McAlister, A. The modification of smoking behavior: Progress and problems. *Addictive Behaviors*, 1976, *1*, 89–102.

Best, J. A., & Bloch, M. Compliance in the control of cigarette smoking. In R. B. Haynes, D. W. Taylor, & D. L. Sackett (Eds.), *Compliance in health care*. Baltimore: Johns Hopkins University Press, 1979.

Blackwell, B. The drug regimen and treatment compliance. In R. B. Haynes, D. W. Taylor, & D. L. Sackett (Eds.), *Compliance in health care*. Baltimore: Johns Hopkins University Press, 1979.

Bower, G. H. Mood and memory. *American Psychologist*, 1981, *31*, 129–148.

Bower, G. H., Black, J. B., & Turner, T. J. Scripts in memory for text. *Cognitive Psychology*, 1979, *11*, 177–220.

Bradshaw, P. W., Ley, P., Kincey, J. A., & Bradshaw, J. Recall of medical advice: Comprehensibility and specificity. *British Journal of Social and Clinical Psychology*, 1975, *14*, 55–62.

Breslow, L. Prospects for improving health through reducing risk factors. *Preventive Medicine*, 1978, *7*, 449–458.

Breslow, L., & Enstrom, J. E. Persistence of health habits and their relationship to mortality. *Preventive Medicine*, 1980, *9*, 469–483.

Brody, D. S. The patient's role in clinical decision-making. *Annals of Internal Medicine*, 1980, *93*, 718–722.

Brownell, K. D., & Stunkard, A. J. Behavior therapy and behavior change: Uncertainties in programs for weight control. *Behaviour Research and Therapy*, 1978, *16*, 301.

Bruch, H. *Eating disorders: Obesity, anorexia nervosa and the patient within.* New York: Basic Books, 1973.

Cacioppo, J. T., & Petty, R. E. Social psychological procedures for cognitive response assessment: The thought-listing technique. In T. V. Merluzzi, C. R. Glass, & M. Genest (Eds.), *Cognitive assessment.* New York: Guilford Press, 1981.

Campbell, D. T., & Stanley, J. C. *Experimental and quasi-experimental design for research.* Chicago: Rand McNally, 1966.

Carter, W. B., Inui, T. S., Kukull, W. A., & Haigh, V. H. Outcome based doctor–patient interaction analysis: II. Identifying effective provider and patient behavior. *Medical Care*, 1982, *20*, 550–566.

Carver, C. S. A cybernetic model of self-attention processes. *Journal of Personality and Social Psychology*, 1979, *37*, 1251–1281.

Carver, C. S., & Scheier, M. F. Control theory: A useful conceptual framework for personality—social, clinical and health psychology. *Psychological Bulletin*, 1982, *92*, 111–135.

Center for Disease Control. *United States immunization survey: 1975.* Atlanta: Author, 1976.

Chrisman, N. J. The health-seeking process: An approach to the natural history of illness. *Culture, Medicine, and Psychiatry*, 1977, *1*, 351–377.

Closson, R., & Kikugawa, C. Noncompliance varies with drug class. *Hospitals*, 1975, *49*, 89–93.

Coates, T. J., & Thoreson, C. E. Treating obesity in children and adolescents: A review. *American Journal of Public Health*, 1978, *68*, 143–150.

Conroy, W. J. Human values, smoking behavior, and public health programs. In M. Rokeach (Ed.), *Understanding human values.* New York: Free Press, 1979.

Cook, T. D., & Campbell, D. T. *Quasi-experimentation: Design and analysis issues for field settings.* Chicago: Rand McNally, 1979.

Cooke, C. J., & Meyers, A. The role of predictor variables in the behavioral treatment of obesity. *Behavioral Assessment*, 1980, *2*, 59–69.

Criqui, M. H., Barrett-Connor, E., Holdbrook, M. J., Austin, M., & Turner, J. D. Clustering of cardiovascular disease risk factors. *Preventive Medicine*, 1980, *9*, 525–533.

Cummings, K. M., Becker, M. H., Kirscht, J. P., & Levin, N. W. Intervention strategies to improve compliance with medical regimens by ambulatory hemodialysis patients. *Journal of Behavioral Medicine*, 1981, *4*, 111–127.

Currey, H., Malcolm, R., Riddle, E., & Schacthe, M. Behavioral treatment of obesity. *Journal of the American Medical Association*, 1977, *237*, 2829–2831.

Dapcich-Miura, E., & Hovell, M. F. Contingency management of adherence to a complex medical regimen in an elderly heart patient. *Behavior Therapy*, 1979, *10*, 193–201.

Davis, B. A., & Roncari, D. Behavioural treatment of obesity. *Journal of the Canadian Medical Association*, 1978, *119*, 1423–1425.

Davis, M. S. Variations in patients' compliance with doctors' advice: Analysis of congruence between survey responses and results of empirical observations. *Journal of Medical Education*, 1966, *41*, 1037–1048.

Davis, M. S. Variations in patients' compliance with doctors' advice: An empirical analysis of patterns of communication. *American Journal of Public Health*, 1968, *58*, 274–288.

Dawber, T. R., Meadors, G. F., & Moore, F. E. Epidemiological approaches to heart disease: The Framingham Study. *American Journal of Public Health*, 1951, *41*, 279–286.

Deci, E. L., & Ryan, R. M. The empirical exploration of intrinsic motivational processes. In

L. Berkowitz (Ed.), *Advances in experimental social psychology* (Vol. 13). New York: Academic Press, 1980.

Delahunt, J., & Curran, J. P. Effectiveness of negative practice and self-control techniques in the reduction of smoking behavior. *Journal of Consulting and Clinical Psychology,* 1976, *44,* 1002–1007.

Dervin, B., Harlock, S., Atwood, R., & Garzona, C. *The human side of information: An exploration in a health communication context.* Paper presented at the annual meeting of the International Communication Association, 1980.

DiMatteo, M. R., Taranta, A., Friedman, H. S., & Prince, L. M. Predicting patient satisfaction from physicians' nonverbal communication skills. *Medical Care,* 1980, *18,* 376–387.

Dimsdale, J. E., Klerman, G., & Shershow, J. C. Conflict in treatment goals between patients and staff. *Social Psychiatry,* 1979, *14,* 1–4.

Dingle, J. H. The ills of man. *Scientific American,* 1973, *229,* 77–84.

Dishman, R. K. Compliance/adherence in health related exercise. *Health Psychology,* 1982, *1,* 237–267.

Dubos, R. *Man, medicine and environment.* London: Pall Mall Press, 1968.

Dunbar, J. M. Assessment of medication compliance: A review. In R. B. Haynes, M. E. Mattson, & T. O. Engebretson (Eds.), *Patient compliance to prescribed antihypertensive medication regimens: A report to the National Heart, Lung and Blood Institute.* Bethesda, Md.: National Heart, Lung and Blood Institute, 1980.

Dunbar, J. M., & Stunkard, A. J. Adherence to diet and drug regimen. In R. Levy, B. Rifkind, B. Dennis, & N. Ernst (Eds.), *Nutrition, lipids, and coronary heart disease.* New York: Raven Press, 1979.

D'Zurilla, T., & Goldfried, M. Problem-solving and behavior modification. *Journal of Abnormal Psychology,* 1971, *78,* 107–126.

Egbert, L. D., Battit, G. E., Welch, C. E., & Bartlett, M. K. Reduction of postoperative pain by encouragement and instruction of patients: A study of doctor–patient rapport. *New England Journal of Medicine,* 1964, *70,* 825–827.

Eisenberg, J. M. Sociologic influences on decision-making by clinicians. *Annals of Internal Medicine,* 1979, *90,* 957–964.

Eisenthal, S., Emery, R., Lazare, A., & Udin, H. "Adherence" and the negotiated approach to patienthood. *Archives of General Psychiatry,* 1979, *36,* 393–398.

Eisenthal, S., & Lazare, A. Evaluation of the initial interview in a walk-in clinic: The clinician's perspective on a "negotiated approach." *Journal of Nervous and Mental Disease,* 1977, *164,* 30–35.

Elling, R., Whittemore, R., & Greene, M. Patient participation in a pediatric program. *Journal of Health and Human Behavior,* 1960, *1,* 183–189.

Engel, G. L. The need for a new medical model: A challenge for biomedicine. *Science,* 1977, *196,* 129–136.

Espenshade, J. Personal communication, September 1982.

Etzioni, A., & Remp, R. Technological "shortcuts" to social change. *Science,* 1972, *175,* 31–38.

Evans, R. I., Henderson, A. H., Hill, P. C., & Raines, B. E. Current psychological, social and educational programs in control and prevention of smoking: A critical methodological review. In A. M. Gotto & R. Paoletti (Eds.), *Atherosclerosis reviews* (Vol. 6). New York: Raven Press, 1979.

Fabrega, H. The need for an ethnomedical science. *Science,* 1975, *189,* 969–975.

Feinstein, A. R., & Ransohoff, D. R. Problems of compliance as a source of bias in data analysis. In L. Lasagna (Ed.), *Patient compliance.* Mount Kisco, N. Y.: Future, 1976.

Festinger, L. A theory of social comparison processes. *Human Relations,* 1954, *7,* 117–140.

Finnerty, F. A., Shaw, L. W., & Himmelsbach, C. K. Hypertension in the inner city: II. Detection and follow-up. *Circulation,* 1973, *47,* 76–78.

Fishbein, M., & Ajzen, I. *Belief, attitude, intention and behavior: An introduction to theory and research.* Reading, Mass.: Addison-Wesley, 1975.

Folkman, S., & Lazarus, R. An analysis of coping in a middle-aged community sample. *Journal of Health and Social Behavior,* 1980, *21,* 219–239.

Fordyce, W. Behavioral concepts in chronic pain and illness. In P. O. Davidson (Ed.), *The behavioral management of anxiety, depression and pain.* New York: Raven Press, 1974.

Foreyt, J. P., & Gotto, A. M. Behavioral treatment of obesity. In A. M. Gotto & R. Paoletti (Eds.), *Atherosclerosis reviews* (Vol. 6). New York: Raven Press, 1979.

Francis, V., Korsch, B. M., & Morris, M. J. Gaps in doctor–patient communication: Patients' responses to medical advice. *New England Journal of Medicine,* 1969, *280,* 535–540.

Freemon, B., Negrete, V., Davis, M., & Korsch, B. Gaps in doctor–patient communication: Doctor–patient interaction analysis. *Pediatric Research,* 1971, *5,* 298–311.

Freidson, E. *Patients' views of medical practice.* New York: Russell Sage Foundation, 1961.

Friedman, H. S. Nonverbal communication between patients and medical practitioners. *Journal of Social Issues,* 1979, *35,* 82–99.

Ganong, W. *Fundamental physiological mechanisms of neuroendocrine function.* Paper presented at the annual meeting of the Academy of Behavioral Medicine Research, Charlottesville, Va., June 1980.

Garb, J. R., & Stunkard, A. J. A further assessment of the effectiveness of TOPS in the control of obesity. *Archives of Internal Medicine,* 1974, *134,* 716–720.

Garrity, T. F. Medical compliance and the clinician–patient relationship: A review. In R. B. Haynes, M. E. Mattson, & T. O. Engebretson (Eds.), *Patient compliance to prescribed antihypertensive medication regimens: A report to the National Heart, Lung and Blood Institute.* Bethesda, Md.: National Heart, Lung and Blood Institute, 1980.

Genest, M., & Turk, D. C. Think-aloud approaches to cognitive assessment. In T. V. Merluzzi, C. R. Glass, & M. Genest (Eds.), *Cognitive assessment.* New York: Guilford Press, 1981.

Glasgow, R. E., & Rosen, G. M. Behavioral bibliotherapy: A review of self-help behavior therapy manuals. *Psychological Bulletin,* 1978, *85,* 1–23.

Glasser, W. *Positive addiction.* New York: Harper & Row, 1976.

Glogow, P. H. Noncompliance: A dilemma. *Sight Saving Review.* Spring 1973, pp. 29–34.

Goetz, A. A., Duff, J. F., & Bernstein, J. E. Health risk appraisal: The estimation of risk. *Health Promotion at the Worksite,* 1980, *95,* 119–126.

Goldfried, M. R. Anxiety reduction through cognitive-behavioral intervention. In P. C. Kendall & S. D. Hollon (Eds.), *Cognitive-behavioral intervention.* New York: Academic Press, 1979.

Green, L. W. Evaluation and measurement: Some dilemmas for health education. *American Journal of Public Health,* 1977, *67,* 155–161.

Greenwald, A. G. Cognitive learning, cognitive response to persuasion, and attitude change. In A. G. Greenwald, T. C. Brock, & T. M. Ostrom (Eds.), *Psychological foundations of health attitudes.* New York: Academic Press, 1968.

Gutmann, M. C., & Meyer, D. The role of social sciences in hypertension control. *Family and Community Health,* 1981, *4,* 63–72.

Gutmann, M. C., Pollock, M. L., Schmidt, D. H., & Dudek, S. Symptom monitoring and attribution by cardiac patients. *Clinical Research,* 1981, *29,* 320A.

Guyton, A. C., Coleman, T. G., Cowley, A. W., Scheel, K. W., Manning, R. O., & Norman, R. A. Arterial pressure regulation. *American Journal of Medicine,* 1972, *52,* 584–594.

Haefner, D. Arousing fear in dental health education. *Journal of Public Health Dentistry,* 1965, *25,* 140–146.

Hall, J. A., Roter, D. L., & Rand, C. S. Communication of affect between patient and physician. *Journal of Health and Social Behavior,* 1981, *22,* 18–30.

Hall, J. H., & Zwemer, J. D. *Prospective medicine.* Indianapolis: Methodist Hospital of Indiana, 1979.

Harrup, T., Hansen, B. A., & Soghikian, K. Clinical methods in smoking cessation: Description and evaluation of a stop smoking clinic. *American Journal of Public Health*, 1979, *69*, 1226–1231.

Hayes-Bautista, D. E. Modifying the treatment: Patient compliance, patient control and medical care. *Social Science and Medicine*, 1976, *10*, 233–238.

Haynes, R. B. A critical review of the 'determinants' of patient compliance with therapeutic regimes. In D. L. Sackett & R. S. Haynes (Eds.), *Compliance with therapeutic regimens*. Baltimore: Johns Hopkins University Press, 1976.

Haynes, R. B. Determinants of compliance: The disease and the mechanics of treatment. In R. B. Haynes, D. W. Taylor, & D. L. Sackett (Eds.), *Compliance in health care*. Baltimore: Johns Hopkins University Press, 1979. (a)

Haynes, R. B. Strategies to improve compliance with referrals, appointments, and prescribed medical regimens. In R. B. Haynes, D. W. Taylor, & D. L. Sackett (Eds.), *Compliance in health care*. Baltimore: Johns Hopkins University Press, 1979. (b)

Haynes, R. B., Sackett, D. L., Gibson, E. S., Hackett, B. C., Taylor, D. W., Roberts, R. S., & Johnson, A. L. Improvement of medication compliance in uncontrolled hypertension. *Lancet*, 1976, *i*, 1265–1268.

Haynes, R. B., Taylor, D. W., & Sackett, D. L. (Eds.). *Compliance in health care*. Baltimore: Johns Hopkins University Press, 1979.

Heinzelmann, F. Factors in prophylaxis behavior in treating rheumatic fever: An exploratory study. *Journal of Health and Human Behavior*, 1962, *3*, 73–81.

Hemminki, E., & Heikkila, J. Elderly people's compliance with prescriptions, and quality of education. *Scandinavian Journal of Social Medicine*, 1975, *3*, 87–92.

Hertroijs, A. R. A study of some factors affecting the attendance of patients in a leprosy control scheme. *International Journal of Leprosy*, 1974, *42*, 419–427.

Hochbaum, G. *Public participation in medical screening programs: A socio-psychological study* (DHEW Publication No. (PHS) 572). Washington, D.C.: U.S. Government Printing Office, 1958.

Hoenig, F., & Ragg, N. The non-attending psychiatric outpatient: An administrative problem. *Medical Care*, 1966, *4*, 96–100.

Hovland, C. I. Effects of the mass media on information. In G. Lindzey (Ed.), *Handbook of social psychology* (Vol. 2). Cambridge, Mass.: Addison-Wesley, 1954.

Hovland, C. I. Reconciling conflicting results derived from experimental and survey studies of attitude change. *American Psychologist*, 1959, *14*, 8–17.

Hovland, C. I., Janis, I. L., & Kelley, H. H. *Communication and persuasion*. New Haven: Yale University Press, 1953.

Hulka, B. S., Cassel, J. C., Kupper, L. L., & Burdette, J. A. Communications, compliance and concordance between physicians and patients with prescribed medication. *American Journal of Public Health*, 1976, *66*, 847–853.

Hulka, B., Kupper, L., Cassel, J., Efird, R., & Burdette, J. Medication use and misuse: Physician-patient discrepancies. *Journal of Chronic Diseases*, 1975, *28*, 7–21.

Hulley, S. B., Rosenman, R. H., Bawol, R. D., & Brand, R. J. Epidemiology as a guide to clinical decisions. *New England Journal of Medicine*, 1980, *302*, 1383–1389.

Hunt, W. A., & Bespalec, D. A. An evaluation of current methods of modifying smoking behavior. *Journal of Clinical Psychology*, 1974, *30*, 431–438.

Hunt, W. A., & Matarazzo, J. D. Three years later: Recent developments in the experimental modification of smoking behavior. *Journal of Clinical Psychology*, 1971, *27*, 455–456.

Hunt, W. A., Matarazzo, J. D., Weiss, S. M., & Gentry, W. D. Associative learning, habit, and health behavior. *Journal of Behavioral Medicine*, 1979, *2*, 111–124.

Inui, T. S., Carter, W. B., Kukull, W. A., & Haigh, V. H. Outcome-based doctor–patient interaction analysis: I. Comparison of techniques. *Medical Care*, 1982, *20*, 535–549.

Inui, T., Yourtee, E., & Williamson, J. Improved outcomes in hypertension after physician tutorials. *Annals of Internal Medicine*, 1976, *84*, 646–651.

Jaccard, J. A. A theoretical analysis of selected factors important to health education strategies. *Health Education Monographs*, 1974, *3*, 152–167.

Janis, I. L. Effects of fear arousal on attitude change: Recent developments in theory and experimental research. In L. Berkowitz (Ed.), *Advances in experimental social psychology* (Vol. 13). New York: Academic Press, 1967.

Janis, I. L., & Leventhal, H. Human reactions to stress. In E. Borgatta & W. Lambert (Eds.), *Handbook of personality theory and research*. Chicago: Rand McNally, 1967.

Janis, I. L., & Rodin, J. Attribution, control and decision making: Social psychology and health care. In G. C. Stone, F. Cohen, & N. E. Adler (Eds.), *Health psychology*. San Francisco: Jossey-Bass, 1979.

Jeffery, R. W., Wing, R. R., & Stunkard, A. J. Behavioral treatment of obesity: The state of the art, 1976. *Behavior Therapy*, 1978, *9*, 189–199.

Jenkins, J. J. Remember that old theory of memory? Well, forget it. *American Psychologist*, 1974, *29*, 785–795.

Johnson, J. E. Stress reduction through sensation information. In I. C. Sarason & C. D. Spielberger (Eds.), *Stress and anxiety* (Vol. 2). Washington, D.C.: Hemisphere, 1975.

Johnson, J. E., & Leventhal, H. The effects of accurate expectations and behavioral instructions on reactions during a noxious medical examination. *Journal of Personality and Social Psychology*, 1974, *29*, 710–718.

Johnson, J.E., Rice, V. H., Fuller, S. S., & Endress, M. P. Sensory information, instruction in a coping strategy and recovery from surgery. *Research in Nursing and Health*, 1978, *1*, 4–17.

Jones, E. E., & Nisbett, R. E. *The actor and the observer: Divergent perceptions of the causes of behavior*. New York: General Learning Press, 1971.

Kadushin, C. *Why people go to psychiatrists*. Chicago: Aldine, 1968.

Kanfer, F. H. The many faces of self-control, or behavior modification changes its focus. In R. B. Stuart (Ed.), *Behavioral self-management: Strategies, techniques and outcomes*. New York: Brunner/Mazel, 1977.

Kanfer, F. H., Cox, L. E., Gruner, J. M., & Karoly, P. Contracts, demand characteristics, and self-control. *Journal of Personality and Social Psychology*, 1974, *30*, 605–619.

Katz, E. The two-step flow of communication: An up-to-date report on an hypothesis. *Public Opinion Quarterly*, 1957, *21*, 61–78.

Kelley, H. H. The processes of causal attribution. *American Psychologist*, 1972, *28*, 107–128.

Kelly, T., Kegeles, S. S., Lund, A. K., & Weisenberg, M. Knowledge and attitudinal effects of a children's dental slide show. *Journal of Preventive Dentistry*, 1976, *3*, 30–34.

Keys, A., Taylor, H. L., Blackburn, H., Brozek, J., & Anderson, J. T. Coronary heart disease among Minnesota business and professional men followed fifteen years. *Circulation*, 1963, *28*, 381–395.

Kingsley, R. G., & Wilson, G. T. Behavior therapy for obesity: A comparative investigation of long-term effects. *Journal of Consulting and Clinical Psychology*, 1977, *45*, 288–298.

Kirschenbaum, D. S., & Tomarkin, A. J. On facing the generalization problem: The study of self-regulatory failure. In P. C. Kendall (Ed.), *Advances in cognitive–behavioral research and theory* (Vol. 1). New York: Academic Press, 1982.

Kirscht, J. P., Becker, M. H., & Eveland, J. P. Psychological and social factors as predictors of medical behavior. *Medical Care*, 1976, *14*, 422–431.

Kirscht, J. P., & Rosenstock, I. M. Patients' problems in following recommendations of health experts. In G. C. Stone, F. Cohen, & N. E. Adler (Eds.), *Health psychology: A handbook*. San Francisco: Jossey-Bass, 1979.

Kleinman, A. *Healers and patients in the context of culture: The interface of anthropology, medicine and psychiatry*. Berkeley: University of California Press, 1980.

Kleinman, J. C., Feldman, J. J., & Monk, M. A. The effects of changes in smoking habits on coronary heart disease mortality. *American Journal of Public Health*, 1979, *69*, 795–802.

Kloster, F. E., Kremkau, E. L., Ritzman, L. W., Rahimtoola, S. H., Rosch, J., & Kanarek, P. H.

Coronary bypass for stable angina: A prospective randomized study. *New England Journal of Medicine*, 1979, *300*, 149–157.

Knapp, J. E. Diet compliance in obesity. *Primary Care*, 1978, *5*, 689–695.

Knowles, J. H. (Ed.). *Doing better and feeling worse: Health in the United States*. New York: Norton, 1977.

Kopel, S., & Arkowitz, H. The role of attribution and self-perception in behavior change: Implications for behavior therapy. *Genetic Psychology Monographs*, 1975, *92*, 175–212.

Korsch, B., Freemon, B., & Negrete, V. Practical implications of doctor–patient interactions: Analysis for pediatric practice. *American Journal of Diseases of Children*, 1971, *121*, 110–114.

Korsch, B., Gozzi, E. K., & Francis, V. Gaps in doctor–patient communication: 1. Doctor–patient interaction and patient satisfaction. *Pediatrics*, 1968, *42*, 855–871.

Lando, H. A comparison of excessive and rapid smoking in the modification of chronic smoking behavior. *Journal of Consulting and Clinical Psychology*, 1975, *43*, 350–355.

Lang, P. J., Melamed, B. G., & Hart, J. A psychophysiological analysis of fear modification using an automated desensitization procedure. *Journal of Abnormal Psychology*, 1970, *76*, 220–234.

Lansky, D. A methodological analysis of research on adherence and weight loss: Reply to Brownell and Stunkard (1978). *Behavior Therapy*, 1981, *12*, 144–149.

Lazarus, R. *Psychological stress and the coping process*. New York: McGraw-Hill, 1966.

Lazarus, R. S., & Launier, R. Stress-related transactions between person and environment. In L. A. Pervin & M. Lewis (Eds.), *Perspectives in interactional psychology*. New York: Plenum, 1978.

Leon, G. R. Current directions in the treatment of obesity. *Psychological Bulletin*, 1976, *83*, 557–578.

Lepper, M. R., & Greene, D. (Eds.). *The hidden costs of reward*. Hillsdale, N.J.: Erlbaum, 1978.

Lerner, M., & Anderson, O. W. *Health progress in the United States: 1900–1960*. Chicago: University of Chicago Press, 1963.

Leventhal, H. Findings and theory in the study of fear communications. In L. Berkowitz (Ed.), *Advances in experimental social psychology* (Vol. 5). New York: Academic Press, 1970.

Leventhal, H. Changing attitudes and habits to reduce risk factors in chronic disease. *American Journal of Cardiology*, 1973, *31*, 571–580.

Leventhal, H. Toward a comprehensive theory of emotion. In L. Berkowitz (Ed.), *Advances in experimental social psychology* (Vol. 13). New York: Academic Press, 1980.

Leventhal, H. The integration of emotion and cognition: A view from the perceptual motor theory of emotion. In M. S. Clarke & S. T. Fiske (Eds.), *Affect and cognition: The seventeenth annual Carnegie Symposium on Cognition*. Hillsdale, N.J.: Erlbaum, 1982.

Leventhal, H. Behavioral medicine: Psychology in health care. In D. Mechanic (Ed.), *Handbook of health care, and the health professions*. New York: Free Press, 1983.

Leventhal, H., Brown, D., Shacham, S., & Engquist, G. Effect of preparatory information about sensations, threat of pain and attention on cold pressor distress. *Journal of Personality and Social Psychology*, 1979, *37*, 688–714.

Leventhal, H., & Cleary, P. D. Behavioral modification of risk factors: Technology or science. In M. L. Pollack & D. H. Schmidt (Eds.), *Heart disease and rehabilitation: State of the art*. Boston: Houghton Mifflin, 1979.

Leventhal, H., & Cleary, P. D. The smoking problem: A review of the research and theory in behavioral risk-reduction. *Psychological Bulletin*, 1980, *88*, 370–405.

Leventhal, H., & Hirschman, R. S. Social psychology and prevention. In G. S. Sanders & J. Suls (Eds.), *Social psychology of health and illness*. Hillsdale, N.J.: Erlbaum, 1982.

Leventhal, H., & Johnson, J. Laboratory and field experimentation into development of a theory of stress reduction. In R. Leonard & P. Wooldridge (Eds.), *Behavioral science and nursing theory*. St. Louis, Mo: C. V. Mosby, 1980.

Leventhal, H., Jones, S., & Trembly, G. Sex differences in attitude and behavior change under conditions of fear and specific instructions. *Journal of Experimental Social Psychology*, 1966, *2*, 387–399.

Leventhal. H., Meyer, D., & Gutmann, M. The role of theory in the study of compliance to high blood pressure regimens. In R. B. Haynes, M. E. Mattson, & T. O. Engebretson (Eds.), *Patient compliance to prescribed antihypertensive medication regimens: A report to the National Heart, Lung and Blood Institute.* Bethesda, Md.: National Heart, Lung and Blood Institute, 1980.)

Leventhal, H., Meyer, D., & Nerenz, D. The common-sense representation of illness danger. In S. Rachman (Ed.), *Medical psychology* (Vol. 2). New York: Pergamon Press, 1980.

Leventhal, H., & Nerenz, D. A model for stress research and some implications for the control of stress disorder. In D. Meichenbaum & M. Jaremko (Eds.), *Stress prevention and management: A cognitive behavioral approach.* New York: Plenum, 1983.

Leventhal, H., Nerenz, D., & Straus, A. Self-regulation and the mechanisms for symptom appraisal. In D. Mechanic (Ed.), *Psychosocial epidemiology.* New York: Neale Watson, 1980.

Leventhal, H., & Niles, P. Persistence of influence for varying durations of exposure to threat stimuli. *Psychological Reports*, 1965, *16*, 223–233.

Leventhal, H., Safer, M., Cleary, P., & Gutmann, M. Cardiovascular risk modification by community-based programs for life-style change: Comments on the Stanford Study. *Journal of Consulting and Clinical Psychology*, 1980, *48*, 150–158.

Leventhal, H., & Singer, R. P. Affect arousal and positioning of recommendations in persuasive communications. *Journal of Personality and Social Psychology*, 1966, *4*, 137–146.

Leventhal, H., Singer, R., & Jones, S. Effects of fear and specificity of recommendations upon attitudes and behavior. *Journal of Personality and Social Psychology*, 1965, *2*, 20–29.

Leventhal, H., & Watts, J. C. Sources of resistance to fear arousing communications on smoking and lung cancer. *Journal of Personality*, 1966, *34*, 155–175.

Leventhal, H., Watts, J. C., & Pagano, F. Effects of fear and instructions on how to cope with danger. *Journal of Personality and Social Psychology*, 1967, *6*, 313–321.

Levine, D. M., Green, L. W., Deeds, S. G., Chwalow, J., Russell, P., & Finlay, J. Health education for hypertensive patients. *Journal of the American Medical Association*, 1979, *241*, 1700–1703.

Levitz, L., & Stunkard, A. J. A therapeutic coalition for obesity: Behavior modification and patient self-help. *American Journal of Psychiatry*, 1974, *131*, 423–427.

Levy, R. L. The role of social support in patient compliance: A selective review. In R. B. Haynes, M. E. Mattson, & T. O. Engebretson (Eds.), *Patient compliance to prescribed antihypertensive medication regimens: A report to the National Heart, Lung and Blood Institute.* Bethesda, Md.: National Heart, Lung and Blood Institute, 1980.

Ley, P. Primacy, rated importance and recall of medical information. *Journal of Health and Social Behavior*, 1972, *13*, 311–317.

Ley, P. Psychological studies of doctor–patient communication. In S. Rachman (Ed.), *Contributions to medical psychology* (Vol. 1). Oxford: Pergamon Press, 1977.

Ley, P., Bradshaw, P. W., Eaves, D., & Walker, C. M. A method for increasing patients' recall of information presented by doctors. *Psychological Medicine*, 1973, *3*, 217–220.

Ley, P., & Spelman, M. S. *Communicating with the patient.* London: Staples Press, 1967.

Ley, P., Whitworth, M. A., Skilbeck, C. E., Woodward, R., Pinset, R. J. F. H., Pike, L. A., Clarkson, M. E., & Clark, P. B. Improving doctor–patient communication in general practice. *Journal of the Royal College of General Practitioners*, 1976, *26*, 720–724.

Lichtenstein, E. Modification of smoking behavior: Good designs—ineffective treatments. *Journal of Consulting and Clinical Psychology*, 1971, *36*, 163–166.

Lichtenstein, E., & Danaher, B .G. Modification of smoking behavior: A critical analysis of theory, research and practice. In M. Hersen, R. M. Eisler, & P. M. Miller (Eds.), *Progress in behavior modification* (Vol. 3). New York: Academic Press, 1975.

Lilienfeld, A. M., & Lilienfeld, D. E. *Foundations of epidemiology* (2nd ed.). New York: Oxford University Press, 1980.

Loro, A. D., Levenkron, J. C., & Fisher, E. B. Critical clinical issues in the behavioral treatment of obesity. *Addictive Behaviors*, 1979, *4*, 383–391.

Louria, D. B., Kidwell, A. P., Lavenhar, M. A., Thind, I. S., & Naje, R. G. Primary and secondary prevention among adults: An analysis with comments on screening and health education. *Preventive Medicine*, 1976, *5*, 549–572.

Lowe, K., & Lutzker, J. R. Increasing compliance to a medical regimen with a juvenile diabetic. *Behavior Therapy,* 1979, *10,* 57–64.

Lund, A. K., Kegeles, S. S., & Weisenberg, M. Motivational techniques for increasing acceptance of preventive health measures. *Medical Care, 1977, 15,* 678–692.

Mahoney, M. J., & Mahoney, K. *Permanent weight control.* New York: Norton, 1976.

Marlatt, G. A., & Gordon, J. R. Determinants of relapse: Implications for the maintenance of behavior change. In P. O. Davidson & S. M. Davidson (Eds.), *Behavioral medicine: Changing health lifestyles.* New York: Brunner/Mazel, 1980.

Marston, A. R., & McFall, R. M. Comparison of behavior modification approaches to smoking reduction. *Journal of Consulting and Clinical Psychology,* 1971, *36,* 153–162.

Marston, M. Compliance with medical regimens: A review of the literature. *Nursing Research,* 1970, *19,* 312–323.

Massaro, D. W. *Experimental psychology and information processing.* Chicago: Rand McNally, 1975.

Mausner, B. An ecological view of cigarette smoking. *Journal of Abnormal Psychology,* 1973, *81,* 115–126.

Mausner, B., & Platt, E. S. *Smoking: A behavioral analysis.* New York: Pergamon Press, 1971.

Mazen, R., & Leventhal, H. The influence of communicator–recipient similarity upon the beliefs of pregnant women. *Journal of Experimental Social Psychology,* 1972, *8,* 289–302.

McFall, R. M., & Hammen, C. L. Motivation, structure, and self-monitoring: Role of nonspecific factors in smoking reduction. *Journal of Consulting and Clinical Psychology,* 1971, *48,* 129–142.

McFall, R. M., & Lillesand, D. B. Behavior rehearsal with modeling and coaching in assertive trainings. *Journal of Abnormal Psychology,* 1971, *77,* 313–323.

McGuire, W. J. Personality and susceptibility to social influence. In E. Borgatta & W. Lambert (Eds.), *Handbook of personality theory and research.* Chicago: Rand McNally, 1968.

McKeown, T. *The role of medicine: Dream, mirage or nemesis.* London: Nuffield Provincial Hospitals Trust, 1976.

McKinlay, J. B. Who is really ignorant—physician or patient? *Journal of Health and Social Behavior,* 1975, *16,* 3–11.

McKinlay, J. B. Social network influences on morbid episodes and the career of help seeking. In L. Eisenberg & A. Keleiniman (Eds.), *The relevance of social science for medicine.* Dordrecht, Holland: D. Reidel, 1981.

McKinlay, J. B., & McKinlay, S. M. Medical measures and the decline of mortality. In P. Conrad & R. Kern (Eds.), *The sociology of health and illness: Critical perspectives.* New York: St. Martin's Press, 1981.

Mechanic, D. Social psychologic factors affecting the presentation of bodily complaints. *New England Journal of Medicine,* 1972, *286,* 1132–1139.

Mechanic, D., & Cleary, P. D. Factors associated with the maintenance of positive health behavior. *Preventive Medicine,* 1980, *9,* 805–814.

Meichenbaum, D. *Cognitive-behavior modification.* New York: Plenum, 1977.

Meyer, D. *The effects of patients' representation of high blood pressure on behavior in treatment.* Unpublished doctoral dissertation, University of Wisconsin–Madison, 1981.

Meyer, D., Leventhal, H., & Gutmann, M. Common-sense models of illness: The example of hypertension. *Health Psychology,* in press.

Miller, N. E., & Dworkin, B. R. Different ways in which learning is involved in homeostasis. In R. S. Thompson, L. H. Hicks, & V. B. Shvyrkov (Eds.), *Neural mechanisms of goal-directed learning.* New York: Academic Press, 1980.

Miller, G. A., Galanter, E., & Pribram, K. H. *Plans and the structure of behavior.* New York: Henry Holt, 1960.

Mischel, W. Toward a cognitive, social learning reconceptualization of personality. *Psychological Review,* 1973, *80,* 252–283.

Mitchell, C., & Stuart, R. B. Weight control and smoking reduction: Friends or enemies? *Canadian Journal of Public Health,* 1979, *70,* 399–404.

Mitchell, J. H. Compliance with medical regimens: An annotated bibliography. *Health Education Monographs*, 1974, 2, 75–87.

Mortimer, E. A. Immunization against infectious diseases. *Science*, 1978, 200, 902–907.

Muehlenhard, C. L. *A comparison of fully automated and semiautomated assertion training*. Unpublished doctoral dissertation, University of Wisconsin–Madison, 1981.

Multiple Risk Factor Intervention Trial Research Group. Multiple risk factor intervention trial: Risk factor changes and mortality results. *Journal of the American Medical Association*, 1982, 248, 1465–1477.

National Institutes of Health. *The public and high blood pressure* (DHHS Publication No. (NIH) 81-2118). Washington, D.C.: U.S. Government Printing Office, 1981.

Neisser, U. *Cognitive psychology*. New York: Appleton-Century-Crofts, 1967.

Nerenz, D. R. *Control of emotional distress in cancer chemotherapy*. Unpublished doctoral dissertation, University of Wisconsin–Madison, 1979.

Nerenz, D. R., & Leventhal, H. Self regulation theory in chronic illness. In T. Burish & L. Bradley (Eds.), *Coping with chronic disease: Research and applications*. New York: Academic Press, 1983.

Nichols, A. B., Ravenscroft, C., Lamphiear, D. E., & Ostrander, L. D. Independence of serum lipid levels and dietary habits. *Journal of the American Medical Association*, 1976, 236, 1948–1953.

Niles, P. *The relationship of susceptibility and anxiety to acceptance of fear arousing communications*. Unpublished doctoral dissertation, Yale University, 1964.

Nilsson, L. G. *Perspectives on memory research*. Hillsdale, N.J.: Erlbaum, 1979.

Norman, D. A. *Memory and attention*. New York: Wiley, 1969.

Ostrom, C. W., Jr. *Time series analysis: Regression techniques*. Beverly Hills, Calif.: Sage, 1978.

Parsons, T. *The social system*. New York: Free Press, 1951.

Paul, G. L. Behavior modification research: Design and tactics. In C. M. Franks (Ed.), *Behavior therapy: Appraisal and status*. New York: McGraw-Hill, 1969.

Pennebaker, J. W. Perceptual and environmental determinants of coughing. *Basic and Applied Social Psychology*, 1980, 1, 83–91.

Pennebaker, J. W., & Skelton, J. A. Selective monitoring of physical sensations. *Journal of Personality and Social Psychology*, 1981, 41, 213–223.

Posner, M. I. *Cognition: An introduction*. Glenview, Ill.: Scott, Foresman, 1973.

Psathas, G. (Ed.). *Everyday language: Studies in ethnomethodology*. New York: Irvington, 1979.

Powers, W. T. Feedback: Beyond behaviorism. *Science*, 1973, 170, 351–356.

Reinhardt, L. C. *Attention and interpretation in control of cold pressor pain and distress*. Unpublished doctoral dissertation, University of Wisconsin–Madison, 1979.

Ringler, K. *Process of coping with cancer chemotherapy*. Unpublished doctoral dissertation, University of Wisconsin–Madison, 1981.

Robbins, L., & Hall, J. H. *How to practice prospective medicine*. Indianapolis: Methodist Hospital of Indiana, 1970.

Rogers, R. W. A protection motivation theory of fear appeals and attitude change. *Journal of Psychology*, 1975, 91, 93–114.

Rogers, R. W. Cognitive and physiological processes in fear appeals and attitude change: A revised theory of protection motivation. In J. Cacioppo & R. Petty (Eds.), *Social psychophysiology*. New York: Guilford Press, 1983.

Rogers, R. W., & Deckner, C. W. Effects of fear appeals and physiological arousal upon emotion, attitudes, and cigarette smoking. *Journal of Personality and Social Psychology*, 1975, 32, 222–230.

Rogers, R. W., Deckner, C. W., & Mewborn, C. R. An expectancy-value theory approach to the long-term modification of smoking behavior. *Journal of Clinical Psychology*, 1978, 34, 563–566.

Rogers, R. W., & Mewborn, C. R. Fear appeal in attitude change: Effects of a threat's noxiousness, probability of occurrence, and the efficacy of coping responses. *Journal of Personality and Social Psychology*, 1976, 34, 54–61.

Romm, F. J., Hulka, B. S., & Mayo, F. Correlates of outcomes in patients with congestive heart failure. *Medical Care*, 1976, *14*, 756–776.

Rosen, G. M. The development and use of nonprescription behavior therapies. *American Psychologist*, 1976, *31*, 139–141.

Rosen, T. J., Terry, N. S., & Leventhal, H. The role of esteem and coping in response to a threat communication. *Journal of Research in Personality*, 1982, *16*, 90–107.

Rosenberg, M. *Conceiving the self.* New York: Basic Books, 1979.

Rosenberg, S. G. Patient education—an educator's view. In D. L. Sackett & R. B. Haynes (Eds.), *Compliance with therapeutic regimens.* Baltimore: Johns Hopkins University Press, 1976.

Rosenman, R. H., Friedman, M., Straus, R., Jenkins, C. D., Zyzanski, S. J., & Wurm, M. Coronary heart disease in the Western Collaborative Group Study. *Journal of Chronic Diseases*, 1970, *23*, 173–190.

Rosenstock, I. M. The health belief model and preventive health behavior. *Health Education Monographs*, 1974, *2*, 354–386. (a)

Rosenstock, I. M. Historical origins of the health belief model. *Health Education Monographs*, 1974, *2*, 328–335. (b)

Rosenstock, I. M. Patients' compliance with health regimes. *Journal of the American Medical Association*, 1975, *234*, 402–403.

Rotter, J. B. *Social learning and clinical psychology.* Englewood Cliffs, N.J.: Prentice-Hall, 1954.

Rozensky, R. H., & Bellack, A. S. Individual differences in self-reinforcement style and performance in self- and therapist-controlled weight reduction programs. *Behaviour Research and Therapy*, 1976, *14*, 357–364.

Russell, M. A. H., Wilson, C., Taylor, C., & Becker, C. D. Effect of general practitioners' advice against smoking. *British Medical Journal*, 1979, *ii*, 231–235.

Sackett, D. L. Patients and therapies: Getting the two together. *New England Journal of Medicine*, 1978, *298*, 278–279.

Sackett, D. L., & Haynes, R. B. (Eds.). *Compliance with therapeutic regimens.* Baltimore: Johns Hopkins University Press, 1976.

Sackett, D. L., Haynes, R. B., Gibson, E. S., Hackett, B. C., Taylor, D. W., Roberts, R. S., & Johnson, A. L. Randomised clinical trial of strategies for improving medication compliance in primary hypertension. *Lancet*, 1975, *i*, 1205–1207.

Sackett, D. L., & Snow, J. C. The magnitude of compliance and noncompliance. In R. B. Haynes, D. W. Taylor, & D. L. Sackett (Eds.), *Compliance in health care.* Baltimore: Johns Hopkins University Press, 1979.

Safer, M. A. An evaluation of the health hazard appraisal based on survey data from a randomly selected population. *Public Health Reports*, 1982, *97*, 31–37.

Safer, M. A., Tharps, Q., Jackson, T., & Leventhal, H. Determinants of three stages of delay in seeking care at a medical clinic. *Medical Care*, 1979, *17*, 11–29.

Schachter, S. Recidivism and self-cure of smoking and obesity. *American Psychologist*, 1982, *37*, 436–444.

Schenkein, J. *Studies in the organization of conversational interaction.* New York: Academic Press, 1979.

Schlesel, R. P., & Kunetsky, M. Immediate and delayed effects of the "five-day plan to stop smoking" including factors affecting recidivism. *Preventive Medicine*, 1977, *6*, 454–461.

Schoenberger, J., Stamler, J., Shekelle, R., & Shekelle, S. Current status of hypertension control in an industrial population. *Journal of the American Medical Association*, 1972, *222*, 559–562.

Schulman, B. A. Active patient orientation and outcomes in hypertensive treatment. *Medical Care*, 1979, *17*, 267–280.

Schwartz, G. E. The brain as a health care system. In G. C. Stone, F. Cohen, & M. E. Adler (Eds.), *Health psychology: A handbook.* San Francisco: Jossey-Bass, 1979. (a)

Schwartz, G. E. Disregulation and systems theory: A biobehavioral framework for biofeedback and behavioral medicine. In N. Birbaumer & H. D. Kimmel (Eds.), *Biofeedback and self-regula-*

tion. Hillsdale, N.J.: Erlbaum, 1979. (b)

Schwartz, J. L. A critical review and evaluation of smoking control methods. *Public Health Reports,* 1969, *84,* 483–506.

Shacham, S. *The effects of imagery monitoring, sensation monitoring, and positive suggestion on pain and distress.* Unpublished doctoral dissertation, University of Wisconsin–Madison, 1979.

Shuval, J. T. *Social functions of medical practice: Doctor–patient relationships in Israel.* San Francisco: Jossey-Bass, 1970.

Singer, R. P. *The effects of fear-arousing communications on attitude change and behavior.* Unpublished doctoral dissertation, University of Connecticut, 1965.

Skipper, J. K. Jr., & Leonard, R. C. Children, stress, and hospitalization: A field experiment. *Journal of Health and Social Behavior,* 1968, *9,* 275–287.

Solomon, R. L., & Corbit, J. D. An opponent process theory of motivation: I. Temporal dynamics of affect. *Psychological Review,* 1974, *81,* 119–145.

Stalonas, P. M., Johnson, W. G., & Christ, M. Behavior modification for obesity: The evaluation of exercise, contingency management, and program adherence. *Journal of Consulting and Clinical Psychology,* 1978, *46,* 463–469.

Steckel, S., & Swain, M. Contracting with patients to improve compliance. *Hospitals,* 1977, *51,* 81–84.

Steele, D. J., & Leventhal, H. *Illness cognition and the provider patient encounter in the treatment of hypertension.* Paper presented at the meeting of the American Psychological Association, Washington, D.C., 1982.

Sternbach, R. A. *Pain patients: Traits and treatment.* New York: Academic Press, 1974.

Stiles, W. B. *Manual for a taxonomy of verbal response modes.* Chapel Hill, N.C.: Institute for Research in Social Science, 1978.

Stiles, W. B., Putnam, S. M., Wolf, M. H., & James, S. A. Interaction exchange structure and patient satisfaction with medical interviews. *Medical Care,* 1979, *17,* 667–681.

Stimson, G. V. Obeying doctor's orders: A view from the other side. *Social Science and Medicine,* 1974, *8,* 97–104.

Stuart, R. B. Behavioral control of overeating. *Behaviour Research and Therapy,* 1967, *5,* 357–365.

Stuart, R. B. A three-dimensional program for the treatment of obesity. *Behaviour Research and Therapy,* 1971, *9,* 177–186.

Stuart, R. B. (Ed.). *Behavioral self-management: Strategies, techniques and outcome.* New York: Brunner/Mazel, 1977.

Stunkard, A. J. From explanation to action in psychosomatic medicine: The case of obesity. *Psychosomatic Medicine,* 1975, *37,* 195–236.

Stunkard, A. J. Behavioral treatment of obesity: Failure to maintain weight loss. In R. B. Stuart (Ed.), *Behavioral self-management: Strategies, techniques and outcome.* New York: Brunner/Mazel, 1977.

Stunkard, A. J. Behavioral medicine and beyond: The example of obesity. In O. F. Pomerleau & J. P. Brady (Eds.), *Behavioral medicine: Theory and practice.* Baltimore: Williams & Wilkins, 1979.

Stunkard, A. J., & Mahoney, M. J. Behavioral treatment of the eating disorders. In H. Leitenberg (Ed.), *Handbook of behavior modification and behavior therapy.* New York: Appleton-Century-Crofts, 1976.

Stunkard, A. J., & Penick, S. B. Behavior modification in the treatment of obesity. *Archives of General Psychiatry,* 1979, *36,* 801–806.

Suchman, E. A. Stages of illness and medical care. *Journal of Health and Human Behavior,* 1965, *6,* 114–128.

Svarstad, B. *The doctor–patient encounter: An observational study of communication and outcome.* Unpublished doctoral dissertation, University of Wisconsin–Madison, 1974.

Svarstad, B. Physician–patient communication and patient conformity with medical advice. In D. Mechanic (Ed.), *The growth of bureaucratic medicine.* New York: Wiley, 1976.

Szasz, T., & Hollender, M. A contribution to the philosophy of medicine: The basic models of the doctor–patient relationship. *Archives of Internal Medicine*, 1956, *97*, 585–592.

Tagliacozzo, D. M., Luskin, D. B., Lashof, J. C., & Ima, K. Nurse intervention and patient behavior. *American Journal of Public Health*, 1974, *64*, 596–603.

Taylor, D. W., Sackett, D. L., & Haynes, R. B. Compliance with antihypertensive drugs. *Annals of the New York Academy of Sciences*, 1978, *304*, 390–403.

Thomas, L. On the science and technology of medicine. In J. H. Knowles (Ed.), *Doing better and feeling worse: Health in the United States*. New York: Norton, 1977.

Thorsen, R. D., Jacobs, D. R., Grimm, R. H., Keys, A., Taylor, H., & Blackburn, H. Preventive cardiology in practice: A device for risk estimation and counseling in coronary disease. *Preventive Medicine*, 1979, *8*, 548–556.

Truett, J., Cornfield, J., & Kannel, W. A multivariate analysis of the risk of coronary heart disease in Framingham. *Journal of Chronic Diseases*, 1967, *20*, 511–524.

U.S. Public Health Service. *Smoking and health: A report of the Surgeon General* (DHEW Publication No. (PHS) 79-50066). Washington, D.C.: U.S. Government Printing Office, 1979.

Veterans Administration Cooperative Study Group on Antihypertensive Agents. Effects of treatment on morbidity in hypertension: I. Results in patients with diastolic blood pressure averaging 115 through 129 mm Hg. *Journal of the American Medical Association*, 1967, *202*, 1028–1034.

Veterans Administration Cooperative Study Group on Antihypertensive Agents. Effects of treatment on morbidity in hypertension: II. Results in patients with diastolic blood pressure averaging 90 through 114 mm Hg. *Journal of the American Medical Association*, 1970, *213*, 1143–1152.

Ward, G. Keynote address, National Conference on High Blood Pressure Control, 1977.

Watts, T. E. The regularity of attendance of male tuberculosis patients diagnosed at Mulago Hospital between January and July in 1968 and in 1970. *Tubercle*, 1972, *53*, 174–181.

Weiss, W. Effects of the mass media of communication. In G. Lindzey & E. Aronson (Eds.), *New handbook of social psychology* (Vol. 5). Reading, Mass.: Addison-Wesley, 1969.

West, C. When the doctor is a "lady": Power, status and gender in physician–patient conversations. In A. Stromberg (Ed.), *Women, health and medicine*. Palo Alto, Calif.: Mayfield, 1982.

Wilson, G. T. Obesity, binge eating, and behavior therapy: Some clinical observations. *Behavior Therapy*, 1976, *7*, 700–701.

Wilson, G. T. Methodological considerations in treatment outcome research on obesity. *Journal of Consulting and Clinical Psychology*, 1978, *46*, 687–702.

Wing, R. R., & Jeffery, R. W. Outpatient treatment of obesity: A comparison of methodology and clinical results. *International Journal of Obesity*, 1979, *3*, 261–279.

Wollersheim, J. P. Effectiveness of group therapy based upon learning principles in the treatment of overweight women. *Journal of Abnormal Psychology*, 1970, *76*, 462–474.

Wolinsky, F. D. *The sociology of health: Principles, professions, issues*. Boston: Little, Brown, 1980.

Wooley, S. C., Blackwell, B., & Winget, C. A learning theory model of chronic illness behavior: Theory, treatment, and research. *Psychosomatic Medicine*, 1978, *40*, 379–401.

Worsley, A. Adolescents' views of obesity. *Food and Nutrition Notes and Reviews*, 1979, *36*, 57–63.

Wynder, E. L., & Hoffmann, D. Tobacco and health. *New England Journal of Medicine*, 1979, *300*, 894–903.

Yates, A. J. *Theory and practice in behavior therapy*. New York: Wiley, 1975.

Zifferblatt, S. M. Increasing patient compliance through the applied analysis of behavior. *Preventive Medicine*, 1975, *4*, 173–182.

Zimmerman, R. *The dental practitioner–patient interaction: Dental health, expectations, and satisfaction*. Paper presented at the meeting of the American Sociological Association, San Francisco, 1982.

Zimmerman, R., Linz, D., Leventhal, H., & Penrod, S. *Development of a disease model upon first screening for hypertension*. Unpublished manuscript, Madison, Wisconsin, 1982.

CHAPTER 11

Community Applications of Behavioral Medicine

John W. Farquhar
Stanford University

Nathan Maccoby
Stanford University

Douglas S. Solomon
Stanford University

INTRODUCTION

The purpose of this chapter is to describe the theory, design, and methods of education and evaluation for community-based education programs. The necessity for behavioral medicine research to include community studies is heightened when the topic under study involves behavioral or psychosocial attributes that affect large proportions of the population, as is the case for the risk factors for many cardiovascular diseases and for many adult cancers. We therefore draw on examples in the field of cardiovascular disease from the Stanford Heart Disease Prevention Program (SHDPP) and similar work in eight other locales in the United States and other countries.

RATIONALE FOR COMMUNITY-BASED STUDIES

A logical sequence for the solution of a public health problem would entail field testing of hypotheses and methods first developed in tightly controlled, basic, small-group studies (clinical research). Both the selection process used in most clinical research studies and the artificial environments of such studies could lead to either an attenuation or an accentuation of the effects achievable within community settings. It is intuitively clear, and it may be predicted from the adoption–diffusion model of Rogers (1983) and social learning theory (Bandura, 1969, 1977, 1978), that the adoption and mainte-nance of innovations in health behavior are affected by social environments. Thus, one might anticipate an intrinsic advantage of educational programs that can affect the work, home, and community environments of an individual, as compared with those programs that are restricted to a single aspect of an individual's environment. However, the contents, intensity, credibility, or quality of health education can be lessened if community-wide methods are used. Considerable efficacy may be intrinsic to clinical settings, but findings in small groups of selected individuals may not be readily generalizable. Community studies must therefore be included in the spectrum of research done in behavioral medicine. Furthermore, community-based studies offer potential cost savings, provide testing of generalizable methods, and provide policy makers with information more germane to their problems than that obtained from clinical research (Farquhar, 1978). Community studies may bypass some of the ethical problems involved in denial to randomized control populations of the possible benefits of educational programs. Finally, such studies allow repeated independent samples of large populations as measures of effects, thus decreasing the risk of sensitization or "contamination" inherent in the repeated surveys of treatment and control cohorts typical of controlled clinical trials.

THEORETICAL BASIS FOR COMMUNITY-BASED HEALTH EDUCATION

A community education program is a highly complex undertaking. It challenges the existing state of knowledge related to education and behavior change. In fact, most theoretical frameworks, having been derived at the level of controlled laboratory study, are not directly applicable to community efforts. Therefore, it is necessary to draw upon several disciplines in order to provide foundations for the planning, implementation, and evaluation of community education.

In addition to the field of community organization, whose concepts can be applied to help create a receptive environment for educational materials and programs, it is necessary to borrow from three perspectives to create the blend needed for success. These are the communication–behavior change (CBC) framework, the social marketing framework, and the community organization framework. The CBC framework is based on a social-psychological perspective relevant to individual and group learning. This perspective is particularly useful in the development of the contents of education materials and the sequence in which they are delivered. The social marketing framework is especially applicable to the practical issues of how to design and distribute educational products. The community organization framework has special applicability to the process of diffusion of communication via organizations and helps establish a basis for long-term maintenance of health education programs.

The Communication–Behavior Change Framework

The CBC framework offers a perspective on how individuals and groups acquire new knowledge, attitudes, and behaviors. This approach to the change process draws on the work of many investigators. These include the early work of Cartwright (1949) on the role of interpersonal influence as a needed trigger for action; the social learning model of Bandura (1977); the "hierarchy of learning" model of Ray and colleagues (Ray, Sawyer, Rothschild, Heeler, Strong, & Reed, 1973); the communication–persuasion model of McGuire (1969); the counterarguing concepts of Roberts and Maccoby (1973); the attitude change model of Fishbein (Ajzen & Fishbein, 1980); the peer influence concepts of Festinger (1954); and the adoption–diffusion model of Rogers (1983). The CBC model, introduced here, emphasizes the features that are relevant to community-based education and health promotion. There are several underlying assumptions implicit in this portrayal of the change process:

1. A need for change and the room for change exist.
2. A large proportion of the population needs to change.
3. Initial and final states are measurable.
4. Education forces have adequate social legitimacy.
5. Interaction among educational elements, peer influence, and diffusion will occur and will magnify effects.
6. Adequate time exists within the design for measurable change to occur.

The CBC framework also contains a postulated idealized sequence of educator–client steps, in which the educator provides information, incentive, skills training, and follow-up support, and the receiver or client learns information, changes attitude, becomes motivated to change, learns skills needed for change, and learns methods of maintenance of change. These steps are rooted in the empirical data derived from the previously cited research, such as the social learning theory (Bandura, 1977).

The Social Marketing Framework

The concept of social marketing (Kotler & Zaltman, 1971) is that marketing principles and techniques—based to a considerable extent on applications of the CBC change model—can be applied to social change programs to improve their effectiveness. In 1982, Kotler defined the concept as follows: "Social marketing is the design, implementation and control of programs seeking to increase the acceptability of a social idea or cause in a target group(s)" (p. 490). The design and implementation of community education programs in general, and the media effects of them in particular, can be viewed as an application of social marketing to community health education.

The marketing process begins with an understanding of the consumer. This understanding directs the creation of products or services, with price, promotion, and distribution organized to attract the consumer with an offer of something of potential value. The marketing process is often divided into these four key elements, the "four P's" of marketing management: "the right *product* backed by the right *promotion* and put in the right *place* at the right *price*" (Kotler & Zaltman, 1971). Each of these four elements is described below as it applies to social marketing.

The "product" element is concerned with designing appropriate products in "packages" that target audiences find desirable and are willing to purchase. Health promotion products may take a tangible form (e.g., a low-cholesterol cookbook) or may be much less tangible (e.g., a TV message to adopt a healthier life style). Products may also be services.

The "promotion" element is concerned with how to make the "product" familiar, acceptable, and even desirable, usually through advertising, personal selling, publicity, and sales promotion.

The "place" element has to do with the provision of adequate and compatible distribution and response channels. Kotler and Zaltman (1971, p. 8) note, "Motivated persons should know where the product can be obtained," and the activity involved is "arranging for accessible outlets which permit the translation of motivations into actions" through well-established patterns of distribution.

The "price" element "represents the costs that the buyer must accept in order to obtain the product." Kotler and Zaltman define price to include "money costs, opportunity costs, energy costs, and psychic costs," and in this fashion includes the notions of "transaction" in his formulation of social marketing. They note that "the marketer's approach to selling a social product is to consider how the rewards for buying the product can be increased relative to the costs, or the costs reduced relative to the rewards" (1971, pp. 9–10).

Although it is clear that semantic analogies can be made between social marketing elements and the CBC elements previously described, it is also clear that the social marketing framework adds to theory and practice by forcing one to consider the practical realities of marketing health promotion products in the complex urban environments of the modern world.

An application of marketing to community health education relies on the health educator's ability to control or arrange the elements of product, promotion, price, and place. It assumes that the social marketer has a clear understanding of consumer attributes and needs and has the requisite flexibility to design and produce needed commodities or services. It further assumes that adequate distribution systems exist for the marketer to reach the target audience. A "place" where the consumer intersects with the "product" is required. A marketing model also assumes that a "transaction" is possible within the context of people's lives, and that they can afford and will pay the "price" of the "product." Finally, it requires knowledge of results of prior actions (the equivalent of sales data) as the basis for product design and system management.

The Community Organization Framework

The following important assumptions can be made regarding community organization's role in community education programs:

1. Mass media education alone is powerful, but its effects may be augmented by community organization.
2. Interpersonal influence can be cheaply enhanced through community organization, multiplying the effects of other educational modalities.
3. Organizations can expand the distribution of educational materials and programs.
4. Organizations can become sponsors of educational programs and can thus increase the likelihood of their persistence.
5. Formation of new organizations will increase the array of groups concerned with health education and health promotion.

A general plan for community organization can be derived from the "development–maintenance" strategy (Spergel, 1969), in which the involvement of the initiating research team and the strategies used evolve as the community assumes a greater role in working toward the overall health care goals. This dual strategy, however, misses an important additional task: The need to provide curricula, training of instructors, and skills training looms large as a requirement not covered under either development or maintenance. Thus, we believe that a hybrid strategy is required, with a phase of "implementation" sandwiched between development and maintenance to cover the educational activities important in a behaviorally oriented project.

The methods by which the three frameworks are used to achieve change within a community project are described in a later section.

DESIGN PROBLEMS AND EVALUATION CHALLENGES OF COMMUNITY-BASED STUDIES

The design constraints of community studies induce such a lengthy list of problems in logistics, execution, and evaluation that the experimenter must often return to remind himself or herself of the issues of generalizability, cost, and policy relevance alluded to earlier to regain needed courage. Since these problems create a need for increased diligence and ingenuity in evaluation, it is not surprising that ancillary evaluation measures have been developed that will enhance the validity and scientific value of these studies (Farquhar, 1978; Flay & Cook, 1981).

Design Problems and Constraints

The issues described below are not given in order of priority; some stand alone, and others are related.

1. Communities are complex and changing systems.
2. If a study requires cooperation of local governments and agencies, will agreements, relationships, and constituents remain stable?
3. People move in and out of communities, thus diluting the impact of planned social change.
4. Random events (such as unemployment related to failure of a particular industry) could envelop one community in ways not shared by the entire region under study.
5. Few suitable communities are available within reach of any particular institution that wishes to initiate a study.
6. Communities within reach are nonetheless relatively remote from the initiating institution, and the distance creates important logistical problems.
7. Blinding of investigators and clients/patients/residents to the treatment modality is clearly impossible.
8. The penetration of educational inputs into a community system is a problem. In a controlled clinical trial, a selected sample excludes the generous proportion of people who are not information seekers but who remain as permanent "dropouts" in a community study.
9. The salience of the program may be low within the population of the community (Flay & Cook, 1981), thus exacerbating the problem of low penetration.
10. The causal chain in a community system is longer and harder to trace than it is in a clinical research study on volunteers. For example, diffusion effects and interaction among varied educational inputs are more likely to occur within a community system.
11. Resource limitations may prevent a single research institution from selecting more than three to six communities for study, and the freedom to randomize is limited due to geographical factors, such as the presence of overlapping mass media influences (Farquhar, 1978). Even if randomization is possible, the small number of communities accessible to a single research institution leads to a serious restriction in interpretation by classical criteria.
12. The common necessity for nonrandom allocation of treatment and control will lead to limitations of causal inference. Campbell and Stanley (1963) and Cook and Campbell (1976, 1979) have described these limitations, and Campbell (1957) has termed the legitimate concerns for rival hypotheses "threats to internal validity." Solutions to these threats have been proposed (Cook & Campbell, 1976, 1979; Farquhar, 1978; Flay & Cook, 1981) and are described below.

Evaluation Challenges and Solutions

The challenge of evaluation is clearly inherent in the complex and murky waters of the community milieu. Clarification of uncertainty can be sought only by increasing the depth, breadth, and sensitivity of analyses and by assessing and deriving inference on the rich tapestry of results produced, often in nonstatistical ways. For example, a strong consistency among independent outcome measures that evaluate the results from a variety of perspectives is persuasive evidence of a real effect. A number of approaches to the problems described above are presented, again not necessarily in order of priority.

1. Randomly assign a rather large number of communities, perhaps at the least 16 (Sherwin, 1978), to treatment and control. This ideal situation is unlikely to be achievable for most experimenters, due to the limitations of resources and geography alluded to earlier.

2. Match and randomly assign a smaller number of communities to treatment and control. As mentioned above, logistical limitations commonly preclude the random assignment.

3. Match a smaller number of nonrandomized community units in order to decrease baseline differences. As an example of this approach, in the Stanford Three Community Study, only 3 of 56 baseline comparisons in salient risk factors between treatment and control samples showed significant statistical differences (Farquhar, Maccoby, Wood, Alexander, Breitrose, Brown, Haskell, McAlister, Meyer, Nash, & Stern, 1977). The effectiveness of the matching process may be increased when the variables to be matched are repeatedly measured over several baseline surveys, but costs frequently preclude this luxury.

4. If close matching is not feasible, then adjustment for baseline differences among communities through covariance analysis may reduce the effect of these differences on outcome measures (Cook & Campbell, 1979; Williams, Fortmann, Farquhar, Mellen, & Varady, 1981).

5. In designs limited to a few units or even a single unit, a "long" baseline may be sought, through use of repeated analyses extending well prior to and following intervention, in order to distinguish treatment effects from long-term secular trends (Glass, Willson, & Gottman, 1975).

6. A nonequivalent dependent variable design (Cook & Campbell, 1979) can be used to strengthen the inference for a causal role of the intervention by testing for the specificity of the intervention. In this maneuver, the experimenter seeks evidence for lack of effect on a dependent variable other than the one that is the object of the experimenter's intervention. Thus one would expect the rate of insurance claims for whiplash to fall in response to a seat-belt campaign, but not the rates of other types of injuries (Flay & Cook, 1981).

7. Seek evidence for a dose–response relationship by partitioning the sample by level of exposure, or by correlating change versus exposure to

education. In the Stanford Three Community Study, such partitioning revealed a surprisingly linear relationship between treatment effect and treatment input (Maccoby, Farquhar, Wood, & Alexander, 1977; see Figure 11.1). As Flay and Cook (1981) point out, such a result in a quasi-experimental design argues strongly against the alternative explanations of regression and historical trend, but it does not address well the rival hypothesis of self-selection, since those who selectively attend to a message could be those who would "spontaneously" change.

8. Seek further evidence for a cause-and-effect role of a specific campaign

FIGURE 11.1. Percentage of change in the Stanford Three Community Study from the first to the second survey in participants' knowledge about dietary risk factors. The groups are ranked from top to bottom, according to our estimation of increasing intensity of educational input. (From Maccoby, N., Farquhar, J. W., Wood, P.D., & Alexander, J. K. Reducing the risk of cardiovascular disease: Effects of a community-based campaign on knowledge and behavior. *Journal of Community Health*, 1977, *3*, 100–114. Reprinted by permission.)

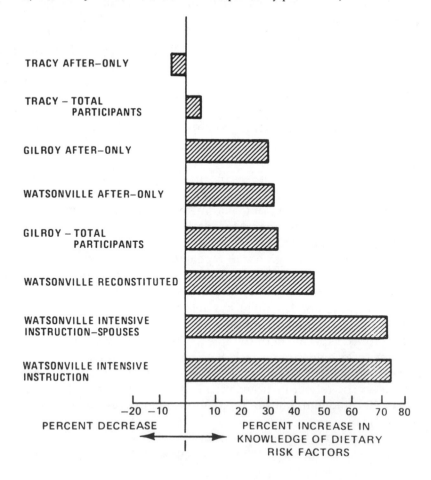

through network analysis (Rogers & Kincaid, 1981). Network analysis traces the path of communication through the social structure of communities. As an example, methods developed by Rogers were applied in the Stanford Three Community Study to demonstrate that one of the observed effects of education was to increase a behavioral characteristic termed "opinion leadership." It was also found that the amount of this change was a function of the extent of educational exposure (Farquhar, 1978; see Figure 11.2). Such generation of opinion leadership was independent of socioeconomic status (Meyer, Maccoby, & Farquhar, 1977). The findings were relevant to causal inference, in that alternative explanations to the specific treatment effect were not evident.

9. Employ path analysis—a method in which causal modeling of complex systems is examined through use of two or more regression equations. This method was also used in the Stanford Three Community Study to assess the likelihood that the changes seen were the result of the specific education given (Farquhar, 1978; Milburn, 1979). This method, however, is quite weak in its role in the study of whether an effect occurred, as it has its principal use in the study of why the effect occurred.

10. Use time-series of trend analysis. Flay and Cook (1981) point out that although the ideal time-series analysis should comprise 40 or 50 measurements to allow formal statistical analysis, an abbreviated time series can add to the internal validity of a study. As an example, in the Stanford Three Community Study, regression analysis employed community rather than subject as the basic experimental unit and the community by time variation as the error term. In this analysis, conclusions derived by the standard method were supported (Williams *et al.*, 1981).

11. Other methods may be used as supplementary analyses—for example, the use of specific markers within an educational communication that will allow the evaluator to identify a causal link between that specific communication and a change in knowledge or behavior; or analyses of unobtrusive measures such as grocery store sales to confirm that changes detected in a population survey are generalizable to the community at large.

In summary, many approaches can enhance understanding not only of the causal links between treatment and effect, but also the process by which change occurs and is maintained. In the sections of this chapter that describe completed or existing studies, further examples of the rich variety of measurement and evaluation are given.

METHODS FOR ACHIEVING CHANGE IN COMMUNITY-BASED STUDIES

This section lists the operational steps needed to design, carry out, and evaluate community-based health education studies. These steps are derived from our decade of experience in carrying out one completed study, the Stan-

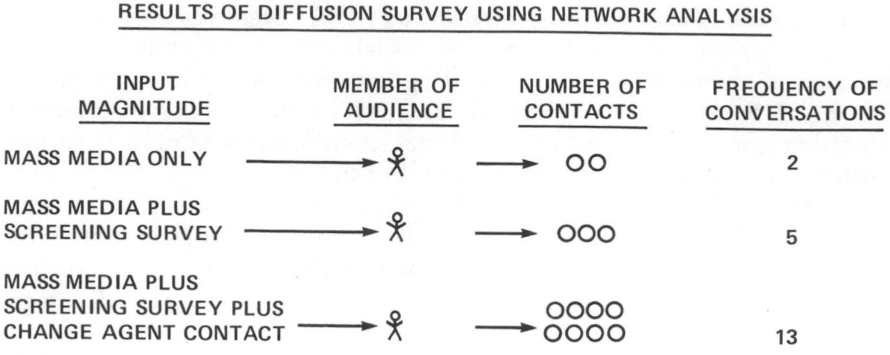

RESULTS OF DIFFUSION SURVEY USING NETWORK ANALYSIS

INPUT MAGNITUDE	MEMBER OF AUDIENCE	NUMBER OF CONTACTS	FREQUENCY OF CONVERSATIONS
MASS MEDIA ONLY ⟶	👤 ⟶	OO	2
MASS MEDIA PLUS SCREENING SURVEY ⟶	👤 ⟶	OOO	5
MASS MEDIA PLUS SCREENING SURVEY PLUS CHANGE AGENT CONTACT ⟶	👤 ⟶	OOOO OOOO	13

FIGURE 11.2. Evidence for variable diffusion and opinion leader status as a result of varied input of health education during the first year of campaigning in the Three Community Study. Intervention recipients who were personally contacted (see bottom of figure) had more conversations about the health issues with a larger number of acquaintances than did recipients of mass media only or of mass media plus the screening survey. (From Farquhar, J. W. The community-based model of life-style intervention trials. *American Journal of Epidemiology*, 1978, *108*, 103–111. Reprinted by permission.)

ford Three Community Study (Farquhar *et al.*, 1977; Maccoby *et al.*, 1977) and in the design and implementation of an ongoing 8-year study, the Stanford Five City Project (Farquhar, 1978; Maccoby & Solomon, 1981). Although the methods described have been derived from studies on cardiovascular disease prevention, there is a high likelihood that they will be relevant to any study in which life style change within a large proportion of the population is the goal.

The methods are described in the temporal sequence in which such activities can often be expected to occur, and information is given on the usual activities before and following the research group's successful application for the funding needed for such studies. The model being described is that of a field demonstration project with a strong evaluation component—the "experimental paradigm" of Flay and Cook (1981). In such a project, a considerable proportion—usually in excess of 50%—of the total cost is assigned to measurement and evaluation.

Initial Planning Phase (Pregrant or Contract)

The project begins as an idea held by one or a few members of the research team. This idea can grow to involve a nucleus of potential principal investigators. This planning group or executive committee must meet for at least 6 months and is responsible for the following sequence of tasks:

1. Clarification of overall research goals, including scientific rationale, and assessment of community need and interest. The ideal sequence, which is unlikely to occur, is that a year-long planning grant is obtained that will allow a final grant proposal to be written with greater assurance.
2. Writing and submission of the grant or contract proposal.
3. Awkward interim waiting period while the community opinion leaders begin to wonder if they have been forgotten. The recruiting process itself may in fact trigger certain community groups to launch programs of the type planned. This can occur in either treatment or control communities, of course.
4. The site visit—convincing those who will award the grant or contract that the study is worthwhile.

Final Project Planning (Postgrant or Contract)

The planning or executive committee is advised to form a larger group of investigators into a steering committee for a minimum of 4 to 6 months of final planning before formal field operations begin. The steps needed here are as follows:

1. Complete the community recruiting phase. Within control communities, this step is one solely of reaffirmation of intent to obtain archival information or survey data.
2. Establish expert groups to complete prefield planning. These tasks include the following:

    a. A survey design and data management group must refine the statistical power calculations, define the survey and evaluation instruments, and hire and train survey and evaluation staff. This process will take 6–12 months, depending on the complexity of the survey.

    b. An education group should establish task force groups assigned to particular educational goals; these groups should produce a set of planning guides that specify the goals recommended by the groups on the basis of current knowledge in various fields.

    c. The steering committee assembles the planning guides to determine whether any additional prefield studies are needed before field operations can begin.

    d. The prefield studies are assigned to either the survey–measurements group or the education group. The two most likely prefield activities will be either survey instrument pretests or pretests of educational methods.

Field Operations

The phase of field operations comprises the major portion of the project and is characterized by the evaluation processes and by the development, implementation, and maintenance phases of community organization, which forms the matrix into which the educational concepts, activities, and products are placed. The educational concepts, in turn, are determined by reference to the CBC model, and the products and their placement largely by the social marketing guidelines. The blend of theoretical frameworks is engrafted onto a data-based management system that is designed to (1) solve problems, (2) be responsive to changing community needs as determined by ongoing surveys and evaluation, and (3) shape the educational inputs by the process of formative evaluation. Examples are given below of each of these activities: (1) the field application of the three major theories or frameworks of community organization, CBC, and social marketing; (2) formative evaluation; (3) data-based management of planning and operating.

Field Application of Community Organization

Following the recruitment and early development activities described above, the three stages of development, implementation, and maintenance are begun, in that order. These are described here.

1. During the first stage, development, there are four processes that take place:

    a. Goal definition: Reviewing relevant literature; using baseline survey data for determining what people need in order to reduce risk in a particular area (information, motivation, skills, etc.); determining the target audience and the most appropriate type of program.

    b. Resources definition: Discovering and assessing existing community resources concerned with a particular risk factor; reviewing the potential for creating new programs within organizations.

    c. Community recruiting: Establishing cooperative relationships with existing organizations to identify key community figures; assessing interest in a particular program; bringing together organizations for cooperative efforts; and matching organizations with program alternatives.

    d. Program definitions: Using community feedback to help design a program to fit the community's and the initiators' needs; using the theoretical framework; compiling the scientific content of the program; beginning formative evaluation of program content and materials; and finally designing and writing the program.

2. Development sets the stage for implementation. During the implementation stage, three types of activities take place:

    a. Materials and program development: Completing the depth and breadth of the scientific content of materials; fixing the program design (e.g., are there group leaders? who trained the leaders?); completing formative evaluation and pretesting of materials; and developing program evaluation materials (questionnaire design, focus groups, etc.).

    b. Consulting with community groups: Helping individual organizations make way for new programs; helping advisory boards become functioning community units; helping community organizations to reorganize to improve health delivery services.

    c. Program field testing: Transferring the program to the community by teaching community program organizers about the program, recruiting leaders, training leaders, recruiting participants, implementing the program, evaluating it, and beginning to redesign and refine the program.

3. The implementation stage merges into the maintenance stage through the continual refinement of programs. Maintenance involves the following steps:

    a. Program monitoring: Monitoring progress of trained personnel (employees of an organization or volunteers).

    b. Program multiplication: Recruiting new organizations to adopt or take part in a program; planning for the future.

    c. Program continuation: Finishing the process of defining the role of a community advisory board; introducing the process of organizing for institutionalization of the program.

The guidelines listed above, though general, define the nature of this hybrid theoretical formulation described earlier. The implementation phase, however, cannot be completed in a vacuum. The next section describes how the vacuum can be filled.

Field Application of the Communication–Behavior Change Framework

Health education programs often will encompass multiple objectives in a population whose members vary greatly in their awareness, knowledge, and behaviors relative to each objective. Planning of an education program therefore requires a division of the audience into smaller units that share relevant characteristics. Rational education decisions (message content, choice of media channel) can then be made, and educational activities can be presented in a logical sequence. Messages can be pinpointed to address the needs of various parts of the total audience at various stages in the matrix by topic area (such as the risk factors for cardiovascular disease). Used in this way, the CBC framework is a helpful organizing scheme for audience segmentation, message design and sequencing, and content of instructional events and community programs.

    One element of the CBC framework is an assumption that individuals go through a series of steps as they gradually adopt the advocated attitudes and/or behavior (but not necessarily in the order listed in Table 11.1). This is called the "hierarchy of effects" concept (McGuire, 1969; Ray *et al.*, 1973). The concept of behavior change as an orderly sequence of steps is admittedly an idealized version of real life and is not always an accurate chronological portrayal of the process of life style change for all people in all areas. For some people, on some topics, the sequence of steps may vary. On some issues, one or two steps will be much more important than others. One message or event may also perform more than one function. However, the model does help planners to develop a clearer picture of the elements needed for action. It can also be used as an evaluation framework to observe

TABLE 11.1. Communication–Behavior Change Model

COMMUNICATION INPUTS	COMMUNICATION FUNCTIONS (FOR THE SENDER)	COMMUNICATION–BEHAVIOR CHANGE OBJECTIVES (FOR THE RECEIVER)
Messages, media, community events, diffusion	1. Gain attention (set the agenda).	1. Become aware.
	2. Provide information.	2. Increase knowledge.
	3. Provide incentives.	3. Increase motivation.
	4. Provide models.	4. Learn and practice skills.
	5. Provide training.	5. Take action, assess outcomes.
	6. Provide cues to action.	6. Maintain action, practice self-management skills.
	7. Provide support, self-management training.	7. Inform and influence members of one's social network.

the shift of population groups over time in the direction of the intended project goals.

In Table 11.1 the steps, or CBC objectives, are listed in the right-hand column. The middle column lists the corresponding communication function required to meet those objectives. The column on the left notes that instructional products and events must be designed, produced and distributed, in sequence, to perform the functions listed. Each step is organized around a postulated need of the audience. A discussion of the communication functions listed in the middle column follows.

Agenda Setting
The function of agenda setting is to gain the public's attention and to focus it on certain specific issues and problems. In the public's mind, the existence of the problem must be established, and an awareness of potential solutions must be promoted. Generally, in a pluralistic society, the mass media play an important agenda-setting role. When attention is brought to an issue either by the mass media or through interpersonal means, and when people begin thinking about it, then the first step in the behavior change process is under way.

Information
Once a particular topic or subject matter is on the public agenda, an educational program must present information in lay terms that makes the issue interesting, understandable, and personally meaningful, and that sets the stage for action. The messages must be retained in a way that predisposes people to act in a different way in the future.

Incentives
Change is more likely when individuals clearly perceive the personal and social benefits of change, which can be enhanced by appropriate communications. Coupons, group recognition, and other external rewards may act as incentives.

Skills Training
Where changes in complex habits of long standing are involved, it may be necessary to provide skills training in how to start making and maintaining changes, both by providing step-by-step instruction and by promoting the availability of self-help and professional resources.

Cues to Action
Ideally, this phase of an overall strategy would provide educational inputs that act as cues to trigger specific actions. Messages would indicate clear paths of action to stimulate the trial adoption of new behaviors.

Assistance in Maintenance
Research on maintenance of behavior change is still in its infancy. We know how to take weight off, but not how to keep it off. We know how to stop smoking, but not always how to stay stopped. There are, however, several theoretical and empirical suggestions. Some of these are discussed later.

At this stage, inputs are required to provide a sense of social support and approval, and to remind people of both the short-term and long-term personal and social benefits of the changes undertaken. Both gaining self-efficacy and learning self-management methods are important aspects of the maintenance phase. It is especially important to note that maintenance of behavior change may well depend heavily on how the initial learning of change takes place.

In health promotion programs with multiple objectives, not everything can be done all at once for everyone. Planners need to have a rational basis for making selections from among competing choices and for sequencing actions over time. The CBC framework can be a general guide. It suggests how to break the large community health promotion tasks down into manageable pieces, and, depending on the current status of various audience segments, helps to pinpoint where to start with which message.

The framework shown in Table 11.1 is an example from the SHDPP. It guides the general planning of educational programs from the perspective of risk factors. Its value is to provide a framework for assessing what people currently know, believe, and do in each behavior change area. This helps place the emphasis where it is most needed—on the sequence of events leading from awareness to action and social support.

This framework shows that planning is organized around specific objectives. In our case, the objectives are changes in risk factor status. Then the communication needs are assessed by noting how the population is distributed along the behavior change stages within each risk factor area. Additional subdivisions are made along other dimensions (e.g., English- or Spanish-speaking, male or female).

In the area of smoking prevention, for example, we find a clear need for a wide variety of programs for various audience segments. Pregnant women, middle-aged men, teenagers who smoke, teenagers who do not smoke—all need and desire different types of interventions, ranging from mass media only to highly intensive group programs. In addition, we have found for virtually all audiences that people are well past the awareness and knowledge phases regarding the health hazards of smoking. Indeed, they are also already highly motivated to quit smoking. The problem is clearly a lack of skills and cues to action to quit smoking and to maintain that behavior. These data, based on formative research, have clearly changed the course of the SHDPP education program.

Given the guidelines above, it is clear that the ideas created and formulated by the set of CBC theories still need the polish and practical transformation into acceptable products and services that can be provided through the principles of the social marketing framework and through formative research. This framework is now discussed.

Field Applications of the Social Marketing Framework

The social marketing framework provides many useful perspectives on the design and implementation of community education programs. Many of the social marketing concepts are similar to those of the CBC model, since the two fields have had a great deal of overlap. However, social marketing, with its roots firmly in the real problems of implementing marketing programs, has developed many distinctive concepts and methodologies that can be borrowed for health education. Each of 10 social marketing concepts having applicability to the design and implementation of social programs is briefly described below. Each poses questions that should be answered by the planners of social change prior to implementation of a program.

The Marketing Philosophy

The marketing philosophy states that the goal of an organization should be to meet consumers' needs and wants. Furthermore, marketing is seen as a process whereby something of value is exchanged among two or more parties because they themselves feel this will best meet their individual needs. The marketing philosophy presents a challenge to those interested in health to insure that they are meeting consumer needs and not, as is often the case, developing health systems that only best serve the needs of the provider. This challenge is better defined in the marketing concept of the "four P's."

The "Four P's" of Marketing

The "four P's" have already been described (Kotler & Zaltman, 1971): product, price, place, and promotion. The challenge to health programs is to design an effective core product and to use marketing techniques to develop it into tangible forms that are desirable to the target audiences. For example, the generic "product" of a health education program is information. Considerable effort must be expended to present this information in a way that will be valued and understood by the target audience.

The "price" of participating in health programs is very often ignored by planners. Since many services are free in prevention programs directed at communities, planners are often surprised at low participation rates. This is often caused by ignoring the full price of participation, which includes time and social and psychological costs. Although face-to-face smoking cessation clinics may be more effective than short courses on television, the price of time and exposure of one's "frailty" to others may make the mediated approach more effective. Therefore, the price of a product or service should be carefully set, based on research involving consumer's perceptions.

"Place" means the distribution system for a product or service. Many social programs in the health area have failed because they did not have adequate distribution systems within easy reach of the target group. Unknowingly, many community health organizations put up barricades limiting the access to their products—for example, limiting the distribution of booklets to those willing to come to an office in person.

"Promotion" of programs and events in community education is perhaps one of the most difficult and least researched areas. A health education program should monitor those who attend community events to determine how attendees heard about the event and what motivated their participation. Researchers are also advised to conduct experiments in promotion. For example, such methods as direct mail flyers, announcements in community group meetings, and letters sent home through school children can be tested as alternative ways to encourage adults to view special educational TV programs.

Hierarchies of Communication Effects

A great deal of the literature on the hierarchy of effects comes from the field of marketing research (Ray et al., 1973). This concept has also had contributions from individuals such as Rogers (1983) and McGuire (1969). This issue has already been discussed above in connection with the CBC framework.

Audience Segmentation

Audience segmentation is an important marketing concept. There is a rich marketing literature on methods of obtaining the best set of audience segmentation variables (Frank, Massy, & Wind, 1972). These methods are applicable to social marketing as well. There are many ways to segment an audience: for example, demographic characteristics, audience needs, mass media use, attitudes, readiness to change, and language. Since health programs have often mistakenly used a single message for all, it is clear that these marketing concepts will be of use in social change programs.

Understanding All Relevant Markets

Marketers are always concerned with the multiple "publics" that are important to the success of a given program. For example, a university-based health education program has four distinct publics: internal publics (i.e., faculty and staff), groups supporting the university (i.e., alumni, foundations), groups consuming the program's offerings (i.e., people in the communities), and groups regulating the program (i.e., government agencies, etc.). Even the groups consuming the program's offerings can be segmented further into the public at large, government organizations, health professionals, and volunteer health agencies. It is important not to forget any of these markets when designing and implementing a program. Many health promotion programs have failed because of lack of cooperation from one or more markets. Formative research can be quite useful in understanding the needs and attitudes of each of these segments prior to the implementation of a program.

Information and Rapid Feedback Systems

Over the years, marketers have learned the importance of rapid feedback systems. Academicians are more used to asking at the end of a program whether or not it succeeded than they are to asking why it succeeded or failed. In complex long-term community education programs, it is essential to devise a system of "guideposts" over time that can be easily measured to insure that the program is on course.

Interpersonal and Mass Communication Interactions

There is a common assumption in the communication and marketing literature that the mass media may be more successful in creating awareness of a program's message, while interpersonal communication may be more effective in motivating behavior change (Rogers, 1983). Therefore, marketers often direct messages through the mass media with the idea of encouraging interpersonal communication; thus, a California grocery chain's campaign theme is "Tell a Friend." Considerable empirical evidence exists for the importance of interpersonal communication in the diffusion of ideas and adoption of innovations (Rogers, 1983). Therefore, the mass media and interpersonal communications should be coupled as an effective social marketing method.

Utilization of Commercial Resources

In virtually every corner of the developed world, there are commercial resources (such as advertising agencies, marketing research companies, distribution companies, etc.) that can be very useful in social programs. These are often ignored by community education programs. The County Health Improvement Program in Pennsylvania uses such commercial resources as a survey research organization and a social marketing advertising firm in implementing their program. Commercial resources should not be ignored, particularly by those programs that are smaller in scale and do not have the resources to assemble all of the talent needed for community health education on their own.

Understanding the Competition

A very simple concept from marketing is to consider the competition for a product or service. While the concept is obvious for commercial companies, the competition is not always evident for social programs. However, for heart disease prevention, there is massive competition from commercial firms that promote unhealthy products, from competing social climates, from competing activities for a person's time, and even from competing heart disease prevention efforts (e.g., quack diets, commercial weight loss firms, etc.). The competition should be understood in great detail, so that a community health promotion program can provide competitive products and services.

Expectations of Success

Commercial marketers and social marketers often diverge in expectations. Marketing's experience tells us that expectations should be modest. Commercial marketers are often quite satisfied with gaining 2% or 3% of a lucrative market. However, social planners often believe that they are failing unless they change everyone overnight. Clearly, some middle ground must be reached. Health promoters should understand all steps in the change process, should assign probabilities of success to each of them, and should realize that the compound probability of success is usually quite small even with high individual probabilities. For example, if there are three steps in a change process (say, knowledge, attitude change, and behavior change), and each step has a 50% probability, then the chance of getting an individual to move through all three stages is $.5 \times .5 \times .5$, or .125. Regardless of which estimation method is used, the key issue is that rapid and substantial change in health habits is not readily achieved, and health education planners must learn to set more realistic goals than is often the case.

Summary

The application of the social marketing framework provides many useful practical guides in the design and implementation of community health education programs. In order to answer the questions social marketing poses, it is first necessary to conduct extensive formative research. The following section provides guidance on the field application of formative research in community health education.

Field Application of Formative Research

"Formative research" is defined as any research designed to provide guidance for educational planners in facilitating the development of appropriate, attractive, and effective educational and community programs. It is also used for monitoring and modifying the progress of an educational program over time. Thus, not only is it used to help design the educational campaign strategies and plan the educational materials, but it is also a vital source of feedback on how well these elements are doing.

Formative research has several purposes, including the following:

1. The collection of baseline data for developing audience profiles and for defining specific audience segments (e.g., answers to "What are the needs, desires, and experiences of the people in the communities as far as risk reduction is concerned?").
2. The provision of information for specific program planning (e.g., answers to "Which of the following five smoking cessation programs would you most like to participate in?").
3. The provision of information for the development of specific media components (e.g., answers to "Which of these booklets looks the most interesting to you? Why?").
4. The process analysis of media events (e.g., answers to "Have you seen this logo? Have you read this booklet we sent you in the mail?").
5. The process analysis of educational programs (e.g., answers to "What have you heard about our programs and activities?").

The project's overall summative evaluation survey can be used to answer many formative questions, of course. For example, knowledge gained by the population as a result of the education program must be assessed, and these data can be used formatively. Parts of this survey can also be designed for specific formative purposes. In addition, small-scale surveys need to be done periodically to gather information between administrations of the large-scale surveys and to assess the impact of particular events or programs. Such formative surveys are necessary for several reasons: (1) the formative data need not have as much precision in confidence intervals as evaluation data must; one would want to know the range of opinions on an issue, but not necessarily the exact proportions of the population responding one way or another. (2) A large number of formative questions are needed; thus many samples may be required to avoid an overload of any one participant. (3) People and events in a community are not stationary, and one would wish to obtain formative measures over time.

Below are some examples of such "minisurveys" from the SHDPP:

1. General health perceptions and motivations. A questionnaire was designed to provide information on personal health priorities, motivations for change, and obstacles to change.
2. Nutrition behavior. This questionnaire provided information on topics

such as food shopping, food preparation, decisions about what to eat, and design and content of an optimum cookbook.
3. Weight loss. This questionnaire determined past experiences with various types of weight loss programs, especially histories of backsliding, and desirable elements of an ideal program.
4. Print preferences and strategy testing. This questionnaire provided guidance in the choice of booklet size and shape and cover color. A second section tested hypotheses on various mechanisms for information delivery.

These four examples all represent the field application of formative research techniques along the lines of the social marketing framework. These formative data are used in program planning, as described in the next section.

Field Application of Data-Based Management

A reasonable way of organizing a community research enterprise is to set up two wings. These two wings, as noted earlier, are (1) a data and measurements group (responsible for assessing change in the dependent variables for summative evaluation), and (2) an education group (responsible for producing change in the independent variables).

Frequent regular meetings of the two major wings of a community-based research study are recommended to guide the progress of the study. Each group receives data on the progress of each wing, and assigns priorities and reformulates policy in accordance with the data received. The education group is advised to create 6-month plans as an overall guide, but to modify these plans as formative data and as community acceptance for programs dictate.

A small executive committee (three to six persons) is also advisable for setting broad policy, monitoring the daily progress of the project, and coordinating the two wings, especially in regard to budgetary and personnel issues. Such a committee should include the principal investigator and the administrator, as well as the heads of the two wings.

EXAMPLES OF COMMUNITY-BASED STUDIES IN CARDIOVASCULAR DISEASE PREVENTION

Two projects, the Stanford Three Community Study (Farquhar et al., 1977; Maccoby et al., 1977) and the Finnish North Karelia Project (Puska, Tuomilehto, Salonen, Nissinen, Virtamo, Björkqvist, Koskela, Neittaanmäki, Takalo, Kottke, Maki, Sipila, & Varvikko, 1981; Puska, Virtamo, Tuomilehto, Mäki, & Neittaanmäki, 1978), were begun in 1972 and were in operation for 3 and 5 years, respectively. Eight comparable multifactor studies with an emphasis on comprehensive educational methods, including the mass media, have since been undertaken in Australia, South Africa, Switzerland, the Federal

Republic of Germany, and the United States. Many other studies are in the planning phase or are under way in Europe (World Health Organization Report, 1977). Although some of these studies will surely be comparable, others either will not have reference communities or will stress methods of detection and clinical management of high-risk individuals rather than comprehensive public health education as the means of changing cardiovascular disease risk.

Three of the four current U.S. studies are now funded by the National Heart, Lung and Blood Institute and are loosely bound in a confederation for sharing evaluation methods. These three are (1) the Stanford Five City Project, begun in 1978 (Farquhar, 1978, in press); (2) the Minnesota Heart Health Study, under the aegis of Dr. Henry Blackburn of Minneapolis, begun in 1980 (Blackburn, in press); and (3) the Pawtucket Heart Health Study, under the aegis of Dr. Richard Carleton of Providence, Rhode Island, begun in 1980 (Carleton, in press). A fourth U.S. study, now partly funded through the State of Pennsylvania Health Department, is under the aegis of Drs. Paul Stolley and Albert Stunkard of the University of Pennsylvania.

Table 11.2 lists the 10 projects of greatest interest in the present context and identifies the years of community education, country of origin, numbers of communities, and numbers of residents. In only one of the 10 studies has random assignment been used, and in this instance (in Switzerland) the random assignment was within two pairs of French- or German-speaking villages, chosen for demographic similarity within each language group.

THE STANFORD THREE COMMUNITY STUDY

The Stanford Three Community Study had as a research objective to begin investigation on the kinds of large-scale primary prevention programs that might be mounted community-wide. The central objective of the project was to observe the changes in information, attitudes, and risk-related behavior that occurred as a consequence of mass media interventions. The project's ultimate goal was to achieve a clinically meaningful reduction in the overall risk of heart disease. This endpoint, the "risk score," is the estimated probability that a person will be the victim of a cardiovascular event over the next 12-year period. The score is derived from an equation based on the Framingham Heart Study (Truett, Cornfield, & Kannel, 1967). Factors entered into the risk equation are age, sex, systolic blood pressure, relative weight, amount of cigarette smoking, and level of cholesterol in the blood. Therefore, the behavior change goals in the Stanford Three Community Study were for participants to achieve their desirable weight; to cut down on or stop smoking; to increase physical activity; and to reduce or modify their consumption of refined sugar, salt, cholesterol, saturated fats, and alcohol.

Both clinical and epidemiological evidence suggested the educational–behavioral approach to risk factor modification. The community education

TABLE 11.2. Description of 10 Community-Based Multifactor Health Education Studies

DESCRIPTION	COUNTRY	YEARS OF EDUCATION	REFERENCE
1. Stanford Three Community Study: three towns, two treatment, one reference, $n=45,000$.	United States (California)	1972–1975	Farquhar, Maccoby, Wood, Alexander, Breitrose, Brown, Haskell, McAlister, Meyer, Nash, & Stern (1977)
2. North Karelia Project: two counties, one treatment, one reference, $n=433,000$.	Finland	1972–1977	Puska, Tuomilehto, Salonen, Nissinen, Virtamo, Björkqvist, Koskela, Neittaanmäki, Takalo, Kottke, Maki, Sipila, & Varvikko (1981)
3. North Coast Project: three towns, two treatment, one reference, $n=70,000$.	Australia	1977–1980	Egger, Fitzgerald, Frape, Monaem, Rubinstein, Tyler, & McKay (1983)
4. Swiss National Research Program: four towns, two treatment, two reference, $n=40,000$.	Switzerland	1978–1980	Gutzwiller, Junod, & Schweizer (1979)
5. South African Study: three towns, two treatment, one reference, $n=$uncertain.	South Africa	1978–	Rossouw, Jooste, Kotze, & Jordaan (1981)
6. Community Health Improvement Project: two counties, one treatment, one reference, $n=224,000$.	United States (Pennsylvania)	1979–	Stolley & Stunkard (1980)
7. Heidelberg Study: two towns, one treatment, one reference, $n=30,000$.	Federal Republic of Germany	1980–	Nüssel (1981)
8. Stanford Five City Project: five cities, two treatment, three reference, $n=330,000$.	United States (California)	1980–1986	Farquhar (1978); Farquhar (in press)
9. Minnesota Heart Health Study: two towns, two cities, two suburbs, paired treatment and reference, $n=356,000$.	United States (Minnesota)	1982–1989	Blackburn (in press)
10. Pawtucket Heart Health Study: two cities, one treatment, one reference, $n=173,000$.	United States (Rhode Island and Massachusetts)	1982–1986	Carleton (in press)

Note. This list is necessarily incomplete and represents projects personally known to us of studies based on communities, including at least one reference area, and involving use of comprehensive public health education and community organization methods. In some instances, the final population sizes have not been determined.

programs were also based on a number of theoretical and research findings, alluded to above (see "Theoretical Basis for Community-Based Health Education"), on how change can be achieved in human behavior and the factors that influence the change process. The special role of these theoretical concepts within the context of the planning of the Stanford Three Community Study is described here.

One research finding that greatly influenced the project design was a formulation of Cartwright (1949). Analyzing household sample survey data on the purchasing of U.S. Savings Bonds, Cartwright found data suggesting that mass media alone were not effective in achieving sales, but that personal solicitation, within the context of the campaign, was. To account for this finding, he posited that in order to influence behavior, it was necessary to stimulate action or behavioral structures in addition to cognitive and motivational ones. Thus, from this perspective, it was seen that the educational success of the Stanford Three Community Study might be enhanced by the addition of an interpersonal element designed to stimulate specific behavior changes linked to cardiovascular health, through interpersonal influence and group processes. It was also decided to build action cues and skills training into the mass media.

Another of the primary theoretical orientations guiding the planning of the education was derived from Bandura's social learning theory (1969, 1977). In a more recent formulation, Bandura (1978) describes a model of reciprocal interaction. According to this conceptual approach, human behavior is regulated by immediate situational influences and by a person's performance skills and anticipations of the consequences for different courses of action, rather than by such global constructs as personality traits. Bandura views the interplay between environment and behavior as a process of reciprocal influence, in which the environment shapes the individual's behavior, but the person also shapes his or her environment. Thus, the person's relationship with his or her environment is an open system, always modifiable by providing the individual with appropriate self-management skills and the motivation to make use of them.

Social learning theory, particularly with the addition of cognitive training for self-control, offered a promising conceptual framework for stimulating community-wide behavior change. We realized, however, that the techniques employed in behavior change typically involved live face-to-face training, either one on one or, at most, in a small group. Although often effective, these training methods would be extremely costly when applied in a community-wide project attempting to reach the entire adult population. Such procedures are cost-effective only when the target population is limited to the 1–2% at "highest risk." Therefore, in the Three Community Study, we decided to rely upon a mass media program as the major educational mechanism for the majority of people, but to supplement it in one town by face-to-face, intensive instruction for a subset of those at higher risk. This latter education method was to be the "gold standard" against which a media-only method could be compared.

The face-to-face behavior modification protocols in the Three Community Study were directly based on social learning theory as explicated by Bandura. This theory was also applied to the media. Since it is evident that skills can be learned by modeling or the practice of observed behavior, it seemed clear that audiovisual portrayals (film and television) and, to a lesser extent, audio media alone (radio and recordings) or visual media alone (slides, pamphlets, billboards, posters, etc.), could constitute appropriate models. Another problem for media, of course, is whether or not the acquired skills will be practiced in the appropriate circumstances. Again, the appropriate cueing for acquired behavior can be learned via mass media. A family picnic scene on film can serve via imagery as a cue for utilizing the acquired knowledge of what kinds of foods to pack in the basket. Listening to a radio statement that gives warnings about how to respond to the advertising of unhealthy products helps remind those listening to such ads of the need to discount false claims. Self-management of behavior involves precisely such self-cueing in the appropriate situation at the appropriate time. If the problem of helping people to learn healthier habits is thought of as involving not only new knowledge and increased motivation, but also the acquisition, performance, and maintenance of such new behaviors in the appropriate settings, the media—if interventions are properly planned, produced, and exhibited—ought to have an excellent chance of being effective.

The vast literature in persuasion and attitude change also contributed to elements of the project's design (Katz, 1957; Katz & Lazarsfeld, 1955; McGuire, 1969). Much of the experimentation in this field has been concerned with temporary rather than with stable change. However, several examples of studies concerned with long-term change exist. Festinger (1954) postulated that pressures to conformity exist in groups and are brought to bear on the individual group member in such a way that he or she will tend to conform to the opinions and behavioral patterns of the other group members. Lumsdaine and Janis (1953), McGuire (1964), and Roberts and Maccoby (1973) formulated and tested some hypotheses on counterarguing and persuasion, aimed at discovering the bases for stable change.

The research design enabled us to compare two California towns (Gilroy and Watsonville) over a 3-year period of education, with one reference town (Tracy). All were independent communities rather than suburbs. They were matched as closely as possible with respect to such characteristics as socioeconomic status, minority–majority distribution, and population size. The total populations of the towns ranged from 13,000 to 15,000. Agriculture, agricultural marketing, and retail trade comprised the main economic base of all three towns. The two treatment communities were within one TV coverage area, but the reference community was well removed from its reach. A narrow range of low mountains separated the two treatment towns, thus diminishing interpersonal communication between them (Farquhar, 1978).

A complete description of the composition of the 12 study groups and response rates observed over the course of the 3 years can be found in Farquhar *et al.* (1977), Fortmann, Williams, Hulley, Haskell, and Farquhar (1981), Maccoby *et al.* (1977), Meyer *et al.* (1977), Meyer, Nash, McAlister, Maccoby, and Farquhar (1980), Stern, Farquhar, Maccoby, and Russell (1976), and Williams *et al.* (1981). An education program was developed for delivery through mass media and interpersonal communication. Gilroy received the mass-media-only treatment. In Watsonville, this campaign was supplemented by the program of intensive instruction. Based on a probability sample of residential addresses (Stern *et al.*, 1976), the study went through the following stages shown in Table 11.3: About 550 subjects per town, aged 35 to 59, were recruited into the study during the initial survey (S1, in the autumn of 1972). A mass media campaign in English and Spanish was begun directly after the baseline survey and continued through August 1973. The first year's campaign was followed by the second survey of the same sample (S2) in the autumn of 1973. This pattern repeated itself through 1974 and 1975. To observe the effects of the measurement process itself, a small independent subsample was interviewed at the time of the second survey in 1974. The Tracy sample was also interviewed at baseline and annually thereafter, but no education programs were introduced.

Individuals falling into the top quartile of risk, stratified by age decade, were defined as being at high risk. In Watsonville only, nine times in the first year two-thirds of these individuals were randomly selected and offered "intensive instruction" in group sessions or individual home counseling. Follow-ups took place in Years 2 and 3. Then the remaining one-third were treated exactly like the non-high-risk portion of the treatment samples (i.e., they received mass media treatment only). Spouses also participated if they wished, even though their risk status did not qualify them for inclusion. The high-risk counterparts in Gilroy and Tracy were identified and observed as subgroups over the course of the study; however, no further supplemental education was offered to those in Gilroy.

Educational Processes in the Three Community Study

Changes in overt human behavior are known to occur through the basic series of intermediary processes outlined earlier in this chapter in the sections on theory and methods; however, the way in which these processes occur may well vary with age, sex, socioeconomic status, current health beliefs, and previous education. These influences are complex; often they are contradictory or negative. The Three Community Study attempted to take into account the full range of potential influences operating at the individual

TABLE 11.3. Study Design and Time Line of the Stanford Three Community Study

	1972	1973	1974		1975
Watsonville (W)	Baseline survey (S1)	• Media campaign • Intensive instruction (II) (2/3 of high-risk participants)	Second survey (S2)	• Media campaign • Intensive instruction (II) Summer follow-up	Third survey (S3)	• Maintenance (low-level) media campaign	Fourth survey (S4)
Gilroy (G)	Baseline survey (S1)	• Media campaign	Second survey (S2)	• Media campaign	Third survey (S3)	• Maintenance (low-level) media campaign	Fourth survey (S4)
Tracy (T)	Baseline survey (S1)		Second survey (S2)		Third survey (S3)		Fourth survey (S4)

Note. From Farquhar, J. W. The community-based model of life-style intervention trials. *American Journal of Epidemiology, 1978, 108,* 103–111. Reprinted by permission.

level, the primary-group level, and the social or macroenvironmental level (DeFleur & Ball-Rokeach, 1974). To do so, considerable attention was paid to audience needs and perceptions, audience segmentation, pretesting, and other formative research methods, as described previously.

The Three Community Study's education program consisted of both a community-wide mass media program and a targeted face-to-face supplementary instruction program for the high-risk subset, as described earlier. The face-to-face instruction program was delivered to 107 subjects and their spouses over a 2½-month period. These individuals received group instruction in nine 90-minute evening sessions conducted by health counselors who had previously received 4 weeks of training in delivery of instruction, based on Bandura's social learning theory. Each client received a personalized approach to his or her particular risk factor levels. During the second and third years, a few letters, telephone calls, and meetings of the groups occurred as reinforcement (Meyer et al., 1980). The general education program employed a variety of media (e.g., TV spots, bus cards, etc.); messages were released to the target audience through the most generally available channels. A broad range of materials was produced—for example, some 50 TV spots, 3 hours of TV programming, over 100 radio spots, several hours of radio programming, weekly newspaper columns, newspaper advertisements and stories, billboards, printed material sent via direct mail to participants, calendars, and other assorted materials. The media programs began 2 months after the initial survey and continued for 9 months in 1973, stopped during the second survey, and then continued for 9 more months in 1974. A reduced educational program continued in 1975. Because the communities had sizable Spanish-speaking populations, specially tailored media materials were presented in Spanish. All broadcast time (TV and radio) was donated by the local stations as part of their public service requirements. The media programs were prepackaged, in that all of the communications were sent by Stanford directly to the distribution channels. The media programs in the two treatment communities differed only insofar as the local media gatekeepers varied their overall placement, publication, or broadcast of the materials made available to them.

The design precluded the use, in the media-only treatment, of any direct interpersonal or quasi-interpersonal communication with the target audience. Thus, many types of events often associated with such public education programs (appearances at public forums, speeches to community groups, participation in celebrations or health fairs, etc.) were not undertaken. The media program also avoided the use of communication opportunities that were idiosyncratic to one town (a popular radio talk show, a TV news feature interview) to keep the media output reaching each town as similar as was practically possible.

A central element of the media campaign was the use of formative evaluation in the design, production, and distribution of messages. The main prefield sources used in message planning were a pretest of the survey on a similar population in Modesto, California (Wood, Stern, Silvers, Reaven, & von der Groeben, 1972); the baseline survey in the target communities; the results of special audience testing; a series of interviews with scientific, professional, and political figures in the towns; marketing data on media usage patterns; results of talks with the owners and managers of local media channels; and, of course, consideration of the very practical limitations imposed by budget and available time. An important prefield study of the face-to-face health counseling methods was done on volunteers from a local industry (Meyer & Henderson, 1974). This study furnished the design and curriculum for the intensive instruction program of the first year's educational program in Watsonville.

Once the field education program was under way, it became necessary to supplement these preliminary data sources with a series of occasional, informal interviews and observations (dubbed "minisurveys" as compared to the annual "surveys"). These were designed to provide media planners with immediate feedback on public response to a particular media event or set of events, so that the ongoing production and distribution process could benefit from the information. For example, in March 1973, we conducted what was then termed an "informal survey" in Gilroy and Watsonville. We interviewed a total of about 80 adults in the two towns in their homes. The aim was to find out about their exposure to, awareness of, and information gained from the campaign to date. Our purpose was to get some indication of the penetration of the materials and, in an experimental sense, to find out whether or not a "treatment" was being applied from the individual subject's point of view. The data gathered led us to conclude that much of the education program had been perceived by the individuals, and that therefore we had passed a "threshold" level of awareness. Further, we believed that we were detecting indications of increased awareness and comprehension of the specific causes of heart disease.

The overall education program can be seen as an orchestration of discrete media events that occurred in many channels but that had common themes, styles, and content. Furthermore, a monitoring mechanism was occasionally activated to provide feedback on both the efficiency and reliability of the distribution system and the public response to current media events. In this way, flexible planning within practical limits was possible; it enabled us to refocus priorities, to reset directions, and in general to modulate the course of the program in directions likely to promote the overall behavioral and physiological endpoints.

Results of the Three Community Study

In general, we found that both the media-only town (Gilroy) and the town with media plus intensive instruction (Watsonville) showed general improvement, in contrast to the no-treatment community (Tracy). The results of the study, after 2 years of education, have been reported (Farquhar *et al.*, 1977).

Figure 11.3 depicts the overall result of education over time, using a multiple-logistic function of cardiovascular risk that incorporates age, sex, plasma cholesterol, systolic blood pressure, and relative weight. In the random samples of participants, there was a small increase in risk in the reference community (T), compared with significant and consistent reductions in risk in the treated cohorts. The lower portion of the figure contains data for high-risk participants; those who had a double treatment of face-to-face instructions plus mass media (W-I.I.) did significantly better than the two media-only cohorts did, largely due to differences in smoking cessation rates. Comparable reduction in risk factors were also observed within the Finnish North Karelia study (Puska *et al.*, 1981), through methods that included a lesser use of media and greater use of education through established health professionals.

Consistent with the Cartwright (1949) formulation, there was considerable success when the mass media programs of the Three Community Study were supplemented by intensive instruction (see Figures 11.1 and 11.3). However, it is also clear that the mass media efforts were quite successful even in the absence of supplemental personal instruction (see Figures 11.1, 11.2, and 11.3). It now seems evident that certain kinds of behavior associated risk reduction (e.g., nutritional behavior) can be learned through exposure to mass media (Farquhar *et al.*, 1977; Maccoby *et al.*, 1977), while others (e.g., cigarette smoking cessation) require a different constellation of media events that contains a considerable amount of skills training. However, we believe that if access to media can be secured, mass media can be designed to provide some of that training and to organize personal instruction systems to augment that mediated training.

Much of the success of the community education program can be attributed to the quality of the media campaign, to the synergistic interaction of multiple educational inputs, and to interpersonal communication stimulated by application of these inputs in a community setting. The media effect was seen in a sample that enjoyed yearly interviews and brief "medical" examinations. Some of the change was probably related to an interaction between media and this attention, although surveying alone had little impact in the control community of Tracy (Maccoby *et al.*, 1977).

In general, the changes in knowledge, behavior, and physiological endpoints observed in the first year of treatment were maintained and considerably improved in the second year of education. Some changes were further extended in the third year, despite a reduced educational program, and most changes were maintained during this year (Meyer *et al.*, 1980; Williams *et al.*, 1981).

The results of both the Stanford and the Finnish studies provide evidence that behavior change for risk reduction can be accomplished through sustained community-based education. However, we have only begun to define the optimal strategy for conducting that education. Intensive face-to-face in-

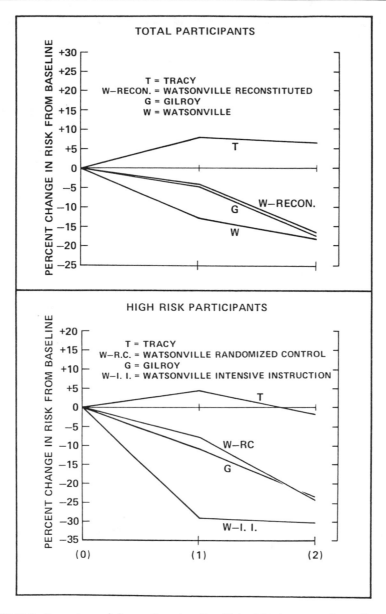

FIGURE 11.3. Percentage of change from baseline (0) in risk of coronary heart disease after 1 and 2 years of health education in various study groups from three communities. Watsonville (W) and Gilroy (G) received intervention, and Tracy (T) served as a control. (From Farquhar, J. W. The community-based model of intervention trials. *American Journal of Epidemiology*, 1978, *108*, 103–111. Reprinted by permission.)

struction and counseling seem important for changing such refractory behavior as cigarette smoking and for inducing rapid change in dietary behavior. Remaining to be learned is the use of these methods to correct obesity and reduce smoking, and how to employ them effectively with limited resources (i.e., by training volunteer instructors). (Although weight reduction did not take place in the two towns in which we intervened, mean weights did not increase, as they did in the reference town; see Williams *et al.*, 1981.) It is clear that the mass media (plus screening survey "attention") can increase knowledge and change dietary behavior. However, we believe that the power of the media can be enhanced if they are used to stimulate and coordinate programs of interpersonal instruction in existing community groups (such as the existing health care system or employee groups) and to deliver some forms of specialized training and counseling.

One of the problems in the use of mass media for helping people to achieve change, such as quitting smoking or reducing fat consumption, is that learning how to modify complex habitual behaviors can be quite difficult. Acquisition of such skills is enhanced when there is feedback on the results of practice. Ideally, there should be initial modeling and then guided practice that is tailored to the needs of individuals. Mass media may not readily provide all of this. They can, however, effectively provide the initial modeling (Lumsdaine, 1961) and encourage the development of community organization and support systems to deliver the necessary guided practice and reinforcement.

In the Three Community Study, a number of behavioral science principles were integrated into the development of the two educational strategies, and we believe that these principles can be applied with even more positive results to the formulation of the overall strategy for the cardiovascular disease prevention program in subsequent larger community projects.

A media-based program can be successful if it integrates the concepts of goals, social support, and social controls, and if it uses existing interpersonal networks as channels for the diffusion of health information. Such a strategy does not use mass communication exclusively, however central the media are to the plan. Although it is possible that in the future the entire effort might be accomplished via the media, the current prudent choice of the "best" strategy for optimum efficiency of community-based risk reduction is a plan that blends a minimal, focused amount of face-to-face instruction with an extensive media campaign strong enough to create the desired outcomes, in part, by itself.

THE STANFORD FIVE CITY PROJECT

The promising results of the Three Community Study prompted the creation of a larger-scale study designed to implement recently developed and more effective behavior change strategies in communities that are larger and more complex. This study, the Stanford Five City Project, was planned after the completion of the first study. It includes the successful elements of the previous study, while enlarging and improving the scope of the project. The chief differences from the Three Community Study are these:

- The new communities are much larger than the previous ones, and the project is designed to last for 9 years.
- The sample of community participants has been broadened to include all people from about age 12 to age 74.
- The larger size of the communities and the longer time span should make possible the detection of differences not only in the risk of heart disease and stroke, but also in cardiovascular morbidity and mortality.
- A major plan for youth education is included.
- Community education efforts are to be encouraged to continue indefinitely through the transfer of skills and knowledge to local groups.
- Finally, the most important element of the current project is its emphasis on generalizability and on the cost-effectiveness that generalizability requires.

A major goal of the Five City Project is to develop a model program that can be subsequently adopted by other communities. Because of this concern for generalizability, the design of the community education program consists of the creation of an organizational plan, the design and production of the mass media materials, the provision of catalytic organizational services, and the training of leaders within the communities who will in turn train others to provide direct services. Stanford has very few full-time coordinators in the communities; all community-level educational activities, such as face-to-face instruction and the facilitation of community action, will ultimately be conducted by existing local groups, although early programs of group instruction may be modeled by the Stanford staff.

Design

As its name suggests, the Five City Project is a quasi-experiment being conducted in five California communities of moderate size, varying in population from 44,000 to 130,000. In each of two of these, a similar educational program is being launched, and in the other three, only measurement is being done. The methods of data collection for evaluative purposes include population surveys as well as a surveillance system for morbidity and mortality. Morbidity and mortality surveillance is being conducted in all five communities, while surveys are being conducted in four, with one reference town being omitted.

Survey Design

The survey design consists of two main elements. In each of the four communities, a survey center has been established; each center is staffed by a nurse supervisor, an interviewer/abstractor, a laboratory technician, and a medical office assistant. Using letters and interpersonal communication strategies, they invite the age-eligible members of a random sample of households to visit the survey center for a comprehensive evaluation. In the initial year of the survey, roughly 600 people in each community visited the centers. This comprised the first independent sample of each community. After an average of 18 months, these same individuals were invited to return to the survey center for a follow-up evaluation. They will be restudied every 2 years and constitute the cohort sample. This cohort has been established in order to study the processes of change in cardiovascular risk and related behaviors over time in individuals. The plan calls for repeated, independent population samples to be drawn and surveyed every 2 years as well. These cross-sectional surveys will show the effects of the education program in the community at large, independent of previous survey experience. The overall study design can be found in Figure 11.4.

Contents of the Survey

The survey at baseline consisted of four main components: the core questionnaire, the formative questionnaire, physiological measures, and biochemical tests. The baseline survey required about 2 hours of participant time; subsequent surveys take 90 minutes.

The core questionnaire was designed to provide a baseline for use in subsequent measuring of the change process in cardiovascular risk, knowledge, attitudes, and behavior. It consisted of these components: demographic

FIGURE 11.4. Design and time sequence of Stanford's Five City Project.

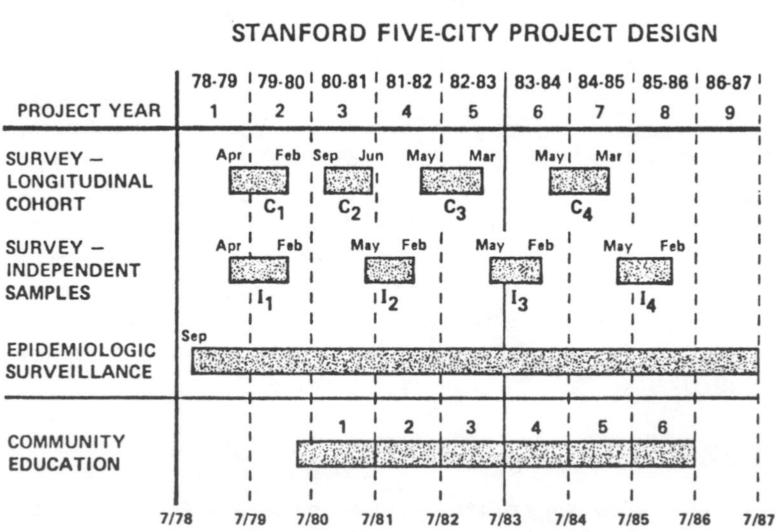

STANFORD FIVE-CITY PROJECT DESIGN

measures; attitude and opinion measures; health knowledge assessment; measures of stress behavior; measures of diet/nutrition and weight behavior; measures of smoking behavior; measures of physical activity; assessment of mass media use and interpersonal communication patterns; assessment of community organization memberships and involvement, and an interpersonal communication network analysis; and a medical history (including medication use and adherence to antihypertensive drug regimens). Finally, a 24-hour dietary recall was administered to a random 40% of the participants, while the others answered a formative evaluation questionnaire. This questionnaire is described in greater detail below.

Physiological measures included blood pressure readings (automated and auscultated), height and weight measurements, and a submaximal exercise test using a calibrated stationary bicycle. The biochemical tests were urinary sodium/potassium and creatinine, blood lipids and lipoproteins, carbon monoxide concentration in expired air, and plasma thiocyanate. The last two tests are indirect measures of smoking exposure.

The Educational Program

The overall goals of the Five City Project are to provide a 15–20% reduction in cardiovascular risk and eventual reductions in morbidity and mortality, due to the interactive nature of the risk factors. For the community as a whole, the goals include reduction of tobacco use by 9%, reduction of body weight by 2%, reduction of blood cholesterol by 4%, and reduction of blood pressure by 7%.

The educational program deals with various combinations of the standard heart disease and stroke risk factors, including nutrition, diet, and weight; stress; physical activity; high blood pressure; and smoking.

As mentioned earlier, the basic overriding concern with the educational program is generalizability and cost-effectiveness. Therefore, Stanford's role is limited to the design and production of the mass media component and contributions to the organization and promotion of community programs, including the training of community leaders. All labor-intensive educational activities are conducted by members of the communities themselves, although some lectures and seminars are using Stanford personnel as speakers or workshop leaders, especially in the initial stages of training.

Mechanisms for Education Delivery

The main mechanisms for education delivery include the mass media, health professionals, and community groups. In addition, a youth education component is designed to provide in-school education.

Many kinds of media are used in the educational program, including radio, TV, newspapers, direct mail, booklets, and posters. The educational program is presented in both English and Spanish, since there is a significant Spanish-speaking group in each city. As in the Three Community Study, the Spanish program is not merely a translation of the English materials. Rather, it is a special effort designed to reflect particular needs, attitudes, and behaviors related to heart disease and stroke in the Spanish-speaking population.

The health professionals component includes continuing education programs for health professionals at all levels; encouragement of health professionals to discuss heart disease prevention methods with their clients and patients; and the use of health system workplaces as distribution channels for our educational materials.

The Three Community Study demonstrated that health education via the mass media could be enhanced by more intensive educational experiences. The Five City Project therefore includes an important community organization component. The purposes of community organization are to obtain community acceptance and support, to enhance risk reduction through the provision of programs, to create changes in organizations that will establish permanent health promotion programs, and to provide policy information to health planners. Risk reduction programs vary in intensity from small-group formats to correspondence courses and are generally developed through collaboration between Stanford's Five City Project staff and local organizations. The most active local organizations to date are the community colleges and the local health departments.

Diversity and Timing of Components

Central to the Five City Project education program is the concern with providing individuals with multiple opportunities and broad encouragement for achieving health behavior change. The mass media serve to alert, motivate, and educate; community programs provide education and training. Individuals may choose from an array of programs for assistance with behavior change and are confronted with multiple reminders of the importance of change. This has been designed on the assumption that different people are likely to desire and use different alternatives at different times. The availability of one alternative supports and augments the others to produce a synergistic educational effect.

An educational program cannot present information on a wide variety of topics at the same time. Therefore, the campaign is designed to present information on several different risk factors in a particular order, designed to present general information first and then to move to more specific information. The order is determined to appeal to the widest variety of people initially and then to address specific needs such as weight loss or smoking cessation. Other important factors are the activities and agendas of community groups. The education program is made flexible enough to adapt to both planned activities of community groups (such as "High Blood Pressure Month" and health fairs) and events that occur with little planning (such as "fun runs" and hospital staff meetings). Finally, the seasons of the year and individual agendas for change play important roles in the scheduling and design of the education effort. For instance, it is very difficult to encourage people to begin running regularly during the rainy season, and it may be useless to do so if they first prefer to do brisk walking—as we have found to be the case in our formative research.

GENERALIZATIONS AND IMPLICATIONS FOR FUTURE COMMUNITY EDUCATION PROGRAMS

Given the assumption we have made in this chapter that community-oriented risk reduction programs have at minimum a moderately important role to play in prevention efforts and at maximum have great potential, it is important to close the chapter with some generalizations based on previous experience about the attributes of successful community programs. There are five main areas of community program planning that may provide useful guidance to future planners: problem analysis and strategy design, community organization, media selection, message design, and evaluation research.

Problem Analysis and Strategy Design

"Problem analysis" is a process of refining the overall goals of a project, based on a great deal of thinking and at least some minimal research. The goal of problem analysis is to create a set of objectives that are highly specific, measurable, and achievable. By "highly specific," it is meant that they must define the details of various desirable outcomes, such as changes in specific knowledge, specific attitudes, self-efficacy, behavioral intentions, information-seeking behavior, and stimulation of interpersonal communication.

It is critical in this stage to break the overall audience down into manageable segments. Different audience segments are likely to have different past experiences, attitudes, and other attributes. Any education group that believes it can be all things to all people is deceiving itself.

As described in a previous section, the phase of problem analysis must also include an analysis of the current status of various audience segments on a hierarchy of change (i.e., knowledge, skills, motivations, etc.). This will prevent wasted efforts designed to change people in a way they have already changed.

Problem analysis also allows us to look for noncommunication obstacles to change if we are going to reach our objectives. For example, we may find that healthy alternative foods (e.g., nonfat yogurt) are not available in these communities, in which case no amount of education is going to achieve behavior change. If we cannot solve this problem by encouraging grocers to select such products, then we might decide that the aim of our messages will be to encourage customers to ask their grocers for these foods. As this example shows, the use of problem analysis and strategy design can drastically alter the course of an educational program and improve its possibilities for success.

Community Organization

The principal perspective required for most prospective community researchers is a retreat from arrogance. No theory, method, media program, or curriculum is of any value if the local outlets do not want it. If the local health professionals are marching to the sound of a different drummer, or if an underfunded, demoralized, and overworked school system has no interest in a "splendid advanced model" of a school health curriculum, then nothing will happen to the education effort being proposed. Community organization, especially the recruiting process (development), must be elevated in importance within the minds of the researchers in order for them to avoid major mistakes. One cannot assume that the community will cooperate passively; a blending of agendas requires true cooperation, and, in turn, the scientists must develop their skills as community organizers in accordance with the principles previously discussed.

Media Selection and Use

Too often, education programs choose media outlets before the goals of the program are specifically defined, and before the necessary cooperative arrangements are made with local media sources. This mistake spawns a large number of superficial programs that cannot provide the kinds of information necessary for guiding specific behavior changes. It is important to match the goals of a component of an overall program with the medium to be used. For example, TV can be used to reach a large audience with a short, relatively low-content informational message, or to encourage people to write or call for more detailed information. Longer formats are necessary if TV is to teach substantial information or skills. It is also important to use different channels for multiple communications that reinforce one another and are coordinated by similar verbal and visual styles. Community organization efforts, such as the use of group settings, should be considered as a medium of communication and should be evaluated and planned along with the other media.

Finally, it is important that messages receive adequate exposure among the target audience. Therefore it is important to monitor the "reach" (number of people reached with at least one message), the "frequency" (number of times the average person is exposed to a message), and the "timing" (time of day the exposure occurs, which is really an element in the other two variables) of the messages. Public service campaigns, which include most community education programs, often do not have any choice in timing and repetition of their messages. However, monitoring the exposure variables and communication with the relevant media outlets can facilitate increased reach and frequency. This monitoring can help explain the success or failure of a campaign.

Message Design

"Message design" is the process of setting specific objectives for each message, generating alternative messages, pretesting the messages, and revising them so that they meet the original objectives. It applies equally to mass media messages as well as to interpersonal messages. These tests must be carried out at early stages of message development. This research need not be expensive or complex. Simply sitting down with a group of five or six individuals who are similar to those in the target population and discussing a potential poster or TV spot can provide a wealth of insights into the creation of more effective messages. Message variables, such as the source, the message itself, the channel, and the receiver, have been investigated (e.g., McGuire, 1969; Schramm, 1972; Zimbardo, Ebbesen, & Maslach, 1977) and should not be ignored by campaign planners. Once messages are generated, they should be subjected to as much pretesting and revision as is practically possible.

Evaluation

By "evaluation," we mean both formative and summative evaluation. Formative evaluation has been discussed earlier; "summative evaluation" is the measure of outcomes—the impact of the total program. We have described many of the evaluative procedures used in the Three Community Study, including both standard statistical methods (Farquhar et al., 1977; Maccoby et al., 1977; Meyer et al., 1980) and ancillary evaluation measures that strengthened the internal validity of the study (Farquhar, 1978; Williams et al., 1981). Most of these methods deal only with the first main question in evaluation: "Did the program work?" Clearly, a highly important question to the policy maker and a principal challenge to community research of a quasi-experimental nature is to increase the sensitivity and breadth of the evaluation instruments used in answering this question.

However, a second question—"Why did it work or fail?"—is also important and is often ignored in risk reduction evaluations. This kind of evaluation is often called "process evaluation." If process evaluation is ignored, the benefits from the program are lessened, since it loses its value as a model for the design of future efforts. Because of this possibility, it is essential to identify a number of steps in the process of change and to measure each of these steps. For example, while the ultimate outcome variable may be a change in the morbidity and mortality that is due to heart disease and stroke, it is also important to measure such stages as success in community organization, increases in knowledge, attitude change, skills learning, and performance and maintenance of these skills. One needs evaluation of the success of achieving stable and meaningful change in community practices and institutions as a measure of success in "leaving behind" a program that runs on its own steam. While one cannot guarantee a totally clear explanation of success or failure, there will be at least some important clues to provide guidance for the development of future efforts. The use of path analysis is one example of how causal links may be traced (Farquhar, 1978; Milburn, 1979). The potential of community-based risk reduction efforts can therefore be enhanced if advanced evaluation methods are used.

REFERENCES

Ajzen, I., & Fishbein, M. *Understanding attitudes and predicting social behavior.* Englewood Cliffs, N.J.: Prentice-Hall, 1980.

Bandura, A. *Principles of behavior modification.* New York: Holt, Rinehart & Winston, 1969.

Bandura, A. *Social learning theory.* Englewood Cliffs, N.J.: Prentice-Hall, 1977.

Bandura, A. The self system in reciprocal determinism. *The American Psychologist,* 1978, *33,* 344–358.

Blackburn, H. The Minnesota Heart Health Program: A research and demonstration project in cardiovascular disease prevention. In J. D. Matarazzo, N. E. Miller, A. J. Herd, & S. M. Weiss (Eds.), *Behavioral health: A handbook of health enhancement and disease prevention.* New York: Wiley, in press.

Campbell, D. T. Factors relevant to the validity of experiment in social settings. *Psychological Bulletin,* 1957, *54,* 297–312.

Campbell, D. T., & Stanley, J. C. *Experimental and quasi-experimental designs for research.* Chicago: Rand McNally, 1963.

Carleton, R. Lay volunteer delivery of community-based cardiovascular risk factor change program: The Pawtucket Experiment. In J. D. Matarazzo, N. E. Miller, A. J. Herd, & S. M. Weiss (Eds.), *Behavioral health: A handbook of health enhancement and disease prevention.* New York: Wiley, in press.

Cartwright, D. Some principles of mass persuasion. *Human Relations,* 1949, *2,* 253–267.

Cook, T. D., & Campbell, D. T. The design and conduct of quasi-experiments and true experiments in field settings. In M. D. Dunnette (Ed.), *Handbook of industrial and organizational psychology.* Chicago: Rand McNally, 1976.

Cook, T. D., & Campbell, D. T. *Quasi-experimentation: Design and analysis for field settings.* Chicago: Rand McNally, 1979.

DeFleur, M. L., & Ball-Rokeach, S. Mass communication and persuasion. In *Theories of mass communication* (3rd ed.). New York: David McKay, 1974.

Egger, G., Fitzgerald, W., Frape, G., Monaem, A., Rubinstein, P., Tyler, C., & McKay, B. Results of a large scale media antismoking campaign: North Coast "Quit For Life" Programme. *British Medical Journal*, 1983, *286*, 1125–1128.

Farquhar, J. W. The community-based model of life-style intervention trials. *American Journal of Epidemiology*, 1978, *108*, 103–111.

Farquhar, J. W. The Stanford Five City Project: An overview. In J. D. Matarazzo, N. E. Miller, A. J. Herd, & S. M. Weiss (Eds.), *Behavioral health: A handbook of health enhancement and disease prevention.* New York: Wiley, in press.

Farquhar, J. W., Maccoby, N., Wood, P. D., Alexander, J. K., Breitrose, H., Brown, B. W., Jr., Haskell, W. L., McAlister, A. L., Meyer, A. J., Nash, J. D., & Stern, M. P. Community education for cardiovascular health. *Lancet*, 1977, *i*, 1192–1195.

Festinger, L. Theory of social comparison processes. *Human Relations*, 1954, *7*, 117–140.

Flay, B. R., & Cook, T. D. The evaluation of media-based prevention campaigns. In R. Rice & W. Paisley (Eds.), *Public communication campaigns.* Beverly Hills, Calif.: Sage, 1981.

Fortmann, S. P., Williams, M. S., Hulley, S. B., Haskell, W. L., & Farquhar, J. W. Effect of health education on dietary behavior: The Stanford Three Community Study. *American Journal of Clinical Nutrition*, 1981, *34*, 2030–2038.

Frank, R. E., Massy, W. J., & Wind, Y. *Market segmentation.* Englewood Cliffs, N.J.: Prentice-Hall, 1972.

Glass, B. F., Willson, V. L., & Gottman, J. M. *Design and analysis of time-series experiments.* Boulder: Colorado Associated University Press, 1975.

Gutzwiller, F., Junod, B., & Schweizer, W. Prevention des maladies cardio-vasculaires. *Les Cahiers Médico-Sociaux*, 1979, *23*, 79–144.

Katz, E. The two-step flow of communication: An up-to-date report on an hypothesis. *Public Opinion Quarterly*, 1957, *21*, 61–78.

Katz, E., & Lazarsfeld, P. F. *Personal influence: The part played by people in the flow of mass communications.* Glencoe, Ill.: Free Press, 1955.

Kotler, P. Social marketing. In *Marketing for nonprofit organizations* (2nd ed.). Englewood Cliffs, N.J.: Prentice-Hall, 1982.

Kotler, P., & Zaltman, G., Social marketing: An approach to planned social change. *Journal of Marketing*, 1971, *35*, 3–12.

Lumsdaine, A. A. (Ed.). *Student response in programmed instruction.* (National Research Council Publication No. 943). Washington, D.C.: National Academy of Sciences, 1961.

Lumsdaine, A. A., & Janis, I. L. Resistance to counterpropaganda produced by one-sided and two-sided communication. *Public Opinion Quarterly*, 1953, *17*, 311–318.

Maccoby, N., Farquhar, J. W., Wood, P. D., & Alexander, J. K. Reducing the risk of cardiovascular disease: Effects of a community-based campaign on knowledge and behavior. *Journal of Community Health*, 1977, *3*, 100–114.

Maccoby, N., & Solomon, D. S. The Stanford community studies in heart disease prevention. In R. Rice & W. Paisley (Eds.), *Public communications campaigns.* Beverly Hills, Calif.: Sage, 1981.

McGuire, W. J. Inducing resistance to persuasion: Some contemporary approaches. In L. Berkowitz (Ed.), *Advances in experimental social psychology* (Vol. 1). New York: Academic Press, 1964.

McGuire, W. J. The nature of attitudes and attitude change. In G. Lindzey & E. Aronson (Eds.), *The handbook of social psychology.* Reading, Mass.: Addison-Wesley, 1969.

Meyer, A. J., & Henderson, J. B. Multiple risk factor reduction in the prevention of cardiovascular disease. *Preventive Medicine*, 1974, *3*, 225–236.

Meyer, A. J., Maccoby, N., & Farquhar, J. W. The role of opinion leadership and the diffusion of innovations in a cardiovascular health education campaign. In D. Nimmo (Ed.), *Communication yearbook I.* New Brunswick, N.J.: Transaction Books, 1977.

Meyer, A. J., Nash, J. D., McAlister, A. L., Maccoby, N., & Farquhar, J. W. Skills training in a cardiovascular health education campaign. *Journal of Consulting and Clinical Psychology*, 1980, *48*, 129–142.

Milburn, M. A. A longitudinal test of the selective exposure hypothesis. *Public Opinion Quarterly,* 1979, *43,* 507–517.

Nüssel, E. Personal communication, 1981.

Puska, P., Tuomilehto, J., Salonen, J., Nissinen, A., Virtamo, J., Björkqvist, S., Koskela, K., Neittaanmäki, L., Takalo, T., Kottke, T., Maki, J., Sipila, P., & Varvikko, P. The North Karelia Project: Evaluation of a comprehensive community programme for control of cardiovascular diseases in 1972–77 in North Karelia, Finland. *Public Health in Europe: WHO/EURO Monograph Series,* Copenhagen, 1981.

Puska, P., Virtamo, J., Tuomilehto, J., Mäki, M., & Neittaanmäki, L. Cardiovascular risk factor changes in three year follow-up of a cohort in connection with a community programme (the North Karelia Project). *Acta Medica Scandinavica,* 1978, *204,* 381–388.

Ray, M. L., Sawyer, A. G., Rothschild, M. L., Heeler, R. M., Strong, E. C., & Reed, J. B. Marketing communication and the hierarchy of effects. In P. Clarke (Ed.), *New models for mass communication research.* Beverly Hills, Calif.: Sage, 1973.

Roberts, D. F., & Maccoby, N. Information processing and persuasion: Counterarguing behavior. In P. Clarke (Ed.), *New models for mass communication research.* Beverly Hills, Calif.: Sage, 1973.

Rogers, E. M. *Diffusion of innovations* (3rd ed.). New York: Free Press, 1983.

Rogers, E. M., & Kincaid, D. L. *Communication networks: Toward a new paradigm for research.* New York: Free Press, 1981.

Rossouw, J. E., Jooste, P. L., Kotze, J. P., & Jordaan, P. C. J. The control of hypertension in two communities: An interim evaluation. *South African Medical Journal,* 1981, *60,* 208–212.

Schramm, W. (Ed.). *What the research says about quality in instructional television.* Honolulu: University Press of Hawaii, 1972.

Sherwin, R. Controlled trials of the diet–heart hypothesis: Some comments on the experimental unit. *American Journal of Epidemiology,* 1978, *108,* 92–99.

Spergel, I. A. *Community problem solving: The delinquency example.* Chicago: University of Chicago Press, 1969.

Stern, M. P., Farquhar, J. W., Maccoby, N., & Russell, S. H. Results of a two-year health education campaign on dietary behavior: The Stanford Three Community Study. *Circulation,* 1976, *54,* 826–833.

Stolley, P., & Stunkard, A. Personal communication, 1980.

Truett, J., Cornfield, J., & Kannel, W. Multivariate analysis of the risk of coronary heart disease in Framingham. *Journal of Chronic Disease,* 1967, *20,* 511–524.

Williams, P. T., Fortmann, S. P., Farquhar, J. W., Mellen, S., & Varady, A. A comparison of statistical methods for evaluating risk factor changes in community-based studies: An example from the Stanford Three Community Study. *Journal of Chronic Diseases,* 1981, *34,* 565–571.

Wood, P. D., Stern, M. P., Silvers, A., Reaven, G. M., & von der Groeben, J. Lipoprotein abnormalities in a free living population of the Central Valley, California. *Circulation,* 1972, *45,* 114–124.

World Health Organization Report. *Comprehensive cardiovascular community control programmes* (WHO meeting in Koli, Finland, August 1976) (ICP/CVD 018). Geneva: Author, 1977.

Zimbardo, P., Ebbesen, E., & Maslach, C. *Influencing attitudes and changing behavior.* Reading, Mass.: Addison-Wesley, 1977.

CHAPTER 12

The Behavioral Treatment of Somatic Disorders

W. Stewart Agras
Stanford University School of Medicine

INTRODUCTION

Defining the Goals of Intervention

As we turn to consider the treatment of somatic disorders by behavior change methods, the individual with disease becomes the focus of our attention. Both assessment and therapy are complicated, however, by the various ways in which behavior and disease may be related. First, behavior may result in disease. This may range from the behavior associated with accidents to the influence of cigarette smoking upon lung cancer or to the influence of a stressed life style—the Type A behavior—upon heart disease. In turn, many environmental factors influence both the predisposing behavior and the biological response. Therapy in such instances is aimed at changing the predisposing behavior in an attempt to prevent or minimize the disease process. Such approaches are less certain, when, as is often the case, the exact linkages between behavior and the disease process are not well understood; thus the exact target behaviors for intervention may not be clear (this area has been discussed in detail in Chapter 3, this volume).

A second pathway involves the influence of the disease process itself upon behavior. Examples include the effect of stigmatizing congenital deformities on childhood development; the sometimes debilitating effects of sick role behavior; and the behavioral responses to a catastrophic illness, such as cancer. Included in the last category may be affective responses, such as anxiety or depression; changes in cognition; and changes in behavior, such as interpersonal withdrawal. Therapy in such instances must form part of the overall medical approach to such conditions and may involve the patient, the family, and members of the treatment team. Closely related to such problems are cases in which the behavioral response is to medical treatment for a somatic disorder. Problems in this area include the effect of fear of medical procedures, faulty adherence to the prescribed regimen (see Chapter 10, this volume), and the variety of beneficial or harmful patient responses to attention by health care workers. Finally, therapy may be directed toward the symptomatic behavior itself, whether it is a motor behavior, such as tension headache, or an autonomic behavior, such as cardiac arrhythmia.

So far, this discussion implicitly assumes that a clear distinction can be made between behavior and somatic disease; however, this may not be the case either for the therapist or for the patient. Take, for example, the tension headache. Here we have somatic muscles that contract in response to particular life situations, often involving interpersonal stresses but sometimes involving concentrated effort. This represents a straightforward behavioral response to a life situation and can hardly be considered to be a disease, even though it may be regarded and treated as a medical disorder. Similar and perhaps even more striking problems arise in the case of pain. A person might very easily learn that complaining of pain can lead to beneficial consequences, such as avoiding situations that cause distress. Here we have a simple verbal behavior as an example of a deficient coping response, and not a disease. However, to the extent that disordered nerves or muscles are added to this situation, we move away from behavior toward disease. Yet in both cases a person may enter the medical system, receive a diagnosis, and be treated as though organic pathology exists.

This confusion between behavior and disease is at the root of many problems in medical care and contributes to some of the poor results obtained with such problems. Even the treatment—in many cases, medication to relieve pain—may complicate the outcome by, for example, reinforcing complaints of pain when medication taking becomes contingent upon such complaints, or by causing unwanted side effects or even addiction. Moreover, some of the environmental causes of the problem are likely to be ignored, and the sufferer will reach a new and less satisfactory adaptation to his or her life problem than if the problem had been treated directly as the behavior it is. In a surprisingly short time, such erstwhile patients become insulted if one suggests that a life problem may be causing what is now considered to be a symptom of a medical disorder. Only a palliative approach is then possible.

These reflections are nothing new, yet the medical profession has not been able to educate the public about such problems and has instead been relying on pain relievers and tranquilizers as the easiest solution, despite the costs and complications of such an approach. One aim of behavioral medicine must, then, be to educate the public about the role of behavior in the genesis of many common problems such as tension headache, and about more appropriate ways to manage such problems, using the best scientific information available.

Uncertainty concerning the etiology of many common conditions makes the choice of an intervention strategy difficult. For example, tension headache may be treated directly, using relaxation or electromyographic feedback—approaches that, as noted later in this chapter, have met with some success. Alternatively, the patient could be taught new skills for better management of the interpersonal situations that elicit the tension headache. Ultimately these different approaches can be compared experimentally, but in the meantime in this case, as in many others, there is little to guide us in choosing among different approaches. For although the development of the field of behavioral medicine has been predicated in part upon the steadily increasing body of information concerning human behavior change—information that has been developed from both basic and applied research conducted during the past 25 years—there is much left to learn.

Human Behavior Change

Theory of Behavior Change

The most comprehensive theoretical approach to the understanding of human behavior is social learning theory (Bandura, 1977). This system, which ties together findings from diverse areas of research, suggests that behavior is developed and maintained by three interacting regulatory influences: stimulus control, reinforcement, and cognitive mediation processes. The first two influences directly affect performance, while cognitive processes appear to modulate the effects of the other two influences. Thus, reinforcement (or reward) is not an automatic strengthener of behavior; rather, its effect is modulated by what is attended to and regarded as salient by the individual whose behavior is being rewarded. Behavior and environment are regarded as reciprocating influences. The environment, particularly the social environment, influences the behavior of an individual. But, just as surely, the behavior of an individual influences the social environment. This dynamic interplay undoubtedly accounts for some of the difficulties involved in predicting behavior, for one can never predict the exact state of a given individual's social environment at any one time.

Research guided by some of the theoretical notions subsumed by social learning theory has led to the identification of a number of procedures that influence behavior. These include the provision of information, therapeutic instructions, feedback as to progress, modeling, reminders, prompts, and cues, all of which precede a particular behavior. In addition, there are procedures that are applied following the appearance of behavior, such as extinction, reinforcement, and punishment. Apart from their use in mediated form, these procedures are embedded within a general therapeutic relationship, which embodies a number of unidentified influences often referred to as "nonspecific factors."

Determining the exact way in which these procedures should be combined for use in a particular situation forms one of the major goals for therapeutic research today. Moreover, by no means all of the active influences upon behavior have been elucidated, and new procedures are being and will continue to be discovered. One example of a relatively new procedure that appears to affect both physiology and behavior is relaxation training. The history of relaxation training is interesting: Closely related meditative techniques have been practiced for centuries, and Jacobson (1938, 1939) began some 40 years ago to study the physiology of relaxation systematically; yet it is only in the last few years that more sophisticated research approaches have begun to clarify the effects of this intriguing procedure. Moreover, as I point out later, little is known about which components of relaxation training are essential in obtaining its beneficial effects.

Behavior change procedures may be classified roughly into two types: those with well-specified procedures, and those with poorly specified procedures whose relationship to behavior change is not well understood. Verbal psychotherapy provides an example of the latter type, while a reinforcement procedure provides an example of the former. However, as noted earlier, reinforcement must be carried out in the context of a human relationship that contains many unspecified behavior change factors. The trend in both behavior change research and practice today is toward the specific and away from the poorly specified.

Phases of Behavior Change

The process of therapeutic behavior change can be divided into four phases: induction, acquisition of behavior, generalization of such behavior, and maintenance. In addition, adequate assessment procedures must be used before and during therapy to define the problem and to monitor the progress of treatment. "Induction" consists of explaining the rationale of therapy, collecting more detailed information concerning the problem behavior, clarifying therapeutic expectations, and detailing the therapeutic procedures to be used. Many studies in the field of verbal psychotherapy and behavior therapy have demonstrated the importance of this (usually too short) phase of therapy (Frank, 1961; Hoehn-Saric, Frank, Imber, Nash, Stone, & Battle, 1964). Removing therapeutic instructions often nullifies the effects of the other procedures used; thus this procedure appears to be a necessary but not a sufficient ingredient for behavior change (Leitenberg, Agras, Barlow, & Oliveau, 1969). Presumably the placebo effect, which is considered in some detail in a later section of this chapter, is engendered largely by this induction process.

The phase of "acquisition" is dominated by the use of the specific procedures outlined earlier to promote and reinforce behavior change. Here the focus is upon teaching the specific skills required by the patient to overcome the problem. Practice of the new skills, often in the form of carefully structured homework, is an essential element for success. Assessment of the problem behavior is nowhere more important than in this phase of therapy; the therapist needs assessment both to define the problem accurately and thus to take the correct therapeutic approach, and to monitor progress and if necessary to change the therapeutic program. Behavioral approaches to treatment are considered by some to be the more or less automatic applications of particular procedures to particular problems. While this may be the case in highly controlled research applications, in clinical practice an individualized approach must be taken to each patient. Thus the therapist must be well versed in the principles of behavior change, skilled in their application, and knowledgeable concerning the research findings.

The phases of "generalization" and "maintenance" of newly acquired behavior call for practice of the behavior under all the circumstances in which it is appropriate. Both generalization and maintenance of behavior require an environment that will reinforce the occurrence of the newly acquired behavior over both the short and the long term. This may call for intervention at various levels. For the individual, it may involve carefully inserting the behavior into the daily schedule, so that it is automatically performed. Self-reminders or automated prompts may also be useful. At the family level, the behavior must be acceptable, must fit into family life, and must be reinforced by family members. At the community level, mediated information and reminders concerning certain classes of health care behavior may help to maintain behaviors acquired in individual therapy. Much remains to be worked out in the areas of generalization and maintenance of behavior, which together form a challenging arena for both basic and applied research at the present time.

Behavioral Assessment

The measurement of the behavior change that results from a therapeutic intervention is important for both research and practice. The situation is, however, complicated in the field of behavioral medicine by the need to measure both physiological and behavioral outcomes in many of the clinical problems addressed. Thus, researchers and clinicians need to become familiar with the advantage and limitations of measures in two very different spheres. Moreover, care must be taken to draw the correct conclusions from each particular measure. For example, although blood pressure may be used as an index of medication taking in hypertensives, it actually reveals little about such behavior, since many variables affect blood pressure levels. On the other hand, the pill count is also an indirect measure of medication taking, with its own peculiarities and limitations.

Measurement in behavioral medicine takes place at many levels: physiological (e.g., blood pressure or heart rate); chemical (e.g., serum cholesterol or urinary catecholamines); behavioral (e.g., assertiveness); and cognitive (e.g., attributions). At each of these levels, there are different methods and frequencies of administration of measures that need to be considered. If one is interested in the chemistry of stress, one must choose between, for example, urinary and serum assays of catecholamines. Moreover, if a behavioral measure is also to be used, then it should follow the same time course as the biochemical measures if physiology and behavior are to be related.

Behavioral Measures

Turning to examine behavioral measurement in more detail, we find an array of measures in use. These vary from complex inventories to more narrowly targeted self-report or direct measures of behavior. While the issue has not been examined for the measures used in behavioral medicine, a recent review suggests that psychological inventories are poor indicators of outcome in the treatment of anxiety-based disorders, as compared with direct behavioral measures or specific self-reports of outcome (Agras & Jacob, 1981). In general, the more specific the measure, the better it is likely to be. Sometimes in the early development of a measure a more global approach is taken, while in subsequent versions better specification occurs. This will probably be the case in the measurement of the so-called Type A and Type B behavior patterns, the former of which appears to be a risk factor for coronary artery disease (Rosenman, Brand, Jenkins, Friedman, Straus, & Wurm, 1975). Classification of persons into one type or the other is achieved either through a standardized interview that is later rated or through a questionnaire method (Jenkins, Rosenman, & Friedman, 1967; Rosenman, Friedman, Straus, Wurm, Kositchek, Hahn, & Werthessen, 1964). While the two different methods of measurement show a modest association, it is not clear which aspects of the Type A behavior are associated with the increased risk of disease. For effective interventions, therefore, the Type A personality must be broken down into its component parts, and the risk associated with each aspect of the behavior pattern must be determined. One example of this involved a factor analysis of the Western Collaborative Group Study data set. This revealed the Type A behavior pattern to consist of five elements: competitive drive, past achievement, impatience, nonjob achievement, and speed (Mathews, Glass, Rosenman, & Bortner, 1977). Only competitive drive and impatience were found to be related to the later development of coronary heart disease.

Not only are the measures themselves important; the site of measurement is also significant. For the most part, problems occur in everyday life, far from the clinic. Yet the bulk of assessment procedures take place in the clinic or office setting. Of late, however, newer methods are being developed to assess both physiology and behavior in circumstances more reflective of everyday life. One of the simplest approaches is self-monitoring of behavior and, to a lesser extent, of such physiological indexes as blood pressure or weight. However, self-monitoring has some special disadvantages. The patient may not observe behavior accurately, may forget to record instances of behavior, or may lose the record. In addition, self-observation may prove to be reactive. Nonetheless, this is a useful and often revealing measure for use by the clinician who wishes to understand both the frequency of problem behavior and the relationship of such behavior to events in everyday life.

Direct observation of problem behavior can be most easily made within an inpatient unit or residential setting. Behavior can also be examined directly in a contrived setting designed to approximate some aspects of real life. Thus couples can enact conflictual communication, and both behavioral and physiological measures can be made. Or mental arithmetic or ice water can be used as stressors in a laboratory setting, and both behavior and physiology can again be observed.

As useful as such measures are, they can only palely reflect the occurrence of behavior in everyday life. The recent advent of microelectronics promises to make more accurate measurement possible. Thus, activity and many physiological indexes can now be measured around the clock or during the working day to provide a more realistic account of behavior. Portable pill containers can record the exit of pills, and can thus measure medication taking better. Posture can be measured during the day. Many of the problems encountered within behavioral medicine, forming as they do a blend of physiological and behavioral problems, may be uniquely measurable with these new electronic devices. We may be entering an era where round-the-clock measures of behavior and physiology will shed new light on old problems.

The direct measurement of the physiological and behavioral changes associated with a particular medical problem need to be supplemented by measurement of additional dimensions for a proper assessment of outcome. One of the more difficult aspects of a problem is to compute the benefits of a treatment in terms of economic changes. While the costs of treatment may be reasonably easy to measure, benefits such as lengthened life and changes in the quality of life are less easy to evaluate in terms of cost, although some advances have been made in this difficult area.

Interpreting the Significance of Research Findings

Given an accurate method of assessment, the importance of a particular outcome to treatment can be estimated in several ways. The most prevalent of these is to rely upon statistically significant differences, with significance usually set at the .05 level, between the mean outcome of two or more groups. Many problems are associated with this method, including the risk of a false negative result due to the use of too-small groups, or the risk of a finding that is statistically significant but clinically meaningless. An even more complicated problem is that such clinical insignificance may in itself be spurious. For example, insufficient treatment to produce clinically significant results might have been used. The fact that this risk is real is underlined by the results of a recent literature survey, which found that the median duration of therapy in controlled studies of behavioral procedures was only 6 weeks (Agras & Berkowitz, 1980). Such brevity is surely likely to be associated with weak effects. Besides the duration of therapy, the population selected for study may also affect outcome. For example, in the case of blood pressure, changes due to therapeutic interventions—whether placebo, antihypertensive medication, or relaxation therapy—are positively associated with the initial level of blood pressure (Jacob, Kraemer, & Agras, 1977). Yet many studies of relaxation therapy have been carried out with essentially normotensive individuals. The resulting small changes in blood pressure give a misleading view of both the statistical and the clinical effectiveness of relaxation therapy.

It is true that small changes in physiological indexes may be clinically significant under some circumstances. For example, small changes in blood pressure or weight across large populations can be associated with sizeable reductions in morbidity and mortality if the changes are maintained for many years. Thus, a clinically insignificant level of change becomes an important change from a public health perspective. Nonetheless, the problem of clinical significance is real. One partial solution to the problem is to preset levels of change that might be regarded as clinically significant, and to ascertain the percentages of participants who meet such criteria in both the experimental and the control groups after treatment. In setting such levels of significance, one might be guided by the research literature, or, in the absence of relevant information, by an experienced clinician. For example, in the case of blood pressure, whether to set a target level (e.g., below 90 mm Hg diastolic) or a change in level (e.g., $-10/-5$ mm Hg) as the criterion for clinical significance will depend partly upon individual predilection and partly upon the purpose of the study. However, the addition of an index of clinical significance might add a new dimension to the understanding of how effective a particular therapeutic strategy really is.

Assessment for the Clinician

So far, the discussion has been mainly concerned with assessment in the service of research. Much of what I have covered is not applicable to the clinic setting, due to the expense of using such measures, and thus the clinician is faced with using more traditional approaches to assessment, albeit in a new way. As noted earlier, behavior is controlled to a larger degree than was apparent in the past by external events largely located in the social environment. The task of the clinician, then, is to use the interview first to specify the problem behaviors in as objective and precise a way as possible, and then to investigate the relationship between such behaviors and current events. Once this has been accomplished, a self-monitoring program can be started to ascertain both the frequency and temporal distribution of the problem behaviors and their relationship to current events.

Goldiamond (1979) has very nicely distinguished between two modes of relating events and behavior. The first, which he calls a "topical" approach, relates antecedents and consequences to the occurrence of behavior. Therapy is directly aimed at the presenting behavior and consists of altering the environmental events that impinge directly upon the behavior. This may include alterations of reinforcement to reduce maladaptive behavior or to strengthen adaptive or competing behavior; alterations in antecedent conditions that lead to the problem behavior; the use of reminders and prompts to promote occurrence of adaptive behavior; or the use of such techniques as relaxation or desensitization to influence the target problem directly. The second or "systemic" approach is one in which the costs and benefits of both maladaptive behavior and its adaptive alternatives are elucidated. In this system, problem behavior is seen as the most rational alternative available to the client. As Goldiamond (1979) points out, one of the problems encountered by therapists attempting to alter such behavior is that there are considerable costs involved in instating new behavior, and that such costs may outweigh the immediate benefits. Thus no behavior change will occur. Among the examples cited by Goldiamond is the following case:

> . . . an interfaith marriage had forced the couple to move away from the wife's own neighborhood, destroying her entire social life in the process. Subsequently, the wife began recurrent vomiting (following bouts of excessive eating), which placed her at medical risk, and was the presenting problem. During treatment, the husband was directed to relieve his wife's confinement with her infant in a dismal flat in which the only sunlit room was the kitchen. The stage was thus set for her to get out and construct a new social life. Thereafter, the presenting symptoms faded away—without direct therapeutic attention to the vomiting or the eating. (1979, p. 391)

Once the initial behavior analysis has been completed and a plan of action has been worked out with the patient (and, if necessary, his or her relatives), then therapy can be started. Self-recording of the problem behavior and life events should continue, so that a determination can be made at any point whether to continue therapy, to end it, or to change to a new procedure. Thus the process of therapy becomes a continued process of problem analysis and solution, engaged in by both the client and the therapist.

Such a behavior analysis may be supplemented in some cases by direct observation of physiological indexes of problem behavior. These may include specific muscular disabilities or spasms; sexual responses to slides or descriptions of sexual activity; physiological responding to stress or particular ideation; and so on. Where they are possible, such objective measures can play an important part in helping both patients and therapists to assess outcome more precisely. One of the problems here is that few therapists can afford the array of equipment necessary to carry out such objective measures. One solution may be for therapists and clinics to specialize in certain problems, thus making particular assessment packages possible. Another solution may be for some clinics to specialize in assessment, thus providing any therapist with the option to purchase their services in particular cases. Whatever the outcome, it is necessary at this point to emphasize the need for continued development of clinical assessment procedures, which in turn can be expected to enhance the efficiency and outcome of therapy.

The Development of Clinical Interventions

One of the problems in developing new and effective clinical procedures is that the research enterprise is scattered across the country in academic "villages"; it takes a "cottage industry" approach, instead of an industrial development and marketing approach, which might be more appropriate (see Agras & Berkowitz, 1980, for a more detailed discussion of this issue). Moreover, academic researchers are rewarded for their published work and not for the power and efficiency of the treatment procedures that they develop. This system does not fit well with the progression of research necessary to produce and continually to refine new treatment procedures.

This progression is outlined in Figure 12.1. The first phase in a therapeutic advance is the development of a novel intervention procedure rooted in a theoretical base, basic laboratory studies, and uncontrolled tests in a series of patients. Here the prepared mind, often disregarding traditional thought and practice, sees the usefulness of basic research and is able to translate the findings of such research into a new therapeutic procedure (Comroe, 1978). The next phase of research involves a short-term randomized comparison with a no-treatment control. Here a successful demonstration of efficacy, replicated by other workers, sets the stage for a burst of research directed either at defining which components of therapy are functional or at testing the effect of additional theoretically derived procedures. As shown in Figure 12.1, the single-case and analogue-population experimental strategies are most useful at this stage. As the findings emerge, improvements in the efficacy of the original therapeutic procedure may be made, and the more effective therapy can then be tested in short-term comparative outcome studies.

Once the short-term effectiveness of a particular procedure has been established, new questions become pertinent, including the evaluation of gen-

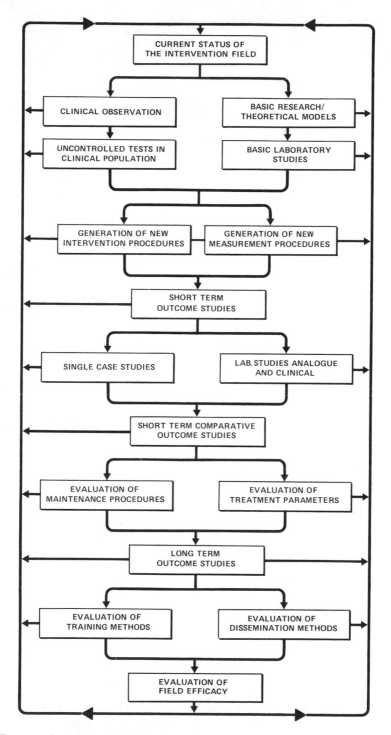

FIGURE 12.1. A flow chart illustrating the necessary progress of clinical research from a clinical or basic science observation to the full development of a treatment procedure.

eralization and maintenance procedures and the evaluation of such treatment parameters as applications in a group or individual format, or with therapists of different levels of training, or in the form of bibliotherapy. As answers to these questions are worked out, the therapeutic procedure, once more refined, is ready for long-term testing. By this time, the procedure may have become quite complex; perhaps it takes the form of a decision tree, in which a particular response to therapy calls for one procedure to be applied, while another response leads to the application of a different procedure. Such issues as the relative cost of different treatments or reductions in morbidity (and even in mortality if appropriate) may become salient at this phase of research. Such studies, since they may require large numbers of participants, may have to be carried out in several centers, denoting the phase of the multicenter clinical trial. To date, no behavioral medicine procedure has been the focus of such a trial; this suggests that the field has not yet advanced to the point of relative certainty concerning the long-term effectiveness of its therapeutic procedures.

Once long-term effectiveness has been established, investigation of the most effective methods of therapist training and ways to disseminate the results to the clinical community become important. Finally, a new question emerges, one that is rarely asked even in well-established fields such as medicine: namely, is the therapy effective in the hands of clinical practitioners? All research is somewhat artificial, and thus the results of a clinical trial may not be generalizable to clinical practice. To establish efficacy in clinical practice, studies of a carefully monitored series of cases treated in the field are needed, so that comparisons of efficacy between the clinic and clinical trials can be made.

In actual practice, the results of research at any one phase of development can close a particular feedback loop, as indicated in Figure 12.1, and can lead to a new direction in research. However, the problem most frequently encountered is that major gaps in research development exist, and thus both clinicians and researchers are less sure of the applicability of a given procedure than they might be. In the following pages, as the chapter moves to a consideration of some of the interventions currently in use in behavioral medicine, the reader should keep this model in mind, so that the actual progress in any one clinical problem or intervention method can be measured against the ideal.

BEHAVIORAL MEDICINE APPLICATIONS

While the field of behavioral medicine is relatively new, the interest in altering behavior or physiology to enhance medical treatment has a long history. Therapeutic applications include patient education, psychotherapy, and hypnosis, as well as the more recently developed behavioral procedures. In addition, the placebo, whether a pill or a procedure, has been found to have a wide range of effects. While it is not possible to provide a comprehensive review of this vast literature, selected controlled studies from each of these areas are presented to give the reader some sense of the usefulness of as wide a variety of procedures applied to as many problem areas as possible.

While therapeutic procedures may be given one or another label in a particular study, it should be remembered that it is what the therapist actually did, not the label used, that is important. The specification of the procedures used is one of the most neglected areas of clinical research. All too often it is unclear what the therapist actually did in a given study. If there is uncertainty about the procedures used, then replication of a particular study becomes difficult, and clinical application becomes impossible. Thus, while various studies are considered here under particular headings, such as ''Psychotherapy'' or ''The Placebo,'' the reader should be alert for the possibility that two procedures considered under different headings may in fact be very similar.

The Placebo

The simplest behavior change procedure in common use may well be the placebo, which has been defined as ''any effect attributable to a pill, potion, or procedure, but not to its pharmacodynamic or specific properties'' (S. Wolf, 1959). The apparent simplicity of the concept is deceptive, in that it refers to changes and events in many structures and processes (e.g., the musculoskeletal system, the cardiovascular system, the central and peripheral nervous systems) at physiological or chemical levels, at the levels of cognition and behavior, and/or at the level of environmental events.

From the viewpoint of psychological theory, the events involved in producing the placebo effect include environmental events (both past and present), therapist activities, and patient variables. Environmental events include such things as the place of therapy and the form of therapy (e.g., pill, injection, or psychological procedure). Moreover, the effects of the present forms of administration are influenced by the past experience of the patient with these events. Therapist activities include such variables as therapeutic instructions, the giving of a therapeutic rationale, persuasiveness, enthusiasm, and reinforcement. Finally, the patient's perception of these events and occurrences will affect expectancy, and, as noted above, such expectancy and other cognitive events are undoubtedly influenced by the past experience. This complex of procedures, both known and unknown, comprises a common basis for all therapies and contributes the nonspecific portion of the total therapeutic effect. The remainder of the effect is then attributable to the specific therapeutic procedures used. From a research viewpoint, placebo controls become extremely important. Thus the blinded, randomized placebo–active drug pharmacological study came into existence.

But in psychological research the situation is more complex than in pharmacological research. Thus a placebo therapy needs to be as credible as the experimental therapy and should be applied with equal enthusiasm by the researchers—a difficult ideal to attain. Lately, however, measures of the credibility of therapy have been devised. As becomes clear, however, very few of the controlled studies to be reviewed have used such control procedures or have assessed the credibility of the treatments used.

There is good evidence that placebo procedures affect a number of behaviors and physiological processes, including postoperative pain (Lasagna, Mosterla, Von Felsinger, & Beecher, 1954), cough (Gravenstein, Devloo, & Beecher, 1954), nausea (Beecher, 1959), and blood pressure (Jacob et al., 1977). In the case of blood pressure, for example, considerable lowering may result from the use of placebos of various kinds. Thus Goldring, Chasis, and Schreiner (1956) found that a supportive relationship with a nurse and irradiation with a machine containing a light bulb produced an impressive lowering of blood pressure. Others have used pills and injections to produce similar effects. Interestingly, as with medication, the extent of the placebo effect on blood pressure is directly related to initial blood pressure levels; thus most of the difference between studies is probably due to differences in mean initial blood pressure, rather than differences between procedures. Moreover, as with most therapies, the effect of the placebo upon blood pressure tends to diminish with time (Taylor, 1978). Whether this decline over time is due to poor adherence to placebo taking or to a deterioration of the placebo effect is not known. We may conclude, however, that the placebo is a therapeutic procedure of broad-gauge effects and a mysterious mechanism of action.

Some of this mystery has, however, been clarified in the case of pain. In a recent study of postoperative dental pain, patients given a morphine antagonist (naloxone) reported more pain than did those given a placebo. Moreover, for those who experienced pain relief with placebo, naloxone led to reports of greater pain when given as a second drug, while no such effect was found in nonresponders to placebo (Levine, Gordon, & Fields, 1978). This strongly suggests that the administration of a placebo to relieve pain releases endogenous substances, endorphins, which in turn reduce pain. This interaction between a psychological procedure and a chemical response is fascinating and may point the way toward understanding of other placebo effects.

While the rudiments of the placebo effect are well known, the use of the placebo for therapeutic goals is by no means adequate. A recent study demonstrated that physicians and nurses greatly underestimated the effectiveness of placebo administration on pain (Goodwin, Goodwin, & Vogel, 1979).

Moreover, the majority of both groups felt that if a patient showed pain reduction after administration of a placebo, then the pain must be due to psychological rather than physiological causes. As we have seen, this is not true. Placebos can relieve physiologically induced pain. Finally, placebos tended to be used for problem patients who were not responding well to pain relief medication. Again, this is a poor use of the placebo, which tends to work better in those individuals who obtain relief from drugs such as morphine. Such misunderstanding of, and misuse of, a potentially powerful therapeutic modality is unfortunate and requires correction.

Hypnosis

Although the therapeutic use of hypnosis was endorsed by the British Medical Association in 1955, by the American Medical Association in 1958, and by the American Psychological Association in 1960, clinicians still tend to regard its use with some suspicion. This may be due in part to the lack of well-controlled clinical studies of its effectiveness, although well-done studies with analogue populations, especially in the area of pain, abound. Adding to the uncertainty is the controversy as to whether the state of hypnosis represents a distinctive alteration of consciousness or is simply a behavioral response to a particular set of instructions (Barber, Spanos, & Chaves, 1974; Hilgard, 1968). As with other psychotherapeutic methods, many of the reported studies do not specify the procedures used in much detail. Thus hypnosis may be used to suggest physiological changes directly; to suggest alteration in the perception of a symptom (e.g., pain); or to enhance insight into the causes of a symptom. For the most part, studies in the area of behavioral medicine use the first two approaches. Although hypnosis has been applied to a wide array of disorders, including pain, skin diseases, asthma, and warts, the bulk of the studies are case reports, uncontrolled series of cases, or laboratory experiments with nonclinical populations. Few well-controlled clinical outcome studies exist, and the results of such studies are less encouraging than the often enthusiastic interpretations of uncontrolled studies (see, e.g., DePiano & Selzberg, 1979, and Weisenberg, 1978, for recent reviews pertinent to this topic).

In one exceptionally well-controlled study, patients with asthma were randomly assigned either to hypnosis or to a relaxation procedure (Research Committee of the British Tuberculosis Association, 1968). Patients were seen monthly and were encouraged to practice either self-hypnosis or relaxation exercises daily. Improvement was measured over the course of a year by means of reports of wheezing and the use of bronchodilators, as well as direct measures of pulmonary function. The proportion of patients with mild wheezing became larger in the hypnosis group than in the relaxation group at the third month of treatment and continued to diverge thereafter. Differences between the groups in the reported use of bronchodilators did not quite reach statistical significance by the end of the trial, although the trend was in favor of the hypnosis group. Measures of lung function showed even less difference between the groups. However, when the slopes of improvement were examined, only the hypnosis group showed a slope significantly greater than zero for the measurement of forced expiratory volume. Further, evidence for the effectiveness of hypnosis was suggested by the finding that patients of physicians who were experienced hypnotists fared better than did the patients of less experienced physicians. Since relaxation itself may produce slight benefits for the asthmatic, differences between the groups may have been minimized. Moreover, since both treatments can be considered as active, these results cannot be attributed to the placebo effect.

That the effects of hypnosis go beyond the placebo effect was shown even more convincingly in a laboratory study of pain (McGlashan, Evans, & Orne, 1969). A total of 24 volunteers, 12 of whom were highly susceptible to hypnosis and 12 who were virtually nonresponsive, took part in the experiment, which included three phases: a no-treatment baseline; hypnotically induced analgesia; and a placebo given with instructions that it would reduce pain. Both objective and subjective measures of ischemic muscle pain were used in each of these phases. Both groups of subjects showed a response to hypnosis and the placebo, although, as might be expected, the response to hypnosis was greater for the susceptible subjects. However, for the latter subjects, the pain relief induced by hypnosis was greater than that induced by the placebo on both subjective and objective measures. This was not true for the nonresponsive group.

These findings suggest that we need to conceptualize the differences between the placebo effect and other therapeutic procedures very carefully. Indeed, the term ''placebo'' may carry with it enough surplus meaning—in terms, for example, of the deception involved—to make it less than useful. Many of the procedures used in administering a placebo are of known effect—for example, therapeutic instructions, or the stimulus conditions associated with previous effective therapy (such as the therapist–patient role), or the sight and swallowing of a pill. Thus when we compare the effects of an active therapy (e.g., hypnosis) with a placebo, we are looking for those effects that go beyond both the known and the unknown ingredients of the placebo effect. To the extent that the procedures responsible for the extra benefit can be identified, then therapy can become less of an art and more of a technology. Clearly, more research is required to illuminate both the procedures and mechanisms associated with the placebo effect, which would then form the necessary minimum package for any therapeutic procedure. In these terms, we must still consider the effective ingredients embodied in the hypnotic procedure to be unclear and the mechanism of action to be uncertain, perhaps largely unknown.

Psychotherapy

Like hypnosis, psychotherapy in one form or another has been practiced for a very long time and in many different forms, from supportive therapy, educational therapy, and psychodynamic therapy to psychoanalytic therapy. These myriad approaches suggest that the procedural specification of psychotherapy might be poor, and this suspicion is shared even by sympathetic observers, such as Fisher and Greenberg (1977), who noted that "the field [of psychoanalysis] is filled with vagueness, appeals to authority rather than evidence, lack[s] specificity in definitions used, and [shows] unreliability in the application of techniques and dynamic conceptualization. . . . It is our conclusion after reading through the literature that a single unified approach to the treatment of patients that can be labeled 'psychoanalysis' does not exist" (p. 315). This, of course, makes evaluation of the efficacy of psychotherapy extremely difficult, since, even more than is the case with hypnosis, the procedures used in most psychotherapy studies are poorly described, and little work has been done to delineate which elements of therapy might be effective. The bulk of the work in the field is uncontrolled, and even those studies that use controls often contain major methodological flaws. Nonetheless, if we define the procedure fairly widely, some applications pertinent to behavioral medicine are apparent. These include the use of psychotherapy in reducing the overuse of medical services, in rehabilitation, in adjustment to medical or surgical procedures, and in classical psychosomatic conditions.

The findings that life events may be associated with illness of many kinds (Rahe, 1967) and that emotional problems can be associated with illness (see Rosen & Wiens, 1979, for a review of this area) suggest that psychotherapy might be effective in reducing the use of medical services. This notion has now been tested in several uncontrolled studies and one controlled study. In the controlled study, patients who were referred to a psychology clinic from a medical clinic, and who were not known patients of any mental health facility, were nonrandomly assigned to one of three groups: psychological evaluation and treatment; psychological evaluation only; and appointment not kept (Rosen & Wiens, 1979). In addition, a "control group" was randomly selected from the patients of the medical clinic who were not referred for psychological services. Of the group receiving assessment, 38% were found to have organic brain damage, while only 2% of the group receiving psychotherapy carried such a diagnosis.

Significant differences in subsequent medical utilization were found between the groups, with a marked reduction in outpatient visits, prescriptions, and diagnostic services for the group receiving psychological assessment and the group receiving assessment and treatment. However, for the group receiving psychotherapy, including psychotherapy visits in the calculation meant that this group received significantly more treatment than the other groups did. Moreover, an inspection of these data suggests that those patients who were not referred for psychological treatment (or who did not keep their appointment for a psychological referral) had a lower baseline use of medical services than did those who were referred and kept their appointments. Nonetheless, the group that simply received a psychological assessment did show an overall reduction in use of medical services, even including the assessment visit.

Although this study has been widely cited as evidence that psychotherapy reduces use of medical services, such a conclusion is not warranted. First, even when the findings are taken at face value, only the group receiving assessment showed an overall reduction in visits. The reason for this may simply have been clarification of the diagnosis in the high proportion of those with organic brain syndrome. Second, the nonrandom nature of allocation to groups appears to have led to the selection of groups with differing baseline use of medical facilities. Thus, comparisons between the groups are meaningless, since the obtained differences may have arisen by chance. This study, in fact, nicely illustrates the difficulties in evaluating psychotherapy research, particularly when the experimental design is seriously flawed.

In other studies usually considered to be within the realm of psychotherapeutic applications, there is some promise of potential usefulness.

Applications to Postoperative Pain

In an excellent study of patient preparation for surgery, Egbert, Battit, Welch, and Bartlett (1964) described the use of a preoperative visit in which explanation and coping strategies were used. The patients were told about the preparation for surgery, the length of the operation, the recovery room, and the probability that they could expect to suffer pain. They were also taught the use of a trapeze to minimize discomfort on movement, as well as the use of relaxation to ease the pain. As compared with a control group, those prepared in this manner received significantly less narcotic medication and were discharged from the hospital some 3 days earlier on the average. The critical procedural elements in this study are not known, although they presumably included information and instructions regarding coping. This study probably has less in common with the usual psychotherapy study and more in common with the older educative psychotherapies (Pratt, 1907) and the newer behaviorally oriented therapies—similarity that has been repeated in subsequent studies with a positive outcome.

Postcoronary Rehabilitation

A recent report suggests that brief group psychotherapy may be of benefit in the rehabilitation of those who have survived myocardial infarctions (Rahe, Ward, & Hayes, 1979). Forty-four postcoronary patients were randomly allocated to either a treatment or a no-treatment condition, and 15 others were added at a later time to the treatment group. Treatment consisted of six group sessions held at biweekly intervals, and was described as "education and discussion," with a focus on behaviors that might be deleterious, such as Type A characteristics, smoking, lack of exercise, and so on. At 6 months after treatment, the treatment group had been hospitalized less than the control group had been for coronary insufficiency, although this advantage was lost at subsequent follow-up. However, at a 3-year follow-up, there was a significant difference in favor of the treatment group in the number of coronary deaths and incidence of reinfarctions. No differences were found in weight loss, smoking, or cholesterol levels between the groups, although reports of some Type A behaviors (such as overwork and time urgency) showed an advantage for the treatment group. Moreover, this group also showed an earlier return to work.

These are encouraging findings, although some difficulties in interpreting the results should be noted. The exact procedures used in the group treatment were not well specified, nor is the mechanism by which the therapy achieved its results clear. It is also possible that extra attention was sufficient to produce the observed results. Nonetheless, replication and extension of these findings are clearly needed.

Peptic Ulcer

The next study to be considered illustrates one of the major flaws of the field of psychotherapy research—namely, that a sequentially developed body of studies does not exist. Isolated studies remain unreplicated and unextended; thus there is little growth in our understanding of these procedures. In 1936, Chappell, Stefano, Rogerson, and Pike conducted a rather well-designed study of the psychotherapeutic treatment of peptic ulcer. The study included 52 patients who had been hospitalized for nonsurgical treatment of peptic ulcer. Of this group, 32 patients were assigned to treatment and 20 to no treatment, although it was not clear whether the assignment was random. Nonetheless, the baseline characteristics of the subjects in each group were similar; some even favored the control group.

Therapy was extensive, in that the experimental group was "trained" 7 days a week for 6 weeks. Training consisted of teaching techniques to control worry (e.g., redirecting thoughts); of limiting discussion of sickness (apparently including advice to the patients' families); of controlling effort (e.g., by "babying themselves"); and of making self-suggestions concerning recovery. The physiological and emotional basis of peptic ulcer was also explained. At the end of therapy, 30 of the 32 treated subjects were essentially without symptoms, while only two of the controls were in comparable condition. Further follow-up showed reasonable maintenance of the results achieved by treatment.

While some problems exist with this study—for example, the results might be due to attention and other nonspecific procedures rather than to the specific procedures used, and it is not clear by what criteria recovery was judged, or who made those judgments—the results are extremely encouraging. Again, follow-up research, as indicated in Figure 12.1, is needed to elaborate upon these results.

Summary

Overall, then, we can conclude that some applications of psychotherapy in the area of behavioral medicine have been encouraging. However, there is no evidence that some procedures, such as the interpretation of psychodynamics, are effective; and although the procedures associated with therapeutic outcome in the studies reviewed are somewhat obscure, success seems to be associated with such factors as the provision of information, support, and fairly well-targeted cognitive or behavior change procedures. It is in this sense that the newer behaviorally oriented therapies are related to psychotherapy studies. For, as soon becomes clear, the effects of some specific procedures in some particular conditions have been elucidated. And although much remains mysterious, at least a beginning has been made in understanding the process of behavior change.

The next section considers the effects of a group of related procedures—meditation–relaxation techniques, which have roots in religious practice and show some similarity and relationship to such procedures as hypnosis. As with the placebo and perhaps hypnosis, we appear to be dealing with procedures that have fairly broad-gauge effects.

Relaxation Training Procedures

Relaxation training procedures include progressive muscular relaxation, metronome-conditioned relaxation, meditation, and autogenic training. The main components of each of these procedures seem to be (1) mental focusing by attending to body sensations, a particular image, or a particular thought; (2) muscular relaxation; and (3) a therapeutic set regarding the aim of the exercise. As can be seen, the procedures appear to have much in common with hypnosis, although direct suggestions to alter bodily sensations or functions are not usually made. The procedures have been applied to a variety of conditions, including essential hypertension and other cardiovascular risk factors, such as elevated serum cholesterol levels; headaches due to excessive muscular tension; insomnia; and asthma. An impressive research literature has begun over the past few years to delineate the clinical utility of these interesting procedures.

Essential Hypertension

The best-worked-out area of application of relaxation training procedures is to essential hypertension (see Agras, 1981, and Seer, 1979, for more extensive reviews). The early uncontrolled work that suggested potential usefulness (e.g., Datey, Deshmukh, Dalvi, & Vinekar, 1969; Jacobson, 1939) has now been extended by randomized controlled studies. The first of the latter was conducted by Patel and North (1975), who randomly allocated 35 patients to treatment and control conditions. Treatment consisted of relaxation training supplemented by feedback of either muscle tension or galvanic skin response, in two sessions a week for 6 weeks, and then biweekly treatment for a further 3 months. In the control condition participants were asked to rest on a couch—an exercise that would, they were told, lower their blood pressure. The end of treatment results showed reductions for those receiving relaxation treatment of 26.1/15 mm Hg and for the control group of 8.9/4.2 mm Hg; as is evident, there was a significant advantage for those treated. The control group was then treated and achieved similar lowering. A subsample of patients underwent stress testing; here relaxation-treated patients showed more rapid recovery from the stressors, as measured by changes in blood pressure, than the control group did. These are impressive findings for a group of hypertensives already receiving medical treatment. One possibility, however, is that the attention control condition aroused less expectancy of improvement than did the relaxation treatment. Did the patients really believe that rest would ameliorate their raised blood pressure?

This question was investigated by Taylor and his colleagues (Taylor, Farquhar, Nelson, & Agras, 1977) in a study of hypertensives who were not showing optimal response to medical treatment. In this study, participants were randomly allocated to three groups: continued medical treatment; medical treatment plus relaxation therapy; and medical treatment plus nondirective psychotherapy. No biofeedback was used. Patients' comments suggested a strong belief in the efficacy of psychotherapy; however, following treatment, only the relaxation-treated group showed significant lowering of blood pressure. This study was later replicated and extended, and the findings were similar (Brauer, Horlick, Nelson, Farquhar, & Agras, 1979). Relaxation therapy was more effective 6 months after treatment than the nonspecific therapy was. However, relaxation therapy taught by tape recordings and without a live therapist was no more effective than was the nonspecific therapy. As in the previous studies, blood pressure reductions over and above the changes induced by antihypertensive medication were of considerable magnitude, averaging 17.8/9.7 mm Hg. Thus we may conclude that relaxation therapy confers at least an immediate clinically significant benefit for essential hypertensives who are not well controlled with medication, and that these benefits are due to the specific procedure of relaxation, over and above the changes due to the placebo effect.

The next question to consider is whether the effects of relaxation therapy persist around the clock and generalize to situations other than that in which training occurred. Persistence of blood pressure lowering across the 24 hours has been demonstrated in one controlled study (Agras, Taylor, Kraemer, Allen, & Schneider, 1980). Five patients with essential hypertension who were not then taking medication were treated on a clinical research ward with intensive relaxation training (nine sessions in 3 days), preceded and followed by a no-treatment baseline. Blood pressure was frequently measured during the day and night, and for those patients who achieved a therapeutic effect from relaxation training, clear evidence of superior lowering of blood pressure on training days than on nontraining days was found. Interestingly, this difference was particularly clear at night when the patients were sleeping, and was of a clinically significant magnitude ($-12.5/-7.3$ mm Hg).

Generalization to the home environment has been examined in only one uncontrolled study (Blackwell, Bloomfield, & Gartside, 1976). Participants in that study measured their blood pressure at home, and small decreases in blood pressure were found both in the treatment and home settings; however, the absence of a control group limits the conclusions that one might draw from this study.

More convincing was a recent controlled study of blood pressure lowering throughout the working day (Southam, Agras, Taylor, & Kraemer, 1982). The participants in this study had been medically treated for essential hypertension for a mean of 5.6 years and had a diastolic blood pressure above 90 mm Hg on the last of three weekly screenings, indicating poor control. In all, 42 persons were randomly allocated to treatment or to repeated assessment with feedback of blood pressure. Posttreatment blood pressures were significantly lower for those receiving treatment, both in the clinic and in repeated blood pressure readings taken by means of a portable monitor during the working day.

Theories can be elaborated at several levels to explain the observed persistence of blood pressure lowering across place and time. For example, at the cognitive–behavioral levels, patients might reduce their activity, worry less, and handle interpersonal situations more effectively and with less emotional arousal. Behavior changes associated with relaxation therapy have not been directly investigated, and only in one study have self-reported changes in behavior been considered (Peters, Benson, & Parker, 1977). In that study, conducted with volunteers in an industrial setting, subjects treated with relaxation therapy showed greater improvement than did those in an untreated control group on self-reported symptoms; on reported performance, including feelings of general fatigue; on self-reports of number of illness days; and on an index of sociability. These findings indicate that more detailed information on the behavior changes accompanying relaxation training is urgently needed. Accompanying such changes may be mediating effects upon sympathetic adrenal activity or circulating cathecholamines (Davidson, Winchester, & Taylor, 1979; Henry & Stephens, 1977).

Finally, we need to examine the maintenance effects of relaxation therapy on blood pressure lowering over months and years. Of the eight controlled studies providing follow-up information, only one showed a return to baseline values at the 1-year follow-up (Surwit, Shapiro, & Good, 1978); moreover,

this study obtained extremely weak initial effects from the relaxation procedure. The remaining studies showed good maintenance from between 4
weeks and 1 year after treatment (Brauer *et al.*, 1979; Friedman & Taub, 1977;
Patel, 1975; Patel & Datey, 1977; Patel & North, 1975; Southam *et al.*, 1982;
Taylor *et al.*, 1977). These are encouraging findings, which, taken together
with the findings concerning immediate outcome and generalization, suggest that relaxation training is a useful adjunctive procedure in the treatment
of essential hypertension. More work investigating the mechanisms of action, generalization, and maintenance of the therapeutic effects is needed;
but, given the lack of complications associated with this treatment, we can
conclude that hypertensives who do not achieve adequate control of blood
pressure with pharmacological agents should be given a trial of relaxation
therapy.

Headache

The second area in which the use of relaxation training appears promising is
the treatment of headache, including tension headache, migraine, and mixed
tension—migraine cases. Since the initial uncontrolled demonstrations of the
potential effectiveness of both relaxation training and electromyographic
feedback in these conditions, the focus of research has been on the elucidation of the relative effectiveness of these two approaches to treatment. The
evidence from some 14 controlled studies now suggests that both treatments
are about equally effective and are superior to either pharmacological or psychological placebo conditions of various types.

In the case of tension headache, for example, Cox, Freundlich, and
Meyer (1975) found that electromyographic feedback from the frontalis muscle and relaxation training were equally effective, and that both were superior
to medication placebo immediately after treatment and at a 4-month follow-
up. These results were true for reduction in muscle tension, for reports of
headache frequency and intensity, and (at follow-up) for the reduction of
medication use. Other studies essentially confirm these findings; Beaky and
Haynes (1979) provide a detailed review of this area. Beaky and Haynes point
out that all the controlled studies to date treat the last element in the chain
that causes headache—namely, the tense muscle—rather than the first element in the chain—namely, the situation leading to muscular tension. It may
be that a treatment based upon an individualized behavior analysis and the
teaching of better interpersonal coping skills would be a preferable and more
successful strategy to use.

In the case of migraine headache, similar conclusions may be drawn.
Thus, in one recent controlled study (Blanchard, Theobald, Williamson, Silver, & Brown, 1978), patients with migraine headache were randomly assigned to either temperature feedback, relaxation training, or a waiting-list
control. The reported duration of headache activity was cut from 17.0 and

14.0 hours a week to 4.8 and 5.2 hours for the groups receiving thermal feedback and relaxation, respectively, while the control group showed no change. Again, these findings are consistent with other studies (see Adams, Feuerstein, & Fowler, 1980). However, it is well to bear in mind that in one study using electromyographic feedback, cases with mixed tension—migraine headaches did less well than those with straightforward tension headaches did (Philips, 1977). Moreover, even to a greater extent than in the case of tension headache, long-term follow-up of treated cases of migraine headache is conspicuously absent from the controlled research literature.

While we may conclude that a useful start has been made toward the development of a psychological treatment of the common problems of tension and migraine headaches, much remains to be done. The maintenance of treatment effects must be better established, and efforts should be made to identify effective treatment procedures for those who fail to do well in therapy. Would biofeedback procedures be useful for those who respond poorly to relaxation training, and vice versa? Since there appear to be no differences between biofeedback and relaxation treatment, then presumably the latter should be the procedure first used when a psychological treatment is chosen for either tension or migraine headache, since it is cheaper and more convenient to use. Other unresolved questions include the relative effectiveness of pharmacological treatment and relaxation (or biofeedback) training, and the effectiveness of combinations of pharmacological and behavioral treatment.

Insomnia

While the number of controlled studies of the use of relaxation procedures in the treatment of sleep-onset insomnia is smaller than in the case of either essential hypertension or headache, enough has been done to suggest that relaxation therapy is a useful treatment procedure in this condition.

As in the case of essential hypertension, idiopathic insomnia represents the set of cases left over when the known causes of insomnia have been excluded. Such causes include sleep disorders secondary to psychological disturbances, circadian rhythm shifts, sleep apnea, and postural myoclonus. A number of hypotheses have been put forward to explain idiopathic insomnia, prominent among which are anxiety and worry; however, evidence for these hypotheses is presently scanty. A further complication is that some half of those persons complaining of sleep disturbances fail to show any electroencephalographic evidence of a sleep deficit (Dement, 1972), and in such cases the term ''pseudoinsomniac'' appears appropriate, although it should be borne in mind that a subtle difference in sleep quality not identifiable by present physiological methods could account for such a condition. Thus the syndrome of idiopathic insomnia is identified by complaints of difficulty in falling asleep and restless sleep, together with findings from polysomnography that are confirmatory of these complaints.

The recent interest in psychological approaches to the treatment of insomnia was sparked in part by the finding that while pharmacological treatment may produce short-term benefits, long-term drug use may compound and worsen the problem; in addition, some of the agents used have addictive potential. One of the best-controlled studies of the use of relaxation training with insomniacs was recently reported by Borkovec, Grayson, O'Brien, and Weerts (1979). In this study pseudoinsomnia was separated from idiopathic insomnia, and both sets of patients were given either relaxation training, attention focusing, or no treatment. Only the idiopathic insomniacs treated with muscular relaxation showed more improvement on both self-reported and electroencephalographic measures of sleep latency than the idiopathic no-treatment group did. Follow-up 12 months after treatment showed that the gains were maintained, although only self-reported measures were used at that time. Thus we can conclude that muscular relaxation training (conducted by tape recording) was responsible for the observed effect, which on the average was a 50–60% reduction in sleep latency. While such an effect is not as large as one might wish, it appears to be of clinical significance.

These findings essentially replicate earlier work (Borkovec & Weerts, 1976; Freedman & Papsdorf, 1976), although these studies did not distinguish between subtypes of insomnia. Clearly the next steps are to achieve a better understanding of the mechanisms by which relaxation achieves its effects in insomnia, and to strengthen the effects of relaxation therapy.

Raynaud Disease

Raynaud disease, a disorder of the vascular system, is characterized by episodic pallor and cyanosis (usually of the fingers, but more rarely affecting the toes). These attacks, which are usually associated with throbbing, aching, and pain, are precipitated by vascular spasm, which in turn seems to be triggered by cold or by emotional upsets. While the first attempts to treat this disorder involved feedback of blood volume flow or skin temperature, a recent study found that relaxation training—in this case, using an autogenic format—was equally effective (Surwit, Pilon, & Fenton, 1978). In this study, 30 patients with Raynaud disease were allocated at random either to autogenic training or to a combination of autogenic training and skin temperature feedback. In addition, half of each group received training in the laboratory, while the other half received training and home practice. Both groups were asked to practice hand warming briefly up to 30 times each day without the assistance of temperature feedback or taped relaxation instructions.

No differences in outcome, either between the two types of treatment or between laboratory and home training, were found. However, both groups showed higher digital temperature in a posttreatment stress test than in a pretreatment test, and both the frequency and the intensity of attacks were reduced. Since half the subjects had treatment delayed by 1 month and were given stress tests before and after the waiting period, a no-treatment control condition was present for the first subjects treated. Treated subjects showed marked superiority in their ability to maintain higher skin temperature in response to the stress test than did subjects in the control group. Thus these findings are attributable to the treatment procedures used, although whether a simpler placebo treatment might have produced similar improvement is not known.

One of the problems in the assessment of the treatment of Raynaud disease is the strong association between seasons and the intensity and frequency of symptoms. Thus, follow-up over 1 or more years is important. In this instance, Surwit and colleagues have provided us with data after a 1-year follow-up (Keefe, Surwit, & Pilon, 1979). Of the original 30 patients, 19 participated in the follow-up study. Interestingly, 86% of those trained in the laboratory took part in the follow-up, while less than half of those trained at home, who therefore received less therapist contact, participated. These findings are reminiscent of those of Brauer et al. (1979), in which essential hypertensives who received relaxation training mainly at home via tapes showed markedly less lowering of blood pressure at a 6-month follow-up than did a group treated by a therapist. Keefe et al. (1979) report two interesting findings. First, participants continued to report reduction in the frequency and intensity of attacks. However, in response to a laboratory stress test, subjects were found to respond as they had before treatment, being unable to maintain the higher finger temperatures in the presence of cold. The reasons for this discrepancy between measures are unclear, and the interpretation of these follow-up data must be regarded as uncertain. Nonetheless, one thing is clear: More effective methods of motivating patients to continue to practice and to enhance maintenance of the physiological effects of training are needed.

In another study from the same group of investigators, three treatments for Raynaud disease were compared: autogenic training, relaxation training, and a combination of autogenic training and skin temperature feedback (Keefe, Surwit, & Pilon, 1980). Patients in all three groups showed improvements that were similar in degree to those obtained in the previous study; however, no differences were found in the efficacy of the three treatments. Unfortunately, the patients treated with the combination of autogenic training and biofeedback may have been less severely affected than those in the other two groups may have been, and a floor effect may have prevented the full effect of the combined treatment from being apparent.

Asthma

As noted earlier, hypnosis has been shown to be superior to relaxation training in the treatment of adult asthmatics. While the research concerning the application of relaxation training to asthma is not directly comparable to the hypnosis work, since the majority of the asthma studies have been done with children, the results are quite compatible with the findings in adults. For the most part, children suffering from asthma improve very little with relaxation training. At the most, statistical significance without clinical effect is achieved (see, e.g., Alexander, Cropp, & Chai, 1979; Erskine-Millis & Schonell, 1981). These results are disappointing, but not entirely out of line with what we know about asthma. Adrenergic agents produce major symptomatic relief in asthmatics that is associated with bronchodilation; yet relaxation therapy presumably blocks or reduces sympathetic nervous system arousal—an effect directly opposite to that of the drugs commonly employed in treatment. Thus, we may conclude that while relaxation therapy may counteract the fear responses shown by asthmatics toward their attacks, no other clinically useful benefits are obtained.

Overview

With relaxation therapy, we have come to the first treatment procedure that is well specified and that has been relatively well researched. As this section indicates, relaxation therapy is a useful adjunct to the pharmacological management of hypertension, useful in the treatment of tension and migraine headaches, and useful in treating insomnia; however, it is not useful in the treatment of asthma. The mechanism of effect may be different in each of the three disorders: sympathetic blockade in hypertension; direct muscle tension reduction in headache; and lowering of central nervous system arousal in insomnia. However, the mechanisms underlying the effectiveness of relaxation therapy are not well understood, and some common pathway may be responsible for the effects across these three rather different conditions.

Other conditions in which relaxation training may be helpful include paroxysmal ventricular tachycardia, irritable bowel syndrome, nausea, and pain tolerance. But as yet there are too few well-controlled studies in these areas to reach firm conclusions.

Up to this point, this discussion has been confined to the effects of procedures that have been developed empirically, rather than having been derived from a theoretical perspective, which in turn is based upon a body of basic knowledge. In the following sections, I discuss the applications of more specific procedures based largely upon social learning theory, as detailed earlier in this chapter (see pp. 481–484)—procedures that include modeling, stimulus control, fading, reinforcement and punishment, systematic desensitization, and various combinations of these therapeutic elements. However, the distinction between the older and newer procedures is becoming somewhat blurred, for two reasons. First, the effectiveness of the less well-defined therapeutic procedures can be understood in part, if not in whole, from a social learning perspective. Second, even the well-specified procedures are embedded in a matrix of less well-specified therapeutic procedures. Here again, however, the research methods and perspective of social learning theory will probably allow us to dissect the unspecified into at least some of its component parts, slowly turning therapy from a clinical art into an applied science. With this in mind, we may now consider the first discrete therapeutic approach—modeling—and some of its applications.

Modeling

Modeling has been most used in behavioral medicine in the reduction of children's fears of impending surgery, extending the work of Bandura (1969), who demonstrated that observing a model interact fearlessly with an animal reduced the observers' fear and avoidance of that animal. One of the advantages of modeling is that it can be accomplished by means of film, videotape, or other media, which are most cost-effective therapeutic modalities (see also "Bibliotherapy," p. 521). Thus, for children awaiting surgery, a film portraying a child entering a hospital, being prepared for surgery, receiving anesthesia, and recovering can be shown. In this way, information concerning a new situation can be presented. Fear arousal can be diminished through symbolic exposure to the fear-evoking situation, and coping skills can be acquired through observation.

In a well-controlled study of the effectiveness of such a procedure, children about to be scheduled for such operations as tonsillectomies or herniorrhaphies were allocated at random either to a group viewing a film showing a child coping with hospitalization or to a group viewing a control film unrelated to the hospital experience (Melamed & Siegel, 1975). Both groups received the usual rather careful explanation and demonstration of many of the hospital procedures by the medical and nursing staff. Immediately after viewing the film, the experimental group showed more physiological arousal (as measured by the palmar sweat index) than the control group did. This was presumably due to the viewing of fear-arousing events by the experimental group. However, both on the evening before surgery and 3 to 4 weeks after surgery, both subjective and physiological indexes of fear were markedly less in the experimental than in the control group. Perhaps even more significant from a clinical viewpoint, fewer experimental subjects received pain medication following surgery, fewer were nauseated or vomited, and more ate solid food earlier. These findings are reminiscent of those of Egbert *et al.* (1964), described earlier (see p. 496). However, they suggest that, at least for children, observation of successful coping adds to the provision of information concerning impending surgery and hospitalization. These results have been replicated and extended (Melamed, Meyer, Gee, & Soule, 1976), indicating a most useful preventive approach to a common and troublesome aspect of pediatric surgery.

Fading

Just as modeling provides information and the opportunity for observational learning prior to engaging in a behavior, so "fading" refers to the slow and systematic alteration of an aspect of the stimulus conditions (cues or signals) governing a particular behavior, in order to enhance performance. This procedure was used by one group of workers to enhance visual acuity in short-sighted subjects (Epstein, Collins, Hanney, & Looney, 1978). The basic procedure was to increase the difficulty of a particular discrimination slightly, following successful identification of a letter. Most of the subjects trained in this way showed greater improvement than did those in an untreated control group. In a second experiment, a multiple-baseline design was used, which demonstrated steady acquisition of improved recognition of letters over successive trials, thus providing further evidence of the effects of training. In addition, a follow-up 2 weeks after treatment showed persistence of improved discrimination. While this experiment provides a nice example of the use of stimulus fading in an area of behavioral medicine, the clinical usefulness of the procedure is questionable. However, given the possibility of regular home practice of this relatively simple procedure, it may be that this experiment points the way toward an adjunctive treatment of myopia, perhaps leading to lessened reliance on corrective lenses.

The second study (Foxx & Brown, 1979) assumed that nicotine levels are one aspect of the stimulus conditions controlling cigarette smoking. Fading in this case consisted of introducing cigarettes containing progressively less nicotine. Subjects smoked their regular brands of cigarettes in the first week of the experiment; a brand containing 30% less nicotine in the second week; a brand with 60% less in the third week; and a brand with 90% less in the fourth week, at which point the subjects were to quit smoking. Subjects were randomly allocated to one of four groups: the fading procedure with and without self-monitoring; self-monitoring alone; and a modified American Cancer Society Stop Smoking Program. The combination of fading and self-monitoring was the most effective condition, with self-reported abstinence rates of 40% at an 18-month posttreatment follow-up, as compared with 10% for the other three groups. The effect of self-monitoring alone is about what might be expected, but the interaction between fading and self-monitoring was unexpected and not immediately explicable.

These examples suggest that changing stimulus conditions by means of fading may have useful applications in a number of specific circumstances in behavioral medicine. Stimulus conditions can, of course, be altered more abruptly; this is usually the case in the treatment of overweight, when clients are advised to put food out of sight, to buy less food, and to eat only in a single place at a distinctively laid table.

Informational Feedback

Informational feedback, which provides an individual with knowledge concerning his or her progress in an endeavor, has for many years been considered an important variable in such areas as training in motor skills (Wolfle, 1951) and programmed instruction (Pressey, 1950). More recently, the contribution of informational feedback to such therapeutic contexts as the treatment of phobia has been elucidated (Leitenberg, Agras, Thompson, & Wright, 1968), while in a behavioral medicine context, the provision of information concerning food intake and weight has been shown to be an important variable in the treatment of anorexia nervosa (see p. 516). The most frequent use of feedback in behavioral medicine has, however, been in the amplification and display of responses in the procedure known as biofeedback.

Biofeedback is aimed at promoting voluntary control of physiological processes that are not normally under self-control, such as aspects of cardiovascular physiology or even somatic muscle contractions. The procedure consists of monitoring a particular physiological function and then amplifying and displaying the responses in a convenient and understandable mode to an individual who is motivated to change the particular behavior. The relative simplicity of the procedure, the availability of good equipment, and the ease of its acceptance in a technologically oriented society has led to widespread use of this procedure before a satisfactory body of evaluative research has been developed.

As we have already seen, biofeedback has been used more or less successfully in several conditions where a simpler procedure, such as relaxation training, is at least equally effective. These conditions include essential hypertension, tension and migraine headache, asthma, and Raynaud disease. As Silver and Blanchard (1978) point out, biofeedback and relaxation training may produce the same state of lowered physiological arousal by inducing relaxation (see also Qualls & Sheehan, 1981). Since these areas have already been covered in some detail, they are not considered further in this section. For the most part, such conditions should be treated with the simpler procedure, relaxation training; however, it should be noted that biofeedback may be helpful for those who do not respond to relaxation training, although this possible use has not yet been investigated. The remaining applications of biofeedback are directed toward voluntary or involuntary musculature, such as the heart or skeletal muscles. It is in these applications that biofeedback may become extremely important (see Ray, Raczynksi, Rogers, & Kimball, 1979, for a detailed review of this area).

Cardiac Arrhythmias

The most frequently investigated arrhythmia has been the premature ventricular contraction (PVC), an arrhythmia that appears to be associated with sudden death. By teaching patients control of heart rate, so that voluntary slowing was possible, Engel and his associates found that some patients could decrease the frequency of PVCs (Engel & Bleecker, 1974; Weiss & Engel, 1971). Control of heart rate was demonstrated in nine patients, using a single-case experimental design, in which instructions to slow heart rate were alternated with instructions to speed up heart rate while providing feedback. Two-thirds of this group of patients showed a reduction in the frequency of PVCs during the laboratory sessions, and the majority of this group also showed some reductions outside the laboratory—reductions that persisted during follow-up periods ranging from 3 to 20 months. Thus this procedure may have clinical application in patients whose cardiac arrhythmias are not well controlled by pharmacological means.

Muscular Rehabilitation

The prime use of biofeedback may well be in the rehabilitation of muscles that have been damaged or disabled as a result of direct injury, of central nervous system damage (e.g., stroke or head injury), or of peripheral nerve damage. Biofeedback can be used to increase the strength of particular muscles or muscle groups or to decrease spasm in an affected muscle.

The earliest controlled study in this area was designed to examine the added effect of biofeedback to physical therapy in 20 adult hemiparetic patients with foot drop (Basmajian, Kukulka, Narayan, & Takebe, 1975). These patients were randomly allocated either to physical therapy training or to such training plus biofeedback. In both cases, therapy was aimed at relieving foot drop and continued for a 5-week period. Following completion of therapy, the group receiving biofeedback training showed a greater range of motion in the affected foot and greater strength in the treated muscles—about double that of the control group in both instances. However, two points obscure the meaning of this study. First, no statistical analysis of the difference between the groups is presented; thus, it is possible that the difference occurred by chance. Indeed, in a study comparing two active treatments, sample sizes of 10 subjects in each group are unlikely to be large enough to allow differences to be detected. Second, more of the patients receiving the combined treatment had had recent strokes, and therefore may have had a better therapeutic outlook than those receiving therapy alone.

A second controlled study with similar patients (Mroczek, Halpern, & McHugh, 1978) showed a similarly uncertain outcome. In this study with nine patients, a cross-over design was used, with two treatments: electromyographic feedback of the affected muscles, or physical therapy. Statistical analysis revealed no differences between the two types of treatment on any measure, although both treatments, separately or combined, showed improvement over baseline measures. However, very little therapist contact was given to the biofeedback group in this study. Patients receiving this treatment were left by themselves with instructions to contract and relax the affected muscles, using feedback to help. Thus we may conclude that the biofeedback treatment was likely to be less costly of therapist time than physical therapy was.

Finally, the efficacy of biofeedback in the treatment of myofascial pain involving the masseter muscle was examined in a controlled study (Dohrmann & Laskin, 1978). A total of 24 patients with this syndrome were randomly assigned either to auditory muscle feedback (16 subjects) or to a control procedure in which patients were told that they would receive a low-grade electrical current through the affected muscles, which would help to relax the muscles and thus to reduce pain. The experimental group showed a steady decrease in electromyographic activity in the affected muscles over the course of treatment, as compared with a much slighter and nonsignificant decrease in the control group. In addition, both the patients' and the examiners' rating of the outcome of treatment strongly favored the biofeedback procedure. This experiment also suggested that the feedback procedure (and not placebo variables) was responsible for the obtained outcome, although no measures of the credibility of the two procedures were obtained. Thus it is possible that patients found the control procedure to be less believable than the treatment procedure.

The question of the specificity of biofeedback effects has, however, been examined in several clinical studies. In the first of these, patients with muscular weakness in the upper arm consequent to a stroke were assigned to varying orders of true electromyographic feedback; to noncontingent feedback from the muscle of the experimenter, unknown to the subject; or to no feedback. No differences were found among these conditions in terms of electromyographic activity. However, when the data were regrouped in a retrospective analysis, older, poorly motivated subjects were found to have benefited from feedback, while the younger, well-motivated subjects did not show improvement (Lee, Hill, Johnson, & Smichorowski, 1976). While these results throw doubt on the specificity of biofeedback effects in muscular disorders, two further studies suggest that a different conclusion may be warranted.

In the first of these studies, 12 subjects, half with muscular weakness due to brain damage and half with muscular weakness due to peripheral nerve damage received two experimental conditions in both of two sessions (Middaugh & Miller, 1980). The first condition consisted of no feedback, while in the second, electromyographic feedback was provided. Electromyographic activity was significantly greater for both types of muscle weakness in the feedback condition when instructions to contract the muscle were given. In the second study, 31 participants with tension headache were randomly assigned either to frontalis electromyographic feedback or to a placebo therapy with demonstrated equal credibility to the biofeedback condition (Holroyd, Andrasik, & Noble, 1980). Those receiving feedback not only demonstrated greater reduction in electromyographic activity of the frontalis muscle than did the control group, but also showed superior reductions in headache severity and duration. Taken together, both these studies (Holroyd *et al.*, 1980; Middaugh & Miller, 1980) suggest that providing feedback concerning muscular activity has specific therapeutic effects.

When one takes an overall view of the efficacy of biofeedback, the conclusion of Ray *et al.* (1977) appears to be justified: ''biofeedback applications have been spreading into various clinical areas while research efforts within individual areas remain at very primitive levels of experimental design. . . . Most areas of biofeedback application are not advanced to the stage where decisions about the scientific efficacy of the treatment procedures can be made'' (p. 35). While there is some evidence for the specificity of effects of feedback procedures in cardiac arrhythmia and muscular disorders, only in the first of these conditions does the use of feedback appear to be superior to other therapeutic approaches, and even this conclusion is based more on lack of evidence to the contrary than on positive experimental evidence. Nonetheless, the area must still be regarded as promising, and certainly is in need of further research development.

Reinforcement

As noted earlier in this chapter, the use of reinforcement is implicit in many therapeutic procedures, even in those not specifically acknowledging its use or its role in behavior change. Many such uses have already been covered in the preceding pages; social reinforcement, for example, often accompanies the use of biofeedback. In this section, a few selected examples of the use of reinforcement are examined, and further uses are discussed in the section entitled ''Therapeutic Packages'' (see pp. 516–518).

The term ''reinforcement'' refers both to a procedure and to a behavioral effect. The basic procedure is to follow a well-defined behavior with a consequence, which in turn leads to an increase in the frequency, strength, and duration of the behavior. Since individuals vary in their preferences, points exchangeable for a variety of goods or events have been extensively used to reinforce behavior. One innovative use of a point system was reported from a pediatric hemodialysis unit (Magrab & Papadopoulou, 1977). Children find even more difficulty than adults do in adhering to the dietary regimen that is part and parcel of renal dialysis. In this study, points exchangeable for a variety of prizes were awarded to children when blood urea nitrogen, potassium, and weight were within the therapeutic range. A reversal design was used to evaluate the effectiveness of the point contingency, and weight gained between sessions showed a clear effect of the contingency. This finding indicated a desirable clinical outcome and lays the groundwork for further investigation of the procedure.

A second study illustrates the use of reinforcement with a larger population; it attempted to increase the use of dental facilities by children from low-income families (Reiss, Piotrowski, & Bailey, 1976). The families of 51 children in need of dental care were allocated at random to either a reminder system involving the use of three prompts to attend the clinic, or a system involving one prompt plus a $5 incentive to attend, in the form of a redeemable coupon. Prompts alone were only moderately effective, although a home visit incorporated within the prompting system led to 60% attendance, while the incentive system led to 67% attendance. However, the cost of the incentive system was only half the cost of the three-prompt system, and thus the former should be the preferred method in practice. This is an intriguing finding, since the savings of staff time and effort more than compensate for the value of the incentives used.

Reinforcement may be used in conjunction with the procedure of contracting with clients for specific behavioral outcomes. Thus, in one study, students deposited items of personal value that they could earn back by fulfilling a contract aimed at increasing exercise (Wysocki, Hall, Iwata, & Riordan, 1979). Participants in this program contracted each week to complete a certain number of aerobic points, and to do the exercise involved in the presence of another participant. In addition, each participant contracted to observe and record the amount of exercise performed by another program participant. Using a multiple-baseline design, the experimenters demonstrated that increases in exercise were related to the reinforcement contract. However, as in the case of other exercise programs, one-third of those taking part dropped out—in this case, during the baseline condition. Self-reported exercise 1 year after termination of the 6-week program showed good maintenance of the exercise habits acquired during the study.

Another instance of reinforcement administered by means of a contract was aimed at diminishing a patient's overuse of medical services; this was described by Taylor, Pfenninger, and Candelaria (1980). The patient, a 30-year-old woman, had made 280 visits to a teaching hospital in 13 years, had seen 159 different members of the medical staff, and had made 146 emergency room visits. Yet, despite her many complaints, little medical cause for her complaints could be found. Following a baseline period of 4 months, a treatment contract was written and agreed upon, in which visits to two health professionals (which the patient enjoyed and during which she was able to discuss her problems) were made contingent upon her not visiting other health professionals without permission and upon her attending a high-school diploma class. Finally, the contract was terminated for 4 months to determine whether permanent changes had been effected.

During the baseline period, the combined costs of outpatient and emergency room visits averaged over $500 per month, an indication of gross overuse of the medical system. When the reinforcement contract was initiated, costs dropped to below half that figure, and eventually to below $100 per month. As an indication of the effectiveness of the contract, costs during the reversal phase rose once more to those seen in the baseline period. This type of therapeutic contract might be useful for many patients who overuse medical facilities, and might be equally useful over the shorter term for the inpatient who is difficult to manage.

The reverse of reinforcement—namely, extinction—may be used to reduce the frequency of an unwanted behavior. In extinction, a behavioral assessment identifies naturally occurring reinforcers that can be removed, and the effect of removing the reinforcement is monitored by direct measurement of the behavior in question. A nice example of the use of extinction—in this case, to eliminate a 9-year-old girl's vomiting in class in a residential school—was provided by M. M. Wolf, Birnbrauer, Williams, and Lawler (1965). Direct observation revealed that after each vomiting episode the child's school teacher returned the girl to her dormitory. Hypothesizing that this escape from classroom work reinforced the rate of vomiting, the authors suggested that the child stay in class following vomiting, and that adaptive behavior (i.e., the absence of vomiting) be reinforced by social attention. Instituting these contingencies led to cessation of the vomiting. In the next school year, vomiting returned when a new teacher instituted the old contingencies. Once more, an extinction procedure led to cessation of the problem behavior.

In another instance, a 17-year-old girl who had been vomiting after meals for 10 years was treated in an inpatient setting (Alford, Blanchard, & Buckley, 1972). Again, social attention was hypothesized to be reinforcing the behavior. During a baseline phase, the nursing staff gave their usual attention to the patient after each vomiting episode while the time elapsed from the end of eating to the beginning of vomiting was measured; this time varied between 1 and 15 minutes. In the second phase of the experiment, the nurses were instructed to leave the room as soon as vomiting began. Almost at once, the latency of vomiting rose to 1 hour, and thereafter for the first time no vomiting occurred. Two brief returns of vomiting were both associated with accidental attention being paid to the patient following a meal; these incidents confirmed the relationship between social attention and the behavior. In a later phase of treatment, the patient began to eat in the presence of others, who had been taught to ignore her should vomiting occur. Similar training sessions were held with the family. A follow-up 7 months after treatment revealed only one occasion of vomiting.

Punishment

The use of aversive procedures carries with it the ethical problem of inflicting possible harm on the client—a risk that is particularly problematic in the unsuspecting or the unwilling. Thus the ideal clients for this treatment are fully informed volunteers with a problem that is resistant to more benign methods of management. In this sense, cigarette smoking may be a perfect problem behavior for an aversive approach, since the behavior carries with it serious health hazards, and since most therapeutic approaches show little more effect than the combination of simple instructions to quit with attention does (Lichtenstein & Keutzer, 1971). Several types of aversive stimuli have been used with cigarette smokers, including electric shock, inhaling of warm smoky air, or rapid smoking. In one study (Lichtenstein, Harris, Birchler, Wahl, & Schmahl, 1973), the latter two procedures, used singly and in combination, were compared with the effects of simple instructions and attention. The aversive treatments were of similar effectiveness and were clearly superior to the control condition, with self-reported abstinence rates of 60% at 6 months after treatment. Contraindications to the use of this treatment include severe lung disease and incipient cardiac failure.

Another arena for the use of aversive procedures has been eating disorders, including obesity and ruminative vomiting. The latter condition is usually manifested by infants who repeatedly regurgitate their food, often leading to a life-threatening state of affairs, with weight loss and dehydration. The only controlled studies of the treatment of this condition have involved the use of punishment procedures, including the application of brief electric shock (Lang & Melamed, 1969). Despite the success of this procedure, some would hesitate to use shock on an already sick infant. To overcome this problem, a later study (Sajwaj, Libet, & Agras, 1974) used lemon juice as the aversive stimulus and examined the effectiveness of this procedure, using a single-case experimental design. More traditional approaches to treatment, such as increased attention to the infant, had failed. Each episode of the abnormal mouthing that preceded regurgitation was quickly followed by a small amount of lemon juice placed in the infant's mouth. This procedure led to a rapid reduction in ruminative vomiting. A brief cessation of the punishment procedure showed a rapid return to baseline levels of vomiting, and when therapy was reinstated, vomiting was suppressed over a 30-day period and satisfactory weight gain occurred. As is the case with the successful use of punishment, the behavior in question was rapidly eliminated; thus the use of the aversive stimulus was limited. In this case, the largest number of applications of lemon juice following a feeding was 12, and, for the most part, between one and four applications were needed.

Cognitive Approaches

The classification of any therapy as "cognitive" or "noncognitive" is, of course, quite arbitrary, in that it is impossible for any psychotherapeutic procedure to bypass human cognition. Moreover, experimental manipulations of therapeutic instructions have shown that all therapeutic approaches are dependent upon the presence of such instructions. One of the first behaviorally oriented therapies, systematic desensitization, relies heavily on cognitive procedures, such as imagining scenes that evoke fear; for the purposes of this chapter, it is especially interesting, since it has been compared with the use of relaxation training in the treatment of asthma. As noted earlier, hypnosis appears to be superior to relaxation training in the treatment of asthma, and detailed studies of the effect of relaxation training alone suggest a statistically but not a clinically significant effect in this disorder.

The first controlled study of the use of systematic desensitization in asthma was reported by Moore (1965), who compared desensitization with either relaxation alone or relaxation accompanied by strong suggestions of improvement. For systematic desensitization, hierarchies based on anxiety-provoking situations associated with asthmatic attacks were constructed, as well as anxiety-provoking situations felt to be central to a particular individual's life circumstances. Treatment then consisted of working through the hierarchies in a relaxed state. Each of 12 asthmatic patients received two of the three treatments in a counterbalanced order. Systematic desensitization was found to be significantly superior to the other two treatments, as shown by improvement in maximum peak respiratory flow. In addition, the number of asthmatic attacks reported each week followed the same trend. It is interesting to note that the two relaxation groups showed maximal positive effects after 4 or 5 weeks and then exhibited a declining trend, while the group treated with desensitization showed a steady improvement over the weeks. One disadvantage of the cross-over design used is that assessment of longer-term effectiveness was impossible, since each subject received two treatments.

This pioneering study was replicated and extended a few years later in a comparison of relaxation therapy and systematic desensitization (Yorkston, McHugh, Brady, Serber, & Sergeant, 1974). The report of this study is particularly noteworthy in that the treatment is described in great detail, including desensitization in the clinic and graded exposure to anxiety-provoking situations at home and at work. Once more, desensitization was found to be superior to relaxation training immediately after treatment on a measure of forced expiratory volume. Even more impressive was the finding at the 2-year follow-up that desensitization was superior in outcome both on clinical ratings and in terms of reduction of medication use.

Given the often-noted influence of thoughts and feelings upon the production and persistence of asthmatic attacks (Luparello, Lyons, Bleecker, & McFadden, 1968), the relative ineffectiveness of relaxation—a finding that must now be regarded as well established—and the effectiveness of a cognitively oriented therapy are of great theoretical interest. It seems very likely that respiratory changes are conditioned both to specific life events and to thoughts concerning those events. Thus the efficacy of desensitization makes particularly good sense. Given the extent of clinical relief produced by desensitization and the theoretical issues involved, this area of treatment would seem to be in further need of research development and clinical application.

Therapeutic Packages

One theme that has been repeatedly sounded in this chapter is that all therapeutic procedures, no matter how simple they appear, contain many components both specified and unspecified. Thus, many of the applications of these procedures to medical conditions have had many components; this trend is nicely illustrated by the recent treatment approaches to anorexia nervosa and obesity. Since the research into the treatment of anorexia nervosa has succeeded in identifying some of the active components of treatment, this discussion begins with a consideration of that uncommon disorder.

Anorexia Nervosa

Most workers now agree that the central feature of anorexia nervosa is a fear of being overweight coupled with a distorted perception of body shape, such that even emaciation can be viewed as fatness. These features are accompanied by weight loss, amenorrhea in the female, and overactivity. Behavioral research to date has focused on the treatment of underweight, a theme ushered in by the pioneering case study of Bachrach and his colleagues (Bachrach, Erwin, & Mohr, 1965). However, in the first experimental attempt to document the role of reinforcement in encouraging weight gain, some rather curious findings emerged (Agras, Barlow, Chapin, Abel, & Leitenberg, 1974). We used a single-case experimental design and found that when reinforcement was introduced, weight gain occurred. Reinforcement in this case was access to ward activities, which was made contingent on small cumulative gains in weight. However, in the next phase of the experiment when reinforcement was removed, weight gain (and caloric intake) continued unabated. The reinstatement of reinforcement in the last experimental phase led to no further increase in the rate of weight gain. These findings suggested that some therapeutic variable other than reinforcement was operating. The patients involved in this phase of the experiment both claimed that once they found they could gain weight, they continued to eat in order to be able to leave the hospital, an environment of which they were not fond. This raised the possibility that negative reinforcement (performing a task to reduce a perceived noxious environmental event or circumstance) was operating in the research environment.

To neutralize negative reinforcement in the next series of studies, patients were admitted to the research facility only if they contracted to stay in the hospital for 12 weeks, whether or not they gained weight. A replication of the original experiment under these conditions now revealed the effect of positive reinforcement, with gains in weight and caloric intake, and slowing in the rate of weight gain following removal of positive reinforcement. Thus, one may conclude that two forms of reinforcement, negative and positive, were active therapeutic ingredients—an excellent example of the discovery of a hidden therapeutic component.

During the baseline condition in the experiments just described, the patients were told their weight each day and given feedback as to the number of calories consumed after each meal. Inspection of caloric and weight data during the baseline period suggested that this feedback might be exerting an influence on eating behavior. Thus, in the next series of experiments, feedback was removed from the baseline condition, and reinforcement was introduced separately from feedback. Under these circumstances, it appeared that reinforcement had no effect on eating behavior until it was combined with informational feedback. Finally, it was demonstrated that large meals (1,500 calories each) led to a larger caloric consumption than did smaller meals (750 calories each) even though a patient never finished all the food at any one sitting. This finding was replicated by other workers, who found that food intake was reduced by about 500 calories per day when smaller meals were served (Elkin, Hersen, Eisler, & Williams, 1973).

This combined group of studies, then, strongly suggests that four procedures lead to weight gain in patients with anorexia nervosa: positive reinforcement, negative reinforcement, informational feedback as to caloric intake and weight gain, and large meals. However, from a clinical viewpoint, even more factors may be added; these include therapeutic instructions and usually the defining of a therapeutic contract (which seems to be necessary in this rather manipulative group of patients), as well as the organization of a carefully planned therapeutic milieu (Agras & Werne, 1981). This package has now been experimentally tested in a further study (Pertschuk, Edwards, & Pomerleau, 1978). These investigators used a variant of the multiple-baseline design, in which patients were allocated to treatment at randomly selected and varying times after admission. Weight gain for those completing treatment was then compared with weight gain for those who had not finished treatment, and a significant difference in favor of the behavioral contract was found. Indeed, patients tended to lose a little weight during the control period, .09 kg/day, as against a mean gain of .32 kg/day during behavioral treatment. All seven patients with anorexia nervosa gained weight during the program, with a range of weight gain from 3.4 kg to 6.01 kg during an average of 24 days of active treatment.

While it appears that a satisfactory program to enable patients with anorexia nervosa to gain weight has been developed and tested, it is also clear that much more needs to be done. The typical patient with anorexia nervosa has many social and skill deficits. At present, no research into the nature or scope of these problems from the viewpoint of applied behavioral science has appeared, nor have controlled studies of interventions in this area been published. This next step in research will undoubtedly prove more vital than the work that has appeared to date, for anorexia nervosa tends to be a long-term chronic condition, and complete rehabilitation is needed to prevent the poor outcome that is presently seen in a substantial number of cases.

Obesity

From the beginning, the behavioral treatment of obesity has consisted of the application of a complex package aimed at altering the eating style of the overweight person, reducing caloric intake, and increasing energy expenditure. The initial theoretical contributions of Ferster and his colleagues (Ferster, Nurnberger, & Levitt, 1962) and the early work of Stuart (1967) have led to the development of a therapy that includes self-monitoring, attempts to change the stimulus control of eating, alterations in eating style, caloric modification, nutritional education, increases in activity, and the systematic use of reinforcement to strengthen many of these behaviors. The experimental literature is now vast and has been well reviewed elsewhere (e.g., Agras & Werne, 1981; Stuart, Mitchell, & Jensen, 1980; Wilson & Brownell, 1980; Wing & Jeffery, 1979); thus a selective approach is taken in this section. The behavioral package outlined above has been demonstrated to be more effective than no treatment (Harris, 1969); than various types of placebo or nonspecific therapy controls (Hagen, 1974; Wollersheim, 1970); than more traditional forms of dietary counseling (Penick, Filion, Fox, & Stunkard, 1971); and than the use of fenfluramine, an appetite suppressant (Ost & Gotestam, 1976).

Notwithstanding these impressive findings for a therapy usually administered in a cost-effective group format, some problems remain. The average weight loss is only 11 pounds per client, with a mean rate of weight loss of about 1 pound per week (Wing & Jeffery, 1979). Moreover, the range of outcomes both within and between studies is quite large, varying from about 7 pounds gained to 47 pounds lost in one large clinical series (Jeffery, Wing, & Stunkard, 1978) and from 2 to 36 pounds lost between studies. Such variation is likely to be a result of two factors. First, "obesity" is a term that undoubtedly spans a variety of disorders, each of which many respond differently to treatment; and second, given that behavioral treatment has many components, different workers may emphasize or include a varying number of therapeutic elements. Thus, at present, as far as short-term outcome is concerned, we must conclude that the behavioral approach has most to offer those whose overweight does not exceed 35 to 50 pounds.

Given the relatively modest outcome of the behavioral approach to the treatment of overweight, it would seem important to discover ways to enhance the immediate outcome of therapy. In a recent study, monetary reinforcement was used to improve performance (Jeffery, Thompson, & Wing, 1978). Participants were asked to contract to deposit $200, to be returned contingent upon either weekly weight loss, reports of caloric restriction, or attendance. Subjects were randomly allocated to one of three groups. In the first, $20 was returned each week when the participant met a preset criterion of 2 pounds lost; for the second group, a similar refund was made for caloric restrictions that would lead to a 2-pound weight loss; while for the third group, $20 was returned for each session attended. In addition, each of the three groups received a standard behavioral program. Those who had been reinforced for attendance only lost an average of 8.6 pounds, while those reinforced for caloric restriction and weight reduction lost 19.4 pounds and 21 pounds, respectively. These are impressive results, at least doubling the efficacy of the standard weight reduction program. However, it is to be noted that not everyone will take part in such a program. Thus, only half of those who agreed to participate attended the first experimental session.

A second approach to the enhancement of weight loss that appeared to be modestly successful involved altering the frequency, but not the overall amount, of contact between therapist and client. Participants were randomly allocated to one of three groups: regular weekly sessions; two additional telephone contacts each week; and two additional personal contacts each week. Those contacted lost more weight than those not contacted (Jeffery et al., 1978).

Even more important than initial outcome in a chronic disorder associated with serious health hazards is the question of maintenance of therapeutic effects. In general, the maintenance of weight loss following behavioral treatment is quite satisfactory. Thus at a mean duration of follow-up of 21 weeks, the average participant had lost an additional pound (Wing & Jeffery, 1979), and studies with follow-up periods of between 1 and 4 years show similar or even better maintenance of weight loss. Thus, in one study in which participants were weighed nearly 4 years after therapy, the initial weight loss of the group as a whole was almost perfectly maintained. However, those who had gained weight during therapy continued to gain weight after treatment. On the other hand, of those who lost weight during treatment, nearly half continued to lose weight in the ensuing years (Graham, Hovell, Taylor, & Siegel, 1979). Unfortunately, in the only 5-year comparison of behavior therapy and more traditional therapy, no differences between treatment modalities were found (Stunkard & Penick, 1979). These data suggest that behavioral approaches to weight management achieve a modest success in terms of long-term weight reduction, but that methods to enhance maintenance are needed.

One method with logical appeal is to provide follow-up or booster sessions after treatment. Kingsley and Wilson (1977) reported that such booster sessions significantly facilitated weight loss up to 9 months after treatment. However, the same researchers were not able to replicate their earlier findings, and another group of investigators failed to find differences in maintenance between a group given three follow-up sessions and one given 10 follow-up sessions in the year following initial treatment (Ashby & Wilson, 1977; Beneke & Paulsen, 1979). Thus, while fairly frequent contact during the follow-up period seems to be a logical clinical approach, there is little experimental support at present for such a procedure.

Similarly conflicting findings have been made for the involvement of family members in weight control programs. In the first study of this procedure, no effect was found either on immediate weight loss or on maintenance of weight loss (Wilson & Brownell, 1978). On the other hand, Brownell, Heckerman, Westlake, Hayes, and Monti (1978) found that weight loss was enhanced at a 6-month follow-up by the involvement of a cooperative spouse. The discrepancy between these studies might be explained by differences in the extent of spouses' involvement. In the latter study, spouses were actively involved, while in the former, they were cast in the role of observers of the treatment process.

Another approach to the improvement of maintenance of weight loss involved the teaching of self-control procedures (Loro, Fisher, & Levenkron, 1979). This was achieved by describing a variety of procedures to the participants and by stressing that foresight and cleverness were needed to arrange one's life so as to minimize temptation and achieve long-term goals. The group treated with this procedure continued to lose weight up to 16 weeks after treatment, while a group treated in more orthodox fashion lost weight and showed good maintenance, but lost no further weight after treatment.

Clearly, more research is required both in the enhancement of initial weight loss and in the maintenance of such losses. In addition, we need a clarification of the therapeutic elements critical for both short-term and long-term success, as well as a better understanding of the process of weight loss. Does alteration of a person's eating behavior (e.g., eating more slowly and taking fewer bites) lead to weight loss, or to better maintenance of weight loss? And if it does, what is the mechanism for that effect? These are examples of the types of questions that must now be settled by further experimental work. Meanwhile, it is fair to say that research into the treatment of overweight is one of the best developed and most active areas in the field of behavioral medicine.

Duodenal Ulcers

The evidence that anxiety and emotional inhibition are associated with the occurrence of duodenal ulcers led one group of researchers to investigate the use of anxiety management and assertiveness training with ulcer patients (Brooks & Richardson, 1980). A total of 22 patients were randomly allocated to treatment and control groups while medical therapy continued for both groups. The therapeutic procedures used were similar to those of Chappell et al. (1938), described earlier in this chapter (see "Psychotherapy"). Thus, patients in the treatment group were given information concerning the role of anxiety in the perpetuation of their symptoms; were taught to identify and change self-defeating thoughts and self-talk; were taught deep muscle relaxation; and finally, were taught how to assert themselves more appropriately. These objectives were accomplished in eight treatment sessions.

At immediate outcome, patients in the treatment group were found to be less anxious than those in the control group, as measured by the State–Trait Anxiety scale; complained of less pain; reported fewer symptomatic days; and used less antacid than those in the control group. Even more impressive were the results at a 42-month follow-up. Five of eight control patients had either had surgical correction of the ulcers or radiographic evidence of recurrence of their ulcers, as compared with only one of the nine patients in the treatment group who were followed up. This difference was statistically significant. This study, taken together with that of Chappell *et al.* (1936), strongly suggests that a treatment procedure aimed at life style changes can be extremely helpful to patients with duodenal ulcers.

Diabetes Mellitus

Nowhere is it clearer that a complex, multiobjective behavior change strategy is needed than in the case of the child with insulin-dependent diabetes. The patient, family, and clinician together face many problems in maintaining optimal control of serum glucose levels. A recent controlled study used a multiple-baseline design across groups to assess the effects of a therapeutic package (Epstein, Beck, Figuera, Farkas, Kazdin, Daneman, & Becker, 1981). Therapy was largely educational in nature, focusing both upon increasing knowledge and skills, and upon enhancing knowledge and skills by instructions, feedback, and reinforcement. Among the topics and skills addressed were insulin adjustment, diet, exercise, self-administration of insulin, stress, and hypoglycemia. Contracts developed between parents and children were used to enhance motivation and performance.

The results of this experiment demonstrated a significant increase from 27% to 39% in urine samples negative for glucose; this figure was further increased to 45% at a 2-month follow-up. This suggests that the program was effective in its major aim, and other data suggest that consumer satisfaction was high—not an easy goal to attain in the management of this difficult disorder.

Bibliotherapy

The use of the written word, with or without illustrations, to change behavior is best conceived of as a type of therapeutic package that may be used alone or with the support of a therapist. Such a package includes therapeutic instructions and rationale; information; and the description of various behavior change procedures, often including the use of self-monitoring and reinforcement (Glasgow & Rosen, 1978). If such a procedure were effective, then savings of therapist time and the accompanying costs would be considerable.

In the area of behavioral medicine, treatment manuals have been used and evaluated fairly extensively in two areas: weight loss and cessation of cigarette smoking. For weight loss, the first treatment manual was developed by Stuart and Davis (1972) and entitled *Slim Chance in a Fat World*. This manual has been evaluated in conjunction both with full therapist attention to clients and with relatively minimal therapist contact. One study found no differences in weight loss between minimal and full therapist contact, while both groups showed weight loss superior to that of a no-treatment group (Lindstrom, Balch, & Reese, 1976). Another use of a well-organized treatment manual is, of course, as an aid to therapists of differing professional background and experience, in order to enlarge the population that can be treated. Balch and Balch (1976) found no differences in outcome among groups treated by a psychologist, a nurse, and a social worker when the Stuart and Davis (1972) manual was used. As in the previous study, weight losses were in the range to be expected from a behavioral treatment approach. In a further study of another manual, no differences were found between minimal-contact and therapist-administered groups, both of which were superior to a no-treatment group and to a placebo group. Maintenance was excellent at a 1-year follow-up, with a trend in favor of the minimal-contact condition (Hanson, Borden, Hall, & Hall, 1976).

Such manuals have also been used on an entirely self-administered basis. In a comparison of self-administration, therapist administration, and no treatment, use of the manual was found to be superior to no treatment. The groups receiving the manuals showed a mean weight loss of up to 15 pounds over the treatment period (Hagen, 1974). Thus, we can conclude that in the treatment of mildly overweight persons, minimal therapist contact combined with the use of a well-designed treatment manual is an effective approach. Moreover, in well-motivated subjects, the manual alone might be expected to produce reasonable results.

This satisfactory outcome has not been repeated in the case of cigarette smoking cessation. Here, although some manuals have led to superior results at immediate outcome, none have been found to be superior to a placebo condition at follow-up (see Glasgow & Rosen, 1978, for a detailed consideration of this literature). This is particularly disappointing, in that many cigarette smokers would like to stop smoking but are not willing to attend clinics to achieve this end. Many other areas in behavioral medicine, such as diet, exercise, medication taking, and stress reduction, are obvious candidates for the use of bibliotherapy. However, at present, although manuals for these areas exist, no carefully controlled tests of such manuals have been carried out. This will undoubtedly become an important area for research in the near future, as will the use of other therapeutic aids, such as audiotapes and videotapes, the latter being particularly useful for the demonstration of specific skills.

OVERVIEW

The fact that clinical research into problems falling within the purview of behavioral medicine is a relatively recent phenomenon is illustrated in Figure 12.2, where the controlled studies referred to in this chapter are graphed by date of publication. As can be seen, less than 10% of the research referred to had appeared by 1960. During the 1960s, controlled clinical studies appeared at a steady but relatively low rate, such that only one-quarter of the total number of studies had appeared by the end of the decade. In the early 1970s, a sudden surge of research began, and shows a continuing acceleration to this day. Two-thirds of the clinical research in the field has appeared since 1973. Given this relatively recent beginning, it should come as no surprise that in most of the areas reviewed in this chapter, there is much uncertainty as to the efficacy and clinical applicability of the procedures used. In no area has research proceeded beyond the beginnings of the progression outlined in Figure 12.1.

Substantial progress has, however, been made in a few areas. Thus, the behavior change packages used in the treatment of overweight have been demonstrated to be more effective (albeit marginally in many instances) than other approaches. However, the process of behavior change is by no means clear: For example, does changing the form of eating behavior lead to weight loss? The research focus is now shifting to the identification of methods to enhance initial weight loss and to maintain that weight loss. Other areas in which progress has been substantial include the application of relaxation training as an adjunctive method of treating essential hypertension, and the application of relaxation training and electromyographic feedback to the treat-

FIGURE 12.2. Developments in the field of behavioral medicine as reflected by the time of appearance of the papers cited in this chapter.

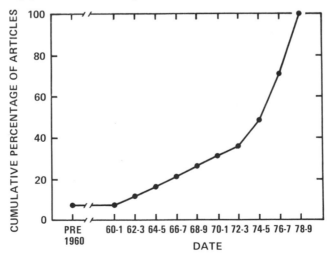

ment of tension and migraine headache. In both these areas, the procedures used appear to have a specific effect over and above the role of nonspecific procedures. Issues of generalization of treatment effect and maintenance have barely been broached in these problems, and the process of behavior change involved in producing the beneficial effects remains obscure.

In other areas, there has been definite progress, but the number and/or the quality of the research studies does not allow such definite conclusions to be drawn. Such areas include the treatment of insomnia by means of relaxation training; the treatment of asthma by means of hypnosis or systematic desensitization; the use of electromyographic feedback in muscular rehabilitation; and methods used to induce weight gain in the patient with anorexia nervosa. Much remains to be done in each of these problems before we can be sure that the methods are definitely superior to prevailing treatments, although in each of these areas the precise definition of the treatment procedures used, coupled with the results of the research published, does much to recommend these methods to the practicing clinician.

Less sure but still promising are the results of research into such problems as cardiac arrhythmias and Raynaud disease. Here the initial studies promote much interest in the procedures, but the paucity of studies suggests that caution as to both the specificity and the clinical utility of effects is in order. Many other areas could be included in this paragraph, but this would simply be a listing of the many applications in which only one or two well-done studies provide a tantalizing glimpse of the progress that might be made over the years to come.

The progress achieved to date has, for the most part, been dependent upon the development of well-defined behavior change procedures compatible with the tenets of social learning theory, although some major exceptions (such as relaxation training) are evident. Even though some studies have suggested that verbal psychotherapy may be successful in the treatment of a particular condition, a closer examination often reveals that such applications have more in common with therapies based on social learning theory (see, e.g., Chappell et al., 1936). Thus most progress is likely to come from applications of well-defined procedures that are derived from social learning theory and investigated according to the research progression outlined earlier.

For the clinician interested in the day-to-day management of the behavior problems encountered in the practice of medicine, the initial therapeutic successes recounted in this and other chapters in this volume suggest that approaches to the understanding of behavior based on social learning theory will be useful in practice. The notions of making as exact a behavior analysis as possible in the clinical setting (with particular assessment of variables that are currently affecting the behavior in question) and of involving the patient actively in the behavior change process (with the use of self-monitoring where applicable) are likely to be of continuing importance. The rapidity of research development, as illustrated in Figure 12.2, also suggests that clinicians will have to change their practices continually and to incorporate new procedures as these are proven superior to the old. This is not always an easy process for clinicians, particularly when the procedures used are technically complex and/or are based on theoretical material with which the clinicians may not be familiar.

The short history and rapid research expansion of behavioral medicine, and the need for applications of behavior change procedures to many medical conditions, have led to high hopes and perhaps even exaggerated expectations for the field. Such, however, is often the fate of a new applied area. Only the establishment of a solid research program will bring to fruition the potential of these new procedural applications for the alleviation of human suffering.

R E F E R E N C E S

Adams, H. E., Feuerstein, M., & Fowler, J. L. Migraine headache: Review of parameters, etiology, and intervention. *Psychological Bulletin*, 1980, *87*, 217–228.

Agras, W. S. Behavioral approaches to the treatment of essential hypertension. *International Journal of Obesity*, 1981, *5* (Suppl. 1), 173–181.

Agras, W. S., Barlow, D. H., Chapin, H. N., Abel, G. G., & Leitenberg, H. Behavior modification of anorexia nervosa. *Archives of General Psychiatry*, 1974, *30*, 279–286.

Agras, W. S., & Berkowitz, R. Clinical research in behavior therapy: Halfway there? *Behavior Therapy*, 1980, *11*, 472–487.

Agras, W. S., & Jacob, R. G. Phobia: Nature and measurement. In M. Mavissakalian & D. H. Barlow (Eds.), *Phobia: Psychological and pharmacological treatment*. New York: Guilford Press, 1981.

Agras, W. S., Taylor, C. B., Kraemer, H. C., Allen, R. A., & Schneider, J. Relaxation training: Twenty-four-hour blood pressure reductions. *Archives of General Psychiatry*, 1980, *37*, 859–865.

Agras, W. S., & Werne, J. Disorders of eating. In S. Turner, K. Calhoun, & H. Adams (Eds.), *Handbook of clinical behavior therapy*. New York: Wiley, 1981.

Alford, G. S., Blanchard, E. B., & Buckley, T. M. Treatment of hysterical vomiting by modification of social contingencies. *Journal of Behavior Therapy and Experimental Psychiatry*, 1972, *3*, 209–212.

Alexander, A. B., Cropp, G. J. A., & Chai, H. Effects of relaxation training on pulmonary mechanics in children with asthma. *Journal of Applied Behavior Analysis*, 1979, *12*, 27–36.

Ashby, W. A., & Wilson, G. T. Behaviour therapy for obesity: Booster sessions and long term maintenance of weight loss. *Behaviour Research and Therapy*, 1977, *15*, 451–464.

Bachrach, A. J., Erwin, W. J., & Mohr, J. F. The control of eating behavior in an anorexic by operant conditioning techniques. In L. P. Ullmann & L. Krasner (Eds.), *Case studies in behavior modification*. New York: Holt, Rinehart & Winston, 1965.

Balch, P., & Balch, K. Establishing a campus wide behavioral weight reduction program through a university student health service: The use and training of health service personnel as behavior weight therapists. *Journal of the American College Health Association*, 1976, *25*, 148–152.

Bandura, A. *Principles of behavior modification*. New York: Holt, Rinehart & Winston, 1969.

Bandura, A. Self efficacy: Toward a unifying theory of behavior change. *Psychological Review*, 1977, *84*, 191–215.

Barber, T. H., Spanos, N. P., & Chaves, J. F. *Hypnotism: Imagination and human potentialities*. New York: Pergamon Press, 1974.

Basmajian, J. V., Kukulka, C. G., Narayan, M. G., & Takebe, K. Biofeedback treatment of foot-drop after stroke compared with standard rehabilitation technique: Effects on voluntary control and strength. *Archives of Physical Medicine and Rehabilitation*, 1975, *56*, 231–236.

Beaky, E. T., & Haynes, S. Behavioral intervention with muscle-contraction headache: A review. *Psychosomatic Medicine*, 1979, *41*, 165–180.

Beecher, H. K. The powerful placebo. *Journal of the American Medical Association*, 1959, *159*, 1602–1606.

Beneke, W., & Paulsen, B. K. Long-term efficacy of a behavior modification program: A comparison of two follow-up maintenance strategies. *Behavior Therapy*, 1979, *10*, 8–13.

Blackwell, B., Bloomfield, S., & Gartside, P. Transcendental meditation in hypertension: Individual response patterns. *Lancet*, 1976, *i*, 223–226.

Blanchard, E. B., Theobald, D., Williamson, D., Silver, B., & Brown, B. Temperature feedback in the treatment of migraine headaches. *Archives of General Psychiatry*, 1978, *35*, 581–588.

Borkovec, T. D., Grayson, J. B., O'Brien, G. T., & Weerts, T. C. Relaxation treatment of pseudo-insomnia and idiopathic insomnia: An electroencephalographic evaluation. *Journal of Applied Behavior Analysis*, 1979, *12*, 37–54.

Borkovec, T. D., & Weerts, T. C. Effects of progressive relaxation on sleep disturbance: An electroencephalographic evaluation. *Psychosomatic Medicine*, 1976, *38*, 173–176.

Brauer, A. P., Horlick, L., Nelson, E., Farquhar, J. W., & Agras, W. S. Relaxation therapy for essential hypertension: a Veterans Administration outpatient study. *Journal of Behavioral Medicine*, 1979, *2*, 21–29.

Brooks, G. R., & Richardson, F. C. Emotional skills training: A treatment program for duodenal ulcer. *Behavior Therapy*, 1980, *11*, 198–207.

Brownell, K. D., Heckerman, C. L., Westlake, R. J., Hayes, S. C., & Monti, P. The effect of couples training and partner cooperativeness in the behavioural treatment of obesity. *Behaviour Research and Therapy*, 1978, *16*, 323–334.

Chappell, M. N., Stefano, J. J., Rogerson, J. S., & Pike, F. H. The value of group psychological procedures in the treatment of peptic ulcer. *American Journal of Digestive Disease and Nutrition*, 1936, *3*, 813–817.

Comroe, J. H. The road from research to new diagnosis and therapy. *Science*, 1978, *200*, 933–937.

Cox, D. J., Freundlich, A., & Meyer, R. Differential effectiveness of electromyographic feedback, verbal relaxation instructions, and medication placebo with tension headaches. *Journal of Consulting and Clinical Psychology*, 1975, *43*, 892–898.

Datey, K. K., Deshmukh, S. N., Dalvi, C. P., & Vinekar, S. L. "Shavason": A yogic exercise in the management of hypertension. *Angiology*, 1969, *20*, 325–333.

Davidson, D. M., Winchester, M. A., & Taylor, C. B. Effects of relaxation therapy on cardiac performance and sympathetic activity in patients with organic heart disease. *Psychosomatic Medicine*, 1979, *41*, 303–309.

Dement, W. C. *Some must watch while some must sleep*. Stanford, Calif.: Stanford Alumni Association, 1972.

DePiano, F. A., & Selzberg, H. C. Clinical applications of hypnosis to three psychosomatic disorders. *Psychological Bulletin*, 1979, *86*, 1223–1235.

Dohrmann, R. J., & Laskin, D. M. An evaluation of electromyographic feedback in the treatment of myofascial pain–dysfunction syndrome. *Journal of the American Dental Association*, 1978, *96*, 656–662.

Egbert, L. D., Battit, G. E., Welch, C. E., & Bartlett, M. D. Reduction of postoperative pain by encouragement and instruction of patients. *New England Journal of Medicine*, 1964, *270*, 825–827.

Elkin, T. E., Hersen, M., Eisler, R. M., & Williams, J. G. Modification of caloric intake in anorexia nervosa: An experimental analysis. *Psychological Reports*, 1973, *32*, 75–78.

Engel, B. T., & Bleecker, E. R. Application of operant conditioning techniques to the control of cardiac arrhythmias. In P. A. Obrist, A. H. Black, J. Berner, & L. V. DiCara (Eds.), *Cardiovascular psychophysiology*. Chicago: Aldine, 1974.

Epstein, L. H., Beck, S., Figuera, J., Farkas, G., Kazdin, A. E., Daneman, D., & Becker, D. The effects of targeting improvements in urine glucose on metabolic control in children with insulin dependent diabetes. *Journal of Applied Behavior Analysis*, 1981, *14*, 365–376.

Epstein, L. H., Collins, F. L., Hanney, H. J., & Looney, R. L. Fading and feedback in the modification of visual acuity. *Journal of Behavioral Medicine*, 1978, *1*, 273–288.

Erskine-Millis, J., & Schonell, M. Relaxation therapy in asthma: A critical review. *Psychosomatic Medicine*, 1981, *43*, 365–371.

Ferster, C. B., Nurnberger, J. I., & Levitt, E. B. The control of eating. *Journal of Mathetics*, 1962, *1*, 87–109.

Fisher, S., & Greenberg, R. P. *The scientific credibility of Freud's theories and therapy*. New York: Basic Books, 1977.

Foxx, R. M., & Brown, R. A. Nicotine fading and self-monitoring for cigarette abstinence or controlled smoking. *Journal of Applied Behavior Analysis*, 1979, *12*, 111–126.

Frank, J. D. *Persuasion and healing*. Baltimore: Johns Hopkins University Press, 1961.

Freedman, R., & Papsdorf, J. D. Biofeedback and progressive relaxation treatment of sleep onset insomnia: A controlled, all night investigation. *Biofeedback and Self-Regulation*, 1976, *1*, 253–271.

Friedman, H., & Taub, H. A. The use of hypnosis and biofeedback procedures for essential hypertension. *International Journal of Clinical and Experimental Hypnosis*, 1977, *25*, 335–347.

Glasgow, R. E., & Rosen, G. M. Behavioral bibliotherapy: A review of self help behavior therapy manuals. *Psychological Bulletin*, 1978, *85*, 1–23.

Goldiamond, I. Behavioral approaches and liaison psychiatry. *Psychiatric Clinics of North America*, 1979, *2*, 379–401.

Goldring, W., Chasis, H., & Schreiner, G. E. Reassurance in the management of benign hypertensive disease. *Circulation*, 1956, *14*, 260–264.

Goodwin, J. S., Goodwin, J. M., & Vogel, A. V. Knowledge and use of placebos by house officers and nurses. *Annals of Internal Medicine*, 1979, *91*, 106–110.

Graham, L. E., Hovell, M. F., Taylor, C. B., & Siegel, W. *Assessment of long-term weight loss maintenance following behavior therapy*. Paper presented at the meeting of the Association for Advancement of Behavior Therapy, San Francisco, 1979.

Gravenstein, J. S., Devloo, R. A., & Beecher, H. K. Effect of antitussive agents on experimental and pathological cough in man. *Journal of Applied Physiology*, 1954, *7*, 119–139.

Hagen, R. L. Group therapy versus bibliotherapy in weight reduction. *Behavior Therapy*, 1974, *5*, 222–234.

Hanson, R. W., Borden, B. L., Hall, S. M., & Hall, R. G. Use of programmed instruction in teaching self-management skills to overweight adults. *Behavior Therapy*, 1976, *7*, 366–373.

Harris, M. B. Self-directed program for weight control: A pilot study. *Journal of Abnormal Psychology*, 1969, *74*, 263–270.

Henry, J. P., & Stephens, P. M. *Stress, health, and the social environment: A sociobiologic approach to medicine*. New York: Springer-Verlag, 1977.

Hilgard, E. R. *The experience of hypnosis*. New York: Harcourt, Brace, and World, 1968.

Hoehn-Saric, R., Frank, J. D., Imber, S. D., Nash, E. H., Stone, A. R., & Battle, C. Systematic preparation of patients for psychotherapy: I. Effects on therapy behavior and outcome. *Journal of Psychiatric Research*, 1964, *2*, 267–274.

Holroyd, K. A., Andrasik, F., & Noble, J. A comparison of EMG biofeedback and a credible pseudotherapy in training tension headache. *Journal of Behavioral Medicine*, 1980, *3*, 29–40.

Jacob, R. G., Kraemer, H. C., & Agras, W. S. Relaxation therapy in the treatment of hypertension: A review. *Archives of General Psychiatry*, 1977, *34*, 1417–1427.

Jacobson, E. *Progressive relaxation*. Chicago: University of Chicago Press, 1938.

Jacobson, E. Variation of blood pressure with skeletal muscle tension and relaxation. *Annals of Internal Medicine*, 1939, *12*, 1194–1212.

Jeffery, R. W., Thompson, P. D., & Wing, R. R. Effects on weight reduction of strong monetary controls for caloric restriction or weight loss. *Behaviour Research and Therapy*, 1978, *16*, 363–369.

Jeffery, R. W., Wing, R. R., & Stunkard, A. J. Behavioral treatment of obesity: The state of the art 1976. *Behavior Therapy*, 1978, *9*, 189–199.

Jenkins, C. D., Rosenman, R. H., & Friedman, M. Development of an objective psychological test for the determination of the coronary prone behavior pattern in employed men. *Journal of Chronic Diseases*, 1967, *20*, 371–379.

Keefe, F. J., Surwit, R. S., & Pilon, R. N. A 1-year follow-up of Raynaud's patients treated with behavioral therapy techniques. *Journal of Behavioral Medicine*, 1979, *2*, 385–392.

Keefe, F. J., Surwit, R. S., & Pilon, R. N. Biofeedback, autogenic training, and progressive relaxation in the treatment of Raynaud's disease: A comparative study. *Journal of Applied Behavior Analysis*, 1980, *13*, 3–12.

Kingsley, R. G., & Wilson, G. T. Behavior therapy for obesity: A comparative investigation of long-term efficacy. *Journal of Consulting and Clinical Psychology*, 1977, *45*, 288–298.

Lang, P. J., & Melamed, B. G. Avoidance conditioning therapy of an infant with chronic ruminative vomiting. *Journal of Abnormal Psychology*, 1969,. *74*, 139–142.

Lasagna, L., Mosterler, F., Von Felsinger, J. M., & Beecher, H. K. A study of the placebo response. *American Journal of Medicine*, 1954, *16*, 770–779.

Lee, K., Hill, E., Johnston, R., & Smichorowski, T. Myofeedback for muscle retraining in hemiplegic patients. *Archives of Physical Medicine and Rehabilitation*, 1976, *57*, 588–591.

Leitenberg, H., Agras, W. S., Barlow, D. H., & Oliveau, D. C. Contribution of selective positive reinforcement and therapeutic instructions to systematic desensitization therapy. *Journal of Abnormal Psychology*, 1969, *74*, 113–119.

Leitenberg, H., Agras, W. S., Thompson, L. E., & Wright, D. E. Feedback in behavior modification: An experimental analysis in two phobic cases. *Journal of Applied Behavior Analysis*, 1968, *1*, 131–137.

Levine, J. D., Gordon, N. C., & Fields, H. L. The mechanism of placebo analgesia. *Lancet*, 1978, *i*, 654–657.

Lichtenstein, E., Harris, D. E., Birchler, G. R., Wahl, J. M., & Schmahl, D. P. Comparison of rapid smoking, warm smoky air, and attention placebo in the modification of smoking behavior. *Journal of Consulting and Clinical Psychology*, 1973, *40*, 92–98.

Lichtenstein, E., & Keutzer, C. S. Modification of smoking behavior: A later look. In R. D. Rubin, H. Fensterheim, A. A. Lazarus, & C. M. Franks (Eds.), *Advances in behavior therapy*. New York: Academic Press, 1971.

Lindstrom, L. L., Balch, P., & Reese, S. In person versus telephone treatment for obesity. *Journal of Behavior Therapy and Experimental Psychiatry*, 1976, *7*, 367–369.

Loro, A. D., Fisher, E. B., & Levenkron, J. C. Comparison of established and innovative weight-reduction treatment procedures. *Journal of Applied Behavior Analysis*, 1979, *12*, 141–155.

Luparello, O. T., Lyons, H. A., Bleecker, E. R., & McFadden, E. R. Influences of suggestion on airway reactivity in asthmatic subjects. *Psychosomatic Medicine*, 1968, *30*, 819–828.

Magrab, P. R., & Papadopoulou, Z. L. The effect of a token economy on dietary compliance for children on hemodialysis. *Journal of Applied Behavior Analysis*, 1977, *10*, 573–578.

Mathews, K. A., Glass, D. C., Rosenman, R. H., & Bortner, R. W. Competitive drive, Pattern A and coronary heart disease: A further analysis of some data from the Western Collaborative Group Study. *Journal of Chronic Disease*, 1977, *301*, 489–498.

McGlashan, T. H., Evans, F. J., & Orne, M. J. The nature of hypnotic analgesia and placebo response to experimental pain. *Psychosomatic Medicine*, 1969, *31*, 227–246.

Melamed, B. G., Meyer, R., Gee, C., & Soule, L. The influence of time and type of preparation on children's adjustment to hospitalization. *Journal of Pediatric Psychology*, 1976, *1*, 31–37.

Melamed, B. G., & Siegel, L. J. Reduction of anxiety in children facing hospitalization and surgery by use of filmed modeling. *Journal of Consulting and Clinical Psychology*, 1975, *43*, 511–521.

Middaugh, S. J., & Miller, M. C. Electromyographic feedback: Effect on voluntary muscle contractions in paretic subjects. *Archives of Physical Medicine and Rehabilitation*, 1980, *61*, 24–29.

Moore, N. Behavior therapy in bronchial asthma: A controlled study. *Journal of Psychosomatic Research*, 1965, *9*, 257–276.

Mroczek, N., Halpern, D., & McHugh, R. Electromyographic feedback and physical therapy for neuromuscular retraining in hemiplegia. *Archives of Physical Medicine and Rehabilitation*, 1978, *59*, 258–267.

Ost, L., & Gotestam, K. G. Behavioral and pharmacological treatments for obesity: An experimental comparison. *Addictive Behaviors*, 1976, *1*, 331–338.

Patel, C. H. Twelve month follow-up of yoga and biofeedback in the management of hypertension. *Lancet*, 1975, *i*, 62–64.

Patel, C. H., & Datey, K. Relaxation and biofeedback techniques in the management of hypertension. *Angiology*, 1977, *27*, 401–405.

Patel, C. H., & North, W. R. Randomized controlled trial of yoga and biofeedback in the management of hypertension. *Lancet*, 1975, *ii*, 93–95.

Penick, S. B., Filion, R., Fox, S., & Stunkard, A. J. Behavior modification in the treatment of obesity. *Psychosomatic Medicine*, 1971, *33*, 49–55.

Pertschuk, M. J., Edwards, N., & Pomerleau, O. F. A multiple baseline approach to behavioral intervention in anorexia nervosa. *Behavior Therapy*, 1978, *9*, 368–376.

Peters, R. K., Benson, H., & Parker, D. Daily relaxation breaks in a working population: 1. Effects on self-reported measures of health, performance, and well-being. *American Journal of Public Health*, 1977, *67*, 946–959.

Philips, C. The modification of tension headache pain using EMG biofeedback. *Behaviour Research and Therapy*, 1977, *15*, 119–129.

Pratt, J. The class method of treating consumption in the homes of the poor. *Journal of the American Medical Association*, 1907, *49*, 755–759.

Pressey, S. S. Development and appraisal of devices providing immediate scoring of objective tests and concomitant self-instruction. *Journal of Psychology*, 1950, *29*, 417–447.

Qualls, P. J., & Sheehan, P. W. Electromyographic biofeedback as a relaxation technique: A critical appraisal and reassessment. *Psychological Bulletin*, 1981, *90*, 21–42.

Rahe, R. H. Longitudinal study of life change and illness onset. *Journal of Psychosomatic Research*, 1967, *10*, 355–372.

Rahe, R. H., Ward, H. W., & Hayes, V. Brief group therapy in myocardial infarction rehabilitation. Three to four year follow-up of a controlled trial. *Psychosomatic Medicine*, 1979, *41*, 229–241.

Ray, W. J., Raczynski, J. M., Rogers, T., & Kimball, W. H. *Evaluation of clinical biofeedback*. New York: Plenum, 1979.

Reiss, M. L., Piotrowski, W. D., & Bailey, J. S. Behavioral community psychology: Encouraging low-income parents to seek dental care for their children. *Journal of Applied Behavior Analysis*, 1976, *9*, 387–398.

Research Committee of the British Tuberculosis Association. Hypnosis for asthma: A controlled trial. *British Medical Journal*, 1968, *iv*, 71–76.

Rosen, J. C., & Wiens, A. N. Changes in medical problems and use of medical services following psychological intervention. *American Psychologist*, 1979, *34*, 420–431.

Rosenman, R. H., Brand, R. J., Jenkins, C. D., Friedman, M., Straus, R., & Wurm, M. Coronary heart disease in the Western Collaborative Group Study: Findings and follow-up experience of 8½ years. *Journal of the American Medical Association*, 1975, *233*, 872–877.

Rosenman, R. H., Friedman, M., Straus, R., Wurm, M., Kositchek, R., Hahn, W., & Werthessen, N. T. A predictive study of coronary heart disease. *Journal of the American Medical Association*, 1964, *189*, 103–110.

Sajwaj, T., Libet, J., & Agras, W. S. Lemon juice therapy: The control of life threatening rumination in a six month old infant. *Journal of Applied Behavior Analysis*, 1974, 7, 557–566.

Seer, P. Psychological control of essential hypertension: Review of the literature and methodological critique. *Psychological Bulletin*, 1979, 86, 1015–1043.

Silver, B. V., & Blanchard, E. G. Biofeedback training in the treatment of psychophysiologic disorders: Or are the machines really necessary? *Journal of Behavioral Medicine*, 1978, 1, 217–239.

Southam, M. A., Agras, W. S., Taylor, C. B., & Kraemer, H. C. Relaxation training: Blood pressure lowering during the working day. *Archives of General Psychiatry*, 1982, 39, 715–717.

Stuart, R. B. Behavioural control of overeating. *Behaviour Research and Therapy*, 1967, 5, 357–365.

Stuart, R. B., & Davis, B. *Slim chance in a fat world: Behavioral control of obesity*. Champaign, Ill.: Research Press, 1972.

Stuart, R. B., Mitchell, C., & Jensen, J. A. Therapeutic options in the management of obesity. In J. A. Bradley & C. K. Prokop (Eds.), *Medical psychology: A new perspective*. New York: Academic Press, 1980.

Stunkard, A. J., & Penick, S. B. Behavior modification in the treatment of obesity: The problem of maintaining weight loss. *Archives of General Psychiatry*, 1979, 36, 801–806.

Surwit, R. S., Pilon, R. N., & Fenton, C. H. Behavioral treatment of Raynaud's disease. *Journal of Behavioral Medicine*, 1978, 1, 323–336.

Surwit, R. S., Shapiro, D., & Good, M. I. Comparison of cardiovascular biofeedback, neuromuscular biofeedback and meditation in the treatment of borderline essential hypertension. *Journal of Consulting and Clinical Psychology*, 1978, 46, 252–263.

Taylor, C. B. Relaxation training and related techniques. In W. S. Agras (Ed.), *Behavior modification: Principles and clinical applications* (2nd ed.). Boston: Little, Brown, 1978.

Taylor, C. B., Farquhar, J. W., Nelson, E., & Agras, W. S. The effects of relaxation therapy upon high blood pressure. *Archives of General Psychiatry*, 1977, 34, 339–342.

Taylor, C. B., Pfenninger, J. L., & Candelaria, T. The use of treatment contracts to reduce medical costs of a difficult patient. *Journal of Behavior Therapy and Experimental Psychiatry*, 1980, 11, 77–82.

Weisenberg, M. Pain and pain control. *Psychological Bulletin*, 1978, 34, 1008–1043.

Weiss, T., & Engel, B. T. Operant conditioning of heart rate in patients with premature ventricular contractions. *Psychosomatic Medicine*, 1971, 33, 301–321.

Wilson, G. T., & Brownell, K. D. Behavior therapy for obesity: Including family members in the treatment process. *Behavior Therapy*, 1978, 9, 943–945.

Wilson, G. T., & Brownell, K. D. Behavior therapy for obesity: An evaluation of treatment outcome. *Advances in Behavior Research and Therapy*, 1980, 3, 49–86.

Wing, R. R., & Jeffery, R. W. Outpatient treatments of obesity: A comparison of methodology and clinical results. *International Journal of Obesity*, 1979, 3, 261–280.

Wolf, M. M., Birnbrauer, J. S., Williams, T., & Lawler, J. A note on the apparent extinction of the vomiting behavior of a retarded child. In L. P. Ullmann, & L. Krasner (Eds.), *Case studies in behavior modification*. New York: Holt, Rinehart & Winston, 1965.

Wolf, S. The pharmacology of placebos. *Pharmacological Review*, 1959, 11, 689–704.

Wolfle, D. Training. In S. S. Stevens (Ed.), *Handbook of experimental psychology*. New York: Wiley, 1951.

Wollersheim, J. P. The effectiveness of group therapy based on learning principles in the treatment of overweight women. *Journal of Abnormal Psychology*, 1970, 76, 462–474.

Wysocki, T., Hall, G., Iwata, B., & Riordan, M. Behavioral management of exercise: Contracting for aerobic points. *Journal of Applied Behavior Analysis*, 1979, 12, 55–64.

Yorkston, N. J., McHugh, R. B., Brady, R., Serber, M., & Sergeant, H. G. S. Verbal desensitization in bronchial asthma. *Journal of Psychosomatic Research*, 1974, 18, 371–376.

AUTHOR INDEX

SUBJECT INDEX

ACTH. *See* Adrenocorticotropic hormone
Accelerated speech and movement in coronary heart disease etiology, 51, 53
Acceleration effects on mice, 133
Acceptability
  in health education, 439, 440
  of medical information to patients, 387
Acculturation, 19, 90
Achievement-oriented motivation, 51, 298
  see also Type A behavior
Acid-secretion role in ulcers and lesions, 178–180, 205
Acne, 43
Action cues in community-based programs, 451, 460
Activity
  active-agent role of patients in compliance, 375, 377, 378, 388–393, 413, 414
  active coping, 62, 106, 107
  active doctor–passive patient roles, 412
  activity–stress ulcers, 186, 210
Acute disease schema, 393
Adaptation
  coping and, 282–325
    coping effects on adaptation, 310–317
  in neuroendocrine response, 264
  types of, 308, 309
Adherence
  compliance as, 371, 372
  to health-related decisions, 359–364
  to medical regimens, patient decision making and, 331, 333, 339, 348, 357
  as self-regulation, 373, 374
  see also Compliance
Adjustment problems, 118
Adoptees, 121
Adoption–diffusion model in health education, 439
Adrenergic mechanisms
  in cardiovascular disease, 234, 235, 240, 242, 251, 254, 259
  in CNS control, 267, 269–271
  electrocardiogram and Q-T interval effects of, 237, 239

Adrenocortical activation in immune responses, 157–161
Adrenocorticotropic hormone, 185, 247, 271
Affect
  affective changes in disease etiology, 46
  compliance and, 402
  in practitioner–patient relationships, 411, 412, 414, 417
Age in gastric lesion studies, 183
Agenda setting in community-based programs, 450
Aggression
  in coping, 313
  in shock studies of gastric lesions, 207, 208
Allergic encephalomylitis in rats, 127
Allografts in mice, 136
Alpha-adrenergic mechanisms in cardiovascular disease, 251
Alternatives
  in decision making, generation of, 334, 351–356, 359, 360
  in patient self-regulation, 373
Ambiguity in appraisal and coping, 293–295, 301, 302
Ambition, 22, 23
Analysis of etiology. *See* Levels of analysis; Methodology
Anaphylactic shock, 136
Anesthesia effects in mice, 133
Anger
  in cancer prognosis, 68
  cooling of, 108
  as coping style, 102–105
  in disease etiology, 42
  in essential hypertension, 249
Angina pectoris, 54
Animal studies
  arthritis, 126
  gastric lesions, 178, 181, 184, 186, 189, 194–198, 200, 201, 206, 209, 210
  immunologically mediated disease, 122–127, 132–138, 140–147, 150–153
  parasitic disease, 125, 127